CELEBRATION SERIES®

THE PIANO ODYSSEY®

HANDBOOK FOR TEACHERS

Cathy Albergo

Reid Alexander

Marvin Blickenstaff

FREDERICK
HARRIS
MUSIC

National Library of Canada Cataloguing in Publication Data

Albergo, Cathy, 1951-
Celebration series : the piano odyssey : handbook for teachers

(Celebration series)
Previous ed. published under title: Handbook for teachers.
Includes index.
ISBN 0-88797-740-5

1. Piano – Instruction and study.
I. Alexander, Reid, 1949-   .
II. Blickenstaff, Marvin.
III. Title.
IV. Title: Handbook for teachers.
V. Series.

MT245.A329 2001   786.2'071   C2001-930051-4

Preface

Since its inception in 1987 and renewal in a second edition in 1994, the *Celebration Series*® has established itself as an internationally acclaimed collection of piano teaching materials. Launched in 2001 and building on the success of previous editions, the *Celebration Series*®, *The Piano Odyssey*® takes advantage of the wealth of new repertoire and the changing interests and needs of teachers. This extensive series, with valuable supporting materials for both student and teacher, is the ideal resource for the development of the complete pianist.

In writing the *Handbook for Teachers,* the authors have affirmed a basic commitment to why it is that teachers teach—to impart to their students not only knowledge but also a joy in learning that will last a lifetime. Together, the *Student Workbooks* and the *Handbook for Teachers* of the *Celebration Series*®, *The Piano Odyssey*® will yield new insights and pleasures as teachers and students explore the repertoire, studies, and recordings in this wide-ranging series. It is my pleasure and privilege to acknowledge the tireless effort and dedication of the authors to furthering the work of teachers.

As we welcome you, the readers, to explore the *Celebration Series*®, *Handbook for Teachers,* we invite you to share with us your impressions and suggestions and become participants in our never-ending quest to improve and extend our publications.

Dr. Trish Sauerbrei
Editor-in-Chief

Table of Contents

Preface 3

Foreword 6

    Introduction to the *Celebration Series®, The Piano Odyssey®* 6

    Organization of the *Handbook for Teachers* 8

Level 1 12

Level 2 37

Level 3 60

Level 4 84

Level 5 108

Level 6 129

Level 7 156

Level 8 183

Level 9 209

Level 10 244

Appendix 1: Composer Catalogue Numbers 282

Composer Index 283

Subject Index 290

Foreword

Introduction to the *Celebration Series®, The Piano Odyssey®*

The *Celebration Series®, The Piano Odyssey®* is a comprehensive compilation of materials for piano teachers and students as well as pianists who play solely for their own enjoyment. The *Celebration Series®*, however, is not a piano method in the traditional sense. Instead, this series encompasses a carefully graded selection of piano literature with supporting teaching materials.

The *Celebration Series®* comprises eleven *Piano Repertoire* albums, ten *Piano Studies/Etudes* albums, eight *Student Workbooks,* compact discs for each of the eleven Levels, and the *Handbook for Teachers.* The material is organized into eleven Levels, as listed in the chart below. Collectively, these publications support the musical training of the eye, ear, mind, and body. To omit any segment would diminish the depth of the student's musical experience.

Piano Repertoire	*Piano Studies/Etudes*	*Student Workbooks*	*Compact Discs*
Introductory Level			Introductory Level
Level 1	Level 1	Level 1	Level 1
Level 2	Level 2	Level 2	Level 2
Level 3	Level 3	Level 3	Level 3
Level 4	Level 4	Level 4	Level 4
Level 5	Level 5	Level 5	Level 5
Level 6	Level 6	Level 6	Level 6
Level 7	Level 7	Level 7	Level 7
Level 8	Level 8	Level 8	Level 8
Level 9	Level 9		Level 9
Level 10	Level 10		Level 10

A major strength of the *Celebration Series®* is its vast selection of repertoire. The 447 pieces contained in the *Piano Repertoire* and *Studies/Etudes* albums present an extensive sampling of styles and composers covering a broad spectrum of piano music from four centuries. In addition, the *Celebration Series®, The Piano Odyssey®* includes compositions by contemporary composers whose works are not regularly found in other collections.

Together, the editing, footnotes, and identification of sources provide students with helpful guidance as their awareness of musical styles matures.

➤ The editing in the *Celebration Series®, The Piano Odyssey®* is tasteful and focuses on the musical growth of the student.

➤ Editorial fingerings help students achieve efficient movement. However, such fingerings are suggestions only. Teachers and students are encouraged to try alternate fingerings to suit individual cases.

➤ Metronome markings suggest an upper and lower setting within an appropriate tempo.

➤ Footnotes below the music include brief suggestions for articulation and examples for the realization of ornaments.

➤ Teachers and students alike will appreciate the scholarship evidenced through clear references to original sources for individual pieces.

The *Piano Repertoire* Albums

There are eleven *Piano Repertoire* albums in the *Celebration Series®, The Piano Odyssey®*:

- Introductory Level: appropriate for students who have completed one to two years of study
- Levels 1, 2, and 3: late elementary through early intermediate
- Levels 4, 5, and 6: intermediate through late intermediate
- Levels 7 and 8: late intermediate to early advanced
- Levels 9 and 10: advanced recital repertoire appropriate for highly skilled high school pianists or college piano majors

The pieces in Levels 1 to 10 are organized (into lists) according to style period or genre.

Although this method of organization was developed for the purpose of The Royal Conservatory of Music examinations, it also provides a useful chronological and style reference. The contents of these lists are briefly explained in the introduction to each section of the *Handbook for Teachers*.

The *Piano Studies/Etudes* Albums

The ten *Piano Studies/Etudes* albums contain numerous etude-like selections that address particular technical challenges, as well as some character pieces and Baroque selections. Each Level includes works which can be used effectively as technique builders, recital or competition pieces, and pieces for enjoyment. Composers range from Bach and Handel to Burgmüller, Heller, Kabalevsky, Shostakovich, and Finney.

This graded series of *Piano Studies/Etudes* is designed to help students gradually master a variety of pianistic challenges. Each piece has a technical focus. While the *Piano Studies/Etudes* complement the *Piano Repertoire* albums, the studies do not necessarily correlate directly with specific repertoire pieces. However, in many instances, a study can be used as preparation for a similar composition in a repertoire album.

The *Student Workbooks*

The eight *Student Workbooks* in the *Celebration Series®, The Piano Odyssey®* are companion volumes to the *Piano Repertoire* albums for Levels 1 through 8. They are written for the student, using language and music terminology appropriate for students at each Level.

For each selection of repertoire, the student's interest and intellect are engaged by an approach of discovery learning: relevant historical and theoretical discussion and hands-on writing and creative experiences lead the student to an understanding of the essence of the music.

The discussions cover a wide range of topics, including:
- biography and style
- form and analysis
- harmony and texture
- rhythmic preparation
- dynamics and articulation
- ornamentation

The *Student Workbooks* may be incorporated into the lesson or serve as at-home enrichment study. Recognizing the different modes by which students learn, the authors have included a variety of activities —aural, visual, and kinesthetic. The wealth of information provided by these *Student Workbooks* can serve as an impetus to the development of musicality when used in conjunction with the *Piano Repertoire* and *Piano Studies/Etudes* albums and the *Celebration Series®* recordings.

The *Celebration Series®, The Piano Odyssey®* Recordings

The compact disc recordings offer representative interpretations of the complete works from the *Piano Repertoire* (Introductory Level through Level 10) and *Piano Studies/ Etudes* (Levels 1 through 10) of the *Celebration Series®, The Piano Odyssey®*. The CDs may be used by students as a reliable reference and inspiration for a polished performance. Teachers will find these professional recordings an invaluable resource for style period performance practice.

The *Handbook for Teachers*

The *Handbook for Teachers* is a comprehensive teaching aid that draws together the *Piano Repertoire* and *Piano Studies/Etudes* albums, the *Student Workbooks,* and the recordings and organizes the material for optimum use in the teaching studio. In addition to a detailed discussion of each selection in the *Piano Repertoire* and *Piano Studies/Etudes* albums, Levels 1–10, the *Handbook for Teachers* also includes suggestions for presenting and teaching the *Celebration Series®, The Piano Odyssey®* from start to finish.

Organization of the *Handbook for Teachers*

The Study Modules

The ten sections of this *Handbook for Teachers* correspond to Levels 1–10 of *Celebration Series®, The Piano Odyssey®*. In the sections covering the first eight Levels, the authors have divided each Level into a number of Study Modules. The Study Modules provide logical points of entry for teacher and student. The purpose of these Modules is to integrate the *Piano Repertoire* albums with the *Piano Studies/Etudes* albums and to organize these compositions into units of study.

In general, the Study Modules represent a gradual increase in difficulty, both within each Module and from one Module to the next. Almost all the Modules include pieces from each style period list in the *Piano Repertoire* album.

The sections covering Levels 9 and 10 are not organized into Modules, but rather according to the order of the *Piano Repertoire* and *Piano Studies/Etudes* albums. A suggested order of difficulty is given for the works from each style period.

The Module Chart

Each Module is presented initially in a chart listing the pieces in the order in which they appear in the *Piano Repertoire* and *Piano Studies/Etudes* albums. The sample chart shown below is taken from Level 3.

The information in the composer and title columns provides teachers with a detailed overview of the compositions contained in the Module. In the Page column, "R" indicates a page number from the *Piano Repertoire* album, "S" a page number from the *Piano Studies/Etudes* album, and "SW" a page number from the *Student Workbook*.

SAMPLE MODULE

Page	List	Composer	Title	Key, Meter and Tempo
R10 SW17	A	Johann Sebastian Bach, attr.	*Polonaise in G Minor, BWV Anh. 119*	G Minor $\frac{3}{4}$ $\quad$ ♩ = 92
R16 SW27	B	Muzio Clementi	*Sonatina, op. 36, no. 1 (Third Movement)*	C Major $\frac{3}{8}$ Vivace
R22 SW37	B	Alexander Gedike	*Sonatina in C Major, op. 36, no. 20*	C Major **C** Allegro moderato
R30 SW57	C	Boris Berlin	*The Haunted Castle*	C Major $\frac{4}{4}$ Andantino
R38 SW73	C	Nancy Telfer	*The Sleeping Dragon*	A Minor $\frac{4}{4}$ Slowly, smoothly
S5		Johann Friedrich Burgmüller	*Arabesque, op. 100, no. 2*	A Minor $\frac{2}{4}$ Allegro scherzando
S9		Carl Czerny	*Study in D Minor, op. 261, no. 53*	D Minor **C** Allegro

Assign first:

Polonaise in G Minor . . . .
Sonatina in C Major . . . .
The Haunted Castle . . . .
Study in D Minor

Assign next when ready:

Arabesque
Sonatina
The Sleeping Dragon

The pieces in this Study Module vary widely in mood. Encourage your students to describe the pieces they study. Discuss the story or picture of the piece, the colors, or feelings. There are no wrong answers. Students will have their own individual perceptions. The goal is to develop musical imagination and sensitivity to the expressive quality of sound.

Order of Assignment

The two lists below the chart—"Assign first" and "Assign next when ready"—give a suggested order in which the pieces in the Module can be assigned.

The authors suggest assigning pieces in the first column (either as a group or individually) before pieces in the second column. Often, pieces listed opposite each other (for example *Polonaise in G Minor* and *Arabesque*) have features in common (such as texture, articulation, or style period). In these cases, the piece in the "Assign first" column helps prepare the student for the piece in the "Assign next when ready" column. Thus, in the sample Module, *Arabesque* can be assigned after the student has completed *Polonaise in G Minor,* and *The Sleeping Dragon* after *The Haunted Castle.*

Pieces without a corresponding follow-up assignment (in this example *Study in D Minor*) are usually lengthier or more difficult, and may take longer for the student to learn.

In developing these chronologies, the authors have made an effort to determine how the pieces might best be assigned to an average student. Points taken into consideration include:
- balance of style periods
- technical difficulties
- common features or stylistic traits between pieces
- sequence from easier to more difficult
- length of time required for a student to complete each piece

The organization of the Study Modules is not meant to be dogmatic. The authors encourage teachers to adjust the order of pieces within the Modules or create their own chronology for assigning the materials in a way which best meets the needs of the individual student. Teachers should also consider whether or not the student will play all pieces in the Study Module and how many pieces the student is accustomed to studying simultaneously.

Discussion of the Study Module

The discussion of each Study Module begins with a short introduction, often covering suggested approaches to the music in the Module. The discussions of individual compositions, presented in Module order, are divided into several categories:
- ➤ *Background Information*
  Historical or stylistic points which may serve as a springboard for further discussion in the lesson or class (beginning in Level 6).
- ➤ *Exploring the Score*
  Ideas for the introduction of pieces; observations and questions which may facilitate discussion between teacher and student.
- ➤ *Practice Suggestions*
  A variety of suggestions for practicing, using terminology a teacher might use while addressing a student in a lesson.
- ➤ *Creative Activities*
  Projects for the student's own compositions, based on concepts and elements discovered in the pieces (Levels 1–8 only).

Much of the discussion of individual pieces, especially in the lower Levels, takes the form of questions a teacher might ask a student as they examine a piece of music together. Often, the answer is given in square brackets following the question.

The brief summary or conclusion at the end of each Level is intended to allow the student and teacher to reflect upon the experience gained through the study of the pieces in the Level and to review common musical characteristics found in those pieces.

In addition, some Levels involve specific learning activities—a *Dance Chart* is introduced in Level 2, and *Musical Tips* in Level 3. These activities encourage students to build their musical knowledge as they learn new pieces. Although these ideas only appear in one Level, teachers are encouraged to apply these concepts in higher Levels as appropriate.

Terminology used in the *Handbook for Teachers*

Blocking is the action of grouping two or more notes into a chord whose tones are sounded simultaneously. Blocked intervals or chords are also known as solid intervals or chords.

Drop and lift describes a wrist motion which facilitates the grouping of two or more notes into one movement or gesture. In executing a two-note slur, for example, the wrist drops to play the first note and lifts to play the second note.

Double 3rds (*double 6ths,* etc.) refers to a succession of solid or blocked parallel intervals played in one hand.

Harmonic analysis is an extremely useful exercise for students. Chords can be labeled in a number of ways, according to the students' experience and knowledge of harmony. Here are some suggestions:
- harmony names (tonic, dominant)
- chord symbols (I, V, i, v)
- chord names (C major, G minor)
- chord abbreviations (C, G, c, g)

Accuracy in playing often improves when students understand the harmonic progression of a passage. Have students name the harmonies aloud while they play.

Out of four, go for three: In a four-measure phrase, the focus of the phrase is often on the third measure. This simple rule of thumb is helpful for students who are learning to feel the shape of a musical phrase.

Throw and lift describes a continuous gesture which groups two or more notes and produces a *staccato* or accented sound. The throwing motion starts with the hand lifted off the key. As you play the first tone or chord, lift the wrist to play succeeding tones. Think of "shaking out" the successive notes, gradually lifting the wrist as you complete the passage. Keep the fingers close to the keys.

The *una corda* pedal (often called the soft pedal) is the left pedal on the piano. *Una corda* means one string. On older instruments, this pedal moved the hammers slightly to the right so that they struck only one string. On modern instruments, this pedal shifts the hammers so that they strike two strings instead of three. The term *tre corde* (or, less frequently, *tutte le corde*) indicates cancellation of the soft pedal.

One of the most important challenges of piano teaching is to ensure that the student, at whatever level of advancement, have access to materials which stimulate and educate. The *Celebration Series®, The Piano Odyssey®* provides a body of materials which furnishes the student with an outstanding selection of the highest quality teaching literature (the *Piano Repertoire* and *Piano Studies/Etudes* albums), guidance and instruction (the *Student Workbooks*), and inspiring performance models (the compact disc recordings).

We trust that this *Handbook for Teachers* will be helpful to you and your students as you explore the wealth of musical material in the *Celebration Series®, The Piano Odyssey®*. We anticipate that your journey through the *Celebration Series®, The Piano Odyssey®* will be exciting and musically rewarding.

Cathy Albergo, Professor of Music
Department of Music, William Rainey Harper College
Palatine, Illinois

Reid Alexander, Professor of Music
School of Music, University of Illinois at Urbana-Champaign
Urbana, Illinois

Marvin Blickenstaff, Artist Faculty
The College of New Jersey, Ewing, New Jersey; Westminster Choir College of Rider University, Princeton, New Jersey; and The New School for Music Study, Princeton, New Jersey

Level 1

The Publications

Level 1 of the *Celebration Series®* includes the following publications:

Piano Repertoire 1
Piano Studies/Etudes 1
Student Workbook 1
Recording of Repertoire and *Studies/Etudes 1*

The Repertoire

Piano Repertoire 1 is divided into three sections or lists.
➤ List A includes a selection of pieces composed during the Baroque period (*ca* 1600 to *ca* 1750) and the Classical period (*ca* 1750 to *ca* 1820).
➤ List B includes a selection of pieces composed during the Romantic era (*ca* 1820 to *ca* 1910) and the 20th century.
➤ List C consists of short pieces for two voices written in imitative style.

Musical Development

The repertoire and studies in Level 1 present musical and technical challenges for late elementary students as they develop control over:

- balance between melody and accompaniment
- shaping a musical phrase
- articulation of two- and three-note phrases
- hand and finger independence
- two- and three-part forms
- chords in root position and inversions
- a variety of *legato* and *staccato* articulations

The pieces in List C are intended to develop hand independence. They provide valuable preparation for Baroque and Classical dances and contrapuntal textures.

The Study Modules

The eight Study Module discussions in Level 1 are organized into the following categories:
Exploring the Score
Practice Suggestions
Creative Activities

Exploring the Score is designed as an interactive exercise between teacher and student. Background information and ideas for presentation of the pieces are provided. Some questions are addressed to the student, as you might ask them during the lesson. **Practice Suggestions** are also directed to the student. The **Creative Activities** act as reinforcement to your students' understanding of a musical concept and can provide a springboard for their improvisation and composition. Please refer to the *Foreword* for an explanation of how to use the *Assign first … Assign next when ready* listing under each module chart.

Musical Tips

As students work through this Level, they will accumulate knowledge about musical style that they can apply to other pieces they study. Your student can use a blank page to write down these points, which are identified as musical tips (**TIP:**). Encourage your students to notate these points and add to the list as they progress from level to level.

The chart below lists the repertoire and studies in Level 1. Page numbers for works in *Piano Repertoire 1* and *Piano Studies/Etudes 1* are found in the first column. Study Module numbers are found to the far right. Study Module groupings of repertoire and studies follow.

Piano Repertoire 1

	Page	Composer	Title	Study Module
List A	R4	Jeremiah Clarke	*Minuet in D Major, T 460*	1
	R5	Christoph Graupner	*Bourrée in D Minor*	2
	R6	Johann Sebastian Bach	*Minuet III in G Major*	8
	R8	Daniel Gottlob Türk	*The Hunting Horns and the Echo*	1
	R9	Johann Wilhelm Hässler	*Minuet in C Major, op. 38, no. 4*	4
	R10	Daniel Gottlob Türk	*Arioso in F Major*	6
	R11	Franz Joseph Haydn	*German Dance in G Major, Hob. IX:22, no. 3*	3
	R12	Wolfgang Amadeus Mozart	*Minuet in F Major, K 2*	7
	R13	Johann Krieger	*Menuet in A Minor*	5

	Page	Composer	Title	Study Module
List B	R14	Cornelius Gurlitt	*The Hunt, op. 117, no. 15*	2
	R15	Alexandr T. Grechaninov	*Fairy Tale, op. 98, no. 1*	7
	R16	Mel. Bonis	*The Sewing Machine*	5
	R18	Alexander Gedike	*Sad Song*	8
	R19	Linda Niamath	*Hallowe'en Night*	4
	R20	Clifford Poole	*Spooks*	3
	R22	Stephen Chatman	*Beaver Boogie*	8
	R23	David Duke	*March (Lydian Mode)*	1
	R24	Vladimir Blok	*Happy Times*	6
	R26	Christopher Norton	*Duet for One*	2
	R27	Anne Crosby	*Robots*	4
	R28	Veronika Krausas	*The Alligator*	8
	R29	Pierre Gallant	*This Old Man*	6
	R30	Vladimir Blok	*The Bear in the Forest, op. 11, no. 6*	1
	R31	Nancy Telfer	*Monté sur un éléphant/Climb up on an Elephant*	5
	R32	Grigori Frid	*The Jolly Fiddler, op. 41, no. 5*	3
	R33	Aleaxnder Gedike	*A Happy Tale, op. 36, no. 31*	7
List C	R34	David Duke, arr.	*She's Like the Swallow*	7
	R35	Irena Garztecka	*A Ball*	6
	R36	Gordon A. MacKinnon	*Swirling Leaves*	5
	R37	Jon George	*Dialogue (Canon)*	3
	R38	Pierre Gallant	*Dorian Invention*	1
	R38	Pierre Gallant	*Sur le pont d'Avignon/On the Bridge at Avignon*	2
	R39	Andrew Markow	*Teapot Invention*	4
	R40	Renée Christopher	*The Snake*	8

Piano Studies/Etudes 1

Page	Composer	Title	Study Module
S4	Linda Niamath	*Robins*	5
S4	Dmitri Kabalevsky	*A Porcupine Dance, op. 89, no. 8*	2
S5	Carl Czerny	*Study in C Major, op. 777, no. 3*	4
S6	Cornelius Gurlitt	*Morning Greeting, op. 117, no. 13*	3
S7	Lajos Papp	*Martellato and Forte–Piano*	1
S8	Theodor Oesten	*Hunting Horns*	2
S9	Alexander Tansman	*Both Ways*	5
S10	Vladimir Ivanovich Rebikov	*The Bear*	7
S12	Linda Niamath	*Kites*	4
S13	Terry Winter Owens	*Prelude for Aries*	6
S14	Paul Sheftel	*Ins and Outs*	3
S15	Jerzy Lefeld	*Little Mouse*	6
S16	Leon Aubry	*Woodland Scene*	8

Level 1 Repertoire and Studies/Etudes – Listed by Study Module

Study Module 1

List	Composer	Title	Page & Book
A	Daniel Gottlob Türk	*The Hunting Horns and the Echo*	R8, SW10
A	Jeremiah Clarke	*Minuet in D Major, T460*	R4, SW4
B	David Duke	*March (Lydian Mode)*	R23, SW42
B	Vladimir Blok	*The Bear in the Forest, op. 11, no. 6*	R30, SW56
C	Pierre Gallant	*Dorian Invention*	R38, SW72
Study	Lajos Papp	*Martellato and Forte–Piano*	S7

Study Module 2

List	Composer	Title	Page & Book
A	Christoph Graupner	*Bourrée in D Minor*	R5, SW6
B	Cornelius Gurlitt	*The Hunt, op. 117, no. 15*	R14, SW24
B	Christopher Norton	*Duet for One*	R26, SW46
C	Pierre Gallant	*Sur le pont d'Avignon/On the Bridge at Avignon*	R38, SW74
Study	Dmitri Kabalevsky	*A Porcupine Dance, op. 89, no. 8*	S4
Study	Theodor Oesten	*Hunting Horns*	S8

Study Module 3

List	Composer	Title	Page & Book
A	Franz Joseph Haydn	*German Dance, Hob. IX:22, no. 3*	R11, SW17
B	Clifford Poole	*Spooks*	R20, SW37
B	Grigori Frid	*The Jolly Fiddler, op. 41, no. 5*	R32, SW60
C	Jon George	*Dialogue (Canon)*	R37, SW70
Study	Cornelius Gurlitt	*Morning Greeting, op. 117, no. 13*	S6
Study	Paul Sheftel	*Ins and Outs*	S14

Study Module 4

List	Composer	Title	Page & Book
A	Johann Wilhelm Hässler	*Minuet in C Major*	R9, SW12
B	Linda Niamath	*Hallowe'en Night*	R19, SW34
B	Anne Crosby	*Robots*	R27, SW49
C	Andrew Markow	*Teapot Invention*	R39, SW76
Study	Carl Czerny	*Study in C Major, op. 777, no. 3*	S5
Study	Linda Niamath	*Kites*	S12

Study Module 5

List	Composer	Title	Page & Book
A	Johann Krieger	*Minuet in A Minor*	R13, SW22
B	Mel. Bonis	*The Sewing Machine*	R16, SW29
B	Nancy Telfer	*Monté sur un éléphant/Climb up on an Elephant*	R31, SW58
C	Gordon A. MacKinnon	*Swirling Leaves*	R36, SW68
Study	Linda Niamath	*Robins*	S4
Study	Alexandre Tansman	*Both Ways*	S9

Study Module 6

List	Composer	Title	Page & Book
A	Daniel Gottlob Türk	*Arioso in F Major*	R10, SW14
B	Vladimir Blok	*Happy Times*	R24, SW44
B	Pierre Gallant, arr.	*This Old Man*	R29, SW54
C	Irena Garztecka.	*A Ball*	R35, SW66
Study	Terry Winter Owens	*Prelude for Aries*	S13
Study	Jerzy Lefeld	*Little Mouse*	S15

Level 1 Repertoire and Studies/Etudes – Listed by Study Module

Study Module 7

List	Composer	Title	Page & Book
A	Wolfgang Amadeus Mozart	*Minuet in F Major, K 2*	R12, SW20
B	Alexandr T. Grechaninov	*Fairy Tale, op. 98, no. 1*	R15, SW26
B	Alexander Gedike	*A Happy Tale, op. 36, no. 31*	R33, SW62
C	David Duke, arr.	*She's Like the Swallow*	R34, SW64
Study	Vladimir Ivanovich Rebikov	*The Bear*	S10

Study Module 8

A	Johann Sebastian Bach	*Minuet III in G Major*	R6, SW8
B	Alexander Gedike	*A Sad Song*	R18, SW31
B	Stephen Chatman	*Beaver Boogie*	R22, SW40
B	Veronika Krausas	*The Alligator*	R28, SW52
C	Renée Christopher	*The Snake*	R40, SW77
Study	Leon Aubry	*Woodland Scene*	S16

STUDY MODULE 1

Page	List	Composer	Title	Key, Meter and Tempo
R4 SW4	A	Jeremiah Clarke	*Minuet in D Major, T 460*	D Major $\frac{3}{4}$ ♩ = 126-138
R8 SW10	A	David Gottlob Türk	*The Hunting Horns and the Echo*	D Major $\frac{4}{4}$ ♩ = 100-116
R23 SW42	B	David Duke	*March (Lydian Mode)*	F Lydian $\frac{4}{8}$ Fast
R30 SW56	B	Vladimir Blok	*The Bear in the Forest, op. 11, no.6*	A Minor $\frac{2}{4}$ Slowly
R38 SW72	C	Pierre Gallant	*Dorian Invention*	D Dorian $\frac{2}{2}$ ♩ = 60-66
S7		Lajos Papp	*Martellato*	E Minor $\frac{2}{4}$ Allegretto
S7		Lajos Papp	*Forte-Piano*	D Minor $\frac{2}{4}$ Allegro

Assign first:

The Hunting Horns and the Echo . . . .
Minuet in D Major . . . .
Dorian Invention
Martellato . . . .

Assign next when ready:

The Bear in the Forest
March (Lydian Mode)

Forte-Piano

Explore the pieces in Module 1 from the standpoint of LH and RH relationships as well as key variety (major, minor, Dorian, and Lydian). In two pieces (*The Hunting Horns and the Echo* and *The Bear in the Forest*), the hands move in parallel motion. In *Minuet in D Major* and *March*, the LH provides accompaniment to the RH melody. *Dorian Invention* is written in canon style. *Martellato* and *Forte-Piano* explore overtone sounds created when one hand silently depresses the keys.

Daniel Gottlob Türk
The Hunting Horns and the Echo (R8, SW10)

Exploring the Score

The favorite orchestral instrument of the 19th century was the horn, for it epitomized a love of the out of doors. Every child has experienced an echo. The dynamics "sell" this piece, and are easily grasped.

➢ You might play an echo game with the student. It could be verbal or musical. Eventually, move the game to the keyboard and play the three-note motives that are echoed at the end of each section. Have the student echo those notes.
➢ Find the appearances of this dotted motive in the score and have the student clap or tap:

➢ Follow this by tapping the entire dotted sequence, mm. 6-8.
➢ As you listen to the *Celebration Series®* recording, have the student point in the score, counting *1 2 3 4*. Feeling the main beats in each measure is crucial to rhythmic success.
➢ Then the student can tap the rhythm of short sections. Emphasize the snappy rhythm of the dotted figures.
➢ Label the sections A and B.

Practice Suggestions

➢ Discuss the fingering and circle the notes where you cross the thumb over. Practice the crossings (mm. 2-3 and 7-8) in the lesson.
➢ Which hand plays almost entirely in stepwise motion? [RH]
➢ Which hand plays the wider intervals? [LH]
➢ Before playing hands together, you may find it helpful to play hands separately.
➢ Feel the short values and dotted figures move to the quarter and half notes. Let the dynamics give the music a feeling of forward movement.

TIP: Short values move to a longer value. ("Shorts move to longs.")

Jeremiah Clarke
Minuet in D Major, T460 (R4, SW4)

Exploring the Score

The minuet dance step was a six-beat sequence. To understand the rhythm of *Minuet in D Major,* compare two-measure units (six beats). The first measure has an active, moving rhythm; the second measure is quarter notes. This suggests a dance gesture of movement or turning (first measure) and toe taps (second measure).

➢ You and your student may wish to choreograph a minuet step that involves a three-beat turn and toe taps. Fit your dance steps to the music as you listen to the *Celebration Series®* recording.
➢ Conduct a search of "first measures" (odd-numbered measures). How many different rhythms do you find? Have the student tap and count those measures.
➢ Position shifts in this piece can be challenging. Mark the fingerings in the score that create a shift of position.

TIP: Composers often write phrases in balanced pairs. The first phrase—a Question—usually ends on a note other than the keynote. The second phrase—the Answer—usually ends on the keynote.

➢ Find the Question and Answer in the A section.

Practice Suggestions

This piece is written in units of two measures. That may be a helpful unit of practice for your first week. Try this routine:

➢ Tap the practice unit. (Each unit has an upbeat.)
➢ Check fingering and notes for any position changes
➢ If you feel you need hands separate practice, play the more difficult part first.
➢ Play hands together slowly, counting aloud.
➢ When you have learned the notes and rhythms well, continue with extra practice on the last line. It is the most difficult.

Vladimir Blok
The Bear in the Forest, op. 11, no. 6 (R30, SW56)
Exploring the Score

The title of the piece can be a helpful guide to interpretation. What does one expect to hear in a piece titled *The Bear in the Forest?*
  – slowly moving sounds?
  – low sounds?
  – grumbling sounds?
➢ Have the student sight-play mm. 1-4 and discuss the mood created. Over half of the piece is already learned!
➢ Label the lines: A A B A1.
  – How is the B section different? What is the LH interval?
  – How is A1 the same? different? Is the LH the same? Can you find a 6th in the LH? [m. 15]
➢ In mm. 9-12, have the student play only downbeat chords. Play the second chord of each phrase louder than the first.
➢ If your student knows five-finger positions, discuss the role of A minor in this piece.

Practice Suggestions

➤ Which five-finger pattern is used in mm. 1–8? [A minor]
➤ In mm. 9-12, listen to the sound of the upper two voices as you divide them between the hands.
   - Then block the RH as written.
   - Finally, play the RH as written, listening carefully for notes held by the thumb.
   - Keep a smooth *legato* in the upper voice when the thumb shifts from C to D.
➤ In mm. 15-16, practice first hands separately, then hands together.

CREATIVE ACTIVITY

Using the A minor pattern and lots of unison playing, create your own piece: Title: *Mr. Hippo Takes a Bath*

David Duke
March (Lydian Mode) (R23, SW42)
Exploring the Score

➤ To set the mood of the piece and experience the *ostinato,* have the student tap the LH rhythm on a tambourine or rhythm sticks as you play the piece.
➤ The next question is an obvious one: "In which measure does the LH *not* play the *ostinato*?"
➤ You may wish to introduce the term Lydian to your student. The Lydian mode is a major scale with a raised fourth tone. The F Lydian mode has no sharps or flats.

Practice Suggestions

➤ Set a slow beat and tap the rhythm of both hands, counting aloud. Which measures have exactly the same rhythm?
➤ Block the RH chords. Practice mm. 5 and 9-10 for a quick move to the second chord. Give special attention to correct fingering.
➤ In m. 3, what triad is outlined by the RH? [F major] Measure 4, RH? [G major] If you know the names of other chords, write them in the score.
➤ Bring out the special rhythmic surprise (syncopation) on beat four in m. 5.
➤ Have fun in m. 14!

CREATIVE ACTIVITIES

Use the following methods to create variations on Duke's *March*:
➤ Change the LH rhythm.
➤ Change the RH melody.
➤ Use steps instead of broken chords.
➤ Make a new dynamic plan.
➤ Play the piece in a different register.

Pierre Gallant
Dorian Invention (R38, SW72)
Exploring the Score

Since this may be the student's first exposure to imitative inventions, explore the texture and sound. Listen to the *Celebration Series®* recording or play the inventions and ask the student to follow the score and listen for the staggered entrances of the melodies. Sight read some inventions as duets, with the student playing one voice and teacher playing the other.

Practice Suggestions

These practice steps will help students hear the canon:
➤ Practice hands separately at a slow tempo. Lift slightly at the end of each phrase.
➤ Play each RH two-measure phrase followed by the LH answer.
➤ Play each two-measure unit as written.
➤ Exaggerate the phrase lifts at the end of each phrase while keeping a smooth *legato* in the other hand.
➤ Practice the entire piece hands together.

Lajos Papp
Martellato and Forte–Piano (S7)

Martellato:
Exploring the Score

For most students, this is a new and fascinating sound experience. Before referring to the score, devise some exploratory experience through which your student can hear the sounds of overtones. [Depress several bass tones silently and continue to hold the keys down while playing a few treble notes with the RH. Lift the RH and listen while holding the LH keys.]
➤ What interval is used in mm. 7-12? [perfect 5th]
➤ What is the dynamic plan?
➤ Does your student know the meaning of *martellato?*
➤ Find the E minor five-finger pattern.

Practice Suggestions

➤ Papp has written the score carefully. It is especially important to observe the rests during practice.
➤ Block the RH melody notes and find the different positions.

STUDY MODULE 2

Page	List	Composer	Title	Key, Meter and Tempo
R5 SW6	A	Christoph Graupner	*Bourrée in D Minor*	D Minor $\frac{2}{2}$ Allegro
R14 SW24	B	Cornelius Gurlitt	*The Hunt, op. 117, no. 15*	C Major $\frac{3}{4}$ Allegretto
R26 SW46	B	Christopher Norton	*Duet for One*	E Minor $\frac{4}{8}$ Calmly
R38 SW74	C	Pierre Gallant, arr.	*Sur le pont d'Avignon / On the Bridge at Avignon*	F Major $\frac{2}{2}$ Andante
S4		Theodor Oesten	*Hunting Horns*	C Major $\frac{6}{8}$ Allegretto
S8		Dmitri Kabalevsky	*A Porcupine Dance, op. 89, no. 8*	C Major $\frac{2}{4}$ Allegretto staccatissimo

Assign first:

Bourrée in D Minor
The Hunt . . . .
Duet for One
A Porcupine Dance . . . .

Assign next when ready:

Hunting Horns

Sur le pont d'Avignon / On the Bridge at Avignon

The pieces in this module provide an opportunity to compare and contrast the use of melody and accompaniment.

➤ Which pieces have melody in both hands? [all except *The Hunt*!]
➤ Which pieces use broken chords? [*The Hunt, A Porcupine Dance, Hunting Horns*]
➤ Which piece has RH melody and LH accompaniment? [*The Hunt*]
➤ Which piece uses imitation between the hands? [*Sur le pont d'Avignon*]
➤ Which piece has a unison melody or parallel motion? [*Hunting Horns*]

Christoph Graupner
Bourrée in D Minor (R5, SW6)
Exploring the Score

This is a typical bourrée with its short upbeat, strong half-note pulse, and brusque character. A bourrée and a minuet live on opposite ends of the dance spectrum. The performance goal is a spirited sound with sharply detached quarter notes.

➤ Which hand is the easier one? Have the student memorize the LH mm. 1-4 in this introductory lesson.
➤ Make a survey of RH downbeats. Each downbeat is slurred into beat two. Some are preceded by an upbeat. One is slurred into beat three.
  – Play all slurred "groups" slightly emphasizing the first note of each group. Did you discover both two-note and three-note groups?
➤ Bracket shifts of position.

➤ The main theme (mm. 1-4) is repeated. Taking into consideration that the performance should respect the repeat marks, how many times will we hear this theme in a performance? [six times]
➤ Students know that *bi-* implies two parts. They can learn the term *binary form,* for this piece is in two equal parts. Binary forms have repeat marks in the middle. Mark the A and B sections in the score. [mm. 1 and 9]
➤ If your student plays the D minor scale, associate that scale with this piece.

Practice Suggestions

➤ Divide the piece into two-measure practice units.

➤ Which LH notes will you play detached? [all quarter notes]

➤ Find places where one hand plays *legato* and the other plays detached.

➤ Before playing, look for the places where the RH lifts. Do you find places where the hands lift together? [e.g., m. 4, third beat]

➤ Play the RH two-note slurs with a drop–lift gesture.

Cornelius Gurlitt
The Hunt, op. 117, no. 15 (R14, SW24)
Exploring the Score

The Hunt is strictly a tonic-dominant piece. Even more unusual is the fact that all chords are played in root position.

➤ Have students listen to a lively performance of the piece as they count downbeats "1 - 2 - 3 - 4."

Gurlitt has written a predictable, four-measure galloping rhythm.

➤ Have the student find the opening RH position. Play and feel the galloping motion. Count only the downbeats aloud: "a1 a2 a3 – 4."

Practice Suggestions

When students can block the positions (I, V, and V7), they are ready for independent practice.

➤ Block each group of four measures before you play. Make special note of the dynamic plan. [*f, mf, p, f*] Listen for those changes in your practice.

➤ Make up a story about *The Hunt.* What is the time of year? Where does this take place? How many hunters are there? What is being hunted?

CREATIVE ACTIVITY

The Hunt uses I and V7 chords in C major. Using Gurlitt's rhythmic plan of "a1- a2 - a3 - 4" compose your own hunting piece using these same chords. You might change one note per measure, create a totally new RH part, or use a combination of blocked and broken chords.

Your title: _____.

Christopher Norton
Duet for One (R26, SW46)
Exploring the Score

What can the student learn about the piece through observing the score?
- – tempo and mood
- – slowly moving melody
- – predictable rhythm in both hands
- – phrases of equal length

➤ Circle the first four RH tones. Circle the repetitions of those same tones. This melodic fragment is like a question that is answered in the next phrase. The circled groups show the form of the piece.

➤ Guide your student to a quickly memorized understanding of the LH *ostinato.*

➤ Turn this piece into a *Duet for Two,* with the teacher playing the RH, the student playing the LH (from memory!).

Practice Suggestions

This tranquil, melodic piece is a duet between and within the hands. Before practicing hands together, you may wish to:

➤ Practice the LH alone with pedal. Your pedal will be most successful if you lift the pedal on beat one, and depress the pedal on beat two (not before!).

➤ Then, practice the RH for fingering and a warm *legato* sound.

➤ If you have played duets previously, you will be familiar with the terms *Primo* and *Secondo.* Your RH is the *Primo* and your LH is the *Secondo.* Be a good *Secondo* player; keep your LH decidedly quieter than the *Primo.*

Pierre Gallant, arr.
Sur le pont d'Avignon/On the Bridge at Avignon (R38, SW74)
Exploring the Score

➤ Most students will know this French folk song. To set the "sound background" for this invention, sing the tune together. Then sing it in canon, guided by Gallant's arrangement.

➤ The student must be able to tap hands together successfully before attempting to play. Measures 3 and 5 present the problems to be solved.

1. Tap the rhythm hands separately.
2. Tap the rhythm hands together and chant:

both   left right both   right

3. Walk the LH rhythm while clapping the RH rhythm.

Practice Suggestions

➤ Tap and count the piece each day before playing on the keyboard.

Dmitri Kabalevsky
A Porcupine Dance, op. 89, no. 8 (S8)

Exploring the Score

What better way could there be to imitate a porcupine's sharp quills than by playing *staccatissimo?*

This *staccato* study features contrary motion with mirror fingering. There are three different hand positions (see mm. 1-3).

➤ Notice that the RH and LH thumbs always play on adjacent white keys.
➤ How does Kabalevsky create interest? [variety of phrase length, dynamic contrast in mm. 9-12]
➤ To help students learn notes and fingering, have them block the hand positions in each measure. Play the entire piece blocked.

Practice Suggestions

You can learn this piece quickly if you know the changes of position.

➤ Block the positions.
➤ How quickly can you memorize those position shifts? Soon you will have the entire piece memorized!

CREATIVE ACTIVITY

Experiment with the blocked chords in *A Porcupine Dance.* Make your own *Dance* by inverting the patterns, repeating notes, playing the chords in a different order, etc.

Your title: _____

Theodor Oesten
Hunting Horns (S4)

Exploring the Score

Compare *Hunting Horns* with Gurlitt's *The Hunt* (R14) already discussed in this module.

➤ What are the similarities (meter, rhythmic figures, tempo)?
➤ The galloping figure in m. 1 is a broken chord. What is the name of this chord?
➤ Circle all dynamic markings in the score. Do you remember *The Hunting Horns and the Echo* (R8) from Study Module 1? Could these *piano* measures represent an echo?

Practice Suggestions

➤ If you block mm. 1-4, you will discover the primary positions shifts of the piece.
➤ The *forte* measures are to be played with great vigor and energy. Listen for a *crescendo* to the top pitch (mm. 2, 6, 14) and to the last note (mm. 9, 11).
➤ After you have mastered the notes and fingering in each hand, practice slowly, hands together.

STUDY MODULE 3

Page	List	Composer	Title	Key, Meter and Tempo
R11 SW17	A	Franz Joseph Haydn	*German Dance, Hob. IX:22, no. 3*	G Major $\frac{3}{4}$ ♩ = 116-126
R20 SW37	B	Clifford Poole	*Spooks*	D Minor $\frac{4}{4}$ Misterioso
R32 SW60	B	Grigori Frid	*The Jolly Fiddler, op. 41, no. 5*	D Major $\frac{2}{4}$ Lively
R37 SW70	C	Jon George	*Dialogue (Canon)*	D Major $\frac{4}{4}$ Simply

STUDY MODULE 3

Page	List	Composer	Title	Key, Meter and Tempo
S6		Cornelius Gurlitt	*Morning Greeting, op. 117, no. 13*	G Major $\frac{3}{8}$ Allegretto
S14		Paul Sheftel	*Ins and Outs*	Modal $\frac{4}{4}$ Not fast

Assign first: **Assign next when ready:**

German Dance
Ins and Outs . . . . *The Jolly Fiddler*
Spooks
Dialogue . . . . *Morning Greeting*

This study module provides an opportunity to focus on a variety of touches. Such issues as arm weight, fast versus slow key attack, different qualities of *staccato, legato* fingering, and expressive slurs can be explored with the student.

Franz Joseph Haydn
German Dance, Hob. IX:22, no. 3 (R11, SW17)
Exploring the Score
Numerous dances are cast in $\frac{3}{4}$ time, yet they have their own unique characteristics. (We would not mistake a waltz for a minuet.) Haydn's *German Dance* may be different from other minuets you have heard, for this is a country dance representing the gusto of peasant folk dance.

➤ Have the student play mm. 1-2 as if they were playing a minuet. In the LH, slur beats one and two and give the other notes elegant detachment.
  – Now play this country dance LH louder, more detached, with more robust energy.
  – Tap the rhythm of the RH mm. 1-2.
➤ Musical Search: find other measures with that same RH rhythm. Do they have the same phrasing (slurs)? Are they found only in the A section?
➤ Why do most students find the B section easier than the A section? [parallel motion]
TIP: Dances of the Baroque and Classical periods are usually in binary form.

➤ Your student knows the term *binary form*. This is another fine example of that form.
➤ *German Dance* provides the student with an excellent example of Question and Answer phrases. Each section is divided into two four-measure phrases.

TIP: Composers often write phrases in balanced pairs. The first phrase—a Question—usually ends on a note other than the keynote. The second phrase—the Answer—usually ends on the keynote. A parallel Answer starts the same as the Question. A contrasting Answer starts differently from the Question.

Practice Suggestions
➤ Practice the RH on a flat surface, with exaggerated lifts at the ends of slurs. Can you play the lifts correctly and observe the fingering?
➤ Add the LH. In the A section, the LH is always detached. In the B section, it slurs and lifts with the RH.
➤ You will be most successful if you practice in two-measure units. Play slowly, perfectly, repeating each unit three times.

Practice Check List:
  – slow practice, steady beat
  – exaggerate the RH lifts
  – follow the fingering in the score

Grigori Frid
The Jolly Fiddler, op. 41, no. 5 (R32, SW60)
Exploring the Score

Imagine a country barn dance with a fiddler tuning up as the dancers gather on the straw-covered floor.

➤ Where do you hear the instruments tuning up?
   What blocked interval is used? [5th]
   What notes are used to represent this tuning up? [E–A–D–G]
   Do you know the pitch of the violin strings? [E–A–D–G]

➤ Mark the ABA form of this piece. You can label the "tuning 5ths" as "X."
   A (mm. 1-8)
   B (mm. 8-16)
   A (mm. 17-26)

➤ Notice that A is composed of the "tuning 5ths" and a melody. Does the B section repeat its tune? [yes]

➤ To instill the rhythm of the A section, try tapping and counting this skeletal version:

➤ Tap these combinations of sixteenth notes found in *The Jolly Fiddler:*

Practice Suggestions

The RH melodies can be blocked in two major five-finger patterns.

➤ Name them. [D major and A major] Label those positions in the score. Notice that the fingering helps you with the position shifts. [mm. 8, 11, 12, 15, 24]

➤ Circle two places where the RH must cross over the LH.

➤ What different touches will be used to play *tenuto, staccato,* and *legato?*

CREATIVE ACTIVITY

Play *The Jolly Fiddler* again and compose your own variation by changing at least one RH melody note in each measure. Keep the LH the same.

Title: *My Jolly Fiddler*

Clifford Poole
Spooks (R20, SW37)
Exploring the Score

Before students see the piece, ask them to improvise "spooky" sounds. Suggest a list:
   – sounds for a dark night (add a bit of wind if you like!)
   – quiet, tip-toe *staccato* notes
   – bones clattering
   – a loud BOO!
   – running from the haunted house

➤ Then find the "sound effects" in Poole's *Spooks.* Label each musical idea with an event or action in your story. Who is singing *mesto espressivo* (m. 17)? [sad or mournfully expressive]

➤ Label the ABA1 sections. [mm. 1, 17, 31]

Practice Suggestions

Which measures of this piece do you not have to practice? (Nearly half of the piece is made of repeated ideas.) Practice similar ideas together.
   – Mm.7-8 are descending four-note groups. Find other groups with descending stepwise motion. [m. 15, mm. 39-40]
   – M. 5 has repeated tones. Find other measures with repeated note figures.

CREATIVE ACTIVITY

Create a spooky piece using some of the musical ideas found in *Spooks.*

Title: *A Visit to the Haunted House*

Jon George
Dialogue (Canon) (R37, SW70)
Exploring the Score

Dialogue is a musical conversation between the hands with dovetailed (overlapping) entrances of each voice.

➤ Which five-finger patterns are played in the RH and LH? [A major and D major] Do the notes go beyond these positions? [LH – no; RH – yes, m. 15 – move to D major]

➤ Measures 10-13 repeat which measures? [mm. 4-8] How are they different? [dynamics and shift of bar line]

Practice Suggestions

To train hand independence, determine a short practice unit and follow these steps:

➤ Establish a slow tempo and tap hands together.
➤ Play on a flat surface, observing the fingerings.
➤ Play on a flat surface, exaggerating phrase lifts.

> Play one hand on the keyboard, and the other on the wood of the piano (or a flat surface).
> Reverse hands.
> Practice hands together.

Paul Sheftel
Ins and Outs (S14)
Exploring the Score

An entire piece based on blocked and broken 5ths!
> Help your student observe the single interval that is used in the piece. Notice that the 5ths are both blocked and broken.
> Why is the piece titled *Ins and Outs*?
> The first line starts with a G – D 5th. Play all blocked 5ths and say "G – In, G – Out," etc. Label this line A.
> What will you say when you play the second line? ["E – In, E – Out," etc.] Label this line B.
> Continue the "In – Out" verbalization for lines 3 and 4 and label the form.

Practice Suggestions

When do you not play *staccato*? [half and whole notes]
> Tap hands together on the keyboard lid, imitating the in and out moves, *staccatos,* and rests.
> Then, play on the keyboard.
> Where do you add pedal?

CREATIVE ACTIVITY

Make up your own *Ins and Outs* by choosing 5ths and moving in and out as you wish.

Title: _____

Cornelius Gurlitt
Morning Greeting, op. 117, no. 13 (S6)
Exploring the Score

Gurlitt once again provides us with a piece entirely built around tonic and dominant harmonies.
> Have the student play bass notes G and D. As you play the RH, the student plays the proper G's and D's, saying "I – V – I" etc.
> In the B section [m. 9] the student moves to D and A. Play and say as before.
> Observe that the beginning is repeated in m. 17.
> This harmonic exercise also leads to an understanding of form. The double bar indicates two-part form *(binary)*, but the repeat of the A section "rounds out" the form. The form is *rounded binary.*

TIP: *Rounded binary* became one of the most important forms of the late 18th century, as it led to sonata form.

> Find and label the two complete G major scales. [mm. 5-8 and 21-24]
> Have the student attempt to play the RH of mm. 1-4 with the LH of mm. 9-12. It sounds odd, but makes its point.

Practice Suggestions

Practice the LH fingering in mm. 1-4 and listen for the *legato* between the double notes.
> Practice the RH accompaniment in mm. 9-12.
> Then, play hands together, both hands *legato.*

STUDY MODULE 4

Page	List	Composer	Title	Key, Meter and Tempo
R9 SW12	A	Johann Wilhelm Hässler	*Minuet in C Major, op. 38, no.4*	C Major $\frac{3}{4}$ Tempo di menuetto
R19 SW34	B	Linda Niamath	*Hallowe'en Night*	A Minor $\frac{3}{4}$ Mysteriously
R27 SW49	B	Anne Crosby	*Robots*	C Major $\frac{4}{4}$ Mechanically
R39 SW76	C	Andrew Markow	*Teapot Invention*	G Major $\frac{2}{4}$ Sprightly
S5		Carl Czerny	*Study in C Major, op. 777, no. 3*	C Major $\frac{3}{4}$ Allegro
S12		Linda Niamath	*Kites*	C Major / G flat Major $\frac{4}{4}$ Smoothly and freely

STUDY MODULE 4

Assign first:

Minuet in C Major
Kites . . . .
Teapot Invention . . . .
Robots

Assign next when ready:

Hallowe'en Night
Study in C Major

Here is an opportunity to nurture a student's imagination. The pieces in this module include two dances (*Minuet* and Czerny's *Study in C Major*) and four "character" pieces with very colorful titles (*Hallowe'en Night, Teapot Invention, Kites,* and *Robots.*) Use your imagination when projecting the music—a gliding minuet, a delicate waltz, a mysterious Hallowe'en piece, a mechanical robot, etc. Make up a musical story for each piece, emphasizing expressive playing.

Johann Wilhelm Hässler
Minuet in C Major (R9, SW12)

Exploring the Score

This graceful minuet uses broken chords and variation to create a light, elegant dance.

➤ Have the student find where the hands "dance" separately, and where they "dance" together.
➤ Which measures are exactly alike? Which measures create a variation by adding notes?
Now the student has a grasp of the form:
    A = mm. 1-8
    A1 = mm. 9-16

TIP: The short–short–long phrase structure (2 + 2 + 4 measures) is an important characteristic of music from the Classical era.

➤ Notice the short–short–long phrase structure in mm. 1-8 (2 + 2 + 4 measures). Look for this same short–short–long phrase structure in the A1 section and in other pieces you have studied.

Practice Suggestions

➤ Block the notes in mm. 1-2 (C chord) and mm. 3-4 (G7 chord). Write the names of the chords in your score. Do the same for mm. 9-12.
➤ Circle the RH ascending E, F, G, and A in mm. 5-6. Bring out this melodic line as you "whisper" the C's.
➤ Try lifting each hand after the downbeat quarter notes in mm. 9-12.
➤ Quarter notes that are not slurred can be played detached.

Linda Niamath
Hallowe'en Night (R19, SW34)

Exploring the Score

A mysterious Hallowe'en atmosphere is created by combining unusual harmonies with pedal and subtle dynamics.

Play *Hallowe'en Night* for the student, or listen to the *Celebration Series*® recording. Help your student list the musical elements that set a Hallowe'en mood in this piece.

➤ Which lines are most alike? What is similar in lines two and four?
➤ Find the secret pattern of notes in mm. 13-15. (**Clue:** How many different notes are there?) What are the intervals between the notes? Notice the unusual fingering for those notes.

Practice Suggestions

➤ When you have mastered the fingerings for mm. 6-8, and the pattern of notes in the last line, this piece is quickly learned. Work on lines two and four first.
➤ The pedal is an important part of the sound of this piece. Listen for the special mysterious sound while holding the pedal in mm. 6-8 and mm. 13-15. Did you hear clear pedal changes on the final chords?
➤ Observe the dynamics with special care.

Anne Crosby
Robots (R27, SW49)

Exploring the Score

Play *Robots* for the student, or listen to the *Celebration Series*® recording.

➤ How does the composer create a mechanical sound?
    articulation?
    rhythm?
    intervals?

Examine the score closely to discover:

➤ What interval is used in line 1?
➤ What makes mm. 1-4 easy to play? [LH plays only white keys; RH plays only black keys except for one chord.] Find and circle the only white key 5th played by the RH.
➤ Where do these measures repeat?
➤ In m. 4, Crosby uses two different whole-tone clusters—CDE and F sharp G sharp A sharp. Can you find other whole-tone clusters? [mm. 6, 10, 11]
➤ Find the chromatic scale.

Practice Suggestions

➤ Watch for clef changes! This piece moves from Low C in m. 1 to High C in m. 12. Circle the clef changes on your music.
➤ Choreograph the hand movements and clef changes on the closed keyboard cover before playing.

CREATIVE ACTIVITY

Using the same elements found in *Robots,* make up your own mechanical robot piece. Use 5ths, whole-tone clusters, and a chromatic scale.

Title: _____

Andrew Markow
Teapot Invention (R39, SW76)
Exploring the Score

Teach the student the familiar song *I'm a Little Teapot.* Allow the student to find the first part of the piece on the piano by ear. Start on C. Then start on G. When the student has successfully found the tune, you could add the imitation quietly:

➤ Observe the score and discuss how Markow has created the piece.
➤ You may wish to introduce the term *canon.*
➤ The independence of hands is challenging. The following rhythm exercise can also become a practice technique, substituting playing for tapping:
  – tap the RH mm. 1-2
  – tap the LH mm. 3-4 (same rhythm)
  – tap mm. 1-4 hands together
  – follow the same procedure for each line

Practice Suggestions

➤ Circle the finger crossings in both the RH and LH. Don't forget m. 4!
➤ Use the steps outlined above for tapping and playing.
➤ Exaggerate the difference between *legato* and *staccato.* That is part of the fun!

Linda Niamath
Kites (S12)
Exploring the Score

➤ Have the student observe the musical flight of this kite. Does it always sail upward? What happens in mm. 9-10?
➤ Does the music require hand crossings?
➤ In mm. 1-4, have the student find the first note of each position. Discovery: they are all C's!
➤ Do the same for mm. 5-6; 9-10, 11-12. Niamath's "secret" in this piece is hands starting on the same letter name.

Practice Suggestions

Before students start their practice on the piece, it is important that they hear a finished performance.

➤ The piece is divided into obvious sections (white keys, black keys). Practice in those sections. Before playing as written, map out the starting notes of each hand as the positions move up and down the piano. Play those starting notes with correct fingering. You might even name the notes: "C – C – C – C – C."
➤ When you are confident with the notes and position changes, work carefully on the dynamics and the changes of tempo *(rit.).*
➤ Where might you pause to watch the kite soar? [*fermatas* in mm. 4, 9, 10]
➤ Make up a story about the kite to match the dynamics and expressive terms in this piece.

CREATIVE ACTIVITY

Create your own musical picture of a kite. In one section you might use only white keys and in another section only black keys. How does your story end?

Title: _____

Carl Czerny
Study in C Major, op. 777, no. 3 (S5)
Exploring the Score

This is a light and playful waltz using I and V7 chords.

➤ Does the RH change positions? [no: stays in a C major five-finger pattern]
➤ Have the student block LH fingers 1 and 5 to discover the consistency of the interval movement 5th–6th–5th–6th–5th.
➤ If your student knows I and V7 chords, use Roman numerals to label the harmonies.
➤ Why does Czerny sometimes write a D, and sometimes an F, in the LH V7 chord? [If the RH plays an F, the LH takes the D, and vise versa.]
➤ What is the form? [binary]

Practice Suggestions

➤ Practice hands together in four-measure sections.
  – Play the RH as written, accompanied by blocked 5ths and 6ths in the LH.
  – Review the I and V(7) chords.
  – Play the RH, accompanied by blocked chords.
  – Play as written.
➤ When you practice the LH, say "down–up–up" to guide your hand gesture. Remember to keep the "oom pah pah" bass light and graceful.
➤ Listen for the long four-measure phrase.

TIP: Remember the rule "Out of Four, Go for Three." In a four-measure phrase, emphasize the third measure to shape the phrase.

CREATIVE ACTIVITY

Make up your own *Waltz* by using the same LH waltz bass and chord pattern as the *Study in C Major*. Create your own RH melody in the C major five-finger pattern. You might create two Question and Answer sets. If you wish, compose a contrasting B section.

Title: *Waltz, op. 1, no. 1*

STUDY MODULE 5

Page	List	Composer	Title	Key, Meter and Tempo
R13 SW22	A	Johann Krieger	*Minuet in A Minor*	A Minor $\frac{3}{4}$ ♩ = 112-126
R16 SW29	B	Mel. Bonis	*The Sewing Machine*	G Major $\frac{2}{2}$ Allegro vivo
R31 SW58	B	Nancy Telfer, arr.	*Monté sur un éléphant / Climb up on an Elephant*	B flat Major $\frac{6}{8}$ Awkwardly
R36 SW68	C	Gordon A. MacKinnon	*Swirling Leaves*	D Minor $\frac{3}{4}$ Andante espressivo
S4		Linda Niamath	*Robins*	A Major $\frac{4}{4}$ Brightly
S9		Alexandre Tansman	*Both Ways*	A Minor $\frac{4}{4}$ Moderato

Assign first:

Minuet in A Minor
The Sewing Machine
Swirling Leaves . . . .
Both Ways . . . .

Assign next when ready:

Monté sur un éléphant / Climb up on an Elephant
Sassy Mood

The pieces in Study Module 5 have descriptive titles. They provide opportunities for expressive playing and "story-telling." Discuss how touch and dynamics support the title (story) of the piece.

Johann Krieger
Minuet in A Minor (R13, SW22)

Exploring the Score

The minuet has been discussed earlier in Level 1. Review the characteristics of this dance form:
  – $\frac{3}{4}$ meter
  – binary form
  – six-beat units

Does the student find those characteristics in *Minuet in A Minor?*

➤ This minuet is remarkable in its constant use of steady quarter notes. Tap the piece on a flat surface, limiting the tapping to the hand that plays only quarter notes. [**Hint:** The hands will alternate.]
➤ The second half is longer than the first half because:
  – new material is introduced in m. 9
  – mm. 1-8 are restated as mm. 17-24

➤ The label for this form is *rounded binary.*

➤ Mm. 1-2 are "twins" to mm. 3-4. They have the same shape, the same rhythm, and even the same fingering. Mm. 9-10 are "twins" to mm. 11-12.

TIP: *Sequence* is the term used to describe a pattern that is repeated on different pitches.

Practice Suggestions

➤ To concentrate on finger numbers and position changes, play hands separately on the keyboard cover, saying finger numbers as you play.
➤ In mm. 1-4, practice only the quarter note movement and then add the dotted half values.
➤ Practice the sequences.
➤ Find measures with eighth notes. Tap them hands together before playing.

Have you noticed the phrase structure: 2 mm. + 2 mm. + 4 mm? This plan happens three times. To achieve the feeling of that phrase structure, try this "breath test"— each phrase must be completed in only one breath:
- Tapping your foot to a steady quarter beat, play the RH as you exhale on the sound of a constant "f-f-f." Take a quick catch-breath before you start a new phrase. The two-measure phrases will be easy to do in one breath. Take a deep breath before you start the four-measure phrase. Remember: one breath per phrase.

Nancy Telfer, arr.
Monté sur un éléphant / Climb up on an Elephant (R31, SW58)
Exploring the Score

Which sounds best suit a piece about an elephant ride?
- low sounds or high sounds?
- light sounds or heavy sounds?
- slow or fast speed?
- a wobbly rhythm or a marching rhythm?

What sounds does Nancy Telfer use?
➤ The student can "elephant walk" around the studio and clap the rhythm of mm. 1-4. How many times is this pattern repeated in the piece?
➤ Label the RH chords in mm. 2-8. [B flat and E flat chords]

Practice Suggestions

➤ Have students swing their arms to a slow dotted-quarter-note pulse to feel the underlying pulse.
➤ Which LH measures may need special practice? [mm. 9-21]
➤ Practice the RH chords for accuracy of notes and fingering. If you have a problem remembering the black keys, circle them.
➤ Remember to use a "drop–lift" gesture on the two-note slurs.

Mel. Bonis
The Sewing Machine (R16, SW29)
Exploring the Score

Why is the LH written with only two repeated tones? [imitates the movement of a sewing machine] The RH moves frequently, like a busy seamstress.
➤ Mark the A and B sections in the music.
➤ Help your student find the position shifts. Play only the first note of each new position.

Practice Suggestions

➤ Are you comfortable with the dotted quarter–eighth rhythm? To practice dotted rhythms, count and clap the following:

1. $\frac{4}{4}$ ♩ ♩ ♩ ♩ | ♩ ♩ ♩ ♩ |

2. $\frac{4}{4}$ ♩ ♫ ♩ ♩ | ♩ ♫ ♩ ♩ |

3. $\frac{4}{4}$ ♩‿♫ ♩ ♩ | ♩‿♫ ♩ ♩ |

4. $\frac{4}{4}$ ♩. ♪♪ ♩ | ♩. ♪♪ ♩ |

➤ Let the LH depress its two keys. Practice the RH shifts (mm. 11-12, 19-20, etc.) against this LH static position.
➤ In mm. 11-16 and 19-30, hold the RH high and the LH low to provide space for both hands.

CREATIVE ACTIVITY

Compose a new piece by using the same LH *ostinato* bass as *The Sewing Machine* and making up your own RH melody. Use the notes of the G major scale.

Title: *Spinning Wheel*

Gordon A. MacKinnon
Swirling Leaves (R36, SW68)
Exploring the Score

One might first think of swirling leaves music as being fast and agitated. This is a slow piece, in which we see the swirling leaves in slow-motion replay.

➤ Observe the score and discuss the musical shape that reflects the title.
➤ Discuss the D minor scale in all three forms— natural, harmonic and melodic. Which form is used in *Swirling Leaves?* [melodic]
➤ Play this piece as a duet with your student, having the student play first the RH and then the LH part.

Level 1

27

Practice Suggestions

➤ Have the student draw the RH phrase shapes in the air, noticing the swirling activity of the lines.
➤ First practice steps might include:
  – circling finger crossings in the score to discover shifts of position
  – tapping the rhythm and lifting at ends of phrases
  – playing each phrase hands together in unison

Linda Niamath
Robins (S4)

Exploring the Score

➤ Looking at the score, what activities of the robin seem to be suggested in the music?
➤ Circle the time signature change in your music.
➤ The rhythm gives the piece a feeling of unpredictability and constant change. Have the student experience the various rhythms before practice begins.

Practice Suggestions

➤ Tap and count the rhythms of this piece. Carefully observe the rests and changing time signature. How long will you hold the tied notes in mm. 6-7?

➤ Draw a ✓ for each lift of the two-note slurs in m. 5. Remember to use a drop–lift gesture for the slurs.

Alexander Tansman
Both Ways (S9)

Exploring the Score

For the student to discover the meaning of the title, discuss the following:

➤ Which hand plays the melody in mm. 1-8? [RH]
➤ Where is the melody in mm. 9-15? [LH]
➤ How are the melodies the same? How are they different?
➤ Play the LH in mm. 1-8. Then play the RH in mm. 9-14. What do you find?
➤ You may wish to write in phrase marks for the melody. Where does it sound natural to take a breath?

Practice Suggestions

➤ Practice the RH melody in mm. 1-8; then play the LH melody in mm. 9-15. Can you play them in unison?
➤ What does the term *marcato* suggest in m. 9?
➤ Practice the chromatic lines hands separately. Can you play them with your eyes closed?

STUDY MODULE 6

Page	List	Composer	Title	Key, Meter and Tempo
R10 SW14	A	Daniel Gottlob Türk	*Arioso in F Major*	F Major $\frac{2}{4}$ Poco adagio
R24 SW44	B	Vladimir Blok	*Happy Times*	D Major / D Minor $\frac{2}{4}$ Allegro
R29 SW54	B	Pierre Gallant, arr.	*This Old Man*	C Major $\frac{2}{2}$ Scherzando
R35 SW66	C	Irena Garztecka	*A Ball*	G Major $\frac{3}{4}$ Allegro
S13		Terry Winter Owens	*Prelude for Aries*	D Minor $\frac{2}{4}$ Moderato
S15		Jerzy Lefeld	*Little Mouse*	C Major $\frac{2}{4}$ Allegretto

Assign first:

Arioso in F Major
Happy Times
This Old Man . . . .
Study in F Major . . . .

Assign next when ready:

A Ball
Little Mouse

Explore the concept of melody in this module. Both *Arioso in F Major* and *Study in F Major* have clear melody and accompaniment textures. In *Happy Times, This Old Man, A Ball,* and *Little Mouse,* the melody either alternates between hands or is divided between the hands.

Daniel Gottlob Türk
Arioso in F Major (R10, SW14)
Exploring the Score

The beauty and tenderness of this piece lie in the expressive two-note slurs at the ends of phrases. The dynamic plan for a two-note slur is determined by tradition: "louder–softer." Words such as "sigh-ing," "swal-low," or the student's two-syllable name can be helpful reinforcement.

TIP: A musical "sigh" has its emphasis on the first note.

In his *Klavierschule,* Türk tells us that the finger should be raised from the key on the last note of a phrase, i.e., on the second treble note of mm. 4, 8, and 12. These measures should thus be phrased:

➤ Have the student locate the two-note slurs. (Do not overlook the eighth-note pairs in m. 7 and the hidden eighth-note pairs in m. 15.) Practice them with an exaggerated dynamic plan. You may wish to associate a "drop-lift" gesture of the wrist with this sound.
➤ Label the A and B sections.
➤ Compare mm. 5-8 and mm. 13-16. How are they alike? different?
➤ Circle the dynamic marking at the beginning of each line. Memorize that dynamic plan.

Practice Suggestions

➤ Practice line 1 and line 3 in two-measure units. (Play each unit three times.) If you need special fingering practice, play on the closed keyboard cover of your piano, saying the RH fingerings aloud.
➤ Practice line 2 and line 4 in two-measure units. Be consistent with RH fingerings.
➤ Practice the LH separately with a *legato* touch.

Vladimir Blok
Happy Times (R24, SW44)
Exploring the Score

One can scarcely imagine a more "happy times" piece! Every note bounces with energy and wit. There are surprises, and even some good belly laughs.

➤ Play the *Celebration Series®* recording. Explore the score with your student, looking for "happy times" clues. Write a list of the student's observations at the top of the score.

➤ Help the student find and mark position shifts.
  - The first page has just one shift of position.
  - The student will recognize the position of mm. 17 and 21.
  - Mm. 19 and 23 are similar to m. 9 (check the LH).
  - Block the 3rds in mm. 25-28.

➤ Blok alternates D major and D minor tonalities. Find at least two examples of the following triads:
  - D major [mm 1-2, 7-8, 17-18, etc.]
  - D minor [mm. 9-10,11-12]
  - B flat major [mm. 19-20, 23-24]

Practice Suggestions

➤ Find the places in the piece where the positions are the same or similar. Regard those as a practice unit.
➤ Then practice in four-measure and eight-measure units.
➤ Observe all expressive signs (*staccato,* two-note slurs, dynamics, etc).

Pierre Gallant, arr.
This Old Man (R29, SW54)

Have your students write the words for this song in the music so they can sing as they play:

This old man, he played one,
He played knick-knack on my thumb,
With a knick-knack paddy-whack,
Give a dog a bone!
This old man came rolling home.

Exploring the Score

➤ As you play or listen to the recording, have the student sing along.
➤ Then have the student sing the tune and tap the rhythm of mm. 8-15 hands together.
➤ Tap the rhythm of mm. 1-7 hands together.
➤ Go through the score and name all of the dynamic and expressive signs. Don't forget the *scherzando.*
➤ Lines 1 and 2 are in C major. What chord is outlined in mm. 1-2? [C].
➤ Find an F minor five-finger pattern. [mm. 10-11]
➤ Can you name the chords in mm. 14-15? [G7 and C]
➤ Play the *Celebration Series®* recording and listen for details of dynamics and articulations. Help students hear the difference between *mezzo piano, piano,* and *pianissimo* as they play.

Practice Suggestions

➤ Have the student first locate and play the melody, making note of the finger numbers that indicate a shift of position.

➤ Play the RH separately in mm. 3-6, observing *tenuto,* two-note slur, *staccato,* and accent marks.
➤ Play the LH separately in mm. 5-7 with *staccatos* and accents. The breath mark (') means to lift or detach the half notes.
➤ Isolate mm. 6-7 for careful practice. The "alto" voice is very busy with its rest, slurs, and lifts.

CREATIVE ACTIVITY

Play the melody for *This Old Man.* Harmonize it with LH I and V7 chords. Make several variations by changing the melody, changing the accompaniment style, or even changing from major to minor.

Title: *Variations on a Familiar Tune*

Irena Garztecka
A Ball (R35, SW66)
Exploring the Score

➤ The rhythms used in this piece are severely limited by the composer. Which rhythmic values are used in *A Ball?* [quarter, dotted half]
➤ Choreograph the rhythm in three different patterns:
  – Tap only the quarter notes moving from hand to hand.
  – Tap only the dotted half notes moving from hand to hand.
  – Tap hands together.
➤ If you think of the first line as a Question and the second as an Answer, how would you "analyze" the form of lines 3 and 4?
➤ Which measures are exactly alike?

Practice Suggestions

➤ In the first week, practice in two-measure units.
  – Tap the rhythm hands together.
  – Block the chords.
  – Play each practice unit three times.
      Did you hear full value on the dotted half?
      Did the *staccatos* "dance"?
  – Write the names of the chords in the score.

Terry Winter Owens
Prelude for Aries (S13)
Exploring the Score

➤ Label the A B A1 sections. [mm. 1-7, 8-16, 17-24]
➤ Owens' notation makes the shaping of the phrases nearly automatic. The peak of each phrase in the A section is a double-stemmed quarter note. (Have your student circle those downbeat tones and discuss "focus of the phrase.") The dynamics add interest and variety.
➤ In the B section, which hand leads and which hand echos?

➤ Can you find the descending sequence in the B section?

Practice Suggestions

➤ Block the hand position shifts for each two-measure unit in the A section. Then block each measure in the B section. Practice playing these blocked positions with the correct dynamics.
➤ How smoothly can you play the *legato* phrases? Play so smoothly that each phrase sounds as if one hand is playing.
➤ You have circled downbeat quarter notes in the A section. Let the first measure of each phrase move towards that melodic goal.

Jerzy Lefeld
Little Mouse (S15)
Exploring the Score

➤ The clever construction of this piece is readily revealed when the student plays a skeleton of only the two notes that fall on beats one and two in each measure.
  – mm. 1-2 outline 5ths
  – mm. 3-4 are descending 3rds divided between the hands
The plan is sometimes reversed and slightly altered, but this skeletal reading approach allows the student full participation in the compositional process.

➤ Help the student determine the plan for playing the scales. [the beginning hand plays four tones, the answering hand plays five tones]
➤ What interval is used for the grace notes? [always a half step below the main tone]
➤ The grace notes are always how far below the main note? [half step]
➤ If necessary, review the abbreviations *m.s. (mano sinistra* – left hand) and *m.d. (mano destra* – right hand)

Practice Suggestions

➤ Each day, practice the outline of the piece by playing only the two "beat notes" in each measure.
➤ As you practice the grace notes, play them *with* their main tone. Later you can play them slightly before the main tone.
➤ Make up a story for this piece. What is the mouse doing? Is there a cat in your story?

CREATIVE ACTIVITY

Using the same musical elements in *Little Mouse* (running 16ths, grace notes, *staccatos,* etc.) make up your own piece about a mouse and a cat. You can even rearrange the order of the sections or invert them to get a different sound.

Title: *Cat and Mouse*

STUDY MODULE 7

Page	List	Composer	Title	Key, Meter and Tempo
R12 SW20	A	Wolfgang Amadeus Mozart	*Minuet in F Major, K 2*	F Major $\frac{3}{4}$ Allegretto
R15 SW26	B	Alexandr T. Grechaninov	*Fairy Tale, op. 98, no. 1*	E Minor $\frac{4}{4}$ Moderato
R33 SW62	B	Alexander Gedike	*A Happy Tale, op. 36, no. 31*	C Major $\frac{2}{4}$ Allegro
R34 SW64	C	David Duke, arr.	*She's Like the Swallow*	D Dorian $\frac{3}{4}$ Allegro
S10		Vladimir Ivanovich Rebikov	*The Bear*	Whole tone $\frac{2}{4}$ Allegretto

Assign first:

Minuet in F Major
A Happy Tale . . . .
The Bear . . . .

Assign next when ready:

Fairy Tale
She's Like the Swallow

The pieces in this module are rich in tonal diversity. *Minuet in F Major* and *A Happy Tale* use major keys to express their light, joyful character. *Fairy Tale* alternates between G major and the surprise cadences on a B major chord. *She's Like the Swallow* is in the Dorian mode and Rebikov used a whole-tone scale when he wrote *The Bear*. Compare and contrast the sounds of these pieces as you discuss major, minor, modes, and whole-tone scales.

Wolfgang Amadeus Mozart
Minuet in F Major, K 2 (R12, SW20)

Exploring the Score

TIP: All dance music makes the downbeat clear to the dancers.

➤ Notice Mozart's downbeat rhythm for most of the piece. These eighth notes announce the downbeat and move the music forward.
➤ Why does Mozart occasionally write ♩ ♩ ? Where does that rhythm occur in the phrase? [At the end of each phrase. The half note is a focal "wrong" or "leaning" note *(appoggiatura)* which resolves into the last note of the measure.] Students readily feel the *appoggiatura*–resolution if they are asked to bow deeply *(appoggiatura)* and straighten up *(resolution)*.
➤ Create a choreography for the *Minuet in F Major:* three measures can have the same step or turn, and the fourth measure can "bow–lift." The student readily learns that the phrase lengths and rhythmic patterns are the same for each phrase.
➤ The most difficult aspect of this piece is the variety of chord shapes and positions in the

eighth-note measures. Try this approach to blocking those harmonies.
Practice in three-measure groups:
  – Play the downbeat tone.
  – Add the next two notes to create the triad.
  – If possible, name the triad and write its name in the score. Also, circle the notes that are played on black keys.
➤ Find the "surprise" chord. [m. 20 – deceptive cadence]
➤ How can you emphasize this musical surprise? [ease into the cadence; observe the *fermata*]

Practice Suggestions

➤ The RH broken chords require special practice. Use the plan outlined above to find the chords.
➤ After covering the chord, release the chord and play the single tone of beat three with the fingering shown. This fingering helps you find the next chord.
➤ Devise your own practice plan for playing blocked chords with the LH.
➤ When you are comfortable with the chords and changes of position, play as written.

Alexander Gedike
A Happy Tale (R33, SW62)
Exploring the Score

The rhythm of this piece is dominated by one motive:

➢ How many times do you see this motive? Notice that the motive is the "kick off" to each four-measure phrase.
➢ Bracket the RH melody in mm. 1-2. Find other measures which have this same pattern. Which two lines are exactly the same? [lines 1 and 3]
➢ The form of the piece could be shown as A A1 A B.

Practice Suggestions

➢ Practice the RH alone in four-measure units. Use a light *staccato* touch on the eighth notes and a *legato* touch for the sixteenths as you shape each phrase.
➢ In the LH, most measures start with a rest. What is the overall rhythmic plan in this hand?

Alexandr T. Grechaninov
Fairy Tale (R15, SW26)
Exploring the Score

Compare this Russian *Fairy Tale* with Gedike's *Happy Tale*.

    – tempo
    – touch
    – mood

If you were to make up a story for each piece, how would the stories differ? Is this a happy or a sad tale?

➢ Help the student find the short–short–long arrangement of phrases in mm. 1-4 and 13-16. What a surprising ending to those phrases! [B major chord]
➢ The section starting in m. 5 is extended. There is emphasis on the D major chord (V of G) which resolves to a single tone G in m. 10, then to that surprising B major chord in m. 12.
➢ The key seems as elusive as the fairy tale. The B major chord seems to ask a question that is never resolved. We might guess that it is the V of E minor, but we'll never know, for the E minor is never stated. In this fairy tale, we are left dangling and are not so sure that they lived "happily ever-after."

Practice Suggestions

➢ Practice in four-measure sections.

➢ When playing hands together, notice the constant movement in contrary motion. Say "start, in, out, in," etc. to help direct the hand moves.
➢ Use the *tenuto* and *diminuendo* markings to help shape the phrases.
➢ The *rallentando* and *fermata* in mm. 15-16 are clues to the musical story. How does the story end for this fairy tale?

David Duke, arr.
She's Like the Swallow (R34, SW64)
Exploring the Score

Imitation and canon have been experienced earlier in this level. To help your student *hear* the canon before playing it, try the following:
➢ The student plays the first phrase of the piece. The teacher answers by playing the same phrase.
➢ The student plays the first phrase again, and the teacher enters in canon as written by Duke.
➢ This sequence is repeated with the student doing all of the playing.
➢ Select other phrases for this activity.

The tonal center of this piece is D with no sharps or flats. This is the D Dorian mode.

Practice Suggestions

➢ Practice the long phrases hands separately.
➢ Practice this piece as a duet with your teacher or a friend, alternating the parts.
➢ Play hands together with a unison melody.
➢ Play as written in canon style, listening for good phrasing and lifts at the ends of phrases.

CREATIVE ACTIVITY

In the key of C major, figure out the melody for *Row, Row, Row Your Boat* by ear and write it out in $\frac{6}{8}$ time. Play the tune first with your RH and then with your LH. Can you play this as a canon by starting the LH two measures later?

Title: _____

Vladimir Ivanovich Rebikov
The Bear (S10)
Exploring the Score

➢ How would you compose a piece called *The Bear*?
    – fast or slow?
    – heavy or light?
    – loud or quiet?
    – high or low?

Does Rebikov use similar ideas to yours?

➤ Notice the easy LH. A constantly repeated pattern is called an *ostinato*.
➤ Label the ABA sections of the piece. [B = double notes in the RH, mm. 11-18] ABA form is called *ternary* because of its three parts.
➤ Make a list of all notes played in the RH and arrange them alphabetically. Play them as if they were a scale. Do you find any half steps in your "scale"? [no] Are they all whole steps? [yes] Use the term *whole tone* to describe the key of the piece. Spell the whole-tone scale used in this piece. [F G A B C sharp D sharp]

Practice Suggestions

➤ Since the LH has been practiced sufficiently in mm. 1-2, play hands together from the first day of practice. However, before playing, check the RH whole-step position.
➤ *Pesante* means to play with a heavy, ponderous touch—like a huge bear walking slowly.
➤ How is the RH different in the second A section? [*staccatos* added]
➤ You may need to practice the RH 3rds in the B section, mm. 11-18. Use correct fingering.
➤ Memorize this piece as soon as you can. Careful— m. 4 and m. 8 are different!

CREATIVE ACTIVITY

Make up your own piece about a bear. Use an *ostinato* bass in the LH and a whole-tone scale in your RH.

Title: _____

STUDY MODULE 8

Page	List	Composer	Title	Key, Meter and Tempo
R6 SW8	A	Johann Sebastian Bach	*Minuet III in G Major*	G Major $\frac{3}{4}$ ♩ = 126-138
R18 SW31	B	Alexander Gedike	*A Sad Song*	D Minor $\frac{2}{4}$ Adagio
R22 SW40	B	Stephen Chatman	*Beaver Boogie*	C Major $\frac{2}{2}$ Boogie Beat
R28 SW52	B	Veronika Krausas	*The Alligator*	A Minor $\frac{6}{4}$ Sneakily
R40 SW77	B	Renée Christopher	*The Snake*	D Minor $\frac{4}{4}$ ♩ = 120-132
S16		Leon Aubry	*Woodland Scene*	G Major $\frac{2}{4}$ Moderato

Assign first:

Minuet III in G Major
A Sad Song . . . .
Beaver Boogie . . . .
Woodland Scene

Assign next when ready:

The Alligator
The Snake

The pieces in Study Module 8 are the most difficult. *Minuet III in G Major* and *Woodland Scene* are two-voice contrapuntal pieces with challenging articulations and phrasing. In *The Alligator* and *The Snake,* the student must interpret a musical picture while dealing with a variety of articulations and musical elements. *Beaver Boogie* offers the challenge of a moving boogie bass line against a jazzy RH melody.

Johann Sebastian Bach
Minuet III in G Major (R6, SW8)
Exploring the Score

Does this minuet share some of the rhythmic or
melodic characteristics of other minuets in this level?
➢ Check the form analysis:
  Line 1: phrase a
  Line 2: phrase b (with sequence)
  Line 3: phrase c
  Line 4 : phrase b1 (phrase b varied at
        higher pitch)
  Line 5: phrase a1 varied
  Line 6: phrase b
➢ Does the term *rounded binary* apply to this piece?
  [yes]

Practice Suggestions

This piece requires the control of developed hand
independence. To achieve that end
➢ work in short practice sections (recommended: two-
  measure units)
➢ use practice steps that involve the following:
  – Tapping and counting, hands together.
  – Playing hands separately, with special focus on
    articulation. (Unmarked quarter notes are played
    detached.)
  – Playing one hand and tapping the other. Listen
    carefully to the articulations.
  – Playing hands together, slowly. Emphasize
    the "lift" of detached notes.

Alexander Gedike
A Sad Song (R18, SW31)
Exploring the Score

➢ As you play or sing the first eight measures, have the
  student draw the contour of the piece in the air. The
  first four measures soar a full octave; the answering
  four measures descend to the tonic note A.
➢ Upon hearing the second half of the piece, your
  student will quickly realize that mm. 9-18 are an
  accompanied version of the melody. Allow the
  student to hear the melody several times. You may
  wish to add words to reinforce the rhythm, or count
  as you sing or play.
➢ The obvious difficulty with this piece is the chordal
  texture and independent voice movement of mm.
  10-15. To help the student realize the independence
  of voices, have the student:
  – Play the melody, mm. 9-12, with the suggested
    fingering.
  – Play the alto part, mm. 9-12, with the LH.
  – Play the RH (soprano and alto), mm. 9-12, divided
    between the hands. Listen for full value alto notes.

– Very slowly, play the RH part, mm. 9-12, as
  written.
➢ Similar practice techniques can be used to gain
  control over the LH, mm. 9-12 and 13-14.

Practice Suggestions

There are three main practice goals for this piece:
1) accurate rhythm (special attention to mm. 5-8)
2) accurate playing of inner voice note values,
  mm. 10-15
3) quietly expressive sound throughout. Follow the
  written dynamics carefully.

➢ Practice the rhythms before playing. Can you tap and
  count each measure perfectly?
➢ You will learn to play mm. 9-18 most quickly and
  accurately if you practice hands separately. The
  special challenge is to hold notes for their full written
  value. Your teacher may have some special practice
  techniques to help you with this practice.
➢ The LH of mm. 16-17 has special phrasing detail.
  Create a slight breath at the end of each slurred
  group.
➢ Your interpretation of the piece will improve if you
  take the time to add words to the melody. Gedike
  was Russian. What words might a Russian child sing
  to this melody?

Veronika Krausas
The Alligator (R28, SW52)
Exploring the Score

➢ With score in hand, listen to the *Celebration Series®*
  recording. Have the student describe the scene
  depicted by the music.
➢ An unusual feature in this piece is the change of
  meter for every measure. Have the student circle the
  meter changes. You may wish to have the student
  write in the counts.
➢ Make special note of the measures that end with
  a rest.
➢ What descriptive effect is achieved by the changing
  meters and rests? [the stop-and-go motions of the
  alligator]
➢ Make a list of graduated dynamics from *pp* to *ff*. Can
  you find all dynamic levels on your list in this piece?

Practice Suggestions

➢ For the octaves, it will help to notice that all the
  downstem notes are played by the LH and the notes
  with upstems by the RH.
➢ Tap the rhythms of this piece on the closed keyboard
  cover.
➢ Which notes are NOT played *staccato*? [tied notes
  and notes longer than a quarter note]

- As you practice each measure, bring out the dynamic contrasts. You need control over five different dynamic levels: *pp p mf f ff*.

Stephen Chatman
Beaver Boogie (R22, SW40)

Exploring the Score

- Here's that word again—*ostinato*. In how many different positions do you find this *ostinato*? [two]
- Have the student play the LH boogie *ostinato*. Emphasize both *staccato* notes at the beginning of each measure. (Students will tend to slur beat two into beat three.)
- The student can practice mm. 3-4 on the closed keyboard cover while you observe. Urge the student to exaggerate the two *staccato* notes.
- Which notes start the RH phrases? [B flat and E flat]
- Compare RH mm. 3-4 with 7-8 and 11-12. They feel the same.
- Compare RH mm. 5-6 with 9-10 and 13-14. They descend, but are all different. That difference becomes a practice assignment.

Practice Suggestions

- As you practice the boogie bass, be careful to play two *staccato* notes in each measure. You might try saying: "off, off, slur it."
- Isolate LH mm. 5 and 6 to practice the LH cross over.
- Give the RH phrases in mm. 5, 9, and 13 special practice for fingering and thumb crossings.

CREATIVE ACTIVITY

Using the same boogie bass line and RH scale as *Beaver Boogie,* make up a new RH melody. It can be totally new or a variation, changing only one or two notes per measure.

Title: _____

Renée Christopher
The Snake (R40, SW77)

Exploring the Score

- Looking at the score, can you see the twisting and turning motion of the snake? Is there more than one snake? Notice how there are more eighth notes in the second half of the piece. What effect does this have? [more intensity, forward motion]
- As one might imagine, the snakes do not stay within a five-finger pattern. They writhe a note or two above and below the pattern. Notice how your fingerings "snake" around the black keys.

- Have you ever seen such an unusual key signature? [B flat and C sharp] Why would a composer use a key signature with a flat and a sharp? [shows the accidentals of D harmonic minor]
- Which note of the scale starts and ends the piece? [A = dominant]
- As in the other Level 1 inventions, this piece is written in imitative style. The LH imitates the RH. Check carefully for any place where the LH does not imitate the RH. [m. 8]

Practice Suggestions

- Find the three different positions in the RH.
- Find the four different positions in the LH.
- Practice the dynamics carefully. You may wish to do this hands separately, making the LH dynamic plan match the preceding plan in the RH.
- Make your *legato* as slithery as possible!

Leon Aubry
Woodland Scene (S16)

Exploring the Score

- Why is this piece included in *Piano Studies/Etudes 1*? Make a list with the student.
  - control of two-note slurs
  - *legato* melody in the RH accompanied by two-note slurs in the LH
  - subtle dynamic variation
- Perhaps your student will benefit from "shadow playing" of these technical challenges.
  - Practice a two-note "drop–lift" on a flat surface.
  - Also on a flat surface, "practice" mm. 3-4 very slowly. The RH plays *legato* and the LH plays an independent "drop–lift."
- Have the student point out all markings in the score indicating a change of sound (including *rit … a tempo*).
- What is the form of this piece? [ABA]
- Can the A section be played in one position? Name that position [G major]
- Can the B section be played in one position?
- What changes does your student find in the B section?

Practice Suggestions

- To prepare for the dynamic levels and changing rhythms of the piece, practice a G major five-finger pattern, hands together up and down, in these ways:
  mf
  mp
  with a *diminuendo*
  with a *crescendo*
  with a *ritardando*

➤ Review the "drop–lift" gesture for the two-note slurs before playing the piece, and "shadow practice" mm. 3-4 and mm. 9-12 on a flat surface for control of RH *legato* and LH two-note slurs.

➤ Play the piece in four-measure units, slowly at first.

CREATIVE ACTIVITY

In *Woodland Scene,* Aubry paints a musical picture. Compose your own piece about animals in a forest and give it a title. Use a G major five-finger pattern and two-note slurs. The music could portray rabbits, deer, or an owl on a moonlit night.

Title: _____

Level 1 SUMMARY

➤ Who were your favorite composers in Level 1?

➤ Which pieces were most challenging technically? What practice techniques did you use to master these technical challenges? Did you use warm-up exercises for any of the pieces?

➤ Which pieces posed rhythmic difficulties? How did you practice the rhythm?

➤ What special practice steps did you use to learn the inventions? How are inventions different from pieces in List A and List B?

➤ What were your favorite "animal" pieces or pieces which could tell a story?

Level 2

The Publications
Level 2 of the *Celebration Series®* includes the following publications:
- *Piano Repertoire 2*
- *Piano Studies/Etudes 2*
- *Student Workbook 2*
- *Recording of Repertoire 2* and *Studies/Etudes 2*

The Repertoire
Piano Repertoire 2 is divided into three sections or lists.
- ➤ List A includes a selection of pieces composed during the Baroque period (*ca* 1600 to *ca* 1750) and the Classical period (*ca* 1750 to *ca* 1820).
- ➤ List B includes a selection of pieces composed during the Romantic era (*ca* 1820 to *ca* 1910) and the twentieth century.
- ➤ List C consists of Inventions, short two-voice compositions written in an imitative style.

Musical Development
Level 2 offers the student a wide range of styles from the late elementary and early intermediate teaching literature. Many of the pieces emphasize two-voice textures in binary or rounded binary form. In most cases, practicing hands separately will be helpful. The repertoire and studies in Level 2 concentrate on:
- balance between melody and accompaniment
- independence of voices
- *legato* and *staccato* articulations
- two- and three-voice textures, both imitative and homophonic
- expressive nuances
- use of the damper pedal
- dance forms from various style periods
- traditional, impressionistic, and contemporary sounds

This level also includes thicker textures using various types of chord figurations. Practicing chords presents opportunities for teaching related skills and musical concepts such as:
- playing triads in inversions
- playing basic cadence patterns
- identifying and labeling each chord

The practice suggestions found in the *Student Workbook* and in the following Study Module discussions will help the student gain control over the various challenges. During the study of Level 2, have the student practice five-finger patterns or scales in conjunction with the key of each piece.

Dance Chart
Many of the pieces in *Piano Repertoire 2* are dances. Encourage students to keep a Dance Chart, adding each new dance they learn. For each dance, list the title, the meter, and the rhythmic characteristics. Here is a list of the dances in Level 2:
- bourrée
- écossaise
- mazurka
- minuet
- quadrille
- waltz

The Study Modules
The six Study Module discussions are organized into the following categories:
- *Exploring the Score*
- *Practice Suggestions*
- *Creative Activities*

Exploring the Score is designed as an interactive exercise between teacher and student. Some questions are addressed to the student, as you might ask them during the lesson. *Practice Suggestions* are directed to the student. The *Creative Activities* act as reinforcement for your students' understanding of a musical concept and can provide a springboard for their creativity and imagination. Please refer to the *Foreword* for an explanation of how to use the *Assign first ... Assign next when ready* listing under each module chart.

Musical Tips
As students work through this Level, they will accumulate knowledge about musical style that they can apply to other pieces they study. These musical "Rules of Thumb" are identified in the discussions as **TIP:** Encourage your students to notate these points, and add to the list as they progress from level to level.

The chart below lists the repertoire and studies in Level 2. Page numbers for works in *Piano Repertoire 2* and *Piano Studies/Etudes 2* are found in the first column. Study Module numbers are found to the far right. Study Module groupings of repertoire and studies follow.

Piano Repertoire 2

	Page	Composer	Title	Study Module
List A	R4	Anon.	*Bourrée in D Minor*	6
	R5	Jean-Philippe Rameau	*Menuet en rondeau/Minuet in Rondo Form*	1
	R6	George Frideric Handel	*Impertinence, HWV 494*	4
	R7	Domenico Scarlatti	*Minuet in C Major*	2
	R8	Franz Joseph Haydn	*Quadrille*	5
	R10	Christian Gottlob Neefe	*Allegretto in C Major*	3
	R11	Daniel Gottlob Türk	*Contentment*	2
	R12	Wolfgang Amadeus Mozart	*Menuetto in C Major*	1
	R13	Franz Schubert	*Écossaise, D299, no. 8*	5
List B	R14	Robert Schumann	*Melody, op. 68, no. 1*	4
	R15	Alexander Gedike	*Military Trumpets, op. 36, no. 53*	4
	R16	Béla Bartók	*Children at Play*	5
	R17	Isak Berkovich	*Mazurka*	5
	R18	Aram Khachaturian	*An Evening Tale*	6
	R20	Boris Berlin	*March of the Goblins*	1
	R21	Dmitri Kabalevsky	*A Little Song, op. 27, no. 2*	3
	R22	Joan Last	*Sailing by Moonlight*	4
	R24	Charles Peerson	*The Mouse in the Coal Bin*	2
	R26	István Szelényi	*Faraway Regions*	6
	R27	Joanne Bender	*Inuit Lullaby*	2
	R28	Linda Niamath	*Penguins*	6
	R29	Christopher Norton	*Chant*	2
	R30	Chee-Hwa Tan	*The Land of Nod*	3
	R32	Janina Garścia	*The Clock*	1
	R33	Nancy Telfer	*Crocodile Teeth*	3
	R34	Nancy Telfer, arr.	*A Sioux Lullaby*	1
List C	R36	Béla Bartók	*Little Dance in Canon Form*	2
	R37	Alexander Gedike	*Fugato, op. 36, no. 40*	3
	R38	Gordon A. McKinnon	*The Argument*	6
	R39	Carleton Elliott	*Canon*	4
	R39	Pierre Gallant	*Jazz Invention No. 1*	5
	R40	Pierre Gallant	*Jazz Invention No. 2*	1
	R40	Cornelius Gurlitt	*Canon*	1

Piano Studies/Etudes 2

Page	Composer	Title	Study Module
S4	Alexander Gedike	*Study in G Major*	4
S5	Henri Bertini	*Study in G Major, op. 166, no. 6*	5
S6	Pál Kadosa	*Study in A Minor*	3
S7	Carl Czerny	*Study in C Major, op. 261, no. 3*	2
S8	Isak Berkovich	*Study in C Major*	1
S9	Veronika Krausas	*Kangaroos*	6
S10	Joan Hansen	*Irish Jig*	3
S11	Linda Niamath	*Butterflies*	3
S12	Aram Khachaturian	*Skipping Rope*	5
S13	Chee-Hwa Tan	*The Wind*	2
S14	Stella Goud	*Moon through the Window*	6
S15	Christopher Norton	*Tram Stop*	4

Level 2 Repertoire and Studies/Etudes – Listed by Study Module

Study Module 1

List	Composer	Title	Page & Book
A	Jean-Philippe Rameau	*Menuet en rondeau/Minuet in Rondo Form*	R5, SW6
A	Wolfgang Amadeus Mozart	*Minuetto in C Major*	R12, SW23
B	Boris Berlin	*March of the Goblins*	R20, SW41
B	Janina Garścia	*The Clock*	R32, SW62
B	Nancy Telfer, arr.	*A Sioux Lullaby*	R34, SW66
C	Pierre Gallant	*Jazz Invention No. 2*	R40, SW75
C	Cornelius Gurlitt	*Canon*	R40, SW77
Study	Isak Berkovich	*Study in C Major*	S8

Study Module 2

List	Composer	Title	Page & Book
A	Domenico Scarlatti	*Minuet in C Major*	R7, SW12
A	Daniel Gottlob Türk	*Contentment*	R11, SW20
B	Charles Peerson	*The Mouse in the Coal Bin*	R24, SW49
B	Joanne Bender	*Inuit Lullaby*	R27, SW54
B	Christopher Norton	*Chant*	R29, SW58
C	Béla Bartok	*Little Dance in Canon Form*	R36, SW68
Study	Carl Czerny	*Study in C Major, op. 261, no. 3*	S7
Study	Chee-Hwa Tan	*The Wind*	S13

Study Module 3

List	Composer	Title	Page & Book
A	Christian Gottlob Neefe	*Allegretto in C Major*	R10, SW17
B	Dmitri Kabalevsky	*A Little Song, op. 27, no. 2*	R21, SW43
B	Chee-Hwa Tan	*The Land of Nod*	R30, SW60
B	Nancy Telfer	*Crocodile Teeth*	R33, SW64
C	Alexander Gedike	*Fugato, op. 36, no. 40*	R37, SW70
Study	Pál Kadosa	*Study in A Minor*	S6
Study	Joan Hansen	*Irish Jig*	S10
Study	Linda Niamath	*Butterflies*	S11

Study Module 4

List	Composer	Title	Page & Book
A	George Frideric Handel	*Impertinence, HWV 494*	R6, SW9
B	Robert Schumann	*Melody, op. 68, no. 1*	R14, SW29
B	Alexander Gedike	*Military Trumpets*	R15, SW31
B	Joan Last	*Sailing by Moonlight*	R22, SW46
C	Carleton Elliott	*Canon*	R39, SW72
Study	Alexander Gedike	*Study in G Major*	S4
Study	Christopher Norton	*Tram Stop*	S15

Study Module 5

List	Composer	Title	Page & Book
A	Franz Joseph Haydn	*Quadrille*	R8, SW15
A	Franz Schubert	*Écossaise, D299, no. 8*	R13, SW26
B	Béla Bartók	*Children at Play*	R16, SW34
B	Isak Berkovich	*Mazurka*	R17, SW37
C	Pierre Gallant	*Jazz Invention No. 1*	R39, SW73
Study	Henri Bertini	*Study in G Major, op. 166, no. 6*	S5
Study	Aram Khachaturian	*Skipping Rope*	S12

Study Module 6

List	Composer	Title	Page & Book
A	Anon.	*Bourrée in D Minor*	R4, SW4
B	Aram Khachaturian	*An Evening Tale*	R18, SW39
B	István Szelényi	*Faraway Regions*	R26, SW52
B	Linda Niamath	*Penguins*	R28, SW56
C	Gordon A. MacKinnon	*The Argument*	R38, SW71
Study	Veronika Krausas	*Kangaroos*	S9
Study	Stella Goud	*Moon through the Window*	S14

STUDY MODULE 1

Page	List	Composer	Title	Key, Meter and Tempo
R5 SW6	A	Jean-Philippe Rameau	*Menuet en rondeau/* *Minuet in Rondo Form*	C Major $\frac{3}{4}$ ♩ = 120-132
R12 SW23	A	Wolfgang Amadeus Mozart	*Menuetto in C Major*	C Major $\frac{3}{4}$ ♩ = 116-126
R20 SW41	B	Boris Berlin	*March of the Goblins*	A Minor $\frac{6}{8}$ In march time
R32 SW62	B	Janina Garścia	*The Clock*	E Minor $\frac{2}{4}$ Allegretto
R34 SW66	B	Nancy Telfer, arr.	*A Sioux Lullaby*	Pentatonic changing meter Very slowly, freely
R40 SW75	C	Pierre Gallant	*Jazz Invention No. 2*	C Major $\frac{4}{4}$ ♩ = 84-96
R40 SW77	C	Cornelius Gurlitt	*Canon*	A Minor $\frac{4}{4}$ Allegretto
S8		Isak Berkovich	*Study in C Major*	C Major $\frac{2}{4}$ Vivo

Assign first:

Menuet en rondeau . . . .
March of the Goblins . . . .
Canon . . . .
A Sioux Lullaby . . . .

Assign next when ready:

Menuetto in C Major
Study in C Major
Jazz Invention No. 2
The Clock

Use the pieces in this module for comparison. Four pieces are in C major; two pieces are in A minor. Three pieces use *ostinato* bass lines. *A Sioux Lullaby* is played only on black keys (pentatonic) and *Jazz Invention* uses a blue note. These elements provide many ideas for discussion and exploration.

Jean-Philippe Rameau
Menuet en rondeau / Minuet in Rondo Form
(R5, SW6)

Exploring the Score

The minuet is a graceful dance with a six-beat dance step sequence.

➤ Label the form. [ABA] The first four measures of the A section can be considered the Question, and mm. 5-8 as the (parallel) Answer.

TIP: Composers often write phrases in balanced pairs. The first phrase (or Question) usually ends on a note other than the keynote. The second phrase (Answer) usually ends on the keynote. A parallel Answer starts the same as the Question. A contrasting Answer starts differently from the Question.

➤ Does the B section have a similar phrase plan?
➤ Divide the A section into four-measure units. In the LH, notice the steady walking rhythm (quarter notes) of the first two measures and the tapping and turning rhythm (half note + quarter) of the next two measures.
➤ Compare the LH rhythm of the next four-measure unit. Did you notice that the rhythmic plan is reversed?
➤ How is this rhythmic plan reflected in the B section?
➤ What is the key of the B section? [G major, V]
➤ Circle the downbeat note of each measure to find the skeletal stepwise motion of the melody.
➤ You may wish to create your own minuet dance steps as you listen and dance to the *Celebration Series®* recording.

Celebration Series® Handbook for Teachers

Practice Suggestions

Practice in two- or four-measure units.

You may want to practice hands separately. Practice the RH *legato* and LH detached before playing hands together.

TIP: It was stylistically correct in Rameau's time to play eighth-note groups with an unequal rhythm, a slight "bending" of the eighths.

➤ Try playing the melody eighth notes in that "bent rhythm" style, as is common in jazz and blues.

Wolfgang Amadeus Mozart
Minuetto in C Major (R12, SW23)
Exploring the Score

Discuss the characteristics of a minuet you find in this piece.
- meter
- pairs of measures
- moderate tempo, clearly defined rhythm

➤ What is the function of the many two-note slurs? [elegant dance quality; dynamic shading]
➤ Compare the LH of mm. 1-4 with mm. 5-8. How does the music change when the LH moves in constant quarter notes? [the phrase is continuous and moves to the cadence in the final measure]
➤ Compare *Menuetto in C Major* with Rameau's *Minuet in Rondo Form* (R5).
- key?
- form?
- six-beat dance step?
- B section in G major? [dominant]
- skeletal step motion in the melody?

TIP: Composers of the Classical period used the *appoggiatura* to create special expression. An *appoggiatura* is a "leaning note," a non-chord tone, played on the downbeat. It resolves up or down a step.

➤ Circle the downbeat *appoggiaturas* in mm. 2, 4, 8, 10, 12, 16 and listen to their tension resolve.
➤ Mozart cleverly places the *appoggiaturas* at the ends of phrases. The resulting phrase plan is: 2mm. + 2mm. + 4mm.

TIP: The short-short-long phrase structure is an important element in early Classical music.

Practice Suggestions

➤ Use the following "practice groups" either hands alone or hands together:

Practice Groups: mm. 1-2, 3-4, 5-8, 9-10, 11-12, 13-16

➤ Pay careful attention to the two-note slurs and *appoggiaturas,* practicing with a "down-up" or drop-lift motion.

Boris Berlin
March of the Goblins (R20, SW41)
Exploring the Score

Let the title of this piece be a guide for your exploration. How does Berlin create the "spooky" mood?

➤ The LH *ostinato* in this piece creates an effective march quality. This is a fine opportunity to introduce the term and engage in a bit of improvisation. The student can play Berlin's LH *ostinato* while the teacher improvises an A minor march tune.
➤ Dynamics are an integral part of this piece. Have the student circle the softest and loudest dynamic markings.

Practice Suggestions

➤ Warm up by playing the A minor five-finger pattern hands together in these different ways:
- *legato*
- *staccato*
- RH *legato*, LH *staccato*; then reversed
- using Berlin's "goblin march" rhythm and touch (see mm. 6-7)
- LH playing the *ostinato*; RH playing the "goblin march" rhythm
➤ Spot practice the double notes in mm. 15-16.

CREATIVE ACTIVITY

Using Berlin's *ostinato* for the march rhythm, make up your own RH. Try using some black keys for a special surprise. Play higher or lower on the keyboard if you like.

Title: *My Goblins March*

Janina Garścia
The Clock (R32, SW62)
Exploring the Score

➤ Have the student find the chime in the piece. What time is it?
➤ What other features of the piece help it sound mechanical? [LH steady tick-tock]
➤ Think of the RH melody as being the tune coming from a musical clock. The mechanism is not in good working order, for the tune starts and stops, and is interrupted by the chimes.

Practice Suggestions

➤ What fingers will you use to play the best "mechanical" tick-tocks?

➤ In mm. 9-12, explore an alternative fingering: play the entire chime (A sharp, D, E, G) with RH 1 2 3 5.

➤ There are some tricky rhythms in the RH, but you have your LH tick-tock to guide you.

Nancy Telfer, arr.
A Sioux Lullaby (R34, SW66)
Exploring the Score

Imagine an Indian village. A mother quietly sings as she rocks her baby to sleep. Here the student has an opportunity to explore music from another culture, in which rhythm is freely conceived and melody and harmony exist outside our world of major and minor.

➤ Students quickly discover an important learning clue as they examine the key signature and notes of the first line. [the piece is *pentatonic*—played only on black keys]

➤ Discuss the rhythm. In line 1, there is no time signature. With the damper pedal down, explore different ways of playing the line. Choose the one that best expresses the lullaby mood of the piece.
 – Circle meter signatures that occur in mm. 2, 4, and 8.
 – Circle the different pairs of notes that comprise the LH *ostinato*.

Practice Suggestions

➤ As you begin practicing, count the RH in a different way by counting the number of beats in an entire phrase. You will find some phrases with six beats, some with five, and none with four! This will help you sense the flow of the phrase and the asymmetric rhythm.

➤ Notice the damper pedal marking. Where is the first lift? [m. 14!] Listen for accurate pedal changes as you play.

Creative Activity

Use only black keys to create your own piece. Play a gently swinging RH melody using the group of three black notes. Your LH *ostinato* can be made from any two black keys.

Title: *Oriental Lullaby*

Pierre Gallant
Jazz Invention No. 2 (R40, SW75)
Exploring the Score

➤ The LH has three positions, built on C, F, and G (I, IV, V). Label these positions in the score.

➤ In jazz, composers often use a lowered 3rd or 7th to create the blues or jazz sound. In the C position, a "blue" note would be E flat. What is an enharmonic name for this note? [D sharp] What are the "blue" notes for the F and G positions?

Practice Suggestions

➤ Take a lesson from old Mr. Rameau (*Menuet en roudeau*, R5) and "bend" the eighth-note rhythms to make a "bluesy" long-short relation. "Swing" the eighth notes by saying "doo-bah, doo-bah".

➤ After you have mastered the opening eighth-note figure, tap and count the rhythm hands together.

➤ In each measure, the fingering of the first four eighth notes deserves special attention. Say these fingerings aloud as you play. (How many times will you say *3 2 1 4*?)

Cornelius Gurlitt
Canon (R40, SW77)
Exploring the Score

The primary goal in playing a canon is to hear both parts simultaneously. This goal is facilitated when the student sings the tune:

➤ Sing the melody with the student. Can the student sing the scale degrees or the *solfege* syllables?

➤ Sing the melody with the student and play the imitative LH.

What is the relationship of E major to A minor? [dominant to tonic]

➤ Have the student block the RH changes of position. Each measure has a shift.

➤ Once the student is comfortable with the RH shifts, play as a duet.
 – At first, play in unison with the student. Then add the imitation very quietly.

Isak Berkovich
Study in C Major (S8)
Exploring the Score

This lively study in C major uses three-note slurs and *staccato* to provide energy and movement. Have the student find measures and lines that are alike:

➤ Compare lines 1 and 2. How are they the same or different?

➤ Can you find two lines that are exactly the same?

➤ Where does the piece change to G major?

➤ Label the form. [AA'BA'].

Practice Suggestions

➤ The three-note figure is played most easily when

the fingers are close to the keys and the hand does a slight left-to-right rotation.

➤ Warm up by playing three-note slurs in each hand in the C major five-finger position as follows, using

a drop-roll-lift gesture to help shape the slurs:
- RH thumb on C. Play: 1 2-3; 2-3-4; 3-4-5; 5-4-3, 4-3-2; 3 2-1
- LH thumb on G. Play the fingerings above.

STUDY MODULE 2

Page	List	Composer	Title	Key, Meter and Tempo
R7 SW12	A	Domenico Scarlatti	*Minuet in C Major*	C Major $\frac{3}{8}$ ♪ = 120-132
R11 SW20	A	Daniel Gottlob Türk	*Contentment*	A Minor $\frac{2}{4}$ Andante tranquillamente
R24 SW49	B	Charles Peerson	*The Mouse in the Coal Bin*	G Minor $\frac{4}{4}$ ♩ = 126-138
R27 SW54	B	Joanne Bender	*Inuit Lullaby*	D Minor $\frac{3}{4}$ Andante espressivo
R29 SW58	B	Christopher Norton	*Chant*	C Major $\frac{4}{4}$ Dynamically
R36 SW68	C	Béla Bartók	*Little Dance in Canon Form*	D Dorian $\frac{4}{4}$ Allegro
S7		Carl Czerny	*Study in C Major, op. 261, no. 3*	C Major $\frac{3}{8}$ Allegro
S13		Chee-Hwa Tan	*The Wind*	A Minor $\frac{4}{4}$ Windily, in a gusting manner

Assign first:

Minuet in C Major . . . .
Inuit Lullaby . . . .
The Wind . . . .
Little Dance in Canon Form . . . .

Assign next when ready:

Contentment
Chant
The Mouse in the Coal Bin
Study in C Major

The pieces in this module describe an activity or scene. There are "singing" pieces, dances (even *Study in C Major* is a waltz), descriptions of nature and animals, and a "mood" piece. The variety of keys includes major, minor, and the Dorian mode and provides opportunities to explore these sonorities.

Domenico Scarlatti
Minuet in C Major (R7, SW12)

Exploring the Score

Predictability is comforting. However, predictability creates the possibility of change and musical surprise. *Minuet in C Major* has nineteen presentations of the basic rhythmic motive. The measures without that motive are easy to find. A more intriguing exploration is to discover how Scarlatti varies the motive.

➤ Compare mm. 1 and 2: skips vs. steps. Mm. 3-4 and 5-6 present the same idea.

➤ Circle the RH downbeats of mm. 1, 3, 5, 7. What plan do you find?

➤ In what ways do mm. 8 and 9 represent contrast? [m. 8 is not in steps; m. 9 "should" start on F to continue the sequence, and is not the same chord shape]

➤ Once Scarlatti breaks the sequence, things are never the same. Find the great variety of shapes and harmonies given to the basic rhythmic motive in the B section. This is truly the writing of a great composer.

➤ Circle the trills. What is their function? [to give special attention to final notes]

➤ Working in two-measure units, block the RH measures that feature the recurring rhythmic motive. Later, add the LH to this practice step.

➤ Play the RH three-note slurs with a *drop-roll-lift* gesture. Create an elegant sound without accent.

➤ The LH contributes its own elegance to this *Minuet* if there is a slight breath between measures.

➤ Mm. 11, 19, and 27 lead to a final resting place. They should be practiced with a *crescendo*.

Daniel Gottlob Türk
Contentment (R11, SW20)
Exploring the Score

What musical elements create the sound of contentment?

➤ Predictability and balance may not have been on your list. Examine the first four measures for the balance created by the short-short-long phrase structure. Does this plan reoccur? [in every line]

➤ How does the B section provide contrast? [dynamics, melody is inverted]

➤ Try playing this piece first as a student/teacher duet to experience phrasing and dynamic differences in each line.

Practice Suggestions

➤ Playing a beautiful *legato* sound is your main goal. Each two-note figure has a special beauty and tenderness. Create a breath between slurred groups.

➤ The "sighs" in mm. 4 and 12 receive special emphasis. Listen for a difference in the sound of the two notes: lean into the first, then gently release the second as your wrist rises.

Charles Peerson
The Mouse in the Coal Bin (R24, SW49)
Exploring the Score

Picture a small mouse exploring and playing in a coal bin. Can you see it walking quietly, sneaking around, climbing on top of the coal, running down and scampering around? How do the following musical events influence your story?

   – the opening *staccatos*

   – the tumbling pairs of eighth notes

   – the quiet middle section

➤ As you discuss the different ideas in the piece, encourage the student to memorize the figures.

➤ Which sections are played in a strict, steady tempo? Which get faster? slower?

➤ In m. 10, what is the meaning of *m.d.* and *m.s.*? [*m.d.* = *mano destra* (RH); *m.s.* = *mano sinistra* (LH)]

➤ This piece is in the key of G minor. First play the G natural minor scale with two flats and then play the G harmonic minor scale by raising the 7th tone to F sharp. Which form of the G minor scale is used in this piece?

➤ How does the B section (mm. 15-27) contrast with the A section? What do you think the mouse is doing?

Practice Suggestions

➤ Practice mm. 11-12 on a flat surface. Make your taps very even. Pretend you are at the keyboard. Play the notes exactly where you feel they would be on the keys.

➤ Play mm. 1-2 and listen for the mouse sneaking around. How much *staccato* and *tenuto* is just right?

➤ Memorize mm. 5-6 and 11-12. Look for black and white key patterns.

CREATIVE ACTIVITY

Make up a piece about a cat and a mouse. Use some of the ideas from Peerson's piece for the chase, for a "sneaky" sound, and even a peace treaty between the two.

Title: *Cat and Mouse*

Joanne Bender
Inuit Lullaby (R27, SW54)
Exploring the Score

In Study Module 1, the student played another folk lullaby: Nancy Telfer's *A Sioux Lullaby* (R34). Each of these pieces creates a special atmosphere of comfort and peace.

➤ Compare the pieces, and discuss what makes each piece a unique experience for performer and listener.

➤ Sing the first three measures with the student until it is memorized. Look for further appearances of that melody. [mm. 7, 13, and a hint in m. 18]

➤ Discuss the prominent use of 5ths in both melody and accompaniment.

➤ Groups of six eighth notes can be divided $2 + 2 + 2$ ($\frac{3}{4}$) or $3 + 3$ ($\frac{6}{8}$). When composers use both types of eighth-note groupings in the same piece it is called *hemiola*. Much of this piece is written in a normal $\frac{3}{4}$. Find where the eighths are grouped $3 + 3$.

➤ The "magic" of the piece lies in the shaping of the melodic line. Each phrase will have its own dynamic plan. If the melody is to imitate song, generous breaths must be taken between phrases.

➤ Practice the RH melody in mm. 1-3 with both hands, playing the LH one octave lower than the right. Listen to the shape of the melody. Take a musical breath at the end of each slurred group.

➤ Tap the RH rhythm in mm. 5-6, counting aloud: *1&2&3&.* This is clearly $\frac{3}{4}$. Tap it again with the LH dotted quarters, counting the eighths *1 2 3 1 2 3.* You now feel the eighth notes grouped in two beats. (*Hemiola!*)

Christopher Norton
Chant (R29, SW58)

Exploring the Score

Rhythm and touch are the primary focus of this jazzy piece.

➤ Tap and count the rhythm of mm. 1-2. Bracket each occurrence of this rhythmic pattern. [mm. 1-2, 3-4, 5-6, 12-13, 16-17, 18-19]

➤ What is the surprise in m. 8? [the first incomplete pattern]

➤ Compare mm. 1-4 with mm. 9-11. In mm.1-4 you feel C as the tonal center. In mm. 9-11 the music shifts to an F tonal center.

➤ Is there any note of the piece not marked with a *staccato,* slur, accent, or *tenuto?*

Practice Suggestions

➤ Tap and count the piece with great energy. Feel the *staccatos* and accents as you tap.

➤ Isolate mm. 9, 11, 13, and 19 for rhythmic and fingering practice.

Béla Bartók
Little Dance in Canon Form (R36, SW68)

Exploring the Score

If your student is not familiar with the term, explain *canon.* Demonstrate the canon of this piece by playing the LH while the student plays the RH.

– play several phrases in unison
– play as a canon, one hand following the other

➤ Bartók places accents on the downbeat of (almost) every measure. Which measures have no downbeat accent? Which measures have the accents on beat 3? Do the accents give the music a dance-like quality?

➤ To establish the tonality of the piece, you may wish to play the D Dorian scale (white keys D to D).

➤ Tapping the rhythm of each hand is a great way to practice a canon. The rhythms are easy. Make your accents in each hand outstanding as you tap hands together. (**Careful:** The accents may be in one hand and not the other!)

➤ "Shadow play" four-measure units on a flat surface. Lift the finger high to make the accents. Lift the hand to create the breath between phrases.

Carl Czerny
Study in C Major, op. 261, no. 3 (S7)

Exploring the Score

➤ At the top of the student's score, make a list of the reasons why Czerny wrote this piece. (How many different technical figures do you find? Did you include the LH held downbeats? Did you mention the waltz?)

➤ Label the A section (mm. 1-8) and B section (mm. 9-16).

➤ Compare lines 1 and 3. Are they the same or different? Careful! Don't let the *8va* sign mislead you.

➤ Block the LH and label the I, IV, and V7 chords.

Practice Suggestions

➤ Before practicing, bracket the finger groups of the scale, mm. 13-14. What is unusual about this fingering? [no groups of 3-2-1] Then:

➤ Practice the LH waltz bass. Why are there two middle C's?

➤ Although there are three different shapes to the sixteenth-note measures, they have a similar dynamic plan: the last note is lifted off quietly. In your practice of those measures:

– play *legato*
– play the final note quieter
– lift at the end of each slur

CREATIVE ACTIVITY

Using the same LH waltz bass, create your own melody. Let the LH chords help guide your RH position and melody.

Title: *Waltzing with Mr. Czerny*

Chee-Hwa Tan
The Wind (S13)
Exploring the Score

Set the mood by first reading the poem. The wind is whirling and swirling, up and down, softer and louder, and finally gusting away in a furious rush!

➤ The goal of this piece is to play "fast like the wind." If the student becomes familiar with the position shifts, that goal is easily attainable.
  – Find the position for mm. 1-4. Where does this position reappear? (Did you include mm. 15 and 17?)
  – Block and name the chords in mm. 5-11.
➤ Circle the time signatures changes.

Practice Suggestions

➤ The most efficient way to learn this piece is to focus on the many shifts of position. Block all positions and practice moving from one position to the next throughout the entire piece.
➤ Set a steady beat. Move from one position to the next, *one beat per position.*
➤ In mm. 5-9, circle the repeated fifth fingers. (If needed, write 5 - 5 in the score.) Practice making these jumps quickly. They are a key to success.
➤ The composer has wisely marked the pedal to give the greatest effect of the blowing wind. Observe her markings very carefully. Listen for clean and complete pedal changes.

STUDY MODULE 3

Page	List	Composer	Title	Key, Meter and Tempo
R10 SW17	A	Christian Gottlob Neefe	*Allegretto in C Major*	C Major $\frac{2}{4}$ ♩ = 84-100
R21 SW43	B	Dmitri Kabalevsky	*A Little Song, op. 27, no. 2*	E Minor $\frac{4}{4}$ Andantino
R30 SW60	B	Chee-Hwa Tan	*The Land of Nod*	G Mixolydian $\frac{3}{4}$ Dreamily drowsy
R33 SW64	B	Nancy Telfer	*Crocodile Teeth*	Chromatic $\frac{4}{4}$ Not too quickly
R37 SW70	C	Alexander Gedike	*Fugato, op. 36, no. 40*	C Major $\frac{4}{4}$ Allegro energico
S6		Pál Kadosa	*Study in A Minor*	A Minor Changing meter Allegretto leggiero
S10		Joan Hansen	*Irish Jig*	G Major $\frac{6}{8}$ With spirit
S11		Linda Niamath	*Butterflies*	G flat Major $\frac{2}{4}$ Delicately

Assign first:

Allegretto in C Major . . . .
Crocodile Teeth . . . .
Study in A Minor . . . .
Butterflies . . . .

Assign next when ready:

A Little Song
The Land of Nod
Fugato
Irish Jig

One of the fascinating aspects of piano music is the variety of ways composers relate the hands. Especially in the Baroque period, the hands were often treated as equal partners, sharing the melodic flow. We see this Baroque style represented in *Fugato,* written by a Russian composer of the Romantic school. Frequently, one hand serves as accompaniment to the other, employing a different rhythm and texture. Most of these pieces are examples of that style. *Study in A Minor* has an accompaniment derived from the more active melodic hand.

Christian Gotlob Neefe
Allegretto in C Major (R10, SW17)
Exploring the Score

Imagine this delicate duet played by violin and cello, or flute and bassoon. The top voice carries the melody in refined articulations and dynamics. The bottom part outlines the phrase structure.

The notation of this piece is typical of the early Classical period and of composers writing for the newly popular fortepiano. We may find the dynamic markings extreme, but they were a display of this new instrument's ability to change dynamic levels. Think of the downbeat markings as an emphasis rather than an accent. Do not overplay either the dynamics or the *staccato*. The difference between *forte* and *piano* is slight.

➤ Play the LH, slurring the pairs of half notes. These pairs provide the clue to the short-short-long (2mm. + 2mm. + 4mm.) phrase structure found repeatedly in the early Classical period.
➤ Find the return of the A section. [m. 17]
➤ Bracket the two-measure sequences in the B section. How could you shape the dynamics to bring out these sequences?

Practice Suggestions

➤ In practicing this piece, the most important goal is to create delicate sound. Let your dynamic range be *mf–mp*.
➤ The sound of the downbeat *staccatos* is also delicate. Imagine trying to play *legato* between the first two notes of the piece, but having only one finger. That is the degree of separation.
➤ Have you marked in the phrasing: 2mm. + 2mm. + 4mm? Listen for those groupings as you practice.
➤ How will your dynamic plan help the listeners hear the sequence, mm. 9-14?

Dmitri Kabalevsky
A Little Song, op. 27, no. 2 (R21, SW43)
Exploring the Score

Kabalevsky has written a hauntingly sad song. The colorful harmonic changes in the second half are a tribute to his creative genius.

➤ Trace the melody through the score. Where does the LH play the melody?
➤ How has Kabalevsky created the sad mood in this piece?
➤ Encourage the student to write lyrics for *A Little Song.*

➤ Each line is a four-measure unit. The first two measures of each line are slightly varied in the following two measures.
➤ Compare lines 1 and 3. The colorful changes in the LH accompaniment are remarkable. Make special note of the tones that are *not* chromatic. Discuss the fingering for these half notes.

Practice Suggestions

Your goal is to create an intensely sad mood. A moderately slow tempo and expressively shaped phrases are your tools.

➤ Find the most important note of each two-measure phrase. Let the dynamics flow to that point of intensity.
➤ The last two measures of each line serve as a variation of the first two measures. Bring out those changes (playing slightly louder or with special emphasis).
➤ Devote special practice to the LH *legato* 3rds, mm. 9-14.
➤ Circle the special *subito piano* surprise in m. 13.
➤ Practice without pedal. The fingers are responsible for the *legato.*

Chee-Hwa Tan
The Land of Nod (R30, SW60)
Exploring the Score

Set the stage for your study of this piece by reading the poem. Then play the piece for the student or listen to the *Celebration Series®* recording. The composer creates a dreamy lullaby over a hypnotic LH pattern.

➤ Discuss whether the entire piece is a dream or whether the child enters *The Land of Nod.*
➤ Name the LH chords. How many different chords did you find? What is the relationship of the quarter note to the chord?
➤ Compare mm. 1-8 with mm. 9-16. In the RH, what remains the same?

Practice Suggestions

➤ "Shadow play" the LH on the closed keyboard cover, with the pedal. As you play each bass note, say "up-down" as a verbal direction to your foot.
➤ Notice the LH-RH contrasting dynamic markings at the beginning. Your LH will tend to play louder because of the moves. Practice the LH twice as soft as the RH.

Nancy Telfer
Crocodile Teeth (R33, SW64)

Exploring the Score

What interval would you select to portray the threat of sharp crocodile teeth? As you examine the score, notice the constant use of the half step. Combining half steps with sharp *staccatos,* Telfer is able to create a most frightening piece.

➤ Use your imagination to create a story to go with this musical picture. Is there a special event represented by the sixteenth notes?
➤ Find the half steps in every measure.
➤ The piece is constructed with great economy of material.
   – Find measures that are like mm. 1-2.
   – Do you see the relationship between m. 3 and m. 7?
   – Compare mm. 13 and 14.

➤ M. 9 uses a four-note chromatic pattern. Where does this pattern repeat?
➤ In your musical story, what happens during the rest in m. 10? What happens on the last sound of the piece?

Practice Suggestions

➤ Practice the piece in groups of similar ideas.
   mm. 1-2; 5-6; 11-12
   mm. 3-4; 7-8
   mm. 9; 14
   mm. 13-14

➤ Then practice in sections.
   mm. 1-4
   mm. 5-8
   mm. 9-10 (the silence is important!)
   mm. 11-15

➤ Let the dynamics help tell your musical story.

Alexander Gedike
Fugato, op. 36, no. 40 (R37, SW70)

Exploring the Score

A *fugato* is a work written in imitative style. In a *fugato,* one expects to find a strict number of voices, and presentations of a theme or "subject" throughout the piece. This *fugato* is mainly written in two voices that converse with each other until they are joined by a third voice in m. 7 and mm. 14-16.

➤ The theme most frequently presented appears first in the LH, mm. 1-4. Find other presentations of this theme. [partial: RH, mm. 5-6; full: RH, mm. 9-12]

➤ The reappearance of the RH theme of mm. 1-4 is cleverly disguised. Can you find it? [LH mm. 9-12]
➤ Discuss how the composer of a fugato or invention creates individuality of voices. [contrasting rhythms, independent articulations.] Notice how seldom Gedike writes the same rhythm and articulation simultaneously in both hands.

Practice Suggestions

➤ Try these steps to gain independence of hands. With each short practice unit (2 mm. or 4 mm.):
   – Play hands separately to hear the sound and feel the shape of each voice.
   – Tap the rhythm hands together, counting aloud.
   – "Shadow play" each unit on a flat surface very slowly. Pay close attention to fingering and exaggerate the slurs and *staccatos.* When you perfect your "shadow play," play the unit on the keyboard.

Pál Kadosa
Study in A Minor (S6)

Exploring the Score

Silly question: *How many notes are in a five-finger pattern?*

Serious question: *When writing a piece using only five-finger patterns, why not use a $\frac{5}{8}$ meter signature?* Kadosa's solution is shown in this study.

➤ Have the student point and follow in the score the shape of the eighth-note patterns: "up-down-up" etc. When the LH plays the eighths in mm. 6-10, what is different? [the shape] What is the same? [the fingering]
➤ Compare the RH of mm. 11-15 with the LH of mm. 6-10 and the RH beginning part. What is the same? What is different?
➤ $\frac{5}{8}$ time is usually divided into 3 + 2 or 2 + 3. Which has Kadosa used?
➤ Notice that the $\frac{1}{4}$ or $\frac{4}{4}$ measures end each section. Count the $\frac{1}{4}$ as two eighths.

Teacher's Note: The metronome marking indicates the beat for an entire measure. The full measure is played at mm. 50-58.

Practice Suggestions

➤ Try this five-finger warm-up in A minor, hands together, playing the pattern up and down twice:
   – *legato, forte; legato, piano*
   – *staccato, forte; staccato, piano*
   – contrary motion, *crescendo-diminuendo*
   – RH twice as fast as the LH, *legato*
   – LH twice as fast as the RH, *legato*

➤ Tap the rhythm of both hands for each section, counting aloud.

➤ Play each section of the piece several times, counting *12 123*.

➤ Listen for light, short *staccatos*. Bounce your hand and fingers quickly but gently. Stay close to the keys.

CREATIVE ACTIVITY

Create your own five-finger study. Choose a minor five-finger pattern, and improvise a melody in $\frac{5}{8}$. Organize the notes in 3 + 2 or 2 + 3 groupings. Add a blocked 5th accompaniment to the melody and play hands together.

Title: _____

Joan Hansen
Irish Jig (S10)
Exploring the Score

This spirited dance gives both hands the opportunity to play the melody.

➤ The four-measure phrase structure provides the outline for the dance:

mm. 1-4	A	RH dances
mm. 5-8	A	LH dances
mm. 9-12	B	RH dances
mm. 13-16	B	LH dances
mm. 17-21	Coda	Dancing together!!

➤ What musical instrument might play the dotted half-note drones?

➤ Look for the *staccatos* and accents. Can you hear the musical hop (upbeat) before the dance begins with an accented downbeat?

Practice Suggestions

➤ Practice in four-measure sections. You may wish to begin with slow practice to make sure you hear the *staccatos* and accents and then gradually increase your tempo.

➤ Notice the places where the fingering changes, sometimes on the same note. Play these passages until they are comfortable.

➤ Feel the difference between the six beat patterns in the A and B sections. The A section tune begins with an upbeat hop. The B section begins with a downbeat accent.

Linda Niamath
Butterflies (S11)
Exploring the Score

A restless butterfly flutters from one blossom to another, taking the time to land only once before flying away. This delicate piece challenges your student to play light, even sixteenths and to paint a musical picture.

➤ At first glance, the key of G flat major may look difficult. Ask the student to find the white keys in the piece. There are none! This piece is played only on the black keys.

➤ To start reading the piece, have the student block the LH notes. The student may profit from naming the intervals: "2nd, 3rd, cluster."

➤ Block the RH positions, mm. 5-8. When the student is secure with the RH shifts, add the LH to that blocking exercise.

➤ Block mm. 9-12 in the same manner: RH alone, then hands together.

➤ Before practice begins, determine that the student can tap the rhythm of mm. 1-4 accurately.

➤ If necessary, explain the *15ma* in the final measure.

➤ By looking at the score, can you tell where the butterfly lands and where it flies away? Where does the butterfly move in short spurts and where does it fly for longer distances?

Practice Suggestions

➤ On the closed keyboard cover, tap the rhythms of measures 1, 3, 4, 9, 12, and 20. You now know all the rhythms in the piece.

➤ Work in four-measure units. Block the hand positions in each measure to discover the hidden black key patterns.

➤ Listen carefully to your pedaling and observe the indicated changes. Notice that the pedal changes with (almost) every LH shift. How does the pedal help paint your musical picture?

CREATIVE ACTIVITY

Using only the black keys, create your own musical story about a butterfly. Think about the butterfly flying higher or lower, landing on a flower, or fluttering in circles. Use dynamics and the pedal to help paint your picture.

Title: *A Day in the Life of a Butterfly*

STUDY MODULE 4

Page	List	Composer	Title	Key, Meter and Tempo
R6 SW9	A	George Frideric Handel	*Impertinence, HWV 494*	G Minor $\frac{2}{2}$ $\quad$ = 76-84
R14 SW29	B	Robert Schumann	*Melody, op. 68, no. 1*	C Major $\frac{4}{4}$ $\quad$ = 80-92
R15 SW31	B	Alexander Gedike	*Military Trumpets*	F Major $\frac{6}{8}$ Allegro vigoroso
R22 SW46	B	Joan Last	*Sailing by Moonlight*	A Minor $\frac{6}{8}$ Andantino con moto
R39 SW72	C	Carleton Elliott	*Canon*	G Minor $\frac{4}{4}$ Moderato
S4		Alexander Gedike	*Study in G Major*	G Major $\frac{2}{4}$ Moderato
S15		Christopher Norton	*Tram Stop*	C Major $\frac{4}{4}$

Assign first:

Impertinence . . . .

Military Trumpets . . . .

Sailing by Moonlight

Study in G Major . . . .

Assign next when ready:

Melody

Tram Stop

Canon

Four of the pieces in this module (*Impertinence, Melody, Canon,* and *Study in G Major*) provide an opportunity to explore a dialogue or a duet between the hands. This can lead to discussions about balance between the hands and how to listen to both parts. *Military Trumpets, Sailing by Moonlight,* and *Tram Stop* suggest colorful musical stories.

George Frideric Handel
Impertinence, HWV 494 (R6, SW9)

Exploring the Score

Listen to the *Celebration Series®* recording of this piece. "Impertinence" can mean rude, bold, saucy, or insulting. Which of these descriptions fit the mood of this two-voice conversation?

The eighth notes have special musical functions in this piece. They form a motive which serves as a unifying device. They also provide energy and forward movement to the sound.
TIP: "Short notes go to longs" is a helpful guide to interpretation.

➤ As students hear the piece (recording or your performance), have them selectively tap only the eighths and their following note. Be sure to include the LH in this tapping exercise. Encourage an energetic *crescendo* in each motive.
➤ Compare mm. 9-10 with mm. 11-12. This repetition is called a *sequence.*
➤ Describe the events of mm. 13-15.

➤ Can you find measures in which the hands have the same rhythm? [mm. 5-8 come close] The hands sound independent of one another because of their contrasting rhythm.
➤ Have the student experience the sound of the piece by playing sections as a student–teacher duet.

Practice Suggestions

➤ During practice, use a *forte* sound and a *legato* touch. This will help you learn fingerings and the coordination of the hands.
➤ Practice in two- or four-measure units:
  – hands separately with special attention to fingerings
  – hands together, slowly, for accuracy of fingering and notes
➤ When you are secure with your *legato* practice, add the articulation. Your teacher will help you decide if you are to detach the quarter notes. (Which articulation gives the music its most "impertinent" sound?)
➤ The time signature (*Alla breve*) suggests that the piece is to be felt in two beats per measure.

Robert Schumann
Melody, op. 68, no. 1 (R14, SW29)
Exploring the Score

This lovely song is a duet. To discover the duet, play the RH as written, and add the LH notes that play directly with the RH (e.g., in m. 1 the LH would play quarter notes C F E C.) Most often, the duet part is parallel to the melody. Can you find examples of contrary motion between melody and LH?

➤ Compare lines that look alike. Are they exactly the same?

➤ Which lines have the feeling of descending motion? which lines ascend?

➤ Discuss the musical goal of the short phrases in mm. 5-7 and 13-15.

Practice Suggestions

➤ Practice the LH alone, listening for the hidden melody. Play the thumb very quietly.

➤ Play the RH-LH duet (notes on beats) without the LH thumb notes.

➤ Practice the RH of mm. 8 and 16 playing one part with each hand. Bring out the top voice.

Alexander Gedike
Military Trumpets (R15, SW31)
Exploring the Score

➤ If you were writing a piece about trumpets, what sounds would you create?
 – Loud or quiet?
 – Accented notes or *legato* lines?
 – Rhythmically precise or flexible?

Compare your ideas with those of this Russian composer.

➤ The opening "fanfare" rhythm occurs throughout the piece. Have the student tap the rhythm of mm. 1-2. Find other presentations of that rhythm.

➤ Teacher and student could tap a performance of the piece: student taps the "solo fanfare" rhythm, while the teacher taps the dotted quarter "trumpet ensemble" response

➤ What is the form of the piece? [ABA1] How does an understanding of the form influence your practice assignment?

➤ Your student may need help with the repeated sixteenth notes. What finger activity plays the notes easily and quickly?

Practice Suggestions

➤ Fast repeated notes usually require a change of fingers in order to produce a crisp even sound.

Practice each repeated-note section listening for accurate rhythms and crisp articulation.

➤ The chords are accented but you must still shape the phrases.
 – If the phrase is two measures long, focus on the downbeat of m. 2.
 – If the phrase is four measures long, focus on the downbeat of m. 3.
 – Isolate these segments for special fingering practice. The fingering is for ease of getting from one chord to another, not for *legato* connection.

CREATIVE ACTIVITY

Make up your own trumpet piece. You may want to use repeated notes and chords as Gedike did. Choose your own key. Make your piece an energetic march.

Title: *Trumpet Fanfare*

Joan Last
Sailing by Moonlight (R22, SW46)
Exploring the Score

Imagine the sounds and the feeling of sailing on a peaceful lake in the moonlight. Words such as "quiet," "gliding," "gentle rocking" come to mind. Bring those words with you as we explore this lovely piece.

➤ The "gentle rocking" is provided by the LH. Have the student play the first measure, using the pedal, and search for the best sound.

➤ Experience "gliding" by playing the RH, mm. 5-8.

➤ To facilitate the reading of the A sections, help your student block the LH and play the RH as written (with that "gliding" sound).

➤ Have the student tap and say this rhythm:

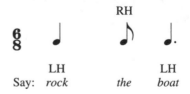

Find that rhythm in the B section, mm. 17-24.

➤ Now say and tap:

➤ The ultimate "quiet" is found at the end. Play the last two measures with your softest sound.

➤ The key of this piece is A minor. What is the final chord? [C Major!] What effect does the major ending have on your sailboat story?

Practice Suggestions

➤ Block the LH chords and practice changing positions while playing the pedal.

➤ Next add the melody and practice in four or eight measure units. When does the pedal change?

➤ Notice how the phrases follow the familiar "short-short-long" grouping. Can you show this phrase structure by the way you shape the dynamics?

Carleton Elliott
Canon (R39, SW72)
Exploring the Score

➤ Look carefully: does the LH play an exact imitation of the RH?

➤ Mark each break in the sound (ends of phrases, rests, *staccatos*) with a check mark in the score. Emphasize these breaks when you "shadow play" or practice the notes.

➤ Teacher and student may wish to experience the canon as a duet. Emphasize the phrase and articulation "lifts."

Practice Suggestions

➤ Play each hand alone, exaggerating the hand lifts at each *staccato,* rest, and slur ending.

➤ Reading from the RH part, play both hands in parallel motion, one octave apart. Exaggerate the hand lifts.

➤ When you practice as written, mm. 5-8 may require special attention. Practice in short units emphasizing the lifts in each hand.

Alexander Gedike
Study in G Major (S4)
Exploring the Score

➤ Have the student play the opening cuckoo bird sounds. The piece is made of *staccatos,* "cuckoos," and _____. [scale fragments and broken chords]

➤ Are there any notes in this piece that are not *staccato?* [final tones]

➤ Find the measures with the broken chords. Can the student label those chords? [m. 12 = D; m. 14 = G; m. 20 = C; m. 23 = D7. The I, IV, V, and V7 of G Major]

➤ How is the B section (m. 9) different? [inverted theme, emphasis on D major]

Practice Suggestions

➤ You may want to do hands separate practice on the scale fragments for correct fingering. (Fingering is always learned most quickly when you play *legato*.)

➤ Practice in four measure units. Notice when the hands play separately and when they are in unison like a duet. Are the unison measures in parallel or contrary motion?

➤ Each phrase begins with an upbeat. Have you marked in your score where each phrase begins?

CREATIVE ACTIVITY

➤ Compose your own variation of this study by changing at least one note or rhythm per measure. You might change the direction of the intervals or even the hand that plays. Have fun and play it a different way each time. Don't forget to include cuckoo calls!

Title _____

Christopher Norton
Tram Stop (S15)
Exploring the Score

Listen as the tram chugs along steadily, lurches—and stops!

➤ Compare mm. 1-7 with mm. 9-15. Are they the same or different? Good news for the student: this is a "half piece" played twice!

➤ Name the RH intervals. They provide the steady rhythm of the tram.

➤ What gives the music the feeling of abrupt stop in mm. 7 and 15? [If the C chord were played on the following downbeat, it would feel more normal.]

Practice Suggestions

➤ How many different rhythms do you find in this piece? [there are only three: mm. 1, 4, 7]

➤ Tap these three rhythms hands together in your lap or on the closed keyboard cover. When you can tap these rhythms accurately, you are ready to play this piece!

➤ Practice in four measures sections, first tapping the rhythms and then playing.

➤ Which LH notes are not *staccato?* [mm. 4, 12] How will you differentiate accented *staccatos* from regular *staccatos?*

STUDY MODULE 5

Page	List	Composer	Title	Key, Meter and Tempo
R8, SW15	A	Franz Joseph Haydn	*Quadrille*	C Major $\frac{3}{8}$ Con spirito
R13 SW26	A	Franz Schubert	*Écossaise, D 299, no. 8*	C Major $\frac{2}{4}$ Allegretto
R16 SW34	B	Béla Bartók	*Children at Play*	C Major $\frac{2}{4}$ Allegro
R17 SW37	B	Isak Berkovich	*Mazurka*	F Major $\frac{3}{4}$ Allegro non troppo
R39 SW73	C	Pierre Gallant	*Jazz Invention No. 1*	C Major $\frac{4}{4}$ Andante
S5		Henri Bertini	*Study in G Major, op. 166, no. 6*	G Major ¢ Andante
S12		Aram Khachaturian	*Skipping Rope*	D Major ¢ Allegro

Assign first:
Écossaise . . . .
Quadrille . . . .
Study in G Major . . . .
Skipping Rope

Assign next when ready:
Jazz Invention No. 1
Mazurka
Children at Play

This module has three wonderful dances. Compare and contrast the dance styles, meters, and rhythms. Which dance is more formal? Remember to add these pieces to your Dance Chart. The other four pieces in this module provide opportunities for technical work in *staccato* versus *legato*, and in the jazz idiom.

Franz Joseph Haydn
Quadrille (R8, SW15)

The quadrille is a dance derived from the elaborate French ballets of the 18th century. Popular in the ballrooms of the early 19th century, the dance was performed by four couples moving in a square. It is often made up of five sections. Listen to the *Celebration Series®* recording of this piece. Do you hear the triple meter? Can you follow the form of repeated sections and contrasting sections?

Exploring the Score

➤ The rhythm of each section is different (see mm. 1, 9, 17, 25). With your student looking at the score, tap one of these rhythms. Can the student find that rhythm in the score? When the student is comfortable with the four different rhythms, trade roles and have the student tap the examples for you to find.
➤ Label the A and B sections of this ternary form (ABA).

➤ What is the key of the A section?
➤ How does Haydn create contrast in the B section? [change of key, change of register, new rhythmic figure]
➤ Amazingly, Haydn uses only the tonic (I) and dominant (V) harmonies in each section. Label the chord with letter names or I and V.

Practice Suggestions

➤ Each eight-measure section makes a logical practice unit. Your practice checklist could include:
  – tap and count
  – check fingering
  – circle fingerings that show change of position
  – decide on the articulation (connected or detached?)
  – slow practice before medium speed
➤ The first note of a short slurred group is the loudest. Play the RH two-note slurs with a drop-lift gesture.
➤ Grace notes give sparkle and emphasis to the notes

they precede. Crush the grace note against the main note, and make a quick *staccato* release.

CREATIVE ACTIVITY

Compose your own eight-measure dance by making up a four-measure Question and a four-measure Answer. Harmonize with tonic and dominant chords. Choose a key and time signature. You may wish to compose a second Question and Answer in a related key. Now you have a dance in ABA form.
Title: *Viennese Dance*

Franz Schubert
Écossaise, D 299, no. 8 (R13, SW26)
Exploring the Score

An écossaise is a country dance in quick $\frac{2}{4}$ meter.

TIP: In the Classical style, the focus of the phrase is often determined by its length. In a two-measure phrase, the focus is often on the downbeat of the second measure; in a four-measure phrase, the focus is usually on the downbeat of the third measure.

➤ In this écossaise, notice that two-measure phrases have their long note on the downbeat of m. 2. Remember? "Short notes go to longs."
➤ The form is an evenly balanced binary (without modulation). Label the A and B sections.
➤ In the B section, help the student "track" the melody: first RH, then LH, etc.
➤ To find the outline of melody and accompaniment, play only the downbeats. The LH downbeats from mm. 1-8 form a strong bass line. Can you memorize it?
➤ Play downbeats again, mm. 1-8, and block the entire LH harmony for each measure. Can you name any of these chords?

Practice Suggestions

➤ It is helpful to practice playing the RH melody with LH blocked chords.
➤ Practice the shifts of position until you can do this easily in rhythm.
➤ To outline the positions in the B section, play only the downbeats.
➤ Shape the two-note slurs. Make the second note quieter than the first.

Belá Bartók
Children at Play (R16, SW34)
Exploring the Score

Sing and play the children's folk song *Ring around the Rosie*. (Notate first six notes—G-G-E-A-G-E.) What intervals are used in this song? [minor third and

major second] These intervals are common to music around the world. Children sing these intervals naturally.

➤ Explore the intervals of the RH melody.
➤ Name the broken chords in mm. 9 and 13.
➤ Name the descending five-finger pattern in mm. 15-16.
➤ Find and circle the hidden melody notes in the LH. **Hint:** They are on the main beats.
➤ Find groups of measures that are repeated.
  Mm. 1-4 are repeated in mm. _____.
  Mm. 9-16 are repeated in mm. _____.

Practice Suggestions

➤ How's your "drop-lift" gesture? You need a good one for this piece!
  – Practice the RH in groups of four measures.
  – Play slowly and exaggerate—the "drop-lift" of the two-note slurs.
➤ When you are confident with the RH articulations, add the LH, playing with a neutral, quiet *legato*.

Isak Berkovich
Mazurka (R17, SW37)
Exploring the Score

A mazurka is a Polish folk dance in triple meter, often with an accent on the second beat. Rhythm is an important feature of this dance. Listen to the *Celebration Series®* recording and discuss the proud character and accented rhythm of this mazurka.

➤ In m. 1, you will find the basic rhythmic motive of this piece. Almost every measure uses this rhythm or a variation. Which measures do not?
➤ Tap and count the RH melody, mm. 1-4, observing the accent on the second beat.
➤ Tap and count the RH rhythmic variation, mm. 9-12.
➤ Notice the consistency of the LH rhythm.
➤ Circle the LH measures that do not use the half note–quarter note rhythm.

Practice Suggestions

➤ All dances have a strong sense of beat. To feel the beat of this mazurka, practice in four-measure units, playing only the notes that fall on beats 1, 2, and 3. Then, follow this by adding in the sixteenths.
➤ Tap each four-measure unit as written.
➤ Once you are comfortable tapping the rhythm, play the dotted rhythms with a sharp rhythmic snap. The short notes should feel as if they belong to the following beat.

Pierre Gallant
Jazz Invention No. 1 (R39, SW73)
Exploring the Score

The accidentals contribute to the jazz flavor of this invention.

➤ Play the piece for your student as written, then without the accidentals. This will illustrate how essential the altered tones are to a jazz vocabulary.
➤ Play a blues scale in C major. [C, E flat, F natural, F sharp, G, B flat, C]
➤ Circle the measures with syncopation, an important jazz element.

Practice Suggestions

Almost every beat is subdivided, and the piece has a constant flow of eighth notes. That makes the rhythm easy.

➤ To solve the coordination problems of a piece with independent hands:
  – Tap the rhythm.
  – "Shadow play" on a flat surface. Observe fingerings carefully.
  – Exaggerate the lifts at ends of phrases.

Henri Bertini
Study in G Major, op. 166, no. 6 (S5)
Exploring the Score

This is a study in two-note slurs and a conversation between the hands. It is the perfect piece in which to practice your two-note slur technique.

➤ Which hand leads in the A section? How does this change in the B section?
➤ Bertini indicates *con pedale.* When do you change the pedal? [every half measure]

Practice Suggestions

➤ To hear the harmonic progressions, block the intervals. Change pedal every half measure.
➤ Listen for the hidden melody on the first and third beats of each measure.
➤ Play broken intervals and listen for the rise and fall of the hidden melody. Use a drop-lift gesture to play the two-note slurs.

Aram Khachaturian
Skipping Rope (S12)
Exploring the Score

➤ Discuss Khachaturian's use of *staccato* and *f* in this piece.
➤ Compare mm. 1-4 with mm. 5-8. What has been changed?
➤ To create a contrasting B section in mm. 9-16, Khachaturian changes the LH accompaniment. Describe that change. How is the RH of the B section similar to the A section?
➤ Mark the ABA_1 form.
➤ The first two RH notes can serve as a model for much of the piece. It is tempting to slur the dotted half notes into the *staccato* quarters. Instead, there should be a slight break *before* each *staccato* upbeat. Practice this articulation with the student before home practice begins.

Practice Suggestions

The challenge of this study is the accurate playing of *legato* and *staccato.*

➤ You may wish to practice the RH separately for the correct performance of the basic motive (Think "hop-land.") Make a break *before* each *staccato* tone.
➤ Measures that combine *staccato* and *legato* (B section) deserve special practice. Play *very* slowly, listening to the contrasting articulations.

STUDY MODULE 6

Page	List	Composer	Title	Key, Meter and Tempo
R4 SW4	A	Anon.	*Bourrée in D Minor*	D Minor $\frac{4}{4}$ Allegro
R18 SW39	B	Aram Khachaturian	*An Evening Tale*	A Minor $\frac{3}{4}$ Andante Cantabile
R26 SW52	B	István Szelényi	*Faraway Regions*	Whole tone **c** Lento armonioso
R28 SW56	B	Linda Niamath	*Penguins*	A flat Major $\frac{4}{4}$ Waddling
R38 SW71	C	Gordon A. MacKinnon	*The Argument*	E Minor $\frac{4}{4}$ Moderato
S9		Veronika Krausas	*Kangaroos*	Atonal $\frac{4}{4}$ Moderato
S14		Stella Goud	*Moon through a Window*	A Minor $\frac{4}{4}$ Dreamily

Assign first:	Assign next when ready:
Bourrée in D Minor	
An Evening Tale	*The Argument*
Faraway Regions	*Moon through the Window*
Penguins	*Kangaroos*

Study Module 6 could be subtitled the "Sound Module." Have students look for examples of whole-tone scales, chromatic scales, *glissandos,* and pedal effects. This module contains the most challenging repertoire in Level 2.

Anon.

Bourrée in D Minor (R4, SW4)

Exploring the Score

A *bourrée* is a vigorous French dance with a short upbeat.

➤ Play several RH measures for the student to hear the upbeat motive. One can see the dancers:

hop   land turn a-round

➤ Notice that the dance turns to smoother gestures in the B section (m. 9). The quarter note is replaced by two eighths, and the movement seems more graceful.
➤ Label the ABA form.
➤ Circle each repetition of rhythm "x" in the A section, and rhythm "y" in the B section:

Practice Suggestions

➤ Divide the piece into short practice units of one or two measures.
➤ A section:
  – Always start your practice unit with the upbeat.
  – If both hands have a quarter note upbeat, play them with equal detachment.
  – LH quarters are detached, even if the RH is *legato.*

➤ B section:
  – Find the three-note rhythmic motive "y" in the RH.

TIP: A composer can increase musical tension by adding ornaments, increasing the rhythmic activity or complexity or increasing the frequency of harmonic changes.

➤ During the Baroque period, performers often added their own ornaments. It would be proper for you to add a *cadential trill* on the third beat of m. 7 and m. 23. Your trill brings attention to the ending of the section.

István Szelényi
Faraway Regions (R26, SW52)
Exploring the Score

➤ *Faraway Regions* is a goldmine of expressive sound. Can you imagine the sound of the piece just by looking at the music?

➤ Szelényi utilizes the whole tone system in this piece. Your student may not have experienced a whole tone scale.
  - Start on C and progress up in whole steps: C, D, E, F sharp, G sharp, A sharp, C. The whole-tone scale has six different notes.
  - A second whole-tone scale can be built starting on C sharp: C sharp, D sharp, F, G, A, B, C sharp.

➤ Szelényi created a special key signature to show the whole-tone scale based on three black keys (F sharp, G sharp, A sharp) and three white keys (C, D, E).

➤ Help the student find the positions for the first measure.

➤ What do the ties over the bar line indicate? [continuing sound]

➤ In mm. 2-3, circle the notes played on black keys. Play those measures.

➤ If one were to label the opening whole tone cluster "x," how many times does "x" appear in the piece? [11]

➤ If one were to label the shape of the sixteenths in m. 10 "y," how many times does "y" appear? [7]

➤ Name the highest pitch in m. 2; in m. 5; in m. 8; in m. 9. Each phrase ascends one whole step higher. As the notes grow higher a step at a time, the rhythm becomes slightly more intense:
  - m. 5-6 have four eighth notes per half measure.
  - m. 8 has five eighth notes per half measure.
  - m. 9 has six eighth notes per half measure.
  - m. 10 has eight sixteenth notes in the first half of the measure

➤ Very slowly, draw large circles in the air. These represent a half note. Feel the pulse at the bottom of the circle. Counting aloud, divide a full swing into *1234*, then *12345*, then *123456*, and finally *1234-1234*. Let this feeling of increasing subdivisions guide the playing of mm. 5-11.

Practice Suggestions

➤ Tap and count the rhythm of this piece on the closed keyboard cover before you play.

➤ For *con pedale*, experiment with long pedals, changing the pedal in mm. 4, 7, 12, and 15. In the final four measures, experiment with holding the LH sounds without the pedal, listening for the delicate release of the RH *staccato* tones.

CREATIVE ACTIVITY

Create your own piece by playing whole-tone scale patterns in different registers of the keyboard. Play black keys with the LH and white keys with the RH, then reverse the pattern. Use the damper pedal and add a title.

Title: *Outer Space*

Aram Khachaturian
An Evening Tale (R18, SW39)
Exploring the Score

The first four measures seem to say "Once upon a time …" and invite the listener in.

➤ Imagine a scene with someone dancing. What happens with the abrupt change in m. 20? Are there trumpets announcing the arrival of someone important? Is this a signal of something ominous or threatening?

➤ The key of the piece is A minor. Is the opening scale natural, harmonic or melodic minor? [melodic minor; F sharp and G sharp are the raised 6th and 7th degrees for melodic minor]

Practice Suggestions

➤ The RH melody is song-like with long *legato* phrases. Play the LH waltz bass lightly, always quieter than the RH.

➤ In mm. 20-26, play the RH repeated notes with a slight *crescendo* toward the dotted half note.

➤ Block the LH in this section to feel the subtle differences between chord shapes.

TIP: Repeated notes are rarely played the same. Change the dynamics on each note to create a sense of movement.

➤ As the waltz concludes in mm. 40-52, the music grows louder, then softer and slower. What happens at the end of this beautiful waltz?

Linda Niamath
Penguins (R28, SW56)

This piece is a clever sound portrait of penguins as they waddle and slide in their snowy playground.

Exploring the Score

➤ How does the LH *ostinato* bass remind you of the waddling penguin?

➤ The chromatic scale passages sound unique because of the tritone interval between the hands. A tritone equals three whole steps and can be written as an augmented fourth or a diminished fifth.

Practice Suggestions

This piece has five sections—three using an *ostinato* and two using chromatic scale patterns. It is a perfect piece to learn in sections:

➤ The *ostinato* sections (mm. 1-7, 10-13, 18-26) are the same except the last section, which is an octave lower. Start with hands separate practice on these passages.

➤ When you are ready to put the hands together on the *ostinato* sections, begin hands separate practice on the two chromatic figures (mm. 8-9 and 14-15). Use consistent fingerings and say the finger numbers aloud.

➤ Next, put the chromatic figures hands together using at least three different speeds, slow-medium-fast. Begin memorizing the *ostinato* sections at this stage.

➤ Memorize the entire piece.

CREATIVE ACTIVITY

Using Niamath's LH *ostinato,* compose a new RH melody based on m. 1-4 of *Penguins.* You may choose to keep your RH melody in a C major five-finger pattern.

Title: _____

Gordon A. MacKinnon
The Argument (R38, SW71)
Exploring the Score

The "argument" is between two parties, each represented by a hand.

➤ The accents in the first theme in mm. 1- 2, let us know that the tempers have flared.

➤ Does the LH entrance begin with the same note? Already we hear disagreement.

➤ What two triads are outlined in mm. 1-2? [E minor, B major]

➤ The B theme in RH, m. 5 is not allowed to finish before the LH enters. Isn't that typical of arguments?

➤ Why is there no LH argument in mm. 8-10? (The RH won!)

Practice Suggestions

The fingering gives the necessary guidance for efficient crossings and changes of position. Follow the fingering carefully.

➤ How long does the hand stay in one position? Examine the hands separately, and bracket the positions. For example, your first bracket would reach from the first note to the end of beat two, m. 2. The next bracket is for one note only.

Veronika Krausas
Kangaroos (S9)
Exploring the Score

Kangaroos is a study in movement. It is natural that this piece hops about the keyboard in *staccato* notes and octave jumps.

➤ Circle all the clef changes.

➤ What interval is used throughout the piece? [half steps]

➤ Most of the piece is limited to the use of three pairs of half steps. They can be labeled by their top tone:

Those labels show the familiar relationship of I, IV, and V.

➤ Circle the half steps that are not on C, F, or G.

➤ Compare mm. 5-6 with mm. 7-8. Did you find the "mirror" image?

Practice Suggestions

If you divide the piece into these sections you will learn it quickly: mm. 1-4, 5-8, and 9-10.

Try this exercise for finding positions. Disregard the rhythm for the moment. "Shadow play" the positions on the closed keyboard cover. Move your hands up and down, imagining that you are playing the actual notes. Identify the type of movements used in each section:

    – one hand crosses over the other
    – hands move in contrary motion
    – hands move in parallel motion

➤ Repeat this exercise on the keyboard cover, adding the accurate rhythm.

➤ Practice in two-measure groups. Memorize each practice unit. (Let accurate dynamics be part of your memory project.)

Stella Goud
Moon through the Window (S14)
Exploring the Score

Goud has written an easy *glissando* exercise, and framed it in silver moonlight. After hearing the piece, ask your student to tell you about the picture portrayed by the A section *glissandos,* and the B section eighth notes.

➤ How many times does the pedal change during the piece?

➤ Where do you play black keys? [LH, mm. 13-14]

➤ Work on the *glissando* technique with your student before home practice begins. Quiet *glissandos* are the easiest. Some students spot a final *glissando* tone accurately, while others find it helpful to turn the hand over at the end of a *glissando* and play the final note in a normal position with finger 2 or 3.

Practice Suggestions

➤ Practice RH *glissandos* with a loose hand. Allow your upper arm to lead, and be sure to let all of the middle fingers help produce the sound.

➤ In mm. 9-15, block the intervals. Write in your choice of fingerings.

Level 2 SUMMARY

➤ How many dances are on your Dance Chart?

➤ What new pieces did you compose for Level 2? You may want to record those pieces before they are lost. With your teacher's help, notate some of the pieces.

➤ Have you learned new technical ideas from the studies? Which studies were easiest for you? Which were the most difficult? How did you solve the technical problems?

Level 3

The Publications
Level 3 of the *Celebration Series®* includes the following publications:

Piano Repertoire 3
Piano Studies/Etudes 3
Student Workbook 3
Recording of Repertoire and *Studies/Etudes 3*

The Repertoire
Piano Repertoire 3 is divided into three lists.

➤ List A includes a selection of pieces composed during the Baroque period (*ca* 1600 to *ca* 1750).

➤ List B includes a selection of pieces composed during the Classical period (*ca* 1750 to *ca* 1820).

➤ List C includes a selection of pieces composed during the Romantic era (*ca* 1820 to *ca* 1910) and the twentieth century.

Musical Development
Level 3 provides a transition from the early intermediate level of piano study to the mid-range of the intermediate repertoire. With these pieces, the student will become further acquainted with Baroque dances and two- and three-part forms. The List B pieces introduce the Classical sonatina with its characteristic figures: scale passages, cadence patterns, and accompaniment styles. List C pieces feature forms and sounds found in the Romantic and Contemporary periods.

Musical Tips
As students work through this level, they will accumulate a growing vocabulary of musical style and performance. The student can keep a notebook of these points, identified in the discussions below as musical tips (**TIPS:**). Encourage your students to add to the list as they progress from level to level.

The Study Modules
The six Study Module discussions in Level 3 are organized into the following categories:

Exploring the Score
Practice Suggestions
Creative Activities

Exploring the Score is designed as an interactive exercise between teacher and student. Questions are addressed to the student, as you might ask them during the lesson. *Practice Suggestions* outline first week practice steps. The *Creative Activities* act as reinforcement for your students' understanding of a musical concept and can provide a springboard for composition and improvisation.

If you have questions regarding the "Assign first ... Assign next when ready" at the bottom of each module chart, please refer to the *Foreword* at the front of this *Handbook*.

The chart below lists the repertoire and studies in Level 3. Page numbers for works in *Piano Repertoire 3* and *Piano Studies/Etudes 3* are found in the first column. Study Module numbers are found to the far right. Study Module groupings of repertoire and studies follow.

Piano Repertoire 3

	Page	Composer	Title	Study Module
List A	R4	Christian Petzold	*Minuet in G Major, BWV Anh. 114*	1
	R6	Christian Petzold	*Minuet in G Minor, BWV Anh. 115*	2
	R8	Henry Purcell	*Hornpipe in B flat Major, Z T683*	6
	R9	Anon., Johann Sebastian Bach, attr.	*Musette in D Major, BWV Anh. 126*	5
	R10	Anon., Johann Sebastian Bach, attr.	*Polonaise in G Minor, BWV Anh. 119*	3
	R11	George Frideric Handel	*Gavotte in G Major, HWV 491*	4
List B	R12	Muzio Clementi	*Sonatina in C Major, op. 36, no. 1 (First Movement)*	1
	R14	Muzio Clementi	*Sonatina in C Major, op. 36, no. 1 (Second Movement)*	2
	R16	Muzio Clementi	*Sonatina in C Major, op. 36, no. 1 (Third Movement)*	3
	R18	Ludwig van Beethoven	*Sonatina in G Major (First Movement)*	4
	R19	Ludwig van Beethoven	*Sonatina in G Major (Second Movement)*	5
	R20	Johann Anton André	*Sonatina in A Minor (Third Movement)*	6
	R22	Alexander Gedike	*Sonatina in C Major, op. 36, no. 20*	3

Piano Repertoire 3

	Page	Composer	Title	Study Module
List C	R23	Pyotr Il'yich Tchaikovsky	*Morning Prayer, op. 39, no. 1*	6
	R24	Alexander T. Grechaninov	*Horse and Rider, op. 98, no. 5*	5
	R26	Alexander T. Grechaninov	*After the Ball, op. 98, no. 13*	4
	R27	Dmitri Kabalevsky	*Clowns, op. 39, no. 20*	6
	R28	Robert Fuchs	*Timid Little Heart*	1
	R29	Béla Bartók	*Play*	1
	R30	Boris Berlin	*The Haunted Castle*	3
	R31	Yashinao Nakada	*The Song of Twilight*	2
	R32	William Lea	*Snoopy*	2
	R33	Petr Eben	*Bird on the Windowsill*	4
	R34	Seymour Bernstein	*The Elegant Toreador*	4
	R36	Ruth Watson Henderson	*Lullaby in Black and White*	5
	R38	Nancy Telfer	*The Sleeping Dragon*	3
	R40	Christopher Norton	*Coconut Rag*	2

Piano Studies/Etudes 3

Page	Composer	Title	Study Module
S4	Sam Raphling	*Bike Ride*	1
S5	Johann F. Burgmüller	*Arabesque, op. 100, no. 2*	3
S6	Christopher Norton	*Inter-city Stomp*	1
S7	Béla Bartók	*Minuet*	4
S8	Samuil Maikapar	*The Young Shepherd's Song, op. 28, no. 3*	6
S9	Carl Czerny	*Study in D Minor, op. 261, no. 53*	3
S10	Daniel Gottlob Türk	*Having Fun*	5
S11	Vladimir Blok	*Two Ants*	5
S12	Cornelius Gurlitt	*Undaunted, op. 197, no. 7*	1
S13	Gem Fitch	*Chinese Kites*	5
S14	Alexandre Tansman	*The Doll*	4
S15	Alexand Gedike	*Study in E Minor, op. 32, no.12*	6
S16	Lorna Paterson	*Rush Hour*	2

Level 3 Repertoire and Studies/Etudes – Listed by Study Module

Study Module 1

List	Composer	Title	Page & Book
A	Christian Petzold	*Minuet in G Major, BWV Anh. 114*	R4, SW4
B	Muzio Clementi	*Sonatina in C Major, op. 36, no. 1 (First Movement)*	R12, SW23
C	Robert Fuchs	*Timid Little Heart*	R28, SW52
C	Béla Bartók	*Play*	R29, SW54
Study	Sam Raphling	*Bike Ride*	S4
Study	Christopher Norton	*Inter-city Stomp*	S6
Study	Cornelius Gurlitt	*Undaunted, op. 197, no. 7*	S12

Study Module 2

List	Composer	Title	Page & Book
A	Christian Petzold	*Minuet in G Minor, BWV Anh. 115*	R6, SW7
B	Muzio Clementi	*Sonatina in C Major, op. 36, no. 1 (Second Movement)*	R14, SW26
C	Yoshinao Nakada	*The Song of Twilight*	R31, SW59
C	William Lea	*Snoopy*	R32, SW61
C	Christopher Norton	*Coconut Rag*	R40, SW76
Study	Lorna Paterson	*Rush Hour*	S16

Level 3 Repertoire and Studies/Etudes – Listed by Study Module

Study Module 3

List	Composer	Title	Page & Book
A	Johann Sebastian Bach, attr.	*Polonaise in G Minor*	R10, SW17
B	Muzio Clementi	*Sonatina, op. 36, no. 1 (Third Movement)*	R16, SW27
B	Alexander Gedike	*Sonatina in C Major, op. 36, no. 20*	R22, SW37
C	Boris Berlin	*The Haunted Castle*	R30, SW57
C	Nancy Telfer	*The Sleeping Dragon*	R38, SW73
Study	Johann Friedrich Burgmüller	*Arabesque, op. 100, no. 2*	S5
Study	Carl Czerny	*Study in D Minor, op. 261, no. 53*	S9

Study Module 4

List	Composer	Title	Page & Book
A	George Frideric Handel	*Gavotte in G Major, HWV 491*	R11, SW20
B	Ludwig van Beethoven	*Sonatina in G Major (First Movement)*	R18, SW29
C	Alexander T. Grechaninov	*After the Ball, op. 98, no. 13*	R26, SW46
C	Petr Eben	*Bird on the Windowsill*	R33, SW63
C	Seymour Bernstein	*The Elegant Toreador*	R34, SW66
Study	Béla Bartók	*Minuet*	S7
Study	Alexander Tansman	*The Doll*	S14

Study Module 5

List	Composer	Title	Page & Book
A	Johann Sebastian Bach	*Musette in D Major*	R9, SW14
B	Ludwig van Beethoven	*Sonatina in G Major (Second Movement: Romanze)*	R19, SW31
C	Alexander T. Grechaninov	*Horse and Rider, op. 98 no. 5*	R24, SW43
C	Ruth Watson Henderson	*Lullaby in Black and White*	R36, SW70
Study	Daniel Gottlob Türk	*Having Fun*	S10
Study	Vladimir Blok	*Two Ants*	S11
Study	Gem Fitch	*Chinese Kites*	S13

Study Module 6

List	Composer	Title	Page & Book
A	Henry Purcell	*Hornpipe in B flat Major, Z T683*	R8, SW11
B	Johann Anton André	*Sonatina in A Minor (Third Movement: Rondo)*	R20, SW34
C	Pyotr Il'yich Tchaikovsky	*Morning Prayer, op. 39, no. 1*	R23, SW40
C	Dmitri Kabalevsky	*Clowns, op. 39, no. 20*	R27, SW49
Study	Samuil Maikapar	*The Young Shepherd's Song, op. 28, no. 3*	S8
Study	Alexander Gedike	*Study in E Minor, op. 32, no. 12*	S15

STUDY MODULE 1

Page	List	Composer	Title	Key, Meter and Tempo
R4 SW4	A	Christian Petzold	*Minuet in G Major, BWV Anh. 114*	G Major $\frac{3}{4}$
R12 SW23	B	Muzio Clementi	*Sonatina in C Major, op. 36, no. 1 (First Movement)*	C Major ¢ Allegro
R28 SW52	C	Robert Fuchs	*Timid Little Heart*	A Minor $\frac{3}{4}$ Etwas bewegt
R29 SW54	C	Béla Bartók	*Play*	C Major $\frac{2}{4}$ Allegretto
S4		Sam Raphling	*Bike Ride*	C Major $\frac{4}{4}$ Easy riding
S6		Christopher Norton	*Inter-city Stomp*	G Minor $\frac{4}{4}$ Lively
S12		Cornelius Gurlitt	*Undaunted, op. 197, no. 7*	G Major $\frac{2}{4}$ Allegretto

Celebration Series® Handbook for Teachers

STUDY MODULE 1

Assign first:	Assign next when ready:
Minuet in G Major	*Sonatina in C Major*
Timid Little Heart	*Undaunted*
Bike Ride	*Play*
Inter-city Stomp	

Contrasts of touch are highlighted in these Study Module 1 pieces. For example, *Minuet in G Major* and *Sonatina in C Major* require independence of hands and careful articulation, whereas *Bike Ride, Play,* and the jazz-like *Inter-city Stomp* use a light *staccato* touch. *Timid Little Heart* and *Undaunted* feature careful balance between RH melody and LH accompaniment.

Christian Petzold, J.S. Bach, attr.
Minuet in G Major, BWV Anh 14 (R4, SW4)

This elegant minuet is a delight to teach. Most students have heard the piece and are eager to add it to their repertoire.

Exploring the Score

The basic minuet dance pattern required six beats to complete. One often finds two-measure phrase groupings that reflect this pattern. Here, imagine that the dance step involved an elegant turn on the eighth-note motive, and a tap of the toe on the repeated quarter notes.

step, turn - a - round and stop, tap, tap

➤ Where do you find two-measure patterns? Bracket them. [examples: mm. 1-2, 3-4]
➤ Where do you find four-measure patterns? Bracket them. [examples: mm. 5-8; 13-16]
➤ Are there one-measure patterns?

Rhythm is the essence of any dance. The basic rhythmic motive in this piece is a group of four eighth notes moving to a downbeat quarter note. Find the places where the music consists solely of this motive. [mm. 5-8; 13-16] Notice the intensity of eighth-note rhythmic activity in mm. 13-16.

TIP: Composers often intensify rhythmic and harmonic activity as they approach a cadence.

➤ Tap the basic rhythmic motive with the student, verbalizing the five-note group.

now - we - go - to   1

➤ Challenge the musical "sleuthing skills" of the student. Find the downbeat stepwise motion that leads to the cadence, mm. 13-16.

What evidence of descending stepwise motion (downbeats or successive beats) can the student find in the second half of the piece?

Practice Suggestions

Choreograph a six-beat dance pattern for *Minuet in G Major.* As you listen to the *Celebration Series®* recording, dance to the music. Include turns and toe-taps.

Divide *Minuet in G Major* into four-measure practice units. Here are several practice steps:

➤ Block the RH. Circle the first finger that represents a position shift. Practice moving the hand from one circled fingering to the next. Did you notice the five-finger positions in mm. 1-2 and 3-4?
➤ Circle the fingerings in the LH that represent

position shifts.
➤ Listen for the eighth-note patterns that could be verbalized as "now we go to 1."
➤ To make the piece sound more like a dance,

detach all quarter notes. Be careful with the downbeat quarter notes—it is tempting to slur them into beat 2.

➤ The LH of mm. 25-26 is written as two voices. Be sure your performance produces full half note values in these measures.

Muzio Clementi
Sonatina in C Major, op. 36, no. 1 (First Movement) (R12, SW23)

Exploring the Score

Sonatina in C Major, op. 36, no. 1 is one of the most famous sonatinas from the Classical period. It belongs on every student's basic list of repertoire. (The other two movements of this sonatina are in Study Modules 2 and 3, respectively.) This first movement has great appeal through its bold Theme 1 and the scales and octave leaps in Theme 2. A few obstacles must be overcome to enjoy playing this piece fully.

➤ What does your student know about this piece from the title "Sonatina"? Review or introduce the terms *exposition, development, recapitulation* and mention contrasting themes and keys. For example, the exposition to the first movement of a sonatina often has two contrasting themes. The second theme is usually in the dominant key. Have the student label the sections.

➤ Where does Theme 2 begin? [m. 8] In what key does it end? [m. 15, G major, dominant]

➤ Ask the student to play the first measure with the sound of a trumpet fanfare: bold, spirited, and with sharply detached quarter notes. Accompany that sound several times with the LH "drum."

➤ Circle the RH downbeats, mm. 8-12. Notice the ascending step motion they create.

➤ Circle the LH downbeats, mm. 9-13. They, too, form ascending step motion.

➤ Play those downbeats hands together. Some students may wish to add the entire RH part.

➤ An alert "musical detective" will see that the LH of mm. 20-23 is a variation of mm. 16-19.

Practice Suggestions

Efficient practice of this piece involves focus on scales and zigzag figures.

Scale figures:

➤ Block mm. 3-4: CM - link – GM. Memorize the patterns blocked. Play them as written.

➤ Block the finger groups of m. 8: 3 notes + 5 notes.

➤ Find those same finger groups in mm. 10, 31, and 33.

Listen for a smooth sound with a slight *crescendo* on these scale measures.

Zigzag figures:

➤ Repeat the fingering sequence 4-2-3-1 for the eighths beginning in m. 6, beat four. Block pairs of fingers or practice as written while saying the fingering aloud. (Compare with m. 30.)

➤ Play and say the fingering aloud for the zigzag patterns in m. 13 and m. 37.

Other practice techniques for these figures include: (a) play *staccato,* (b) play in dotted rhythms, (c) play slowly and *legato.*

CREATIVE ACTIVITIES

Using the melody of Clementi's *Sonatina in C Major* (First Movement), make your own arrangement trying different LH accompaniment styles, such as an LH *Alberti* bass in eighth notes or a LH duet (countermelody) in quarter notes. Remember to add dynamics and rests.

Title: *Variations on Sonatina in C Major*

Robert Fuchs
Timid Little Heart (R28, SW52)

Exploring the Score

The title of this piece invites the student's interpretive involvement. The teacher can guide discussion—the student will have plentiful input. The descending motion of the phrases might express sadness or loss.

Notice how the composer starts each four-measure phrase with a suspended dissonant tone and lets the phrase fall from there. The primary interpretive element for the RH is to play an expressive "exhalation" on the first tone of each phrase—a poignant, deep tone, more a *tenuto* feel than dynamic accent. A slightly less intense approach is appropriate for the dissonances occurring in the third measure of each phrase.

➤ What is the formal plan? [A, mm. 1-8; B, mm. 9-16] Key? [A minor]

➤ The A features two four-measure units. How is the B section organized? [2 + 2 + 4]

➤ Can you find descending step motion that could imply sadness or resignation?

➤ What harmony does Fuchs begin with in m. 1? E7, V7]

Often the third beat in the RH is tied to the following downbeat. The missing downbeat is supplied by the LH.

➤ Circle the tied notes in the score.

➤ Mark upbeats that have accents. [mm. 8 and 10]

Practice Suggestions

This composition is a study in shaping phrases. How expressively can you play the RH phrases?

Your responsibility while learning this piece is to be faithful to four areas: rhythm (be careful with the RH tied values!), proper phrasing, dynamic marks, and pedaling. These steps will help you:

➤ First, block each LH measure before playing hands together.
➤ Observe the release of the LH on each third beat. The RH should be heard by itself on beat three.
➤ To develop this coordination, practice this exercise:

➤ Work for a singing *legato* tone. Lift between each RH phrase, just as you would take a breath at the end of a sentence.
➤ To achieve the dynamic plan, observe the *crescendo–diminuendo* in mm. 9-16 (B section).
➤ When pedaling, always press the damper pedal just as you play the first note of each measure (not before!) and release at the end of the second beat. Listen for unblurred harmony changes.

CREATIVE ACTIVITY

Using the LH (mm. 1-8) of *Timid Little Heart,* improvise a different RH melody. Once you settle on a musical idea, notate it on staff paper. Remember to play in $\frac{3}{4}$ meter!
Title: *Dream Waltz*

Béla Bartók
Play (R29, SW54)
Exploring the Score

How does Bartók achieve a playful quality in this piece?
➤ What kind of play does the phrasing suggest? [jumping, bouncing a ball]
➤ Play the opening four measures of this piece with the LH chords on the *downbeats*. Then play Bartók's version (LH on beat two) and discuss why his version sounds better.
➤ Circle all the dynamic markings and discuss how they contribute to the playful quality of the piece.

➤ Does the playful activity gradually end or suddenly come to a stop? [rhythmic augmentation occurs in mm. 49-52; compare with mm. 17-18]

Practice Suggestions

➤ Start your practice with the keyboard cover closed. The issue is lift *vs.* slur. In mm. 1-4, the hands lift together three times. In m. 3, the LH releases while the RH plays a *legato* phrase. Practice this on the keyboard cover, exaggerating the lifts. When you have mastered that coordination, consider yourself "home free."
➤ Play mm. 19-20 and 23-24 with a relaxed arm and hand. You can master this through slow practice. These repeated-note measures sound best when played with a slight *crescendo*.

Sam Raphling
Bike Ride (S4)
Exploring the Score

➤ As the student hears the sound of *Bike Ride,* ask about the relation of title to sound. Is it a bright day? Is the rider in a good mood? Where do horns honk?
➤ Do a Rhythm Search: How many different one-measure rhythms can you find in the RH? As your list grows, tap and count them.
➤ How many *different* blocked 5ths can you find in the LH? [two: mm. 5 and 7] Can you find examples of blocked 6ths in the RH and LH?

Practice Suggestions

➤ Consider mm. 1-2 to be the A theme. Find other A's. [mm. 3-4; 7-8; 18-19] Practice them as a group, playing accurately their slight differences.
➤ Play the *staccatos* with gentle hand bounces, keeping the wrist loose. Play the repeated eighth notes in a *single* bounce by letting the finger and hand "rebound" on the first note.
➤ Circle all accent marks. Make special note of places where the accent is in one hand only.
➤ Spot practice the LH in mm. 12-14 and listen for the held bass C.

Christopher Norton
Inter-city Stomp (S6)
Exploring the Score

What student can resist the forward drive of this dance? This is the rock beat so compelling to young people. Your student will have no rhythmic problems here—the LH is a built-in drumbeat!

- How does Norton create the "stomp" effect? [repeated LH pitches]
- Help your student memorize the rhythm of the first five measures. Note the four RH eighth-note patterns, and the beats of their entrance: beat one, beat two, beat two, beat one, beat four.
- What descending five-finger pattern is used in the RH in m. 1? [G minor without the A]
- What interval does Norton use for musical contrast? [fourth] Find the appearances of fourths—do not overlook the chords at the end!

Practice Suggestions

- Tap a steady beat in the LH and let the RH enter with the eighth-note pattern on the proper beat. Counting aloud is a "must."
- Practice the *staccato* eighth notes by letting the hand bounce from the wrist. When you play at performance tempo, you may find it easier to keep your fingers close to the keys.

CREATIVE ACTIVITY

Create a different RH melody using the same LH repeated notes (G and E flat) you played in *Inter-city Stomp*. Give your piece a title.

Title: _____

Cornelius Gurlitt
Undaunted, op. 197, no. 7 (S12)
Exploring the Score

Beauty can be created from simple elements. *Undaunted* employs limited resources, yet the result is a lovely, sensitive expression.

- Speculate on Gurlitt's choice of title for the piece.
- Both hands are written without shifts of position, and the LH moves in constant eighth notes. How does Gurlitt create contrast? [B section, mm. 17-24, changes focus to the dominant and has a slight rhythmic variation]

Practice Suggestions

- Dynamic shading is important to the successful study of this piece. The ends of phrases must be quieter, tapered. Compare the endings of the phrases in mm. 2 and 4 with m. 8. In mm. 2 and 4 the phrase ends "up," and in m. 8 gravity pulls the phrase down. Will the endings sound exactly alike? Experiment with the dynamics until you have found the shape that sounds most musical.
- Practice the LH alone, listening for a quiet thumb. Lean slightly on the downbeats, and listen to the resulting bass line. Blocking the LH intervals will help you secure this part.
- When playing hands together, listen carefully to balance the melody and accompaniment. Give the melody a rich, singing tone.

STUDY MODULE 2

Page	List	Composer	Title	Key, Meter and Tempo
R6 SW7	A	Christian Petzold	*Minuet in G Minor, BWV Anh. 115*	G Minor $\frac{3}{4}$ ♩ = 116
R14 SW26	B	Muzio Clementi	*Sonatina in C Major, op. 36, no. 1 (Second Movement)*	F Major $\frac{3}{4}$ Andante
R31 SW59	C	Yoshinao Nakada	*The Song of Twilight*	A Major ¢ Quietly
R32 SW61	C	William Lea	*Snoopy*	C Major $\frac{4}{4}$ Very lively
R40 SW76	C	Christopher Norton	*Coconut Rag*	F Blues ¢ Brightly
S16		Lorna Paterson	*Rush Hour*	C Major $\frac{4}{4}$ ♩ = 126

STUDY MODULE 2

Assign first:	Assign next when ready:
Sonatina in C Major	*Minuet in G Minor*
Rush Hour	*Snoopy*
The Song of Twilight	*Coconut Rag*

The pieces in Study Module 2 present an opportunity to study a variety of LH styles. What type of LH accompaniment or melody is used in each of these pieces?

    Minuet in G Minor [countermelody]
    Sonatina in C Major (Second Movement) [broken chord]
    Snoopy [contrary motion melody]
    The Song of Twilight [LH chords and double notes]
    Rush Hour [countermelody, chords]
    Coconut Rag [LH open fifths]

Christian Petzold, Johann Sebastian Bach, attr.
Minuet in G Minor, BWV Anh. 115 (R6, SW7)
Exploring the Score

➤ Compare this minuet with the *Minuet in G Major* on page 4 of *Piano Repertoire 3*. Once again we have an elegant dance featuring two- and four-measure phrases. In what other ways are the two dances similar? How are they different? Can you create dance steps for this minuet?

➤ To explore the rhythmic vocabulary of $\frac{3}{4}$ meter, have students list the different one-measure patterns of quarters and eighths in this piece:

➤ Use words to reinforce the concept that short notes move the music forward to longer values:

    step now you go to **here** now you go to **here**

➤ To reveal the descending melodic line, circle the downbeat melody notes in mm. 1-9.

➤ Explore different articulation options for the melody. Listen to the *Celebration Series®* recording for examples. Choose an articulation pattern and add markings to the scores.

Practice Suggestions

➤ Determine phrasing and articulation through hands separate practice.

➤ Practice hands together first in four-measure units, then in eight-measure units. Watch the fingering very carefully. The first week of practice can be without ornaments.

TIP: Baroque ornaments are played on the beat.

➤ Play the first note of each RH ornament with the LH. Observe the realizations of ornaments shown in the footnotes.

➤ How many different types of ornaments are used in this *Minuet?*

Muzio Clementi
Sonatina in C Major, op. 36, no. 1
(Second Movement) (R14, SW26)

This beautiful movement can seem deceptively simple at first glance: the quietly rolling LH accompaniment and the many repeated RH tones make it look easy on the page. The challenge is to keep the LH subdued so the melody can soar, and to make the repeated tones of the melody sound subtle and charming.

Exploring the Score

➤ Play the first four measures for the student: a lovely melody from just one chord! Let the student play the LH in mm. 1-2 as you play the RH. Work on a quiet, smooth sound, setting a model for the remainder of the movement.

➤ Find the return of the main theme (m. 19) and play with the student again. Relish the surprising E flat.

- With pencil in hand, the student can block the LH chords and write their names in the score. How many different types of LH triads can you recognize between m. 1 and m. 12?

Practice Suggestions

- Divide the piece into practice sections of two or four measures. Some two-measure groupings will start in the middle of a measure. [m. 4, m. 6, m. 10]
- Practice the LH broken chords with small wrist circles. Let the elbow "float."
- From m. 4 into m. 5, play F-D in the RH as a single falling 3rd. Shape the two notes as a "sigh." Now play the pitches as written: F- F- F-D. Lift the wrist slightly on the repeated notes to create a *diminuendo*.

TIP: A musical "sigh" has its emphasis on the first note.

- In m. 9 and 23, listen to the descending stepwise motion by playing one blocked 3rd on each beat. Throughout this movement, play the repeated 3rds and 6ths with a down-up-up wrist motion. Keep the fingers close to the keys, and try to project the top note of the thirds.
- Isolate the RH trills for practice with the LH. [mm. 3, 21, 25]
- Only one measure of this piece does not have triplet subdivision. Continue to feel the triplets in m. 12 to avoid rushing.
- As you become familiar with this beautiful middle movement, listen for a *dolce* RH melody against a smooth LH accompaniment. Take time to breathe at the end of the phrases.

Yoshinao Nakada
The Song of Twilight (R31, SW59)
Exploring the Score

What sounds paint a picture of twilight? Consider tempo, register, and dynamics. What type of harmonies are soothing and peaceful? Would your melody contain mostly steps or wide intervals? Perhaps you and the student could begin an improvisation about twilight sounds. (See Creative Activity below.) Assist the student in finding the elements of sound used by Nakada in *The Song of Twilight*.

- The student can play the LH (or lowest LH tones) as you quietly add pedal and play the RH. Create a memorable atmosphere. Where are you? What is the time of year? What are the pictures conjured by those sounds?

- In mm. 9-12 the bass is static. These four measures constitute a hidden B section: the LH movement is different, as is the RH rhythm.
- Where is the texture not *legato*? How do the *staccato* quarter notes in m. 12 affect the twilight scene?

Practice Suggestions

- First practice the rhythm by tapping hands together.
- Pedal helps create the twilight atmosphere. Practice the LH with pedal before playing hands together. Listen for clear pedal changes where marked.
- Shape the LH sound with a subtle emphasis on the first interval (or chord) of each pair. Think "more-less, more-less."
- The note values get longer as you move through each phrase. Begin each phrase with a feeling of motion, then relax and breathe before starting the next one.

CREATIVE ACTIVITY

Using only black keys, create your own twilight mood. Use long pedals and shimmering, quiet sounds.

Title: *Summer Evening*

William Lea
Snoopy (R32, SW61)
Exploring the Score

Listen to the *Celebration Series*® recording and have the student make up a story to go with the music. The story could reflect dynamic contrasts, position shifts, and articulation.

- What creates humor in this piece? If the student exaggerates those elements, the performance will be highly successful.
- Much of the piece features contrary motion. Have your student find many examples.
- The B section has little contrary motion, and the LH has wide, zig-zag *staccato* intervals. Mark the B section in the score. [mm. 17-24]

Practice Suggestions

- Practice the grace note rolls until they are clean, and end with an accented G. (Pretend you are impatiently drumming your fingers on a table!) How many different C's begin each grace note pattern?
- Practice mm. 6-8 in these short groups. Repeat a minimum of three times. Notice the contrary motion.

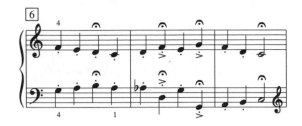

➤ Memorize the LH in mm. 17-22. Notice the alternating Ds and Cs on the downbeats.
➤ Play the RH, mm. 17-22, with careful attention to the articulation. Play hands together, focusing on the RH notes that are marked *staccato*.
➤ Where are quarter notes marked *tenuto* and not *staccato*? [mm. 23-24]

CREATIVE ACTIVITY

Use some of the surprise elements (accents, contrasting dynamics, and grace note rolls) from Lea's *Snoopy* to create your own piece of musical humor. Limit yourself to four-note patterns. Give a title to your piece.

Title: _____

Christopher Norton
Coconut Rag (R40, SW76)
Exploring the Score

Coconut Rag is in the key of F, but notice the many accidentals not associated with F major. The A flats, E flats, and B are part of the F blues scale.

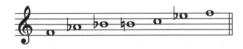

➤ Have your student play the scale, and encourage a bit of improvisation to create the blues feeling.
➤ "Bending" the rhythm is typical of this style.

In *Coconut Rag,* which part of the scale is assigned chiefly to the LH? which part to the RH?
➤ Syncopation is an important characteristic of blues and jazz. Explore the many places where Norton utilizes off-beat accents.
➤ Tap and count the A section, using "scat syllables" for the eighth notes.

Play the RH for those measures, emphasizing DOO in true blues style.

➤ Mark the ABA form in the score.
➤ Be a musical detective: find the 4ths. [the melodic ideas constantly outline a 4th]

Practice Suggestions

➤ Before playing, practice tapping four-measure groups, saying *DOO-bah* on pairs of eighth notes.
➤ Moving about the room, let your feet be the LH rhythm and your clapping hands the RH. Memorize the rhythm two measures at a time, until you can move to entire eight-measure groups.
➤ "Feel" the downbeat rests by clapping or tapping on the rest in mm. 4, 8, 10, 20, 22, and 26.

Lorna Paterson
Rush Hour (S16)
Exploring the Score

The title suggests a very busy time in the city. Everyone is in a hurry, streets and public transportation are crowded, and people are desperate to be someplace else.

➤ How does Paterson create an atmosphere of nervousness and tension? [constant, agitated eighth-note motion with unpredictable angularity; unfamiliar harmonies; *staccatos*]
➤ Compare mm. 1-2 with mm. 11-12. The hands reverse their rhythmic role.
➤ Notice the three-eighth-note pattern in mm. 4-5 and mm. 8-9.

➤ Does your student know the abbreviations *m.d.* and *m.s.* found in m. 13? [*mano destra*—RH; *mano sinistra*—LH]

Practice Suggestions

➤ Tap and count the two-handed rhythm pattern in m. 1 until it is secure. Find all of the measures that use this pattern. Do the same with the patterns found in mm. 4-5 and m. 11.
➤ Select measures that you think are "fingering challenges." Practice those measures *legato* and say the finger numbers aloud as you play. (Be sure to include m. 13.)

➤ If your hand is large enough, block the notes in m. 10 and memorize the positions.

➤ As you put the sections together, keep the eighth notes steady. This may involve slow practice, for it is easy to rush in mm. 1-3 only to find that you must slow down in mm. 4-6.

➤ Isolate passages that have consecutive eighth notes in one hand. [mm. 4, 6, 8, 10, 13]. Practice the *staccatos* with quick hand bounces, keeping the fingers close to the keys. Maintain a loose wrist and elbow.

STUDY MODULE 3

Page	List	Composer	Title	Key, Meter and Tempo
R10 SW17	A	Johann Sebastian Bach, attr.	*Polonaise in G Minor, BWV Anh. 119*	G Minor $\frac{3}{4}$ ♩ = 92
R16 SW27	B	Muzio Clementi	*Sonatina, op. 36, no. 1 (Third Movement)*	C Major $\frac{3}{8}$ Vivace
R22 SW37	B	Alexander Gedike	*Sonatina in C Major, op. 36, no. 20*	C Major 𝄴 Allegro moderato
R30 SW57	C	Boris Berlin	*The Haunted Castle*	C Major $\frac{4}{4}$ Andantino
R38 SW73	C	Nancy Telfer	*The Sleeping Dragon*	A Minor $\frac{4}{4}$ Slowly, smoothly
S5		Johann Friedrich Burgmüller	*Arabesque, op. 100, no. 2*	A Minor $\frac{2}{4}$ Allegro scherzando
S9		Carl Czerny	*Study in D Minor, op. 261, no. 53*	D Minor 𝄴 Allegro

Assign first:

Polonaise in G Minor . . . .
Sonatina in C Major . . . .
The Haunted Castle . . . .
Study in D Minor

Assign next when ready:

Arabesque
Sonatina
The Sleeping Dragon

The pieces in this Study Module vary widely in mood. Encourage your students to describe the pieces they study. Discuss the story or picture of the piece, the colors, or feelings. There are no wrong answers. Students will have their own individual perceptions. The goal is to develop musical imagination and sensitivity to the expressive quality of sound.

Johann Sebastian Bach, attr.
Polonaise in G Minor, BWV Anh. 119 (R10, SW17)
Exploring the Score

➤ Tap the RH rhythm of mm. 1-2, and ask the student to memorize it immediately. With some percussion instrument in hand (drum, tambourine, or a product of your creative invention), have the student walk to a steady, stately beat and tap out the RH rhythm. Head high, back straight—it's time for a stately procession around the studio!

➤ Have the student memorize the rhythm of mm. 3-4, then walk to a four-measure unit.

➤ Discuss the rhythmic groupings using sixteenths. How many different patterns do you find? Which is most frequently used?

➤ The shorter values move the music to the next beat. Where do you find the sixteenths moving the music to beat two? to beat three? to beat one?

➤ Circle the downbeats of mm. 1, 2, 3: G, A, B flat.

They form three ascending steps. Find the hidden "foreshadowing" of those three steps in m. 1. Can you find their reverse in m. 4? Find the downbeat step motion in mm. 7-10.

Practice Suggestions

You may find this traditional learning approach will be helpful with *Polonaise in G Minor.*

➤ Tap and count two measure units.
➤ Play the RH slowly. You have several things to accomplish:
   (a) correct notes
   (b) correct rhythm
   (c) articulation (detaching quarter and eighth notes not written slurred)
   (d) saying the finger numbers written in the score aloud.

Do not proceed to the next two steps until you have played the RH perfectly three times.

➤ Play the LH (if needed) for fingering security.
➤ Play hands together, slowly, with a firm sound, and accurately.

Muzio Clementi
Sonatina, op. 36, no. 1 (Third Movement)
(R16, SW27)

Exploring the Score

Discuss features that give this movement its vibrant energy. One consideration is that the RH plays in the bright treble register. Notice how many of the musical figures ascend or feature high tones. In those tones are brightness, life, and energy. What else makes this movement exciting?

For students with fluent scale technique, this is an exciting piece to play. Beautiful scale playing involves good hand shape, a relaxed arm, and fingers close to the keys. As your student plays scales, encourage this comfortable and efficient approach.

Notice the ways in which the changes of accompaniment style help define the form. As one would expect from a Classical period composer, Clementi writes in balanced phrases.

TIP: Composers often write phrases in balanced pairs. The first phrase—a Question—usually ends on a note other than the keynote. The second phrase—the Answer—usually ends on the keynote. A parallel Answer starts the same as the Question. A contrasting Answer starts differently from the Question.

➤ Find the Question and Answer phrases. Is the Answer (mm. 5-8) parallel or contrasting? [parallel, starts the same as m. 1 but ends on C instead of G]
➤ From m. 1-21 Clementi writes only I (tonic) and V (dominant) harmonies. Label them in the score.

Listen for contrasting dynamics as you play—the dynamics are a key element in this piece.

Practice Suggestions

➤ The LH part provides another opportunity to block and identify chords. When playing the accompaniment as written, keep it quiet but clear. Play with a loose flexible wrist.
➤ You may wish to practice the scale passages without the LH. To learn the fingerings, it is helpful to bracket the finger sets in the score.

➤ Listen carefully to the repeated notes when you play the motive from m. 1, which is repeated many times. Both notes are played with a light wrist bounce. Do not slur beat three into the following downbeat.

CREATIVE ACTIVITIES

This may be an opportunity for your students to compose their own sonatina exposition in C major. Try these approaches:

➤ Create a Theme 1 (consider writing an eight-measure Question and Answer). Limit the rhythm to quarter and half notes and the melodic range to a five-finger pattern.
➤ Create a contrasting Theme 2 (another eight measures). Insert some repeated notes and eighth notes.
➤ Let the LH accompaniment of one theme be chordal, and the accompaniment of the other theme single tones. Can Theme 2 be in the dominant?

Title: *Sonatina,* op. 1, no. 1

Alexander Gedike
Sonatina in C Major, op. 36, no. 20 (R22, SW37)
Exploring the Score

If sonatinas and sonatas are studies in contrasts, this lively *Sonatina in C Major* certainly fills the bill.

➤ Explore the contrasts:
  – dynamics
  – rhythmic figures
  – LH accompaniment styles
  – character of the main themes: compare mm. 1-2 with mm. 5-6.

➤ As with several pieces in previous modules, this sonatina invites orchestration. Have your student decide which instruments play the following:

  – The opening three accented chords
    _____.

  – The answering piano *staccato* notes
    _____.

  – The Theme II *legato* motives
    _____.

Voilà! An entire orchestra at our fingertips!

Practice Suggestions

➤ Theme I is a four-measure Question and Answer. It is restated in mm. 13-16. The "mini-development" in mm. 9-12 is derived from Theme I. Isolate those measures for practice. Give special attention to dynamic contrasts.
➤ Theme II (mm. 5-8) has some rhythmic surprises. Tap these measures before playing at the keyboard.
➤ Most students find it helpful to block the LH *Alberti* bass (mm. 5-8, 17-20). Block the LH alone before combining hands together.

CREATIVE ACTIVITY

Improvise different answers to the musical question posed in mm. 1-2 of Gedike's *Sonatina in C Major.* Your answers can be either parallel or contrasting.

Boris Berlin
The Haunted Castle (R30, SW57)
Exploring the Score

Have students listen to the *Celebration Series®* recording with their eyes closed, imagining the scene this music evokes. Discuss the musical elements Berlin uses to create a mysterious, other-worldly effect:
  – keyboard range
  – damper pedal
  – *staccato* articulation with pedal
  – chords other than major and minor
  – whole-tone scale

Practice Suggestions

Touch and tone are of primary importance. Each sound contributes to a convincing interpretation. Use the performance on the *Celebration Series®* recording as a model. Experiment with different *staccato* touches to create a similar sound on your piano.

CREATIVE ACTIVITY

Berlin's *Haunted Castle* paints a vivid musical picture. Using chords other than major and minor, create a piece that tells a story about another haunted place. Give your piece a title.
Title: _____

Nancy Telfer
The Sleeping Dragon (R38, SW73)
Exploring the Score

This piece opens the doors of musical imagination and sound exploration. Ask the student a few leading questions and make suggestions concerning tone quality, but step back and allow the student's imagination to guide the interpretation.
➤ As the piece opens, is the dragon walking to its cave or is it asleep?
➤ What happens to the dragon in mm. 35-41?
➤ Prior to the first week of practice, guide the student's fingering of the double thirds, RH mm. 1-6. Play both voices *legato*.
➤ Block the position shifts in the B section: mm. 15-16, 21-22, and 23-24. Can the student detect a relationship between the first position and the second?

Practice Suggestions

Legato 3rds are always a challenge to play.

➤ In mm. 1-2, follow the fingering exactly and "feel" the connection moving from 3rd to 3rd.
➤ Isolate the RH chromatic 3rds in mm. 31-34 for special fingering practice.

Johann Friedrich Burgmüller
Arabesque, op. 100, no. 2 (S5)
Exploring the Score

Everyone loves *Arabesque.* What makes it such a student favorite?
  – sixteenths sound difficult, but are easy to play (no crossings)
  – there are only two patterns of sixteenths
  – rhythm is predictable and strong
  – LH chords feel comfortable
  – hands are rhythmically coordinated
  – ending sounds big

➤ Circle the chord tones in the RH mm. 3-6.
➤ Where does Burgmüller use syncopation? [mm. 8 and 24]

Practice Suggestions

➤ When working out the notes and rhythm it will help greatly to tap the syncopated measures.
➤ Use words such as "Mis-sis-sip-pi mud" to reinforce the even rhythm of the sixteenth-note patterns.

Try these suggestions for learning the LH sixteenth notes:
➤ Block the LH sixteenth note positions in mm. 11-16.
➤ Then play as written (LH alone) listening for evenness of sound and lifting on the ending eighth note of each slur.
➤ Practice the same measures hands together at a minimum of three speeds: slow, medium, fast.

Carl Czerny
Study in D Minor, op. 261, no. 53 (S9)

Exploring the Score

This study is much like a broken-chord version of a chorale.
➤ Have the student discover the "chorale" phrases by playing the chords in blocked form.

➤ Notice that this piece uses a 2 + 2 + 4 measure phrase structure.
➤ Write in your dynamic plan for the "chorale" phrases.

Practice Suggestions

Experiment with different ways to create evenness of sixteenths. Do you play most evenly when there is only finger activity and no movement of the hand? Is it more even and consistent when you tip your hand in the direction of the notes? Evenness and dynamics are the issues.

STUDY MODULE 4

Page	List	Composer	Title	Key, Meter and Tempo
R11 SW20	A	George Frideric Handel	*Gavotte in G Major, HWV 491*	G Major $\frac{4}{4}$ ♩ = 138
R18 SW29	B	Ludwig van Beethoven	*Sonatina in G Major (First Movement)*	G Major **C** Moderato
R26 SW46	C	Alexander T. Grechaninov	*After the Ball, op. 98, no. 13*	B Minor $\frac{3}{4}$ Tempo di mazurka
R33 SW63	C	Petr Eben	*Bird on the Windowsill*	C Major **C** Poco agitato
R34 SW66	C	Seymour Bernstein	*The Elegant Toreador*	C Major ¢ Flirtatiously
S7		Béla Bartók	*Minuet*	C Major $\frac{3}{4}$ Andante
S14		Alexander Tansman	*The Doll*	A Minor **C** Assez vif

Assign first:

Gavotte in G Major ....
The Elegant Toreador ....
Minuet ....
The Doll

Assign next when ready:

Sonatina in G Major
Bird on the Windowsill
After the Ball

Notice the programmatic titles. Music often paints descriptive pictures. Encourage the students to make a "program" or story for each piece. Even the *Gavotte in G Major* evokes images of ballrooms, formal attire, and palaces. In addition, ask students to compare the three dances in this module: *Gavotte*, *Minuet*, and *After the Ball*. As you move through Level 3, encourage your students to continue their chart of musical TIPS.

George Frideric Handel
Gavotte in G Major, HWV 491 (R11, SW20)

Exploring the Score

A gavotte is a 17th-century French dance characterized by an upbeat of two quarter notes and phrases that begin and end in the middle of the measure. However, Handel writes this *Gavotte* with a simpler upbeat pattern. Find all the occurrences of this motive:

The quarter note is the goal of this pattern. The longest value (dotted half note) is the goal of the entire phrase.

➤ Have your student draw the phrase shapes in the air while listening to this piece. Which phrases ascend? Which descend? Notice the up–down pairing of the phrases. You and the student may wish to choreograph the *Gavotte*. As the music ascends, move away. As the music descends, approach one another again.

➤ Compare the direction of the bass and treble lines. Where do they move in contrary motion? In parallel motion? (More ideas for your studio choreography!)

TIP: Most Baroque dances are in *binary form*. The two parts are separated by a double bar. The A section modulates to the dominant key, and the B section returns to the tonic key.

Practice Suggestions

In the Baroque period, articulation was a primary means of defining meter and mood. The LH lines of many keyboard dances imitate the bowing of a cello or the tonguing of a bassoon.

➤ Let your "cello" LH dictate the degree of detachment you will use on the RH quarters.

➤ The descending two-note slur patterns in the RH may deserve some special fingering practice. Try this fingering on several different scales. Let the LH join in on the fun, and play an ascending scale with the same fingerings and patterns.

➤ The rhythmic goal of each phrase is its final note, the dotted half note. Experiment with different ways to shape the phrases. Some sound best with a *crescendo* to the long note. Others sound better if the tension resolves at the end of the phrase. Notate your decisions in the score.

Ludwig van Beethoven
Sonatina in G Major (First Movement)
(R18, SW29)

Music scholars have determined that this piece was not written by Beethoven. The composer is unknown. However, we shall continue to teach this "Beethoven" *Sonatina in G Major* for its charming elegance and for its musical benefit.

Exploring the Score

The primary rhythmic motion of the opening is in half notes. One could well imagine in Viennese society that this represents:

stand   bow   stand

The emphasis is on the change of harmony.

➤ Note how the RH makes this "bow" more intense.

➤ Be a musical sleuth and find the hidden step motion in the themes.

What step motion can you find in mm. 5-7? Mm. 9-15 are a "step motion goldmine." Is there step motion in the LH?

➤ Discuss lengths of phrases. Are they all two-measure phrases? Most composers would follow a short idea (mm. 1-2, 3-4) with a longer phrase. Is that true of this composer?

TIP: Short-short-long phrase structure is an important characteristic of music from the Classical era.

What sonata-allegro formal elements are *not* found in this movement? [no Theme II; no modulation to V] The *coda* is of unusual length. Compare the length of the exposition with the *coda.*

Practice Suggestions

➤ Plan the dynamics of your opening "bow" so that the stress is on the middle (dominant) harmony.
➤ The small notes, mm. 1, 3, 5, 6, etc., are played on the beat and are "crushed" with the following principal tone.
➤ Articulate the two-note slurs (m. 2, etc.) by playing the second eighth note lightly.
➤ Write in your LH fingering choices, mm. 5-8.
➤ In mm. 7-8, does it sound best to play the LH *legato* or detached? You decide.
➤ Separate the quarter notes from the descending eighths in RH mm. 13-16.

Alexander Grechaninov
After the Ball, op. 98, no. 13 (R26, SW46)
Exploring the Score

➤ Grechaninov's marking, *Tempo di mazurka,* suggests the dance background of *After the Ball.* Most mazurkas have dotted rhythms, syncopation, and a stress on the second or third beat. How many of these elements are present in this piece?
➤ The form of the piece is obvious, yet a label is difficult. It can not be called binary or rounded binary because the first part is not repeated. It is not ternary (ABA) because the second half is repeated.

None of the musical forms we have defined quite match Grechaninov's clever way of structuring this piece.

➤ Mention has been made of short-short-long phrases in the Classical style. Grechaninov uses that plan in the A section. Is that plan found in the B section?
➤ List ways in which the B section is contrasting. (Make special note of the LH.)

Practice Suggestions

How many different dynamic marks does Grechaninov use? Listen carefully for these different volume levels as you practice.

➤ The one-measure motives at the beginning are a unifying device in the piece. Execute a gentle phrase-lift at the end of each slur. Be sure your listener can distinguish two one-measure phrases and a longer two-measure phrase in the first four measures.
➤ Use the damper pedal to create a blended texture in the A sections.
➤ Highlight the articulation difference between hands in mm. 9-14. Avoid the pedal here.

Petr Eben
Bird on the Windowsill (R33, SW63)
Exploring the Score

The success of this "touch piece" depends primarily on articulation. What actions of the "bird on the windowsill" might these articulations describe?

➤ Have your student list at least four different touches found in this piece. [accented *staccato, staccato, tenuto, legato*]
➤ As an in-lesson experience, have the student practice some of those touches on the closed keyboard cover. Mm. 6-7 are the most difficult of the piece. Guide the first days of practice on those measures. [**Hint:** Emphasize the lifts.]

Practice Suggestions

➤ Divide the piece into sections for practice: mm. 1-5, mm. 6-7, mm 8-10 (downbeat only)
➤ Play mm. 6-7 on a flat surface very slowly, exaggerating the lift after each slur, *staccato,* and *tenuto.*
➤ You may wish to write in extra "reminder" fingerings as you practice. With your teacher's guidance, you may even wish to change some of the printed fingerings. Be consistent in using the fingering you determine to be the best one.

Seymour Bernstein
The Elegant Toreador (R34, SW66)
Exploring the Score

This piece is filled with humor, Latin flavor, and surprise. It is our expense-free trip to a Spanish bullfight.

➤ Away from the piano, have the student play the opening measures on a rhythm instrument (tambourine, castanets). Memorize that rhythm. Your student can continue using the castanets as you play the opening sounds on the piano. Add the main theme, mm. 4-7, to the student's Latin *ostinato*.

➤ Devise a "program" (story) for mm. 5-12: the *subito forte* of m. 4 and its quick fade-out; the shaped motives of mm. 7-8. Is only the toreador present, or are ladies involved? Is the bull introduced in this piece? What gesture from the toreador is represented by the *glissando* in m. 12?

➤ Harmonic analysis will help the student learn the piece quickly. Do you find harmonies other than I and V7?

Practice Suggestions

➤ Tap and count the rhythm before playing. Be sure to feel the rest on beat two.

➤ Practice the changing RH fingers, mm. 4-5.

➤ The dynamics of mm. 4-7 are crucial to a fine performance of the piece. Observe the details of dynamics from your first week of practice.

➤ Spot practice m. 12, playing the printed quarter notes in rhythm *without* the *glissando*. Repeat, adding the *glissando* while maintaining the underlying pulse.

CREATIVE ACTIVITY

Create your own Spanish song in the lesson. As your teacher or another student plays the rhythm of the first four measures on a rhythm instrument, improvise a RH Spanish melody using Bernstein's ideas as a model.

Title: *In Old Madrid*

Béla Bartók
Minuet (S7)
Exploring the Score

Your student has played minuets previously. The unusual feature that Bartók brings to this piece is the elegant "duet" sound of the sixths. (Imagine the piece played on recorders or flutes!) Compare the other minuets of Level 3 and their use of eighth notes moving to a downbeat. [*Piano Repertoire*, pp. 4 and 6]

➤ Your student has learned to associate Baroque dances with binary form. This piece lacks the

obvious repeat double bars in the middle. Help the student discover the formal design:

A = mm. 1-8
A1 = mm. 9-16
Coda = mm. 17-22

➤ Previous discussions have focused on the two-measure minuet dance step. Bartók writes many two-measure phrases here. The student can mark them in the score.

➤ Have the student look for four-measure units. Are there any one-measure units?

TIP: Composers usually use a combination of phrase lengths in a single composition (two- and four-measure phrases are most common). Pieces that use the same phrase length throughout are very rare.

Notice how the LH melody in the *coda* is related to the opening RH motive.

➤ Discuss the elements of unity. [use of repeated motives, use of sixths]

➤ How does Bartók create interest through contrast? [variety of phrase lengths]

Practice Suggestions

This minuet will help you develop a comfortable hand *staccato* on consecutive sixths. Here are two preparatory drills. Maintain a rounded hand position and keep the wrist free of tension. Practice the following example hands separately, then together.

CREATIVE ACTIVITY

Using the same LH as Bartók, make your own variation of this minuet by changing at least one RH beat per measure. Change the direction of the sixths, the rhythm, or even the interval. Experiment with the first eight measures by playing something different each time.

Title: _____

Alexander Tansman
The Doll (S14)
Exploring the Score

After playing part of the piece for the student, ask about the doll. What is the doll doing? Why is this piece chosen for the *Piano Studies/Etudes*? What will you learn technically from the piece? [RH phrasing, LH control, sixteenth-note upbeat patterns]

➤ Each phrase begins with a sixteenth upbeat. In the lesson, have the student experience that pattern (with LH answer) by tapping on the keyboard cover and counting aloud. Did the LH release exactly on the next beat?

➤ Although no slurs are printed beyond m. 4, the articulation patterns set up by the initial measures may be assumed throughout. Agree on the places where longer slurs might be appropriate, and mark them.

➤ Another pattern of sixteenths appears in mm. 4, 8, and 15. Guide a successful experience with that

rhythm prior to the student's first day of practice.

Practice Suggestions

➤ The RH has fingering challenges in the second half of the piece. Practice mm. 9-16 very slowly at first. Can you see a fingering sequence in mm. 10 and 11? [4-2-3 repeated]. Watch out for the last measure!

➤ In mm. 10, 12, and 16, circle the beats where the RH and LH play together. These rhythmic surprises feel different and can be tricky.

STUDY MODULE 5

Page	List	Composer	Title	Key, Meter and Tempo
R9 SW14	A	Johann Sebastian Bach, attr.	*Musette in D Major, BWV Anh. 126*	D Major $\frac{2}{4}$ $\quad \downarrow = 80$
R19 SW31	B	Ludwig van Beethoven	*Sonatina in G Major (Second Movement: Romanze)*	G Major $\frac{6}{8}$ $\quad \downarrow . = 76$
R24 SW43	C	Alexander Grechaninov	*Horse and Rider, op. 98, no. 5*	G Major $\frac{6}{8}$ Allegro
R36 SW70	C	Ruth Watson Henderson	*Lullaby in Black and White*	C Minor $\frac{6}{8}$ Gently
S10		Daniel Gottlob Türk	*Having Fun*	B flat Major $\frac{2}{4}$ Allegro
S11		Vladimir Blok	*Two Ants*	G Major $\frac{2}{4}$ Allegretto
S13		Gem Fitch	*Chinese Kites*	Pentatonic $\frac{4}{4}$ Playfully

Assign first:

Musette in D Major
Having Fun . . . .
Horse and Rider . . . .
Chinese Kites . . . .

Assign next when ready:

Romanze
Lullaby in Black and White
Two Ants

The pieces in Study Module 5 emphasize a variety of touches and articulations. The *Musette in D Major* requires careful hand coordination for shifts and articulations. The Beethoven *Romanze* has long melodic lines that require *legato* fingerings. *Horse and Rider, Two Ants,* and *Chinese Kites* include many *staccato* articulations.

Johann Sebastian Bach, attr.
Musette in D Major, BWV Anh. 126 (R9, SW14)
Exploring the Score

Musette in D Major is one of the most famous pieces in the early intermediate repertoire. *Musette* is the name given to the French bagpipe of the 17th and 18th centuries. All pieces bearing this title have one style feature in common: a bagpipe drone. In this piece the drone is not the usual blocked 5th, but bouncing LH octaves.

➤ The opening drone is on a D octave. Where does this change? [m. 9, to the note A)] What is the key relationship of these two drones? [tonic-dominant]

➤ Find the rhythmic surprise in mm. 13 and 15.

➤ The student can quickly learn to play the opening two measures. The teacher can answer with mm. 3-4.

➤ Switch parts. What is the position for mm. 3-4? [D major]

> Assist the student with the hand shifts of the B section, mm. 9-20. Each measure has its own RH location.

Practice Suggestions

The position shifts between mm. 2-3 and mm. 4-5 need special practice. Your upper arms will help you shift quickly.
> Block the two RH D major five-finger positions (mm. 1, 3). Practice shifting from the higher position to the lower position, then back up. Next, practice shifting from the higher position to just the lower F sharp (finger 3). When shifting up, aim for just the high A (finger 5).
> Use a similar approach for the LH shifts in mm. 1-8. (Consider putting thumb on the left hand D, m. 4.)
> Give special practice to the position shifts in the B section, mm. 9-20, as well as the chromaticism and syncopation, mm. 13-16.
> The LH octaves are always played detached.

Ludwig van Beethoven
Sonatina in G Major (Second Movement: Romanze) (R19, SW31)

Exploring the Score

It is interesting to compare this *Romanze* movement with the first movement of the sonatina, studied in Module 4. Notice the similarity of formal structure, including the extended *coda*.

Compare the first eight measures of each movement.
> Compare LH harmonies, mm. 1-2, mm. 5-6. [same harmonies]
> Do both sections end in the tonic? [yes]
> What are the highest and lowest pitches in the RH?

Draw the student's attention to the relationship between tonic and dominant harmonies.

TIP: When harmony alternates between tonic and dominant, the stress is usually on the dominant.

Now look for contrasting themes, keys, and textures in the *Romanze* movement.

> Where was the thematic material of the *coda* first presented?
> Find examples of short-short-long phrase structures (2 + 2 + 4 measures).
> Find a six-measure emphasis on the dominant. [mm. 16-21]
> Name and label the I, IV, and V7 chords in this piece.

Practice Suggestions

As you become familiar with this beautiful *Romanze,* listen to the rise and fall of the RH melody over the gentle LH accompaniment. A *Romanze* generally has a tender quality. How can you avoid making this piece sound like a dance? [LH accompaniment very quiet; RH elegantly phrased, lovely *legato*]
> With your teacher, decide on phrasing and articulations for RH eighth notes that are not slurred or marked *staccato*.
> Practice the LH with fingers close to the keys. Avoid a *staccato* sound on the blocked intervals.
> Each phrase of the opening section has three harmonies. To provide contrast, bring out the middle harmony in each phrase.
> Compare the LH notation of mm. 1-2 with mm. 3-4. Hold the bass line dotted quarter notes in mm. 3-4.
> In mm. 17-19, keep the RH rhythm steady. Play the top note of the LH rolled chords with the RH downbeat.

Alexander Grechaninov
Horse and Rider, op. 98, no. 5 (R24, SW43)
Exploring the Score

Picture a young child riding on a rocking horse as you listen to the *Celebration Series®* recording of *Horse and Rider.*
> How does Grechaninov create a galloping or rocking effect?
> What happens on the second page that results in the marking but *"All's well that ends well."*?
> How many measures of this piece do you not need to practice? (Find the repeated sections.)

Practice Suggestions
> For hand coordination and rhythm practice, tap the opening eight measures in a moderate tempo.
> Which measures are most unusual and will need special practice? (Consider mm.15-18 and the "scale measures.")
> The galloping effect is the result of observing correct rhythm and the accent marks. Does your sound match that of the *Celebration Series®* recording?

Ruth Watson Henderson
Lullaby in Black and White (R36, SW70)
Exploring the Score

Your student will immediately be able to relate the title to the score.
> Discuss the sensation of rocking. Which meter(s) best capture the feeling of rocking? Which tempi suggest rocking—rocking a cradle, rocking in a chair,

swinging in a hammock? Now look at the marking on Henderson's score: **6/8**, "Gently."

➤ How does the rocking motion of Henderson's *Lullaby* compare with Grechaninov's *Horse and Rider*? Which motion is more gentle and which is more active?

➤ Even the word "rocking" implies "long-short." Find "long-short" (quarter-eighth) in the score. Henderson uses two versions of the **6/8** rhythm:

♪ ♪ ♪ ♩   ♪

♩   ♪ ♩   ♪

➤ Which hand is "white" and which hand is "black"?
➤ Be a Musical Detective:
  – How much of the piece repeats? [mm.1-10 repeated in mm. 19-28]
  – Analyze the intervals used in m. 1. [LH plays a 5th, RH plays a 4th]
  – How many measures remain true to that arrangement?
  – Compare mm. 1-2 with mm. 5-6: Are the pitches the same? [yes, but turned upside down]
  – What is this called? [inversion]
  – Circle the LH "surprise" of a sixth. [m. 29] Can you explain why the composer wrote that unique interval? [to complete the step motion F-G-A started in mm. 27-28 while retaining the sound of C]

Practice Suggestions

➤ Tap and count the two-handed rhythm, feeling the rocking motion. Watch out for the surprise in m. 18! [hemiola]
➤ Block the positions hands together. Notice that the LH is almost always in a C or F position. Also, the hands are usually separated by a minor third. This knowledge will help you memorize the piece.

CREATIVE ACTIVITY

Make up your own *Lullaby*. Use the rhythms you played in Henderson's piece. You can arrange the hands on white and black keys, play all blacks, or make a wonderful white key lullaby. What intervals will you use?

Title: *Gentle Song*

Daniel Gottlob Türk
Having Fun (S10)

Türk was a renowned teacher and composer of instructional materials. In this piece he provides the student with a variety of broken, zigzag shapes.

Practice Suggestions

The motion for zigzag patterns should come from the forearm. Rotate the forearm back and forth, tipping the hand from side to side as if you were turning a doorknob. Practice this movement on the closed keyboard cover. For the different patterns in this piece, devise practice steps that incorporate forearm rotation.

The RH figures of mm. 7-8 and 14-16 are unpredictable. Divide the sixteenth-note passages into short groups, ending on the thumb. Practice each group several times.

Vladimir Blok
Two Ants (S11)

Exploring the Score

How would you, as a composer, depict two ants? Their movements seem agitated, unpredictable, and frantic. We often see ants crawling over one another. As you look at the score, discuss with your student the issues of direction and unpredictability.

➤ To enter this unusual world, a composer might select unusual intervals and harmonies.
➤ Notice the words used by the composer to guide your interpretation: *leggiero, più mosso, rit., meno mosso.*
➤ Before the student begins practice, make sure that the rhythm is experienced accurately.

Practice Suggestions

➤ The rhythm of this composition is tricky. Be sure you can tap and count a practice section before playing. Count the rests on beat two carefully, especially in mm. 1-2, 4, and similar places.
➤ Decide on an articulation for the opening eighth-note pairs. Is it most "ant-like" to play these pairs slightly detached or connected? The choice is left to you.
➤ You can learn this piece quickly if you block hand positions.

Gem Fitch
Chinese Kites (S13)

Exploring the Score

The key signature has six sharps! This piece is easier, however, than it looks.

➤ Do you play any white keys in *Chinese Kites*? [no, there are none!] Knowing that the piece is limited to black keys will help you read it.

TIP: Pentatonic is the term used for a five-note (black-key) scale. Composers often use pentatonic sounds to imitate music of the Far East.

➤ To begin work on the rhythm, have the student set a steady beat and point to main beats in the score saying *1 - 2 - 3 - 4.*
➤ Repeat this exercise, pointing and saying beats and "ands." *1 & 2 & 3 & 4 &*
➤ Play the rhythm on the closed keyboard cover. Continue counting.
➤ Two chords can be played on all black keys: E flat minor–D sharp minor and F sharp major. Label the chord in m. 9.

Does the student know the meaning of the abbreviations *m.s.* and *m.d.?* See the discussion of Lorna Paterson's *Rush Hour* in Study Module 2 of this Level.

Practice Suggestions

Chinese Kites is unique because all the notes are written using the treble clef. Notice how the stems of notes are beamed: up-stems always indicate the RH and down-stems are played by the LH.
➤ Use the RH to play notes with up-stems. Use the LH to play notes with down-stems. Tap on a flat surface at first and then play on the keyboard.
➤ Notice that all eighth notes are played *staccato,* including those at the ends of slurred groups.
➤ In this study, the hands are very close together. The *staccato* articulations help clear the way for the opposite hand.
➤ Use the damper pedal on the final RH *glissando.*

CREATIVE ACTIVITY

Improvise a short piece using the black note pentatonic scale from *Chinese Kites.* If you create a slow piece, use the damper pedal.

Title: *Chinese Pagoda*

STUDY MODULE 6

Page	List	Composer	Title	Key, Meter and Tempo
R8 SW11	A	Henry Purcell	*Hornpipe in B flat Major, Z T683*	B flat Major $\frac{3}{4}$ ♩ = 88
R20 SW34	B	Johann Anton André	*Sonatina in A Minor (Third Movement: Rondo)*	A Minor $\frac{2}{4}$ Allegretto
R23 SW40	C	Pyotr Il'yich Tchaikovsky	*Morning Prayer, op. 39, no. 1*	G Major $\frac{3}{4}$ Andante
R28 SW49	C	Dmitri Kabalevsky	*Clowns, op. 39, no. 20*	A Minor $\frac{2}{4}$ Allegro
S8		Samuil Maikapar	*The Young Shepherd's Song, op. 28, no. 3*	G Major 𝄵 Allegro non troppo
S15		Alexander Gedike	*Study in E Minor, op. 32, no. 12*	E Minor $\frac{2}{4}$ Moderato quasi andantino

Assign first:

Study in E Minor . . . .
Hornpipe in B flat Major . . . .
The Young Shepherd's Song . . . .

Assign next when ready:

Sonatina in A Minor
Morning Prayer
Clowns

Students will have the opportunity to explore stylistic contrasts from the Baroque to the 20th century. As each piece is studied, ask your student to list the musical elements that are characteristic of the style period.

Most of the Baroque dances studied up to this point have had a predominantly two-voice texture. Many pieces in this module have a three- or even four-voice texture (e.g., *Morning Prayer*). *Hornpipe in B flat Major* has two voices yet remains one of the more challenging pieces in this module because of its rhythm.

Henry Purcell
Hornpipe in B flat Major, Z T683 (R8, SW11)
Exploring the Score

The hornpipe was a solo dance of British origin, with the accompaniment of bagpipes and fiddles. What a jolly scene!

➤ Although there are no *staccato* markings in the score, the "kick" of the dance step is represented by the unmarked eighths in beat three. Have the student experience that articulation in the lesson.

➤ As you play the piece for the student, separate the second and third beats. Treat the last note of beat two as a *staccato,* and detach the following two eighth notes.

➤ Circle the RH melodic notes on the first and third beats of mm. 1-4. The LH part parallels this descending stepwise line. Find the ascending stepwise movement in mm. 9-12.

➤ Compare the LH in mm. 1-4 with mm. 9-12. The final five notes are the same in each group. Notice the mirror image of the first six notes found in mm. 9-11.

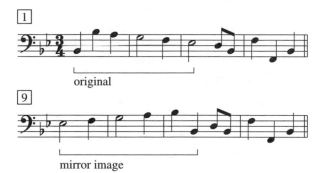

original

mirror image

Practice Suggestions

➤ For rhythmic reinforcement, tap the rhythms, counting in sixteenth-note subdivisions.

➤ Before playing hands together, practice the RH alone in mm. 1-4 to achieve the proper phrasing. In each measure, do the following

    – slur beats one and two together, lifting *lightly* from the last note of the slur

    – play both eighth notes in beat three *staccato*

    – combine steps 1 and 2 for each measure

    – finally, play hands together

Johann Anton André
Sonatina in A Minor (Third Movement: Rondo)
(R20, SW34)
Exploring the Score

TIP: In a typical three-movement sonata structure of the Classical period, the expected plan is:

Movement One:	dramatic, filled with contrast
Movement Two:	(change of key) slow, lyrical
Movement Three:	light-hearted; often in rondo form

This movement is a third-movement rondo. Does it convey the expected light-hearted mood? Discuss the way André imbues this movement with humor and joy (in spite of its minor key!) Consider tempo, articulation, harmony.

The harmonies of mm. 1-8 are so surprising, we should grin with delight when we hear them.

    mm. 1-4 are clearly in A minor

    mm. 5-6 suddenly shift to E minor

    mm. 7-8 do an abrupt about-face and land in C major!

Notice the reference to A minor in m. 14, and then back to C major again in m. 16!

➤ Rondos feature contrasting sections and returns to the opening theme. Help your student map out the form of this piece. If one considers the repeats, the form might look like this:

    A A B B transition A C (Coda)

    m. 1 1 9 9 17   21 28

Practice Suggestions

➤ Each day during your first week of practice, play the RH alone to secure accuracy of articulation. Then play hands together, working in two-measure units.

➤ Check the LH eighth notes, mm. 13-14, for fingering and articulation. The combination of contrasting touches in both hands will require spot practice.

➤ Did you notice the held half notes in LH mm. 9-10, 28-29, and 32-34? Those measures may require special practice.

Pyotr Il'yich Tchaikovsky
Morning Prayer, op. 39, no. 1 (R23, SW40)
Exploring the Score

➤ How does Tchaikovsky create a reverent atmosphere? [hymn-like four-part texture]

➤ What tone quality is appropriate for the opening of *Morning Prayer?* [sustained *legato,* projected melody]

➤ What is the effect of the *forte* and accent markings in mm. 7, 12, and 16-17? [harmonic surprise, special emotional tension]

➤ Have the student find measures in which two voices in the same hand move independently. Discuss practice steps that will result in control of those independently moving voices.

Practice Suggestions

Playing four notes exactly together is a challenge. Try these practice tips:

➤ Play each chord with a slight arm push to the bottom of the keys.

➤ To bring out the top (soprano) voice, first play each melody note alone (with a full tone); then play the remaining chord tones together quietly. Keep that sound in your mind's ear. Play with a relaxed hand and arm.

Playing two independent voices in one hand is also a challenge. Practice the LH in mm. 16-21 this way:
➤ Divide the two voices between the hands, RH playing the upper tenor voice, LH playing the bass repeated G's.
➤ Then play both voices slowly as written. The blocked intervals are coordinated most easily if you push gently with the arm. Listen for the *legato* tenor voice.

Practice the syncopated pedaling in mm. 1-4. Remember that the foot *lifts* as you *play* each chord, not before.

Pedal

Dmitri Kabalevsky
Clowns (R27, SW49)
Exploring the Score

If you wrote a piece about a clown, what would it sound like? Are clowns always happy and energetic? What is behind that funny face?
➤ How does Kabalevsky create the mood in this famous piece? Help your student make a list. You might include:
  – tempo
  – LH intervals and *staccato* articulation "happy–sad" abrupt changes from major to minor
  – unpredictable lengths of groupings
➤ What tone quality is appropriate for the opening of this piece? Should the hands be equal in volume?
➤ Each four-measure unit features a pair of chromatic tones:
    mm. 1-4: C sharp–C
    mm. 5-8: G sharp–G
    mm. 9-12: A–A flat
    mm. 13-16: (LH) E-D sharp
    mm. 17-21: C sharp–C
    mm. 22-24: G sharp–G

Ask your student to find this chromatic "clue" and circle the skeletal chromaticism in each phrase.

➤ Why the teeter-totter between major and minor in the main motive? Does the change in m. 9 strike you as being humorous or sad?
➤ In mm. 13-16 there seems to be a repeated attempt to get somewhere or do something. What is your story for those measures?
➤ Most students learn this piece quickly because of the infrequent shifts of position. During the lesson, help your student block out the piece in position shifts.

Practice Suggestions

➤ At the beginning of each day's practice, review the blocked positions for each four-measure unit.
➤ As you practice slowly, play very sharp *staccatos* in both hands, and emphasize the accents.
➤ Listen for the subtle changes from major to minor.
➤ Notice the three different articulations Kabalevsky indicates in mm. 13-16.
➤ The most difficult moment of this piece is the final three chords. Study those chords and practice slowly.

Samuil Maikapar
The Young Shepherd's Song, op. 28, no. 3 (S8)
Exploring the Score

This is truly a finger study. It has a joyous mood, and the *staccatos* often evoke the feeling of dance. Explore with your student the two technical figures in *Young Shepherd's Song*. [four-note patterns and a "short trill" sixteenth-note figure]

Practice Suggestions

The quickest way to learn this piece is to isolate the two technical figures.
➤ Find all the sixteenth-note patterns of four descending notes. Practice them hands together, keeping a flexible wrist.
➤ Find the short sixteenth-note "trill" figures. Practice them hands separately at first.

CREATIVE ACTIVITY

Using Maikapar's four-note patterns and trill figures, compose your own piece. The RH or LH can play alone, play hands together, play *legato* or *staccato*, parallel or contrary motion. Be creative and find ways to vary the patterns.

Title: *Shepherd's Flute*

Alexander Gedike
Study in E Minor, op. 32, no. 12 (S15)
Exploring the Score

Although Gedike was a late-Romantic composer, he creates phrases here in which the final note is the goal, as was the case in much Baroque music. The exception and contrast occurs in the B section, mm. 13-23. Here the phrase focus is on the penultimate beat.

➢ Listen to the *Celebration Series®* recording.
➢ Give the piece a title that fits its mysterious mood.

Practice Suggestions

➢ Tap the rhythms hands together. Did you hear even sixteenths divided between the hands?
➢ Play in short practice sections. Practice the sequences in mm. 13-20 slowly, phrase by phrase. Do you spot the rising chromatic bass line?
➢ Decide on a dynamic plan for the phrases.

Level 3 SUMMARY

➢ Several **Musical Tips** occur throughout Level 3 discussions. How many different ideas did you list on your Chart of Musical Tips? Remember these musical concepts and apply them as you begin work in the next album.
➢ *Repertoire Piano 3* includes seven sonatina movements. Compare the movements and look for examples of the following: blocked or broken chord accompaniment, scale passages, Question-and-Answer phrases, coda, and sequence.
➢ Many of the pieces from the 19th and 20th centuries are programmatic in nature. Titles often indicate a story, a character, a place, or an animal. How did the titles *The Sleeping Dragon, Clowns,* and *The Haunted Castle* influence your study and performance of those pieces?
➢ Which pieces in this level were your favorites and why? Which pieces were the most challenging for you? Recall the ways in which you met the challenges successfully.

Level 4

The Publications

Level 4 of the *Celebration Series®* includes the following publications:
Piano Repertoire 4
Piano Studies/Etudes 4
Student Workbook 4
Recording of Repertoire and *Studies/Etudes 4*

The Repertoire

Piano Repertoire 4 is divided into three lists.

➤ List A includes a selection of pieces composed during the Baroque period (*ca* 1600 to *ca* 1750).

➤ List B includes a selection of pieces composed during the Classical period (*ca* 1750 to *ca* 1820) as well as pieces in the Classical style written during the nineteenth and twentieth centuries.

➤ List C includes a selection of pieces composed during the Romantic era (*ca* 1820 to *ca* 1910) and the twentieth century.

The repertoire and studies represent the intermediate level of piano study. The range of composers and combination of well-known teaching pieces with less familiar repertoire make this collection an enjoyable experience for both teacher and student.

Students are encouraged to add to their Dance Chart begun in Level 2, listing the title and rhythmic characteristics of each dance studied.

Musical Development

The wide variety of repertoire pieces and technical studies in Level 4 provides materials through which the intermediate-level student can experience significant musical and technical growth. The three-voice textures require control of balance and projection of melody over accompaniment. Accompaniment styles range from the independent lines of the Baroque repertoire to a variety of figures in the Classical sonatinas.

For the first time in the *Celebration Series®*, the sonatina movements present a complete sonata-allegro form with contrasting themes in the exposition and a true development section. The Romantic selections focus on melody, balance, and

expression. They include several pieces in triple meter including the ever-popular waltz. Challenging rhythmic experiences in this level include constantly changing meters (*Changing Bars* by István Szelényi) and the use of *hemiola* (David Duke's *Barcarole*).

The Study Modules

Level 4 is divided into six Study Modules. The discussions of the individual pieces in each Study Module are organized under the following headings:
Exploring the Score
Practice Suggestions
Creative Activities

Exploring the Score is designed as an interactive exercise between teacher and student. These sections include questions you might address to the student during lessons. ***Practice Suggestions*** are largely directed to the student. The ***Creative Activities*** act as reinforcement for your students' understanding of a musical concept and can provide a springboard for their composition and improvisation.

The six Study Modules suggest an order of difficulty. Please refer to the discussion of ***Order of Assignment*** in the Foreword, p. 9, if you have questions regarding the columns "Assign first" and "Assign next when ready" found below each Study Module Chart.

Musical Tips

As students work through this Level, they will accumulate general information about musical style that can be applied to other pieces. Your student can use a blank page to notate these points, which are identified as musical tips (**TIP:**).

The chart on the opposite page lists the repertoire and studies in Level 4. Page numbers for works in *Piano Repertoire 4* and *Piano Studies/Etudes 4* are found in the first column. Study Module numbers are found to the far right. Study Module groupings of repertoire and studies follow.

Piano Repertoire 4

	Page	Composer	Title	Study Module
List A	R4	Anon., J.S. Bach, attr.	*Minuet in D Minor, BWV Anh. 132*	4
	R5	William Babell	*Rigadoon in A Minor*	2
	R6	George Frideric Handel	*Bourrée in G Major*	3
	R7	Georg Philipp Telemann	*Fantasia in E Minor, TWV 33:21*	1
	R8	Domenico Scarlatti	*Aria in D Minor, L 423/K 32*	6
	R9	C.P.E. Bach	*March in D Major, BWV Anh. 122*	5
List B	R10	Muzio Clementi	*Sonatina in G Major, op. 36, no. 2 (Second Movement)*	1
	R12	Muzio Clementi	*Sonatina in G Major, op. 36, no. 2 (Third Movement)*	2
	R15	Franz Joseph Haydn	*Sonata in F Major, Hob. XVI:9 (Third Movement: Scherzo)*	5
	R16	Anton Diabelli	*Sonatina in F Major, op. 168, no. 1*	3
	R18	Tobias Haslinger	*Sonatina in C Major (First Movement)*	4
	R20	Cornelius Gurlitt	*Sonatina in G Major, op. 188, no. 3*	6
	R22	Erkki Melartin	*Sonatina in B flat Major*	6
List C	R24	Carl Maria von Weber	*Waltz in G Major, op. 4, no. 2*	5
	R25	Felix Mendelssohn	*Romance in G Minor*	3
	R26	Robert Schumann	*The Wild Horseman, op. 68, no. 8*	5
	R27	Alexandre Tansman	*Melody*	1
	R28	Béla Bartók	*Children's Game*	1
	R30	Boris Berlin	*Monkeys in the Tree*	2
	R32	Marcel Poot	*Across the Channel*	6
	R34	Robert Benedict	*Shallows*	2
	R35	David Duke	*Barcarole*	4
	R36	István Szelényi	*Changing Bars*	4
	R38	Stephen Chatman	*Game of Hypnosis*	3
	R40	Christopher Norton	*Play It Again*	6

Piano Studies/Etudes 4

Page	Composer	Title	Study Module
S4	Carl Czerny	*Study in G Major, op. 599, no. 45*	3
S5	Alexander Gedike	*Study in G Major, op. 36, no. 26*	6
S6	Carl Czerny	*Study in B flat Major, op. 599, no. 83*	5
S7	Árpád Balázs	*Game*	1
S8	Stephen Heller	*The Avalanche, op. 45, no. 2*	4
S10	Johann Friedrich Burgmüller	*The Wagtail, op. 100, no. 11*	3
S11	Judith Snowdon	*Adults*	3
S12	Clifford Crawley	*You're Joking!*	6
S13	Johann Friedrich Burgmüller	*Progress, op. 100, no. 6*	5
S14	Jean-Baptiste Duvernoy	*Study C Major, op. 176, no. 24*	4
S15	Alexandre Tansman	*Skating*	6
S16	David Karp	*Sailing Along*	1
S18	Lorna Paterson	*Scherzo*	5
S19	Béla Bartók	*Syncopated Dance*	2
S20	Christopher Norton	*Blues No. 1*	2

Level 4 Repertoire and Studies/Etudes – Listed by Study Module

Study Module 1

List	Composer	Title	Page & Book
A	Georg Philipp Telemann	*Fantasia in E Minor, TWV 33:21*	R7, SW13
B	Muzio Clementi	*Sonatina in G Major, op. 36, no. 2 (Second Movement)*	R10, SW22
C	Alexandre Tansman	*Melody*	R27, SW54
C	Béla Bartók	*Children's Game*	R28, SW56
Study	Árpád Balázs	*Game*	S7
Study	David Karp	*Sailing Along*	S16

Study Module 2

List	Composer	Title	Page & Book
A	William Babell	*Rigadoon in A Minor*	R5, SW7
B	Muzio Clementi	*Sonatina, op. 36, no. 2 (Third Movement)*	R12, SW28
C	Boris Berlin	*Monkeys in the Tree*	R30, SW59
C	Robert Benedict	*Shallows*	R34, SW65
Study	Béla Bartók	*Syncopated Dance*	S19
Study	Christopher Norton	*Blues No. 1*	S20

Study Module 3

List	Composer	Title	Page & Book
A	George Frideric Handel	*Bourrée in G Major*	R6, SW10
B	Anton Diabelli	*Sonatina in F Major, op. 168, no. 1*	R16, SW31
C	Felix Mendelssohn	*Romance in G Minor*	R25, SW48
C	Stephen Chatman	*Game of Hypnosis*	R38, SW74
Study	Carl Czerny	*Study in G Major, op. 599, no. 45*	S4
Study	Johann Friedrich Burgmüller	*The Wagtail, op. 100, no. 11*	S10
Study	Judith Snowdon	*Adults*	S11

Study Module 4

List	Composer	Title	Page & Book
A	J.S. Bach, attr.	*Minuet in D Minor, BWV Anh. 132*	R4, SW4
B	Tobias Haslinger	*Sonatina in C Major*	R18, SW36
C	David Duke	*Barcarole*	R35, SW68
C	István Szelényi	*Changing Bars*	R36, SW71
Study	Stephen Heller	*The Avalanche*	S8
Study	Jean-Baptiste Duvernoy	*Study C Major, op. 176, no. 24*	S14

Study Module 5

List	Composer	Title	Page & Book
A	C.P.E. Bach	*March in D Major, BWV Anh. 122*	R9, SW18
B	Franz Joseph Haydn	*Sonata in F Major, Hob. XVI:9 (Third Movement: Scherzo)*	R15, SW28
C	Carl Maria von Weber	*Waltz in G Major, op. 4, no. 2*	R24, SW46
C	Robert Schumann	*The Wild Horseman, op. 68, no. 8*	R26, SW51
Study	Carl Czerny	*Study in B flat Major, op. 599, no. 83*	S6
Study	Johann Friedrich Burgmüller	*Progress, op. 100, no. 6*	S13
Study	Lorna Paterson	*Scherzo*	S18

Study Module 6

List	Composer	Title	Page & Book
A	Domenico Scarlatti	*Aria in D Minor, L 423/K 32*	R8, SW15
B	Cornelius Gurlitt	*Sonatina in G Major, op 188, no. 3 (First Movement)*	R20, SW39
B	Erkki Melartin	*Sonatina*	R22, SW43
C	Marcel Poot	*Across the Channel*	R32, SW62
C	Christopher Norton	*Play It Again*	R40, SW76
Study	Alexander Gedike	*Study in G Major, op. 36, no. 26*	S5
Study	Clifford Crawley	*You're Joking!*	S12
Study	Alexandre Tansman	*Skating*	S15

STUDY MODULE 1

Page	List	Composer	Title	Key, Meter and Tempo
R7 SW13	A	Georg Philipp Telemann	*Fantasia in E Minor, TWV 33:21*	E Minor **C** Very fast
R10 SW22	B	Muzio Clementi	*Sonatina in G Major, op. 36, no. 2 (Second Movement)*	C Major **¾** Allegretto
R27 SW54	C	Alexandre Tansman	*Melody*	A Minor **C** Moderato
R28 SW56	C	Béla Bartók	*Children's Game*	D Minor **²⁄₄** Allegretto
S7		Árpád Balázs	*Game*	D Dorian **²⁄₄** Allegro e leggermente
S16		David Karp	*Sailing Along*	Whole tone **⁶⁄₈** Allegro

Assign first:

Sonatina in G Major . . . .
Game . . . .
Sailing Along . . . .

Assign next when ready:

Fantasia in E Minor
Children's Game
Melody

The pieces in Module 1 are highly contrasting. For example, the consistent dotted rhythm in Clementi's *Sonatina in G Major* can be compared with the unifying eighth-note motion of Tansman's *Melody*. Also, compare the two musical games by Bartók and Balázs. How does each composition portray its musical game? The keys selected by the composers provide further discussion. Three pieces are in minor keys. What are the tonal centers for the remaining three?

Georg Philipp Telemann
Fantasia in E Minor, TWV 33:21 (R7, SW13)
Exploring the Score

The term *fantasy* or *fantasia* has been used in keyboard composition for centuries. However, even in a given style period, the term held different meanings for different composers. The footnote indicates that this is the third section of a larger composition, revealing that Telemann's fantasies are sectional.

Note the tempo marking: *Very fast.* This is a robust, energetic dance. How will you articulate *Fantasy in E Minor* to emphasize the dance quality? Experiment with the articulation. Find the best sound for a dance.

Consider the phrase organization:

➤ Telemann uses a half note to end RH groups. In the opening section, the groups are 1m. + 1m. + 2mm. This "short + short + long" gives fine balance to mm. 1-4.

➤ The B section, mm. 5-10, feels strangely off balance. Why? [a six-measure section] What are the groupings? [2mm + 1m. + 1m. + 2mm.]

➤ *Fantasy in E Minor* is cast in *rounded binary form.* The B section is "rounded out" by a return of the opening A theme. If you mark in the score the A, B, A sections and circle the double bar repeat signs, you have a picture of *rounded binary form.*

➤ If your student plays harmonic minor scales, the D sharp in mm. 4 and 10 is easily explained.

➤ What harmonies are outlined in the final cadence (second ending)? [IV-V-I]

Practice Suggestions

The musical goal is to create the effect of a bright, energetic dance.

➤ Decide on the articulation. Edit your score, writing in the slurs and *staccatos.*

➤ Use a drop-lift motion when two eighths are slurred to a quarter.

Muzio Clementi
Sonatina in G Major, op. 36, no. 2
(Second Movement) (R10, SW22)
Exploring the Score

When you first see this movement, what is its most striking feature? [constant dotted rhythm—very unusual for a second movement.] What mood is established by the dotted figures and the *Allegretto* tempo?

➤ To clarify the *ternary form,* have the student mark the A B A sections. In which key does each section end?

➤ In the A section (mm. 1-8), notice the four-measure phrase groups so common to the Classical era. Discuss the variety of smaller groupings found in these standard phrases.

➤ Can you find the unusual phrase groupings in the B section (mm. 9-16)?
  – Mm. 9-10 establish a two-measure pattern.
  – Mm. 11-12 start as if they were a two-measure sequential repetition, but the phrase extends all the way to m. 16. Circle the notes on the main beats of RH mm. 12-14. What do you see? [ascending G major scale]. The dynamic markings will help the phrase move through to its high point, then come back down.

➤ Compare mm. 21-24 with mm. 25-28. Why did Clementi add this extra repetition? [to emphasize the ending of the movement]

Compare the harmonies of mm. 1-2 and mm. 5-6. Both sets employ I and V harmonies, but the progressions are shaped differently. Play these measures, listening carefully to the harmonic changes. In mm. 1-2, the V pushes across the bar line to I. In mm. 5-6, the tension of the V7 is released on the third beat (I). Discuss the effect of these different harmonic formulas.

Harmonic rhythm refers to the rate at which harmonies change. In this movement the accompanying quarter and half notes signal the changes of harmonies.

➤ Find the measures where the harmonic rhythm is: **half note–quarter note.**

➤ Find the unusual measures where the harmonic rhythm is: **quarter note–half note.**

➤ The music intensifies when the harmonic rhythm is: **quarter note–quarter note–quarter note.** These measures lead to important cadences at the end of each section.

TIP: Composers frequently approach a cadence with an increase of harmonic and rhythmic intensity.

Practice Suggestions
➤ When the LH has the dotted rhythms (mm. 5-6, 21-23, and 25-26) match the *legato* quality to that of the RH.

➤ Spot practice the RH double 3rds in mm. 5-6 and similar places. Listen for the *legato* connection and think "drop-lift" for proper phrasing. Be careful not to play the *fz* with too much accent. Maintain the *dolce* (sweetly) sound indicated on the score.

➤ Which measures have no dotted rhythm? [mm. 8 and 28] To maintain a steady pulse in these cadential measures, think of four background sixteenth notes for every quarter note.

CREATIVE ACTIVITY
Compose a four-measure RH tune using only the dotted rhythm from Clementi's sonatina movement. Label this melody "a." Compose a contrasting four-measure LH melody that avoids the dotted figure. Label this melody "b." Add I, IV and V chord accompaniments to both melodies. Combine these melodies to form a composition with two or three sections–for example "ab," "aba," or "ba."
Title: *Variation on a Theme by Clementi*

Alexandre Tansman
Melody (R27, SW54)
Exploring the Score

If one can speak of delicious harmonies, then this piece is a feast. Tansman has given us a rare and beautiful experience.

➤ Play the piece for the student or listen to the *Celebration Series®* recording.

➤ Block the chords in two-measure units. Circle the one chord in each unit you find most interesting and colorful. Put a box around your favorite chord of the entire piece. You now have a road map for the shape of each phrase and a focal point for the entire piece.

➤ The pedal is the "seasoning" in this delicious feast. Discuss the timing of pedal changes.

➤ Play only the melody to experience the four-measure phrase groupings.

➤ To highlight the balance between melody and accompaniment, have the student play the blocked intervals from beats one and three, divided between the hands:

Listen to the balance of melody and accompaniment when you use both hands. Now practice achieving that sound with the RH alone.

Practice Suggestions

➤ Block the chords in two-measure units. Practice the pedal changes as you block the chords.

➤ You have circled the colorful harmonies in each unit. When you play in blocked chords, listen to the shape of the four-measure phrases and play those harmonies with tender emphasis.

➤ In each half measure, play the half note alone with a rich tone quality, followed by the four eighth notes, *pianissimo*. Listen for this clear balance of sound when you play it as written.

Béla Bartók
Children's Game (R28, SW56)
Exploring the Score

Listen to the *Celebration Series®* recording of this piece with special attention to articulation. What playful gestures are suggested through the music? For example, where might two children be running after each other? [mm. 9-10] Can you find other moments of "musical tag"?

➤ Mark the form in the score. Notice that each large section (mm. 1-26, 27-52, 53-73) is divided into two contrasting sub-sections.

➤ Bartok was a master at varying his accompaniments. Compare his treatment of melody and accompaniment in mm. 1-8, 27-34, and 53-60. What stays the same? [melody]. What changes? [accompaniment and dynamics] Do a similar comparison of mm. 13-20, 39-46, and 61-68.

➤ Notice the *Adagio ppp* cadence measures, which are always alike. What role do they play in the *Children's Game?* The tonality of the piece is D minor, but these cadences end with an open 5th on A. It is rare when a piece does not end on the tonic note. The final cadence leaves the listener with an incomplete feeling, as if the game is to continue.

Devise a tapping activity in which the student taps and counts aloud, emphasizing the slurred groups:

1 AND 2 AND 1 and 2 rest, 1 AND 2 and 1 - 2

Continue this activity for mm. 13-18.

Practice Suggestions

Much of your practice will be focused on the coordination between hands, as there is an abundance of opposing articulations.

➤ First, find passages where the hands have the same articulation, e.g. mm. 5-8, 11-12, 43-46.

➤ Challenge: mm. 13-16. Observe RH lifts.

➤ Next challenge: mm. 1-4. Practice this first on a flat surface ... slowly! Did you hear a slight accent on the beginning of each short slurred group?

➤ Final challenge: mm. 18-21.

➤ Use damper pedal where marked.

Árpád Balázs
Game (S7)
Exploring the Score

Pieces depicting play often include humorous surprises. Find the surprises in this piece. (Check both rhythm and dynamics.) Circle the places you find *most* surprising.

➤ How many different technical ideas do you find? [broken intervals, blocked chords, *staccatos*]

➤ If you marked the sections in the score, what would be the form of this piece?

A: mm. 1-4
A1: mm. 5-8
B: mm. 9-14
C: mm. 15-22 (starts like A, ends like a Coda)

➤ What is the key of the piece? (Tonal center on D, but no flats or sharps.) You are experiencing the sound of the Dorian mode, D to D (d, e, f, g, a, b, c, d) through most of the piece.

➤ In m. 18, the RH triad leaves the listener with the final sound of D major. Does the ending suggest the game is over or continuing?

Practice Suggestions

➤ For mm. 1, 9-10, 19-21, write the basic eighth-note counting (*1 & 2 &*) in the score. Tap and count these measures until they are perfect. Which measure has downbeat eighth-note rests in both hands? [m. 10]

➤ How will you finger mm. 9-10?

➤ Spot practice the two different technical figures (broken intervals, blocked chords).

David Karp
Sailing Along (S16)
Exploring the Score

If your student does not know about the *whole tone scale,* this is a perfect introduction because it contains the two possibilities for the whole-tone scale:

The sound of a whole-tone piece is one of unresolved suspension—no tone is tonic.

➤ Conduct a search for the two whole-tone scales.

➤ What happens to our pleasant day of sailing in the last line?

Practice Suggestions

Find the following musical elements and isolate them for spot practice:

- *staccato* whole-tone scales
- *legato* whole-tone scales
- pedaled clusters
- C major RH five-note cluster (C, D, E, F, G) played in the bass clef
- forearm clusters on white keys

As you practice, be aware of the different combinations of *staccato* and *legato.*

CREATIVE ACTIVITY

Using the two whole-tone scales in Karp's *Sailing Along,* create your own piece. Use different registers of the keyboard, ascending and descending. Add damper pedal.
Title: *Outer Space*

STUDY MODULE 2

Page	List	Composer	Title	Key, Meter and Tempo
R5 SW7	A	William Babell	*Rigadoon in A Minor*	A Minor ¢ ♩ = 96
R12 SW28	B	Muzio Clementi	*Sonatina, op. 36, no. 2 (Third Movement)*	G Major $\frac{3}{8}$ Allegro
R30 SW59	C	Boris Berlin	*Monkeys in the Tree*	G Major $\frac{3}{4}$ Lively
R34 SW65	C	Robert Benedict	*Shallows*	D Minor $\frac{4}{4}$ Andantino e rubato
S19		Béla Bartók	*Syncopated Dance*	D Minor ¢ Allegro deciso
S20		Christopher Norton	*Blues No. 1*	C Major $\frac{4}{4}$ Steady four

Assign first:

Rigadoon . . . .
Syncopated Dance . . . .
Blues No. 1 . . . .

Assign next when ready:

Sonatina
Monkeys in the Tree
Shallows

Comparison often leads to insight. Use the following questions to compare the pieces in Study Module 2.

Which pieces are bold and strongly rhythmic?

Which pieces have a unifying rhythmic motive?

Which pieces have a unifying technical figure?

Which piece is the longest? What is its form?

In which piece(s) does the LH use a broken chord bass figure?

In which piece is elegance of expression and pedaling important?

Which piece has a jazz feel?

William Babell
Rigadoon in A Minor (R5, SW7)
Exploring the Score

It is helpful to know that a *Rigadoon* was a lively, vigorous dance. In mm. 9-10 one can hear:

with a hey! hey! hey! and a ho! ho! ho!

That spirit is the goal of the performance. The piece is divided into sections:
➤ Which section uses imitative two-part writing? [A = mm. 1-8]
➤ Which section has melody and accompaniment? [B = mm. 9-20]
➤ What is Babell's formal plan? [A B A]
➤ Where do you find four-measure phrases? six-measure phrases?

Investigate the dynamic plan and tonal center:

➤ Can you find examples of a call and echo effect? How does this match the phrasing?
➤ The key of this piece is A minor. What is the last chord of the piece?

TIP: In a minor key, a major 3rd used in the final chord is called a *Picardy third*. This device was primarily used during the Baroque period.

Practice Suggestions

➤ When practicing mm. 1-4, you may wish to play hands separately to check fingerings and LH rests.
➤ The footnote suggests detaching most quarter notes. Listen carefully for this articulation. Lean into the first note of each two-note slur for contrast.

➤ When playing at performance tempo, remember that the piece is in cut time. Feel two half-note pulses per measure.

Muzio Clementi
Sonatina in G Major, op. 36, no. 2
(Third Movement) (R12, SW28)
Exploring the Score

For the student with fluent scale technique, this piece is a joy to play. The movement is filled with contrast. How many different ideas can you find?
➤ melody starting with repeated notes
➤ melody ending with repeated notes
➤ ascending scales
➤ descending scales
➤ zigzag patterns
➤ melodies accompanied by:
  – broken chords
  – broken octaves
  – slurred falling intervals with two bounces on the lower note

Find and label the three big sections in the score:
    A = mm. 1-31
    transition to B = mm. 32-40
    B = mm. 41-74
    A1 = mm. 75-end

TIP: In the Classical style, the focus of the phrase is often determined by its length. In a two-measure phrase, the focus is often on the downbeat of the second measure; in a four-measure phrase, the focus is usually on the downbeat of the third measure.

As you become familiar with the movement, compare phrase lengths.
  – most of the phrases are four measures long
  – look for two-measure phrases
  – find examples of phrases extended to emphasize the end of a section

Practice Suggestions

The challenge is to shape the RH. The LH remains a quiet partner in the background.
➤ Play the RH melody while blocking the LH.
➤ Always use subtle dynamics to give repeated tones in the melody a sense of forward motion (e.g., mm. 1, 5, 71-73) .
➤ The most difficult RH figure is the zigzag motion found in the B section (mm. 50, 52). Practice these passages with hand rotation. Try dotted rhythm practice, too. Can you see inner voice steps that move in contrary motion with the LH?
➤ What are the components of good scale playing? [curved fingers, quiet wrist, fingers close to the keys] Each day as you practice the scale passages, strive to make your scale playing more even and beautiful.

Boris Berlin
Monkeys in the Tree (R30, SW59)
Exploring the Score

The composer has created his delightful picture of monkeys from one technical figure.
➤ Have the student find the clef changes on the score. The frequent shifts up or down an octave may be a clue to the title. [monkeys jump and swing]
➤ Label the AABA form.
➤ Discuss dynamics in the B section, mm. 20-31. Are different-size monkeys playing in this tree? Which measures could sound like a large baboon? Where does the RH play in the bass clef, *m.d.* (*mano destra* = RH)? [mm. 3, 13, 22, etc.]
➤ Find the stepwise motion skeleton around which the main figure is built.

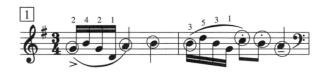

Does the LH also employ stepwise motion?
➤ Berlin repeats his figure frequently, sometimes in a different octave. Have the student circle the measures with contrasting material.
➤ Discuss the use of hand rotation to play the sixteenth-note figure.
➤ Circle the time signature changes.

Practice Suggestions

➤ Spot practice the main figure in all the octaves in which it appears.

➤ Isolate the contrasting measures (the B section) for practice.
➤ There are many quick changes of position. Follow these steps to master the shifts:
  - Play the measure immediately before the shift of position.
  - As you play the last note of that measure, *say the name of the first note* in the new position.
  - Play that exercise again and visually spot the new note as you say it, well before you play it.

Robert Benedict
Shallows (R34, SW65)
Exploring the Score

➤ Have the student listen (with eyes closed) to your performance of the piece or to the *Celebration Series®* recording. What pictures come to mind as you hear the piece?
➤ For initial presentation, a teacher–student duet could take place at the lesson, with the student playing LH and the teacher adding the RH. Shape the phrases beautifully so the student will experience the finished performance sound.
➤ Discuss the frequent use of fermatas in *Shallows*. What effect do they have on the flow of the piece and the resulting mood?
➤ Mm. 1-4 and 19-24 frame the body of the piece. Compare these phrases. Find the subtle differences.
➤ Guide the student through an exploration of the melody:
  - The first phrase is five measures long (mm. 5-9.) After descending from A to D (mm. 5-6), the melody soars up to C, then descends again before coming to rest on B.
  - Look at the melody in mm. 10-13. Have you seen it before?
  - Where are the melodic lines in mm. 12-15 and mm. 16-18? Upon which pitches do these inner lines come to rest? [B and E]
➤ Have the student play the LH blocked chords. They are grouped in two-measure pairs. Make special note of the tones that move.

Practice Suggestions

➤ Review the LH triads. Listen to the inner voice movement. Find other places for hands separate practice.
➤ The LH of mm. 7-8 is a three-voice texture. Say the finger numbers of the moving quarter notes as you read these measures.
➤ Circle the change of time signatures in mm. 8 and 9. Keep the same quarter note pulse.
➤ Watch and listen for the B naturals in mm. 8-9!

Let the *Celebration Series*® recording guide your sound. Did the tempo of that performance influence your practice?

CREATIVE ACTIVITY

Borrow the LH accompaniment (mm. 1-4) of *Shallows*. Improvise different RH melodies over this accompaniment. Write down your favorite melody.

Title: _____

Béla Bartók
Syncopated Dance (S19)
Exploring the Score

All of the rhythms used in this piece can be found in the first two measures.

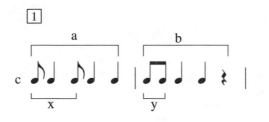

➤ Find and label other measures that have the complete "a" rhythm.
➤ Find and label measures that use the "x" syncopated rhythm twice.
➤ "Y" is a pair of eighths. Find measures you could label as "2y." Did you find the "3y"?
➤ The ends of phrases are marked by rests. Knowing this, how many measures are in the first phrase? [2] the second? [3] the third? [5] Discuss how Bartók creates longer phrases with such limited material.

Practice Suggestions

Rhythm is the driving force in *Syncopated Dance*.
➤ Tap the rhythm hands together.
➤ Play the RH while tapping the LH. Reverse the roles.
➤ In mm. 4-5 and 9-10, what blocked intervals are in each hand? What makes the LH easier?

As you play hands together, look for the measures that have parallel motion between the hands and measures that represent contrary motion.

Listen carefully for a difference between *staccatos* and *tenutos*.

Christopher Norton
Blues No. 1 (S20)
Exploring the Score

The long tones in the bass give you the clue to the basic harmonic progression of this blues piece: I, IV, (I), V, I.
➤ Memorize the rhythm of m. 1. Play and say *1 & 2 & 3 & rest*. It is customary to "swing" the eighth notes in a blues style. Play the first note of each eighth-note pair a bit longer than the second.
➤ Play the LH, m. 3, and say: *(1) & 2 & 3 &*.
➤ Add LH m. 4 to m. 3, saying the rhythm. When that rhythm is mastered, you are ready to tap entire sections.

Listen to the *Celebration Series*® recording. Does the performer "bend" the eighth notes in blues style?

Practice Suggestions

An effective performance of this blues piece requires steady pulse and accurate articulations.
➤ Tap and count before playing, especially if you plan to swing the eighth notes.
➤ To learn notes and position shifts quickly, block the intervals in each hand and practice slowly.
➤ Observe the articulations. Norton's slurs suggest the importance of notes on the beat. Lean into the slurs and make the first note of each eighth-note pair louder than the second.
➤ Where is the loudest dynamic level?

STUDY MODULE 3

Page	List	Composer	Title	Key, Meter and Tempo
R6 SW10	A	George Frideric Handel	*Bourrée in G Major*	G Major $\frac{4}{4}$ $\quad \downarrow = 132$
R16 SW31	B	Anton Diabelli	*Sonatina in F Major, op. 168, no. 1 (First Movement)*	F Major **c** Moderato cantabile
R25 SW48	C	Felix Mendelssohn	*Romance in G Minor*	G Minor $\frac{3}{4}$ Andante
R38 SW74		Stephen Chatman	*Game of Hypnosis*	Chance, no meter $\downarrow = 60$
S4		Carl Czerny	*Study in G Major, op. 599, no. 45*	G Major $\frac{2}{4}$ Allegretto
S10		Johann Friedrich Burgmüller	*The Wagtail, op. 100, no. 11*	C Major $\frac{2}{4}$ Allegretto
S11		Judith Snowdon	*Adults*	F Major $\frac{4}{4}$ With energy

Assign first:

Study in G Major . . . .
Adults . . . .
Bourrée . . . .
Sonatina in F Major

Assign next when ready:

The Wagtail
Game of Hypnosis
Romance in G Minor

Study Module 3 presents a microcosm of keyboard styles and technical approaches. Handel's *Bourrée in G Major* and Diabelli's *Sonatina in F Major* require careful articulation and facile finger technique. Mendelssohn's *Romance in G Minor* employs a variety of subtle expressive touches, sensitive balance, and careful pedaling. Both the Diabelli and Mendelssohn provide the opportunity to explore the melodic effects of the *appoggiatura*. Chatman's *Game of Hypnosis* uses contemporary sounds and allows the performer to determine the sequence of musical events. The three studies provide students with new experiences of hand *staccato* employing both chromatic and broken- chord patterns.

George Frideric Handel
Bourrée in G Major (R6, SW10)
Exploring the Score

A *bourrée* is a robust, fast dance in duple meter. Each phrase starts with an upbeat. A fine interpretation of this piece will be energetic, full-toned, with strongly detached quarter notes.

Mark a check at the end of each phrase. Do the new phrases start with an upbeat?

Relate the direction of the phrases to the movements of the dancers:
- mm. 1-2 move in one direction (ascend)
- mm. 3-4 reverse direction
- mm. 5-7 are an exciting drive upward to reach their goal (m. 8).

- mm. 9-14 are shorter units (contrast)
- mm. 15-21 are a relentless search for their final goal (m. 22)

Is this dance in binary form?

TIP: Virtually all dances in the Baroque period are in binary form. The A section shifts to the dominant key, and the B section returns to the tonic key.

Analyze the score. Identify:
- the key at the beginning [G major: I]
- the key at the end of the A section [D major: V]
- the key at the end of the piece [G major – I]
- all the places where Handel's melody includes an ascending or descending run of four stepwise eighth notes (Don't be fooled by the way the notes are beamed!)

It is important to know the lengths of the phrases in order to shape them appropriately.

TIP: Baroque phrases tend to push forward to their final note. The longer the phrase, the more the intensity accumulates.

Practice Suggestions:

➤ A delightful feature of this *bourrée* is the use of syncopation. Emphasize half notes on beat 2.

TIP: In the Baroque period, syncopations were highlighted by using a detached articulation before the syncopation.

➤ Play *legato* until the fingerings are comfortable and secure.
➤ Coordinating your two hands may be challenging. Work very slowly, repeating each small practice unit until secure.
➤ Play sharply detached quarter notes to improve your dance interpretation.
➤ The dynamics in the score are helpful editorial suggestions.

TIP: Sequences often get louder as they progress higher.

Anton Diabelli
Sonatina in F Major, op. 168, no. 1
(First Movement) (R16, SW31)
Exploring the Score
The opening theme's tender expression is created by the *appoggiatura*. An *appoggiatura* is a non-chord tone that falls on a strong beat. Lean on these non-chord tones for dynamic emphasis; resolve quietly to the chord tone that follows.

➤ Find the downbeat *appoggiaturas* in the opening theme. Investigate the variety of approaches to the *appoggiaturas*—from below, from above, by step, by leap.
➤ Because each *appoggiatura* is approached differently, each deserves a unique sound. Which one should have the most stress?
➤ You may use *rubato* to add expression to an *appoggiatura*.

Analyze the score:
  – Exposition [mm. 1-12]
      theme 1 [I, F major]
      theme 2 [V, C major]
  – Development [mm. 13-24, cadence on V7]
  – Recapitulation [mm. 25-38]
      theme 1 [I, F major]
      theme 2 [I, F major]

➤ Compare themes 1 and 2 (mm. 1-7, 8-12). How do they differ? [accompaniment, melody, articulation]
➤ Which harmony in the development section is most surprising and has the most tension? How will you emphasize this?

Practice Suggestions

➤ How many of the LH harmonies can you name? Block the chords to identify them, then write their names in the score.
➤ You will learn the LH shifts and fingerings fastest if you practice moving from one blocked chord to another.
➤ Because there is such intensity of expression in the RH, make your LH sound like a neutral background.

Felix Mendelssohn
Romance in G Minor (R25, SW48)

A romance is a short, lyrical, expressive song.

Exploring the Score
A musical sigh is associated with falling pitches, especially two-note slurs. Mendelssohn intensifies his musical sigh by using a dotted rhythm.

➤ Find the outline of the sigh. [D–A, B flat–F sharp]
➤ Experiment with the dynamics to find an appropriate shape for the sigh.
➤ Look for variations of the sighing figure. [mm. 4, 8, 10, etc.]
➤ Discuss the term *appoggiatura* and point out the examples in mm. 12, 16, and 18. Listen to the interpretation of these sighing figures on the *Celebration Series*® recording.
➤ The dotted rhythm can be labeled the "x" motive. The eighth-note scale figures can be "y." Notice the balance Mendelssohn achieves between "x" and "y."

Practice Suggestions

The score is marked *con pedale*, but the many rests and the frequent step motion indicate that there are no long, connecting pedals. Touches of pedal are used for color. Practice first without the pedal. Then add short pedals to enhance the color of a harmony.

Pedal suggestions for the first four measures are included in the *Student Workbook* for this level.

Stephen Chatman
Game of Hypnosis (R38, SW74)

This is an example of chance (aleatory) music, in which chance or improvisation is an important element. This contemporary compositional technique became important after 1945.

Exploring the Score

Before playing, compare each "musical event" on the page:
➢ Are the eight pitches the same for each event? [yes]
➢ Does the register between events ever change? [no]
➢ Is the low whole note always the same? [yes, except for the final note]
➢ Does each group have the same number of beats? [no]

Practice Suggestions

There are eleven musical events in this piece. Read the composer's directions at the bottom of the page (R38). The metronome marking and the quarter notes in the events indicate that there is a steady beat pervading the piece. Survey each event, counting the number of quarter-note beats that precede the whole note G. Can you find the longest event? [4 beats]

For technical reinforcement, play the grace note patterns *slowly*, *staccato* and without pedal to maintain a clear articulation.

CREATIVE ACTIVITY

Using the same pitches in Chatman's *Game of Hypnosis*, create your own "chance" piece using at least five musical units. Use the damper pedal. Title: *Game of Chance*

Carl Czerny
Study in G Major, op. 599, no. 45 (S4)
Exploring the Score

The piece is organized into four eight-measure groups:
➢ Label the sections. [A, A1, B, A2]
➢ Where does the LH have the melody? [B section]
➢ Which two A sections are most alike? [A and A1]

Practice Suggestions

What two technical patterns did Czerny combine in this study? [arpeggiated four-note chords (open hand position) and scales (closed hand position)]
Arpeggiated four-note chords are made easier if you:

➢ Avoid holding your hand stretched tensely over the whole octave. Let your wrist carry your hand (and fingers!) to the right as you play up the arpeggiation.
➢ Make wise fingering choices. If the top RH interval is a fourth, play 3-5. If the top RH interval is a third, play 4-5. Pay special attention to the LH fingering in m. 24.

Spot practice all RH sixteenth-note passages. You may want to use short groups of 4 + 1 at first.

Johann Friedrich Burgmüller
The Wagtail, op. 100, no. 11 (S10)

A wagtail is a small bird with a long tail that wags up and down. Through the musical figures, one hears the bird chirp and the tail bobbing.

Exploring the Score

Most of the harmonies are easily named:

➢ Write in the score the chord names you know. Remember to look for inversions.
➢ How many inversions of the C major triad can you find?
➢ Discuss and illustrate the benefits of practicing in blocked chords.

Practice Suggestions

The goal of the piece is clean playing through bright *staccatos* and a light sound.
➢ Practice the triads in blocked form.
➢ Give careful attention to the fingering. Circle the sixteenth notes played by the second finger, or write the fingering in the music.
➢ Use a down-up wrist gesture to shape the three-note slurs.

Judith Snowdon
Adults (S11)
Exploring the Score

What makes this music sound like adults? Is their activity busy or calm? What might the *szforzando* markings represent in this music picture?
➢ How many sections are there? [three] Label the sections [A, B, A]
➢ Which chords sound *bitonal* (two different harmonies)? [half notes in mm. 2, 4]
➢ What is the quality of the B section chords? [major]

In this étude, the goal is to play a clear, sharp *staccato*.

➤ The *staccato* chromatic eighth notes and chords require different technical approaches. Play the single tones with a "finger scratch" close to the key. Play the four repeated chords with a slight lifting of the wrist.

➤ To learn the fingerings of the chromatic figures, first play *legato,* then *staccato.*

➤ Use the metronome to build the tempo. Practice five incremental speeds:
quarter = 60, 76, 90, 104, 120

Listen for the dynamic levels indicated by the composer.

STUDY MODULE 4

Page	List	Composer	Title	Key, Meter and Tempo
R4 SW4	A	J.S. Bach, attr.	*Minuet in D Minor, BWV Anh. 132*	D Minor $\frac{3}{4}$ ♩ = 104
R18 SW36	B	Tobias Haslinger	*Sonatina in C Major (First Movement)*	C Major **C** Allegro moderato
R35 SW68	C	David Duke	*Barcarole*	C Major $\frac{6}{8}$ Slowly
R36 SW71	C	István Szelényi	*Changing Bars*	A Minor, mixed meter Molto allegro
S8		Stephen Heller	*The Avalanche, op, 45, no. 2*	A Minor $\frac{2}{4}$ Allegro vivace
S14		Jean-Baptiste Duvernoy	*Study in C Major, op. 176, no. 24*	C Major $\frac{2}{4}$ Allegretto

Assign first:

Minuet in D Minor . . . .
Changing Bars . . . .
Study in C Major . . . .

Assign next when ready:

Sonatina in C Major
Barcarole
The Avalanche

Diversity of rhythmic figures is a notable feature of this Study Module. In *Changing Bars,* Szelényi uses a different meter signature in each measure. The two studies highlight different rhythmic and technical figures: *staccato* 6ths and 3rds in *Study in C Major* and triplet eighth-note patterns and pedaled chordal patterns in *The Avalanche.* Help students create preparatory drills using these elements.

Anon., J.S. Bach, attr.
Minuet in D Minor, BWV Anh. 132 (R4, SW4)

Exploring the Score

This piece has a variety of melodic figures and rhythms. Find the basic unifying elements using the following "x" and "y" rhythms:

Minuet discussions in earlier levels have focused on the two-measure or six-beat unit for the dance steps. Consider having your student create a movement pattern for this minuet.

➤ Where do you find six-beat units? [at the beginning of each section: mm. 1-2, 3-4 and mm. 9-10, 11-12]

➤ What is the phrase length of the remaining measures? [four measures] **TIP:** "Short-short-long" phrase organization is frequently found in works by Baroque composers. The "long" phrase moves forward to the cadence. (Please refer to the *Student Workbook* for further discussion of cadences and binary form in this piece.)

Practice Suggestions

➤ When practicing, observe carefully the fingerings and articulations. Most RH quarter notes are played detached. Are there phrases which need no hands separate practice?

➤ Baroque music moves steadily forward to the final cadence of a section. As you practice mm. 5-8 and mm. 13-16, insert the energy of a *crescendo* so that the arrivals in mm. 8 and 16 are clear.

TIP: In the Baroque period, changes of direction and wide leaps were often highlighted by a break in the sound.

➤ Find the leaps in mm. 9-12 and emphasize them by using detached articulations.

Tobias Haslinger
Sonatina in C Major (First Movement) (R18, SW36)
Exploring the Score

A discussion of contrasts in this movement could be limitless. Almost every measure holds a new delight for our ears and minds. Discuss the sonata form of this movement. Mark your findings in the score. Compare your formal analysis with this chart:

Exposition:	Theme 1a: mm. 1-8
	Theme 1b: mm. 8-12
	Bridge: mm. 12-16
	Theme 2 / Coda: mm. 16-24
Development:	mm. 25-40
Recapitulation:	follows the same plan as the Exposition.

➤ How does one determine that the new theme in m. 8 is not Theme 2? [Theme 2 must be in the dominant.]

➤ Find elements of contrast within each of the themes. Notice the important role played by the LH in creating contrast.

➤ Notice the frequent use of tonic and dominant harmonies in the LH.

Practice Suggestions

➤ Focus your attention on the contrasting elements in the *Sonatina*. With your teacher, devise practice plans around the following:
  – contrasting melodic fragments
  – contrasting dynamics
  – changes in accompaniment style
  – varieties of texture
  – contrasting articulation

As you work towards performance, the most important thing to accomplish is contrast of themes. It may be helpful to give titles to the themes, e.g., Theme 1a "March," Theme 1b "Violins," etc.

CREATIVE ACTIVITY

Using Haslinger's *Sonatina in C Major* as a guide, compose a four-measure melody and notate it on staff paper. Write a simple LH tonic-dominant accompaniment for your melody. Now, create variations of your melody by altering rhythms, adding notes, or changing the accompaniment style. Give your piece a title.

Title: _____

David Duke
Barcarole (R35, SW68)
A barcarole is a Venetian boat song in $\frac{6}{8}$ or $\frac{12}{8}$ with a rocking rhythm.

Exploring the Score

Make a list of musical genres that use $\frac{6}{8}$ meter. Here is a start:
  – galloping and hunting pieces
  – boat or water pieces
  – some dances, e.g., *gigue*
  – some lullabies

Next, discuss the title *Barcarole,* and have the student create a rocking movement with torso and arms as you play the opening chords.

Composers use harmony to create expression. Note the colorful chords in Duke's *Barcarole.*
➤ How many different chords are used in the LH pattern, mm. 1-2? [five]
➤ Play the pattern and listen to the changing sound quality. Can you label each chord with a color?
➤ Composers use *8va* as an indication to play an octave above or below the printed note. Notice Duke's use of *15ma* above the RH in m. 7. What does it tell you? [play two octaves higher than written].
➤ Imagine a picture for mm. 7-8. Play these measures a little slower, with a distant sound.

Have the student listen to the *Celebration Series®* recording and feel the gently rocking movement in beat groups of three. Where does this change? [mm. 9-10—the chords are grouped in two's, 1-2, 3-4, 5-6]
TIP: Hemiola is the rhythmic shift from 3 + 3 to 2 + 2 + 2).

Practice Suggestions

➤ Practice the LH chords, mm. 1-6, with pedal. Listen for clean changes of harmonies.

➤ Notice in mm. 7-8 how Duke creates a special effect in the upper register by marking the notes *staccato* over a held damper pedal. To appreciate that special effect, first play the *staccatos* in mm. 7-8 *without* damper pedal. Then repeat with pedal.
➤ When practicing the chords in mm. 9-10, cover the new chord silently before playing: Play/release, (cover), play/release, (cover), etc.

CREATIVE ACTIVITY

Choose a chord pattern to play in a barcarole rhythm, such as:

$$\begin{array}{cccc} \text{I} & \text{V} & \text{V} & \text{I} \\ \text{or: I} & \text{IV} & \text{V} & \text{V} \\ \text{or: I} & \text{vi} & \text{vi} & \text{I} \end{array}$$

Write a simple melody above your chords.

Title: *Boat Song*

István Szelényi
Changing Bars (R36, SW71)
Exploring the Score

This piece was inspired by the unusual folk dance rhythms of Hungarian peasants. One can imagine the LH drone played on a primitive bagpipe, with the rhythm accented by drums and tambourines. The RH dance tune may have been inspired by a fiddler.

➤ With a percussion instrument, have the student play the LH while counting aloud the number of eighth notes in each measure.
➤ What interval is always used in the LH? [perfect 5th]
➤ On which RH beats does Szelényi place accents? Is there a pattern to the use of accents?
➤ Where can you find RH slurs that cross the bar line? How does this affect the phrasing?
➤ The two *crescendo* markings provide clues to the organization of this piece. The first leads to the *fortissimo* climax at m. 15. The second leads to a return of the "A theme" at m. 29.
➤ Notice the lack of any dynamic mark in the last ten bars. What dynamic level do you want to hear as the piece ends?

Practice Suggestions

To experience the changing meters, try these practice steps:
   1. Tap the rhythm hands together, emphasizing the phrase groupings and RH accents.

2. Play the RH alone, counting aloud in eighth notes.
3. Count through the entire piece but play *only* the $\frac{4}{8}$ measures.
4. Repeat step 3, playing *only* the $\frac{3}{8}$ measures.
5. Repeat step 3, playing *only* the downbeats.

CREATIVE ACTIVITY

Create several short eighth-note motives. Each one should have a different shape. For example:
   – two notes downward
   – three notes repeated
   – four notes zigzag
   – five notes upward

➤ Number each motive and write them on staff paper. Play the motives in random order. You can play them in the same position, or move them around the keyboard.
➤ For an accompaniment, play a LH blocked 5th at the beginning of each motive.
➤ When you find an order of motives you especially like, notate your composition.

Title: *Hungarian Dance*

Stephen Heller
The Avalanche, op. 45, no. 2 (S8)
Exploring the Score

Students enjoy playing *The Avalanche*. It sounds advanced, yet is relatively easy to learn and play. One rhythmic motive dominates the study:

➤ Why do all of the half notes have an accent? [the culmination of the triplet movement]

Practice Suggestions

The triplets move forward rhythmically and dynamically to the accented half notes.
➤ Block the triplet figures to learn notes and fingerings.
➤ Play as written, emphasizing a *crescendo* through the triplets.
➤ The chords in mm. 18-20 and 22-24 include both repeated and moving notes. Play the RH melodic notes *legato*, with the fingering 3-4-5. Play the RH chords, releasing fingers 1 and 2. Project the melody.

In mm. 51-53 the hands move in contrary motion using different phrasing. These measures will need careful practice:

➤ Play the RH alone following the marked *cresc.* to *sf.*
➤ Play the LH alone listening for a true *legato* line.
➤ Play hands together accurately, using at least three different speeds: slow, medium, and fast.

The last five measures have many rests. Count these measures carefully.

Jean-Baptiste Duvernoy
Study in C Major, op. 176, no. 24 (S14)

Exploring the Score

In this study, Duvernoy confronts the student with a basic technical challenge: double note repeated tones. Carefully guide the student's technique before home practice begins.

Duvernoy wrote this study using four-measure groups.
➤ Find the phrase groupings. Did you find one eight-measure phrase? [mm. 9-16]

➤ The RH melodic sixths and thirds in mm. 1-8 repeat in mm. 17-24. How does the accompaniment change? Which presentation do you like the most?
➤ Notice the new challenge starting in m.17. (Your RH has an opportunity to teach the LH how to play the *staccato* notes!)

Practice Suggestions

Find a technique that will keep the arm and hand loose and relaxed. (Consecutive down motions will cause tightness.) Practice this study first on the closed keyboard cover in these contrasting ways:

➤ Play several lines without using an up or down movement of the wrist.
➤ Compare the feeling as you play again using a continuous wrist movement for each measure. Say "drop and lift-ing" as you play to describe the movement of your wrist:

drop   and   lift - ng

Which movement makes this study easier to play?

STUDY MODULE 5

Page	List	Composer	Title	Key, Meter and Tempo
R9 SW18	A	C.P.E. Bach	*March in D Major,* *BWV Anh. 122*	D Major ¢ ♩ = 126
R15 SW28	B	Franz Joseph Haydn	*Sonata in F Major,* *Hob. XVI:9 (Third Movement: Scherzo)*	F Major 2/4 ♩ = 92
R24 SW46	C	Carl Maria von Weber	*Waltz in G Major, op. 4, no. 2*	G Major 3/4 Allegretto
R26 SW51	C	Robert Schumann	*The Wild Horseman,* *op. 68, no. 8*	A Minor 6/8 Allegro
S6		Carl Czerny	*Study in B flat Major,* *op. 599, no, 83*	B flat Major 6/8 Allegro
S13		Johann Friedrich Burgmüller	*Progress, op. 100, no. 6*	C Major ¢ Allegro
S18		Lorna Paterson	*Scherzo*	C Major 4/4 Allegro con brio

Assign first:

March in D Major
Scherzo . . . .
Study in B flat Major . . . .
Progress. . . . .

Assign next when ready:

Sonata in F Major
Waltz in G Major
The Wild Horseman

STUDY MODULE 5

This Study Module contains well-known piano pieces, favorites of students and teachers. The module provides excellent examples of the stylistic characteristics of the four major style periods: Baroque, Classical, Romantic, and twentieth century. Ask students to list style characteristics for each piece. Consider the variety of forms, titles, key centers, meter and tempo markings present in this collection. Would a piece titled *The Wild Horseman* have been written in the Baroque period? Would a *March* be written in any of the style periods? Contrast the two pieces, each with the title *Scherzo,* written two hundred years apart. Developing a list of style characteristics allows students to compare pieces within a given style period as well as pieces from two different periods.

C.P.E. Bach
March in D Major, BWV Anh. 122 (R9, SW18)
Exploring the Score

Listen to the *Celebration Series*® recording of this piece. At the top of the score, have your student make a list of elements that make this piece a convincing march. The list might include:

- strong beat
- drum roll at ends of sections
- constant, marching quarter notes in the LH

➤ Although syncopations are not associated with a march, they are an attractive feature of this piece. Have the student circle the syncopated notes (long tones on beat two).
➤ Circle the RH downbeat tones in mm. 14-17. Bach's plan is obvious. [step motion]
➤ Find more step motion, mm. 18-20.

Practice Suggestions

➤ Independent movement of the hands is important in this piece. For special practice, isolate measures where the hands play similar figures:
- the 4ths in mm. 1-2 and 10-11
- the motive in mm. 4-5
- the 4th, 3rd, 2nd in m. 7
- the stream of eighth notes at the cadences

➤ Find the passages in which fingering plays a crucial role. Practice these measures hands separately, saying the finger numbers aloud.
➤ When do fingers change on repeated notes?

Find and mark the sequences in mm. 13-16 and 17-19. How will you play the dynamics to reflect the sequences?

TIP: Sequences are often played louder if they are higher than the original phrase, and softer if they are lower.

Franz Joseph Haydn
Sonata in F Major, Hob. XVI:9
(Third Movement: Scherzo) (R15, SW28)
Exploring the Score

Haydn wrote approximately sixty-two sonatas over the course of his career. His early sonatas were given the titles of *Divertimento* or *Partita.* Often all of their short movements were in the same key.

➤ Discuss the meaning of *scherzo.* [joking, playful] In spite of the fact that his music is often very humorous, Haydn seldom used this term. He must have felt this movement had special qualities of playfulness. Can your student suggest Haydn's reasons for the title?
➤ This is a fine example of *rounded binary form.* Label the sections. [A section returns m. 16]
➤ Compare the two A sections. Are they *exactly* the same? [see LH downbeat, mm. 7 and 23]
➤ Notice Haydn's use of upbeats. Which eighth-note upbeats are slurred? not slurred? Do they create slightly different moods?
➤ Is the familiar "short notes go to long notes" idea appropriate with these phrases?

Practice Suggestions

Follow these steps to learn this piece quickly:
➤ Decide on and mark the articulation for all upbeat eighth notes *before* playing.
➤ Divide the A section into four-measure units. Pay special attention to RH fingering, especially on the double thirds in mm. 3-4. When the RH is secure, add the LH.
➤ Find all zigzag patterns and practice them using forearm rotation.
➤ Give special practice to RH mm. 14-15 for fingerings and the wide stretch.
➤ When you are comfortable with the B section RH, add the LH in blocked intervals.
➤ Remember, "short notes go to long notes." Plan and listen for dynamic shaping in your phrases.

Carl Maria von Weber
Waltz in G Major, op. 4, no. 2 (R24, SW46)

Exploring the Score

➤ Have the student compare the Trio with the rest of the piece. How is it different? [key, rhythm, texture, LH accompaniment]

➤ Next, focus on the balance and variety of phrase structure. The entire piece is constructed from four-measure units, but Weber uses different combinations and subdivisions to create variety. For example, mm. 1-4 have a 1 + 1 + 2 measure construction, but mm. 17-20 constitute one flowing unit.

➤ Where does the LH have the melody? [mm. 9-12] How does the composer use dynamic marks to remind us?

Practice Suggestions

➤ The RH fingering of mm. 21-24 deserves attention. Analyze which fingers provide the *legato* connection. Practice RH alone, emphasizing the finger lifts in the *non-legato* voice.

➤ Play the LH waltz accompaniment with a light touch. Use a down-up-up motion to keep the second and third beats quiet.

➤ With your teacher, discuss pedaling for this piece.

Robert Schumann
The Wild Horseman, op. 68, no. 8 (R26, SW51)

Exploring the Score

The Wild Horseman is one of the most famous pieces from Schumann's *Album for the Young,* op. 68. Your student may be familiar with this character piece. If not, play it for the student. Why does everyone like *The Wild Horseman?*

Romantic composers often used ternary (ABA) form in their short character pieces. The double bar lines on the score make the sections easy to identify.

➤ What are the contrasts between the A and B sections? [location of melody; A minor vs. F major]

➤ In what ways are the sections alike?

➤ Look at the harmonic progression in each section. What two chords are used? [I and V]

Have your student find the unison relationship between the top notes of the LH and the RH in mm. 2-3. Does the LH receive this same "assistance" when it has the melody?

Practice Suggestions

➤ Block the RH galloping melody. In mm. 1-2, how many shifts of position did you play? In mm. 3-4, how many shifts did you play? When you are confident of these position shifts, you have conquered the RH of the A section.

➤ In mm. 9-16, block the LH positions. How often do you shift position?

➤ To achieve the required "wild" sound, you must create an intense *crescendo* on the ascending eighths. Practice hands together, exaggerating the *sfz* in each phrase.

➤ Listen for crisp, pointed *staccatos.* Play the chords with a quick wrist bounce and a "grabbing" motion of the fingertips.

➤ Spot practice mm. 12 and 16. The contrary motion makes these measures challenging.

Carl Czerny
Study in B flat Major, op. 599, no. 83 (S6)

In Study Module 4, you played a *staccato* study by Duvernoy. Apply your skill of playing repeated notes (lifting the wrist) to this study.

Practice Suggestions

This piece sounds best when there is *great* dynamic difference between melody and accompaniment. Much of your practice will be devoted to gaining dynamic control over the accompaniment chords.

➤ In the A section, play each group of LH eighth notes in one hand gesture. Try a "drop-lift-ing" wrist motion.

➤ In the B section, practice the RH chords with the "drop-lift-ing" wrist motion.

➤ "Crush" the RH melodic grace and eighth notes together with the corresponding LH note. Lift off quickly with a slight twist of the hand.

Johann Friedrich Burgmüller
Progress, op. 100, no. 6 (S13)

Exploring the Score

We often associate "progress" with playing scales upwards on the keyboard. Burgmüller reinforces that association.

➤ Have the student find all examples of "progressing up the keyboard."

➤ Check the B section, m. 9. "What goes up must come down!"

➤ A casual glance might not reveal the actual interval relationship between the hands. Does your student see the placement of hands a tenth apart for each scale?

Practice Suggestions

As preparation, play several white key scales with hands a tenth apart. The fingering relationship is the same as if you were playing the scales an octave apart. Then:

- ➤ Isolate each of the scale passages. Accurate fingering is your goal.
- ➤ To learn the notes and fingerings of mm. 3-4, block the intervals formed by pairs of eighth notes. Practice *legato* before playing *staccato*.
- ➤ In the B section, block the eighth-note pairs at first (with correct fingering!) When playing as written, use a "drop-lift" technique for the two-note slurs. Make sure the second eighth note is a light *staccato*.
- ➤ Spot practice the one contrary motion scale in m. 8.

CREATIVE ACTIVITY

Use these three elements:
1. Hands together scales separated by a 10th.
2. Contrary motion scales.
3. Broken triads played *staccato*.

Create your own short technical study patterned after Burgmüller's *Progress*.

Title: *More Progress*

Lorna Paterson
Scherzo (S18)
Exploring the Score

Compare the *Scherzo* by Haydn (in this same module) with Paterson's *Scherzo*. The pieces were written nearly two hundred years apart, but you may find similarities.
- – duple meter
- – zigzag motion in both hands
- – bright tempo

This piece is a study in hand relationships. Find where:
- – hands alternate [mm. 7, 17]
- – hands play in unison rhythm [mm. 9, 16]
- – hands cross [mm. 4, 8]
- – RH plays in the bass clef [mm. 7-8, 17]
- – RH plays off-beat accents [mm. 6]
- – LH plays on-beat accents [mm. 10, 12, 18]

Circle and name the RH notes in m. 8. [**Hint:** Bass clef low C.]

Practice Suggestions

This piece is fun to play on a flat surface because the hands have such different activities. When you "shadow play" the piece, simulate the exact distances between hands, the exact spot for the high and low crossovers, and the positions of the final two measures. The more exact you are with space relationships, the more accurately you will play. Do not forget to include accents, *ritardandos, diminuendos, crescendos,* etc. in your "shadow play" performance.

STUDY MODULE 6

Page	List	Composer	Title	Key, Meter and Tempo
R8 SW15	A	Domenico Scarlatti	*Aria in D Minor, L 423, K 32*	D Minor $\frac{3}{8}$ ♪ = 84
R20 SW39	B	Cornelius Gurlitt	*Sonatina in G Major, op. 188, no. 3 (First Movement)*	G Major $\frac{3}{8}$ Allegretto
R22 SW43	B	Erkki Melartin	*Sonatina*	G Minor $\frac{3}{4}$ Tempo di menuetto
R32 SW62	C	Marcel Poot	*Across the Channel*	C Major $\frac{2}{4}$ ♩ = 96
R40 SW76	C	Christopher Norton	*Play It Again*	F Major $\frac{4}{4}$ Steadily
S5		Alexander Gedike	*Study in G Major, op. 36, no. 26*	G Major $\frac{2}{4}$ Allegro marziale
S12		Clifford Crawley	*You're Joking!*	D Minor ¢ Vivo
S15		Alexandre Tansman	*Skating*	C Major $\frac{4}{4}$ Assez vif

STUDY MODULE 6

Assign first:	Assign next when ready:
Study in G Major	Skating
Sonatina in G Major	Sonatina
You're Joking!	Play It Again
Sonata in D Minor	Across the Channel

Study Module 6 contains some of the most challenging compositions in Level 4, including two sonatinas. Sonatinas of the Classical and Romantic periods focus on a single concept: contrast. When students see, hear, discuss, and label elements of contrast in the music, their performances take on a new sense of musical insight. The sonatinas by Gurlitt and Melartin in Study Module 6 display obvious contrasts of form, melody, key, articulation, and dynamics. Use the following discussions as a springboard for comparing these two works.

Pieces by Post, Norton, Tansman, and Crawley provide an interesting combination of 20th-century styles, each strikingly different from the other.

Domenico Scarlatti
Aria in D Minor, L 423, K 32 (R8, SW15)
Exploring the Score

Domenico Scarlatti's compositions were influenced by the dances and guitar music of Portugal and Spain. The 32nd-note flourishes imitate the strumming of a guitar. This rhythmic figure gives each phrase an energetic "kick-off." Listen to the *Celebration Series*® recording for the guitar-like flourishes. Does the performer roll the LH chords? Notice the performer's emphasis on non-chord tones (e.g., *appoggiatura* C sharp in m. 2).

The 32nd-note flourishes initiate two-measure phrases. Can you find places in the piece that are *not* written in two-measure groupings? [mm. 13-16]

Practice Suggestions

➤ Most of the phrases in this piece are two-measure groupings. The 32nd note "strum" provides the energy that propels the remainder of the phrase. Practice the two-measure phrases with a slight *diminuendo.*

➤ The two-note slur (*appoggiatura* and resolution) at the end of each short phrase has its own special "sigh-ing" dynamic plan. Insert slight breaks before and after each two-note slur.

➤ Look carefully for phrases that are *not* the typical two-measure units. Find an appropriate dynamic plan for those phrases.

➤ Isolate each RH trill for special practice.

TIP: In Baroque music, a contrasting texture of *legato* and detached note values is desirable. In general, the slower note values may be played detached. Which note values will you play detached?

Cornelius Gurlitt
Sonatina in G Major, op. 188, no. 3
(First Movement) (R20, SW39)
Exploring the Score

Most sonatinas feature contrasting themes. An unusual feature of this movement is the lyricism of both its themes.

➤ Play the opening and enjoy the swaying motion of the theme.

➤ Play the LH theme starting in m. 17. Notice how it sways, too.

➤ The drum-roll sixteenths beginning in m. 9 provide vivid contrast.

➤ A development section usually reworks one of the themes. This development (m. 37) is very different. What is the source of m. 37-38? [m. 35-36!] The drum-roll figure also finds its way into this section.

Practice Suggestions

➤ Practice the measures of sixteenth notes first. To learn fingerings, you may wish to practice hands separately.

➤ Listen to the horn-like duet in the LH at mm. 15-24, 62-71. Keep the RH light and moving forward with a slight down–up gesture in each measure

➤ Listen to the shape of both short and long phrases. Taper slightly at the ends of slurs.

Erkki Melartin
Sonatina (R22, SW43)

Erkki Melartin was a Finnish composer. This *Sonatina* is written in the style of a minuet.

Exploring the Score

This *Sonatina* has several unusual features. Perhaps the student can point them out:
- the minuet-like rhythm and tempo
- the traditional Theme 2 replaced by a restatement of Theme 1 in the LH—without a change of key!
- first section ends in—the tonic!
- the "development" is made of new material

Label the sections of the piece, using your own innovative designations. ["Theme RH," "Theme LH," "Closing"]
- ➤ Discuss the tempo and touch that are required to make the opening convey an elegant dance.
- ➤ The opening eight-measure section is constructed from a two-measure sequence pattern. Melartin has indicated the dynamic plan for the two-measure units. They cannot all be alike, however. Which of the two-measure units will be loudest or most intense? In a musical structure of four units, shape is provided by a dynamic focus on the third unit— in this case, mm. 6-7.

TIP: "Out of four, go for three."

Discuss the repetition of ideas in the B section ("development"). The effect is one of familiarity and ease.

Practice Suggestions

To speed the learning process:
- ➤ Practice the RH alone in mm. 1-8, focusing on the detailed articulations.
- ➤ Then tackle the same melody in the LH, m. 10.
- ➤ Tap the unison rhythms in mm. 21-35 before playing. Then play HT being careful with the tied note values. Good and consistent fingerings will help!
- ➤ Listen for the full value of half notes in mm. 16-20 and m. 52 to the end.

Marcel Poot
Across the Channel (R32, SW62)
Exploring the Score

Marcel Poot was a Belgian composer. What country does he describe as "across the channel"? [England] Think of the sober-faced, smartly uniformed guards in front of Buckingham Palace, and the clicking of their feet on the pavement as they march back and forth.

Now you have a mental picture to help you convey the spirit of this spritely military march (*Alla marcia!*).
- ➤ For most of the first page, the LH is a marching *ostinato*. Let the student describe the movement from one chord to the next. Can you hear the marching feet on the cobblestones?
- ➤ What instrument might be imitated in the RH?
- ➤ As the student hears the second page, a new part of the story can develop. Why does the piece fade away?
- ➤ Look at the *Student Workbook* article for another possible interpretation of Poot's story.

Practice Suggestions
- ➤ Tap and count slowly to secure the coordination between the hands. Exaggerate the RH articulation as you tap.
- ➤ Which sections would you choose as your practice units?
- ➤ This is a great piece for metronome practice. Choose at least three different speeds: slow, medium, fast.
- ➤ Your goal is to play the piece with military precision. Short groups of sixteenths are to be played "clipped," almost with the technique of grace notes.

Christopher Norton
Play It Again (R40, SW76)
Exploring the Score

Teachers work tirelessly to help students achieve an accurate reading of a score. Infrequently we confront a piece in which an accurate reading of the score is not the correct interpretation. In *Play It Again* Norton has written a blues, a style in which one "bends" or slightly swings the eighth notes. The bending is subtle, with the beat note slightly longer and more emphasized than the "and."

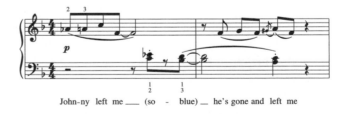

John-ny left me ___ (so - blue) ___ he's gone and left me

The LH off-beat notes ("so – blue") are to be played casually, almost lazily. Your student might enjoy counting in "scat syllables" instead of the traditional numbers. Use *DOO* for the beat notes and *bah* for the "ands."

Doo-bah Doo bah   (bah - bah)

Practice Suggestions

➤ As a warmup to learning this piece, play an F blues scales in the RH.

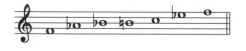

➤ Work on the "bent" blues rhythm as you play this scale. (Swing the eighth notes.)
➤ Sing or "scat" the rhythms in this piece until they feel natural, then play.

Alexander Gedike
Study in G Major, op. 36, no. 26 (S5)
Exploring the Score

Use this study as a summary of several studies in *Piano Studies/Etudes 4*. Identify the following technical figures and find those same figures in other studies. What different hand and wrist motions are used for each figure?
- sixteenth-note tetrachords (finger technique for single tones)
- broken chords (hand rotation)
- blocked *staccato* intervals (hand *staccato*)

➤ This piece has three eight-measure sections. Label the ABA form. What are the contrasts in the B section? The B section ends in what key? [D major]
➤ Each eight-measure section is divided in two-measure units. In a two-measure phrase, the focus is often on the downbeat of the second measure. Does this apply here?

Practice Suggestions

The purpose of this study is to explore tetrachords, broken chords, and blocked intervals.
➤ How many different tetrachord positions do you find?
➤ Identify and label as many blocked chords as you can. (The chord tones are played by both hands.)
➤ Use loose forearm rotation on the combination of double and single notes in the RH, mm. 7 and 23. Isolate these passages for extra practice.

Clifford Crawley
You're Joking! (S12)
Exploring the Score

This is a humorous piece. Which moments sound particularly funny?
➤ *The non-legato* marking means everything is played *staccato*. Where does the composer mark slurs in the music? Do the slurs contribute to the joke?
➤ Assist the student in finding a way to count the piece slowly and accurately.
➤ Find repetitions of mm. 1-2. Is the idea transposed? [mm. 15-16]
➤ *You're Joking!* features several sequences. How many can you find?

Practice Suggestions

➤ Try using "opposites" to help you learn the piece: alternate each day between *legato* and *staccato* practice as well as slow and fast.
➤ Practice in two-measure, then four-measure groups.
➤ Say the fingering aloud during initial practice. What will your RH fingering be for m. 8? Write it in.
➤ Keep the hand and arm loose when playing *staccato*.

Alexandre Tansman
Skating (S15)
Exploring the Score

Some pieces have a limited number of musical ideas, which facilitates the learning of the piece. Other pieces have a wide variety of technical and rhythmic figures, making them more complicated to master.
➤ *Skating* is laid out conveniently on the page, as each line has its unique technical challenge.
➤ Can you see the changes in the sixteenth-note patterns from line to line? Use your own terminology to identify the quick changes of direction, the hand extensions that immediately become a scale pattern, etc.
➤ Tansman writes beautiful, descriptive music. The music, in its finished form, glides across the keyboard. With the student, devise ways to practice the various figures.

Practice Suggestions

This piece is primarily a study in rotation. Each change of direction is reflected in a movement of the hand. Practice the different figures with that challenge in mind. Try these "tests" of control on your sixteenths:
➤ Practice *staccato*.
➤ Practice in dotted rhythms.
➤ Stop at the beginning and end of patterns that move by step. Prepare for the next note with a lifted finger.

➤ Stop on each downbeat and think through the gestures used for the remainder of the measure.
➤ Isolate the RH zigzag patterns in mm. 10-11. Use forearm rotation to play the larger intervals. Keep the thumb loose and light.

Level 4 SUMMARY

Level 4 has presented opportunities for much musical growth—new forms, new composers, new styles, and new experiences with notation.

➤ What are the titles of the Baroque dances in List A? Is your Dance Chart updated and current?
➤ Were all of the dances in binary form?
➤ Some of the pieces in *Piano Repertoire 4* have two voices played by the same hand. How do you practice two voices in the same hand?
➤ Seven sonatina movements are included in List B. Compare the forms of the first movements, the second movements, and the third movements.
➤ List twentieth-century composers in this level. Which pieces explored new contemporary sounds and unusual notation? Which were your favorites? Which piece presented the most challenge?

Level 5

The Publications
Level 5 of the *Celebration Series®* includes the following publications:
- *Piano Repertoire 5*
- *Piano Studies/Etudes 5*
- *Student Workbook 5*
- *Recording of Repertoire* and *Studies/Etudes 5*

The Repertoire
Piano Repertoire 5 is divided into three lists.
➤ List A includes a selection of pieces composed during the Baroque period (*ca* 1600 to *ca* 1750).
➤ List B includes a selection of pieces composed during the Classical period (*ca* 1750 to *ca* 1820).
➤ List C includes a selection of pieces composed during the Romantic era (*ca* 1820 to *ca* 1910) and the twentieth century.

In Level 2, students began a Dance Chart listing the title and rhythmic characteristics of each dance studied. Students are urged to add the dances encountered in Level 5 to that list.

Musical Development
An expanding musical vocabulary is associated with the pieces in Level 5. In the discussions below, the following terms are used:
➤ Forms and formal practices: *divertimento, binary, rounded binary, sonata-allegro, rondo, sonata rondo*
➤ Compositional practices: *sequence, pentascale, ostinato, bitonality, twelve-tone row*
➤ Ornaments: *mordent, cadential trill*
➤ Expressive devices: *rubato, portando, appoggiatura*
➤ Dances: *Allemande, Rigaudon, Mazurka, Waltz, Jig*

The Study Modules
The five Study Module discussions are organized into categories:
- *Exploring the Score*
- *Practice Suggestions*
- *Creative Activities*

Exploring the Score is designed as an interactive exercise between teacher and student. These activities and questions are for use during the introduction of the piece to the student, prior to the first week of practice, helping to open the student's mind, eyes, ears, and hands to the new repertoire. The *Practice Suggestions* assist the student in the early period of study on a piece. They explore ways to solve challenging rhythms; facilitate technical solutions for speed, accuracy, and fingering; and suggest steps to efficient practice. The *Creative Activities* act as reinforcement for your students' understanding of a musical concept and can provide a springboard for their creativity and improvisation.

Musical Tips
As students work through this Level, they will accumulate information about musical style that can be applied generally. Your student can use a blank page to notate these points, which are identified as musical tips (**TIP:**). Encourage your students to find application for these "musical rules of thumb," and to add to the growing list as they progress from level to level.

The five Study Modules suggest an order of difficulty. Please refer to the discussion of **Order of Assignment** in the Foreword, p. 9, if you have questions regarding the columns "Assign first" and "Assign next when ready" found below each Study Module Chart.

The following chart lists the repertoire and studies in Level 5. Page numbers for works in *Piano Repertoire 5* and *Piano Studies/Etudes 5* are found in the first column. Study Module numbers are found to the far right. Study Module groupings of repertoire and studies follow.

Piano Repertoire 5

	Page	Composer	Title	Study Module
List A	4	J.S. Bach	*Little Prelude in C Major, BWV 939*	1
	5	J.S. Bach	*Allemande in G Minor, BWV 836*	4
	6	Jean-Phillippe Rameau	*Deux Rigaudons / Two Rigadoons*	5
	8	Christoph Graupner	*Intrada in C Major*	2
	10	Georg Philipp Telemann	*Fantasia in C Minor, TWV 33:35*	3
	11	Domenico Zipoli	*Verso in E Minor*	2
List B	12	Carl Philipp Emanuel Bach	*La Caroline, Wq 117/39, H98*	2
	14	Franz Joseph Haydn	*Divertimento in G Major, Hob. XVI:8 (First Movement)*	1
	16	Muzio Clementi	*Sonatina in G Major, op. 36, no. 5 (Third Movement)*	5
	20	Ludwig van Beethoven	*Sonatina in F Major (First Movement)*	3
	22	Ludwig van Beethoven	*Sonatina in F Major (Second Movement)*	4
List C	25	Robert Schumann	*A Little Romance, op. 68, no. 19*	5
	26	Pyotr Il'yich Tchaikovsky	*Mazurka, op. 39, no. 11*	3
	28	Edvard Grieg	*Waltz, op. 12, no. 2*	4
	30	Béla Bartók	*Jest*	1
	32	Jean Coulthard	*Star Gazing*	4
	34	Herbert Haufrecht	*Tick-Tock Toccata*	5
	36	George Fiala	*Postlude (à la Shostakovich), op. 7, no. 6*	5
	37	Christopher Norton	*Dreaming*	3
	38	Violet Archer	*Jig*	2
	40	Larysa Kuzmenko	*Romance*	1

Piano Studies/Etudes 5

Page	Composer	Title	Study Module
4	Johann Christoph Friedrich Bach	*Allegro in C Major*	2
5	Dmitri Kabalevsky	*Prelude, op. 39, no. 19*	1
6	Antoine Henry Lemoine	*Study in A flat Major, op. 37, no. 44*	3
8	Ludmilla Eurina	*Blues "Mignon"*	5
9	Johann Friedrich Burgmüller	*Sweet Sorrow, op. 100, no. 16*	2
10	Johann Friedrich Burgmüller	*The Hunt, op. 100, no. 9*	4
12	Jenö Takács	*The Little Fly*	4
14	Carl Albert Loeschhorn	*Study in D Minor, op. 65, no. 40*	4
16	Stephen Heller	*Study in D Major, op. 125, no. 12*	3
17	Alexander Gedike	*Study in C Major, op. 32, no. 16*	1
18	Pál Kadosa	*Vivo*	3
19	Vladimir Ivanovich Rebikov	*In the Forest, op. 51, no. 4*	1
20	Samuil Maikapar	*Staccato Prelude, op. 31, no. 6*	2

Summary of the Study Modules

Study Module 1

List	Composer	Title	Page & Book
A	J.S. Bach	*Little Prelude in C Major, BWV 939*	R4, SW4
B	Franz Joseph Haydn	*Divertimento in G Major, Hob. XVI:8*	R14, SW27
C	Béla Bartók	*Jest*	R30, SW49
C	Larysa Kuzmenko	*Romance*	R40, SW68
Study	Dmitri Kabalevsky	*Prelude, op. 39, no. 19*	S5
Study	Alexander Gedike	*Study in C Major, op. 32, no. 16*	S17
Study	Vladimir Ivanovich Rebikov	*In the Forest, op. 51, no. 4*	S19

Study Module 2

List	Composer	Title	Page & Book
A	Christoph Graupner	*Intrada in C Major*	R8, SW15
A	Domenico Zipoli	*Verso in E Minor*	R11, SW21
B	Carl Philipp Emanuel Bach	*La Caroline, Wq 117/39, H98*	R12, SW24
C	Violet Archer	*Jig*	R38, SW65
Study	Johann Christoph Friedrich Bach	*Allegro in C Major*	S4
Study	Johann Friedrich Burgmüller	*Sweet Sorrow, op. 100, no. 16*	S9
Study	Samuil Maikapar	*Staccato Prelude, op. 31, no. 6*	S20

Study Module 3

List	Composer	Title	Page & Book
A	Georg Philipp Telemann	*Fantasia in C Minor, TWV 33:35*	R10, SW18
B	Ludwig van Beethoven	*Sonatina in F Major (First Movement)*	R20, SW34
C	Pyotr Il'yich Tchaikovsky	*Mazurka, op. 39, no. 11*	R26, SW44
C	Christopher Norton	*Dreaming*	R37, SW62
Study	Antoine Henry Lemoine	*Study in A flat Major, op. 37, no. 44*	S6
Study	Stephen Heller	*Study in D Major, op. 125, no. 12*	S16
Study	Pál Kadosa	*Vivo*	S18

Study Module 4

List	Composer	Title	Page & Book
A	Johann Sebastian Bach	*Allemande in G Minor, BWV 836*	R5, SW8
B	Ludwig van Beethoven	*Sonatina in F Major (Second Movement: Rondo)*	R22, SW37
C	Edvard Grieg	*Waltz, op. 12, no. 2*	R28, SW47
C	Jean Coulthard	*Star Gazing*	R32, SW52
Study	Johann Friedrich Burgmüller	*The Hunt, op. 100, no. 9*	S10
Study	Jenö Takács	*The Little Fly*	S12
Study	Carl Albert Loeschhorn	*Study in D Minor, op. 65, no. 40*	S14

Study Module 5

List	Composer	Title	Page & Book
A	Jean-Philippe Rameau	*Deux rigaudons / Two Rigadoons*	R6, SW12
B	Muzio Clementi	*Sonatina in G Major, op. 36, no. 5 (Third Movement: Rondo)*	R16, SW31
C	Robert Schumann	*A Little Romance, op. 68, no. 19*	R25, SW41
C	Herbert Haufrecht	*Tick-Tock Toccata*	R34, SW55
C	George Fiala	*Postlude (à la Shostakovich), op. 7, no. 6*	R36, SW58
Study	Ludmilla Eurina	*Blues "Mignon"*	S8

STUDY MODULE 1

Page	List	Composer	Title	Key, Meter and Tempo
R4 SW4	A	Johann Sebastian Bach	*Little Prelude in C Major, BWV 939*	C Major **C** ♩ = 100
R14 SW27	B	Franz Joseph Haydn	*Divertimento in G Major, Hob. XVI:8*	G Major **2/4** Allegro
R30 SW49	C	Béla Bartók	*Jest*	D Major **2/4** Allegramente
R40 SW68	C	Larysa Kuzmenko	*Romance*	F sharp Minor **3/4** Tempo rubato
S5		Dmitri Kabalevsky	*Prelude, op. 39, no. 19*	G Minor **C** Moderato
S17		Alexander Gedike	*Study in C Major, op. 32, no. 16*	C Major **2/4** Allegro moderato
S19		Vladimir Ivanovich Rebikov	*In the Forest, op. 51, no. 4*	Bitonal, free Allegretto

Assign first:

Little Prelude in C Major . . . .
Divertimento in G Major
Jest . . . .
Romance . . . .

Assign next when ready:

Prelude

Study in C Major
In the Forest

The pianist has the distinct advantage (and challenge!) of being able to produce both melody and accompaniment simultaneously. Study Module 1 presents music that can serve as the basis for a continuing investigation into the intriguing, constantly varied relationship between these two. Often, it is the change of accompaniment style and texture that determines a new section in a form. Notice that most of these composers use one accompaniment style throughout. The notable exception is the Haydn sonata movement.

J.S. Bach
Little Prelude in C Major, BWV 939 (R4, SW4)
Exploring the Score

One immediately recognizes in this piece the "warm-up," improvisational character of a prelude. Bach establishes the main chords of the key, creates a dominant pedal point in the bass, and leads into the final cadence with a flourish. One could scarcely imagine a more convincing way to establish the key of C major.

➤ Help the student analyze the main harmonies. Notice how the first four measures clearly identify the key of C major, outlining I, IV, V, I.
➤ Why does Bach need accidentals in this short prelude? Here you have the opportunity to discuss "borrowed dominants" (secondary dominants). The B flat in m. 1 transforms the C major triad into the V7 of IV. The F sharp of m. 5 helps create the V7 of V. Explore with your student the many measures in

which the fourth beat presents the dominant of the harmony in the next measure.
➤ Discuss the basic shape of the main eighth-note figure. [arpeggiated triad followed by a three-note "tail"] Notice how many times this figure is used in the prelude. It is a unifying element in the piece. How does Bach create contrast in this prelude?

TIP: A composer can increase musical tension by adding ornaments, increasing the rhythmic activity, or increasing the frequency of harmonic changes.

➤ Discuss the purpose of the mordent in mm. 9-11. [brings attention to the G and intensifies rhythmic movement]
➤ What musical purpose is served by the sudden use of sixteenths in m. 14? [intensification of movement towards the cadence]

Practice Suggestions

➤ Circle the opening eighth rest in the RH. This is the primary clue to the phrasing: each unit begins on the second eighth of the measure. (Notice the LH entrance in m. 4.) Therefore, the following articulations are possible for this prelude:

Try these various articulations and decide which projects the musical figure best.

➤ Practice the fingering indicated for the mordent.
➤ Now practice each mordent against the eighth notes in the RH. The mordent should finish before the second eighth, sounding like a sixteenth-note triplet.

Franz Joseph Haydn
Divertimento in G Major, Hob. XVI:8
(First Movement) (R14, SW27)

Exploring the Score

In the previous discussion (Bach's *Prelude in C Major*) the student explored ways in which Bach unified his piece.

➤ In this Haydn movement, explore the different ways in which Haydn creates contrast:
– contrasting rhythms
– contrasting phrase lengths
– contrasting melodies
– contrasting keys

TIP: In the Classical style, one of the primary elements of composition is contrast.

➤ This piece is the first movement of one of Haydn's earliest sonatas, although the original title was *Divertimento*. Discuss the meaning of the term *divertimento*. It might be of interest to know that all movements of this *Divertimento* are in G major.

➤ This "sonata" was written for harpsichord, which means that the dynamic indications in the score are editorial suggestions. Discuss the editor's choices of dynamics, and allow the student to explore other dynamic plans.
➤ Locate the major sections (Exposition, Development, and Recapitulation), and label the tonal centers.

Practice Suggestions

➤ To reinforce the principle of contrast, find and practice:
– the dotted rhythms
– triplet motives
– LH melodies
– parallel movement between the hands
– one-measure groupings
– two-measure phrases
– any four-measure phrases?

Béla Bartók
Jest (R30, SW49)

Exploring the Score

➤ Find the elements of repetition in the piece and determine the form. Would you label it Theme and Variations, or A, A1, A2?
➤ Discuss the ways in which Bartók creates the variations.
– Does each "variation" …
… have a four-measure introduction? [not at m. 33]
… start in D major? [not in m. 35]
… have the same seven-measure (!) theme? [yes]
… have a different accompaniment?

➤ How does Bartók change the ending to conclude the piece?
➤ Notice the two-measure insertion of quarter-note chords marked *piano, poco rall.* Help the student decide what this might signify in the jest. What words might you set to those quarter notes to give them significance? [*just in fun … tip-toe here … slow-ing down*]
➤ What musical elements does Bartók use to make this piece sound humorous?

Practice Suggestions

Bartók marks his scores meticulously. Nearly every note in this piece has an indicated articulation, and the accuracy of articulation becomes a practice focus.

➤ In the first days of practice, play mm. 5-16, RH alone, with special attention to each *staccato* and slur. In mm. 6, 8, and 15, play the two-note slur with a "down-up" gesture and a "louder-softer" dynamic plan. Make an articulation break after the second note.

➤ Playing hands together in m. 5 is easy because the hands release their *staccato* notes together. Measure 6 is more challenging because the hands have very different articulations. Practice this measure carefully, and *exaggerate the lifting gesture in each hand*. To master this complicated coordination, you may wish to practice as follows:

➤ Compare mm. 12-13, 28-29, 44-45. Which articulation is slightly different? [44-45 has *legato* LH, pedal]

➤ The quarter notes in these surprise measures are long, but detached. This "sticky" sound is called *portato*. There is approximately a sixteenth note of silence between the chords. Make the third chord of each set the same length as the previous two.

➤ It is tempting to play mm. 14-17 too fast. The *a tempo* indication means you should play at exactly the same tempo you set in m. 1.

CREATIVE ACTIVITY

Use Bartók's LH pattern found in m. 17.
Create your own RH using the articulations found in mm. 5-6.

Title: *Hungarian Dance*

Larysa Kuzmenko
Romance (R40, SW68)
Exploring the Score

➤ Look for all of the markings that contribute to the expressive quality of this piece.

➤ The composer suggests *Tempo rubato*. As you play through *Romance* or listen to the *Celebration Series®*

recording, where do you find opportunities to employ *rubato* other than the *rit. ... a tempo* indications in the score? [suggestion: four-measure phrases can employ a slight *ritardando* as they end]

➤ Label the form of the piece. [A = mm. 1-8; B = mm. 9-16; A1 = mm. 17-end]

➤ The A section has a feeling of descending motion. Find the descending bass line in mm. 2-9 and have the student play that long, flowing scale. Find a similar bass descent in the A1 section.

➤ The B section phrases are in pairs, and the harmonies of the first two pairs are surprising. Can you find a common tone that links the harmonies of each pair? For example, the chords in mm. 9-10 are A major and C major. The common tone is an E.

Practice Suggestions

The composer marked slurs and phrases carefully. It is important to observe these groupings. Between slurred groups there should be a slight phrase breath. The LH groupings are most easily overlooked.

➤ Practice the LH with special attention to the slurs. Notice that the fingerings often help create those breaks.

➤ In such a highly expressive piece, the dynamics become a crucial factor for effective interpretation. Focus your practice on dynamic shading.

➤ In performance, savor each phrase as if it were a line from a beautifully written poem.

Dmitri Kabalevsky
Prelude, op. 39, no. 19 (S5)
Exploring the Score

➤ Ask your student to identify the five-finger patterns in the LH. It is clear that Kabalevsky was intent on limiting his accompaniment to these two pentachords. The RH emerges from the five-finger pattern as a broken chord and then takes on a life of its own in a quasi-improvisational style.

➤ Discuss the form of *Prelude*. In what ways does the opening G minor section differ from the return to G minor?

➤ This is a study in hand independence. Locate the few measures in which the hands play in parallel motion at the octave.

➤ Where are the most intense moments of the piece? [mm. 9-10; 17] Which register of the piano is used at these climactic points? [high]

➤ Take special note of the printed fingerings. These often mark shifts of position or hand shape and may require special practice.

➤ The composer slurs the LH pattern in one-measure groupings. Practice a slight break between measures to make that phrasing clear.

➤ When practicing hands together, emphasize the lifting gesture.

➤ The dynamics are the key to a successful performance of this piece. Plan dynamics carefully and listen for dynamic fluctuation in your practice.

CREATIVE ACTIVITY

For your LH, select a five-finger pattern similar to what you have found in the Kabalevsky. Improvise a RH melody based on that five-finger pattern.

Title: *Russian Daydream*

Alexander Gedike
Study in C Major, op. 32, no. 16 (S17)
Exploring the Score

➤ Why did Gedike write this piece? [for the three-note "drop-and-lift" gesture and to exercise fingers 2-3-4]

➤ Before home practice begins, work with the student on an exaggeration of the "drop-and-lift" gesture. This gesture will be refined as the speed increases.

➤ Almost all measures have a repeated tone linking the two beats. Find the measures in which there are no repeated tones.

Practice Suggestions

TIP: Short slurred groups of notes have their stress on the first note.

➤ Circle the beats in which the LH starts the three-note motive with finger 1.

➤ Exaggerate the "drop-and-lift" gesture at first. As you gradually increase speed, this motion will be smaller and less noticeable.

➤ Special caution: When the motive ascends, listen for a light eighth note at the end of the motive. The first sixteenth on the beat note is always played loudest. Each repetition of this three-note motive has a "louder-quieter" dynamic plan.

➤ Gedike writes articulation slurs, but does not indicate longer phrase groupings. As you become familiar with the piece, mark the phrases in the score. (**Hint:** Your performance of the piece will have more interest if you project a variety of phrase lengths.)

Vladimir Ivanovich Rebikov
In the Forest, op. 51, no. 4 (S19)
Exploring the Score

This piece encourages the student to explore issues of pedaling, balance, subtle dynamic shading, and phrasing. Rebikov has notated the score in a most surprising manner: no meter signature, no key signature, no bar lines, no pedal markings, articulation slurs but no phrasings, and very few dynamic indications. Listen to the *Celebration Series®* recording of this study. The composer invites us to wander through his magical forest of sound.

➤ Discuss the notation of the piece with the student. What musical decisions led Rebikov to decide on this notation? Does the absence of bar lines create a look of "wandering" on the page? Does this notation invite you, the performer, to engage more fully in the interpretation?

➤ Are there any white keys played by the LH? Any black keys played by the RH? Discuss the meaning of the term *bitonality*.

➤ Which note value indicates the end of a phrase? [half note] Find the short eight-beat phrases, and the long sixteen-beat phrases.

➤ Is there an identifiable form to this piece? [see the change of LH pattern]

Practice Suggestions

➤ Play with the pedal from the beginning days of practice. Let the pedal maintain the mystery of being lost in the forest, allowing bits of sunlight to penetrate your sound world. Explore pedal changes that do not lift completely to the top, yet help clarify the bitonal sound. The half notes at ends of phrases will receive the clearest pedal change.

➤ The LH is an *ostinato* accompaniment, the ever-present forest surrounding us. Play the LH quieter than the RH melody.

➤ The RH slurs have a dynamic plan: play the first note slightly louder than the last note.

➤ Let each phrase swell slightly to its mid-point, then subtly *diminuendo* to its close.

CREATIVE ACTIVITY

Create a LH *ostinato* using a white key broken chord. Improvise a bitonal RH by playing only on black keys. Create interest by changing articulations and dynamics.

Title: *View from a Submarine*

STUDY MODULE 2

Page	List	Composer	Title	Key, Meter and Tempo
R8 SW15	A	Christoph Graupner	*Intrada in C Major*	C Major **C** ♩ = 152
R11 SW21	A	Domenico Zipoli	*Verso in E Minor*	E Minor **3/8** ♪ = 138
R12 SW24	B	Carl Philipp Emanuel Bach	*La Caroline, Wq 117/39, H98*	A Minor **2/4** Allegro ma con tenerezza
R38 SW65	C	Violet Archer	*Jig*	Dorian **6/8** Lively
S4		Johann Christoph Friedrich Bach	*Allegro in C Major*	C Major **¢** ♩ = 92
S9		Johann Friedrich Burgmüller	*Sweet Sorrow, op. 100, no. 16*	G Minor **C** Allegro moderato
S20		Samuil Maikapar	*Staccato Prelude, op. 31, no. 6*	G Major **2/4** Allegretto

Assign first:

Intrada in C Major . . . .
Allegro in C Major . . . .
La Caroline . . . .
Staccato Prelude

Assign next when ready:

Jig
Verso in E Minor
Sweet Sorrow

Only one time signature is duplicated in this Study Module. As the student works on these pieces, fruitful discussions can take place comparing similar, yet different, meters. For instance, what are the differences between 2/4, ¢, and 6/8? How does music in 3/8 and 3/4 sound different? Is there a difference in rhythmic groupings when comparing 4/4, (**C**), and ¢?

Christoph Graupner
Intrada in C Major (R8, SW15)
Exploring the Score

From the bracketed first phrase below, one sees Graupner's use of a 4th to form his musical ideas:

➤ Find the 4ths in the melody. Is there a pattern to their positioning within each four-measure phrase?

➤ The opening motive is repeated frequently, but not always with the tones C-G-G. Find the motive in other keys, and label those keys.

➤ Where does the student find figures not derived from the first four measures?

➤ Discuss rounded binary form and find these characteristics in *Intrada*:
   – double bar separating the two sections
   – cadence on the dominant at the double bar
   – new material in the B section
   – return of the opening A material in the second half of the B section

Practice Suggestions

➤ The footnote in the score suggests that the quarter notes be played detached. Imagine the RH as a trumpet fanfare, and the LH as drum beats. Let that image help you determine the articulation.

TIP: In Baroque music, a contrasting texture of *legato* and detached note values is desirable. In general, the slower note values may be played detached.

➤ Analyze the use of fourths and the patterns in both LH and RH. Challenge: How quickly can that understanding of construction lead to a memorized performance?

TIP: Most Baroque harpsichords and organs had two manuals (keyboards). The manuals could contrast dynamically, allowing the performer to create an echo effect or change of color.

➤ Observe the echo effects in mm. 13-20.

Domenico Zipoli
Verso in E Minor (R11, SW21)
Exploring the Score

Zipoli writes three main configurations of sixteenth notes in *Verso in E Minor:*

➤ The student can label these motives as "x," "y," "z" and find their repetitions and imitations.

➤ Although this piece cannot be classified as a fugue, it is highly imitative, and it was written to be played on the organ. Would the entrances of the imitations be heard clearly on that instrument? [yes] This may influence your choice of dynamics for voice entrances. Each entrance must be heard. Knowing that we hear top voices more easily than lower voices, special care should be given to the RH dynamic level when the LH entries occur.

Practice Suggestions

➤ It is standard practice to separate phrases by breaths and articulation breaks. Play through hands separately and mark in the score where the musical idea is completed and followed by a breath. Notice that your decisions placed a break before each entrance of the "x," "y," and "z" motives.

TIP: A rule of Baroque articulation suggests that a syncopated tone is preceded by a breath.

Find the syncopations, and mark a break before each of those tones, e.g., RH m. 14, LH m. 15.

➤ When learning an imitative composition, a useful procedure is to practice hands separately, allowing your ear and hand to become thoroughly acquainted with each voice. Incorporating that idea, do the following:
  – select short practice segments of one or two measures
  – play hands separately with special attention to articulation and fingering
  – practice each segment hands together as slowly as necessary for perfect accuracy

C.P.E. Bach
La Caroline, Wq 117/39, H98 (R12, SW24)
Exploring the Score

The key word to the interpretation of this piece is Bach's indication *con tenerezza* (with tenderness). *La Caroline* is an example of C.P.E. Bach's *Empfindsamer Stil,* sensitive style.

TIP: A musical "sigh" has its emphasis on the first note.

➤ Have the student find the "sighs" (*legato* two- and three-note descending groups). Create your own lyrics to reinforce the musical inflection.

➤ C.P.E. Bach's pieces in *Empfindsamer Stil* frequently are highly ornamented. Make a survey of the different ornaments.
  – Ornaments that end a slur (mm. 6, 8, 12). These are to be played with special lightness and tenderness.
  – Cadential ornaments (m. 19). These can be played broadly, to emphasize the ending of the section.
  – Ornaments that enhance the harmony (mm. 9, 10). The B's are *appoggiaturas* in the harmony, and require a slight stress.
  – Ornaments that emphasize a beat (m. 30).
  – Double-function ornaments (mm. 33, 35). One function of this ornament is to end the "sigh" motive. The other function is to link the "sigh" to the next phrase.

Practice Suggestions

This piece requires a sensitive touch and carefully controlled dynamics.

➤ Isolate slurred notes and practice their dynamic plan ("sighs").
➤ There are no slurs in the opening four measures, but consider slurring the RH half notes from mm. 1-4 as one idea.
➤ LH repeated tones also require subtle dynamics. The sensitive sound of each measure is enhanced when the repeated tones are played with a slight *diminuendo*.

Violet Archer
Jig (R38, SW65)
Exploring the Score

This piece was inspired by traditional French-Canadian fiddle music. Fiddlers often tap their feet as they play. In *Jig,* the LH imitates foot tapping and the RH plays the fiddle tune.

➤ How many different LH "foot-tapping 5ths" (rhythms and articulations) can you find? [dotted half note, dotted quarter note, *staccato* eighth note, etc.]
➤ As you play over this piece with the student or listen to the *Celebration Series®* recording, you become immediately aware of harmonic surprises. Our ears expect a B flat in m.1, and the E flat of m. 2 sounds out of place. The piece has a D tonal center, but it is neither major nor minor. Welcome to the world of the Dorian mode! Through the Dorian mode, the composer is able to create the sound and spirit of folk instruments. The E flat may even represent an out-of-tune bagpipe.
➤ Label the ABACA sections of this piece.
➤ As the student becomes familiar with the features and sound of each section, a discussion of the choreography of this dance can take place.
  - How would the student choreograph the change of movement in m. 9?
  - What is suggested by the loud chords in mm. 25 and 29?

Practice Suggestions

➤ Notice that the composer writes very few beat accents in the RH. The RH phrases often have a *crescendo/diminuendo* marking. Archer implies that the RH portrays the swirling of the dancers. Play these phrases fluidly, in contrast to the angular beat of the (LH) foot-tapping.
➤ Notice how many slurs end with a *staccato* note.

Play the ends of short slurs and phrases lightly throughout the piece.
➤ Experiment with adding pedal to warm up the sound of the chords in mm. 25 and 29. Lift off abruptly (but lightly!) on the first eighth note of mm. 26 and 30.

CREATIVE ACTIVITY

Using the same LH 5ths in mm. 1-8, create your own jig melody. Use the dorian mode (white keys D to D).

Title: *Dublin Dance*

Johann Christoph Friedrich Bach
Allegro in C Major (S4)
Exploring the Score

➤ If a student ever needed justification for scale practice, this is it! Have the student count the number of one octave scales found in the piece. How many different starting tones are there?
➤ What is the basic fingering plan for the scales?
➤ In which measures does Bach avoid an octave scale?
➤ One might assume that a motivic piece written in J.C.F. Bach's day would employ *sequences*. Assist your student in locating the sequences. [compare mm. 1-2 with 3-4; m. 5 with m. 6; m. 17 with m. 18]

Practice Suggestions

➤ Practice the scales with special attention to the consistent fingering pattern.
➤ Devise different ways to practice the scales: dotted rhythms, *staccato,* each note twice, etc.
➤ Practice the *appoggiatura* in mm. 8 and 12. Then add the LH of the preceding measure. Be sure your counting remains steady for both measures.

Johann Friedrich Burgmüller
Sweet Sorrow, op. 100, no. 16 (S9)
Exploring the Score

➤ Burgmüller's op. 100 is a set of études. Discuss possible reasons why Burgmüller wrote this study and why he gave it the title *Sweet Sorrow.* [broken-chord accompaniment, balance between hands, minor key, descending *legato* melody]

TIP: A guiding principle of piano playing suggests that the hands play at contrasting dynamic levels: melody projected, accompaniment in the background.

This principle may explain the creation of this piece—Burgmüller presents a dynamic challenge. Can the LH be so controlled and quiet that it does not extinguish the long melodic tones in the RH?

Practice Suggestions

➤ Practice slowly at first, with a ringing *forte* melody and a *pianissimo* accompaniment. Notice those measures in which the LH has the melody.

➤ In mm. 9 and 11, play the two RH voices with two hands, listening for a clear upper voice shadowed quietly by the lower. Try to match this two-handed balance when playing both notes in one hand.

➤ Where are the two dynamic peaks in this piece? How will your *sf* and *forte* sounds vary at these loudest moments? [mm. 7 and 13]

Samuil Maikapar
Staccato Prelude, op. 31, no. 6 (S20)
Exploring the Score

This piece presents the student with the challenge of playing *staccato* 6ths and 3rds while changing positions frequently.

Have the student trace the moves in the LH. Can you find measures where the LH does more than just play an accompaniment? [mm. 12, 14] Explain *m.s.* = *mano sinistra* (LH) and *m.d.* = *mano destra* (RH).

Are all the phrases four measures in length? [No. The second phrase is extended (mm. 5-10). The last line has a $\frac{3}{4}$ measure and a cadential tag.]

Practice Suggestions

➤ Choose pairs of sixths (changing pitches), and practice a quick move to the second pitch, as if the first were a grace note. Maintain a relaxed arm as you play.

➤ Let the LH participate in this drill. Play the exercise hands together. The goal is to observe what the hand does naturally as it moves quickly from one open position to a second position.

➤ Repeat the exercise, but add the repeated 6th as found in the opening measures of the piece. A loose wrist promotes ease and speed in this technical gesture.

CREATIVE ACTIVITY
Make up your own technical drill using *staccato* sixths.

STUDY MODULE 3

Page	List	Composer	Title	Key, Meter and Tempo
R10 SW18	A	Georg Philipp Telemann	*Fantasia in C Minor, TWV 33:35*	C Minor **C** Moderato
R20 SW34	B	Ludwig van Beethoven	*Sonatina in F Major (First Movement)*	F Major $\frac{2}{4}$ Allegro assai
R26 SW44	C	Pyotr Il'yich Tchaikovsky	*Mazurka, op. 39, no. 11*	D Minor $\frac{3}{4}$ Allegro non troppo
R37 SW62	C	Christopher Norton	*Dreaming*	C Major $\frac{3}{4}$ Dreamily
S6		Antoine Henry Lemoine	*Study in A flat Major, op. 37, no. 44*	A flat Major **C** Andantino
S16		Stephen Heller	*Study in D Major, op. 125, no. 12*	D Major $\frac{2}{4}$ Moderato preciso
S18		Pál Kadosa	*Vivo*	E Minor $\frac{3}{8} + \frac{2}{4}$ Vivo

Assign first:

Fantasia in C Minor . . . .
Mazurka . . . .
Study in D Major . . . .
Study in A flat Major

Assign next when ready:

Sonatina in F Major
Dreaming
Vivo

In music, emotion, expressiveness, and mood are created through numerous musical elements combined in different ways: dynamics, rhythm, melody, texture, etc. In Study Module 3, the student can explore the relationship between touch (articulation) and mood. In Telemann's *Fantasia,* the dance-like quality is a result of brightly detached eighth notes. Beethoven's *Sonatina in F Major* is brought to life through the swooping sixteenth runs (*legato*) and the contrasting, detached eighths. *Mazurka* by Tchaikovsky employs a variety of articulations to heighten the dance quality. Norton's *Dreaming* would be impossible without the smoothly flowing *legato* quality. Lemoine and Heller write "touch" études, and Kadosa's alternating rhythms are distinguished by different touches.

Georg Philipp Telemann
Fantasia in C Minor, TWV 33:35 (R10, SW18)

Exploring the Score

➤ With your student, listen carefully to the *Celebration Series*® recording of this piece as a model of articulation. How does the performer articulate the tones that are not slurred in the score? Were they detached like one might expect?

➤ This piece is highly imitative. The LH usually imitates a RH idea. Can the student find places where the RH imitates a LH motive? [mm. 6, 8]

➤ In Telemann's time, this piece would have been performed on a harpsichord. Knowing that dynamic accents were impossible on the harpsichord, how does Telemann make beats one and three clear and prominent? [slurs, rhythmic and harmonic emphasis]

➤ Does this piece have the formal requirements of *binary form*? [repeat marks separating the two parts; cadence in the dominant at the end of the first section, final cadence in the tonic]

➤ Discuss the placement of the trills. These two ornaments are excellent examples of *cadential trills.*

Practice Suggestions

Achieving independence of hands in imitative compositions is a difficult technical challenge. Here are some practice steps to help you master the independent articulations in this piece:

➤ Play m. 1 RH alone, observing the articulation. (The note ending the slur has the same detachment as the notes following.)

➤ Practice this same articulation drill in the LH.
➤ Practice the articulation drill hands together.
➤ Isolate m. 1 beats two and three for very slow practice, hands together. Emphasize the *staccato* "lifts." The hands have opposite articulations, except for the final eighth of beat three.
➤ Use this same slow practice procedure for m. 2, beats one to three.

Ludwig van Beethoven
Sonatina in F Major (First Movement) (R20, SW34)

The second movement of this sonatina is discussed in Study Module 4.

Exploring the Score

Recent scholarship has determined that this sonatina was not composed by Beethoven. We will, however, continue to label it as Beethoven's *Sonatina in F Major.* Its musical value is indisputable.

➤ This movement has many of the characteristics of *sonata-allegro form.* Assist the student in finding the following:

Exposition and Development (see below for a discussion of the unusual Recapitulation)

Theme 1a [m. 1]
Theme 1b [m. 9]
Cadence in the dominant [m. 18]
Coda [m. 60]

➤ The Recapitulation: Frequently, sonatas and sonatinas that use the main theme as the primary material for the development do not restate that theme to announce the recapitulation. In this sonatina, the recapitulation starts in m. 51 with Theme 1b.

➤ Sonatinas commonly present a second theme in the dominant key. In this sonatina, there is no theme in C major. The composer uses the material of Theme 1b for modulation to the cadence in the dominant.

➤ Traditionally no new thematic material is introduced in the Development section of a sonatina. Can the student find "new material" in the Development? [m. 21 motive; m. 28 descending eighths]

➤ The thematic material in the coda is not new. Where did it first appear? [Development]

Practice Suggestions

➤ Identify the different types of sixteenth-note figures in each hand. [broken-chord pattern, scalar passage, five-finger pattern, chromatic fragment, trill-like figure] Isolate each pattern for hands separate practice.

➤ Keep the LH thumb light in sixteenth-note passages. Listen to the bass line created by the lower notes in broken-chord and zigzag patterns.

➤ Listen for the LH *legato* connection in mm. 13-16 and 55-58.

➤ Play the small notes mm. 9-10, etc. "crushed" with their principal tone, on the beat.

Pyotr Il'yich Tchaikovsky
Mazurka, op. 39, no. 11 (R26, SW44)
Exploring the Score

➤ The opening motive is evocative of a dance step:

step   and turn

➤ Assist the student in discovering the ABA form. Mark it in the score. [mm. 1-8, 19-34, 35-52]

➤ Tchaikovsky writes this mazurka with balanced, predictable four-measure phrases. The score, however, is marked with numerous articulation slurs. Your student may wish to draw in the larger four-measure units.

➤ Notice the Question and Answer phrasing in the A section:
m.1 motive ascends (Question); m. 2 motive descends (Question)
mm. 1-4 (Question) find their Answer in mm. 5-8

➤ Help the student with an outline of keys:
A section start in _____. [D minor]
A section ends in _____. [F major]
B section is in_____. [C major]
The piece ends in _____. [D minor]

➤ A mazurka is always in $\frac{3}{4}$, but there are rhythmic surprises within that meter. Discuss the emphasis Tchaikovsky gives to the second beat. Are there accents on the third beat? Do you find that the A section emphasizes the second beat, and the B section emphasizes the third beat?

Practice Suggestions

➤ Practice the first eight measures hands separately with careful attention to RH articulation.

➤ Isolate the LH accompaniment and practice the pedaling as indicated. This is an example of straight or direct pedaling.

➤ Slowly practice hands together in small sections, listening to the details of articulation and pedaling.

Christopher Norton
Dreaming (R37, SW62)
Exploring the Score

Traditional triads are made of 3rds. This piece allows students to experience the luscious sounds of extended harmonies used in jazz.

TIP: Jazz composers stack 3rds on triads to create 7th, 9th, and even 11th chords.

➤ Construct some 7th and 9th chords, and then observe the harmonies in the first four measures.
m. 1: CMaj7
m. 2: G9
m. 3: E flat 9
m. 4: C9

➤ Discuss the composer's choice of meter. Why is $\frac{3}{4}$ a proper vehicle for the mood of this piece? What is the effect of the one measure in $\frac{2}{4}$? [suggests rocking, swaying, floating]

➤ Assist the student in finding the two sections of the piece. They can be labeled A and A1(m. 17).

Practice Suggestions

➤ To capture the floating mood, play only downbeat chords in mm.1-8. The phrases consist of pairs of measures; the first downbeat is played slightly louder than the second. Listen for that dynamic relationship in your practice.

➤ The grace-note slide, into the downbeat of m. 1, helps set the lazy, dreamy mood. Play that grace note chord reluctantly.

➤ Note the change of phrase structure and emphasis in mm. 9-12. Practice your dynamic plan for those measures.

➤ Although sixteenth notes appear in almost every phrase, they should assist in setting the mood. Play them with the same feeling of laziness you used with the opening grace-note chord.

CREATIVE ACTIVITY

Explore the construction of 7th, 9th, and 11th chords. Play a favorite folk tune or hymn tune using those extended harmonies.

Antoine Henry Lemoine
Study in A flat Major, op. 37, no. 44 (S6)
Exploring the Score

➤ With the ringing sound of the three accented quarter notes in each measure, this study could be subtitled "The Bells." The challenge is to make the three "bell tones" sound as if they were played by one hand.

➤ By blocking the first half of each measure, the student will be able to quickly hear the harmonic progressions. How many different dominant 7th chords can you find? Do they resolve as expected?

Practice Suggestions

➤ To gain control over the LH shifts, play the LH alone.

➤ Then using both hands and pedal, play only the quarter notes. The downbeat serves as a harmonic foundation. The treble notes (RH-LH-RH) are the melody and should sound with equal intensity. The listener should not hear a difference in the melody when comparing m. 1 with m. 4.

➤ Practice two- and four-measure segments playing the LH as written and blocking the RH chords.

Stephen Heller
Study in D Major, op. 125, no. 12 (S16)
Exploring the Score

The primary considerations for the student are the variety of touches and the quick thirty-second-note "flip."

➤ How many different touches can be found in the score? In addition to *staccato* and *legato*, find the accented notes and the "sticky" *portato* tones.

➤ Help the student block and identify chords, especially in the LH. Notice the ascending chromatic bass line in mm. 13-17.

➤ Can you hear the completion of the ascending left-hand motive in m. 1? [the four-note pattern ends on D, played by RH thumb in m. 2] Now trace this motive in mm. 9-12. Where is the fourth note? [played by finger 5 in RH]

Practice Suggestions

➤ The most difficult aspect of this piece for many students is to create a light, clear rendition of the thirty-second-note figure. Here is a suggested practice technique for m. 2:
  – Place the LH thumb on the D.
  – Lift the 4th finger side of the hand so that the 4th finger is off the key.
  – Imagine that the 4th finger must play a very *staccato* A; play a very quick A–D by rotating the hand.
  – If you play each thirty-second note as if it were *staccato,* the lightness and speed of the figure will be easier.

➤ Compare the rhythm of mm. 1-2 with mm. 27-28. Can you describe the similarity?

Pál Kadosa
Vivo (S18)

Pál Kadosa and his teacher Béla Bartók were devoted to the folk music of their native Hungary. Mixed meters are a prominent characteristic of Eastern European folk music.

Exploring the Score

This study has two time signatures: $\frac{3}{8}$ and $\frac{2}{4}$. The meters are combined to create a prevailing rhythmic formula.

➤ How many measures comprise the basic melodic pattern? [three: $\frac{3}{8}$, $\frac{2}{4}$, $\frac{3}{8}$]

➤ Bracket any measures that do not follow that formula.

➤ The LH changes pitch every three measures. Discuss with the student the way in which the LH supports the basic rhythmic formula of $\frac{3}{8}$, $\frac{2}{4}$, $\frac{3}{8}$. In performance, emphasize the changing bass notes.

Practice Suggestions

➤ With both hands, tap the rhythm of the repeating three-measure pattern until it is comfortable.

➤ What is the pattern of articulation for the RH melody? Practice that varied articulation on a flat surface prior to playing on the keyboard.

➤ Each measure of the repeating pattern uses a different combination of LH and RH touches. Isolate each measure for slow practice, focusing on the sound and feel of the opposing touches.

STUDY MODULE 4

Page	List	Composer	Title	Key, Meter and Tempo
R5 SW8	A	Johann Sebastian Bach	*Allemande in G Minor, BWV 836*	G Minor **C** ♩ = 76
R22 SW37	B	Ludwig van Beethoven	*Sonatina in F Major (Second Movement: Rondo)*	F Major $\frac{2}{4}$ Allegro
R28 SW47	C	Edvard Grieg	*Waltz, op. 12, no. 2*	A Minor $\frac{3}{4}$ Allegro moderato
R32 SW52	C	Jean Coulthard	*Star Gazing*	Atonal, free Quite slowly
S10		Johann Friedrich Burgmüller	*The Hunt, op. 100, no. 9*	C Major $\frac{6}{8}$ Allegro vivace
S12		Jenö Takács	*The Little Fly*	Bitonal $\frac{4}{4}$ Moderato
S14		Carl Albert Loeschhorn	*Study in D Minor, op. 65, no. 40*	D Minor $\frac{2}{4}$ Allegro

Assign first:

Study in D Minor . . . .
Sonatina in F Major
Waltz . . . .
Star Gazing . . . .

Assign next when ready:

Allemande in G Minor

The Hunt
The Little Fly

A work of art must have form, and that form creates unity and variety. Study Module 4 provides material for discussion of different forms and how those forms reflect the period in which they were written. *Star Gazing* would not have been written by Mozart, in part because of the form. The *Allemande in G Minor* would not have been the product of a Romantic composer, again because of the form. Pursue this discussion with your student until an association of form and period become working information.

J.S. Bach
Allemande in G Minor, BWV 836 (R5, SW8)
Exploring the Score

In the seventeenth and eighteenth centuries, dance steps determined a great deal about the music: meter, tempo, upbeat pattern, and characteristic rhythmic figures. Musicians familiar with these characteristic rhythms and their associated steps could identify common dances by ear.

➤ What are the characteristics of an allemande? [duple meter, moderate tempo, upbeat] Notice that the shorter phrases start with an eighth-note upbeat.

TIP: Most Baroque dances are in binary form. The A section modulates to the dominant key, and the B section returns from the dominant key back to the tonic.

➤ Have the student label the keys established at the cadences in mm. 5 and 13.

➤ Notice the unusual, asymmetrical measure numbers (5 and 13) for the ends of sections. Help the student analyze how Bach creates the five-measure phrase in the A section. How many measures are in each phrase of the second part of the piece?

➤ There are no slurs in the score. Student and teacher can plan the articulation together.

Practice Suggestions:

The music suggests a generous sprinkling of detached notes, especially on eighth-note upbeats that imitate the "hop-land" dance step.

Celebration Series® Handbook for Teachers

The slurs on beats one and three strengthen their important role in the meter.

➤ Tap the main theme in m. 1, then in m. 10-11. Notice that the rhythm of the main theme is altered slightly when it reappears in mm. 10-11. The upbeat is now a sixteenth note leading to beat 3, and there are two dotted-eighth-sixteenth rhythms.
➤ The B section contains a substantial sequence. Isolate each pattern in the sequence separately before playing the whole passage.
➤ The dynamics indicated in the B section will highlight the sequence as it builds to the high point in m. 8.

Ludwig van Beethoven
Sonatina in F Major (Second Movement: Rondo) (R22, SW37)
A discussion of this sonatina's first movement can be found in Study Module 3.

Exploring the Score

➤ Your student may not be aware that rondo forms can vary considerably. Have the student find reappearances of the main theme in this movement. [mm. 29 and 75] It is unusual for a rondo to employ the many repetitions found here. In addition, the first sixteen measures represent an eight-measure period that is repeated. The composer didn't want his listeners to miss a thing!
➤ Rondos often have a bright, joyful mood. The staccatos in this piece help create that mood. How does the mood change in the C section (m. 37)? What is the key?
➤ Notice the change of accompaniment in the B section (m. 17). Contrast plays an important role in music of the Classical era. How else does the composer create contrast in this rondo?

Practice Suggestions

TIP: "Short notes go to longs" is a frequently used interpretation guideline. That rule can bring life to the A theme:

TIP: Short slurred groups of notes have their stress on the first note.

Notice how this adds rhythmic variety and surprise to mm. 2-3 and 7.

➤ When notes are not slurred, they can be lightly detached. Compare the difference in sound between mm. 37-40 and mm. 41-45.
➤ When hands together practice begins, work very slowly at first, focusing on the sound and feel of the contrasting articulations in each hand.
➤ Spot practice the RH chromatic scale in mm. 27-28. Block the sets of fingers.

Edvard Grieg
Waltz, op. 12, no. 2 (R28, SW47)
Exploring the Score

Rhythmic clarity and predictability are provided through the consistent waltz bass in this popular piece. A close look at the melody reveals constant change and variation of ideas.

➤ Compare mm. 3-6 with mm. 7-10. The LH is a consistent waltz bass. Find the measures in which the RH has a downbeat stress. In the RH, which measures have no downbeat? Where does Grieg write a RH stress on beat two? On beat three?
➤ New material is presented in m. 11. What has changed? [texture, melody, rhythmic figures]
➤ Discuss the pattern (mm. 11-12) and sequence (mm. 13-14) and the fragmentation (mm. 15, 16).
➤ Have your student play LH downbeats from mm.11-16 to discover the consistent I-V relationships.
➤ List the contrasts found in the B section (m. 37-70) and the coda (71-79)

Practice Suggestions

➤ Look carefully at mm. 3-10. The LH is consistent but the RH is extremely varied in its touches. Question: Which notes are connected? Answer: Very few!
  - None in mm. 3-4.
  - Only the grace note in m. 5.
  - The slurs in mm. 7, 8.

Practice the RH slowly to gain control over Grieg's articulations.

➤ Practice the LH melody in the B section for similar control.
➤ Many waltzes use short pedals to emphasize the downbeat. Grieg employs that idea in this piece. Practice a "direct pedal" on beat one, lifting on beat two. If you hold the pedal too long, your careful work on RH articulations can be undermined.
➤ What is the purpose of the pedal in mm. 12-17? [connecting the measures] This pedal effect can be realized best if you depress the pedal on beat three, releasing immediately on the following downbeat.

Simple waltzes often use only the primary triads of I, IV, V. Using those harmonies, create a LH waltz bass. Add a RH melody using chord tones.

Title: *Let's Dance!*

Jean Coulthard
Star Gazing (R32, SW52)
Exploring the Score

Star Gazing is a musical description of the beauty, grandeur, and mystery of the stars.

➤ Ask the student to find measures that are freely floating, giving a sense of the timeless expanse of the universe. Now find the parts that have a steady beat. What aspect of the night sky might these rhythmic sections represent?

➤ The four "star point" measures (mm. 2, 7, 12, 17) are to have a random sound, played very freely. Illustrate various interpretations of the "star points," making each tone an equal *pianissimo*.

➤ The random sound of the "star points" is created in part because each measure uses all twelve chromatic tones.

Refer to the twelve-tone rows used by Jean Coulthard in the *Student Workbook* of this level.

CREATIVE ACTIVITY

Write out your own twelve-tone row. You may intentionally create major and minor chords in your row, or you may intentionally avoid them. Play some of the tones together to create cluster chords. Play some of the tones separately to form melodic motives. Use the tones in the order you have composed. You may also use the tones backwards.

Your title: _____

Johann Friedrich Burgmüller
The Hunt, op. 100, no. 9 (S10)
Exploring the Score

The Hunt was written by Burgmüller as a technical exercise, but it is programmatic in its depiction of a "romantic" scene: the outdoors, sportsmen on horses chasing their game.

➤ One would like to ask Burgmüller about the meaning of the *dolente* [sad] section (mm. 29-36.) Does your student have suggestions for the "program" of these measures?

➤ Have the student list the different technical ideas in the piece. They could be assigned letters, numbers, or names.

Practice Suggestions

➤ Practice this chord inversion exercise to master quick chord releases and shifts to the next inversion.

play shift   play shift   play shift

➤ The LH melody (top tones) starting in m. 5 is to be played *legato*.

➤ The RH figure of m. 5 involves a lifting gesture. Practice the Gs on a flat surface, trying two different fingerings:
    5 1 1   and   5 1 2
Which fingering is easiest for your hand/arm?

➤ The RH 3rds, in mm. 13-20, should be played *legato*. Two of these 3rds have a common tone. That tone must be lifted in order to repeat the tone. Its partner must provide the *legato* connection.

Jenö Takács
The Little Fly (S12)
Exploring the Score

The buzzing sound in this piece is created by a clever mixture of white and black keys.

➤ Have the student quickly examine the score to discover that …
    – the LH plays only black keys
    – the RH plays only white keys
    – the RH plays groups of three descending steps (only!)

➤ Explore the "stop and go" groupings of beats. The fly always "rests" for two beats before moving on. Is there a pattern to the number of beats it stays in flight before stopping? [no] Why not? [to depict the unpredictability of a fly's flight]

➤ Look for the dynamic plan of the piece. The short "hairpin" *crescendo* and *decrescendo* markings will add an appropriate nervous quality to the performance.

➤ Discuss the use of triplets in the final line.

Practice Suggestions

➤ Block each beat to secure the notes. Memorize changes in note patterns or fingerings early in the learning process.

➤ To avoid colliding hands, keep the LH wrist higher than normal and play further in on the keys. Your fingers may be straighter than usual.

➤ A convincing interpretation of this piece demands perfectly even sixteenth notes. Practice the basic pattern of sixteenths on a flat surface and listen for evenness.

➤ Experiment with the pedal, the quiet sound, and relatively fast sixteenth notes to make a convincing buzzing sound.

CREATIVE ACTIVITY

Think of some insect (other than a fly). Create a piece depicting that insect using unusual combinations of white and black keys. Let both hands participate.

Your title: _____

Carl Albert Loeschhorn
Study in D Minor, op. 65, no. 40 (S14)

Exploring the Score

The technical challenge of this piece lies in the sixteenth-note figures that frequently change direction.

➤ Help your student find the variety of figures.

➤ Count the number of beats in the opening phrases, and comment on the unusual asymmetry of 3 + 5. Does the student find other examples of asymmetrical groupings?

Practice Suggestions

➤ Label the ABAC Coda form. Use these sections as your practice units.

➤ Count the number of measures of new material that must be learned. Repetitions of ideas (some an octave higher) reduce the new material to very few measures.

➤ Practice each different sixteenth-note figure identified above.

➤ Isolate the zigzag pattern of broken thirds in mm. 32-35. Practice the RH alone using a rotation movement of the hand.

STUDY MODULE 5

Page	List	Composer	Title	Key, Meter and Tempo
R6 SW12	A	Jean-Philippe Rameau	*Deux rigaudons / Two Rigadoons*	E Minor ¢ ♩ = 76
R16 SW31	B	Muzio Clementi	*Sonatina in G Major, op. 36, no. 5 (Third Movement: Rondo)*	G Major $\frac{2}{4}$ Allegro
R25 SW41	C	Robert Schumann	*A Little Romance, op. 68, no. 19*	A Minor 𝄴 Nicht schnell
R34 SW55	C	Herbert Haufrecht	*Tick-Tock Toccata*	C Major $\frac{2}{8}$ Allegretto
R36 SW58	C	George Fiala	*Postlude (à la Shostakovich), op. 7, no. 6*	E flat Minor $\frac{2}{4}$ Adagietto
S8		Ludmilla Eurina	*Blues "Mignon"*	C Major $\frac{2}{4}$ Adagio

Assign first:
Deux rigaudons . . . .
Sonatina in G Major
A Little Romance . . . .
Blues "Mignon"

Assign next when ready:
Tick-Tock Toccata

Postlude

TIP: "Music either dances or it sings."
Perhaps the statement is a bit simplistic, but the thought is profound: music either emphasizes the rhythmic element, or it emphasizes the melodic element. These emphases can change within a composition, even within a given phrase. As your student explores the pieces in Study Module 5, discuss the main emphasis of each composition, of each section. Does the piece "sing," or does it "dance"?

Jean-Philippe Rameau
Deux rigaudons / Two Rigadoons (R6, SW12)
Exploring the Score

A *rigaudon* (or rigadoon) is a lively seventeenth-century dance of French origin with a swinging pulse of two beats per measure. It was popular both as a courtly dance and as a folk dance.

➢ Have the student compare these *rigaudons* with the Bach *Allemande* (R5, Module 4). Both are in duple meter and have an upbeat. Can the student find differences?

➢ The *rigaudon* incorporated jumping movements in its dance steps. Find the downbeats that invite a hearty leap. Bright *staccato* quarter notes may help to evoke the dance steps effectively.

➢ Find the similarities between the two rigaudons. [upbeat pattern; "jumping" downbeats]

➢ Find the contrasting elements in *Rigaudon II*. [key, tune, LH]

➢ Discuss the LH of *Rigaudon I*. Where does the LH imitate the RH, and where is it a parallel partner to the RH?

➢ *Rigaudon II* is written in two-measure phrases. Note the contrast between mm. 17-18 and 19-20. Which phrase sounds best with a *legato* interpretation? [mm. 19-20—parallel step motion] Which phrase sounds best with detached quarter notes? [mm. 17-18—"jumping" movement of the bass]

➢ Is the remainder of *Rigaudon II* written in two-measure units?

➢ Notice the extension (variation) found in mm. 33-36.

Practice Suggestions

➢ The opening LH imitates the RH statement. Practice hands separately to establish the fingering. Then practice the figure in unison before playing the imitation.

➢ Isolate mm. 9-14 for LH spot practice For how many beats do you hold the bass B (m. 8) and D sharp (m. 12)?

➢ A similar LH challenge occurs in *Rigaudon II,* mm. 29-32. Practice slowly, with careful attention to the length of notes.

➢ *Practice Rigaudon II* in two-measure sections. Make special note of position shifts.

➢ Isolate each ornament. Experiment with the fingering that works best for you and write in your choice of fingering. Then practice the measure before and after the ornament.

Muzio Clementi
Sonatina in G Major, op. 36, no. 5
(Third Movement: Rondo) (R16, SW31)
Exploring the Score

Rondo forms can easily become long movements with their contrasting sections and returns to the A theme.

➢ The student may be interested in comparing this rondo by Clementi with the Beethoven rondo discussed in the previous Study Module and found in R22. What is similar? Where are the differences?

➢ The movement would sound quite complete if one played only mm. 1-58.

    A section mm. 1-16
    B section mm. 17-28
    A section mm. 29-44
    Coda   mm. 45-58

The lengthy two-page C section adds an entirely new dimension to the movement. In Classical period rondos, an extended C section acts much like the development in sonata form. The repeated eighths of the C section (mm. 59-72) are melodic. They need to flow in a long phrase. To find that phrase, have the student do the following:

    ... play only the beat notes
    ... mark in the phrases (two measures? four measures?)
    ... write in a dynamic plan for the phrases

Practice Suggestions

There are two main technical considerations in this movement:

    1) clear, even sixteenth notes
    2) repeated eighth notes

Add to your collection of practice techniques for passage work by saying something as you play:

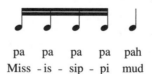

pa   pa   pa   pa   pah
Miss – is – sip – pi mud

(Create lyrics of your own if you wish.)

➢ The issue of repeated eighth notes is first found in the LH.

➢ Avoid playing the two eighths alike. The downbeat is the focus; the second eighth is a very light rebound.

Robert Schumann
A Little Romance, **op. 68, no. 19** (R25, SW41)

Exploring the Score

How is the title reflected in the music? Perhaps the unison melody suggests a musical duet or romance between the hands.

Schumann's use of dynamics deserves special attention.

➤ Have the student follow Schumann's dynamics while listening to the *Celebration Series®* recording or your own performance. Lyrics could be added to the melody, describing the dynamic contour:

➤ Make special mention of the dynamic changes at mm. 9 and 12.
➤ Compare the dynamic plan of mm. 1-2 with mm. 13-14.

Practice Suggestions

It is a rare occasion when hands play a unison melody throughout a piece. This arrangement of melody requires special control of the accompaniment, as both hands have melody and accompaniment.

➤ Limit the practicing to one- or two-measure units. Observe all fingerings, and slowly play all notes, using this approach:
  – Play the melody notes firmly and loudly (relaxed arm).
  – Play the accompaniment chords quietly with totally relaxed muscles in the hand.
➤ Be sensitive to the difference in muscle response when you play melody and when you play accompaniment.
➤ As the footnote suggests, *nicht schnell* means "not fast." However, there is a restlessness created by the ever-changing dynamics and the arrangement of melody and accompaniment. Maintain the energy throughout your performance. Pedal carefully according to the changing harmonies.

Herbert Haufrecht
Tick-Tock Toccata (R34, SW55)

Exploring the Score

When one hears the opening "tick-tock," no clue is given as to the coming subdivisions. The composer has the choice of duple eighths or triplet eighths.

➤ Discuss with the student Haufrecht's choice of the triplet subdivision. Do triplet subdivisions create a greater sense of forward movement? Another "composer" thought of triplet subdivisions: *Hickory, dickory, dock; the mouse ran up the clock.*
➤ The composer writes the groups of three eighths in stepwise motion. The student can play the game of Identify the Scale, listing the scales in which that combination of notes could be found. Example:

Found in: _____ [E major, A major, C sharp minor, A melodic minor]

➤ Play this "game" in m. 17. These notes are taken from two different melodic minor scales.

Practice Suggestions

TIP: Double notes are most easily played with an arm "push."

➤ Allow the arm to play the main beats. The fingers "scratch" the single *staccato* notes.
➤ The entire piece is played *staccato.* Use a light touch and relaxed arm to keep the *staccatos* light.
➤ Isolate mm. 17-20 for hands separate and then hands together practice.

George Fiala
Postlude (à la Shostakovich), op. 7, no. 6
(R36, SW58)

Exploring the Score

➤ Why Shostakovich? Fiala was born in Kiev where he studied at the Tchaikovsky Conservatory. As a student, Fiala was influenced by works of Shostakovich, which feature harmonic surprises, such as found in m. 7 of *Postlude*. Here the melody's B flat is expected, but the harmony of G minor is a surprise.

➤ The texture of this piece is typical of much piano repertoire from the eighteenth, nineteenth, and twentieth centuries. The melody is in the top voice, a bass line provides important polarity to the sound, and the harmony is created in the inner voices. This list also implies a hierarchy of dynamic importance: melody (most prominent), bass line (next loudest), harmony (quietest). You may wish to formulate this dynamic hierarchy into a practice plan for the student.

➤ One could also imagine this piece played by a string quartet, with the melody performed by the first violin. Note the important role the "cello" plays, as it anchors the harmony in the bass line.

Practice Suggestions

➤ Isolate the LH, listening for a fuller tone on the half notes. Play the upper notes with less arm weight.

➤ Practice the melody, shaping each phrase so that it has a focal point. Play with a rich *legato* and aim for the *malinconico* (melancholy) mood indicated by the composer.

➤ The 7ths in the RH of mm. 16-20 create a totally new color. Bring out the top note of these intervals.

Ludmilla Eurina
Blues "Mignon" (S8)

Exploring the Score

This piece illustrates that effective jazz composition is not limited to North Americans. Ludmilla Eurina is a native of Ukraine.

➤ The RH creates an improvised effect, resulting in a variety of rhythms for the student to master. Explore these in the lesson before home practice begins.

➤ The left hand has a "walking bass." Notice how the bass line meanders its way from one harmonic note (C, F, G) to another. How are the main chord tones usually approached? [by half step] What effect does this have?

Practice Suggestions

The RH rhythms are most easily practiced when felt against a consistent eighth-note beat in the LH.

➤ Tap eighth notes in the LH to these groupings in the RH:
  – measures that start with a dotted figure (1, 2, 5, 9, 11, 12, 13). As you practice each measure, first tap four eighth notes and then introduce the RH.
  – half measures that begin with a triplet
  – mm. 1-4; mm. 5-7; mm. 10-11; mm. 13-15

➤ Tap the LH and play short groups of measures in the RH.

➤ As would also apply to Beethoven, remember that short slurred groups start with a slightly accented sound.

➤ This piece can be played successfully without pedal. If touches of pedal are added, consider pedaling only on LH quarter notes.

Level 5 SUMMARY

To the Student:
In what ways have you grown as a musician through your experiences with the pieces in Level 5?

➤ What new forms have you experienced? (binary? rounded binary?)

➤ What Baroque ornaments have you added to your list?

➤ Was this your first experience playing a Rigaudon? an Allemande? a Jig? Blues?

➤ What new words have you added to your musical vocabulary? (*appoggiatura*? *dolente*? twelve-tone row?)

➤ Which were your favorite pieces …
    … from the Baroque period?
    … from the Classical period?
    … from the Romantic period?

➤ What piece created the most vivid pictures in your imagination?

➤ And what piece seemed to you the strangest of all?

Level 6

The Publications

Level 6 of the *Celebration Series*® includes the following publications:

Piano Repertoire 6
Piano Studies/Etudes 6
Student Workbook 6
Recording of Repertoire and *Studies/Etudes 6*

The Repertoire

Piano Repertoire 6 is divided into three lists.

➤ List A includes a selection of pieces composed during the Baroque period (*ca* 1600 to *ca* 1750).

➤ List B includes a selection of pieces composed during the Classical period (*ca* 1750 to *ca* 1820).

➤ List C includes a selection of pieces composed during the Romantic era (*ca* 1820 to *ca* 1910) and the twentieth century.

Musical Development

Level 6 provides a wide variety of late intermediate repertoire and technical studies representing the four major style periods. Students will continue their musical growth as they become acquainted with Baroque dances, Classical sonatinas and sonatas, Romantic character pieces, and contemporary sounds.

Literature from the Baroque period ranges from two- and three-part dances (minuet, bourrée, allemande, and sarabande) to J. S. Bach's *Little Prelude in D Minor, BWV 926* from the *Wilhelm Friedemann Bach Notebook* and the *Minuetto, L31, K83* by Domenico Scarlatti.

Six sonata and sonatina movements from the Classical period provide students with an opportunity to explore *sonata-allegro* form and to compare the various approaches taken to this form. Topics for student–teacher discussions include the form in general, the number of themes, key relationships and modulations, and how composers create contrast.

The Romantic and twentieth-century repertoire provides opportunities for students to interpret character pieces portraying a specific mood or style, and to explore a larger and more diverse harmonic palette. In this repertoire, students will need greater hand and finger independence and will further develop their pedal technique.

The organization of practice time becomes an increasingly important consideration as students progress into the upper intermediate and advanced levels of the *Celebration Series*® (Levels 6-10). Here are some suggestions to students for daily practice:

➤ Practice at times when you are fresh and alert. When possible, schedule more than one practice session each day.

➤ Organize your practice session(s) by deciding on areas of focus.

➤ Articulate your practice goals.

➤ Evaluate your own playing by listening to taped practice performances.

➤ Practice all parts of the assignment daily, but if you cannot practice a segment of the assignment one day, begin the next day's practice with that task.

The Study Modules

The five Study Module discussions are organized into categories:

Background Information
Exploring the Score
Practice Suggestions
Creative Activities

Background Information provides relevant historical information. *Exploring the Score* is designed as an interactive exercise between teacher and student. These sections include questions you might address to the student during lessons. *Practice Suggestions* are largely directed to the student. The *Creative Activities* act as reinforcement for your students' understanding of a musical concept and can provide a springboard for their creativity and imagination.

Please refer to the *Foreword* for an explanation of how to use the suggested order of assignments within each Module.

Musical Tips

As students work through this Level, they will accumulate general information about musical style that can be applied to other pieces. Your student can use a blank page to notate these points, which are identified as musical tips (**TIP:**).

The chart on the following page lists the repertoire and studies in Level 6. Page numbers for works in *Piano Repertoire 6* and *Piano Studies/Etudes 6* are found in the first column. Study Module numbers are found to the far right. Study Module groupings of repertoire and studies follow.

Piano Repertoire 6

	Page	Composer	Title	Study Module
List A	R4	Johann Sebastian Bach	*Little Prelude in D Minor, BWV 926*	5
	R6	George Frideric Handel	*Allemande in A Minor, HWV 478*	3
	R8	Gottfreid Heinrich Stölzel	*Minuet in G Minor*	1
	R9	Domenico Zipoli	*Sarabanda in G Minor*	4
	R10	Johann Ludwig Krebs	*Bourrée in A Minor*	2
	R12	Domenico Scarlatti	*Sonata in A Major, LS 31, K 83 (Second Movement: Minuetto)*	6
List B	R13	Franz Joseph Haydn	*Sonata in G Major, Hob. XVI:G1 (First Movement)*	5
	R16	Jan Ladislav Dussek	*Sonatina in G Major, op. 20, no. 1 (First Movement)*	2
	R18	Muzio Clementi	*Sonatina in F Major, op. 36, no. 4 (First Movement)*	3
	R22	Muzio Clementi	*Sonatina in F Major, op. 36, no. 4 (Second Movement)*	4
	R24	Muzio Clementi	*Sonatina in F Major, op. 36, no. 4 (Third Movement)*	4
	R27	Ludwig van Beethoven	*Bagatelle, op. 119, no. 9*	1
	R28	Anton Diabelli	*Sonatina in F Major, op. 168, no. 1 (Third Movement)*	6
List C	R30	Franz Schubert	*Sentimental Waltz, op. 50, no. 13*	6
	R31	Robert Schumann	*Waltz in A Minor, op. 124, no. 4*	4
	R32	Edvard Grieg	*Arietta, op. 12, no. 1*	3
	R33	Vladimir Ivanovich Rebikov	*Miniature Waltz, op. 10, no. 10*	1
	R34	Dimitri Kabalevsky	*Warrior's Dance, op. 27, no. 19*	6
	R36	Paul Creston	*Pastoral Dance, op. 24, no. 4*	5
	R38	Robert Starer	*Bright Orange*	1
	R40	Bohdana Filtz	*An Ancient Tale*	5
	R42	Dale Reubart	*March of the Buffoons*	5
	R44	Leonard Bernstein	*For Susanna Kyle*	3
	R45	Pierre Gallant	*Sarabande*	3
	R46	André Previn	*Roundup*	6
	R47	Miroslav Lebeda	*Miniature*	2
	R48	Douglas Finch	*Cancan*	5

Piano Studies/Etudes 6

Page	Composer	Title	Study Module
S4	Johann Sebastian Bach	*Prelude in C Minor, BWV 999*	5
S6	Dmitri Kabalevsky	*Toccatina, op. 27, no. 12*	1
S8	George Frideric Handel	*Entrée in G Minor, HWV 453*	3
S10	Cornelius Gurlitt	*Study in E Minor, op. 132, no. 1*	4
S11	Stephen Heller	*Barcarole, op. 138, no. 5*	6
S12	Ruth Watson Henderson	*Toccatina*	3
S14	Henri Bertini	*Study in E Minor, op. 29, no. 14*	6
S15	Stephen Heller	*Fluttering Leaves, op. 46, no. 11*	4
S16	Dmitri Shostakovich	*Dance*	1
S18	Stephen Heller	*Abenddämmerung/Dusk, op. 138, no. 3*	2
S20	Ross Lee Finney	*Playing Ball*	4
S22	Robert Fuchs	*A Little Song, op. 47, no. 4*	2
S24	Génari Karganov	*Game of Patience, op. 25, no. 2*	2

Summary of the Study Modules

Study Module 1

List	Composer	Title	Page & Book
A	Gottfried Heinrich Stölzel	*Minuet in G Minor*	R8, SW10
B	Ludwig van Beethoven	*Bagatelle, op. 119, no. 9*	R27, SW40
C	Vladimir Ivanovich Rebikov	*Miniature Waltz, op. 10, no. 10*	R33, SW55
C	Robert Starer	*Bright Orange*	R38, SW63
Study	Dmitri Kabalevsky	*Toccatina, op. 27, no. 12*	S6
Study	Dmitri Shostakovich	*Dance*	S16

Study Module 2

List	Composer	Title	Page & Book
A	Johann Ludwig Krebs	*Bourrée in A Minor*	R10, SW17
B	Jan Ladislav Dussek	*Sonatina in G Major, op. 20, no. 1 (First Movement)*	R16, SW27
C	Miroslav Lebeda	*Miniature*	R47, SW81
Study	Stephen Heller	*Abenddämmerung / Dusk, op. 138, no. 3*	S18
Study	Robert Fuchs	*A Little Song, op. 47, no. 4*	S22
Study	Génari Karganov	*Game of Patience, op. 25, no. 2*	S24

Study Module 3

List	Composer	Title	Page & Book
A	George Frideric Handel	*Allemande in A Minor, HWV 478*	R6, SW7
B	Muzio Clementi	*Sonatina in F Major, op. 36, no. 4 (First Movement)*	R18, SW31
C	Edvard Grieg	*Arietta, op. 12, no. 1*	R32, SW52
C	Leonard Bernstein	*For Susanna Kyle*	R44, SW72
C	Pierre Gallant	*Sarabande*	R45, SW75
Study	George Frideric Handel	*Entrée in G Minor, HWV 453*	S8
Study	Ruth Watson Henderson	*Toccatina*	S12

Study Module 4

List	Composer	Title	Page & Book
A	Domenico Zipoli	*Sarabanda*	R9, SW13
B	Muzio Clementi	*Sonatina in F Major, op. 36, no. 4 (Second Movement)*	R22, SW34
B	Muzio Clementi	*Sonatina in F Major, op. 36, no. 4 (Third Movement)*	R24, SW36
C	Robert Schumann	*Waltz in A Minor, op. 124, no. 4*	R31, SW49
Study	Cornelius Gurlitt	*Study in E Minor, op. 132, no. 1*	S10
Study	Stephen Heller	*Fluttering Leaves, op. 46, no. 11*	S15
Study	Ross Lee Finney	*Playing Ball*	S20

Study Module 5

List	Composer	Title	Page & Book
A	Johann Sebastian Bach	*Little Prelude in D Minor, BWV 926*	R4, SW4
B	Franz Joseph Haydn	*Divertimento in G Major, Hob. XVI:G1 (First Movement)*	R13, SW23
C	Paul Creston	*Pastoral Dance, op. 24, no. 4*	R36, SW60
C	Bohdana Filtz	*An Ancient Tale*	R40, SW66
C	Dale Reubart	*March of the Buffoons*	R42, SW69
C	Douglas Finch	*Cancan*	R48, SW84
Study	Johann Sebastian Bach	*Prelude in C Minor, BWV 999*	S4

Study Module 6

List	Composer	Title	Page & Book
A	Domenico Scarlatti	*Sonata in A Major, LS 31, K 83 (Second Movement: Minuetto)*	R12, SW20
B	Anton Diabelli	*Sonatina in F Major, op. 168, no. 1 (Third Movement)*	R28, SW43
C	Franz Schubert	*Sentimental Waltz, op. 50, no. 13*	R30, SW45
C	Dmitri Kabalevsky	*Warrior's Dance, op. 27, no. 19*	R34, SW58
C	André Previn	*Roundup*	R46, SW78
Study	Stephen Heller	*Barcarole, op. 138, no. 5*	S11
Study	Henri Bertini	*Study in E Minor, op. 29, no. 14*	S14

STUDY MODULE 1

Page	List	Composer	Title	Key, Meter and Tempo
R8 SW10	A	Gottfried Heinrich Stölzel	*Minuet in G Minor*	G Minor $\frac{3}{4}$ ♩ = 126
R27 SW40	B	Ludwig van Beethoven	*Bagatelle, op. 119, no. 9*	A Minor $\frac{3}{4}$ Vivace moderato
R33 SW55	C	Vladimir Ivanovich Rebikov	*Miniature Waltz, op. 10, no. 10*	B Minor $\frac{3}{4}$ Moderato
R38 SW63		Robert Starer	*Bright Orange*	C Major $\frac{2}{4}$ Fast and light
S6		Dmitri Kabalevsky	*Toccatina, op. 27, no. 12*	A Minor $\frac{2}{4}$ Allegretto marcato
S16		Dmitri Shostakovich	*Dance*	D Major $\frac{2}{4}$ Allegretto giocoso

Assign first:

Minuet in G Minor . . . .
Miniature Waltz . . . .
Dance. . . . .

Assign next when ready:

Bagatelle
Bright Orange
Toccatina

Study Module 1 contains some of the easiest pieces in *Piano Repertoire 6*. Each piece portrays a vivid character and is representative of its style period. Discuss the mood, character, and elements of contrast in the pieces your students study. The musical understanding they gain will stimulate insightful performances. Notice the variety of minor tonalities. This would be an excellent opportunity to discuss relative and parallel key relationships.

Gottfried Heinrich Stölzel
Minuet in G Minor (R8, SW10)

Exploring the Score

➤ Performers in Stölzel's day combined *legato* and *staccato* touches to project an elegant minuet character. Listen to the *Celebration Series*® recording of this minuet, making note of the articulations used by the performer. What articulation do you hear for most of the eighth notes? quarter notes?

➤ Explore the possibilities for variety of touch with your student. The different articulations might include *legato, tenuto, staccato,* and *portato*. Create exercises to develop control of articulation. (see suggestion below).

➤ The choice of keys in this piece is interesting and somewhat unusual. In what key does the second section (m. 13) begin? [G Major, parallel major!]

➤ How does Stölzel add emphasis to the opening downbeats? [chords]

➤ There are examples of skeletal stepwise motion throughout this piece. Notice the RH ascending stepwise on the downbeats of mm. 1-3. Can you find the RH step motion in mm. 13-19? [on downbeats]

➤ Where does Stölzel use descending stepwise motion in the LH?

Practice Suggestions

➤ Devise exercises (based on a Hanon study or a five-finger pattern) to explore different articulation options for eighth notes such as all *staccato*, two-note slurs, or a combination of the two:

➤ How will you play consecutive quarter notes (e.g., m. 3)? [detached touch]

➤ After making your articulation decisions, notate them in the score.

➤ As you practice, feel the forward movement of this minuet. Note the phrase structure of 4 + 8 in mm. 1-12.

➤ How will your practice reflect the phrase patterns of the B section? [all 4-measure units]

Ludwig van Beethoven
Bagatelle, op. 119, no. 9 (R27, SW40)
Background Information

Bagatelle is a French term meaning a "trifle" or a short piece. The term was first used in François Couperin's *Les bagatelles*. The compositions in Opus 119 are the easiest of Beethoven's three sets of bagatelles (Opp. 33, 119, 126). Opus 119 was written during the same period as Beethoven's last three piano sonatas (Opp. 109, 110, 111).

Exploring the Score

➤ What is the form of this piece? [rounded binary; second section features a complete restatement of the opening section]

➤ As you analyze the harmonies, notice which measures are *not* tonic and dominant. What effect does the B flat first inversion chord have in m. 3 of the A theme? [It provides harmonic variety and color.]

➤ What is the label for this B flat chord? [Neapolitan] The Neapolitan 6th chord is a major chord built on the lowered second scale degree, played in first inversion.

Practice Suggestions

The RH ascending arpeggio figure in mm. 1-2 will need special attention. Try these steps:

➤ Play slowly, saying the fingering aloud.

➤ Practice the passage starting and stopping on each thumb.

➤ Practice these fragments before stringing them together:
   – the first two eighths
   – the next four eighths
   – the last three eighths plus quarter note C

➤ Change the articulation and practice the eighth notes *staccato*. Also practice using dotted rhythms.

➤ Use the damper pedal as marked for *legato* connection.

➤ Take time to enjoy the surprising dynamics and colorful harmonies in mm. 3-4 and 7-8. Breathe between phrases.

Vladimir Ivanovich Rebikov
Miniature Waltz, op. 10, no. 10 (R33, SW55)
Background Information

Vladimir Rebikov is sometimes called the father of Russian impressionism or modernism. The many miniatures he wrote for keyboard instruction frequently make use of the whole-tone scale and augmented triads.

Exploring the Score

In the waltz style, composers often avoid the traditional "oom-pah-pah" emphasis on the first beat:

➤ How does Rebikov avoid an over-emphasis on the downbeat in *Miniature Waltz*? [LH does not play on downbeats in mm. 1-9]

➤ Where does the LH look more like a traditional waltz figure? [mm. 17-23]

How does Rebikov create variety in the texture?

➤ Compare mm. 1-2 with 3-4. Which measure is a written out elaboration? [RH, m. 3]

➤ Compare mm. 1-4 with mm. 10-13. What remains the same? [the melody]

➤ Before practice begins, review the phrase organization. Where is the five-measure phrase. [mm. 5-9] What is its effect?

Practice Suggestions

A successful performance highlights the melody with subdued accompaniment and a pedal that does not blur stepwise passages. As you practice, try these steps:

➤ Play the melody (whether RH or LH) with a singing *legato* tone.

➤ What does the term *sotto* mean in m. 2? ["under"; position the LH under the RH]

➤ As you play hands together, listen for the projection of the RH and shape the melodic phrases. Notice that RH half notes are the goal of each phrase. Taper the ends of slurs.

➤ In the first seven measures, pedal on beat two, lifting on beat three. Use this approach in similar passages (mm. 10-16, mm. 26 to the end).

➤ How will you pedal mm. 17-21? [Pedal with the RH melody in mind.]

➤ In your final performance, how will you acknowledge the *fermata* over the final rest in m. 33?

Robert Starer
Bright Orange (R38, SW63)
Background Information

Born in Austria, Robert Starer immigrated to the United States after World War II. A prolific and distinguished composer, he taught composition in New York at the Juilliard School and at Brooklyn College. In his two volumes of *Sketches in Color,* he employs different compositional techniques, including polytonality, jazz, and twelve-tone writing.

Exploring the Score

➤ Think about the color bright orange and describe the images and moods that come to mind. Listen to the *Celebration Series*® recording while following the score. Discuss the student's reaction to Starer's musical depiction of bright orange, with its fast, light feeling and syncopated jazz sounds. Is *Bright Orange* the color you would pick for this composition?

➤ Find different ways in which Starer creates syncopation:
  – accents and *tenuto* marks on weak beats
  – rests *before* emphasized tones on weak beats
  – LH chords on weak beats

➤ Notice Starer's use of B flats, B naturals, and F sharps until m. 33. What functions do the three accidentals have? [e.g., B flat: m. 8, lowered seventh in C major; m. 23, root of B flat major triad, etc.]

➤ Find a B flat in the RH played against B natural in the LH. [mm. 12, 30] The combination of the major and minor 3rds creates a jazz effect.

➤ Most LH triads occur in root position. How many can you identify?

➤ How many triads are not in root position? [only one, C] What inversion? [second, C6/4]

➤ Notice Starer's use of melodic upbeat patterns.

Practice Suggestions

➤ Tap and count the rhythm before playing the notes of each practice section. Find measures and phrases that have the same rhythm. Pay special attention to the rhythm in mm. 28-36. As you gain confidence and security with the rhythm, capture the character of "bright orange" with your tapping.

➤ You may find it helpful to tap and count with the metronome set to a quarter-note pulse. As you tap, "feel" the rests on second beats (listening for the metronome tick).

➤ As you play hands together, exaggerate the dynamic and accent markings.

CREATIVE ACTIVITY

Choose blocked triads from Starer's *Bright Orange* to accompany a melody you create. Restrict yourself to the rhythms and chords in mm. 1-7.

Title: *Bright Blue*

Dmitri Kabalevsky
Toccatina, op. 27, no. 12 (S6)
Exploring the Score

The term *toccatina* ("little toccata") is derived from the word *toccare,* meaning to touch. In what ways is Kavalevsky's *Toccatina* a "touch piece"?

➤ Which hand has the melody? [LH] Which RH notes imitate the LH melody? [top notes of chords]

➤ Name the position of the RH chords. [first inversion] Does the position ever change? [see mm. 31-34]

➤ In mm. 29-34, Kabalevsky changes the relationship of the RH and LH from parallel to contrary motion. Notice that this change precedes the return of the A section.

➤ How many different articulation marks can you find in the score? Does the RH ever play *legato*?

Practice Suggestions

The obvious challenge in *Toccatina* is keeping the RH chords light while correctly articulating and projecting the LH melody.

➤ Begin by blocking the positions hands together in quarter notes (line the RH up with the LH). Play slowly, with a full tone.

➤ Practice the RH alone. Keep the wrist and forearm loose. When playing three consecutive chords, use one arm gesture; lift the wrist slightly on the third chord.

➤ How does the performer on the *Celebration Series*® recording play the LH notes marked without slurs?

➤ How will the *cantando* marking in m. 1 affect your performance?

CREATIVE ACTIVITY

Create your own variation of *Toccatina* by playing the melody with the RH and the chords with the LH. (You may wish to select only your favorite phrases.)

Title: *Little Toccatina*

Dmitri Shostakovich
Dance (S16)
Practice Suggestions

This dance is a study in mechanical, perpetual motion. Find examples of each of these different sixteenth-note patterns in the score:
  – four notes ascending/decending by step
  – full octave scales
  – zigzag patterns
  – broken chords

➤ Isolate similar RH patterns and practice them as a group. Then practice two- or four-measure groups slowly, hands together.

➤ Make a decision about dynamic shaping. Will you use *crescendo* and *diminuendo* to follow the natural phrase shape, or a more mechanical, uninflected sound?

STUDY MODULE 2

Page	List	Composer	Title	Key, Meter and Tempo
R10 SW17	A	Johann Ludwig Krebs	*Bourrée in A Minor*	A Minor **C** ♩ = 63
R16 SW27	B	Jan Ladislav Dussek	*Sonatina in G Major, op. 20, no. 1 (First Movement)*	G Major **C** Allegro non tanto
R47 SW81	C	Miroslav Lebeda	*Miniature*	ends in D Major $\frac{4}{4}$ Allegro
S18	C	Stephen Heller	*Abenddämmerung / Dusk, op. 138, no. 3*	D Minor $\frac{3}{4}$ Lento con espressione
S22		Robert Fuchs	*A Little Song, op. 47, no. 4*	C Major $\frac{6}{8}$ Slowly, singing
S24		Génari Karganov	*Game of Patience, op. 25, no. 2*	D Major $\frac{6}{8}$ Animato

Assign first:
Bourrée in A Minor . . . .
A Little Song . . . .
Game of Patience . . . .

Assign next when ready:
Sonatina in G Major
Abenddämmerung / Dusk
Miniature

Study Module 2 provides the opportunity to contrast fast and slow *tempi* in the context of four different style periods. Discuss with your student the different ways that Baroque, Classical, Romantic, and 20th-century composers indicate tempo. One characteristic distinguishing the Baroque era from the other style periods is the lack of tempo markings. With a modern Baroque score it is most often the editor, not the composer, who chose the tempo marking. Use this module as an opportunity to review with students the Italian origins of tempo markings, which were integrated at a time when Italian musicians held prominent posts throughout Europe. Examine the tempo markings used in this Study Module as well as elsewhere in this level.

Johann Ludwig Krebs
Bourrée in A Minor (R10, SW17)

Background Information

Krebs was a student of J.S. Bach and later worked with him as a singer, keyboard player, and copyist. His music combines the contrapuntal style of J.S. Bach with the newer sound of Bach's son, C.P.E. Bach.

Exploring the Score

Originating in France, the lively *bourrée* is in a quick duple meter, with a strong half-note pulse and a short upbeat. Which of these features are present in this *Bourrée?*

➤ Notice that *Bourrée in A Minor* uses a rounded binary form:

    A   mm. 1-12
    B + A1   mm. 13-24; mm. 25-32

➤ Notice how Krebs uses the opening motive to mark the important moments in the form. The rhythm of this motive dominates the entire piece.

and

Krebs' harmonies move around the circle of 5ths in a modulating sequence. Find the following harmonies in the A section:

A minor	m. 1
D minor	m. 3
G major	m. 4
C major	m. ?
F major	m. ?
B minor	m. ?
E major	m. ?
A minor	m. ?
D minor	m. ?
G major	m. ?
Cadence in C major	m. 12

➤ Find the sequences in the B section. [mm. 17-22] What tonalities does Krebs use in these measures?

➤ Discuss the articulation of this lively dance. Which notes will be played detached?

TIP: Quarter notes before and after slurs should be detached.

Practice Suggestions

➤ Decide on the phrasing and articulation for both hands before beginning your practice.

➤ Practice short sections hands separately. (This will establish accurate fingering and articulation, and help you to hear melodic patterns.)

➤ Feel groupings of "two eighth notes–quarter note" throughout. Use the eighth notes to move forward to the longer note values.

➤ You may wish to isolate the RH in mm. 29-30 for special practice.

Jan Ladislav Dussek
Sonatina in G Major, op. 20, no. 1
(First Movement) (R16, SW27)
Background Information
Dussek received his musical training in Bohemia and traveled all over Europe as a celebrated virtuoso pianist. Known as "le beau Dussek" for his good looks, he was credited by his contemporaries as being the first pianist to display his profile by sitting with his right side to the audience. Like Chopin, he wrote mostly for the piano.

Exploring the Score
Many piano pieces from the Classical period seem to be inspired by instrumental sounds. With a bit of imagination, you can hear piano pieces played by a full orchestra—a theme in the strings may be answered by a flute or clarinet, with the brass providing contrast. As you listen to the *Celebration Series®* recording of this piece, assign orchestral instruments to various themes.

What elements of the form make this movement uncharacteristic of a Classical sonatina first movement? [lacks a clear modulation to the dominant before the second theme and uses a written-out repeat of the exposition instead of the customary double bar and repeat sign]

Exposition:	mm. 1-16
1st theme:	mm. 1-4
2nd theme:	mm. 5-8 (stays in the tonic)
repeat of exposition:	mm. 9-16
Development	mm. 17-24
Recapitulation	mm. 25-34
Coda	mm. 34-end

Practice Suggestions
➤ The active LH Alberti bass can overpower the RH melody if you are not careful. Use a lighter touch for the LH, aided by a relaxed, rotating LH with fingers close to the keys.

➤ The LH repeated notes in mm. 1-3 imitate strings. These notes should support the melody and provide a steady pulse without being overpowering.

➤ For RH slurred 6ths, give preference to the *legato* upper voice.

➤ Isolate RH double 3rds for special practice.

Your practice checklist is:
- Clarity of articulation
- Balance of melody and accompaniment
- Repeated notes not too loud

Miroslav Lebeda
Miniature (R47, SW81)
Background Information
Lebeda spent his early life in the Czech Republic, where he graduated from the Conservatory of Music in Prague and the Prague Academy of Music. Before immigrating to the United States, he was an opera and orchestra conductor in Prague and served as Director of the State School of Music.

Exploring the Score
What musical elements provide the playful (*scherzando*) charm of this delightful *Miniature?*
- Variety of articulation
- Large skips
- *Allegro* tempo
- Wide range of dynamic marks and descriptive indications

➤ Mark the form. [ABA1; A section (mm. 1-8) varied in mm. 17-24]

➤ Which intervals are emphasized in each section? [4ths prominent in A, 2nds and 3rds in B]

➤ Within each section, compare the phrases. What are the textural differences between mm. 1-4 and 5-8? between mm. 9-12 and 13-16?

➤ What is the final harmony? [D major]

Practice Suggestions
➤ Circle the clef changes in your music to make the score easier to read.

➤ Each day, tap the rhythm of the piece using the metronome set at 192 to the quarter note.

➤ Practice slowly in short segments at first. Build up to the *Allegro* tempo incrementally, gradually increasing your tempo over time. If you reach the indicated tempo (192-208) you will be guaranteed an exciting performance!

➤ Follow the damper pedal markings exactly. Often the pedal mark supports a RH shift (under a slur mark) that otherwise could not be played *legato* by the fingers alone.

➤ The articulation and performance indications in the score are essential to an engagingly playful performance. Follow them faithfully.

Stephen Heller
Abenddämmerung / Dusk, op. 138, no. 3 (S18)

Exploring the Score

With its descriptive title and wide range of harmonic and dynamic colors, this piece invites a programmatic approach. Listen to the *Celebration Series®* recording. Why would a composition about twilight have a section of *fortissimo* octaves and chords? How do the dynamic changes at the end affect the scene?

There are two main melodic elements: the LH melody in mm. 2-5 and the RH repeated-note motive in m. 6:

(come   to   me)

➤ Find all appearances of these two elements. How do they change during the piece?

➤ Explore the tone quality of each section. Decide on the balance of sound between the hands, the use of pedal, and the articulation (especially for the repeated-note motive).

➤ Assist your student in finding the diminished 7th chords in mm. 6, 14, 27, and 31. Play those chords and their resolution. Do the two chords have common tones? Are there examples of half steps connecting the chords?

➤ How does the C7 chord in m. 8 resolve? [F major, relative to D minor] The A7 in m. 16?

➤ It is normal for a V7 to have more tension than the tonic (I chord) resolution. Is that the dynamic plan for these V7-I chords?

➤ How does the key signature change from D minor to D major, in m. 21, affect the scene?

Practice Suggestions

➤ When reading the first few measures, you will immediately notice the close proximity of the hands. During practice, position the LH over the RH. You will create more room for the RH if you play the LH closer to the fallboard.

➤ As indicated in the score, use the damper pedal on the opening repeated notes to obtain a rich

tone. Then adopt frequent pedal changes to create a clear LH melody.

➤ Plan your dynamic levels carefully. Make a world of difference between your most delicate *p* sound and your most powerful *ff* color in m. 31. How will you interpret *fp*?

CREATIVE ACTIVITY

Think of the last sunset you saw. Where were you? What were the colors? Improvise a short piece that describes those colors and the evening mood. Use some of the elements from Heller's *Abenddämmerung* (for example, single RH repeated notes and an ascending LH melody). Be sure to include damper pedal.

Title: *Distant Sunset*

Robert Fuchs
A Little Song, op. 47, no. 4 (S22)

Background Information

Fuchs was born in Austria and spent much of his life in Vienna teaching at the Vienna Conservatory. His students included the famous composers Jean Sibelius, Gustav Mahler, and Hugo Wolf. Fuchs' character pieces for piano reflect the influence of Robert Schumann.

Exploring the Score

➤ *Little Song* contains a hidden melodic duet. To discover this duet, have the student play several phrases of the RH melody, and then add the LH melody a 6th below (notated with upstems).

➤ Find the repetitions of mm. 1-4. Where is the repetition of mm. 13-16? [mm. 31-34] The student may enjoy tabulating the number of measures of "new" material that need to be learned.

➤ Mark the sections in your music: A (mm. 1-8), A1 (mm. 9-16), B (mm. 17-26), A1 (mm. 27-34).

Practice Suggestions

➤ Play the duet, using the fingering you would use when playing the complete LH. You may use the damper pedal.

➤ Practice the LH alone, listening actively for the difference between melodic notes and softer accompanying tones.

➤ How will the LH sound different in mm. 17-20?

➤ This piece is marked *con pedale*. When will you change the pedal? [when the harmony changes, usually beats one and four] Are there beats that need no pedal? [stepwise motion in mm. 2 and 6]

➤ As you play the complete texture, listen for the peak of each phrase.

CREATIVE ACTIVITY

Follow these steps to write your own *Little Song:*

➢ Make up a simple melody using only quarter notes.
➢ Find a chord to harmonize each note of your melody. Play the harmony as broken chords under the melody notes. (Use Fuchs' composition as a guide.)

Title: *Little Duet*

Génari Karganov
Game of Patience, op. 25, no. 2 (S24)
Exploring the Score

The title of the piece and the musical score appear totally incongruous until one reads the footnote at the bottom of the page. The music is very animated, filled with accents and frequent dynamic surprises. The composer must have had a very lively card game in mind!

➢ How quickly can your student tap mm. 1-8 and mm. 21-28? Have some fun with the tapping and experience the excitement of the piece from this introductory experience.
➢ The ABA form of the piece is very clear. Mark it on the score. Within the A sections (mm. 1-8, 21-28), notice the repetitions and variations of the first four measures.

➢ Find the two measures where the eighth notes are grouped in twos instead of threes [mm. 17 and 19]. What is this change of rhythmic emphasis called? [*hemiola*] Circle these measures, then tap and count, saying *12-12-12.*

Practice Suggestions

➢ You will learn this piece quickly if you tap the rhythms (watch the *hemiola* in mm. 17-20) and block the positions.
➢ Play the repeated chords in mm. 1-2 and 5-6 with a loose wrist and forearm. Group the chords into a single gesture, lifting the wrist slightly on the third chord. Avoid successive down motions of the arm, which can cause unnecessary tension.
➢ Mm. 9-12 are easily learned if you block each main beat. When you play these measures as written, phrase the eighth notes in groups of three.
➢ Practice the contrasting touches of mm. 13-16 on the closed keyboard cover. Then play on the keyboard, isolating just the slurred notes at first, then just the *staccato* notes. (The hands will alternate.) Play hands together very slowly, listening for the contrasting articulations.
➢ Practice mm. 17-20 saying *12 12 12 123 123.*

STUDY MODULE 3

Page	List	Composer	Title	Key, Meter and Tempo
R6 SW7	A	George Frideric Handel	*Allemande in A Minor, HWV 478*	A Minor ¢ ♩ = 66
R18 SW31	B	Muzio Clementi	*Sonatina in F Major, op. 36, no. 4 (First Movement)*	F Major ¾ Con spirito
R32 SW52	C	Edvard Grieg	*Arietta, op. 12, no. 1*	E flat Major ²⁄₄ Poco andante e sostenuto
R44 SW72	C	Leonard Bernstein	*For Susanna Kyle*	C Major ¾ Peacefully
R45 SW75	C	Pierre Gallant	*Sarabande*	D Mixolydian ¾ Slowly
S8		George Frideric Handel	*Entrée in G Minor, HWV 453*	G Minor ¢ Andante
S12		Ruth Watson Henderson	*Toccatina*	A Minor ¢ Vivace

STUDY MODULE 3

Assign first:	Assign next when ready:
Entrée in G Minor	*Allemande in A Minor*
Sonatina in F Major	
Toccatina	*Arietta*
Sarabande	*For Susanna Kyle*

The challenges of Study Module 3 range from independent hands in two compositions by Handel to the subtle melodic shape and tone colors in Grieg's *Arietta* and Gallant's *Sarabande*. In the Handel compositions *(Allemande in A Minor* and *Entrée in G Minor)*, the two voices are equal partners, each with its own melodic line, rhythm, and dynamic shape. These pieces require hand independence and planned articulation to bring out each separate voice.

The use of melody and accompaniment can be compared in the Clementi, Gallant, Grieg, and Henderson compositions. With the Clementi and Gallant pieces, the texture clearly distinguishes melody from accompaniment, while in the works by Grieg and Henderson, the melody and accompaniment are entwined. While these latter two compositions differ in mood and style, in both pieces the student must discover the melody and highlight it by means of touch and dynamics. The texture of Henderson's *Toccatina* has two parts, while Grieg's *Arietta* has three layers of sound: an upper melody, a bass line, and an inner-voice accompaniment.

George Frideric Handel
Allemande in A Minor, HWV 478 (R6, SW7)
Background Information

Baroque dances are usually in binary form. The A section modulates to the dominant key (or the relative major) and the B section returns to the tonic key. Most allemandes have a short upbeat and are in duple meter. Does Handel's *Allemande in A Minor* fit the definition of a typical baroque allemande? [yes]

Exploring the Score

The absence of phrase and articulation markings in the score provides an opportunity for a discussion about the functions of articulation:

➢ Articulation helps to communicate the mood of a piece. For example, you might play a lively dance with mostly detached notes.
➢ Articulation can be used to highlight independence of voices. This is one reason for giving each voice its own distinct articulation.
➢ Articulation can be used to highlight important beats. For example, a downbeat might be preceded by a break in sound and slurred to the following note.

Plan an articulation according to these suggestions, and mark the articulation in the score. (The performance on the *Celebration Series*® recording illustrates one possible approach to dynamics and articulation.)

Practice Suggestions

➢ As you practice, use articulation that you and your teacher added to the score at the lesson.
➢ Apply consistent fingerings, and write in additional reminder fingerings when necessary.
➢ Practice in short sections, first hands alone and then hands together.
➢ Listen for clarity in the 32nd-note figures beginning in m. 14.
➢ Add ornaments after you can play hands together consistently and accurately. Begin trills from the note above the printed note.

Muzio Clementi
Sonatina in F Major, op. 36, no. 4
(First Movement) (R18, SW31)
Exploring the Score

Imagine this is a Classical symphony. What is the character of this opening movement? Can you imagine the LH octave figure played by low strings, punctuated with timpani strokes? Is there a different character between mm. 1-2 and mm. 3-4? What instrument comes in at m. 4?

➢ Label the exposition, development, and recapitulation, as well as the first and second themes. Measure for measure, compare the exposition and recapitulation. Which is longer? What differences occur?
➢ Discuss the contrast between the 1st theme (mm. 1-17) and 2nd theme (mm. 18-30). Which

theme is more homophonic (melody and accompaniment)? In which theme does the LH imitate the rhythm of the RH?

➤ Find other ways by which Clementi creates variety and contrast. For example, compare the scale figures at the end of the exposition and recapitulation.

➤ In development sections, composers often move further away from the home key. What harmonies are outlined in this development (mm. 31-47)? Can you find A major? The A major chord acts as the V (dominant) of D minor—the relative minor of F major. Note Clementi's use of D minor in mm. 35 and 37.

➤ How does Clementi prepare the listener for the return of F major in m. 48? [the long dominant pedal point on bass C, mm. 43-46]

➤ Where does the RH repeated note figure in the development first appear? [m. 18, second theme]

➤ Can you find an example of a sequence in the development? [compare mm. 38-39 with mm. 40-41]

Extra credit assignment: Find the V7 harmonies of each of those important landmarks in the development: V7 of Dm; V7 of Gm; V7 of C; V7 of F.

Practice Suggestions

➤ Play the RH alone in four-bar segments, listening to the shape of each phrase. Let the dissonant G sharp be the melodic goal of the first four measures.

➤ How will you want repeated note figures to sound in the second theme? [short notes go to long notes—the eighth notes are upbeats into a quarter note downbeat]

➤ The LH accompaniment in this piece can easily become heavy if played *legato*. You may wish to lean into the first eighth note and play the others slightly detached. Keep the thumb light.

➤ In mm. 31-33, think of the repeated notes in pairs to make the underlying pulse clearer.

➤ Compare the RH notes and fingering in mm. 35 and 37.

➤ To learn positions and fingerings of the development quickly, block the interval outlines, especially mm. 37-42. Then play as written, giving special attention to frequent fingering changes.

➤ In zigzag figures (m. 37-42), use forearm rotation in the RH. When playing the smaller intervals, the rotation must be more subtle.

➤ Which measures have major scales to rehearse hands alone? [mm. 28-29, 69-70]

Edvard Grieg
Arietta, op. 12, no. 1 (R32, SW52)
Background Information

Grieg based much of his music on Norwegian folk melodies. His several sets of *Lyric Pieces* for piano represent a stunning variety of moods and textures, perhaps rivaled only by Felix Mendelssohn's *Songs without Words*. An arietta is a short song for voice and accompaniment.

Exploring the Score

Begin the student's experience of this beautiful piece by sharing the music. Play as a teacher–student duet (student playing only the melody an octave higher) or have the student play the melody along with the *Celebration Series*® recording. The goal of this initial experience is for the student to leave the lesson saying, "I love the Grieg!" After hearing the piece, the student will easily identify its A A1 form.

As the student experiences the melody, make note of Grieg's expressive dynamic markings. He shows the focal point of each two-measure phrase. Each short slurred group in mm. 5-8 is a musical sigh. Have the student demonstrate the "loud-quiet" shaping in the lesson.

➤ How does Grieg identify shapes of phrases? [*cresc.* and *dim.* marks above the RH]

➤ Listen to the harmonic tension and resolution in mm. 10, 12, 20, 22. How will you treat these moments rhythmically and dynamically? [stretch the downbeat, play the resolution more quietly than the downbeat]

➤ Where does musical material repeat? [mm. 5-6, 7-8] To enhance the musical interest, vary your performance subtly when the music from mm. 5-6 returns in mm. 7-8. [softer, different rhythmic nuances]

➤ How does the performer on the *Celebration Series*® recording communicate that the final measure is the ending of the piece?

Practice Suggestions

Dynamics are the clues to the interpretation of this piece. Focus your practice on dynamic control.

➤ Play only the melody and bass line. Listen for a *crescendo–diminuendo* pattern in each two-measure phrase. Shape the two-note slurs in mm. 5-8.

➤ Play only the inner sixteenth notes, smoothly and quietly.

➤ Isolate mm. 9, 11, 19, and 21 for RH practice. Follow the fingering and listen for a very *legato* top voice.

➤ Finally, combine the bass and melody with the inner sixteenth notes. Listen to the balance. Are the melody tones clearly heard?

Leonard Bernstein
For Susanna Kyle (R44, SW72)

Background Information

Leonard Bernstein composed four sets of birthday celebration pieces for solo piano. Many were composed during the 1940s, before Bernstein became conductor of the New York Philharmonic Orchestra. Collectively, they represent musical portraits of family, friends, teachers, and fellow musicians, including famous twenieth-century composers such as Aaron Copland and William Schuman. The influence of many styles, including jazz, can be heard in Bernstein's cycle of "anniversaries."

For Susanna Kyle is the last composition in the collection entitled *Five Anniversaries. Susanna Kyle* was dedicated to the daughter of Bernstein's friend, Betty Comden, with whom he collaborated on some musical theater productions.

Exploring the Score

Play through *For Susanna Kyle* for your student or listen to a recording of the piece together. Does it sound like a lullaby? What adjectives come to mind to describe the mood of the music? Your list might include: calm, peaceful, restful, serene.

➤ Notice the changing meter. Mark the time signatures in the score.
➤ What is constant about the meter? [underlying quarter note pulse]
➤ Notice the LH phrase groupings in mm. 12-13. [2 beats + 2 beats + 2 beats] What is this change in rhythmic organization called? [*hemiola*]
➤ Where are mm. 1-6 transposed? [mm. 15-20]
➤ Bernstein uses many colorful harmonic "extensions" including 7th and 9th chords. For example, the harmony in m. 20 is a G sharp minor 7 chord. What other chords can you identify?

Practice Suggestions

Your performance goal is to create a peaceful atmosphere that will reflect the tranquil mood of this charming piece.

➤ The RH is a mixture of two-note slurs and longer phrases. Play the two-note slurs using very gentle lifts on the second tone. Let the wrist move upward to facilitate a tapered (not sudden or abrupt) sound.
➤ Much of the LH is written in two voices. Explore fingerings that will permit the smoothest *legato* possible, always holding tones for their full rhythmic value.
➤ Even though *con pedale* is not marked, you will want to include the damper pedal for *legato* connection. Practice with damper pedal.
➤ Use the *una corda* pedal for the softest moments (*ppp*).

Pierre Gallant
Sarabande (R45, SW75)

Background Information

Gallant studied composition at the University of Toronto and earned an Associate Diploma (ARCT) from The Royal Conservatory of Music in Toronto. An active accompanist and lecturer, he teaches composition, piano, and theory at The Royal Conservatory, where he has been a faculty member since 1979.

Exploring the Score

➤ The sarabande is a slow-moving dance with an emphasis on the second beat. Gallant's LH pattern is constructed to show a clear downbeat, as well as a stress on beat two.
➤ Explore the rhythm of the melody. Find the section where the melody focuses solely on the downbeat. [mm. 13-21]
➤ Where does the harmonic texture change? [mm. 15-20]
➤ Gallant uses harmonies associated with the jazz tradition. Can you identify the LH major 7th chords in mm. 1-8 that occur on beat 2? [G major 7, F major 7] What other LH chords can you identify?

Practice Suggestions

➤ In mm. 1-5, first play the LH alone with damper pedal. Notice the two different lengths of bass notes and the corresponding pedalings. The reason for the difference lies in the RH melody. Melodic tones must be clear, not blurred by the pedal.
➤ Your clue to pedaling for the remainder of the piece lies in the value of the downbeat bass tone. Measures 2 and 3 serve as your model.
➤ Several markings in the score provide clues to the expressive nature of the melody. The most important is *cantabile*. As you practice hands together, immerse yourself in the tonal colors, listening for proper balance between the singing melody, inner chords, and bass tones.

CREATIVE ACTIVITY

Using the LH (mm. 1-8) of Pierre Gallant's *Sarabande,* improvise a RH melody to create your own sarabande. Feel free to change some of the harmonies. Notate your best ideas.

Title: *Slow Dance*

George Frideric Handel
Entrée in G Minor, HWV 453 (S8)
Exploring the Score

Discuss why this piece is a fitting selection for the Studies volume. What are the technical challenges of the piece? [the variety of figures and the lack of exact repetition]

Begin your study with a visual analysis.
➤ Identify the key and meter.
➤ Label the form. [Binary] Label the cadences (mm. 5, 7, 12, 17, 17) and their keys.
➤ Look for repeated patterns and figures. For example, there is a sequence in mm. 11-12.

Practice Suggestions

Use these questions for a teacher–student discussion about practice strategies for this study:
➤ Will you begin by tapping the rhythm?
➤ What are your goals for practicing hands separately initially? At what point should you begin hands together practice?
➤ How will you determine the appropriate practice segments? Will you practice the sections in order or group similar passages together?
➤ When will you deal with the articulation? What guidelines will you use to make articulation decisions?
➤ How will you practice the trills? Look for opportunities to add ornamentation. Experiment with trills at the cadences.

➤ How will you practice the sixteenth notes in order to achieve an even sound in both hands? Pay special attention to the LH in mm. 12-15.

Ruth Watson Henderson
Toccatina (S12)
Exploring the Score

You may have played Kabalevsky's *Toccatina* in Study Module 1. A toccata or a toccatina is a fast, technical piece. The challenges in this toccatina include short melodic fragments, changes of position, and alternating and interlocking hands. You may want to compare the two toccatinas for similarities and differences.

Practice Suggestions

➤ Circle the first note of each LH position. [mm. 1, 11, 17, 21, etc.] Divide the piece into practice sections according to LH position.
➤ Play the RH alone. Are all the RH notes melody tones?
➤ Play hands together in sections (without pedal). Keep the LH above the RH, toward the back of the keys. Play the RH louder than the LH.
➤ Observe the long note values written in each hand, and listen for dynamic nuances.
➤ Add damper pedal as marked.

STUDY MODULE 4

Page	List	Composer	Title	Key, Meter and Tempo
R9 SW13	A	Domenico Zipoli	*Sarabanda*	G Minor $\frac{3}{4}$ Largo
R22 SW34	B	Muzio Clementi	*Sonatina in F Major, op. 36, no. 4 (Second Movement)*	B flat Major $\frac{2}{4}$ Andante con espressione
R24 SW36	B	Muzio Clementi	*Sonatina in F Major, op. 36, no. 4 (Third Movement)*	F Major $\frac{2}{4}$ Allegro vivace
R31 SW49	C	Robert Schumann	*Waltz in A Minor, op. 124, no. 4*	A Minor $\frac{3}{4}$ Lebhaft
S10		Cornelius Gurlitt	*Study in E Minor, op. 132, no. 1*	E Minor $\frac{3}{4}$ con moto
S15		Stephen Heller	*Fluttering Leaves, op. 46, no. 11*	B Minor $\frac{2}{4}$ Andantino
S20		Ross Lee Finney	*Playing Ball*	Bitonal $\frac{2}{4}$ Gaily

Assign first:	Assign next when ready:
Sarabanda	
Sonatina in F Major	*Sonatina in F Major*
Study in E Minor	*Waltz in A Minor*
Playing Ball	*Fluttering Leaves*

Study Module 4 provides examples of the variety of moods that can be created with major and minor tonalities. Four pieces in this Study Module are in minor keys and Finney's *Playing Ball* juxtaposes unrelated major chords. The inclusion of a variety of forms representing different style periods (*Sarabanda, Sonatina, Waltz,* etc.) can lead to comparison and further insights. The waltz bass found in Schumann's *Waltz in A Minor, op. 124, no. 4,* and Gurlitt's *Study in E Minor, op. 132, no. 1,* may be a new technical challenge for the student.

Domenico Zipoli
Sarabanda in G Minor (R9, SW13)
Exploring the Score

A sarabande is a slow, dignified binary dance in triple meter. You may want to compare this *Sarabanda* with Gallant's *Sarabande* in Study Module 3. What typical sarabande characteristics can you find in each?

➤ How does Zipoli emphasize the second beat? [LH half notes in mm. 2-4, RH half notes in mm. 6-7, RH eighth notes in mm. 12-15]
➤ Is the form binary? [yes]
➤ Find examples of sequences. [e. g., RH, mm. 1-3; LH, mm. 6-7]

Discuss Baroque articulation principles before home practice begins.
– play wide skips detached
– play single eighth-note upbeats detached (e. g., mm. 2, 4, 12-15)
– play stepwise motion *legato*

Practice Suggestions

The LH plays two voices throughout. An important focus in practice will be to make the voices sound independent of one another.

➤ First, divide the LH part between the hands, playing the upper notes in the RH and the lower notes in the LH. Can you create articulation independence? (Remember that wider skips can be detached.)
➤ Notice the rhythmic independence of the voices. Rhythmic values are of great importance. Hold longer values their full duration. [mm. 2-4, 10, etc.]
➤ Where do the two voices move in parallel motion? contrary motion? Measures with contrary motion will be more difficult and require careful fingering. [e.g., m. 8]
➤ Isolate the LH sequences for special practice. [mm. 6-7]

➤ In the RH, experiment with adding additional ornaments (e.g., cadential trill m. 20, beat 2)

Muzio Clementi
Sonatina in F Major, op. 36, no. 4
(Second Movement) (R22, SW34)
Exploring the Score

The sixteenth notes on the first page might lead one to think that this is a fast movement. What clues from the opening measures indicate that this is a very expressive (almost pleading), contemplative movement? [*andante con espressione,* longer note values, expressive dynamic markings]

➤ Experience the sound of mm. 1-8 by playing for the student or sharing it as a teacher–student duet.
➤ Similarly, play mm. 17-20, keeping the same tempo of the opening. Shape the phrases.

Discuss how Clementi creates variety in this movement:

➤ Where does the opening accompaniment of single repeated tones change to broken octave eighth notes? broken octave sixteenth notes? [mm. 9 and 35 respectively]
➤ Can you find examples of melodic elaboration or variation? Compare mm. 3-4 with 11-12, and mm. 5-6 with 13-14 and 31-32.
➤ What is the opening phrase structure? [2 + 2 + 4] Can you find an example of a six-measure phrase? [mm. 21-26]
➤ Half-cadences end on the dominant (V) and leave listeners expecting more. Perfect or authentic cadences end on the tonic (I) and sound more conclusive. Where does Clementi use a half-cadence? [mm. 8, 34] Can you find the authentic cadences in B flat major? [mm. 16, 46]

➢ You have probably experienced the common cadential progression, IV-V7-I. Notice how Clementi uses a ii6 chord in the perfect cadences (mm. 15, 45) instead of a IV chord. This is a common substitution [ii6-V7-I replaces IV-V7-I].

TIP: The ii6 chord often substitutes for the IV chord. In B flat major, the IV chord would be E flat major, spelled E flat–G–B flat. The ii6 chord is spelled E flat–G–C.

Practice Suggestions

A successful performance of this movement will include careful balance between melody (RH) and accompaniment (LH), beautiful shaping of phrases, and delicate pedaling. Notice how Clementi uses *sf* and accent marks to show sighing motives and phrase shapes. Avoid a harsh sound on the *sf* tones. The *sf* is not meant to be a forceful sound.

TIP: A musical "sigh" has its emphasis on the first note.

➢ Composers intend that there will be a slight lift (musical breath) at the end of each slur. Mark the musical breaths in the first two lines of the music as a reminder.
➢ Notice that the more melodic LH lines have slurs. When should the LH lift?
➢ Use only touches of damper pedal, always maintaining a very clear sound, never blurring stepwise motion.

Muzio Clementi
Sonatina in F Major, op. 36, no. 4
(Third Movement) (R24, SW36)
The final movement of a Classical sonatina or sonata is usually light-hearted, even humorous.

TIP: In a typical three-movement sonata structure of the Classical period, the expected plan is:

Movement I: dramatic, filled with contrast
Movement II: (change of key) slow, lyrical
Movement III: light-hearted; often in rondo form

Exploring the Score

How is the mood of this third movement different from that of the sonatina's second movement? The mood of this rondo is very "up-beat" (literally!). The movement is a musical romp from beginning to end.

Rondo form is characterized by multiple returns of a main or "rondo" theme: usually ABACA or ABACABA. What is the form of this rondo? [ABA with the B section acting like a development] This rondo is unique because it lacks the traditional thematic contrast. It is highly unified by the triplet subdivisions.

Sonatinas generally exhibit many kinds of contrast. Compare mm. 1-4, 5-7, 8-9, 10-11. You may notice:
  – change of accompaniment
  – change of register
  – change of RH figure
  – changing lengths of ideas

➢ Composers frequently place the dynamic peak in the third measure of a four-measure phrase ("out of four, go for three"). How does Clementi highlight the intensity of the dominant harmony in m. 3? [*cresc.* in m. 2, *forte* in m. 3, *and* the impact of a four-voice dominant chord on the downbeat]
➢ Using accidentals as a guide, identify changes of key in this rondo.
➢ How does Clementi develop material in the B section? Why do mm. 27-29 sound familiar? [m. 27 is an inversion of m. 1; compare the descending RH melody in m. 28 to m. 5; contrast the RH downbeat of m. 29 to mm. 4 and 6]

Practice Suggestions

Playing the constant sixteenth notes evenly is a formidable task. When the LH has solo imitations of the RH, in mm. 36-41, maintaining evenness is especially challenging. In your practice, observe the following suggestions:

➢ Use consistent fingerings in sixteenth passages. Alternate *legato* and *staccato* touches to develop clarity. [playing *legato* will feel easier after *staccato*] Listen for even sixteenths at all times.
➢ Practice at a variety of tempi, gradually increasing speed. At performance tempo, feel the forward motion in each phrase. De-emphasizing downbeats will help you create a longer line.
➢ Block the broken chord figures in mm. 42-45 to learn the notes, then play as written, rotating your hand in the direction of the line.
➢ The ornaments will need special practice.
  – Begin the turns in mm. 21-22 and 24 from above the printed note.
  – Practice a measured RH trill in mm. 30, 35, and 39 against the LH.

Robert Schumann
Waltz in A Minor, op. 124, no. 4 (R31, SW49)
Exploring the Score

Listen to the *Celebration Series®* recording and ask the student for impressions and reactions. There are many unusual features about this waltz. In your discussion, consider the following:
➢ We usually think of a phrase as rising and then falling. Schumann writes an opening phrase

(mm. 1-8) that falls and then rises. The contour seems "backwards." Does Schumann use this phrase shape throughout the waltz?

➤ What feeling or mood is generated by the combination of minor key and falling phrase? [great sadness, resignation] Is this what you expect with a waltz? [Note that Chopin also wrote "sad" waltzes].

➤ Most Romantic melodies fall nicely within a singing range. What is the range of this melody? [nearly two octaves, from the opening A to the B flat in m. 16]

➤ What is the phrase structure? [3 + 2 + 3, then 3 + 5] How does Schumann organize the phrases in mm. 17-28?

➤ The contrasting section of a piece in a minor key is usually in the relative major key. In this piece we would expect C major. What key does Schumann use? [F major!] What notes do the A minor and F major triads have in common? [A and C]

TIP: Romantic composers frequently highlighted the relationship between keys and harmonies with common tones.

➤ A single pitch can be harmonized many ways. Compare mm. 1, 17, and 21. Each starts with the same A but the effect is quite different.

➤ Can you identify the very special harmonic sound of m. 1? The chord sounds like an F7 chord (F, A, C, E flat) but the E flat is spelled as a D sharp. The D sharp creates an augmented 6th above the unusual opening bass note, F. The tension created by these two notes is resolved in the next measure: D sharp resolves upward to E, F downward to E. Chords spelled like this are called augmented 6th chords. Very few pieces begin with this chord.

Practice Suggestions

➤ Notice the LH fingering: whenever possible, reserve the fifth finger for downbeat tones.

➤ Letting your elbow lead, make a graceful arc as your hand moves from the low downbeat notes to the higher chords.

➤ In general, pedal on beat one and lift on beat three. When the LH moves by step, (e.g., m. 8), pedal *each beat.*

➤ Isolate the RH octaves in mm. 21-28 for spot practice. Play as *legato* as possible using damper pedal for connection.

Cornelius Gurlitt
Study in E Minor, op. 132, no. 1 (S10)
Exploring the Score

Discuss reasons why Gurlitt may have written this étude. What are the technical challenges? Your list might include: the LH shifts, the variety of LH chord shapes, and the wide RH leaps.

➤ How long is each section? [8 measures] Label the A A1 B A1 form on the score.

➤ In what key does the B section begin? [G major, relative of E minor]

Practice Suggestions

Here are some tips for LH practice:

➤ Plan your fingering carefully. When possible, avoid using the fifth finger on the bottom note of LH chords.

➤ Practice slowly. Imagine the feel of the second beat chord before you play.

➤ Move the hand and arm in a natural arc.

➤ Use each third-beat rest to position the LH for the next downbeat.

The RH plays a variety of figures:

➤ Use a rocking motion (forearm rotation) for the wide intervals in mm. 1-3.

➤ Circle the RH finger substitutions (mm. 3-4, 11-12, 27-28). Practice these measures slowly, focusing on the *legato* connection in the upper voice.

➤ When the RH plays two voices (for example, mm. 3-4 and 7-8) hold each note for its proper value.

➤ Use a "waltz pedal" to connect beats one and two in the LH. Release the pedal on beat three.

Stephen Heller
Fluttering Leaves, op. 46, no. 11 (S15)
Exploring the Score

Heller did not write a note without an underlying challenge. In *Fluttering Leaves,* the issue is balancing melody with accompaniment, but an accompaniment that is divided between the hands! The *legato* accompaniment must sound as if one hand is playing. The gymnastics of shifting back and forth is the real test.

Practice Suggestions

The obvious "étude" aspect of the piece is the constant crossing movements:

➤ Take care to observe the *m.d.* (RH) and *m.s.* (LH) indications in m. 1. This division of hands can be applied throughout. [Composers frequently use *m.s.* and *m.d.* in the score to indicate hand placement. *M.s.* is the abbreviation for *mano sinistra,* or LH. *M.d.* is *main droite* (French) or *mano destra* (Italian) for the RH.]

➤ First, block the alternating hand positions on the piano keyboard cover to simulate the crossing movements. Notice how the motion resembles a "pawing" gesture.

➤ In mm. 1-14, depress the pedal on beat one, and lift for the last two sixteenth notes of the measure (the "and" of two).

➤ Why would Heller put *tenuto* markings over the RH downbeat eighth notes in mm. 1-2? [The eighth notes must be held long enough to be caught in the pedal change, and they must project above the accompanying sixteenth notes.] Apply this *tenuto* marking throughout the piece.

➤ How will you play the quarter notes marked with slurs and *staccatos* in mm. 26-27? [slightly detached and with touches of damper pedal]

In your performance, shape the alternating rising and falling RH melodic figures to suggest the swaying motion of a falling leaf.

Ross Lee Finney
Playing Ball (S20)
Background Information

American composer Ross Lee Finney was a student of Alban Berg and Nadia Boulanger. A Pulitzer Prize winner, he was influential in modern composition and electronic music and was composer in residence at the University of Michigan from 1949 to 1973. His students include George Crumb and Roger Reynolds.

Exploring the Score

Like J. S. Bach's *Fifteen Two-Part Inventions,* each of *Finney's Twenty-Four Inventions* explores a particular way to combine notes and musical elements. This study uses two elements: LH stepwise motion and RH

chords. Analyze the chords:
➤ Are they all major chords? [no, see mm. 11 and 18]
➤ Are they all in root position? [yes]
➤ Are the rhythmic patterns consistent? [no, but there is some repetition, for example, in mm. 1-4 and mm. 13-16]

There are many accidentals in the LH part. What scales are represented? Name as many as you can.

Practice Suggestions

➤ As a preliminary exercise, play all of the major triads hands together, moving up and down the keyboard chromatically (C, D flat, D, E flat, E, F, etc.). Repeat the exercise using minor triads.

➤ Practice the RH of *Playing Ball* alone, being sure to differentiate between *staccato* and *tenuto* chords. Chords that move by 3rds will require extra drill and repetition.

➤ Next, block the sixteenth-note figures to find finger groupings. Isolate for spot practice the scales you discovered when exploring the score.

➤ As you play hands together, exaggerate dynamics and articulations. Drill one shift at a time in mm. 10, 17, 31-32.

CREATIVE ACTIVITY

Compose your own piece using elements of *Playing Ball*. Be sure to include RH chords and LH sixteenth-note patterns. You may use fragments of Finney's composition to get you going. Remember to play in a quick tempo!

Title: *Playing Games*

STUDY MODULE 5

Page	List	Composer	Title	Key, Meter and Tempo
R4 SW4	A	Johann Sebastian Bach	*Little Prelude in D Minor, BWV 926*	D Minor $\frac{3}{4}$ ♩ = 112
R13 SW23	B	Franz Joseph Haydn	*Divertimento in G Major, Hob. XVI:G1 (First Movement)*	G Major $\frac{2}{4}$ Allegro
R36 SW60	C	Paul Creston	*Pastoral Dance, op. 24, no. 4*	F Lydian $\frac{6}{8}$ Lyrically
R40 SW66	C	Bohdana Filtz	*An Ancient Tale*	A Major $\frac{3}{4}$ Andantino
R42 SW69	C	Dale Reubart	*March of the Buffoons*	C Major 𝄴 Marziale
R48 SW84	C	Douglas Finch	*Cancan*	C Major $\frac{4}{4}$ Lively
S4		Johann Sebastian Bach	*Prelude in C Minor, BWV 999*	C Minor $\frac{3}{4}$ ♩ = 104

STUDY MODULE 5

Assign first:

Prelude in C Minor . . . .
Divertimento in G Major
An Ancient Tale . . . .
March of the Buffoons . . . .

Assign next when ready:

Little Prelude in D Minor

Pastoral Dance

Cancan

Beginning with Bach's *Little Prelude in D Minor* and Haydn's *Sonata in G Major*, the pieces in this study module include a variety of beat subdivisions. Compare tempi, meters, and rhythmic variety among these compositions. The two dances, *Cancan* by Douglas Finch and *Pastoral Dance* by Paul Creston, also invite comparison through contrast of mood. The two Bach preludes both feature RH broken-chord figuration.

Johann Sebastian Bach
Little Prelude in D Minor, BWV 926 (R4, SW4)
Background Information

Bach's *Little Prelude in D Minor* is from the *Wilhelm Friedemann Bach Notebook,* created by Bach for the instruction of his nine-year-old son. Compiled over a period of several years, this notebook is historically significant because of its contents. In addition to several short preludes and instructional pieces, it contains the Two- and Three-part inventions, eleven preludes that became part of *The Well-Tempered Clavier (Book One),* and a table showing ornaments and their realization.

Exploring the Score

Most Baroque preludes focus on one theme or motive. This *Little Prelude* is based on a broken-chord pattern. The arrangement of the chord tones in the RH of mm. 1-6 gives emphasis to the low pitch. This creates a feeling of $\frac{6}{8}$ rather than $\frac{3}{4}$. This ambiguity of meter in the opening may be intentional, as it lends tension to the piece. The single bass note in each of these measures propels the music forward as if there were only one beat to the measure. Help students to be aware of the large pulse patterns of the music. Think in two-measure units and feel the flowing motion from downbeat to downbeat.

➤ As mentioned above, the RH figure often looks as if it were written in $\frac{6}{8}$. Are there places where the RH is obviously in $\frac{3}{4}$?

➤ Where does Bach use a pedal point? [mm. 1-6, mm. 21-24]

➤ The A7 harmony of mm. 21-24 would normally resolve to its tonic, D minor. How does Bach resolve the harmony in m. 25? [B flat major]. What is this type of harmonic surprise called? [deceptive cadence]

➤ How many different types of ornaments are there?

➤ Notice how the *"cadenza"* outburst of sixteenth notes in m. 39 leads us to the dominant chord in m. 43.

➤ Notice the rhythmic groupings in mm. 39-42. Like the opening, the patterns confuse our feeling of beat and pulse.

Practice Suggestions

➤ Play the piece with blocked chords to hear the harmonies. Let the harmonic structure of the music be your guide when adding phrasing and dynamic shape.

➤ The trills in mm. 16 and 18 are challenging. How will you practice these? Playing a shorter three-note ornament (main note, upper note, main note), instead of four notes, is possible and slightly easier.

Your practice checklist for baroque ornaments is:
  – What tone will you begin on?
  – How many notes will you play in the ornament?
  – Is the first note clearly *on the beat?*

The cadenza-like section (mm. 39-42) will also need special attention.
  – Before playing, set your metronome to the quarter-note pulse. Count and tap mm. 38-44 to establish a correct relationship between eighths and sixteenths.
  – Map out logical practice groupings in these measures by comparing the different types of sixteenth-note motion. Mark divisions between the hands.
  – Say the fingering aloud during practice.
  – In practice units, alternate between *staccato* and *legato* practice.

Franz Joseph Haydn
Divertimento in G Major, Hob. XVI:G1
(First Movement) (R13, SW23)

Exploring the Score

Haydn's early sonatas (called *divertimenti*) were written for harpsichord and had no dynamic indications. Thus, the dynamic marks for this *Divertimento in G Major* are editorial. Are there other dynamics you would like to write in the score? For example, is there echo material that could be played softer? Are there possible *forte* moments you would want to mark? Will the dynamic level for the recapitulation, in m. 58, be the same as m. 1 or slightly different to announce the return?

The number and form of the movements vary among these early sonatas. Label the sections and themes of this movement.

Exposition	mm. 1-28
theme 1	mm. 1–7
bridge	mm. 8-12
theme 2	mm. 13-22
closing theme	mm. 22-28
Development	mm. 29-57
Recapitulation	mm. 58-80
theme 1	mm. 58-64
theme 2	mm. 65-74
closing theme	mm. 74-80

➤ This movement illustrates Haydn's concentration on tonic-dominant key contrast rather than thematic contrast. By m. 12 of the exposition, the expected modulation to the dominant key (D major) has already taken place. Strictly speaking, one would expect to hear a contrasting second theme at m. 13. What did Haydn do instead? [repeats the first theme in the new key]

➤ Examine the contour of the themes. Do they descend or ascend? [mostly descend] Find the ascending motives. [mm. 9, 18, 22, etc.] They can be given special emphasis.

➤ What is the length of the opening phrase? [5 + 2] As you read through the exposition, mark Haydn's larger phrase groups in the music. Is the phrase structure the same in the recapitulation?

➤ In a development section, material from the exposition is varied and reorganized. The music usually travels through several keys before returning to the tonic. Trace material in this development section back to the exposition.

➤ What keys can you identify in the development?

Practice Suggestions

➤ Haydn uses a great variety of pulse subdivisions in this movement. To prepare, tap combinations of eighth, sixteenth, thirty-second, and triplet sixteenth notes over a steady eighth-note pulse.

➤ Take out the magnifying glass and carefully observe Haydn's articulation markings. Remember that wedge or stroke marks indicate a *staccato* touch. Your practice checklist should include:
- Which eighth notes will be played *staccato? legato?* [mm. 1, 4, 8]
- Do scalar passages sound even and *legato?*
- What technical motion will you use for the LH broken intervals? [gentle wrist rotation]
- Are you lifting after each slur?
- Are the short two-note slurs articulated with a "down-up" or "drop-lift" motion?

TIP: Short slurred groups of notes have their stress on the first note.

➤ The goal of your practice is to give character and definition to each musical idea. Which themes or ideas are tender and expressive? Which are bold and vigorous?

Paul Creston
Pastoral Dance (R36, SW60)

Background Information

The son of poor Italian immigrants, Paul Creston (born Giusseppe Guttovergi) was almost entirely self-taught, yet became one of America's most widely performed composers. He wrote in an accessible, conservative style and considered his greatest "teachers" to be Bach, Scarlatti, Chopin, Debussy, and Ravel. Rhythm was of great interest to Creston, who wrote two books on the subject. His music often emphasizes shifting subdivisions of regular meters.

"Pastoral" implies the contentment and peace found in nature. The typical rhythm associated with a pastoral work is a lilting $\frac{6}{8}$. Other famous examples of pastoral movements are in Handel's *Messiah* and Beethoven's *Pastoral Symphony*, his sixth.

Exploring the Score

Have the student leave the piano bench and swing or sway to the $\frac{6}{8}$ meter while listening to the *Celebration Series®* recording. How does the performer capture the *very quietly and liltingly* indication? How does the damper pedal affect the sound? [the opening phrase units sound as if they are written in $\frac{12}{8}$]

As you explore further:
➤ What is the typical phrase length? [two measures]
➤ What mode does Creston use? Notice in mm. 1-8 that the tonal center is F but that there are no B flats. This is F Lydian (F to F on the keyboard playing all white notes). A Lydian scale sounds like a major scale with the fourth note raised one half step.

➤ Now look at the remainder of the piece. When Creston moves to other tonal centers, does he continue to use the Lydian sound?

Mm. 9-12:   Uses G sharps? (raised fourth of D scale) [No]

Mm. 13-15:   Uses G naturals? (raised fourth of D flat scale) [Yes]

Practice Suggestions

➤ The LH has very large reaches. Practice the LH alone with pedal to achieve a *legato* sound. Experiment with moving the arm into playing position so that forearm and hand remain in a straight line.

➤ Observe the contrasting slurs, LH and RH, in mm. 14-15. Which hand frequently lifts? [LH]

➤ Be careful not to "dot" the RH downbeat eighth notes in mm. 6 and 28.

➤ Watch the accidentals in mm. 20-22. Notice that the parallel 3rds are always a major 3rd apart.

CREATIVE ACTIVITY

Creston's *Pastorale Dance* uses the Lydian mode:

➤ Play several major scales and then convert each to the Lydian mode. Remember to raise the fourth tone by a half step.

➤ Take your favorite Lydian mode and use the ideas in Creston's piece to explore the Lydian sound.

➤ Start by using the same LH as Creston and then create a new melody.

Title: *Lydian Dance*

Bohdana Filtz
An Ancient Tale (R40, SW66)
Background Information

Filtz is a Ukrainian composer. Her compositions include works for piano, symphony orchestra, voice, violin, and children's choirs. She lives in Kiev, teaching, composing, and writing about Ukrainian music.

Exploring the Score

The *Celebration Series*® recording and a teacher–student discussion of musical imagery will help students appreciate the colors of this expressive musical picture. To draw the student into the sound of *An Ancient Tale,* sight-read mm. 1-6 as a duet, with the student playing only the melody, with damper pedal.

➤ Notice the dynamic arch form of the entire piece (one long *cresc. – dim.*). How does Filtz prepare for the *ff* in m. 15? [increased rhythmic activity, ascending LH lines]

➤ What effect does the composer create with the quiet ending?

➤ Although the piece is not titled "Sarabande," do you see or hear characteristics of a sarabande? [slow tempo, emphasis on second beat]

➤ Discover the tonal centers Filtz creates:

m. 1 A major   I (tonic)

m. 5 F sharp minor   vi (relative minor)

m. 6 D major   IV (subdominant)

➤ Mark other important key areas and their relationship to the key of A major in your score.

Practice Suggestions

➤ Proper pedaling is essential for the *legato* connection of tones. Be careful to hold the damper pedal through entire measures so marked (not lifting on beat two).

➤ Isolate the ascending LH arpeggio figures in mm. 13-14 for fingering security and full sound leading to the *ff* in m. 15.

➤ Above all, the RH melody must project and sing (note the *cantabile* indication in the score).

➤ As you play, what dynamic levels do you hear? Are you planning ahead for the *ff* dynamic peak in m. 15?

Dale Reubart
March of the Buffoons (R42, SW69)
Background Information

Reubart was professor of piano at the University of British Columbia. Since his early retirement in 1986, he has been able to devote more time to composition. His music is essentially tonal and neoclassical. As a composer he is largely self-taught, although he credits a number of mentors and colleagues with leaving significant impressions on his style and technique.

Exploring the Score

Most marches are in duple meter with regular phrase lengths. Marches also have a marked rhythm emphasizing strong beats. Does this piece have these standard march characteristics?

➤ There are no phrase markings in the score. Have the student play, sing, or tap the opening six measures. What grouping of measures do you feel? [two measures]

➤ As the student taps the rhythm of the piece, find the measures in which the rhythm is the same. Conclusion: the rhythm is a predictable duple meter march, but there is subtle variation of rhythm in many of the measures. Could this reflect the unpredictable movements of the buffoons (clowns)?

➤ Throughout the piece, Reubart uses a variety of articulations and note values. The slurred notes provide both contrast to the *staccatos* and emphasis to many third beats.

➤ How does Reubart create a humorous, clown-like atmosphere? What mental pictures do the *glissandos* in mm. 23-24 and mm. 27-28 conjure in the student's mind?

Practice Suggestions

Determine your practice units (two measures or four measures). In the first days of practice, use this practice routine for those units:
- tap the rhythm
- play first on the closed keyboard cover (observe fingerings carefully)
- at the keyboard, play the unit slowly, several times
- observe every *staccato,* slur, and accent mark
- evaluate: did you play "perfectly"?
- maintain a steady pulse throughout

➤ Some two-note slurs are marked with an accent. How will you play these? [faster key descent]
➤ Practice the *glissando* measures by playing just the quarter notes at first, in a steady pulse. When you add the *glissando,* be sure you reach beat four in time.

Douglas Finch
Cancan (R48, SW84)
Background Information

Finch was born in Winnipeg and earned his master's degree from the Juilliard School, where he received composition coaching from David Diamond and Roger Sessions. He has had a multi-faceted career as a concert pianist, composer, and university professor.

Exploring the Score

The cancan was a high-kicking dance, popular in French stage show routines. How does this music imitate the vigorous movements of the cancan?

Notice the great variety of musical textures in Finch's *Cancan*. Find examples of:
- RH melody and LH accompaniment [mm. 1-4]
- LH melody and RH accompaniment [mm. 5-8]
- parallel octaves between the hands [mm. 9-10]
- imitation between the hands [mm. 11-13]

Practice Suggestions

➤ Notice Finch's *sempre staccato* marking. During your first week of practice, slowly play each two-measure practice unit *legato* to establish fingering and the feel of the intervals.
➤ Devise a special practice plan for mm. 3-4 and 16-17. You could block the notes of each beat. (Did you discover Finch's plan? These measures descend in stepwise motion.)
➤ Mark the hand crossings in your music (mm. 11-13 and mm. 18-21). Choreograph the crossings by playing only the first note of each group. Notice the plan: one hand starts on a white key, the other on a black.

Johann Sebastian Bach
Prelude in C Minor, BWV 999 (S4)
Background Information

Bach wrote many short preludes for instructional purposes. Several of these, like the D minor prelude that began this study module, are in the notebook Bach wrote for his son Wilhelm Friedemann. The little preludes provide material for learning a variety of musical textures from the Baroque period. Modern editions often include eighteen preludes organized in sub-groups of six. This particular prelude was actually written for lute, although the piece is often included in many keyboard collections of Bach's *Little Preludes.* The lute was an early stringed instrument, similar to a guitar, but with a round (pear-shaped) body instead of the guitar's flat back.

Exploring the Score

➤ During the lesson, have the student block the chords.
➤ Find the chords that have a "dissonant" or unresolved quality. Name and label as many of the chords as you can. Mark the downbeat bass notes that are also the chord roots. Where is the D pedal point? [mm. 17-32, interrupted by E flat in m. 23]
➤ After the long D pedal point, Bach creates additional tension by delaying the arrival of the expected G major tonality. When does the RH actually arrive at G major? [m. 34, 2nd beat]
➤ Trace the G pedal point that begins in m. 33. What is unusual about the ending? [the piece ends in G major!]
➤ Knowing that this prelude was originally written for lute, what performance tempo will you choose? [not too fast]

Practice Suggestions

This study is an exercise in articulating RH and LH broken chords. It is a prime candidate for blocking practice. When you begin your practice, try this arrangement of notes to learn the RH chords and to feel the rhythm:

beat 1 – LH downbeat note
beat 2 – RH blocked chord
beat 3 – LH 8ths as written

As you practice the entire piece:
➤ The detached LH can sound like a plucked lute.
➤ Listen for *even* RH sixteenth notes.
➤ Phrases tend to grow towards chords that create harmonic tension (dissonance). Plan your dynamics accordingly.

TIP: Baroque composers heightened musical tension in several ways: adding ornaments; increasing the rhythmic activity; increasing the frequency of harmonic changes.

STUDY MODULE 6

Page	List	Composer	Title	Key, Meter and Tempo
R12 SW20	A	Domenico Scarlatti	*Sonata in A Major, LS 31, K 83 (Second Movement: Minuetto)*	A Major $\frac{3}{8}$ ♪ = 158
R28 SW43	B	Anton Diabelli	*Sonatina in F Major, op. 168, no. 1 (Third Movement: Rondo)*	F Major $\frac{6}{8}$ Allegretto
R30 SW45	C	Franz Schubert	*Sentimental Waltz, op. 50, no. 13*	A Major $\frac{3}{4}$ ♩ = 126
R34 SW58	C	Dmitri Kabalevsky	*Warrior's Dance, op. 27, no. 19*	F Minor ¢ Allegro energico
R46 SW78	C	André Previn	*Roundup*	C Major $\frac{4}{4}$ With energy
S11		Stephen Heller	*Barcarole, op. 138, no. 5*	B Minor $\frac{6}{8}$ Lento, con morbidezza
S14		Henri Bertini	*Study in E Minor, op. 29, no. 14*	E Minor ¢ Allegro

Assign first:

Minuetto
Study in E Minor . . . .
Sentimental Waltz . . . .
Roundup. . . . .

Assign next when ready:

Sonatina in F Major
Barcarole
Warrior's Dance

Concert artists often select recital programs that include a diversity of styles and moods. These more difficult pieces in Study Module 6 would make a wonderfully diverse recital program. They reflect the changing styles of piano repertoire from the Baroque era into the early 20th century and include some prominent composers from these style periods. Many piano recitals include a composition by a lesser-known composer. The music of André Previn and Henri Bertini provides that variety.

Domenico Scarlatti
Sonata in A Major, LS 31, K 83
(Second Movement: Minuetto) (R12, SW20)

Background Information

Scarlatti held several musical posts in Italy before being called to serve as court musician to the King of Portugal. One of his many duties there was to teach the young Princess, who proved to be a talented harpsichordist. When she married the heir to the Spanish throne in 1729, Scarlatti moved to Spain with her court. There he spent the rest of his life, composing, conducting, and teaching.

The influence of Spanish and Portuguese dances and guitar music is often evident in Scarlatti's harpsichord compositions. His sonatas—over 550 of them—were cast in a single-movement binary form. Scarlatti's shorter keyboard works carried names such as *Minuetto, Aria,* and *Pastoral.*

Exploring the Score

➤ What is the form of this *Minuetto?* [binary]
➤ Compare this *Minuetto* to the Stölzel *Minuet in G Minor* in Study Module 1 or other minuets in the *Celebration Series®.* Consider meter, form, and phrase lengths.
➤ Notice the placement of the *mp* markings. What function do these editorial dynamics serve? [the *mp* markings indicate an echo effect for repeated material]

TIP: Many Baroque composers wrote for harpsichords or organs with more than one manual or keyboard. The manuals could be set to produce different sounds, contrasting in timbre or dynamic level. Moving from a louder to a quieter keyboard during a piece would yield an effect referred to as "terraced dynamics."

Listen to the *Celebration Series®* recording for ideas on articulation. What articulations will give this *Minuetto* the most effective dance quality? General guidelines would include:
- wide leaps are played detached
- stepwise motion is played *legato*
- lifting at the bar line gives definition to the downbeat.

Practice Suggestions

This *Minuetto* develops hand independence. When do the hands move in parallel motion? contrary motion? [contrary motion measures tend to be more difficult]

During practice, edit your score.
- ➤ Since most of the notes will be played detached, you could write in only the *legato* slurs.
- ➤ Look for the **mp** markings and find all appearances of "statement—echo." Play each as marked.
- ➤ Decide on your practice units. (Many could end with the "echo.") Before playing each practice unit:
  - check fingerings
  - "hear" the articulation you have planned
  - play slowly, *forte* and *legato* one time
  - play slowly with your planned dynamics and articulations two more times.

- ➤ Experiment with adding RH trills in cadential mm. 18 and 36.

Anton Diabelli
Sonatina in F Major, op. 168, no. 1
(Third Movement: Rondo) (R28, SW43)
Background Information

Diabelli was an Austrian composer, teacher, and music publisher (Franz Schubert's publisher). His piano sonatinas are among his best-known compositions.

Exploring the Score

TIP: Third movement rondos are meant to be light and humorous.

Play through the piece for your student or listen to the *Celebration Series®* recording together. Find the elements of humor which Diabelli has created. Bass clef ideas often represent buffoonery. What other ideas contribute to the bright, cheerful, and humorous quality of this movement?
- hand crossings into bass clef
- conversational, operatic duet element [RH in mm. 16-24, 40-48]
- major key and *allegretto* tempo
- detached RH scales
- use of upper register of the piano
- extended Coda—never wants to finish!

Label the rondo form:

A	mm. 1-8
B	mm. 9-15
C	mm. 16-23
Codetta	mm. 24-32
A1	mm. 33-39
C1	mm. 40-48
Coda	mm. 49-end

What chords in the score can you identify? Write the chord letter names in the score.

Practice Suggestions

- ➤ Study the articulation. Diabelli marks the RH articulations with precision, clearly distinguishing *legato* and *staccato* (wedges) passages. With few exceptions, the LH is left unmarked. To provide an unobtrusive accompaniment, play the LH with a flowing *legato*.
- ➤ To learn this movement quickly and efficiently, follow these steps:
  1) Divide the score into four-measure units.
  2) Practice the RH. Make special note of fingerings and articulations.
  3) Block the LH.
  4) Play the RH as written accompanied by the LH blocked harmonies.
  5) Then, play as written. Listen for the articulation contrast between the RH and LH.

- ➤ Visualize the destination or jump for each hand crossing. Try each with your eyes closed.
- ➤ The repeated chords in the LH are challenging and require a relaxed forearm and wrist. Notice the slur in m. 16 (followed by *simile*). Group three successive chords into a single gesture: drop into the first chord, then gradually lift your forearm as you play the remaining chords with gentle hand bounces.
- ➤ Your goal is a lively and spirited interpretation. What images will you associate with each section? Be creative!

Franz Schubert
Sentimental Waltz, op. 50, no. 13 (R30, SW45)

Schubert was only 31 when he died, but he made a magnificent contribution to the music world. Brahms loved Schubert's music and commented many years after Schubert's death, "Where else is there a genius like his?" In Viennese society during Schubert's life, the dance was a prominent social event. Schubert was frequently commissioned to compose music for such dances. He could easily improvise a piano solo or duet part for a waltz. Indeed, the use of triple meter pervades many of his larger works for solo piano.

Exploring the Score

The memorable sounds of *Sentimental Waltz* are the harmonic colors. The LH plays a typical waltz figure and the RH creates an emphasis on beat three. Two aspects of Schubert's RH are important for the student to hear:

1) The RH is written primarily as a duet. Notice that some of the eighth-note groups occur in the soprano, and some in the alto. This shift creates a subtlety that is a tribute to Schubert's genius.

2) When the downbeat and third beat are different notes, the downbeat consistently represents a dissonance (suspension) and the third beat creates the resolution. Schubert's accents on downbeat half notes are for the purpose of harmonic emphasis. The third beat is the harmonic resolution, but has tension of its own, because the tie across the bar line creates a rhythmic emphasis.

One can always expect breathtaking harmonic surprises in Schubert's music. Let us examine the harmonic plan:

➤ Name the key at the beginning. [A major]
➤ Name the harmony in m. 19. [C sharp major]
➤ Did Schubert modulate to C sharp major? [no]
➤ Is there a common tone linkage between A and C sharp? [yes; the C sharp]
➤ Where does Schubert leave the C sharp tonality? [m. 29]
➤ Is there a common tone between m. 28 and 29? [yes; C sharp]

This may be your student's first experience playing in C sharp major. (Let's hear it for Schubert!)

Practice Suggestions

➤ In the LH, start by improvising I-IV-I6/4-V7-I chords in A major using a waltz rhythm with jump bass and damper pedal. If you do not know the pattern, play mm. 1-18!
➤ Next, play the I and V7 chords in C sharp major (mm. 19-28).
➤ Practice the RH alone. Focus on *legato* fingering and shaping the melody. The RH accents are more for harmonic purposes rather than rhythmic placement. These intervals include the non-chord tone that needs to resolve on the third beat.
➤ How will you play RH quarter notes marked *staccato* over the LH *non-staccato* accompaniment (mm. 22, 26, 36)? [both hands can use the same touch]
➤ *Con pedale:* Pedal as the harmony changes. Often the pedal will change on beat three or two. Avoid blurring *staccato* articulations.

CREATIVE ACTIVITY

Using Schubert's bass line (mm. 1-9) from *Sentimental Waltz,* improvise a RH melody using mostly notes from the LH chords. Notate your favorite improvisation.

Title: *Romantic Waltz*

Dmitri Kabalevsky
Warrior's Dance, op. 27, no. 19   (R34, SW58)
Exploring the Score

How would a Russian composer convey traits of a "musical warrior"? Some possibilities might include: a strong rhythmic motive, *forte* dynamics, the strength of unison melodies, minor tonality, and bass sounds. What do you see in this dance that resembles the spirit of Kabalevsky's warrior world?

Notice the opening rhythmic motive in m. 1. How many times can you find this rhythm?

How is *Warrior's Dance* similar to a miniature set of variations? Notice how Kabalevsky varies material based on the rhythm in m. 1. In m. 5, the theme is presented in imitation. In m. 15, the hands play in unison. Where else can you find use of this rhythmic theme? [Hint: Look at mm. 10, 19 and 23.]

Practice Suggestions

➤ How will you play eighth notes marked without slurs? [slightly detached]
➤ Isolate the RH in mm. 19-22 for clarity of articulation and phrasing of two voices.
➤ During practice, focus on projecting precise rhythm and striking dynamic contrasts. Which measures sound like a full orchestra playing *(tutti)* as distinct from the soloist? Where does the LH have drumbeats? [bass notes, mm. 18-22]
➤ Isolate the scale passages in mm. 13-14 and 23-24 for special practice.
➤ Add damper pedal where marked.

André Previn
Roundup (R46, SW78)
Background Information

Previn, former conductor of the London Symphony Orchestra and Pittsburgh Symphony Orchestra, is also a distinguished pianist, composer, and arranger. *Roundup* is from his collection of twenty pieces titled *Impressions*.

Exploring the Score

How is the impression of a roundup (or rodeo) conveyed by the music? [use of syncopation, use of perfect 5ths] The music successfully captures a mood of celebration.

➤ Examine the score to discover the musical ideas and their repetition:
  - The opening idea (A) features syncopation in both hands and open 5ths in the LH. How many measures of "A" do you find? How many black keys will you play in the A measures?
  - The B idea provides the contrast of *legato* and stepwise motion. Count the number of "B" measures. Which hand plays only white keys? black keys? (If your student does not know the term *bitonality,* this is a fine opportunity to introduce that concept.) The five black keys form the *pentatonic* scale.

➤ Are mm. 15 and 16 more closely related to A or to B?

Practice Suggestions

➤ A special challenge is the combination of *staccato* and *legato* touch in the opening measure. Tap this measure to experience the wonderful syncopated feeling. [the opening tune has a true rodeo flair with its "hip" on the syncopation and "hoo-ray!" on the last two notes of m. 1]

➤ Listen for the striking contrast of *forte* and *piano.* Bring these dynamics out during practice.

➤ Notice the close proximity of the hands in the bi-tonal measures. Practice each hand separately to learn the patterns, then practice hands together positioning the RH under the LH.

Stephen Heller
Barcarole, op. 138, no. 5 (S11)
Background Information

Heller was born in Hungary but made his career in Paris, where he settled in 1838. A contemporary of Chopin and Schumann—he contributed to Schumann's *Neue Zeitschrift für Musik (New Chronicle for Music)*—he earned a living as a teacher, composer, and writer. His piano compositions included pieces of all kinds: character pieces and etudes for students, operatic transcriptions and fantasies, nocturnes, waltzes, and scherzos.

A barcarole is usually in $\frac{6}{8}$ meter and imitates the gentle movement of a Venetian gondola. You may want to compare this *Barcarole* with compositions of the same title by composers Duke *(Piano Repertoire 4)* and Tchaikovsky *(Piano Repertoire 9).*

Exploring the Score

What are the technical challenges of this barcarole? [balance of melody and accompaniment, projection of varied dynamic levels, mastery of a shifting LH, and fluent pedaling]

➤ Ask the student to memorize the rhythm of the LH—in two seconds! As the student swings to the $\frac{6}{8}$ rhythm just memorized, the feeling of a barcarole is being experienced. How does Heller create the rhythmic lilt? [by emphasizing beats two and five]

➤ Without a doubt, this is the only barcarole ever written with the performance directive *Lento, con morbidezza.* How will this marking affect your interpretation and performance?

Consider the phrasing:

➤ Where are the longest groups of slurred notes? [mm. 23-24]

➤ What are the shortest slurred groups? [two-note slurs]

Short slurs indicate articulation. Emphasize the first note of the group. Longer slurs indicate *legato* groups. Notice the *staccato* and accent markings within the longer slurs in mm. 9, 14, and 19. Why are these articulations present? [they help broaden the *rit.* and heighten the effect of the *cresc.*]

To avoid the blur of scale passages, have your student try frequent pedal changes during the lesson by changing on each LH event, i.e., four times per measure. When the scales are in the higher register (e.g., m. 9), such frequent pedal changes may not be necessary.

Practice Suggestions

➤ The opening half-measure motive is a contrast to the later scale passages. Practice the RH sixteenths alone for absolute security of notes, fingerings, and rhythms. When combining hands, follow the flow and energy of the RH line.

➤ How does the damper pedal contribute to a rocking-boat effect? For a smooth, "seamless" sound, practice the LH alone with pedal. Most pedal changes will be on the low bass notes.

➤ Listen for each dynamic marking: *piano, pianissimo, mezzo piano, mezzo forte, fortepiano,* and, *sforzando.* How does the performer on the *Celebration Series®* recording interpret these dynamic marks?

CREATIVE ACTIVITY

Using the rocking motion of Heller's *Barcarole,* write your own composition. Use a $\frac{6}{8}$ time signature and simple harmonies (perhaps limited to tonic and dominant chords). Imagine an Italian gondolier singing your melody!

Title: *Boat Song*

Henri Bertini
Study in E Minor, op. 29, no. 14 (S14)
Practice Suggestions

This is an exercise in playing short chromatic figures:

➤ Figure out the fingering of each seven-note group (six triplet eighths + quarter). Notice that the ascending patterns are chromatic scales *except* for the first two tones, which form a whole step.

➤ Isolate each chromatic figure for hands alone practice. Keep the fingers close to the keys.

➤ Isolate the RH zigzag passage in mm. 13-14 and mm. 21-22 for special practice. Try grouping the notes into short gestures of the wrist and forearm. Pause and relax your hand every time you land on finger 5. Try the same procedure with a pause on the thumb.

➤ Listen carefully when playing two independent voices in one hand (RH, mm. 9-13; LH, mm. 13-14). Be sure to hold the long notes for their full value.

Level 6 SUMMARY

➤ Which Baroque pieces contain two voices? three voices? How did you practice to become fluent with the increased number of voices?

➤ Did you listen to the recording of each repertoire piece or study you learned? What aspects of the recorded performances did you like?

➤ Compare the titles of List B with those from List C. Many of the latter titles suggest a mood or scene. How do the composers of sonatinas express moods through the music? Is one mood consistent throughout a piece, or does the mood change within a piece?

Level 7

The Publications

Level 7 of the *Celebration Series®* includes the following publications:

Piano Repertoire 7
Piano Studies/Etudes 7
Student Workbook 7
Recording of Repertoire and *Studies/Etudes 7*

The Repertoire

Piano Repertoire 7 is divided into three lists.

➢ List A includes a selection of pieces composed during the Baroque period (*ca* 1600 to *ca* 1750).

➢ List B includes a selection of pieces composed during the Classical period (*ca* 1750 to *ca* 1820).

➢ List C includes a selection of pieces composed during the Romantic era (Part 1) (*ca* 1820 to *ca* 1910) and the twentieth century (Part 2).

Musical Development

Piano Repertoire 7 and *Piano Studies/Etudes 7* represent the progression from late intermediate to early advanced materials. The Baroque compositions require independence of hands and skill in the performance of ornaments. Bach's *Two-Part Inventions* are introduced here for the first time in the *Celebration Series®*. The sonata movements from the Classical period demand fluency of scale figures and control of accompaniment patterns. For the interpretation of both List B and List C pieces, balance of melody and accompaniment are fundamental considerations. Romantic and 20th-century compositions employ greater chromaticism, modality, changing meters, and dynamic extremes. Clearly, this is material to foster musical growth.

The Study Modules

The six Study Module discussions are organized into the following categories:

Background Information
Exploring the Score
Practice Suggestions
Creative Activities

Background Information provides relevant historical information. *Exploring the Score* is designed as an interactive exercise between teacher and student. These sections include questions and observations to stimulate discussion during lessons. *Practice Suggestions* are directed to the student and are especially appropriate for the first week of practice. The *Creative Activities* act as reinforcement for a student's understanding of a musical concept and can provide a springboard for creativity and imagination. Please refer to the *Foreword* for an explanation of how to use the suggested order of assignment within each Module.

Musical Tips

As students work through this Level, they will accumulate general information about musical style that can be applied to other pieces. Your student can use a blank page to notate these points, which are identified as musical tips (**TIP:**).

The chart below lists the repertoire and studies in Level 7. Page numbers for works in *Piano Repertoire 7* and *Piano Studies/Etudes 7* are found in the first column. Study Module numbers are found to the far right. Study Module groupings of repertoire and studies follow.

Piano Repertoire 7

	Page	Composer	Title	Study Module
List A	R4	Johann Sebastian Bach	*Invention No. 1 in C Major, BWV 772*	4
	R6	Georg Philipp Telemann	*Solo in F Major, TWV 32: 4 (Second Movement: Bourrée)*	1
	R8	George Frideric Handel	*Suite No. 8 in G Major, HWV 441 (Fourth Movement: Aria)*	2
	R10	François Couperin	*Allemande in D Minor*	6
	R12	Johann Sebastian Bach	*French Suite No. 5 in G Major, BWV 816 (Fourth Movement: Gavotte)*	3
	R14	Joseph-Hector Fiocco	*Suite in G Major, op. 1, no. 1 (Second Movement)*	5
List B	R16	Franz Joseph Haydn	*Sonata in C Major, Hob. XVI:1 (Second Movement)*	1
	R18	Ludwig van Beethoven	*Bagatelle, op. 119, no. 1*	4
	R20	Oskar Bolck	*Sonatina, op. 59, no. 2 (Third Movement)*	2
	R22	Muzio Clementi	*Sonatina in C Major, op. 36, no. 3 (First Movement)*	5
	R25	Ludwig van Beethoven	*Für Elise, WoO 59*	6
	R28	Friedrich Kuhlau	*Sonatina in C Major, op. 55, no. 3 (First Movement)*	3
List C Part 1	R31	Frédéric Chopin	*Prelude in E Minor, op. 28, no. 4*	2
	R32	Felix Mendelssohn	*Venetian Boat Song, op. 30, no. 6*	6
	R34	Vladimir Ivanovich Rebikov	*Waltz*	4
	R36	Edvard Grieg	*Elfin Dance, op. 12, no. 4*	3
	R38	Arthur L. Benjamin	*Romance-Impromptu*	1
	R40	Viktor Kossenko	*Melody, op. 15, no. 11*	5
	R42	Johannes Brahms	*Waltz in G sharp Minor, op. 39, no. 3*	1
List C Part 2	R43	Clermont Pépin	*Berceuse*	5
	R44	Béla Bartók	*Pentatonic Tune*	1
	R46	Stephen Chatman	*Ginger Snaps*	2
	R48	Alexina Louie	*Shooting Stars*	3
	R50	Dmitri Kabalevsky	*Rondo-Toccata, op. 60, no. 4*	4
	R54	Rhené Jaque	*Lutin/Goblin*	6

Piano Studies/Etudes 7

Page	Composer	Title	Study Module
S4	Henri Bertini	*Etude in E Minor, op. 29, no. 16*	2
S6	Samuil Maikapar	*Toccatina, op. 8, no. 1*	5
S8	Stephen Heller	*Grief, op. 47, no. 15*	1
S10	Jenö Takács	*In a Great Hurry, op. 95, no. 3*	3
S12	Stephen Chatman	*Kitten*	5
S14	Henri Bertini	*Etude in C Minor, op. 29, no. 7*	3
S15	Cornelius Gurlitt	*Study in G Major, op. 132, no. 7*	2
S16	Jacob Schmitt	*Study in G Major, op. 3, no. 3*	4
S17	Johann Sebastian Bach	*Little Prelude in F Major, BWV 927*	1
S18	Árpád Balázs	*A Sort of Rondo*	4
S20	Robert Schumann	*Fantastic Dance, op. 124, no. 5*	6
S22	Dmitri Kabalevsky	*Dance, op. 27, no. 27*	6
S24	Dmitri Kabalevsky	*Etude, op. 27, no. 3*	2

Summary of the Study Modules

Study Module 1

List	Composer	Title	Page & Book
A	Georg Philipp Telemann	*Solo in F Major, TWV 32: 4 (Second Movement: Bourrée)*	R6, SW8
B	Franz Joseph Haydn	*Sonata in C Major, Hob. XVI:1 (Second Movement)*	R16, SW26
C1	Arthur L. Benjamin	*Romance-Impromptu*	R38, SW57
C1	Johannes Brahms	*Waltz in G sharp Minor, op. 39, no. 3*	R42, SW62
C2	Béla Bartók	*Pentatonic Tune*	R44, SW69
	Stephen Heller	*Grief, op. 47, no. 15*	S8
	Johann Sebastian Bach	*Little Prelude in F Major, BWV 927*	S17

Study Module 2

List	Composer	Title	Page & Book
A	George Frideric Handel	*Suite No. 8 in G Major, HWV 441 (Fourth Movement: Aria)*	R8, SW12
B	Oskar Bolck	*Sonatina, op. 59, no. 2 (Third Movement)*	R20, SW33
C1	Frédéric Chopin	*Prelude in E Minor, op. 28, no. 4*	R31, SW46
C2	Stephen Chatman	*Ginger Snaps*	R46, SW73
	Henri Bertini	*Etude in E Minor, op. 29, no. 16*	S4
	Cornelius Gurlitt	*Study in G Major, op. 132, no. 7*	S15
	Dmitri Kabalevsky	*Study, op. 27, no. 3*	S24

Study Module 3

List	Composer	Title	Page & Book
A	Johann Sebastian Bach	*French Suite No. 5 in G Major, BWV 816 (Fourth Movement: Gavotte)*	R12, SW19
B	Friedrich Kuhlau	*Sonatina in C Major, op. 55, no. 3 (First Movement)*	R28, SW43
C1	Edvard Grieg	*Elfin Dance, op. 12, no. 4*	R36, SW54
C2	Alexina Louie	*Shooting Stars*	R48, SW76
	Jenö Takács	*In a Great Hurry, op. 95, no. 3*	S10
	Henri Bertini	*Etude in C Minor, op. 29, no. 7*	S14

Study Module 4

List	Composer	Title	Page & Book
A	Johann Sebastian Bach	*Invention No. 1 in C Major, BWV 772*	R4, SW4
B	Ludwig van Beethoven	*Bagatelle, op. 119, no. 1*	R18, SW30
C	Vladimir Ivanovich Rebikov	*Waltz*	R34, SW51
C2	Dmitri Kabalevsky	*Rondo-Toccata, op. 60, no. 4*	R50, SW79
	Jacob Schmitt	*Study in G Major, op. 3, no. 3*	S16
	Árpád Balázs	*A Sort of Rondo*	S18

Study Module 5

List	Composer	Title	Page & Book
A	Joseph-Hector Fiocco	*Suite in G Major, op. 1, no. 1 (Second Movement)*	R14, SW23
B	Muzio Clementi	*Sonatina in C Major, op. 36, no. 3 (First Movement)*	R22, SW36
C	Viktor Kossenko	*Melody, op. 15, no. 11*	R40, SW59
C2	Clermont Pépin	*Berceuse*	R43, SW65
	Samuil Maikapar	*Toccatina, op. 8, no. 1*	S6
	Stephen Chatman	*Kitten*	S12

Study Module 6

List	Composer	Title	Page & Book
A	François Couperin	*Allemande in D Minor*	R10, SW15
B	Ludwig van Beethoven	*Für Elise, WoO 59*	R25, SW39
C	Felix Mendelssohn	*Venetian Boat Song, op. 30, no. 6*	R32, SW48
C2	Rhené Jaque	*Lutin / Goblin*	R54, SW82
	Robert Schumann	*Fantastic Dance, op. 124, no. 5*	S20
	Dmitri Kabalevsky	*Dance, op. 27, no. 27*	S22

STUDY MODULE 1

Page	List	Composer	Title	Key, Meter and Tempo
R6 SW8	A	Georg Philipp Telemann	*Solo in F Major, TWV 32: 4 (Second Movement: Bourrée)*	F Major $\frac{4}{4}$ ♩ = 144-160
R16 SW26	B	Franz Joseph Haydn	*Sonata in C Major, Hob. XVI:1 (Second Movement)*	C Major $\frac{4}{4}$ Adagio
R38 SW57	C	Arthur L. Benjamin	*Romance-Impromptu*	G Major $\frac{2}{4}$ Andante semplice
R42 SW62	C	Johannes Brahms	*Waltz in G sharp Minor, op. 39, no. 3*	G sharp Minor $\frac{3}{4}$ Tempo di valse
R44 SW69	C2	Béla Bartók	*Pentatonic Tune*	Pentatonic $\frac{2}{4}$ Allegro scherzando
S8		Stephen Heller	*Grief, op. 47, no. 15*	F Minor $\frac{4}{4}$ Adagio ma non troppo
S17		Johann Sebastian Bach	*Little Prelude in F Major, BWV 927*	F Major $\frac{4}{4}$ ♩ = 100-112

Assign first:

Little Prelude in F Major . . . .
Sonata in C Major
Waltz . . . .
Pentatonic Tune . . . .

Assign next when ready:

Solo in F Major

Grief
Romance

The variety of keys and musical styles in this module provide a wide range of colors, textures, and forms. Major and minor tonalities are represented, as well as pentatonic sounds. Two pieces are contrapuntal *(Bourrée* and *Little Prelude in F Major)* while others explore LH and RH melodies with a variety of accompaniment styles. Rhythmic challenges include several pieces with triplet figures, and one with two-against-three *(Grief)*. Two pieces are dances *(Bourrée* and *Waltz)*. Here is a true palette of styles and colors rich with elements to explore.

Georg Philipp Telemann
Solo in F Major, TWV 32: 4
(Second Movement: Bourrée) (R6, SW8)
Exploring the Score

➤ A bourrée is a lively 17th-century French dance. Less complex rhythmically than other French Baroque dances, a typical bourrée is in duple meter and has an upbeat, usually two eighth notes or a quarter note.

➤ What is the upbeat that begins this piece? Do all the phrases start with this quarter-note upbeat? [no] Place a check ✓ over each quarter-note upbeat in the score. [mm. 1, 5, 19, 23, etc.]

➤ How is the upbeat to m. 31 and m. 33 different? [three eighth notes].

➤ Which phrases start on the beat? [mm. 9-12, 16-18, etc.] Place an X over each downbeat starting point in the score. You now have a map of phrase beginnings for this piece.

➤ Identify the form, and label the keys used in each section.

TIP: Virtually all dances in the Baroque period are in binary form. The A section shifts to the dominant key, and the B section returns to the tonic key.

➤ A remarkable thing about this dance is the variety of rhythms played by the RH. There are at least eight different figures. Find these rhythms and label them with the following letters: (Each figure appears at least twice)

a = four quarter notes (m. 1)
b = syncopation (m. 2)
c = upbeat pairs of eighth notes (m. 3)
d = groups of four eighth notes (m. 5)
e = two quarter notes and one half note (m. 9)
f = quarter, two eighth notes, two quarter notes (m. 13)
g = two eighth notes and three quarter notes (m. 23)
h = four eighth notes and two quarter notes (m. 27)

➤ Find examples of sequences. [mm. 5-8 and 23-26]

➤ Most bourrées feature a half-note pulse and have a time signature of $\frac{2}{2}$, or *alla breve*. Listen to the *Celebration Series®* recording of this piece. Does it feel more like two beats per measure *(alla breve)* or four beats per measure (common time)?

Practice Suggestions

A successful performance of this dance relies upon accurate phrasing and articulation.

TIP: In the Baroque period, syncopations were highlighted with a detached articulation before the long note.

➤ Find and play the syncopated rhythms. [mm. 2, 20, etc.] Detach the quarter notes in these measures.
➤ Carefully practice one phrase at a time, following your phrasing map of ✓'s and X's. Most quarter and half notes should be played slightly detached.
➤ Articulate the RH slurs clearly.
➤ To give more rhythmic definition and to experiment with articulation, you may wish to slur the first two eighth notes in a group of four eighth notes.
➤ Played as marked, dynamics will help to highlight the melodic sequences. A lighter touch in quieter passages will help you bring out the contrast.

Franz Joseph Haydn
Sonata in C Major, Hob. XVI:1
(Second Movement) (R16, SW26)

Exploring the Score

This elegant *Adagio* movement is in simple binary form. Find the modulations through the dominant [mm. 5-8] and subdominant [mm. 11-13].

➤ Label the A and B sections and the different melodic patterns found in each.
  Pattern #1 A: mm. 1-2, B: mm. 9-10
  Pattern #2 A: mm. 3-5, B: mm. 11-13
  Pattern #3 A: mm. 5-6, B: mm. 14-15
  Pattern #4 A: mm. 7-8, B: mm. 16-17
➤ An important teaching element for this movement is helping the student with phrase focus. Identify the large phrases and then discuss how to find the focus (**Hint:** This is often signaled by a change of harmony or by an ornament). The great variety of phrase lengths arising from the initial motive also provides for interesting discussion and exploration.
➤ Circle the first note of each beat in m. 7 to discover the descending melodic line.
➤ The Level 6 discussion of the first movement of *Divertimento in G Major, Hob. XVI:G1* referred to the lack of dynamic markings in Haydn's early sonatas. Explore possibilities for adding dynamics to this movement. Consider phrase lengths as well as harmonic and melodic motion as you make your decisions.

Practice Suggestions

➤ Accurate and consistent fingering is the key to success in this piece. Practice in two-measure segments and circle any essential finger numbers.
➤ The RH triplets should be played *legato* and flowing.
➤ Almost every downbeat is preceded by an eighth-note upbeat. Remember to play the upbeats detached.
➤ Play the LH repeated tones as close to *legato* as possible.
➤ Choose a dynamic plan that draws attention to:
  – melodic repetitions (mm. 5-6, mm. 14-15)
  – the longest and harmonically most interesting phrase in the movement (mm. 11-13)

Arthur L. Benjamin
Romance-Impromptu (R38, SW57)
Background Information

Arthur Benjamin was born in Sydney, Australia, but received his advanced training at the Royal College of Music (RCM) in London. In 1926 he joined the faculty at the RCM, where Benjamin Britten was one of his students. Benjamin was greatly influenced by American jazz, and hearing Gershwin's *Rhapsody in Blue* had an effect on his 1927 *Piano Concertina*. Another influence was Latin American music. Benjamin's well known *Jamaican Rumba (2 Jamaican Pieces,* 1938), for two pianos, is a piece that helped establish his reputation as a composer.

Exploring the Score

This may be the only piece in all piano literature given the title of *Romance-Impromptu*. Both words were used as titles of character pieces in the 19th century. As you listen to the *Celebration Series®* recording, discuss why Benjamin may have used this unusual title for the piece.

➤ The rhythmic motive in the LH creates a constant throbbing effect:

con pedale

➤ Find three places where this LH rhythmic pattern is altered. [mm. 17-18; 25-26; 35-39] Notice that each of these rhythmic changes occurs just before a cadence and section change.

- The melody is eight measures. Label the ABCA1 sections of this piece.
- Discover the descending line in the LH (G, F sharp, E, D, C, B, A) moving in contrary motion to the RH ascending melody.
- Compare the A and C sections. How are they related? [C is an inversion of A!]

Practice Suggestions

- You may wish to practice the LH separately to achieve security of notes and fingerings. Work in segments that coincide with the RH phrases. Be sure to observe the LH tied values in mm. 17-18, 25-26.
- When you are confident with the LH, add the RH. Use your most convincing *legato* touch.
- Benjamin has written dynamics to guide the shaping of the phrases. In phrases without dynamic indications, write in your own plan.
- Listen carefully for balance between the gently throbbing LH and the singing RH.

Johannes Brahms
Waltz in G sharp Minor, op. 39, no. 3 (R42, SW62)
Exploring the Score

As the footnote in the score informs us, the *Waltzes, op. 39* exist in three versions. Encourage your student to listen to a recording of the complete opus 39. This short and hauntingly lovely waltz provides a memorable introduction to the music of Brahms.

- Label the A and B sections of the piece.
- Explore the RH melodies in each section. How does Brahms change the articulation and phrasing?
- How does the LH waltz bass change in the B section? Why are two of the chords rolled? [to lengthen the third beat slightly in anticipation of the following downbeat]

Extra Credit Assignment: With your student, listen to a recording of the duet version of this *Waltz* from op. 39. How is the solo texture distributed between the four hands of two pianists?

Practice Suggestions

The secret to this piece is being totally secure with the LH. Then you will be free to turn your attention to the varied articulations of the RH melody.

- What LH fingerings will give you greatest ease and efficiency? As you practice the LH, listen for the light lilt provided by beats two and three.
- When you put the hands together in each section, work slowly at first to gain control. To develop

fluency, pause on beat two, taking time to prepare your move through the bar line into the next measure. (Think *1–2–hold–&3&1–2–hold–&3 &1, etc.*)
- M. 8 (first ending) makes an abrupt harmonic shift back to G sharp minor. The small *crescendo-decrescendo* marking on beat three is a hint for you to stretch the rhythm and highlight this chord. As you make this transition, listen carefully to the half-step progression in the upper voice (F sharp, F double sharp, G sharp)
- Plan how you will make use of *rubato* in other transitions and at the end of the piece.
- Set a tempo which will allow you to feel the dance rhythm and flow.

CREATIVE ACTIVITY

Transpose Brahms' LH bass line of the A section to G minor. Now compose your own eight-measure melody with first and second endings.

Title: *Waltz in G Minor*

Béla Bartók
Pentatonic Tune (R44, SW69)
Exploring the Score

Bartók is well known for using Hungarian folk tunes in his compositions. In this piece, he alternates between a rhythmic theme and a folk tune with chordal accompaniment.

- Label the eight-measure sections as either "Rhythm" (A) or "Melody" (B). What is the surprise at m. 41? [Bartók combines both Rhythm and Melody in the final section.]
- Compare the melody and accompaniment figures in the "Melody" sections. How does Bartók change the accompaniment to create variations?
- Label the form of this piece ABA1B1A2B2 coda.
- The LH uses a white-key pentatonic scale with the following tones: D E G A B. Are there any other notes than these in the LH? [no]

Practice Suggestions

Notice that every note is marked with either a *staccato, tenuto,* or accent. Bartók sometimes adds accents and *sforzando* markings to the grace note beats. The piece has a wide palette of dynamic colors.

- Practice in eight-measure sections very slowly at first, taking time to observe each articulation and dynamic marking.
- How will your performance tempo help create a *scherzando* or playful mood?

Stephen Heller
Grief, op. 47, no. 15 (S8)

Background Information

Heller wrote many études and short pieces for the piano. His opp. 45, 46, and 47 are among his best-known pieces. Like the majority of Mendelssohn's *Songs without Words,* the titles of the études were not written by Heller but were added later by others to fit the mood and character of the pieces.

Exploring the Score

➤ What is the mood of a piece titled *Grief?* There are several elements in the piece that contribute to that mood:
  - the key
  - the tempo
  - the bass-line melody
  - the two-against-three rhythms, which are more expressive than just a long-short triplet.
➤ A look at the score will reveal two primary elements of this study:
  - constant triplet broken-chord accompaniment
  - *legato* melody with duple rhythm.

This combination of rhythms produces the challenge of two against three. Find and circle each occurrence of two against three.
➤ The key of the piece is E minor. What is the surprise ending? [E major] Does the ending signify a change of mood? [the grief may have been assuaged]
➤ You may wish to make up lyrics to the main melodies. The first two LH phrases could be "Oh, how pain-ful; My heart is break-ing."

Practice Suggestions

➤ Before you practice, tap the two-against-three rhythm on the closed keyboard cover, switching so that each hand taps both parts. Be sure that you are secure in this rhythm. It helps to diagram the rhythm as follows:

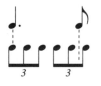

➤ Begin practice by blocking the triplet harmonies in one hand and playing the melody in the other hand.
➤ Isolate mm. 21-24 for special attention to the RH double-stemmed notes. These accented notes are most easily projected if the finger is lifted before striking the key. Once the RH is secure, listen for the balance between the RH and LH melodic lines in these measures.

Johann Sebastian Bach
Little Prelude in F Major, BWV 927 (S17)

Background Information

Bach presented the *Wilhelm Friedemann Bach Notebook* to his son on his tenth birthday, November 22, 1720. This instruction book contains short preludes and inventions as well as several preludes from *The Well-Tempered Clavier.*

Exploring the Score

Discover the harmonic progression in mm. 1-2 by blocking half-measures, hands together. [I-IV-V7-I: (the root of the V7 chord is implied)]

➤ In m. 2, notice the pedal point F (non-chord tone) in the first two beats.
➤ Where else can you find I-IV-V-I patterns? [mm. 3-4!]
➤ Compare mm. 1-2 with 3-4. How does Bach change the texture? [hands are reversed]

➤ How quickly can your student memorize the LH scale lines, mm. 5-7?

➤ Have the student block the RH of mm. 5-8 to discover the suspensions and their resolutions. (On the first and third beats, the third sixteenth note is "held over" from the previous chord.)
➤ Bach finds ingenious ways to intensify the music as it approaches the final cadence. Notice:
  - dominant pedal point (LH), mm. 10-12.
  - irregular groupings of ascending sixteenths, mm. 13-14
  - widens the distance between the two hands at m. 14. (Often, the climax of a Baroque piece occurs when the hands are farthest apart.)
  - harmonic intensification of the final measure.

Practice Suggestions

➤ Play the sixteenth notes as blocked chords. Use accurate fingerings.
➤ Practice the sixteenth notes as written with a rocking motion of the hand.
➤ In mm. 5-8, practice the LH eighth notes *legato* to learn the fingerings. Say the finger numbers aloud as you play. Then practice with a *staccato* touch.

STUDY MODULE 2

Page	List	Composer	Title	Key, Meter and Tempo
R8 SW12	A	George Frideric Handel	*Suite No. 8 in G Major, HWV 441 (Fourth Movement: Aria)*	G Major $\frac{4}{4}$ Presto
R20 SW33	B	Oskar Bolck	*Sonatina, op. 59, no. 2 (Third Movement)*	G Major $\frac{3}{8}$ Allegro vivo
R31 SW46	C	Frédéric Chopin	*Prelude in E Minor, op. 28, no. 4*	E Minor $\frac{4}{4}$ Largo
R46 SW73	C2	Stephen Chatman	*Ginger Snaps*	Bitonal $\frac{4}{4}$ Spicy
S4		Henri Bertini	*Etude in E Minor, op. 29, no. 16*	E Minor $\frac{3}{4}$ Allegro
S15		Cornelius Gurlitt	*Study in G Major, op. 132, no. 7*	G Major $\frac{3}{4}$ Moderato cantando
S24		Dmitri Kabalevsky	*Etude, op. 27, no. 3*	A Minor $\frac{4}{4}$ Allegro vivace

Assign first:

Suite No. 8 in G Major
Sonatina . . . .
Prelude in E Minor . . . .
Ginger Snaps . . . .

Assign next when ready:

Etude in E Minor
Study in G Major
Etude

We often explore the many ways composers provide contrast through keys, forms, and dynamics. In this module, it is interesting to explore how these composers use rhythm to provide both unity and contrast. The steady rhythms of repeated note patterns *(Prelude, Ginger Snaps)*, short rhythmic motives *(Ginger Snaps, Etude)*, waltz style bass lines *(Study in G Major* and *Study in E Minor)*, and the pattern of steady eighths against running sixteenths *(Aria, Sonatina, Etude)* all provide the basis for discussing unity and contrast.

George Frideric Handel
Suite No. 8 in G Major, HWV 441
(Fourth Movement: Aria) (R8, SW12)

Exploring the Score

Baroque composers often imitated other instruments and ensembles in their keyboard works. This aria is imitative of a solo instrument with accompaniment. The RH solo line is often very florid, while the LH plays a steady accompaniment.

➤ Play the opening RH motive in mm. 1-2. List the characteristics of this musical idea. [Upbeat of three sixteenths; descending zigzag pattern; closing two-note slur]

➤ In mm. 3-4, find the sequence that uses the sixteenth notes from the opening motive. Bracket the motives, and notice the pattern: two beats + two beats + four beats (short, short, long).

➤ Find other short and long patterns formed from this motive. This will guide your phrasing.

➤ Check Handel's choice of form. Is this a typical binary dance with a modulation to the dominant? [yes]

Practice Suggestions

➤ To hear the hidden duet between the hands, play the LH as written, and RH upbeat sixteenths, then the stepwise pattern of notes falling directly on the eighth pulses.

➤ Remember to articulate the entrances of the main motive clearly. In m. 3, for example, indicate two appearances of the motive by a slight break.

➤ To give emphasis to the duple meter, you may wish to slur the first two notes in each LH group of four eighth notes.

TIP: The first of two slurred notes, in a series of detached notes, sounds emphasized because of its slightly added length—we hear it a bit longer. Therefore, if you want to show the downbeat without accenting, slur the downbeat note to the second note, and detach the rest of the group.

➤ Remember to play the RH octave leaps with a detached touch, followed with a two-note slur.

TIP: In the performance practice of the Baroque period, wide leaps were highlighted by a slight break.

➤ Practice without the trills at first. Add them when you are comfortable with notes and rhythms.

Oskar Bolck
Sonatina, op. 59, no. 2
(Third Movement) (R20, SW33)

Oskar Bolck was a 19th-century German composer who studied at the Leipzig Conservatory with Moscheles. He was active as a theater conductor in various German towns, and as a teacher at Riga, where his opera *Pierre und Robin* was produced (1876).

Exploring the Score

This is an excellent example of sonata-allegro form in a third movement. Label each section and the main themes in the score.

Exposition	Theme 1	mm. 1-16
	Theme 2	mm. 17-32
Development		mm. 33-70
Recapitulation	Theme 1	mm. 71-86
	Theme 2	mm. 87-102
Coda		mm. 103-106

➤ In the exposition and recapitulation, each theme is eight measures long. How does Bolck extend each theme? [repeats it one octave lower (1st) or higher (2nd)]

➤ Compare and contrast Themes 1 and 2. What are the similarities? the differences?

➤ The development begins in what key? [D major – dominant] Some careful musical sleuthing may reveal motives and figures in the development that cannot be found in the exposition. What do you find? Look for changes in articulation and dynamics, dotted quarter notes, and clef changes.

Practice Suggestions

➤ Practice the exposition and recapitulation in eight-measure units with special attention to fingering and articulation. You may wish to block LH chords at first.

➤ Theme 1: contrast the *legato* scale runs and the detached chords.

➤ Theme 2: feel the four-measure phrase. Remember, "Out of four, go for three." (Bring out the third measure as indicated by the composer.)

➤ The LH in the development is unpredictable. Practice it by itself until the fingerings, shifts (watch the clef changes!), and rhythms are secure.

➤ Carefully practice the measures with sustained and moving voices in the same hand (mm. 37-38, 55-56, 63-68). Listen for the held note. Maintain a relaxed hand and wrist.

Frédéric Chopin
Prelude in E Minor, op. 28, no. 4 (R31, SW46)
Background Information

Chopin's set of twenty-four preludes, Opus 28 was inspired by Bach's *Well-Tempered Clavier,* with preludes in each major and minor key. Unlike Bach, Chopin's key arrangement followed the circle of 5ths (C major, A minor, G major, E minor, etc.) whereas Bach used an ascending chromatic order (C major, C minor, C sharp major, etc.). Notice that the key of this prelude, E minor, is no. 4 in Chopin's key sequence. Encourage your student to listen to a recording of the entire Opus 28 collection.

Exploring the Score

This short prelude is an excellent example of Chopin's use of long melodic lines over a colorful chordal accompaniment.

➤ Listen to the *Celebration Series®* recording of this prelude.
  - What mood is created by the minor key, throbbing chromatic chordal accompaniment, and the repeated two-note motive of the melody?
  - Where are the points of greatest harmonic tension and release?
  - Where is the loudest moment in the piece? How does Chopin build to that climax?
  - Does the performer pedal each harmonic change?
  - Discuss the RH phrase lengths and how to shape them.

➤ Many of the LH harmonies are difficult to label because of their chromatic motion. The progression of the piece is guided by the descending bass line that slowly moves from the tonic to the dominant (B). Find the two appearances of this descent to B.

➤ Look for descending chromatic motion in the middle and upper voices of the LH chords. Does the movement in these lines coincide with the movement in the bass? [no]. Highlighting the half-step motion in all three voices of the LH will help you create a sense of relentless flow.

➤ After the bass line descends to B, Chopin emphasizes the B further by repeating C-B in mm. 10-12 and 18-24. Compare these measures. Does the pattern of C-B repetition change? [in mm. 18-24, the rate of change slows down] What effect does this have?

➤ Notice the B flat in m. 24. By circling the dominant note completely (C-B-B flat-B) Chopin has put even greater focus on it, which intensifies the final resolution to the tonic.

➤ Help the student discover the great harmonic surprise in m. 21. The ear has been prepared for an E minor chord by the B7 in m. 20, but Chopin avoids that cadence until the final chord of the piece. If the student does not know the term "deceptive cadence," this is a golden opportunity for learning.

➤ How will you make decisions on pedaling? [LH chord changes]

Practice Suggestions

➤ Start your practice by following the LH bass descent from G down to B. Analyze the different chord colors Chopin writes on each LH pitch.

➤ Practice the LH with pedal, changing it cleanly with *every* half-step descent. Mark in the score where you feel special harmonic tension, and label the chords that represent the release of that tension.

➤ Practice the RH two-note sigh figure, feeling the motion across the bar line. Focus on the dynamic relationship between the notes and use the most expressive *legato* sound possible.

➤ Practice hands together by first blocking the LH chords (only the harmonic changes) against the RH. Use the damper pedal.

➤ Isolate the RH turn in m. 16 (play with the LH part) as well as the two-against-three rhythm in m. 18 for special practice.

➤ How will you bring out the deceptive cadence in m. 21?

➤ Aim for a sad, somber tone quality on the final cadence. Do you hear all the pitches?

Stephen Chatman
Ginger Snaps (R46, SW73)
Background Information

Chatman's composition teachers have included William Bolcolm, Ross Lee Finney, and Karlheinz Stockhausen. The recipient of numerous awards and grants, Chatman has been commissioned by the Canada Council, the National Endowment for the Arts, the CBC, the Ontario Arts Council, and the Banff Centre. As well as orchestral and chamber works, he has written band, choral, and keyboard compositions for students and amateur ensembles. Chatman currently resides in Vancouver, where he is a professor of composition and orchestration at the University of British Columbia.

Exploring the Score

Want to add some spice to your student's musical diet? This piece provides the perfect recipe!

➤ Tap along as you listen to the *Celebration Series®* recording. (Remember to snap your fingers on the rests.) Enjoy the lively, crisp, syncopated rhythms of this piece.

➤ How many one-measure rhythmic patterns can you find? [mm. 1, 3, 9, 21, 22] Label these five rhythmic patterns as A, B, C, D, and E.

➤ As you explore the score, label each occurrence of these rhythmic patterns. Which patterns occur most frequently? [A = 13 times; C = 9 times] Which patterns are used only twice? [B – compare m. 3 with m. 7; C – m. 21 with 23] Which pattern occurs only once? [E – m. 22]

➤ The key signature might lead you to assume the piece is in C major or A minor. Does this piece sound like it is in either of those keys? Chatman's use of many different chords means we don't hear any one tonality emphasized. This piece is polytonal.

➤ In which position does Chatman write the chords? [root position] Are most of the chords major or minor? [major] Find the minor chords. [mm. 3, 7, 25, 27]

➤ In mm. 1-4, the hands move by 2nds. The movements of the chords change in mm. 17-20, as they move first by 3rds, then by augmented 4ths (tritone), and finally by a 6th. Notice the rhythmic "accommodation" made by the composer for those wider shifts: the preceding note value is lengthened.

➤ Speculate on Chatman's reason for writing a LH pedal point in mm. 9-12 and 13-16.

Practice Suggestions

➤ Before practicing the chords, make sure you are in total command of the four different rhythmic patterns. Tap each pattern before playing at the keyboard.

➤ It may help to make up and chant lyrics for each of these patterns. Pattern A might be "Gin-ger Snaps"; pattern B = "(yes), spi-cy coo-kies"; pattern C = "Gin-ger Snaps, oh" etc. Make up your own lyrics for each pattern and tap and chant the rhythms of the piece!

➤ On the closed keyboard cover, say the rhythm and "shadow play" the direction of the chords. Choose a tempo that allows you to see the chord changes accurately. Do the chords move in parallel or contrary motion? [contrary; m. 30 is an isolated exception]

➤ Slowly play mm. 1-4 and 17-20 and say the direction your hands move. [start-same-in; start-same-out, etc.]

➤ Practice at a slow tempo that allows accurate playing of notes and rhythms. Gradually increase the tempo to a "spicy" degree!

CREATIVE ACTIVITY

Using root-position chords in each hand, improvise your own chord piece. Create an interesting rhythmic pattern and then start the hands either a whole step or a half step apart. Experiment with different registers of the keyboard.

Title: *Mexican Salsa!*

Henri Bertini
Etude in E Minor, op. 29, no. 16 (S4)
Exploring the Score

Staccato practice is an excellent way to improve finger dexterity and speed. Bertini provides the student with an exercise concentrating on RH *staccato* scales.

➤ Check the score:
- Are all RH eighth notes *staccato?* [yes]
- Are all other values (quarters and dotted quarters) played full value? [yes]
- Is the LH marked with any special articulation? [no]

➤ Label the form of the piece. [A: mm. 1-16; B: mm. 17-32; A: mm. 33-48]
- What are the keys of these sections? How are they related?

➤ Notice the constant bass note in each section. These bass notes create a pedal point.

➤ Analyze and label the I IV 6/4 and V7 chords in each section.

Practice Suggestions

➤ Your warm-up for this study can include:
- five-finger patterns in E minor and G major, *legato* and *staccato*
- G major scale, *legato* and *staccato*

- E minor scale (harmonic and melodic forms), *legato* and *staccato*
- i iv6/4 V6/5 I chord progression in E minor and G major. After playing your familiar chord progression, practice Bertini's version, keeping the bottom note E or G as a pedal point.

CREATIVE ACTIVITY

Compose your own study. Use primary chords (I-IV-V) in the LH and eighth-note patterns in your RH.
- Choose a favorite major or minor key. Warm up in that key by playing the scale and the I, IV 6/4, I, V6/5, I chord progression.
- Decide on the order of chords you wish to use during the piece. You may choose the same pattern that Bertini used if you wish.
- Compose two eight-measure sections of melody and accompaniment. (Each eight-measure section may include a four-measure question phrase and a four-measure answer.)

Title: *Study in* _____

Cornelius Gurlitt
Study in G Major, op. 132, no. 7 (S15)
Exploring the Score

With its rich harmonic color and flowing rhythm, this piece could be subtitled *Valse élégante.*

➤ Gurlitt uses eighth-note motion effectively in this piece. Notice the way the short notes move forward to the following downbeat ("shorts go to longs"). The result is charming and elegant.

➤ A change of rhythm occurs in mm. 13-15. Which beat is emphasized by the movement of the eighth notes? [beat 3]

➤ While the RH flows forward with its moving eighth notes, the LH plays the traditional waltz bass role of downbeat emphasis with relaxation on beats two and three.

➤ Name the chords in mm. 1-8.

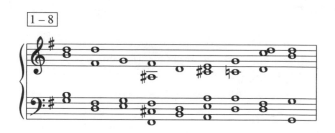

➤ Find pairs of chords that have a dominant-tonic relationship. (The F sharp and A major chords are secondary dominants within the key of G major.)

Practice Suggestions

➤ In mm. 1-8, there is one harmony per measure. In mm. 13-15, 17-18, and 21-22, there are two harmonies per measure. How will this harmonic rhythm affect the pedaling?

➤ Give each RH voice its own dynamic level. As you practice, listen for the louder soprano voice and the softer alto voice.

➤ Circle the finger substitution in m. 3. Where else will you use a substitution? [mm. 11 and 27] Practice these measures alone, listening for the tied values and *legato* inner voice.

➤ The LH downbeat notes create a bass line. Give each of these low notes a slight emphasis.

➤ Take time at the beginning and ends of phrases. Tasteful *rubato* will add elegance to this little waltz.

Dmitri Kabalevsky
Etude, op. 27, no. 3 (S24)
Exploring the Score

This study removes the drudgery of scale practice— there is not a dull moment in the piece!

Analyze the scales. Look for:
  - full-octave scales
  - scales that are less than an octave
  - scales that are more than an octave by one note
  - scales that are more than an octave by several octaves

➤ Are the fingerings in the score the ones that you would choose for these scales?

Practice Suggestions

➤ Isolate the different scale fragments. As you practice, focus on:
  - consistent fingering
  - Kabalevsky's dynamic plan
  - smooth motions of your arm and wrist

➤ Practice the LH two-note slurs. Use a drop-lift hand motion and make a break in sound between each slur.

➤ What is the RH finger pattern for mm. 15-16? [always 1-4]

➤ Lift the damper pedal sharply on the "and" of the first and third beats as marked to avoid blurring RH stepwise motion. Pedal each final chord in mm. 17-18.

STUDY MODULE 3

Page	List	Composer	Title	Key, Meter and Tempo
R12 SW19	A	Johann Sebastian Bach	*French Suite No. 5 in G Major, BWV 816* (Fourth Movement: Gavotte)	G Major ¢ ♩ = 84-92
R28 SW43	B	Friedrich Kuhlau	*Sonatina in C Major, op. 55, no. 3* (First Movement)	C Major $\frac{4}{4}$ Allegro con spirito
R36 SW54	C1	Edvard Grieg	*Elfin Dance, op. 12, no. 4*	E Minor $\frac{3}{4}$ Molto allegro e sempre staccato
R48 SW76	C2	Alexina Louie	*Shooting Stars*	Whole tone $\frac{4}{4}$ ♩ = 69-72
S10		Jenö Takács	*In a Great Hurry, op. 95, no. 3*	Atonal $\frac{2}{4}$ Presto Scherzando
S14		Henri Bertini	*Etude in C Minor, op. 29, no. 7*	C Minor $\frac{4}{4}$ Allegro

Assign first:	Assign next when ready:
French Suite No. 5 in G Major (Fourth Movement: Gavotte)	
Sonatina in C Major	
Elfin Dance	*Shooting Stars*
Etude in C Minor	*In a Great Hurry*

STUDY MODULE 3

This module provides material for comparison and contrast. Four pieces use rhythm as a primary element, either as a dance or unifying pattern (*Gavotte, Elfin Dance, Sonatina in C Major, Etude in C Minor*). Three pieces tell a musical story or paint a musical picture (*Elfin Dance, Shooting Stars, In a Great Hurry*). One can also explore a variety of tonalities in this module—G major/G minor, C major/C minor, whole tone, and atonal.

Johann Sebastian Bach
French Suite No. 5 in G Major, BWV 816
(Fourth Movement: Gavotte) (R12, SW19)

Background Information

Bach's numerous keyboard works include a number of dance suites. Dances and national styles that were popular in the Baroque era are represented in each suite. The best known are the *English Suites, French Suites,* and the *Partitas.* The *French Suite No. 5 in G Major* has seven movements: *Allemande, Courante, Sarabande, Gavotte* (this piece), *Bourrée, Loure,* and *Gigue.* Encourage your students to listen to a recording of the complete work.

Exploring the Score

A gavotte is a 17th-century French dance, usually in a moderate $\frac{2}{2}$ meter, with an upbeat of two quarter notes. The phrases begin and end in the middle of the measure. As you explore the score, discuss how this gavotte fits the description.

➤ The rhythm of the opening motive gives a feeling of "up-up-down" or "short-short-long" to the line. Remember that the upbeats always go to the downbeats. Grouping these lines into four-measure phrases helps give a sense of forward movement and flow. Find and mark the four-measure phrases.

➤ Where is the motive inverted or turned upside down? [mm. 8-9, 16-17]

➤ Label the binary form and keys at the cadences.

TIP: Virtually all dances in the Baroque period are in binary form. The A section shifts to the dominant key, and the B section returns to the tonic key.

Practice Suggestions

Wise and consistent fingering and clear articulation are the initial goals of your practice.

➤ Practice each four measure section slowly, hands separately if needed.

➤ Quarter notes should be played detached.

➤ It is very important to project the characteristic gavotte rhythm. Bring out the "up-up-down" motive wherever it occurs. Did you find the LH motive in mm. 12-15?

➤ In slurred parallel 6ths (e.g., m. 11), give priority to the *legato* of the top voice.

➤ In its day, the gavotte could express a great variety of affects—tender, graceful, joyful, serious. What mood or character will your performance convey?

Friedrich Kuhlau
Sonatina in C Major, op. 55, no. 3
(First Movement) (R28, SW43)

Exploring the Score

Friedrich Kuhlau's sonatinas provide excellent examples of variety and contrast in sonata form.

➤ Label the form of this sonatina movement.

Exposition	Theme 1	mm. 1-8
	bridge	mm. 9-12
	Theme 2	mm. 13-20
	codetta	mm. 21-24
Development		mm. 25-35
Recapitulation	bridge	mm. 36-52
	Theme 2	mm. 53-57

➤ Three ideas characterize the two main themes of the exposition: "x" (mm. 1-2), "y" (mm. 9-10), and "z" (mm. 13-14). Label "x," "y," and "z" throughout the movement.

➤ What is the mood or character of each of the themes?

➤ Name the key of each theme. There is a feeling of arrival in m. 20. What key is confirmed here? [G major]

➤ Which theme is used (exclusively) in the development? [Theme 1]

➤ In mm. 33-35, there is a written-in *ritardando.* What effect does this create? [highlights end of development section, creates anticipation of recapitulation through dominant preparation]

➤ Why would Kuhlau avoid Theme 1 in the recapitulation? [Theme 1 was used throughout the development]

➤ Compare mm. 13-16 with mm. 40-45, and m. 20 with m. 49. How are they alike? How are they different?

➤ What is the musical purpose of the coda? [confirmation of C major tonality]

➤ Have you played other sonatina movements in which the beginning of the recapitulation was not clear?

Practice Suggestions

Practice in short sections checking for the following elements:

- crisp and even scale passages with accurate fingering
- dynamic contrast
- steady tempo and rhythmic accuracy (including rests)
- syncopations in mm. 13-16 and 40-45
- balance between RH melody and LH accompaniment.

Edvard Grieg
Elfin Dance, op. 12, no. 4 (R36, SW54)
Background Information

Edvard Grieg, a Norwegian composer, is perhaps most famous for his ten sets of character pieces which he titled *Lyric Pieces*. It is believed that he wrote the titles before writing the pieces. Therefore, each piece reflects the character, mood, or story depicted in the title.

Exploring the Score

An elf is a creature from a fantasy world, small in size, mischievous, playful and believed to haunt hills and wild places. As you listen to the *Celebration Series®* recording, use your imagination to create a musical story for this playful piece.

➤ Label the form: A (mm. 1-16); B (mm. 17-30); A (mm. 31-38); B (mm. 39-52) A (mm. 53-64); coda (mm. 65-72)

➤ There are two rhythmic motives in this piece:
  - *staccato* quarter notes
  - running eighth notes

Play the first two measures and locate both motives. Look through the score. Are there any measures that do not contain these motives? [only the coda, which has fragments of the motives]

➤ In mm. 3-4, the melody is primarily in the RH. Where is the melody in mm. 7 and 8?

➤ What is the mood or character of the A sections? [playful, light] Of the B sections? [mysterious, sense of drama, building tension]

➤ Find the sequences in the B sections. How do they contribute to the sense of drama?

➤ In the B sections, block the RH intervals of mm. 19-20, 23-26. Notice the contrary motion between the lower voices of the RH and LH. Now block mm. 27-28 and notice the movement of the voices. Can you see the parallel motion?

Practice Suggestions

➤ The secret to this piece lies in the ability to convey a sense of the elfin character, drama, and mystery. Establish a mood and character for the A and B sections.

➤ In the opening measures, notice that up-stem notes are to be played by the RH and down-stem notes by the LH.

➤ Make the *staccatos* sound as light and crisp as possible. Use firm fingers and stay close to the keys.

➤ Practice slowly at first, bringing out the RH or LH melodies over the *staccato* chords. Listen carefully for the dynamic contrasts.

Alexina Louie
Shooting Stars (R48, SW76)

Alexina Louie enjoys a successful composing career, having written major works for most of Canada's leading performers, ensembles, and orchestras. Her unique musical style is an expressive blend of east and west. Louie's imaginative piano works are very atmospheric and often feature improvisatory passages and colorful bell-like sonorities.

Exploring the Score

This piece provides a wonderful opportunity for students to display their creativity and paint a colorful musical picture.

➤ What comes to mind when you imagine shooting stars? [night sky, shimmering moonlight, twinkling stars, flashes of light, etc.] Listen to the *Celebration Series®* recording, to hear the elements you imagined.

➤ This piece makes use of non-traditional scale structures. Find the whole-tone scale in mm. 1-2 and 15-16. What scale does the LH play in mm. 19-24? [pentatonic]

➤ In a visually complex score like this, repetitions of the same sonority can look very different. Play the last chord in m. 2. Now compare those notes with the notes in mm. 3 and 4. Now look at the rolled chords in mm. 5-7. What do you notice?

➤ Compare mm. 11 and 12. Are the notes the same or different?

➤ Map the dynamic plan for this piece. Where is the sky calm? Where do you hear the shooting stars?

Practice Suggestions

➤ Before you play, write the counting in the score and tap each measure in rhythm. Counting eighth notes (*1 & 2 &*, etc.) will help at first.

➤ In mm. 5-7 and 22-25, gently roll the chords. Let the left hand bring out the *tenuto* points of light.

➤ In mm. 8-14, watch for notes affected by accidentals that appear earlier in the measure. Write in reminders if necessary. Block these measures until the positions are secure, then play as written with the *accelerando–ritardando*.

➤ In mm. 19-21, play the *tremolos* gently to reflect the shimmering starlight. Observe the *crescendo* and *diminuendo* markings carefully.

➤ The pedal is an essential element of tone color in this piece. Observe the markings for both the damper and *una corda* pedals. How will the term *tre corde* affect your pedaling in m. 8? [*tre corde* means "three strings," a direction to lift the soft pedal]

CREATIVE ACTIVITY

Compose your own whole-tone piece. Decide which whole-tone scale you will use. Use the damper pedal, dynamic contrasts, and some tone clusters to paint a musical picture.

Title: *Moonbeams*

Jenö Takács
In a Great Hurry, op. 95, no. 3 (S10)
Exploring the Score

Takács is a wonderfully inventive composer. In this piece, he expresses the breathless agitation of someone in a hurry.

➤ Listen to the *Celebration Series®* recording while you read the score. How does Takács create this frantic feeling? [fast tempo, short motives (mm. 1-2, 13-14), unpredictable new figures, sudden dynamic changes]
➤ In mm. 33-38, Takács repeats the opening material with a different mood *(Andante tranquillo)*. Create a story that accounts for this contrast.

Practice Suggestions
➤ With its speed and numerous technical figures, this piece resembles a *toccata,* or "touch piece." Isolate each different idea, practicing the touch, articulation, and fingering required. Use your very sharpest *staccato* touch.

➤ Isolate the chromatic lines of mm. 3 and 6 for secure fingering and hand coordination.

CREATIVE ACTIVITY

Compose your own piece based on agitated movements. Use *staccato* broken chords, chromatic scale fragments, and a fast tempo.

Title: *I Can't Find It!*

Henri Bertini
Etude in C Minor, op. 29, no. 7 (S14)
Practice Suggestions

From our disciplined practice, we think we have control over scales and arpeggio figures until we encounter the creativity of a composer like Bertini. With few exceptions, the figures in this piece are unlike anything from your warm-up routine, yet they are drawn directly from the key of C minor.
➤ Look through the piece to determine which figures will be most challenging. (Changes of direction are more difficult than consistent scale lines.) Devise several practice approaches for those more difficult figures. The RH patterns can be divided into:
– scale lines
– arpeggios or broken chords
– zigzag patterns
Isolate each figure for special practice.

➤ Practice hands together slowly in short sections, gradually increasing the tempo as you become more secure.

STUDY MODULE 4

Page	List	Composer	Title	Key, Meter and Tempo
R4 SW4	A	Johann Sebastian Bach	*Invention No. 1 in C Major, BWV 772*	C Major $\frac{4}{4}$ ♩ = 76-84
R18 SW30	B	Ludwig van Beethoven	*Bagatelle, op. 119, no. 1*	G Minor $\frac{3}{4}$ Allegretto
R34 SW51	C1	Vladimir Ivanovich Rebikov	*Waltz*	F sharp Minor $\frac{3}{4}$ Moderato sempre cantabile
R50 SW79	C2	Dmitri Kabalevsky	*Rondo-Toccata, op. 60, no. 4*	A Minor $\frac{2}{4}$ Allegro scherzando
S16		Jacob Schmitt	*Study in G Major, op. 3, no. 3*	G Major $\frac{6}{8}$ Allegretto
S18		Árpád Balázs	*A Sort of Rondo*	E tonal center $\frac{2}{4}$ Vivo

Assign first:

Invention No. 1 in C Major
Bagatelle . . . .
Study in G Major . . . .
Rondo-Toccata

Assign next when ready:

Waltz
A Sort of Rondo

Discuss the forms of the pieces in this module and the way musical ideas are used. Bach's *Invention No. 1 in C Major* uses a single subject or motive as the basis for the entire piece. Two rondos *(Rondo-Toccata, A Sort of Rondo)* and three ternary form pieces *(Bagatelle, Waltz, Study in G Major)* show us how composers use contrasting themes for variety.

Johann Sebastian Bach
Invention No. 1 in C Major, BWV 772 (R4, SW4)
Background Information

The *Wilhelm Friedemann Bach Notebook* includes early versions of some of the *Inventions* and *Sinfonias.* A revised version of these pieces appears in a manuscript dating from 1723, but they were not published until 1801, long after Bach's death. The title page of the 1723 manuscript suggests that the *Inventions* were written as examples of ways to combine two independent voices, and for the development of *legato (cantabile)* touch. The *Inventions* and *Sinfonias* are arranged in ascending key order, with fifteen pieces in each set. Your student may be interested in exploring which keys are *not* included, and speculating on the reason Bach avoided certain keys.

Exploring the Score

As this may be your student's first Bach *Invention,* take time to explore the fascinating way Bach weaves together the two voices of this composition.

➤ Put brackets around the opening RH subject in m. 1. (You might use a colored pencil.) Then label the running sixteenths as figure "x" and the eighth notes as figure "y."

➤ Similarly, put brackets and the "x" and "y" labels on the LH subject in m. 7. Continue through the score, bracketing complete statements of the subject. Label the "x" and "y" motives in the subjects you have bracketed.

➤ Can you find appearances of the "x" or "y" motive that are not part of a complete statement of the subject? [e.g., LH mm. 1, 2]

➤ Analyze the sixteenth-note movement in the RH, m. 3. How do those sixteenths relate to the "x" motive of m. 1? [m. 3 is an inversion of m. 1] Find other inversions of the "x" motive.

➤ Can you find any figures that do not relate directly to the opening motive?

➤ Which part of this invention is easiest to play? [mm. 15-18] Do these measures represent musical tension or musical relaxation?

➤ Look for the important cadences in the piece. Hint: Scan the LH for occurrences of an octave leap followed by a rising 4th or falling 5th. Play these; they sound like an "arrival" (cadence) in the key of the last note. [mm. 6-7, G major (dominant of C major); mm. 14-15, A minor (relative minor of C major), mm. 21-22, C major (home!)]. This effectively divides the invention into three sections of approximately equal length. Notice that, in two cases, the RH includes an ornament in the beat before the arrival. [cadence]

TIP: The cadential trill was so common that performers often added one even if it was not indicated in the score.

➤ How can you make these arrival points especially clear? [slight broadening, *crescendo*]

Practice Suggestions

➤ Use the cadence points to divide the piece into three convenient practice sections. [mm. 1-6, 7-14, 15-23].

➤ Once you have decided on an articulation plan, use it to play every entrance of the subject or its parts.

➤ Make a slight break in sound before entrances of the "x" and "y" motives.

➤ Both "x" and "y" figures need a sense of forward motion, usually to the final tone.

➤ The first note of each ornament should be heard on the beat, played with the corresponding LH note. Isolate each ornament for hands together practice.

➤ Play the invention as a LH–RH duet with your teacher. If a keyboard with recording features is available, record one hand, then play the other hand with the recording to experience the full texture.

Ludwig van Beethoven
Bagatelle, op. 119, no. 1 (R18, SW30)
Background Information

The French word *bagatelle* means a "trifle." Therefore, a composition titled "bagatelle" is a short piece. Beethoven wrote three sets of bagatelles: Opus 33, Opus 199, and Opus 126. His bagatelles are thought to count among his most experimental compositions, as if they were a "proving ground" for compositional ideas. They are short, often humorous, and filled with musical surprises.

Exploring the Score

➤ Engage in a literal "sight-reading" of the score. Without hearing or playing the piece, glean as much information as you can by looking at the music.
  – Can you see the sections? (Check m. 17 and m. 37.)
  – Are there key changes? major or minor?
  – Which section seems to have the shortest musical ideas? the longest?
  – Do you see any musical surprises?
  – What role does the LH play in providing contrast to the sound?
  – Hum the melody as you tap the A section (mm. 1-16). Did you see and hear the plan of 2mm. + 2mm. + 4mm.?
  – How long is the phrase beginning in m. 45?
  – Can you find the phrase groupings for the remainder of the piece (mm. 53-end)?

➤ Beethoven often experimented with form. This piece is an example. Label the form of the *Bagatelle:* A (mm. 1-16); B (mm 17-32); bridge (mm. 33-36) A1 (mm. 37-51) coda (mm. 52-74).

➤ What are the keys of the A and B sections? (G minor/E flat major) Notice that Beethoven could easily move from G minor to E flat major even though they are not related keys because of the two common tones in their triads! [G and B flat]

➤ Compare the A sections and discuss Beethoven's variation technique.

➤ Compare and contrast the mood and touch of the A and B themes. [A is light, *staccato*, lively; B is *legato*, lyrical with warm harmonies, and pedal] The A section dances; the B section sings!

➤ What is the surprise ending in the Coda? [G major] (In truth, the final line is actually written in C minor with dominant G7 chords. Perhaps the reason for ending in G major is its ambiguity—will we stay here? or will we resolve to C minor?)

Practice Suggestions

Success with this piece depends on accurate realization of the articulations and touches.

➤ Practice in eight-measure sections, listening to dynamics and articulations.

➤ In this piece, a dynamic plan that provides a *crescendo* to ascending notes and a *diminuendo* to falling pitches sounds very natural. This is especially true of Beethoven's A section. Listen for changing dynamics as the notes rise and fall.

➤ In the A sections, look for patterns and sequences to help shape the phrasing.

➤ Use RH *legato* fingerings in the B section.

➤ When 2-note slurs are marked or seem to be implied by the melodic writing, play with a gentle "down-up" motion of the wrist. Keep the LH thumb light. Listen to the bass line.

➤ Play at first without the pedal and then add the pedal as marked.

Vladimir Ivanovich Rebikov
Waltz (R34, SW51)
Exploring the Score

➤ As you listen to the *Celebration Series*® recording of this piece, immerse yourself in the mood. What words describe your reactions to these sounds? [sad, melancholy]

➤ How does the key of F sharp minor contribute to this mood? [There are no "happy" pieces in F sharp minor!]

➤ The subtle elegance of this piece is remarkable. As you sway to the rhythm of the first two measures, feel the lift of the second beat as if your feet had left the ground. Gravity pulls you to solid footing on the downbeat of m. 2.

➤ Label the A (mm.1-16), B (mm 17-32), A (mm. 33-48) form of the piece.

➤ The A section divides into a series of hypnotic two-measure units. In each, the rhythm and your dynamic inflection should press toward the harmonic change at the downbeat of the second measure, then *diminuendo* to its resolution. Does Rebikov remain with this phrase plan in the B section? [no; he creates four-measure units]

➤ In the B section, find and play the melody. [occurs in both LH and RH]

➤ Devise techniques for voicing melodies in both the RH and LH before home practice begins.

Practice Suggestions

Your practice of this piece will be most productive if you first dance to the music. No one will see you, so sway your arms, bend your knees, swirl and turn as you enjoy the wonderful lilt of this piece.

➤ It is this feeling of movement that must be captured in sound. As you danced, you may have found yourself slightly lingering on the second beat dotted quarter notes. Great! (Rebikov writes *sempre rubato.*) Work that rhythmic nuance into your performance. Let "musical gravity" pull the first measures of phrases to the downbeat of the second measures.

➤ The voicing of melodies needs careful consideration. How will you project the melody over the accompaniment? What fingering helps most to bring out the LH melody? Did you notice Rebikov's dynamic markings in m. 17?

➤ Isolate passages with RH melodies, listening for the top note of blocked intervals and chords. At mm. 21-24, it may be helpful to divide the RH part between the hands to model the desired balance. Try to reproduce the same sound when playing all the notes in the RH.

➤ Notice the detailed pedal indications in mm. 17-20.

Dmitri Kabalevsky
Rondo-Toccata, op. 60, no. 4 (R50, SW79)
Exploring the Score

This toccata is an excellent example of a "touch" piece because it explores various articulations.

➤ *Rondo-Toccata* is from a set of *Four Rondos,* in which Kabalevsky creates four different styles of music, all cast in rondo form. When labeling the form, first find the appearances of the A sections. [m. 1, m. 33, m. 65, m. 97] Notice their even distribution throughout the piece. Next, label the B and C sections. [ABACABA]

➤ Is the entire piece played *staccato?* Find the section in which a *legato* or *portato* touch might be appropriate.

➤ How much of the piece features unison writing?

Practice Suggestions

➤ Use your knowledge of the rondo form to organize your practice. Practice each section separately.

➤ In the A sections, pay special attention to the LH broken chords and subtle changes to the patterns. Play the notes of each LH measure with a circular gesture controlled by the upper arm. Keep the wrist loose and avoid consecutive down motions of the forearm. Listen for balance between melody and accompaniment.

➤ In the B section, practice the unison melody first. Then add the repeated thumb notes [pedal point] very lightly.

➤ Notice the special emphasis on the "arrival" tones in the C section.

CREATIVE ACTIVITY

Compose your own ABA *Toccata.* Use two different ideas: *staccato* five-finger patterns, and accented broken chords. Create an accompaniment for each idea.

Your title: _____

Jacob Schmitt
Study in G Major, op. 3, no. 3 (S16)
At last! A piece in which you play a scale, hands together, three octaves! All that scale practice is now justified!

Exploring the Score

➤ Schmitt's purpose in writing this exercise is not the three-octave scale, but rather the difficult changes of direction which employ the weak fingers (LH) and passing under of the thumb (RH).

➤ A most helpful discussion at the lesson could focus on the ingredients that create clear, smooth, efficient playing of these technical challenges.
 - Will fingers be close to the key or striking from a distance?
 - What is the role of the wrist?
 - What is the role of the forearm?
 - Can you suggest a variety of practice techniques?

Practice Suggestions

➤ Smooth-sounding sixteenth notes and careful articulations are important. How will you divide the sixteenth notes into practice groups?
 - Isolate the RH *staccatos* and two-note slurs in mm. 1-7 for hands alone practice.
 - Then practice the LH alone in mm. 8-12, focusing on tied values and holding the tones for their full value.

Árpád Balázs
A Sort of Rondo (S18)
Exploring the Score

➤ *A Sort of Rondo* is an unmistakable dance. Create some ways your student might experience the rhythm of the piece:
 - tap the rhythms while listening to the recording
 - tap the RH rhythm on a drum or tambourine
 - memorize the RH rhythm of mm. 1-2 and find other appearances of that rhythmic motive.
 - memorize instantaneously the rhythm of the B section's LH accompaniment

- This piece is indeed a rondo. Label the form: ABACA Coda.
- Determine which intervals are most closely associated with each section.
- There is no key or mode in this piece. The tonal center for the A sections is E. What are the tonal centers for the B and C sections? [B flat and F]
- What interval is used most frequently in mm. 1-4? [4th – sometimes perfect and sometimes augmented]
- How many different 4ths can you find? (Do not forget the intervals rising above the Bass E in the LH in mm. 1, 19, etc.)

Practice Suggestions
- Tap the rhythms of each section hands together on the closed keyboard cover.
- As you practice each section, look and think intervallically. That will facilitate accurate reading.
- Follow the fingering carefully, especially the LH fingering substitution, and unusual crossings that allow for a *legato* touch in m. 3. In the RH, let the wrist and hand follow the direction of the fingers. Avoid reaching for notes with an extended hand.
- Notice Baláz's careful phrasing. Practice each section slowly, first hands alone, with special attention to articulations, ties, and phrasing.

STUDY MODULE 5

Page	List	Composer	Title	Key, Meter and Tempo
R14 SW23	A	Joseph-Hector Fiocco	*Suite in G Major, op. 1, no. 1 (Second Movement)*	G Major $\frac{2}{4}$ ♪ = 69-76
R22 SW36	B	Muzio Clementi	*Sonatina in C Major, op. 36, no. 3 (First Movement)*	C Major $\frac{4}{4}$ Spiritoso
R40 SW59	C1	Viktor Kossenko	*Melody, op. 15, no. 11*	G sharp Minor $\frac{3}{4}$ Andantino cantabile
R43 SW65	C2	Clermont Pépin	*Berceuse*	F tonal center $\frac{2}{4}$ Andante
S6		Samuil Maikapar	*Toccatina, op. 8, no. 1*	C tonal center $\frac{4}{4}$ Allegro vivace
S12		Stephen Chatman	*Kitten*	Atonal $\frac{6}{8}$ Playfully

Assign first:
Suite in G Major . . . .
Sonatina in C Major . . . .
Melody . . . .

Assign next when ready:
Berceuse
Kitten
Toccatina

This module provides an opportunity to compare the different ways composers use accompaniment figures to support a melody. *Suite in G Major* and *Sonatina in C Major* both use chordal or broken chord bass lines. *Berceuse* and *Toccatina* use triplets and running sixteenth notes, respectively. Is there a melody and accompaniment in *Kitten*?

Joseph-Hector Fiocco
Suite in G Major, op. 1, no. 1 (Second Movement)
(R14, SW23)

Background Information

Joseph-Hector Fiocco was born in Belgium but was of Italian descent. He was an organist and church musician at the Antwerp Cathedral.

Exploring the Score

Suite in G Major (Second Movement) is a piece of true elegance and nobility. One can imagine the melody being played by an oboe, accompanied by stately strings. The spirit of the piece makes it suitable for use in a sacred service.

➤ Explore the elements which create that special elegance:
  – the tempo
  – the predictable yet colorful harmonies
  – the comfortable predictability of sequences
  – the flowing triplets
  – the stately *legato* of the duple subdivisions
  – the ornamentation

➤ Find examples of each of these elements, and discuss their effect.

➤ Fiocco masterfully combines duple and triplet subdivisions in this movement. Each has its character and role to play. The triplets create a musical flow. The duples provided a stately "holding back" and give opportunity for *legato* playing.

➤ A syncopation is usually preceded by a slight break in the sound. In this movement, the break happens naturally when the preceding note and the syncopation note are on the same pitch. Do you find other places where it is desirable to have a slight break in the sound? (Consider ends of phrases.)

➤ The varied ornaments are carefully realized in the footnotes at the bottom of the pages. Close examination reveals that the ornaments have different functions:
  – to emphasize a beat: mm. 1, 2, 4, etc.
  – to emphasize a harmony: mm. 22, 34
  – to end a phrase elegantly: m. 13
  – to move the phrase forward: mm. 8, 21, 25, etc.

Discuss these varied functions and explore the sound that is most suitable for each ornament. The *Celebration Series®* recording will provide an additional model.

➤ Fiocco frequently repeats an idea in sequence. Find examples of sequential writing [mm. 5-8; 9-11; 14-17; 18-20] and discuss an appropriate dynamic plan.

➤ Before the student can begin effective practice of this movement, rhythmic security with the subdivisions must be established. Find and mark each instance of duple sixteenths in the RH. [mm. 15, 17, 21, 25-29, 33]

Practice Suggestions

➤ As a preparatory rhythmic exercise, tap steady eighth notes in the LH against diminishing note values in the RH. Start with quarter notes in RH for several beats, then switch to eighths, then sixteenths, and finally triplet sixteenths.

➤ Practice in short sections (without the ornaments). Feel the forward flow of the triplets and the elegant "pulling back" of the duple sixteenths.

➤ Practice each ornament using the realizations in the footnotes. Work to produce a sound that matches its musical function. Remember that the ornaments should blend into the line rather than stand out.

➤ Give elegant stress to the syncopations.

➤ Listen for a singing melodic line (aria) soaring above the chordal accompaniment (orchestra).

Muzio Clementi
Sonatina in C Major, op. 36, no. 3,
(First Movement) (R22, SW36)

Background Information

Clementi wrote a wide variety of preludes, waltzes, exercises, sonatas, and the *Gradus ad Parnassum*. The *Six Sonatinas* of Opus 36 are his best-known works.

Exploring the Score

Creating contrast was a priority for a Classical composer writing a sonatina. The sonata-allegro form provided a perfect vehicle for presenting such contrast. This movement is an excellent example of sonata-allegro form with a short development section.

➤ Find and label the form and themes of this movement.

Exposition:	Theme 1	mm. 1-12
	Theme 2	mm. 13-26
Development		mm. 27-35
Recapitulation	Theme 1	mm. 36-48
	Theme 2	mm. 49-64

➤ The two main themes of the exposition have contrasting character. Compare and contrast these two themes. [Theme 1 is spirited and lively; Theme 2 is *dolce* or sweet and lyrical] Make up a story or create characters that reflect the mood and style of these two themes. Is it a dialogue between two people? What story could be imagined?

➤ What is the origin of the materials used in the development? [An inversion of Theme 1 opens the development]

➤ How does Clementi extend the theme in mm. 42-45?

➤ Why does the recapitulation start an octave lower than the exposition?

➤ Compare mm. 12-13 with mm. 48-49. What are the key relationships?

Practice Suggestions

➤ From the beginning, focus your practice on the sound. Where is the sound delicate? bold? How does the LH help establish mood?

➤ Within each section or theme, practice the following elements individually:
- running sixteenth-note figures
- broken-chord eighth-note figures
- *Alberti* bass or broken-chord bass lines
- ornaments

➤ Many students have difficulty maintaining a steady tempo throughout this piece. Practicing with the metronome is often helpful. Also, practice moving from one area of the piece to another, to see if you can maintain a steady tempo throughout.

Viktor Kossenko
Melody, op. 15, no. 11 (R40, SW59)

Background Information

Kossenko was a late-Romantic Ukrainian composer. In 1929 he became a professor of composition and piano at the Kiev Conservatory.

Exploring the Score

Melody is an eloquent and expressive soliloquy.

➤ Why would someone choose to write a piece in G sharp minor? To the composer, it represents darkness and is exactly the right key for this somber, melancholy expression.

➤ Notice Kossenko's meticulous phrasing. Every nuance is shown in the score. Every phrase is filled with expression. In spite of the many short articulated groups, the phrases flow in large units of four measures.

➤ Label the form: A (mm. 1-8); A1 (mm. 9-14); A2 (mm. 15-23) Look at the phrase lengths within each section. Why is the A1 section shorter?

➤ In general, there is an arch form to the sound. The piece rises to the top of the second page, then Kossenko uses a series of descending sequences in mm. 17-18 to bring the intensity back down for a final statement of the opening phrase. This arch is a picture of the emotional flow of the piece.

➤ Spell all three forms of the G sharp minor scale—natural, harmonic, and melodic. Does this help explain the F double sharps?

➤ Compare the third beat of m. 1 with the downbeat of m. 5. What are the differences? How would you label the two chords? Which one is minor? major?

➤ Spell the V7 chord in G sharp minor. Can you find it in the score?

Practice Suggestions

➤ Before practicing this piece, warm up in G sharp minor by playing the scales and primary chord progression.

➤ Read through each hand separately, marking any accidentals that might be overlooked.

➤ Work to bring a unique sound and experience to each appearance of the theme. What subtly contrasted effects do you want to create?

➤ Let your ear be your guide for pedaling. Listen to the *Celebration Series®* recording and mark the pedaling you hear in your score. Follow these pedal guidelines and change the pedal:
- with changes of harmony
- to avoid blurring melodic pitches
- between phrases

➤ Listen carefully for balance between melody and accompaniment, both between the hands and when melody and harmony appear in the same hand.

➤ Within each section, let the sixteenth notes carry the music forward across the bar lines. When the rhythmic motion clearly dies down (mm. 8, 14) take time to breathe before beginning the next phrase.

➤ In general, emphasize the first note of slurred groups.

Clermont Pépin
Berceuse (R43, SW65)

Background Information

A native of Quebec, Clermont Pépin studied music in Montreal, Philadelphia, Toronto, and Paris. He has enjoyed a prominent career as a composer and administrator and has written more than eighty works for a range of musical ensembles. Pépin's compositions have been performed in North America, Europe, South America, and Japan. In 1981, he was named to the Order of Canada in recognition of his contribution to the advancement of music.

Exploring the Score

A berceuse is a lullaby. When one pictures the scene of a lullaby, there are two essential characters: the mother and the baby. Some lullabies seem to focus on the child's peaceful sleep; others on the mother's song. Some lullabies show a mother's fear for what may befall the child. These considerations can be helpful as you explore Pépin's *Berceuse*.

➤ The LH portrays the rocking of the cradle. Is the rocking predictable? [yes] How does the composer make the swaying motion clear to the listener? [downbeats contain the lowest tone of the figure and the only blocked interval of the measure]

➤ Just as the baby and the parent are separate individuals, the LH and RH rhythms are basically independent of each other. Review two-against-three patterns by tapping and listening to gain or regain a threshold comfort level.

➤ Notice the repetitive RH rhythm and the predictable phrase groupings. How does Pepin create variety? [subtle harmonic changes in LH, wider intervals in RH to create intensity]

➤ Help your student write lyrics to the melody. ["my sweet and dear-est one …"] Can the lyrics reflect the rising tension of mm. 13-16?

➤ The form is difficult to label in this short piece because it continues to flow without references back to previous material. The form of such pieces is sometimes labeled "through-composed."

➤ A stable harmonic ending resolves the uncertainty of this lullaby. What chord is heard at the end?

➤ Listen to the *Celebration Series*® recording. When does the performer change the pedal?

Practice Suggestions

Accurate rhythms are essential. Tap the following rhythm line hands together on the closed keyboard cover. Count carefully and listen for two against three.

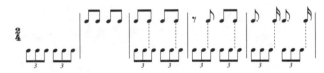

You might follow this practice plan in short sections:
- Play the LH downbeats. Read accidentals carefully. Is there any change of pitch other than a half step?
- Play the LH downbeats with the RH melody.
- Play the entire LH pattern.
- Combine the LH and RH as written. Project the melody with a rich, singing tone.

➤ Reflect on the song of the mother and work to convey her mood in your RH. Composing appropriate lyrics to the RH melody will help the expressiveness of your performance.

Samuil Maikapar
Toccatina, op. 8, no. 1 (S6)
Practice Suggestions

➤ There are no slow toccatas. Speed and clarity are essential in this piece.

➤ There are several different patterns of sixteenth notes. Practice each type separately.

Figure	Practice Method
Zigzag patterns	Rotate the hand
Scales	Divide between the hands *staccato;* then *legato;* then each note twice
Alternating hands	Slap hands on a flat surface, moving from slow to faster; both hands *legato;* one hand *legato,* the other *staccato*
m. 2 *staccato* sixteenths	Play *staccato* notes with a lifted finger; Play "trill" sixteenths from the surface of the key

➤ Keep your fingers close to the keys for the slurred sixteenth notes, and play with a smooth sound. Because of its weak rhythmic position, do not accent the first RH note.

➤ Anticipate the hand crossings in mm. 6-7 and similar places.

➤ Block the texture one beat at a time in mm. 8-12 and mm. 25-31, then play as written.

➤ The *Allegro vivace* marking means this study goes like the wind! How will you gradually increase your tempo? [incremental metronome practice in short sections]

Stephen Chatman
Kitten (S12)
Exploring the Score

Listen to the *Celebration Series*® recording of this piece. What do you hear that relates to the title *Kitten?* Let your imagination create a story for this music.

➤ Study the score closely. The more you look, the more patterns you will find! Identify:
- Most frequently used intervals. [M2, P5]
- RH five-finger positions.
- LH scale patterns.
- Repeated or transposed sections. [e.g., at m. 6 everything moves up a 5th]
- Number of measures in each section. [look for one-measure extensions]
- Measures where the LH plays black keys. [five]
- The dynamic pattern. Does it relate to position shifts?

➤ Find and compare the two sections that use extended pedal. How are they different?

➤ In the *senza pedale* sections, the LH (white keys) plays below the RH (m. 19 is the exception). In the pedaled sections, the LH crosses over the RH *(m.s. sopra)*.

➤ Discuss the dynamics, which play a crucial role in the total effect of the piece. The dynamic marking most easily overlooked is the *crescendo*. Circle each *crescendo* marking in the score.

Practice Suggestions

Let your first focus be on keyboard location. Practice on the closed keyboard cover, and shadow play the piece. Imagine that you can see through the wood of the keyboard cover and play the position shifts as accurately as possible.

➤ Next, block and hold the RH tones in m. 1 while playing the LH of mm. 1-5 as written. Do the same for mm. 6-8, 10-11, and 12-14. Mark the moments in the music when the hands cross. Decide which hand will be over or under.

➤ Isolate the technical challenge in the RH: are the dotted half notes still sounding after you play the *staccato* 5th?

- ➤ Practice each section separately, as written.
- ➤ As you play the entire piece, listen for *staccato* on every eighth note.
- ➤ The markings in the LH of mm. 12-14 and 20-23 indicate an extended, lingering sound. Debussy and Ravel use this indication for sounds that have no definite finish. Notice that these signs are used only when the pedal is held.
- ➤ Follow the performance indications carefully, looking for **sfz**, accents, dynamics, and tempo changes.

CREATIVE ACTIVITY

Using the same musical elements found in *Kitten,* create your own piece about a kitten and a ball of string. You might use: 2nds, 5ths, *staccato* touch, one hand on white keys and one hand on black keys, sudden dynamic changes, etc. First imagine your story and then use the musical elements to paint your picture.
Title: *Playful Kitten*

STUDY MODULE 6

Page	List	Composer	Title	Key, Meter and Tempo
R10 SW15	A	François Couperin	*Allemande in D Minor*	D Minor $\frac{4}{4}$ Legerement/Lightly
R25 SW39	B	Ludwig van Beethoven	*Für Elise, WoO 59*	A Minor $\frac{3}{8}$ Poco moto
R32 SW48	C1	Felix Mendelssohn	*Venetian Boat Song, op. 30, no. 6*	F sharp Minor $\frac{6}{8}$ Allegretto tranquillo
R54 SW82	C2	Rhené Jaque	*Lutin / Goblin*	Atonal $\frac{3}{4}$ Allegro
S20		Robert Schumann	*Fantastic Dance, op. 124, no. 5*	E Minor $\frac{2}{4}$ Sehr rasch
S22		Dmitri Kabalevsky	*Dance, op. 27, no. 27*	D Minor $\frac{2}{4}$ Moderato scherzando

Assign first:

Allemande in D Minor
Für Elise
Fantastic Dance . . . .
Dance. . . . .

Assign next when ready:

Venetian Boat Song
Lutin

Music either sings or dances, and there are excellent examples of both styles in this module. The pieces are colorful and dramatic. Two lovely songs (*Für Elise, Venetian Boat Song*) challenge the student to listen to balance and to play a beautiful *legato* melody over an active bass line. The dances (*Allemande, Dance, and Fantastic Dance*) provide rhythmic and technical challenges. Explore the rich sounds of the minor keys and discuss how a musical picture results from the composer's unique combination of form, texture, melody, and rhythm.

François Couperin
Allemande in D Minor (R10, SW15)
Background Information

For over half a century, a member of the Couperin family held the post of organist at the church of Saint-Gervais in Paris. François Couperin, known in his day as *Le grand,* or "The Great," served at this church and later at the court of Louis XIV. Couperin wrote twenty-seven harpsichord suites, which he called *ordres,* as well as the famous *L'Art de Toucher le Clavecin (The Art of Playing the Harpsichord.)* The *Allemande in D Minor* comes from this important treatise.

Exploring the Score

Imagine that you have been requested to write a keyboard piece in Baroque style.

➤ What stylistic characteristics would you employ to imitate a Baroque composer?
  - strict number of voices
  - independent rhythms and figures between hands
  - imitation
  - strong sense of downbeat, perhaps prepared by a lengthy upbeat pattern
  - ornaments, especially cadential trills
  - binary form with the requisite modulation
  - consistency of figure throughout
  - keyboard range limited to four octaves

Have the student check over the list to see if Couperin was successful in writing a Baroque composition!

➤ Find the binary form and label the keys in the score. The modern "rules" for writing key signatures did not gain universal acceptance until late in the eighteenth century. In many cases, key signatures were written with fewer sharps or flats and more accidentals in the course of the composition. Couperin's *Allemande* is clearly in D minor, though it lacks the usual B flat key signature.

➤ Look for figures that are repeated, for example:
  - ornaments followed by a descending 3rd
  - four-beat phrases (RH, mm. 1-3)
  - imitation between the hands
  - broken 3rds (mm. 9-11)

➤ Notice how Couperin uses high pitches to build to the cadence in m. 6 and to the climax of the piece on the downbeat of m. 12. Passages like this would have been very dramatic in Couperin's time because the performer's hands were near the highest and lowest notes of the keyboard. (On a modern piano, too, the climax of a piece often occurs when the hands are farthest apart.)

Practice Suggestions

Some students might find this piece difficult to learn because of the constantly changing figuration. The following practice suggestions may be helpful:

➤ Practice the sixteenth-note figures in four-beat units, hands separately.

➤ Study each figure carefully. Note the shape and melodic movement:
  - mostly stepwise
  - mostly zigzag
  - wide variety of intervals

➤ Practice each figure at least five times. Challenge yourself to memorize the figure.

➤ Circle skeletal stepwise motion in the melody. Use these circles as visual and musical goals.

➤ Practice the ornaments separately following the realizations provided, and experiment with different fingerings.

➤ Practice each phrase first without the ornaments, then add them one by one into the context of the line. Each ornament begins on the beat. For Couperin, the ornaments were an integral part of the melodic line and should be played lightly.

Ludwig van Beethoven
Für Elise, WoO 59 (R25, SW39)
Background Information

This piece is a universal student favorite. The dedication "For Elise" is thought to be a dedication to the daughter of Beethoven's physician. Many scholars now believe that the title may have been misread by the publisher and that the piece was actually dedicated to Therese Malfatti, a friend of Beethoven.

Exploring the Score

The popularity of this piece is due in part to the fact that the A section is readily accessible and aurally familiar to most students. Teachers, however, know of the more technically demanding sections that follow.

➤ Label the Rondo form and keys:
  - A   mm. 1-22 A minor
  - B   mm. 23-29 F major
  - bridge 1   mm. 30-37
  - A   mm. 38-58 A minor
  - C   mm. 59-76 A minor
  - bridge 2   mm. 77-82
  - A   mm. 83-103 A minor

➤ How does Beethoven create contrast between the sections? Consider:
  - contrast of accompaniment styles
  - contrast of melody and figure
  - contrast of mood
  - contrast of key

➤ Only one section establishes a new key, and that key is unexpected within the A minor family. Find the section and name the key. Can you justify its relation to A minor? [The tonic triads of F major and A minor share two common tones.]

➤ With the metronome ticking eighth notes, have the student tap eighths for two measures, then sixteenths, then triplet sixteenths, then thirty-second notes. Highlight these important rhythmic changes on the score.

Practice Suggestions

Each section of the rondo requires a special practice approach.

A sections:

➤ Listen for a delicate balance between the hands. In mm. 2-4 and similar measures the LH sixteenth notes make a *diminuendo* while the RH sixteenths flow into each downbeat.

➤ It is easy to lose track of the rhythm in mm. 13-15 and 50-52 because of the repeated intervals. Tap or conduct these measures while counting until they are totally secure.

B section:

➤ Block the LH chords and intervals to secure the notes and fingerings.

➤ Listen to the balance between melody and accompaniment. Try playing the LH twice as soft as the RH. Be sure to keep a steady tempo.

Bridge no. 1:

➤ Block the RH intervals in mm. 30 and 32. On the last four notes of these measures, consider using fingers 1-5-2-5. Use wrist notation to help with tempo and even sound.

➤ The speed at which you can play this passage will determine the tempo for the entire piece. Practice with the metronome to help keep the thirty-second notes in tempo. Start slowly and increase the tempo gradually.

C section:

➤ Listen for steady LH repeated notes.

➤ Sink into the keys with a loose wrist as you play the RH chords. Listen for a rich, full tone and project the top note of each chord or interval.

➤ Listen for proper balance when playing hands together. Carefully follow the dynamic plan and let the LH support the climaxes in mm. 62 and 71. Take a little time to highlight the B flat surprise in m. 71.

Bridge no. 2:

➤ Isolate the arpeggios and chromatic scale for special practice. Drill the arpeggios in "impulses" of 3 + 1 to secure the shifts. Keep the thumb and wrist free of tension.

➤ With the metronome ticking eighth notes, practice switching from triplet to duple sixteenths, as in mm. 81-82.

Felix Mendelssohn
Venetian Boat Song, op. 30, no. 6 (R32, SW48)
Exploring the Score

Extended melodic lines are one characteristic of 19th-century piano music. In this *barcarolle* or boat song, the combination of eight-measure phrases with the constant, hypnotic, rocking accompaniment paints a most effective musical scene of a gondola ride through the canals of Venice.

➤ What key would you select for a *Venetian Boat Song?* Mendelssohn's choice is surprising, for F sharp minor is associated with a dark and foreboding mood. As a result, there is not a "happy" note in the entire piece. As you study the piece, be sensitive to mood and color in this highly expressive work by Mendelssohn.

➤ The A section melody (mm. 7-14) is repeated (mm. 15-21). The ends of phrases feature the tones E sharp and G sharp (m. 13, m. 20), but they sound radically different. How? [m. 13 cries out in anguish; m. 20 is resigned]

➤ Notice the forshadowing of those E sharps and G sharps in the introduction (mm. 3-4). Why does Mendelssohn give those two notes such prominence? [they surround the tonic F sharp]

➤ A good, musical sleuth will be able to find other appearances of E sharp and G sharp. [mm. 22-23; mm. 29-30; m. 42] The trills in mm. 46 and 50 feature only the leading tone; its partner has disappeared.

➤ Listen carefully to a recording of this boat song. What nuance does the performer give to the LH accompaniment figure? Does the LH downbeat receive any dynamic emphasis? On the recording, do you hear the dramatic climax in mm. 29-30?

➤ Name the harmony at the climax in mm. 29-30. [C sharp major—the V] The tension of the dominant seeks resolution on its tonic, F sharp. Where does Mendelssohn finally write an F sharp chord (root position)? [m. 39, and ultimately in m. 43—thirteen measures later!]

➤ Compare the melodic contours of the A section and the B section. What differences do you find? [A section melody is undulating up and down; B section melody moves in one direction]

Practice Suggestions

➤ Model the sound of the LH accompaniment by dividing the figure between the hands. Create the

Celebration Series® Handbook for Teachers

strongest impulse on the downbeats, and let the other tones sound as reverberations of the downbeat energy. Create this same sound when playing the LH alone.

➤ Explore different fingerings in the LH until you have found the ones that give you the most ease and create the smoothest sound.

➤ The LH top tones in mm. 5-6 and 13-14 provide a short countermelody. Bring out these notes. Change the damper pedal with the stepwise motion as marked.

➤ The dynamic contour of the melody follows the contour of the pitches. Plan your dynamics to stress the highest pitches.

➤ Play the RH alone, in mm. 39-40, listening for the tied value and *legato* inner voice. Consider the following fingering for the inner voice in m. 39: 1-4-3-2-1-2.

➤ Project the top tones of the chords in mm. 43-45 (F sharp, E, D, C sharp). Find these same notes in the LH, mm. 44-46.

CREATIVE ACTIVITY

Using the LH rocking motion of Mendelssohn's *Venetian Boat Song* as a guide, write your own Boat Song. Use a $\frac{6}{8}$ time signature and simple harmonies (perhaps limited to tonic and dominant chords). Imagine an Italian gondolier singing your melody!

Title: _____

Rhené Jaque
Lutin / Goblin (R54, SW82)
Background Information

Quebec composer Rhené Jaque was born Marguerite Marie Alice Cartier. After joining the sisters of the Holy Names of Jesus and Mary, she continued her music studies at *École Vincent d'Indy*, where she later became a teacher of violin and theory. Jaque has composed numerous atonal teaching pieces intended for young pianists and violinists, as well as chamber music and other works for piano, organ, voice, orchestra, and choir.

Exploring the Score

Listen to the *Celebration Series*® recording while you read the score. List the musical elements used to depict a mischievous goblin. [sudden dynamic changes, tempo changes, *staccato, ostinatos,* bass register]

➤ Our rhythmic training focuses nearly exclusively on a steady beat. As a result, we find the quick changes of tempo indicated in this score to be a special challenge. If an electronic metronome is available, have the student follow the score and

tap or conduct quarter notes, while you change the metronome back and forth between 144 and 120.

➤ Look for repetition of phrases or patterns. [examples: m. 2 is a repeat of m. 1; RH "melody" mm. 11-14, is played by LH in mm. 26-29; mm. 42-43 is a varied repeat of mm. 40-41]

➤ The moods within this piece change abruptly. Find the lyrical melodic passages [mm. 3-5, 7-9, 20-25, 26-29 (LH), 31-33, 35-37] What character will you give them?

Practice Suggestions

➤ Using the metronome, devise a way to practice the tempo shift from mm. 120 to 144. Then, tap and count without the metronome. Record yourself as you tap the tempo shifts, then check your accuracy against the metronome.

➤ If a digital piano or computer sequencer is available, use the recording features to create a "click track" that incorporates all the tempo changes in the piece. At various learning stages, tap or play along with your recording, which can be sped up or slowed down as needed.

➤ Fingerings and rhythmic accuracy are straightforward and should not be a serious challenge in this piece. Focus your practice instead on accuracy of dynamics, articulation, and tempo shifts

➤ Practice very slowly in short sections, following all score markings. Increase your speed gradually.

➤ Use the rapid changes of tempo, dynamics, and articulations to help you depict the good-natured humor of this mischievous goblin.

Robert Schumann
Fantastic Dance, op. 124, no. 5 (S20)
Exploring the Score

Listen to the *Celebration Series*® recording and label the two main sections A and B. Do the sections repeat?

➤ The A section is very rhythmic, with driving triplets divided between the hands. The B section also has triplets. How is the B section different?

Practice Suggestions

A Section:
➤ Tap a steady eighth note pulse and say the number of notes in the subdivisions: *1-2-3, 1-2-3;* then *1-2-3-4,* and even *1-2.*

➤ Block the three-note positions of the triplets in mm. 1-3. (notice the symmetrical fingering).

➤ Play as written, letting the arm drop into the first note of each group.

B Section:
➢ First practice the LH separately, concentrating on a *legato* melody and phrasing.
➢ Play hands together, blocking the RH chords. Use damper pedal, changing with most eighth notes.
➢ Play hands together as written.

Dmitri Kabalevsky
***Dance,* op. 27, no. 27** (S22)
This playful dance is an exercise in *staccato* double 3rds.

Practice Suggestions
➢ Warm up by playing:
  – RH mm. 28-29: three times
  – RH mm. 1-4: three times
  – LH mm. 24-27: three times.
➢ Practice in short sections with a light *staccato* touch. Start slowly and gradually increase your tempo.

Level 7 SUMMARY
➢ Compare pieces with the same name: prelude, sonatina, toccata, waltz, dance. What similarities or differences can you find?
➢ In addition to opus numbers, you will notice that composers' works are often categorized by abbreviations such as BWV, TWV, HWV, and WoO. What do these letters mean? With which composers are these letters associated? (Hint: See the appendix of this book for more information on these abbreviations.)
➢ Music is often called the universal language. How many different countries are represented by the composers in Level 7?

Level 8

The Publications

Level 8 of the *Celebration Series®* includes the following publications:

Piano Repertoire 8
Piano Studies/Etudes 8
Student Workbook 8
Recording of Repertoire and *Studies/Etudes 8*

The Repertoire

Piano Repertoire 8 is divided into four sections or lists.

➤ List A includes a selection of pieces composed during the Baroque period (*ca* 1600 to *ca* 1750).
➤ List B pieces are from the Classical period (*ca* 1750 to *ca* 1820).
➤ List C includes a selection of pieces composed during the Romantic era (*ca* 1820 to *ca* 1910).
➤ List D pieces were composed during the late nineteenth century and the twentieth century.

Musical Development

The repertoire and studies from Level 8 represent an early advanced level and serve as preparation for the advanced Levels 9 and 10. The four style periods are represented equally, and provide the student further experience with those historical styles. The studies are repertoire pieces with a special technical emphasis, and further enhance the student's musical growth.

Our students often do not feel the same progress that we sense in their development. To document that development, have students reserve a cassette tape for their own recordings of Level 8 pieces. Goal: A minimum of two pieces from each Study Module is to be recorded on the tape. (Higher Goal: One piece from each List and one Study from each Module.) Play the tape from time to time, hearing finished performances from earlier Study Modules. At the end of Level 8, the cassette tape can provide tangible evidence of the student's progress.

The organization of practice time becomes an increasingly important consideration as students progress into more advanced levels. These suggestions may be helpful:

➤ Practice at times when you are fresh and alert. When possible, schedule more than one practice session each day.

➤ Practice all of the assignment daily. (If a portion of the assignment is not covered, begin the next day's practice with that material.)
➤ Make daily practice goals and write them down.
➤ Evaluate your own playing by listening to taped practice performances.

The Study Modules

The five Study Module discussions are organized into the following categories:

Background Information
Exploring the Score
Practice Suggestions
Creative Activities

Background Information provides a historical setting for the piece. **Exploring the Score** is designed as an interactive discussion between teacher and student. These observations and questions provide ideas for the introduction of a piece, prior to the first week of practice, helping to open the student's mind, eyes, ears, and hands to the new repertoire. The **Practice Suggestions** are to assist the student in the early weeks of study on a piece, exploring ways to solve challenging rhythms; to facilitate technical solutions for speed, accuracy, and fingering; and to increase practice efficiency. The **Creative Activities** act as reinforcement of a musical concept and provide a springboard for the student's creativity and improvisation.

The six study modules suggest an order of difficulty. Please refer to the discussion of **Order of Assignment** in the Foreword, p. 9, if you have questions regarding the column "Assign first" and "Assign next when ready" found below each Study Module Chart.

The following chart lists the repertoire and studies in Level 8. The page numbers in the first column indicate the location of the piece in *Piano Repertoire 8* and *Piano Studies/Etudes 8*. The column on the right indicates the Study Module groupings.

Piano Repertoire 8

	Page	Composer	Title	Study Module
List A	R4	Johann Sebastian Bach	*Little Prelude in E Minor, BWV 938*	4
	R6	Johann Sebastian Bach	*Little Prelude in D Major, BWV 936*	6
	R8	Georg Philipp Telemann	*Fantasia in D Minor, TWV 33:2*	2
	R11	Johann Sebastian Bach	*Invention No. 6 in E Major, BWV 777*	3
	R14	Giovanni Battista Pescetti	*Sonata in C Minor (Third Movement)*	1
List B	R16	Franz Joseph Haydn	*Sonata in G Major, Hob. XVI:27 (Third Movement: Finale)*	3
	R20	Domenico Cimarosa	*Sonata in B flat Major*	2
	R24	Muzio Clementi	*Sonatina in G Major, op. 36, no. 5 (First Movement)*	1
	R28	Ludwig van Beethoven	*Sonata in G Major, op. 49, no. 2 (First Movement)*	4
	R32	Ludwig van Beethoven	*Sonata in G Major, op. 49, no. 2 (Second Movement)*	5
	R36	Friedrich Kuhlau	*Sonata in A Major, op. 59, no. 1 (First Movement)*	6
List C	R41	Frédéric Chopin	*Prelude in B Minor, op. 28, no. 6*	1
	R42	Edvard Grieg	*Puck, op. 71, no. 3*	5
	R45	Robert Schumann	*An Important Event, op. 15, no. 6*	2
	R46	Felix Mendelssohn	*Andante sostenuto, op. 72, no. 2*	6
	R48	Bedřich Smetana	*Song, op. 2, no. 2*	5
	R50	Franz Liszt	*Consolation No. 1*	3
	R51	John Field	*Nocturne No. 5 in B flat Major, H 37*	5
	R54	Vasili Sergeievich Kalinnikov	*Chanson triste / A Sad Song*	4
List D	R56	Octavio Pinto	*Roda-roda!*	2
	R58	Béla Bartók	*Evening at the Village*	1
	R60	Alexina Louie	*O Moon*	6
	R62	Astor Piazzolla	*Milonga del ángel*	1
	R65	Robert Starer	*Pink*	3
	R66	Robert Starer	*Crimson*	3
	R68	Claude Debussy	*Page d'album / Album Leaf*	5
	R69	Larysa Kuzmenko	*Mysterious Summer's Night*	4
	R70	Oscar Peterson	*The Gentle Waltz*	4

Piano Studies/Etudes 8

Page	Composer	Title	Study Module
S4	Edvard Grieg	*Little Bird, op. 43, no. 4*	2
S6	George Frideric Handel	*Capriccio, HWV 483*	5
S8	Jenö Takács	*Toccatina, op. 95, no. 12*	4
S11	Mario Tarenghi	*Dance of the Marionettes*	6
S14	Johann Friedrich Burgmüller	*Morning Bell, op. 109, no. 9*	3
S16	Johann Friedrich Burgmüller	*The Gypsies, op. 109, no. 4*	5
S18	Stella Goud	*Spider on the Ceiling*	6
S20	Stephen Heller	*Etude in E Major, op. 47, no. 16*	1
S22	Albert Loeschhorn	*Song of the Waterfall*	1
S24	Samuel Dolin	*Little Toccata*	4
S26	Stephen Heller	*Etude in D Minor, op. 45, no. 15*	3
S28	Pál Kadosa	*Allegro, op. 23/f, no. 5*	6
S30	Dmitri Kabalevsky	*Etude, op. 27, no. 24*	2

Level 8 Repertoire and Studies/Etudes – Listed by Study Module

Study Module 1

List	Composer	Title	Page & Book
A	Giovanni Battista Pescetti	Sonata in C Minor (Third Movement)	R14, SW18
B	Muzio Clementi	Sonatina in G Major, op. 36, no. 5 (First Movement)	R24, SW29
C	Frédéric Chopin	Prelude in B Minor, op. 28, no. 6	R41, SW42
D	Béla Bartók	Evening at the Village	R58, SW71
D	Astor Piazzolla	Milonga del ángel	R62, SW78
	Stephen Heller	Etude in E Major, op. 47, no. 16	S20
	Albert Loeschhorn	Song of the Waterfall	S22

Study Module 2

List	Composer	Title	Page & Book
A	Georg Philipp Telemann	Fantasia in D Minor, TWV 33:2	R8, SW10
B	Domenico Cimarosa	Sonata in B flat Major	R20, SW25
C	Robert Schumann	An Important Event, op. 15, no. 6	R45, SW48
D	Octavio Pinto	Roda-roda!	R56, SW68
	Edvard Grieg	Little Bird, op. 43, no. 4	S4
	Dmitri Kabalevsky	Etude, op. 27, no. 24	S30

Study Module 3

List	Composer	Title	Page & Book
A	Johann Sebastian Bach	Invention No. 6 in E Major, BWV 777	R11, SW14
B	Franz Joseph Haydn	Sonata in G Major, Hob. XV:27 (Third Movement: Finale)	R16, SW21
C	Franz Liszt	Consolation No. 1	R50, SW59
D	Robert Starer	Pink	R65, SW81
D	Robert Starer	Crimson	R66, SW83
	Johann Friedrich Burgmüller	Morning Bell, op. 109, no. 9	S14
	Stephen Heller	Etude in D Minor, op. 45, no. 15	S26

Study Module 4

List	Composer	Title	Page & Book
A	Johann Sebastian Bach	Little Prelude in E Minor, BWV 938	R4, SW4
B	Ludwig van Beethoven	Sonata in G Major, op. 49, no. 2 (First Movement)	R28, SW32
C	Vasili Sergeievich Kalinnikov	Chanson triste / A Sad Song	R54, SW65
D	Larysa Kuzmenko	Mysterious Summer's Night	R69, SW89
D	Oscar Peterson	The Gentle Waltz	R70, SW92
	Jenö Takács	Toccatina, op. 95, no. 12	S8
	Samuel Dolin	Little Toccata	S24

Study Module 5

List	Composer	Title	Page & Book
B	Ludwig van Beethoven	Sonata in G Major, op. 49, no. 2 (Second Movement)	R32, SW35
C	Edvard Grieg	Puck, op. 71, no.3	R42, SW45
C	Bedrich Smetana	Song, op. 2, no. 2	R48, SW55
C	John Field	Nocturne No. 5 in B flat Major, H 37	R51, SW61
D	Claude Debussy	Page d'album / Album Leaf	R68, SW86
	George Frideric Handel	Capriccio, HWV 483	S6
	Johann Friedrich Burgmüller	The Gypsies, op. 109, no. 4	S16

Study Module 6

List	Composer	Title	Page & Book
A	Johann Sebastian Bach	Little Prelude in D Major, BWV 936	R6, SW7
B	Friedrich Kuhlau	Sonata in A Major, op. 59, no. 1 (First Movement)	R36, SW38
C	Felix Mendelssohn	Andante sostenuto, op. 72, no. 2	R46, SW51
D	Alexina Louie	O Moon	R60, SW75
	Mario Tarenghi	Dance of the Marionettes	S11
	Stella Goud	Spider on the Ceiling	S18
	Pál Kadosa	Allegro, op. 23/f, no. 5	S28

STUDY MODULE 1

Page	List	Composer	Title	Key, Meter and Tempo
R6 SW18	A	Giovanni Battista Pescetti	*Sonata in C Minor (Third Movement)*	C Minor $\frac{2}{4}$ Presto
R24 SW29	B	Muzio Clementi	*Sonatina in G Major, op. 36, no. 5 (First Movement)*	G Major ¢ Presto
R41 SW42	C	Frédéric Chopin	*Prelude in B Minor, op. 28, no. 6*	B Minor $\frac{3}{4}$ Lento assai
R58 SW71	D	Béla Bartók	*Evening at the Village*	E Minor $\frac{4}{4}$ Lento, rubato
R62 SW78	D	Astor Piazzolla	*Milonga del ángel*	B Minor ¢ ♩ = 104
S20		Stephen Heller	*Etude in E Major, op. 47, no. 16*	E Major ¢ Andantino
S22		Carl Albert Loeschhorn	*Song of the Waterfall*	D Minor $\frac{3}{4}$ Allegro

Assign first:

Sonata in C Minor . . . .
Sonatina in G Major
Prelude in B Minor . . . .
Evening at the Village . . . .

Assign next when ready:

Song of the Waterfall

Etude in E Major
Milonga del ángel

Composers create a balance between unity and contrast. Often, those elements are readily perceived through the form: ABA, sonata-allegro form, rondo. These forms, especially prominent in the 18th and 19th centuries, have inherent unity and contrast. Another aspect of unity is found in the pieces of Study Module 1: unity of rhythm. Notice the constant triplets in the Pescetti and Clementi movements, and the unity of sixteenths in Loeschhorn's *Song of the Waterfall*. Compare the LH of the Heller and the RH of the Chopin: constant eighth-note movement. The LH motives of Piazzolla's *Milonga del ángel* and Chopin's *Prelude in B Minor* are similar in rhythm and in direction. They serve as a unifying factor. Bartók uses rhythm for both unity and contrast.

Have the student record a minimum of two pieces from this study module. Reserve the tape for recording of favorite pieces from the successive modules.

Giovanni Battista Pescetti
Sonata in C Minor (Third Movement) (R14, SW18)
Background Information

Pescetti was a younger Italian contemporary of Bach. In contrast to his German contemporaries, he wrote keyboard music in a light, non-imitative style. Pescetti composed two collections of harpsichord sonatas. The first was published in 1737; the second, dating from around 1756, remained in manuscript.

Exploring the Score

➤ How many different rhythms do you find in this piece? The constant use of triplets gives this final sonata movement the feeling of a driving *tarantella*.

➤ How many different melodic figures do you find?
    a. broken-chord plus scale figure (mm. 1-4)
    b. descending broken triad (mm. 9-13)
    c. descending scale (m. 14)
    d. "turn" figure (m. 54-55)

➤ How does the LH accompaniment reflect the changing RH figures?

➤ The double bar at the end of m. 23 and the key of that measure suggest binary form. Find the return of the A section [m. 32] and compare measure by measure the similarities and differences with the opening section.

> What is the function of the "new" section starting m. 54? [closing – coda]
> What is the overall form? Check your answer with the chart below:

A	a	mm. 1-8
	b	mm. 9-23
B		mm. 24-31
A1	a	mm. 32-39
	b	mm. 40-53
coda		mm. 54-73

> What is the function of the trill in m. 53? [brings the A1 section to a close]

Practice Suggestions

> You have found the different figures written by Pescetti. Practice all of the "a" figures, then all of the "b" figures, etc. Pay special attention to fingerings.
> Mark the "lifts" at the end of each phrase. Are there other articulations you wish to notate in the score? Remember: Baroque music honors consistency. Example: If you break at the end of m. 10 (two-measure unit), you will also break after m. 12.

Muzio Clementi
Sonatina in G Major, op. 36, no. 5 (First Movement) (R24, SW29)
Background Information

In his sonatinas, Clementi provides a wealth of experiences in classical figures, melodic writing, and accompaniment styles. The rhythm of this movement is unusual for a classical sonatina, with its unchanging use of triplet subdivision. It must have been a challenging project for Clementi to write a sonatina movement without rhythmic variety!

Exploring the Score

> Find the few beats that are not subdivided into triplets. Why does Clementi stop the triplet motion at these points (mm. 34, 50, 58, 84)?
> In the Classical period, the performer was instructed to start a short slurred group with a slight accent. Note how this adds interest to the rhythmic structure: some accents fall on weak beats, others on strong beats.
> Label the sections of sonata form in your score. Compare your analysis with the following:

Exposition	mm. 1-34
1st theme	mm. 1-15
bridge	mm. 16-23
2nd theme	mm. 24-34
Development	mm. 35-50
Recapitulation	mm. 51-end
1st theme	mm. 51-65
bridge	mm. 66-73
2nd theme	mm. 74 to end

> How does Clementi create a contrasting second theme? [He moves the accompanying triplets to the RH.]
> Do you find evidence of both the first and second themes in the development?

Practice Suggestions

> Play the broken-chord triplets with a slight rotation of the hand, keeping the fingers close to the keys.
> The triplets are constant, yet some are accompaniments and others are the primary solo material. Practice the contrasting sound needed for the different functions of the triplets.
> Plan the articulation for the quarter notes. What effect do you want to create?

Frédéric Chopin
Prelude in B Minor, op. 28, no. 6 (R41, SW42)
Background Information

J.S. Bach was the first composer to write a set of preludes (and fugues) in each of the twenty-four major and minor keys. Chopin uses the circle of fifths as an organizing principle in his cycle of twenty-four preludes. A major-key prelude is followed by one in its relative minor key. Each piece explores the color and mood of its key.

Exploring the Score

> What mood is created by the choice of B minor for this prelude? What other musical features contribute to this mood?
> What effect does Chopin achieve with the ascending LH sixteenth notes? Name those chords. [m. 1, B minor; m. 5, G major; m. 13, C major]
> Where does the RH have the melody? [mm. 7, 8]
> Make a survey of phrase lengths. Notice how the opening three phrases form a short-short-long pattern.
> In m.18, Chopin creates a wonderful harmonic surprise (deceptive cadence). How can this be emphasized? [slight delay of the downbeat; special emphasis on the LH G]

Practice Suggestions

> This pieces requires total independence of the hands. Chopin carefully marks the sound of the two-note RH accompaniment. Practice the RH alone, exploring the fingering and wrist motion that best produces the "sobbing" effect.
> Note Chopin's consistent dynamic markings that show the focus of the LH melody as the downbeat of m. 2 (the longest value of the phrase), not the highest pitch of m. 1. Special LH practice of Chopin's dynamic plan may be helpful.
> Mm. 6-8 may pose a special reading challenge. Practice the RH alone. Look for the half steps.

Belá Bartók
Evening at the Village (R58, SW71)
Background Information

Bartók immersed himself in the study of the folk music of his native Hungary and surrounding countries. He integrated these melodies and the sounds of the folk instruments and their dance rhythms into his compositions. *Evening at the Village* is an example of Bartók's use of folk material, and the creative way he writes colorful accompaniments. Bartók frequently writes *rubato* or *ad libitum* when he quotes or imitates a folk song, indicating the freedom with which these melodies were sung. The dances are often marked to be played in strict rhythm.

Exploring the Score

➢ The form is seen readily in the score. Mark which sections are "song" and which are "dance."

➢ There are three sections of "song," and two sections of "dance," but no section is an exact repeat. Discuss Bartók's variation technique.

➢ The variations of the A section (song) become thicker in texture. The variation of B (dance) is more intense. The piece ends quietly. Suggest a "program" that makes sense of these musical features.

Practice Suggestions

➢ The articulation is of great importance, as it imitates the inflection of speech. Compose lyrics to the A section melody. Let your words reflect the articulation patterns.

➢ Is there any accented note that is not preceded with a slight break in sound? [no]

➢ Isolate LH mm. 30-40 for special practice. Create your own exercises for securing the chord changes.

CREATIVE ACTIVITY

Bartók creates interest and delight in his alternation of "song" and "dance." Select other opposites for your own composition, e.g. night and day, winter and summer, cold and hot. Create a piece in ABAB form in which you contrast opposites.

Title _____

Astor Piazzolla
Milonga del ángel (R62, SW78)
Background Information

The name of Astor Piazzolla is inextricably linked with the tango and an accordion-like instrument, the *bandoneon*. Piazzolla was born in Argentina, but spent his childhood in New York. During the 50s and 60s, he became a very popular tango performer in Argentina. He received a government scholarship to study composition in France under the famous Nadia Boulanger. The *milonga* was a popular Argentinean dance in the late decades of the 19th century and became one of the sources for the modern tango.

Exploring the Score

➢ To capture the flavor of the *milonga* and tango, listen to the *Celebration Series®* recording of this piece. Search for other recordings of tango music to provide background for the study of this piece.

➢ Mark the sections with A, A1 [m. 17], B [m. 33], C [m. 45], and A2 [m. 61]. Notice the changes of key signature marking the C and A2 sections.

➢ How does Piazzolla vary the accompaniment in the different sections?

➢ "Edit" the score by writing in the phrases. In which sections do you find predictable phrase lengths, and in which sections do you find irregular phrase lengths?

Practice Suggestions

➢ Practice the different rhythms in this piece before playing. Pay special attention to mm. 22-24, 33-44.

➢ The opening phrases are in four-measure units. Make m. 3 the focus of each phrase.

TIP: The usual peak of a four-measure phrase is in the third measure.

➢ The LH broken chord accompaniments must have their own dynamic plan. Do you think it sounds best to play each broken chord with a *crescendo* or with a *diminuendo*?

➢ There are wide stretches throughout much of the piece. Use these guidelines to help deal with those stretches:
   a. Capture low bass tones with the pedal.
   b. Let the arm move the hand into position. Avoid unnecessary stretching of the fingers.
   c. Roll the wide LH chords of mm. 13, 40, and 42.
   d. Explore places where the RH can play the top tone of a LH figure, e.g. mm. 4-8.

➢ The notation indicates that the beginning will be pedaled in full measure units. However, the B section (m. 33) must have a pedal change on nearly every event. Listen carefully to the recording of this piece for ideas on pedaling.

Stephen Heller
Etude in E Major, op. 47, no. 16 (S20)

Exploring the Score

This piece is a study in melodic shaping and projection.

➤ There are three distinct themes in the piece, each with its different combination of melody and accompaniment. Find them, and discuss their differences.

[A = mm. 1-4; B = mm. 5-9; C = mm. 10-15]

Practice Suggestions

The basic practice goal is to project the melody much louder than the accompaniment.

➤ Start with the easiest texture, mm. 1-4.
➤ Practice the texture of mm. 5-8 hands separately, bringing out the top tone of each hand.
➤ When practicing m. 12, play the melodic tone first (loudly) and add the accompanying tones (quietly).

Albert Loeschhorn
Song of the Waterfall (S22)

Practice Suggestions

Fingering of the broken chords is your clue to success. Some decisions will need to be made: if the sixteenth-note group begins with finger 3, the fingering is 3531; if finger 2 starts the beat, the spacing of the chord will determine if the fingering is 2421 or 2521.

➤ Successful practice is based on consistent fingering. Write in your fingering decisions.
➤ Block each chord and say aloud the first two finger numbers as you play.

CREATIVE ACTIVITY

Loeschhorn creates the illusion of a waterfall with his descending broken chords. Turn that idea around and create a piece in which the movement sweeps upward. Compose your piece in the key of D minor. Title: *Waves*

STUDY MODULE 2

Page	List	Composer	Title	Key, Meter and Tempo
R8 SW10	A	Georg Philipp Telemann	*Fantasia in D Minor, TWV 33:2*	D Minor ¢ Presto
R20 SW25	B	Domenico Cimarosa	*Sonata in B flat Major*	B flat Major C Allegro
R45 SW48	C	Robert Schumann	*An Important Event, op. 15, no. 6*	A Major 3/4 ♩ = 96
R56 SW68	D	Octavio Pinto	*Roda-roda!*	D Major 4/4 With much life
S4		Edvard Grieg	*Little Bird, op. 43, no. 4*	D Minor 6/8 Allegro, leggiero
S30		Dmitri Kabalevsky	*Etude, op. 27, no. 24*	F Major 4/4 Allegro marcato

Assign first:

Fantasia in D Minor. . . . .
Sonata in B flat Major . . . .
An Important Event. . . . .

Assign next when ready:

Etude
Little Bird
Roda-roda!

Do you sometimes wonder how a composer chooses the key for a piece? The answer may vary among composers, although most seem to have their own strong sense of a key's color and mood. As you compare the pieces in Study Module 2, which ones are bold and forthright? What are the keys associated with that mood? Find the pieces in a major key, and label the mood. The exploration into key color has unending fascination for the music student.

Which pieces from Module 2 will the student choose to record?

Georg Phillip Telemann
Fantasia in D Minor, TWV 33:2 (R8, SW10)

Background Information

The Baroque fantasia had no specified form, and, as the title suggests, could be highly improvisatory in nature. Telemann's thirty-six fantasies are sectional compositions, and always include a repeat of the opening section.

Exploring the Score

In *Fantasia in D Minor,* Telemann uses the interval of an octave as a unifying idea. In mm. 1-2, both hands travel through an octave. Find the different octave patterns in mm. 26-29, 38, and 91-94.

One interesting aspect of this piece is the exchange of materials between the hands.
➤ Find where the hands trade the musical ideas found in mm. 4-5 [mm. 18-19] and mm. 38-41 [mm. 58-61].
➤ Many of Telemann's keyboard *Fantasies* have a slow B section. The *Adagio* in this piece consists of diminished 7th chords and dominant chords resolving to their tonics. Which chords have greatest tension? Which chords have least tension?
➤ Analyze the harmonies of the *Adagio*. How many examples of V-I can you find?

Practice Suggestions

Although this piece is organized around one idea, it is full of contrast.
➤ Orchestrate the piece, assigning different motives to the full orchestra or to solo instruments. You may wish to sequence these ideas on a keyboard or computer, or use digital sounds to create the orchestral effects. For example:
  – the opening motive mm. 1-3 might represent the full orchestra. Use the same full sound for other statements of this descending broken chord motive.
  – the ascending broken chord in mm. 38-41 could imitate a solo instrument.
➤ Locate the sequences, and plan appropriate dynamics.
➤ In the *Adagio,* explore ways to add interest to the repeated motives and chords by using subtle variations in dynamics.
➤ The half note and whole note chords are to be arpeggiated (or rolled) from bottom to top.
➤ The footnote in the score will assist you with the realization of the ornament.

Domenico Cimarosa
Sonata in B flat Major (R20, SW25)

Background Information

The absence of double bars in this movement indicates that this "sonata" does not conform to the principles of exposition-development-recapitulation as practiced by the Viennese Classical composers. This piece is a sonata in that it is to be *played* ("sonare"), as opposed to *sung* ("cantare"). Cimarosa employs Classical keyboard figures such as the *Alberti* bass. This Italian style greatly influenced the Austrian composers.

Exploring the Score

Every piece has form.
➤ Help the student locate the different figures ("themes") used and label them with numbers or letters.
➤ Find the main cadence points. [m. 18, F major; m. 26, B flat major; m. 46, B flat major]
➤ Note the circle of fifths modulation, mm. 34-38.
➤ Discuss articulation. In earlier keyboard music, a basic articulation rule was to play stepwise motion *legato* and wider intervals detached.

Practice Suggestions

➤ Locate the main motives Cimarosa employs, and plan an articulation for each motive, giving life and identity to each.
➤ Composers of this period were fascinated with the dynamic possibilities of the pianoforte. Bring variety and contrast to your performance by planning dynamic contrasts for repeated motives.
➤ All single small notes (e.g., mm. 2, 4) are played as sixteenth notes on the beat (see footnote in the score).
➤ The turns that first appear in m. 5 are played on the beat.
➤ Rotation technique will help you to master much of the RH figuration with comfort and efficiency. Keep the thumb light in mm. 11-12 and similar passages. Will you need rotation in the LH?

Robert Schumann
An Important Event, op. 15, no. 6 (R45, SW48)

Exploring the Score

An "important event" for a student studying this piece would be hearing the entire *Kinderscenen* with score in hand. Invite the student to enter into Schumann's fantasy world of childhood scenes, and discuss the pictures that result from hearing each piece. Remember that in Schumann's day there were kings and horse-drawn coaches.
➤ Discuss the ways in which Schumann creates the sound of a *very* important event.

Practice Suggestions

➤ Accuracy of chord playing will be enhanced by practicing slowly, covering each new chord position before playing.

- ➤ Determine the dynamic focus of each phrase.
- ➤ In preparation for the LH octaves, play only the LH thumb. Allow the thumb to be the "eye" of the hand when playing the octaves.
- ➤ The LH octaves of the B section sound best when they reflect the dynamics of the RH. Practice the descending octaves with a *diminuendo,* the ascending octaves with a *crescendo.*
- ➤ Technically, the most difficult aspect of this piece is to play the dotted rhythm with spark and snap. Play the sixteenth-quarter-note figure in a single arm gesture, with a wrist "lift" on the quarter note. Avoid consecutive downward motions of the arm.
- ➤ Schumann indicates that the piece is played *con pedale.* In the A section, the harmonies change on each beat. Change the pedal accordingly. In the B section, clarify the bass line by avoiding the pedal on the second beats; pedal only on beats one and three.

Octavio Pinto
Roda-roda! (R56, SW68)
Background Information

Octavio Pinto was a well-known Brazilian composer noted for his writing of miniatures. Another composition, *Salta, Salta (Hobby-horse),* from his *Scenas Infantis (Scenes from Childhood)* is in *Piano Repertoire 9.*

Exploring the Score

- ➤ Demonstrate the piece for the student, or listen to the *Celebration Series®* recording. How does the music represent the happy innocence of children playing "ring-around-the-rosie?"
- ➤ The changes of key signature quickly identify the ABA form of the piece. Mark the form in the score.
- ➤ In the A section, the RH is organized around two major five-finger patterns. [D and G]
- ➤ In the B section, the prevailing motive is three descending steps. Find examples of that motive and circle them in the score.

Practice Suggestions

- ➤ Articulation is the primary element of contrast between the A and B sections. Let your practice emphasize the detached quality of the A section and the *legato* B section.
- ➤ In the A section, there is only one RH slur. Pinto implies that the other RH notes are played slightly detached.
- ➤ Practice the LH of the A section for security and accuracy of the chords, and quick register changes.
- ➤ The RH blocked intervals mm. 15-18 may require special practice to learn the fingerings. Practice each interval with a slight "arm push."

Edvard Grieg
Little Bird, op. 43, no. 4 (S4)
Background Information

Much of Edvard Grieg's compositional output was based on folk music of his native Norway. Over a period of thirty-eight years, Grieg wrote sixty-six pieces under the general title *Lyric Pieces.* Published in ten different books, the *Lyric Pieces* are outstanding examples of Romantic character pieces.

Exploring the Score

- ➤ With the following questions as your "listening guide," listen to the *Celebration Series®* recording of Grieg's *Little Bird.*
  - a. Does the performer use pedal? Where? (Mark that pedaling in your score.)
  - b. Are the 32nd notes clear and well coordinated between the hands?
  - c. What is the loudest measure in that performance?
  - d. What image is evoked as you hear the 32nds in the bass (mm. 9, 29)?
- ➤ How many different intervals does Grieg use for his "bird calls" (32nds)?
- ➤ The form of this piece is rounded binary with coda. Agree or disagree.

Practice Suggestions

The trill figure (bird call) is to be played lightly and clearly. Explore these different approaches in your practice:
- ➤ play the first note of each figure with a lifted finger
- ➤ play the last note of each figure with a wrist lift
- ➤ try alternative fingerings: RH 23132

Dmitri Kabalevsky
Etude, op. 27, no. 24 (S30)
Exploring the Score

Stated simply, composers combine single pitches into melodies and figures. The results of those combinations are:
- scales
- broken chords
- arpeggios
- repeated tones

In this étude, Kabalevsky uses all of these figures except repeated tones.

- ➤ Find examples of unison (i.e., at the octave) triplets.
  - in the A section, mm. 1-14, unison triplets are rare.
  - in the B section, mm. 15-37, unison writing is the norm.

Practice Suggestions

➤ Practice the B section. You may wish to block the chords first.
  - Where will you use finger 4? Notate your decision in the score.
  - Write the names of the chords in the score.
➤ As you read the A section (slowly, accurately), be especially alert to the use of finger 1. If needed, circle the crucial locations of finger 1.
➤ Before playing hands together in mm. 11-12, practice hands separately until you have the figure memorized.

➤ Make special note of the long *crescendo* in the B section, m. 18 to m. 35.

CREATIVE ACTIVITY

Make up a warm-up drill in which you use the different elements found in Kabalevsky's étude: broken chords, scales, and arpeggios. Put the ideas together so that they are continuous and sound like a formulated piece. Create an ending to your drill. Then (are you ready for this?) … transpose your drill to other keys!

STUDY MODULE 3

Page	List	Composer	Title	Key, Meter and Tempo
R11 SW14	A	Johann Sebastian Bach	*Invention No. 6 in E Major, BWV 777*	E Major $\frac{3}{8}$ ♪ = 92
R16 SW21	B	Franz Joseph Haydn	*Sonata in G Major, Hob. XVI:27 (Third Movement: Finale)*	G Major $\frac{2}{4}$ Presto
R50 SW59	C	Franz Liszt	*Consolation No. 1*	E Major **C** Andante con moto
R65 SW81	D	Robert Starer	*Pink*	F Major $\frac{3}{4}$ Not too fast
R66 SW83	D	Robert Starer	*Crimson*	C Major $\frac{7}{8}$ Fast and hard
S14		Johann Friedrich Burgmüller	*Morning Bell, op. 109, no. 9*	A flat Major $\frac{3}{4}$ Andante sostenuto
S26		Stephen Heller	*Etude in D Minor, op. 45, no. 15*	D Minor $\frac{3}{4}$ Poco, maestoso

Assign first:

Invention No. 6 in E Major
Sonata in G Major (Finale) . . . .
Consolation No. 1 . . . .
Crimson . . . .

Assign next when ready:

Etude in D Minor
Morning Bell
Pink

"Music either sings, or it dances." This is a simple statement, yet one that stimulates us to look and listen carefully, asking, "Is the emphasis on the melody, or is it on the rhythm?" Study Module 3 reveals a variety of approaches to the melody/rhythm dichotomy. In some of the pieces (Starer's *Pink* and Haydn's *Sonata in G Major*) the melody is clear. In Bach's *Invention No. 6 in E Major*, both hands are melodic in the opening subject, but the thirty-second-note motive is rhythmic. Some of the pieces have rhythmic focus (Starer's *Crimson*, and Heller's *Etude in D Minor*). The pendulum swings in a fascinating manner.

Celebration Series® Handbook for Teachers

Johann Sebastian Bach
Invention No. 6 in E Major, BWV 777 (R11, SW14)

Background Information

Bach's stated performance goals in writing the *Inventions* were for students to learn to play "cleanly" in two parts, and develop a *cantabile* (singing) style of playing. In all of the *Inventions,* the hands are treated as equal partners, sharing both subject (thematic) and accompanying material. The inventions vary in character from tuneful themes to dance ideas. Each creates its own mood, quite possibly inspired by the key.

Exploring the Score

The unique aspect of this invention lies in the fact that the subject is "two-handed." It is a texture of contrary motion between two voices.

➤ Bracket all appearances of this contrary motion subject.
➤ The fascination of the opening eight measures lies in the contrary motion of the voices. Have the student look for further examples of contrary motion.
➤ In the main subject, both hands flow in eighth-note motion, but notice how voice independence is achieved. [one hand plays on the beat, the other hand plays off-beat]
➤ When the opening contrary motion material is not present, modulation is taking place. Find the key established at m. 20 [B major] and at m. 42 [G sharp minor].
➤ Discuss the use of sequences in mm. 9-17, 33-42, 51-58. Notice how each two-measure pattern is varied and extended on its third appearance.

Practice Suggestions

➤ If the thirty-second-note motive is followed by a slight break, the sound is dance-like.

Practice these motives hands separately, with an articulation break between each three-note group.

➤ Give special attention to the fingerings of the 32nd-note motives. Circle and practice the fingerings that need your greatest attention.
➤ Develop a dynamic plan for the piece. Look to the melodic patterns and sequences for clues. Consider chord progressions as well. (e.g., the intensity of mm. 39-40 creates a harmonic focal point.)

CREATIVE ACTIVITY

➤ Using Bach's contrary motion idea, play hands together on the scales of C, F, and G inward and outward. Find some way to give the hands independence, as was accomplished by Bach's rhythm.
➤ Repeat that activity, but improvise some linking material between the scales. Round out the sound of your "scale exercise" with an ending.
➤ Transpose your piece using the scales of E, A, and B.

Franz Joseph Haydn
Sonata in G Major, Hob. XVI:27
(Third Movement: Finale) (R16, SW21)

Background Information

One of the joys of playing Haydn sonatas is experiencing his creative use of form. This movement is no exception. Is it a rondo? A set of variations? The frequent use of repeat marks would indicate the latter. The frequent return of the opening theme would indicate the former. Let's explore the score.

Exploring the Score

Mm. 1-24 form the foundation of this movement. This is an example of rounded binary form: two-part form with a complete return of the opening idea [mm. 1-8] in the second half [mm. 17-24]. Mm. 9-16 create a mini-development of the opening eight measures.

➤ Explore other rounded binary forms in this movement. [mm. 25-48, mm. 49-72] Did the student find the written out rounded binary of mm. 105-152?
➤ With so much emphasis on the theme of mm. 1-16, how does Haydn create variety in this movement? [Each reappearance of the theme is varied.] Where does Haydn begin a new theme? [m. 49]
➤ The slur (mm. 2, 4, etc.) is used frequently to show an *appoggiatura* [non-chord tone] and its resolution [chord tone]. Which is the louder tone? [the *appoggiatura*]
➤ Analyze phrase lengths. Do you find examples of balanced phrases? Can you find examples of short-short-long groupings (2mm. + 2mm. + 4mm.)?
➤ Label the sections/variations.
　　　Theme: mm 1-24
　　　Var. 1: mm. 25-48
　　　Var. 2: mm. 49-72
　　　Var. 3: mm. 73-104
　　　Var. 4: mm. 105-152

➤ Discuss the ways in which each variation is different.

Practice Suggestions

A proper performance of this movement is achieved when the score is realized in every detail: rests, articulation (*legato vs* detached), clearly articulated fingers, accurate rhythm, and lively tempo. Develop a practice plan that will accomplish each of these goals.

Franz Liszt
Consolation No. 1 (R50, SW59)
Background Information

Liszt's accomplishments as a pianist are legendary. Besides being regarded as the greatest pianist who ever lived, he had incomparable sight-reading and memory skills. The catalogue of his compositions includes great numbers of solo piano, orchestral, and vocal works. Liszt's *Six Consolations* are noteworthy for their lovely melodies and colorful harmonies. They avoid the virtuosic display found frequently in his solo piano works.

Exploring the Score

➤ One tone pervades this work. It is present in every measure, sometimes appearing in every chord. Find that tone. [B]

➤ The off-beat rhythm of mm. 1-2 becomes clear after playing mm. 5-6: the "missing beats" of mm. 1-2 are the B's that appear prominently in mm. 5-6.

➤ Compare mm. 9-12 with mm. 13-16. The notes are written on the same lines and spaces, but the change of accidentals results in a completely altered harmonic effect.

➤ The three most prominent chords of the piece are E (the tonic of the piece), G sharp minor (m. 9), and G major (m. 13). What single tone do those three chords have in common? [B!]

Practice Suggestions

➤ In the A sections (mm. 1-8 and 17-end), the bass line acts in partnership with the melody. Play the melody and the bass line together (without the inner harmony) to hear that relationship. Listen carefully for these exterior voices when you play the full texture.

➤ In the B section, the half notes receive the expressive emphasis.

➤ The LH is your guide to the pedal. Pedal each LH event, observing the LH rests (no pedal).

Robert Starer
Pink (R65, SW81)
Background Information

Robert Starer was born in Vienna and studied at the State Academy in Vienna before pursuing further musical studies in Jerusalem and at the Juilliard School. He has lived in New York City since 1947, and has held teaching positions at The Juilliard School, Brooklyn College, and the Graduate Center of the City University of New York. *Sketches in Color* appear in two sets. The title of each piece is a color, and these short works explore the moods evoked by their titles. Starer employs a wide range of 20th-century techniques and harmonic practices in these pieces.

Exploring the Score

This piece is especially effective when the student understands the phrase structure and communicates those phrases in the performance. The ends of phrases can be shown with a slight *rubato* extension (*rit.* and breath).

➤ Find the long phrases. Mark them in the score.
   mm. 1-4
   mm. 5-9
   mm. 10-13
   mm. 13-17
   mm. 18-22
   mm. 23-28

➤ Starer's dynamic markings show the focus of each phrase.

➤ How many different meters do you find in the score? How does the change of meter serve Starer's musical goals? [$\frac{3}{4}$ is associated with the opening melodic gesture and often ends the long phrase; $\frac{2}{4}$ moves the music through the phrase and is clarified by the LH two-note slurs]

➤ As you hear this piece, how do the sounds evoke the feeling of the color pink? Discuss how you might have written a "pink piece" differently.

Practice Suggestions

➤ Make the dynamic shaping of the phrases a high priority. Follow the composer's indications carefully.

➤ Practice the LH separately. Goals: (a) hold the long notes full value, (b) play each downbeat with a slight emphasis. (The last LH tone of each phrase should be barely audible.)

➤ How can you make the endings of the long phrases clear to the listener? [slight break between phrases, slight extension of the final beat of the phrase, very quiet LH final tone]

Robert Starer
Crimson (R66, SW83)
Exploring the Score

➤ A $\frac{7}{8}$ meter can be felt as 3 + 4 or 4 + 3. Examine the score to determine which grouping Starer preferred for *Crimson*.

➤ There are three basic ideas in this short piece:

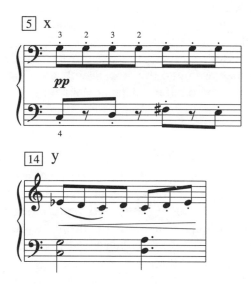

Discuss the differences between the motives. [articulation, LH texture and rhythm, single hand *vs* hands together, dynamics] Mark the appearances of "Intro," "x," and "y" in the score.

➤ Which idea is played loudest?
➤ Is Starer's sound similar to your idea of crimson?

Practice Suggestions

➤ Say aloud and very fast *1234123/1234123*.
➤ Practice the RH of m. 5 saying *1234123*.
➤ What will be the best fingering for m. 5? Consider: 3232321 or 4321321.
➤ In mm. 14-15, create a two-note slur effect in the LH. Play *legato* 5ths. Notice the special RH articulation of this "y" idea.
➤ Tap both hands on the closed keyboard cover before playing hands together. Isolate mm. 21-24 and 36-42 to master the LH articulations.

Johann Friedrich Burgmüller
Morning Bell, op. 109, no. 9 (S14)
Background Information

Burgmüller was born into the tradition of north German romanticism. He lived for many years in France, and his works also bear the influence of that lighter style of composition. His many compositions for piano students combine technical challenge with an evocative title and picturesque sound.

Exploring the Score

➤ As you demonstrate the piece or listen to the *Celebration Series®* recording, locate the morning bell. [LH crossing to the treble E flat] The student may be surprised to find the bell only in the A sections, mm. 1-8 and 25-35.
➤ The texture of the B section (mm. 9-24) changes in both hands. Describe the RH change. [B section

features two voices in a dialogue or duet] And how does the LH change? [thicker texture of full triads]
➤ Assist the student with a harmonic analysis. The goal is to discover where the harmonies change. [only at the beginnings of measures]

Practice Suggestions

A section:
➤ Block the RH harmonies, and practice the LH cross-overs from bass to "bell." Experiment with the tone and dynamic level that gives the most evocative bell sound.
➤ Practice the RH alone for *legato* connections in the melody and for a quiet accompaniment. To model the balance between the two voices, first distribute them between the two hands, then try to reproduce the same sound when playing both voices with the RH.

B section:
➤ The RH in mm. 9-16 is a duet. Train your ear to hear both parts. Practice the alto voice with the LH and the soprano voice with the RH. Try singing one part as you play the other.
➤ When the RH duet plays blocked intervals (mm. 17-19), bring out the soprano.
➤ Label the LH chords, mm. 9-18. Say the names of those chords as you play. Use wise fingerings on those chords. For efficient hand movement, avoid using a finger 5 on the bottom tone of a chord when possible.
➤ Burgmüller indicates that the sixteenths of mm. 21-24 can be played rather freely (*dim. e poco riten.; rall. e dim.*). Use the fingerings indicated and do not rush.
➤ Find the loudest moment of the piece. [*ff* possible means as loudly as possible]

Stephen Heller
Etude in D Minor, op. 45, no. 15 (S26)
Exploring the Score

The challenge of this piece is to play a huge sound and full-handed chords with a sharply dotted rhythm. The entire piece focuses on that idea.

➤ The amount of repeated material results in less than a page of music to learn. Mark the form in your music:

A	mm. 1-8
A	mm. 9-16
A1	mm. 17-24
Bridge	mm. 25-30
A	mm. 31-38
Coda	mm. 38 to end

➤ The harmonic vocabulary of this piece includes major, minor, dominant seventh, and diminished seventh chords. Have the student listen for the distinctive colors of those harmonies, and label them in the score.

➤ Before home practice begins, help the student explore ways to produce the biggest tone that is not harsh. The components are speed of key and a relaxed arm. It is helpful to think "in" rather than "down" when playing the chords.

Practice Suggestions

➤ On a flat surface (closed keyboard cover) and with the fingers clustered together, practice a quick "throw-lift" of the hand and wrist. The "throw" initiates the movement; the "lift" is a relaxed reaction in the wrist. There will be two sounds for one gesture.

➤ Practice the dotted figures on a flat surface, using this "throw-lift" gesture.

➤ For security with shifts, practice moving quickly from one position to the next, silently covering each new chord before playing. Maintain a tension-free arm and elbow. Think "play-shift-relax, play-shift-relax."

CREATIVE ACTIVITY

Start a composition with the chords D minor, C major, B flat major, A major. Play loud octaves in both hands on the root of the chord, low on the keyboard. Holding the octave in the pedal, answer with full, two-handed octave chords in the treble. You're on your way! Continue the idea until you have a composition entitled *Warrior's Song*.

STUDY MODULE 4

Page	List	Composer	Title	Key, Meter and Tempo
R4 SW4	A	Johann Sebastian Bach	*Little Prelude in E Minor, BWV 938*	E Major $\frac{3}{8}$ ♪ = 138
R28 SW32	B	Ludwig van Beethoven	*Sonata in G Major, op. 49, no. 2 (First Movement)*	G Major ¢ Allegro ma non troppo
R54 SW65	C	Vasili Sergeievich Kalinnikov	*Chanson triste / A Sad Song*	G Minor $\frac{5}{4}$ Andante
R69 SW89	D	Larysa Kuzmenko	*Mysterious Summer's Night*	F Minor $\frac{4}{4}$ Andante
R70 SW92	D	Oscar Peterson	*The Gentle Waltz*	C Major $\frac{3}{4}$ Almost hesitant
S8		Jenö Takács	*Toccatina, op. 95, no. 12*	Bitonal $\frac{2}{2}$ Molto vivace
S24		Samuel Dolin	*Little Toccata*	A Minor $\frac{2}{2}$ Allegro

Assign first:

Little Prelude in E Minor . . . .
Sonata in G Major
Chanson triste . . . .
The Gentle Waltz . . . .

Assign next when ready:

Little Toccata

Mysterious Summer's Night
Toccatina

Musicians often speak of texture, making reference to the number of voices in a section, the thickness of chords, the formation of the accompaniment, etc. Study Module 4 provides study materials for a discussion of texture. Where (and why) is the texture thin? thick? In what pieces does the composer change the texture? What is the effect?

Johann Sebastian Bach
Little Prelude in E Minor, BWV 938 (R4, SW4)
Background Information

The *Little Preludes* were written by Bach for the instruction of his son Wilhelm Friedemann and other students. According to Johann Forkel, Bach's earliest biographer, these instructional pieces were written to drill the various ornaments and to provide examples of different musical styles. *Little Prelude in E Minor* is clearly a dance, closely resembling the quick-paced *passepied.*

Exploring the Score

➤ Bach was a masterful composer of independent voices. The use of rhythm in this prelude helps the voices remain independent. Can you find any measures in which both hands have the *same* rhythm? How does the melodic movement help maintain independence?

➤ Articulation can also foster independence of voices. The eighth notes of this piece help create the feeling of a lively dance and can be detached.

➤ Find eighth notes that move by step. [mm. 9-11, etc.; mm. 33-38] In Baroque pieces, these are usually played *legato*. Listen to the *Celebration Series*® recording for ideas on eighth-note articulations.

➤ How many different sixteenth-note figures do you find? (Bach usually limits the material used in a given piece. This prelude has unusual variety.)

➤ Name the keys of the main cadences. [m. 20 = B; m. 32 = A minor; m. 48 = E minor] How are these keys related to the key of the piece? [V, iv, i]

➤ Find examples of pattern and sequences, e.g., mm. 5-8, mm.13-16.

Practice Suggestions

➤ Practice in four-measure groups, hands separately, to establish fingering, articulation, correct realization of ornaments (see footnotes in the score).

➤ Practice slowly to ensure accuracy in this initial experience with the piece.

➤ Use a firm touch and loud dynamic level to facilitate the development of strong muscle memory.

➤ Notice and label chord outlines, scale fragments, and "hidden" bass lines (e.g., mm. 10-18) to enhance the intellectual, aural, and visual components of memorizing.

Ludwig van Beethoven
Sonata in G Major, op. 49, no. 2
(First Movement) (R28, SW32)
Background Information

The two op. 49 piano sonatas count among Beethoven's early works, dating from the mid-1790s. Unlike other Beethoven sonatas, this work appeared in print without dynamic markings. Speculation exists that a family member may have taken the manuscript from Beethoven's apartment and published it without his consent. Although the sonata may not have been completely finished, there is no question about its authenticity.

Exploring the Score

➤ The student can label the sections in the score. Find...

    Exposition [mm. 1-52]
        1st theme [mm. 1-14]
        bridge [mm.15-20]
        2nd theme [mm.21-35]
        closing theme [mm. 36-48]
        codetta [mm. 49-52]
    Development [mm. 53-66]
    Recapitulation [mm. 67-end]

➤ In the recapitulation, find and label the repetition of themes from the exposition.

➤ Many of Beethoven's sonatas have extended development sections. Compare the length of this development with the exposition and recapitulation. What elements from the exposition are used in this (short) development?

➤ Beethoven's accompaniments provide variety of texture, supporting the lyricism of a theme or increasing the intensity of the drama. Discuss the various accompaniment patterns and the effect they create.

➤ There are no sixteenth notes in this movement, yet there is rhythmic variety. Find duple subdivisions. Find triplet subdivisions. Can you draw generalizations concerning the effect created by the duple eighths as opposed to the triplet eighths? [duples are used to create lyricism; triplets are used to create forward movement, drive, drama]

Practice Suggestions

To speed up the learning process, try learning the piece "backwards":

1) From the end of the movement, find the last musical idea and label it #1. [chords of mm. 121-122]
    – Determine the fingering.
    – Analyze the chords.
    – Tap and count.
    – Play three or more times accurately and slowly.

2) Find the next-to-last musical idea and label it #2.
[mm. 116-120]
– Determine the fingering.
– Analyze the harmonies.
– Check the rhythm (tap and count).
– Drill the RH fingering.
– Block the LH chords.
– Play three or more times accurately and slowly.
3) Mark the next practice unit as #3. [mm. 110-115]
Follow similar practice steps.
4) Continue moving toward the beginning of the
piece, phrase by phrase.

Vasili Sergeievich Kalinnikov
Chanson triste / A Sad Song (R54, SW65)
Exploring the Score

The beauty of Kalinnikov's *Chanson triste* is created
through the combination of unusual meter, minor
key, and "sighing" melody.
➢ In $\frac{5}{4}$ one hears the meter as either 3 + 2 or 2 + 3.
Explore Kalinnikov's construction of the five beats.
[The LH provides unmistakable clues.]
➢ Make a list of the contrasts between the B section
[m. 9] and the A section. [key, range, phrase
structure]
➢ Kalinnikov frequently writes grace note figures.
Why? [to emphasize special notes and beats]
These grace notes are played before the beat.

Practice Suggestions

➢ Kalinnikov is generous with the dynamic
indications. Make dynamics an important part of
the practice plan.
➢ The pedaling has been marked with great care.
Follow the indications in order to achieve the
intended sound.
➢ Aim for a subtle flexibility in the melodic line,
remembering that this piece imitates song.
Breathe between phrases, and add touches of
rubato where appropriate.

CREATIVE ACTIVITY

Create your own Sad Song. Select a minor key, and
create a melodic shape that descends. Give your
piece a descriptive title.

Title: _____

Larysa Kuzmenko
Mysterious Summer's Night (R69, SW89)

Listen to the *Celebration Series®* recordings of
Mysterious Summer's Night and John Field's *Nocturne
in B flat Major,* another "night piece" discussed in the
next module. What similarities do you find in these
two expressions of a night mood? What is different
about the pieces?

Exploring the Score

A quick perusal of the score, especially the LH
accompaniment, reveals the ABA form.
➢ Find and label the ABA form. [A mm. 1-8;
B mm. 9-16; A1 mm. 17-24]
➢ What differences do you find between the two A
sections? [different keys] The piece starts in the
key of _____ [A minor] and ends in the key of
_____ [F minor]. Make special note of that,
because it is rare that a piece would begin and
end in different keys.
➢ Observe where Kuzmenko places the longer
values in the RH. How does the mood change
when the main notes occur on beat one (B
section) as opposed to beat three (A section)?
[The A section phrases seem to hover in the air, as
if asking a question. The B section phrases make a
bold statement.]
➢ Discuss phrase construction. Where are the short
one-measure phrases? [A section] Where do you
find longer four-measure phrases? [B section]

Practice Suggestions

➢ Pieces with frequent use of accidentals can be
difficult to read. You will learn this piece quickly if
you practice the challenging measures individually
or in pairs. For learning efficiency, each practice
unit should be repeated three to five times.
➢ The dynamic plan of each phrase, long or short, is
crucial to the successful interpretation of this
piece. Practice the RH for beautiful *legato* (follow
the fingerings) and listen carefully for the dynamic
plan of each phrase.
➢ The composer suggests *con pedale,* yet marks only
one pedal, at the very end of the piece. Listen
carefully for harmonic changes. They are your
pedal indications.

CREATIVE ACTIVITY

After hearing both pieces by Kuzmenko and Field,
you have models for a night mood. Decide on a key
that is especially dark and moody. Find a LH
accompaniment that evokes quiet and peace. Let
your ear guide your hand as you improvise a melody.

Your title:_____

Oscar Peterson
The Gentle Waltz (R70, SW92)
Background Information

A native of Montreal, Oscar Peterson is one of the foremost jazz pianists. His *The Gentle Waltz* serves as an exploration into jazz harmonies, which use added tones called extensions. (9ths, 11ths, and 13ths)

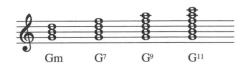

When properly voiced, one or more notes will be omitted from an extended chord. For example, the 3rd is ordinarily omitted from a dominant eleventh chord to avoid the dissonance created by the 11th.

Chord extensions can be chromatically altered: 9ths can be raised or lowered, 11ths can be raised, and 13ths can be lowered. Chord symbols will also be affected. This piece contains many minor seventh chords with a lowered 5th, and many dominant seventh chords with both diatonic and lowered 9ths.

Exploring the Score

➤ The chords give this piece its unique jazz flavor. When a minor seventh chord has a lowered 5th, the chord becomes a half-diminished seventh. Are all the seventh chords half-diminished in this piece? When 9ths are added to dominant seventh chords, are they altered?

➤ In many jazz "standards" (songs written by George Gershwin, Cole Porter, Jerome Kern and others) the formal structure is AABA, with each section being eight measures long. How does this waltz differ from this formal plan? [Each section is sixteen measures long, with a four-measure bridge at m. 29]

➤ In what ways does the B section contrast the A section? [rhythm changes, LH has melodic interest]

➤ Here is a typical jazz waltz rhythm:

♪♩ ♪♩

➤ What rhythms does Peterson use in this waltz?

Practice Suggestions

➤ To gain an understanding of the melodic contour, play the low bass note of each measure with the quarter and half notes of the melody. (Omit the sixteenth notes and inner harmonies.)

➤ Isolate the different rhythmic patterns for security. Watch the syncopations in mm. 18, 20, 26-28.

➤ Practice measure by measure, projecting the RH longer melodic tones, and adding the inner harmonies very quietly. Work on the balance. Notice how frequently Peterson assists in the control of the sound by allowing the melodic tone to speak first, and then adding the colorful harmonies.

➤ Start the sixteenth notes quietly, as they are filler tones linking one melody note to the next.

Jenö Takács
Toccatina, op. 95, no. 12 (S8)
Background Information

Jenö Takács is a Hungarian composer who has enjoyed a truly international career, teaching in Egypt, the Philippines, Switzerland, and in the United States at the University of Cincinnati. This study is typical of Takács' use of 20th-century compositional techniques.

Exploring the Score

➤ The RH and LH have different key signatures at the beginning of the piece. What effect does this create?

➤ Circle the places where the LH plays white keys.

➤ Make a list of the different figures Takács writes in the piece: alternating hands, four-note groups, four sixteenths with LH playing the beat note, RH sixteenths; LH quarters.

➤ These figures reveal the form of the piece. Mark the form with A, B, C, etc. Are any sections repeated?

    A = mm. 1-16
    B = mm. 17-26
    C = mm. 27-35
    D = mm. 36-end

➤ The A section is marked *senza pedale*. Note Takács' use of the pedal in other sections.

Practice Suggestions

➤ Each figure is its own technical challenge. Create two or three different ways to practice each figure.

➤ You may find it helpful to include practicing on a flat surface (e.g., the closed keyboard cover). Practice for the evenness of alternating hands (A section) and four-note groups (B and C sections). Listen carefully for perfect rhythm as your finger tips touch the wood surface.

➤ For quicker security with notes and fingering, block the various figures hands separately, then together. Observe how the hands and fingers move from one group of notes to the next.

Samuel Dolin

Little Toccata (S24)

Background Information

The title toccata has been used in keyboard composition since the early Baroque period. A toccata exploits fast finger work and often has little melodic interest. A Baroque toccata has contrasting sections; some contain highly florid figuration, while others are slow, fugal sections. Toccatas of the 19th and 20th centuries focus on speed and virtuosic skill.

Exploring the Score

➤ This piece has a perpetual motion of eighth notes. Can you find any measure that is not filled with eight eighth notes?

➤ Compare the RH and LH parts. Which hand has more rhythmic and melodic interest? [LH] When does the LH play repeated notes? [mm. 21-31]. When do the hands "share" the texture? [mm. 13-16, 50-53]

Practice Suggestions

➤ Divide the piece into practice sections based on changes in figuration. (Some sections will be very short!) Practice similar measures together (e.g., mm. 2, 4, 5, 17, 19).

➤ Become comfortable with the fingerings of repeated notes. Compare m. 1 with m. 13. Give mm. 32-36 special attention.

➤ Pay special attention to passages in which the hands have different articulations. Practice very slowly, exaggerating the different touches.

STUDY MODULE 5

Page	List	Composer	Title	Key, Meter and Tempo
R32 SW35	B	Ludwig van Beethoven	*Sonata in G Major, op. 49, no. 2 (Second Movement)*	G Major $\frac{3}{4}$ Tempo di Menuetto
R42 SW45	C	Edvard Grieg	*Puck, op. 71, no. 3*	E flat Minor ¢ Allegro molto
R48 SW55	C	Bedřich Smetana	*Song, op. 2, no. 2*	A Minor $\frac{2}{4}$ Moderato
R51 SW61	C	John Field	*Nocturne No. 5 in B flat Major, H 37*	B flat Major $\frac{2}{8}$ Andante cantabile
R68 SW66	D	Claude Debussy	*Page d'album / Album Leaf*	F Major $\frac{3}{4}$ Modéré
S6		George Frideric Handel	*Capriccio, HWV 483*	G Minor C $\quad$ ♩ = 76
S16		Johann Friedrich Burgmüller	*The Gypsies, op. 109, no. 4*	C Minor C Allegro non troppo

Assign first:

Capriccio
Sonata in G Major . . . .
Puck . . . .
Nocturne No. 5 in B flat Major . . . .

Assign next when ready:

Song
The Gypsies
Page d'album / Album Leaf

At the beginning of this level, the student was encouraged to record favorite pieces from each Study Module. Review those choices of repertoire with the student. If the selected repertoire has not included a wide variety of styles, this would be an opportunity to round out the stylistic scope of the recordings.

Ludwig van Beethoven
Sonata in G Major, **op. 49, no. 2**
(Second Movement) (R32, SW35)

Exploring the Score

In this sonata movement, Beethoven makes reference to the minuet, through both tempo and the dance-like dotted rhythm. When writing a minuet or scherzo, however, he normally used binary form. This rather lengthy movement has no double bars, and leaves the issue of form open for exploration.

➤ This movement has the formal features of a rondo. Label the sections.

A	mm. 1-20
B	mm. 21-47
A	mm. 48-67
C	mm. 68-87
A	mm. 87-107
coda	mm. 108-120

➤ Discuss the contrasting mood and musical features of each section.
➤ The first eight measures of the theme use only tonic and dominant harmonies. Help the student analyze these harmonies and determine if the tonic measures are more intense or less intense than the dominant measures. [less intense]

Practice Suggestions

➤ Be precise with the rhythm of the dotted figure. Never allow the sixteenth to sound like part of a triplet. Playing the rhythm accurately will create the proper dance effect.
➤ In the A section, the LH sound is easily learned by omitting the thumb and playing only beat notes. Emphasize the blocked 3rds and play the bass note with a light touch. When you add the LH thumb, play it with special lightness, as it is the least important part of the accompaniment texture.
➤ The hands must be perfectly coordinated in the sixteenths of mm. 28-34. Slow practice and careful listening are your best practice allies.
➤ In the C section, mm. 68-71 imitate wind instruments. Let your "winds" play with bold detachment. Answer the winds with contrasting *legato* "string" sounds in mm. 72-75.

Edvard Grieg
Puck, **op. 71, no. 3** (R42, SW45)

Background Information

Puck, inspired by the Shakespeare character from *A Midsummer Night's Dream,* is one of Grieg's most famous *Lyric Pieces.* As one might imagine, the mood is whimsical and mischievous. (For additional background information on Grieg and the *Lyric Pieces,* see the discussion of *Little Bird* in Module 2.)

Exploring the Score

➤ How does Grieg achieve a whimsical, mischievous character? What role do tempo, articulation, dynamics, and chord quality (major, minor, diminished) play in establishing character?
➤ Grieg organizes the entire piece around two ideas:

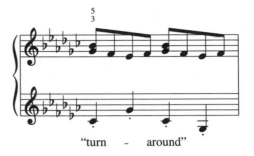

"turn - around"

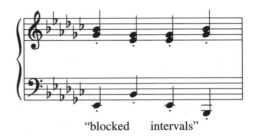

"blocked intervals"

Look for those two motives as you explore the score.

➤ Many 19th-century character pieces were written in ABA form. This piece has the look of ABA. As you label the sections of the piece, consider the following chart:

A	=	mm. 1-20
B1	=	mm. 21-36
B2	=	mm. 37-48
transition	=	mm. 49-61
A1	=	mm. 62-end

➤ Notice the repeat mark written before m. 21. With that repeat, the B section receives additional emphasis.
➤ Explore the way Grieg builds tension from m. 21 to m. 36. Other than the *crescendo,* what devices does he use? [ascending chord sequences, phrases are shortened]
➤ The home tonality is E flat minor. Can you find places where Grieg exclusively uses major chords? Diminished chords?
➤ Chromatic movement tends to blur the sense of a tonal center. Notice the half-step relationship between the end of the B section (mm. 47-48, E major) and the return of the A section (m. 62, E flat minor). Can you find other chromatic relationships? [B to B flat, in mm. 48-53; chromatic scale leading to the return of the A section in mm. 53-62]

Practice Suggestions

Blocking the chords of the A section is a quick way to gain control over the shifts of position.

➤ Block the first two RH chords (E flat minor and F major). Notice the half-step movement:

➤ Block the next two chords (A flat minor and B flat major). Can you find half steps between the chords?

➤ Block hands together mm. 11-14. Name the chords. Find the relationships between chords.

➤ The middle section (mm. 21-36) is dominated by the color of the diminished 7th (a chord made of minor 3rds). The passage is much easier than it looks, because the top tone is the only voice that moves.

➤ Practice the downbeat chords of mm. 23, 27, 29, 31, 33, 34, 35, 36. These are the crucial position shifts.

➤ Practice each chord sequence, holding the repeated tones as tied notes. Be aware of the top-note fingerings.

➤ Much of the mischievous character of this piece is portrayed through dynamics. Capitalize on Grieg's sudden dynamic contrasts.

➤ This piece knows no lazy *staccatos*. Practice for the shortest sound.

Bedřich Smetana
Song, op. 2, no. 2 (R48, SW55)
Background Information

Smetana was the first great nationalist composer of Czechoslovakia (now the Czech Republic). He was active as a teacher, composer, and conductor. His piano compositions focus on Czech and Bohemian dances and scenes of nature inspired by the landscape of his homeland.

Exploring the Score

➤ *Song, op. 2, no. 2* has characteristics typical of many Romantic piano works. The primary feature is a flowing melody supported by a strong bass line. (Note the double stemming of the bass.) Filling out the texture are sixteenth-note broken chords that complete the harmonies. Does this basic texture remain constant throughout the piece?

➤ To discover the form of the piece, play the melody and the bass line. Note the symmetry of eight-measure phrases:

    A = mm. 1-8
    A1 = mm. 9-16
    B = mm. 17-24
    A2 = mm. 25-end

➤ Does the melody of the A section rise or fall? (Falling intervals are associated with sadness or sorrow.)

➤ Playing melody and bass in the B section also reveals its structure: each melodic phrase rises, while the bass descends a full octave scale.

➤ The return of the A section (m. 25) is marked *con tristezza* (with sadness). How is this section different from the opening? [soprano-alto duet]

➤ How does the performer on the *Celebration Series®* recording interpret *con tristezza*?

Practice Suggestions

➤ Play the melody with both hands an octave apart. Notice the consistent two-measure phrase construction. Exaggerate the dynamic inflection to the downbeat of each second measure.

➤ Each day, spend part of your practice playing just melody and bass. This polarity is an important characteristic of the sound.

➤ Try this practice technique to gain control over the balance:

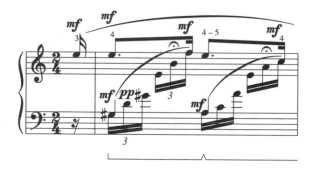

John Field
Nocturne No. 5 in B flat Major, H 37 (R51, SW61)
Background Information

Although Chopin is the most famous composer of *nocturnes*, the first piano pieces with this title were written by the Irish composer John Field. Notice the similarity of LH accompaniment figure in this nocturne to the accompaniments in many Chopin nocturnes, especially his first, op. 9, no. 1.

Exploring the Score

➤ Look for textural contrasts and repeated material. Your student will quickly identify mm. 18-21 and mm. 38-43 as contrasts to the prevailing texture, and the return of the opening theme in m. 23. These are crucial elements in the form.

➤ Finding the restatement of the A theme in m. 9 puts the formal puzzle together.

A = mm. 1-17
Closing material = mm. 18-22
A1 = mm. 23-37
Closing material = mm. 38-43

➤ In what ways does Field change the A section when it reappears in m. 23?

➤ Listen to some examples of *coloratura* singing—the style found in the works of Bellini, Donizetti, Rossini—to help the student understand the effect of improvised elaboration found in the return of the main theme, especially mm. 24 and 28.

Practice Suggestions

On a piano, the tone fades after the hammer strikes the string. When one plays melodies with long note values, it is important to match the dynamic level of a new tone to the faded level of the previous note. Try this exercise:

➤ Play a five-finger pattern of whole notes, starting *forte*. Each new note is to match the faded dynamic level of the previous tone. Listen carefully.

The following example shows dynamic levels for the RH notes in mm. 1-2:

➤ Practice each RH phrase without pedal. Listen for dynamic shading and *legato* sound.

➤ In each phrase, identify the focus and the softest tone.

➤ Add the LH and the damper pedal.

➤ Practice mm. 42-43 hands separately until the fingerings are secure.

➤ Mathematically speaking, only the first of the small notes in m. 28 plays directly with the LH. An artistic performance of these notes would play the rising intervals a bit slower than the falling tones. You may think of the groupings of the small notes as 2 + 3 + 3.

Claude Debussy
Page d'album / Album Leaf (R68, SW86)

Background Information

Debussy's musical style emphasizes color and atmosphere. The composer wrote this brief, elegant waltz in 1915 and later presented it at a wartime benefit concert in 1917. Published in 1933, it is a simple but effective representation of Debussy's highly original approach to composition.

Exploring the Score

➤ The harmonic language of this short piece exemplifies Debussy's style. Find examples of the following:
  - seventh and ninth chord sonorities
  - pedal points
  - subtle chromatic shifts between chords

➤ Discuss ways in which Debussy clearly creates a waltz effect [LH mm. 8-13; 21-30] and where he disguises the $\frac{3}{4}$ meter [RH mm. 7-8; LH mm. 19-20].

➤ What was Debussy's favorite interval when writing this piece? [falling 3rds prevail]

➤ Have your student look up the French terms in a dictionary and write the translations on the score.

Practice Suggestions

➤ Each hand has its challenges in this piece. Before practicing hands together, you should master the following:

➤ LH ease with fingerings and shifts. Of special challenge are mm. 1-13 and mm. 19-20.

➤ LH two-note slurs. The second note is noticeably quieter than the first.

➤ LH and pedal. The low tones are your signal for a pedal change.

➤ RH mm. 23-30: The alto is the melody. To establish a model for that sound, you may wish to play the alto with the LH and the upper tones with the RH. Bring out that alto melody. Then create that same sound playing the RH as written.

George Frideric Handel
Capriccio, HWV 483 (S6)

Exploring the Score

➤ How many different figures does Handel use in this piece?
  - broken octave chords (x)
  - descending scales (y)
  - zigzag patterns (z)

Label the x, y, and z figures in the score.

➤ In much of the piece, the hands play opposing figures. Can you find places where both hands play the same figure?

Practice Suggestions

➤ The zigzag (z) patterns are challenging. Which hand has (nearly) exclusive use of the zigzag patterns? Begin by practicing only those patterns. Be especially observant of and consistent with the fingerings.

➤ The RH zigzag patterns are always accompanied by a broken chord in the LH. Practice these passages hands together, slowly and carefully.

➤ Play the descending scales (y) next. Analyze the finger groupings. On your score, bracket the groups. Above the bracket, write the number of fingers in each group. Here are some examples:

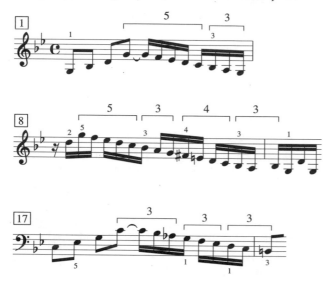

➤ Now you are ready to practice short sections, hands together.

Johann Friedrich Burgmüller
The Gypsies, op. 109, no. 4 (S16)
Exploring the Score

➤ After listening to a recording of this piece, discuss which musical elements Burgmüller uses to create the flavor of gypsy music and personality. [sudden and extreme changes of dynamics, strong rhythmic pulse, off-beat accents]

➤ What are the musical and technical issues in this piece that place it in *Piano Studies/Etudes 8*? [note the great variety of figures, especially on the second page]

➤ Make a list of the contrasts found in *The Gypsies.* Did your list include contrast of keys?

Practice Suggestions

➤ Practice the opening *staccato* chords slowly. Learn correct fingerings from the first day of practice. At a slow tempo, you should be able to cover each new position before playing.

➤ Isolate for special practice the measures in which the hands have different articulations, e.g., mm. 7-8, 22, 38-40.

➤ The rhythm poses no special challenge. However, the off-beat accents may need attention. Note the many accents on beats 2 and 3. (Can you find *any* accents on downbeats?)

STUDY MODULE 6

Page	List	Composer	Title	Key, Meter and Tempo
R6 SW7	A	Johann Sebastian Bach	*Little Prelude in D Major, BWV 936*	D Major $\frac{2}{4}$ ♩ = 60
R36 SW38	B	Friedrich Kuhlau	*Sonata in A Major, op. 59, no. 1 (First Movement)*	A Major **c** Allegro
R46 SW51	C	Felix Mendelssohn	*Andante sostenuto, op. 72, no. 2*	E flat Major $\frac{2}{4}$ Andante sostenuto
R60 SW75	D	Alexina Louie	*O Moon*	Atonal, free Senza misura
S11		Mario Tarenghi	*Dance of the Marionettes*	A Minor $\frac{2}{4}$ Allegretto sostenuto
S18		Stella Goud	*Spider on the Ceiling*	Chromatic $\frac{8}{8}$ With fearful apprehension
S28		Pál Kadosa	*Allegro, op. 23/f, no. 5*	C Major $\frac{2}{4}$ Allegro

STUDY MODULE 6

Assign first:	Assign next when ready:
Little Prelude in D Major	*Dance of the Marionettes*
Sonata in A Major	
Andante sostenuto	*O Moon*
Spider on the Ceiling	*Allegro*

Study Module 6 provides an opportunity for teacher and student to review style period characteristics. Have the student develop a chart to record personal impressions and points made in discussions pertaining to the style periods. How is Bach's *Little Prelude* typical of the Baroque period? What Romantic period characteristics are found in the Mendelssohn piece? Kadosa, Goud, and Louie wrote in the last half of the 20th century. How do their pieces represent recent trends in composition?

Johann Sebastian Bach
Little Prelude in D Major, BWV 936 (R6, SW7)
Background Information

As was mentioned in Study Module 4, Bach wrote the *Little Preludes* for student instruction. Through its unusual texture, this prelude acquaints students with the style and sound of a trio sonata, a popular chamber music form in the Baroque era. Trio sonatas featured two solo instruments plus an accompaniment. The accompaniment, known as the *continuo,* was played by two performers. The bass line was played on a cello or other bass instrument, while the harmonies were "realized" by a keyboard player on an instrument such as a harpsichord or organ. This explains why a *trio* sonata was played by *four* performers!

Exploring the Score

➤ Look through the score for the trio sonata texture. The two melodic lines played by the RH in the opening represent the two soloists. The LH consistently plays the accompanying bass line. One can well imagine a cello playing the LH part, with a separate bow stroke for each note.

➤ The two RH voices are clearly notated except when there is a single line of sixteenth notes. When the RH plays steady sixteenth notes, one can imagine the lower tones being played by one instrument, with the second instrument answering in the upper tones.

➤ This prelude is in binary (two-part) form. What is the key at the double bar? [A major – dominant] Baroque binary structure required a modulation to the dominant.

Practice Suggestions

➤ For "ear education," practice the RH part divided between the hands, observing carefully the lengths of longer tones. This sound must be reproduced eventually by one hand.

➤ Articulation plays an important role in both hands.
  – The "cello" LH will be lightly detached throughout.
  – The RH syncopated notes are preceded by a slight break.
  – The RH "sigh" motives (downbeats of mm. 3-7) are preceded by a slight break.

➤ The trio sonata effect will be clear if steady sixteenth-note passages are slurred in groups of low notes and high notes.

CREATIVE ACTIVITY

Experiment with your own trio sonata texture. Create an ostinato (your cello) in the LH, such as C-B-A-G.

Play a RH melody in quarter notes and half notes. Create an alto duet with an independent rhythm.

Friedrich Kuhlau
Sonata in A Major, op. 59, no. 1 (First Movement)
(R36, SW38)
Exploring the Score

A great experience with Classical literature awaits the student who studies this movement. The music is filled with variety, wide keyboard range, figures that fit the hand well, and colorful changes of tonal center.

➤ Creating musical variety and contrast was at the heart of Classical period composition. Discuss the ways in which Kuhlau creates variety in both melody and accompaniment in this movement.

➤ Find the main formal outline of the movement.
> Exposition [mm. 1-36]
> Development [mm. 37-66]
> Recapitulation [mm. 67-90]

➤ Often in Classical sonatas, the recapitulation is longer than the exposition. Compare these two parts to determine how Kuhlau *shortens* this recapitulation. You may have found:

Exposition		Recapitulation	
1st theme	mm. 1-8	1st theme	mm. 67-73
bridge	mm. 9-20	bridge	mm. 73-76
2nd theme	mm. 21-28	2nd theme	mm. 77-84
closing theme	mm. 28-30	closing theme	mm. 84-90

➤ One of the biggest surprises in this movement is the change of key at the beginning of the development. From the harmony of m. 36 (E7), we expect to hear A major in m. 37. The F major is most surprising. Kuhlau's trick was to start the melody of the RH in m. 37 on A, the common tone between F major and A major.

➤ As you study the development, identify the source of each theme and figure.

➤ Do a "dynamic search." Which themes are to be played loudly? quietly?

➤ Compare the endings of the exposition and recapitulation for dynamic contrast.

Practice Suggestions

➤ Each theme, each phrase, has its own special expression created through dynamics, articulation, and relationship of RH to LH. From the beginning, work on one phrase at a time and focus your practice on its unique sound and character.

➤ This movement can achieve great effect if dynamic nuance is convincingly projected.

➤ Create your own exercises based on mm. 13 and 47.

➤ Exaggerate the *diminuendo* of the opening "sigh" in m. 1. The second note should be barely audible. Can you find other places to use the same approach?

Felix Mendelssohn
Andante sostenuto, op. 72, no. 2 (R46, SW51)
Exploring the Score

Much of Mendelssohn's music exemplifies the nineteenth-century love affair with melody. This piece can be considered a solo piano setting of a song.

➤ Play the melody with the student and discuss the phrase structure. In the beginning one hears a "question-answer" pairing of phrases. Where are phrases repeated? Do you find examples of sequences?

➤ Can the student find repeated sections, or is the form of the piece "through-composed"?

➤ Mendelssohn starts the piece with an introduction. What harmonies are used to establish the key of E flat major in mm. 1-4? Is there a closing section to balance the introduction?

Practice Suggestions

➤ From the first day of practice, give careful attention to Mendelssohn's phrasing and articulation markings. The dynamic nuance of short slurred groups is especially important.

➤ The LH plays an important role. Find the LH "duet" to the RH melody in mm. 5-14. Practice the duet, leaving out the "filler" sixteenth notes.

➤ In other sections of the piece, practice bringing out the low bass tone to define the harmonies and support the texture.

Alexina Louie
O Moon (R60, SW75)
Background Information

Alexina Louie enjoys a successful composing career, having written major works for most of Canada's leading performers, ensembles, and orchestras. Her unique musical style is an expressive blend of east and west. Louie's imaginative piano works are very atmospheric and often feature improvisatory passages and colorful bell-like sonorities.

Exploring the Score

We seldom have experiences in music when time is suspended: no pulse and no forward movement.

➤ Why might a piece with this title be given the tempo indication *senza misura?* (without measure, without strict time). [gravity has disappeared; everything floats]

➤ Discuss the time relationships in *O Moon.* Notice the indications at the end of each line; these serve as a pacing guide for performing the first page.

➤ Even in the measured section of the piece notice the many markings that continue to prevent us from feeling a steady beat.

➤ Find the following "building blocks" from which the composer creates the sonority.
  – series of major chords
  – quartal chords (chords made of 4ths)
  – accumulations of whole steps
  – chords made of black keys
  – chords made of white keys

Practice Suggestions

➤ Practice each of the sonorities found in the series listed above. Then "assemble" the piece and enjoy the experience of creating a world without gravity.

CREATIVE ACTIVITY

With this piece, you are learning about quartal harmonies. Their sound can be bold and strident, or, as in *O Moon,* they can be filled with mystery and wonder. They can be played blocked or arpeggiated. As you experiment with quartal harmonies, decide on a mood you wish to create. You may wish to use the chords with well-defined rhythm, or create a floating, unmetered sound.

Your title:_____

Mario Tarenghi
Dance of the Marionettes (S11)
Exploring the Score

The explicit instruction *senza espressione* is almost never indicated in a piece of music. Ordinarily, we do just the opposite, trying to invest our performances with great expression.

➤ Discuss why the composer would request no expression.
➤ How does Tarenghi achieve a mechanical effect in the music? [repeated notes, *staccatos,* no pedal, accents]
➤ Can you give a label to the form?
    A = mm. 1-34
    B = mm. 35-62
    A1 = mm. 63-82
    Coda = mm. 83-end
➤ What contrasts do you find in the B section? [imitative entrances of opening theme, colorful harmonies, sixteenth-note broken chords, pedal]

Practice Suggestions

➤ Practice m. 1 until the desired amount of accent is achieved. Slur the downbeat eighth note into the *staccato* notes. Avoid stretching to reach finger 5; let the elbow move the LH hand in and out of position quickly.
➤ Emphasize the RH accented notes.

➤ Mm. 36-52 are most easily learned if you name the harmonies. Write the names of the chords in the score. Block the harmonies as you name them. The fingerings are, of course, very important.

Stella Goud
Spider on the Ceiling (S18)
Exploring the Score

The expression marking "*With fearful apprehension*" and the dramatic ending of the piece indicate that there is a "program" to the piece.

➤ Develop a story line for the piece. You might start with the final two lines. What is crawling higher and higher and comes crashing to the floor? How would you describe the first page? Notice that the LH of mm. 3-6 is compressed into two measures at mm. 11-12. Why?

Practice Suggestions

➤ The RH repeats the same figure until the final descending chromatic line. An efficient fingering is most important. Practice hands separately until you are confident with this line.
➤ Practice the LH melody concentrating on articulation, dynamics, and portraying your musical story.
➤ Practice the final chromatic scale hands separately. What is your fingering plan? Then practice hands together. Start with a few notes at first, then gradually add on until the entire scale is mastered.
➤ The composer has indicated half pedal throughout. Find a pedal depth that creates a mysterious ringing sound. "Ride" the pedal and flutter it when necessary to prevent a muddy build-up of sound.

Pál Kadosa
Allegro, op. 23/f, no. 5 (S28)
Exploring the Score

➤ A quick look at the first line reveals much about this piece:
    – the piece is a virtual *staccato* étude
    – the basic technical gesture in each hand consists of repeated tones against stepwise motion
    – the rhythm is primarily eighth notes and quarter notes
➤ Find the places where eighth notes move in 3rds against the repeated notes, as in m. 7
➤ There is a different key in each hand in mm. 16-22. Mark in the score the different keys or patterns represented.

Practice Suggestions

➤ To achieve control over the prevailing figure, practice the moving notes *legato* without the repeated tones.

➤ Add the repeated tones and play them very *staccato.* The moving tones are to be played with a contrasting *legato.* Play slowly!

➤ When you practice all tones *staccato,* give a slight arm impulse to each downbeat. Play with a relaxed arm.

Level 8 SUMMARY

To the Student:

Level 8 is rich in musical experience. As you close the covers on these books, reserve time for reflection.

➤ In what ways have you grown musically?

➤ In what areas have you improved technically?

➤ What do you know now about the style periods that you did not know as you entered this level?

➤ List one or two pieces from each style period that were favorites.

➤ How many Level 8 pieces did you memorize?

If you have recorded pieces from each Study Module, now is the time to sit back, listen, and celebrate!

Celebration Series® Handbook for Teachers

Level 9

The Publications
Level 9 of the *Celebration Series®* includes the following publications:
Piano Repertoire 9
Piano Studies/Etudes 9
Recording of Repertoire and *Studies/Etudes 9*

The Repertoire
Piano Repertoire 9 is divided into four lists:
➤ List A includes a selection of pieces composed during the Baroque period (*ca* 1600 to *ca* 1750).
➤ List B pieces are from the Classical period (*ca* 1750 to *ca* 1820).
➤ List C includes a selection of pieces composed during the Romantic era (*ca* 1820 to *ca* 1910).
➤ List D pieces were composed during the late 19th century and the 20th century.

Musical Development
In Level 9, the student's musical horizons are expanded. This level includes two *Sinfonias* by J.S. Bach and sonata movements by C.P.E. Bach, Haydn, Mozart, and Beethoven. Romantic repertoire includes two works by Chopin (a waltz and a mazurka) and character pieces by Mendelssohn and Grieg, among others. The 20th century is represented by works of Claude Debussy, Joaquín Turina, Dmitri Kabalevsky, Alexina Louie, Clermont Pépin, Gabriel Grovlez, Ewart Bartley, Rodion Konstantinovich Shchedrin, Octavio Pinto, Harold Arlen, and Jean Sibelius. Even a casual perusal of the Level 9 *Repertoire* and *Studies/Etudes 9* indicates that this is difficult music representing considerable musical accomplishment by the student. There are new challenges for the hand (facility and control), the ear (hearing three simultaneous parts, delicate balances, subtle articulations), and the mind (harmonies and form).

Preparation of the Student
The preceding levels of the *Celebration Series®* provide a gradual, thorough preparation for Level 9. Technical preparation has included:
- independence of hands
- balance of melody and accompaniment
- voicing within a hand
- scale and arpeggio figures
- figures with irregular changes of direction
- variety of chord shapes and blocked intervals, leaps, and accompaniment figures
- execution of ornaments

From the earliest levels of the *Celebration Series®*, students have been exposed to repertoire from four centuries, selected and edited to support a growing awareness of style. They have experienced:
- thin textures and independent lines of the Baroque era
- the homophonic style and balanced, shaped phrases of the Classical era
- the wider palette of Romantic harmony and expression
- challenges of stylistic variety, dissonance, and intense expression in 20th-century literature

Organization of Level 9
The preceding levels have been divided into Study Modules of increasing difficulty, integrating repertoire from the four major style periods with pieces from the *Piano Studies/Etudes* album. The discussion of Level 9 is not divided into Study Modules, but rather follows the four Lists of *Piano Repertoire 9* (A, B, C, and D). The pieces are discussed in the order in which they appear in the album.

For each list, there is a suggested order of difficulty, a brief discussion of general style characteristics, and a detailed consideration of each piece under the following headings:
- **Background Information:** stylistic or biographical information
- **Exploring the Score:** suggested material for student–teacher discussions
- **Practice Suggestions:** addressed to the student to assist in the beginning weeks of practice

Teachers can determine the order of repertoire assigned, based on the individual student's needs and program of study. Teachers are encouraged to formulate units of study, integrating pieces of contrasting style periods from the *Piano Repertoire* album and the *Piano Studies/Etudes* album.

The *Celebration Series®* does not include a student workbook for Level 9. It is our hope that the following discussions will facilitate your teaching of this repertoire, provide material for fruitful discussions between you and your students, and increase their musical enjoyment and awareness.

The Studies/Etudes
The studies are discussed separately at the end of this section. The pieces in the *Piano Studies/Etudes* album are similar in purpose to the Chopin *Etudes*. Although each piece has a specific technical focus, these studies have noteworthy musical value and can be considered as repertoire.

The Recordings

The *Celebration Series®* recording of all pieces in this Level is a valuable teaching resource. This professional recording provides a musical sound model, a pedagogical element that words cannot communicate. Listening to the recording with the student can stimulate discussion on topics such as articulation, balance and dynamics, expressive timing *(rubato)*, and pedaling. Listening to recordings should be a regular part of the student's assignment.

The following chart lists the repertoire and studies in Level 9 according to the order presented in *Piano Repertoire 9* and *Piano Studies/Etudes 9*. Page numbers for works in *Piano Repertoire 9* and *Piano Studies/Etudes 9* are found in the first column.

Piano Repertoire 9

Page	Composer	Title
List A – Baroque Repertoire		
R4	Johann Sebastian Bach	*Sinfonia No. 6 in E Major, BWV 792*
R6	Johann Sebastian Bach	*Sinfonia No. 11 in G Minor, BWV 797*
R8	Domenico Scarlatti	*Sonata in C Major, L 104, K 159*
R11	Domenico Scarlatti	*Sonata in D Minor, L 413, K 9*
R14	Domenico Scarlatti	*Sonata in D Major, L 463, K 430*
R17	Johann Sebastian Bach	*Prelude and Fugue in C Minor, BWV 847*
R22	Louis-Claude Daquin	*Le coucou (Rondeau)*
List B – Classical Repertoire		
R25	Carl Philipp Emanuel Bach	*Sonata in C Minor, Wq 48/4, H 27 (Third Movement)*
R28	Wolfgang Amadeus Mozart	*Fantasia in D Minor, K 397 (385g)*
R32	Wolfgang Amadeus Mozart	*Sonata in C Major, K 330 (300h) (Second Movement)*
R35	Franz Joseph Haydn	*Sonata in E Minor, Hob. XVI:34 (First Movement)*
R40	Franz Joseph Haydn	*Sonata in E Minor, Hob. XVI:34 (Second Movement)*
R43	Franz Joseph Haydn	*Sonata in E Minor, Hob. XVI:34 (Third Movement)*
R47	Ludwig van Beethoven	*Sonata in G Major, op. 79 (Presto alla tedesca)*
R52	Ludwig van Beethoven	*Rondo in C Major, op. 51, no. 1*
List C – Romantic Repertoire		
R60	Robert Schumann	*Herberge / The Wayside Inn, op. 82, no. 6*
R63	Franz Schubert	*Impromptu, op. 142, no. 2*
R67	Felix Mendelssohn	*Lost Happiness, op. 38, no. 2*
R70	Frédéric Chopin	*Waltz, op. posth. 70, no. 2*
R74	Frédéric Chopin	*Mazurka, op. posth. 67, no. 4*
R76	Johannes Brahms	*Intermezzo, op. 76, no. 7*
R78	Edvard Grieg	*Notturno, op. 54, no. 4*
R82	Pyotr Il'yich Tchaikovsky	*June (Barcarole), op. 37a, no. 6*
List D – Late Romantic and Impressionistic		
R87	Joaquín Turina	*Sacro-Monte, op. 55, no. 5*
R90	Claude Debussy	*La fille aux cheveux de lin*
R92	Gabriel Grovlez	*La sarabande*
R95	Jean Sibelius	*Romance, op. 24, no. 9*
R100	Octavio Pinto	*Salta, Salta*
R102	Dmitri Kabalevsky	*Variations in D Major, op. 40, no. 1*
R109	Ewart Bartley	*Dance No. 1*
R114	Alexina Louie	*Distant Memories*
R118	Rodion Konstantinovich Shchedrin	*Humoreske*
R122	Harold Arlen, arr. Shearing	*Over the Rainbow*
R124	Clermont Pépin	*Le nez / The Nose*

Piano Studies/Etudes 9

Page	Composer	Title
S4	Johann Baptist Cramer	*Study no. 1: Study in E Minor, op. 39, no. 2*
S6	Hermann Berens	*Study no. 2: Study in A Minor, op. 61, no. 13*
S8	Hermann Berens	*Study no. 3: Study in F Major, op. 61, no. 8*
S10	Carl Czerny	*Study no. 4: Study in C Major, op. 533, no. 1*
S12	Stephen Heller	*Study no. 5: Study in G Major, op. 47, no. 24*
S14	Felix Mendelssohn	*Study no. 6: Song without Words, op. 102, no. 3*
S16	Moritz Moszkowski	*Study no. 7: Study in E flat Major, op. 91, no. 6*
S18	Hermann Berens	*Study no. 8: Study in F Major, op. 61, no. 10*
S20	Niels Gade	*Study no. 9: Scherzo, op. 19, no. 2*
S22	Béla Bartók	*Study no. 10: Bagatelle, op. 6, no. 2*
S24	Jean-Baptiste Duvernoy	*Study no. 11: Study in C Major, op. 120, no. 10*
S26	George Frideric Handel	*Study no. 12: Suite No. 8 in F Minor (Allemande and Gigue), HWV 433*
S30	Moritz Moszkowski	*Study no. 13: Study in E Flat Major, op. 91, no. 17*

LIST A – BAROQUE REPERTOIRE
Suggested Order of Difficulty Repertoire

Page	Composer	Title
R22	Louis-Claude Daquin	*Le coucou (Rondeau)*
R17	Johann Sebastian Bach	*Prelude in C Minor, BWV 847*
R11	Domenico Scarlatti	*Sonata in D Minor, L 413, K 9*
R8	Domenico Scarlatti	*Sonata in C Major, L 104, K 159*
R4	Johann Sebastian Bach	*Sinfonia No. 6 in E Major, BWV 792*
R14	Domenico Scarlatti	*Sonata in D Major, L 463, K 430*
R6	Johann Sebastian Bach	*Sinfonia No. 11 in G Minor, BWV 797*
R20	Johann Sebastian Bach	*Fugue in C Minor, BWV 847*

These pieces, written by composers from Germany, France, and Italy, were written for the harpsichord. When you play them on a modern piano, your primary challenge is tonal clarity and rhythmic precision. For that reason, the pedal is rarely used.

Baroque works require special attention to touch and articulation. The artists heard on the *Celebration Series®* recording make effective use of detached and *staccato* articulations. A contrasting mixture of *legato* and detached touches is highly desirable. In general, use detached articulation:
- to articulate skips and leaps
- to imitate bass instruments (cello, bassoon, etc.)
- before emphasized notes such as syncopations, downbeats, and *appoggiaturas*
- for eighth notes when contrasted with sixteenth notes
- to highlight energetic and joyful moods

In addition, questions and challenges you may encounter with Baroque repertoire include:
➢ What is the character of the piece? Is it a dance, aria, orchestral or instrumental piece, or a programmatic piece?
➢ Identify the subject, countersubject, motive, or themes of the piece. Also, identify sections and label the form. Label the key, modulations, and cadences. In Baroque music, the arrival at a new key or tonal center is an important event that should be emphasized.
➢ Decide on the articulation for each theme or idea. Remember to plan different articulations for contrasting ideas. Consistency of articulation is important in the Baroque style.
➢ Isolate each different musical idea for special practice with emphasis on fingering, articulations, and phrasing.
➢ What is the best fingering for executing phrasing and articulation? Mark your fingering choices in the score.
➢ Identify sequences. Will you use sequential fingering?
➢ Examine phrase lengths. Are there patterns of short and long phrases?
➢ What is the dynamic plan? Will you use terraced dynamics? How will your dynamic plan emphasize the contrasting textures (e.g., echo effects, *solo* and *tutti* effects)?
➢ Where is the greatest harmonic and tonal tension in the piece?
➢ To hear contrapuntal lines, play each voice separately, combine pairs of voices, then play all voices together.
➢ Isolate ornaments and practice their realization before playing them in context.

The discussions below follow the order of appearance in *Piano Repertoire 9*, not order of difficulty.

Johann Sebastian Bach
Sinfonia No. 6 in E Major, BWV 792 (R4)
Background Information

In 1720, J.S. Bach began compiling an instructional notebook to use with his nine-year old son, Wilhelm Friedemann. The famous *Clavier-Büchlein* included ornament charts, short preludes, eleven of the preludes from Book I of *The Well-Tempered Clavier,* and the first versions of the works now known as the *Two- and Three-part Inventions.* Bach originally titled them "Praeambula" and "Fantasias." When he later revised the pieces and grouped them in a separate collection, they were renamed "Inventions" and "Sinfonias." The present-day tradition of referring to the Sinfonias as "Three-part Inventions" was initiated by Forkel, Bach's first biographer.

Exploring the Score

➢ Bach creates variety through his manipulation of texture. This is a three-part invention, yet not every measure has three voices represented. Find measures in which the texture is reduced to two voices.
➢ A single measure of ascending and descending eighth notes comprises the subject:

➢ Look through the score for the close relationship between the subject and subsequent eighth-note groups. These eighth note groups can be:
  – statements of the subject [e.g., mm. 2, 3]
  – inversions of the subject [e.g., m. 17]
  – fragmentation and extension of the subject [e.g., mm. 4, 5]
➢ In mm. 11-15, notice the eighth-note groups which are not derived from the subject. With this change of figure, Bach draws attention to the new tonal center of C sharp minor, the relative minor of E major. This section ends with the first statement of the subject in inversion (m. 17), cascading to a cadence in the dominant, B major.
➢ Find the two instances where Bach simultaneously states the subject and its inversion. [mm. 35, 37] You may wish to compare these measures with the two-part *Invention No. 6 in E Major* (Level 8), in which the subject features voices in contrary motion.
➢ Circle the bass line in mm. 37-41 [D sharp – E – F sharp – G sharp – A – B – E]. The bass ascends to the dominant (B) before resolving to the tonic (E).
➢ Notice the increased rhythmic activity in m. 38 (sixteenth notes). What effect does this have on the listener?
➢ Before home practice begins, first play this piece as a student–teacher duet, each person playing one hand.

Practice Suggestions

➢ Label all appearances of the subject ("S") and practice them with the indicated fingering.
➢ Label all appearances of the subject in inversion ("S-I") and practice with attention to the fingering.
➢ Find extensions of the subject (mm. 4-5, 8, 27-28) and label them "S-X." Practice them to achieve the feeling of two-beat groups.
➢ Practice the eighth-note groups in mm. 11-15. Emphasize each beat when playing these measures.
➢ Through most of the piece, the RH plays two of the three voices. Practice the accompanying longer values, giving special attention to their length. For example, in mm. 3-5, hear the clear, independent movement of the alto and soprano.

Johann Sebastian Bach
Sinfonia No. 11 in G Minor, BWV 797 (R6)
Exploring the Score

Each Invention and Sinfonia is different in the formulation of the subject and the way Bach develops that material. His creativity is remarkable. This graceful subject passes from hand to hand in quick succession, and one has the impression that the subject is not fully presented until it appears in all three voices.

➢ The subject combines a descending broken triad and an octave leap (RH, m. 1). Identify the subject presentations throughout the score. Is the final skip always an octave?
➢ What is your preferred articulation for the subject? You may wish to listen to several recordings of the Sinfonias to compare different ideas. One effective articulation is to detach slightly before and after the third beat.

➢ From m. 1 to m. 23, the subject is ever-present. Then, in m. 24, two surprising changes occur: the bottom voice is held for six measures, creating a pedal point, and the sixteenth motion is upward. Find the other pedal point in the piece. [m. 57-65]
➢ Notice the change of sixteenth-note motion at m. 36. Chart Bach's sequential use of the circle of 5ths in mm. 36-40.
➢ In a G minor piece, one would expect to find references to closely related keys such as the relative major (B flat major) and the dominant (D minor). Can you locate those areas? [m. 16, m. 30]
➢ Melodic "skeletons" of descending stepwise motion occur frequently in this piece. Follow the descending scale in the top voice at the beginning of the piece:

a full octave in mm. 1-8! Find the similar scale at the end of the piece. Look for examples of patterns like this in other voices.

Practice Suggestions

➤ Determine the articulation of the subject before beginning practice.

➤ It is important to realize that the subject starts on the second sixteenth of a measure. Use special caution on measures that have a beginning sixteenth; that downbeat finishes the previous idea. The subject begins on the second tone of the measure.

➤ The most efficient and musical way to achieve control over a three-voice texture is to divide the piece into practice segments. Play each voice alone, listening for musical shaping and with careful attention to fingering and articulation. Then combine pairs of voices, leaving the playing of the complete three-voice texture until last.

Domenico Scarlatti
Sonata in C Major, L 104, K 159 (R8)
Sonata in D Minor, L 413, K 9 (R11)
Sonata in D Major, L 463, K 430 (R14)

Background Information on Scarlatti and his Sonatas

Domenico Scarlatti was born in Naples. He traveled widely throughout Italy and held posts in Venice and Rome. Sometime after 1719, he became maestro of the chapel at the royal court of Portugal in Lisbon and gave keyboard lessons to Maria Barbara, daughter of King John V. When Maria Barbara married the heir to the Spanish throne in 1729, Scarlatti moved to Spain with her court. He spent the rest of his life there, composing, conducting, and teaching.

Scarlatti is most famous for his 555 keyboard sonatas, many of which were written for the gifted Maria Barbara. Although these sonatas are all in one movement and feature an extended binary form, they have remarkable variety and color and are highly original. Scarlatti's sonatas often reveal their Spanish influence, imitating instruments, rhythms, and dances from his adopted country. In some sonatas you can hear guitars, trumpet fanfares, hunting horns, or castanets. Scarlatti does not shy away from dissonance, either. There are moments in some sonatas where the performer plays fistfuls of notes, creating an intense sound. The sonatas often show a very athletic approach to the keyboard, with fast hand crossings and wide shifts of position. Ralph Kirkpatrick, the renowned Scarlatti scholar, suggests

that approximately 388 sonatas are grouped in pairs, both with the same tonal center, and another twelve sonatas form sets of three.

When played on a modern piano, Scarlatti's sonatas require the same clarity and precision as the other List A compositions by Daquin and Bach. Follow the articulation guidelines and practice suggestions presented at the beginning of the List A discussion.

Sonata in C Major, L 104, K 159 (R8)
Exploring the Score

This sonata shows the influence of the Spanish *jota* (pronounced "ho-tah"), a fast dance in triple time, performed to the accompaniment of castanets.

➤ What instruments can you imagine playing the opening measures of this piece?

➤ Look for thick textures and dissonant harmonies (for example, mm. 26-40).

➤ Compare mm. 1-25 with mm. 42-62. What has changed? [The rising eighth notes in mm. 17-19 outline a G major triad. In mm. 56-58, the top notes stay on C.] Why do you think Scarlatti made those changes? [Scarlatti was unable to complete the corresponding C major triad because the highest tone on the harpsichord was F.]

➤ Most phrases are two measures long. Find the longer phrases. What effect do they have?

➤ The editorial dynamics reflect echo phrasing, which was possible on a two-manual harpsichord.

Practice Suggestions

➤ Scarlatti writes slurs to emphasize the relationship between dissonance and resolution. The first note of the slur (beat note) is to be played louder.

➤ Eighth notes not marked with slurs can be played *staccato*.

➤ The double 3rds of mm. 13, 16, etc. can be performed two different ways. Practice these options and decide which one fits the character of the piece best:
  1. Play all double 3rds with a sharp *staccato*.
  2. Emphasize the downbeat of each measure with a *legato* connection between the first two eighths:

➤ Play the quarter–eighth–quarter–eighth LH rhythm detached.

➤ Using the realization indicated in the footnotes, practice the trills with fingers close to the keys. Use a "scratching" action of the fingertips.

Sonata in D Minor, L 413, K 9 (R11)
Exploring the Score

➤ If one were to compare a Scarlatti sonata with a Bach invention, the sheer number of different musical ideas in the Scarlatti would contrast the limited material Bach uses. Look through this sonata and find the many different rhythms and figures employed.

➤ Is the outline of keys what you would expect to find in a binary form? [yes: D minor, F major, D minor] Where is the first appearance of the relative major? [m. 16]

➤ As you listen to the *Celebration Series®* recording of this piece, make special note of the articulation. Does the performer follow the Baroque articulation guidelines presented earlier? Discuss the articulation that you find most effective.

Practice Suggestions

➤ A successful performance of this piece relies on appropriate articulation. Decide on the articulation of each musical idea and notate your decisions in the score. Follow them carefully as you practice.

➤ Set the metronome for a moderately slow eighth-note pulse to practice the scales. Make careful distinction between eighth notes, sixteenth notes, and thirty-second notes.

Sonata in D Major, L 463, K 430 (R14)
Exploring the Score

➤ This sonata is an example of Scarlatti's challenging keyboard writing (notice the shifts in mm. 19-24 and similar passages).

➤ There are no phrasing or articulation marks in the score. How will the sixteenth notes of m. 1 sound different from the eighths of m. 2? How will you contrast the downbeat "sighs" of mm. 19-25 with the octave E–C sharp?

Practice Suggestions

The following suggestions will assist you in developing a consistent approach to phrasing and articulation in this sonata.

- Eighth notes that repeat or skip can be played *staccato.*
- Pairs of stepwise eighth notes on downbeats can be slurred. [drop-lift motion]
- Detach all octaves.
- Slur the sixteenths.

➤ Pay special attention to passages containing independent voices in one hand (RH, mm. 26-28, 63-66, 93-95).

➤ On large leaps, the upper arm leads the motion. Analyze how each leap is approached, what kind of preparation is needed, and how many notes are involved in the grouping. The faster you play, the more you will loosely "throw" the hand.

➤ What is your translation of the directive *Non presto ma a tempo di ballo?*

Johann Sebastian Bach
Prelude and Fugue in C Minor, BWV 847
(R17, R20)
Background Information

In Bach's time, tuning systems for keyboard instruments used acoustically pure intervals. Because of this, certain keys sounded intolerably out of tune. Experiments with a tempered tuning system employed slight modifications of the intervals and made it possible for composers to write in all keys. Bach celebrated this new tuning in his monumental two-volume collection, *The Well-Tempered Clavier.* Each volume contains a prelude and fugue in each major and minor key. *The Well-Tempered Clavier* was not written for a specific instrument. The use of the term *clavier* simply implies keyboard instruments in general.

Each prelude or fugue in *The Well-Tempered Clavier* generally deals with one musical idea. Bach creates contrast within pieces by modulating to different keys and varying the texture. The arrival at a new key or tonal center is an important event. These internal cadences should be stressed because they represent landmarks in the journey through the composition. Most of the preludes are in a free-voiced style, with textures ranging from single lines to a fuller, thicker sound. In contrast, the fugues are written in strict contrapuntal style for a specific number of voices or parts.

Prelude and Fugue in C Minor, BWV 847 (R17)
Exploring the Score

This prelude consists of a rhythmic, motoric section (mm. 1-24) and a free, improvisatory section (mm. 25-38). Bach guides the improvisatory section with three changes of tempi. These tempo indications are rare in Bach's keyboard works.

➤ Bach defines the key at the beginning before exploring related harmonies. In mm. 1-4, find the i-iv-V-i harmonic progression.

➤ Circle the descending stepwise motion in mm. 5-19.

➤ The arrival on the LH G in m. 21 has special harmonic importance because it establishes the tension of the dominant pedal point. How long does that G remain in the bass?

➤ Mm. 28-34 are based on a skeleton of four descending steps in the top voice. In mm. 28-29, find E-flat – D – C – B flat. In mm. 30-34, find three statements of A flat – G – F – E flat (E natural).

- ➤ Notice the intensity of stepwise motion in m. 36. This intensity is preparing for the arrival of the final cadence.
- ➤ Play and name the first bass note of each measure. Which notes are most often repeated? [C and G] What function do those notes play in the key?

Practice Suggestions

- ➤ Block the sixteenth-note figures to learn fingerings and position shifts. For example, play just the boxed notes:

- ➤ In mm. 1-24, all measures but one contain two statements of a pattern lasting one-half measure. Make special note of m. 18, where the pattern changes within the measure.
- ➤ Between mm. 29 and 33, the patterns shift constantly. Practice slowly in half-measure units to gain security.
- ➤ Practice the sixteenth-note figures in different rhythms.
- ➤ Listen to different recordings to get ideas about tempo and articulation choices, use of pedal, and projection of mood and character.

Fugue in C Minor, BWV 847 (R20)
Exploring the Score

- ➤ Find and bracket all complete statements of the two-measure subject. How many do you find? [eight]
- ➤ Many fugue subjects, including this one, have a contrasting companion melody called a *countersubject*. A countersubject is a consistently appearing accompaniment to the subject, and rarely appears without the subject. As you locate statements of the subject, find the accompanying countersubject.
- ➤ Help the student decide on an articulation for the countersubject that establishes its independence from the subject.
- ➤ Passages containing only fragments of the subject or no subject at all are known as *episodes*. Episodes often contain sequences. Locate the six episodes in this fugue. Are they similar or different?
- ➤ What keys are established in mm. 13, 17, and 22? How do these keys relate to C minor? [E flat major –relative major; G minor–dominant; C minor–tonic]

Practice Suggestions

The opening motive of this fugue is distinctive and the presentations of the subject are easy to follow. Articulation is a major factor in establishing independence of the three voices. Listen to several recordings of this fugue. How do the performers articulate the various themes? Is each voice clear?

- ➤ Because the subject and countersubject appear together, each must have a contrasting, independent articulation. Be consistent with your articulation decisions. As a general guideline, detach the eighth notes of the subject and slur the eighth notes of the countersubject.

- ➤ Divide the fugue into two-measure practice units. For each unit:
  - Play each voice separately. Pencil in your articulation decisions and any needed fingerings.
  - Combine pairs of voices: S and A; S and T; A and T. Did you play the articulation and fingering accurately?
  - Combine the three voices.

Louis-Claude Daquin
Le coucou (Rondeau) (R22)
Background Information

With François Couperin and Jean-Philippe Rameau as foremost composers and performers, the late Baroque French harpsichord school achieved a level of refinement and skill respected throughout Europe. Many German composers traveled to France to study. German monarchs and nobles employed French composers and performers at their courts.

French harpsichord music was noted for its emphasis on dance and its elaborate ornamentation. A typical French suite consisted of a mixture of dances and programmatic pieces from which performers selected a group of movements for a given performance.

The *rondeau* was a favored form. In a *rondeau*, repetitions of the theme or refrain are separated by contrasting sections called couplets (A c1 A c2 A).

From 1727 until his death, Louis-Claude Daquin was organist at St. Paul in Paris. He composed harpsichord and organ music, chamber pieces, and a cantata, *La rose*. *Le coucou* is a well-known example of harpsichord music of this period. Notice the programmatic imitation of a cuckoo's call (the falling LH 3rds).

Exploring the Score

Find the different sections of this piece and make a diagram of the form. Use these questions to help determine the order of the sections:

➤ What measure do you play after the first ending in m. 23 the first time? [m. 24] the second time? [m. 43]
➤ To which measure do you return after the *Da Capo* in mm. 42 and 69? [m. 1]
➤ How many times do you play mm. 24-42 and mm. 43-69? [once]
➤ What is the key of each section?

Practice Suggestions

➤ Listen to the *Celebration Series*® recording to help you determine correct articulation.
➤ Determine a precise articulation for the cuckoo motive (*staccato* eighth note, full value quarter note).
➤ Isolate the RH ornaments using the footnotes as a guide, then play them in context within each phrase.
➤ Practice the RH sixteenth notes with wrist rotation to help maintain control and even sounds.

LIST B – CLASSICAL REPERTOIRE
Suggested Order of Difficulty

Page	Composer	Title
R28	Wolfgang Amadeus Mozart	*Fantasia in D Minor, K 397 (385g)*
R32	Wolfgang Amadeus Mozart	*Sonata in C Major, K 330 (300h) (Second Movement)*
R25	Carl Philipp Emanuel Bach	*Sonata in C Minor, Wq 48/4, H 27 (Third Movement)*
R52	Ludwig van Beethoven	*Rondo in C Major, op. 51, no. 1*
R35	Franz Joseph Haydn	*Sonata in E Minor, Hob. XVI:34 (First Movement)*
R40	Franz Joseph Haydn	*Sonata in E Minor, Hob. XVI:34 (Second Movement)*
R43	Franz Joseph Haydn	*Sonata in E Minor, Hob. XVI:34 (Third Movement)*
R47	Ludwig van Beethoven	*Sonata in G Major, op. 79 (First Movement)*

In the Classical style, contrast is a principal element. Classical composers used forms with contrasting sections (ternary form, sonata form, rondo) featuring contrasting themes, keys, textures, and accompaniment patterns. Music of the Classical period has a strong harmonic orientation and makes greater use of homophonic texture (melody supported by harmonic accompaniment) than was common during the Baroque era. Some harmonies have a natural tension and receive dynamic stress. Non-chord tones in the melody are a primary means of expression with a dynamic stress on the non-chord tone.

The phrase is the standard unit of construction. Classical music is often described in terms of language: phrases, sentences, punctuation, inflection, accent, and emphasis.

During the Classical period, the harpsichord gradually gave way to the fortepiano, an instrument on which the performer could create a wide variety of dynamic inflections—sudden and grand or refined and sensitive. Haydn's early sonatas were written for the harpsichord. His later sonatas have numerous dynamic markings and were written for the fortepiano. Mozart also demonstrated a strong preference for the fortepiano.

However, in comparison to the modern piano, the early piano had a small sound and limited sustaining power. Beethoven in particular was never satisfied with the contemporary instrument, and piano makers in Vienna strove to make improvements so that the instrument could withstand his forceful playing. Innovations in the first half of the nineteenth century, such as the use of heavier strings, cross-stringing, and the cast-iron frame, laid the foundation for the modern piano.

Dynamic control is one of the challenges in performing Classical music. The scores of Classical composers include specific dynamic markings (*piano, forte, sforzando, crescendo, diminuendo*) and slurs. The ends of phrases are usually tapered. The balance between melody and accompaniment also requires dynamic control. The performer should determine a dynamic plan for every phrase and for every smaller group of notes within a phrase.

Use these questions to help your student explore the construction of each piece:

➤ What is the form of the piece?
➤ How does the composer create contrasting sections?
➤ Where do the phrases begin and end? Is this phrase part of a larger unit?
➤ Where is the focal point of each phrase? Is this created through rhythm, melody, harmony, or a combination of elements?

Carl Philipp Emanuel Bach
Sonata in C Minor, Wq 48/4, H 27
(Third Movement) (R25)
Background Information
C.P.E. Bach was the second surviving son of Johann Sebastian Bach and the most famous musician among his sons. He served as chamber musician (accompanist) to Frederick the Great of Prussia for approximately thirty years. During the latter part of his life, he was employed as a church musician in Hamburg. C.P.E. Bach's most lasting achievement was his treatise, *Essay on the True Art of Playing Keyboard Instruments,* which is still used today as a reference to understand keyboard performance practices of the latter part of the 18th century.

This *Presto* is the last movement of a sonata from Bach's *Sei sonate per cembalo.* The term *cembalo* refers to harpsichord. Bach's use of the *f* and *p* marking implies that he intended the piece to be played on a two-manual instrument.

Exploring the Score
A quick glance at the score reveals Bach's interest in imitation and in variety of figures.
➢ Look for the points of imitation.
➢ Compare the opening section (mm. 1-16) with the return (mm. 49-60). What makes the ending shorter?
➢ Find the inversions of the opening subject. [e.g., m. 36]
➢ Find the skeletal stepwise progression in all of the *piano* measures. Then find the source of that motion (and the reason for the "echo") in the two measures preceding the *piano.*
➢ Note the stepwise direction of the chord motion, mm. 37-46.
➢ What key is established at the double bar, m. 16? [E flat major, the relative major] What is the key at the cadence in m. 36? [G minor, the dominant]
➢ The extended passage of mm. 25-30 is an example of a composer using part of the circle of 5ths. Each measure represents one key. Name the harmonies.

Practice Suggestions
➢ How will you articulate this music? Locate the points of imitation and practice both hands with the same inflection. [mm. 1-2, 3-4, 17-18, etc.]
➢ Play sixteenth notes with precision and clarity, and eighth notes *staccato.*
➢ Experiment with sequential fingering when dealing with repeated patterns.
➢ Where is the point of greatest harmonic tension? [mm. 46-47] What treatment will you give these measures?

Wolfgang Amadeus Mozart
Fantasia in D Minor, K 397 (385g) (R28)
Background Information
This *Fantasia* was most likely written during 1782 in Vienna. Scholarly research indicates that the final ten measures were not written by Mozart but were added for the publication of the *Fantasia* in 1804, after Mozart's death. The cadence on V in m. 97 (the last measure penned by Mozart) suggests that the piece may have been intended as an introduction to an ensuing movement.

A fantasia has the spirit of improvisation and usually features highly contrasting sections. Many other important composers wrote works bearing this title, including Bach, Schubert, Schumann, Mendelssohn, Chopin, and Liszt.

Exploring the Score
➢ The *Fantasia in D Minor* is a favorite Mozart work among pianists because of its graphic emotional contrasts. Each section has a compelling role to play in this musical portrayal of life's drama. Do the following descriptions match your impressions of the opening pages?
  – The opening broken chords are dark and menacing, as if lifting the curtain on this "piano tragedy."
  – Measures 12-19 are plaintively pleading.
  – Measures 20-22 have the relentless quality of Fate knocking on our door.
  – Measures 23-27 are a frantic flight.

➢ Discuss the other sections and give labels to the character of the music.
➢ Use the tempo markings as a guide to examining the various sections of this *Fantasia:*
  – How many sections are indicated by a change of tempo? [seven]
  – Is the opening *Andante* repeated?
  – How many *Adagio* sections are there?
  – Does each *Adagio* section begin with the same musical material?
  – How many *Presto* sections are there?
  – Of the seven sections, which is the longest? [*Allegretto*]
  – Which sections suggest free improvisation?
  – Which sections are in major and which are in minor?

Practice Suggestions
➢ The goal of your performance is vivid expressivity. Steep yourself in the music's drama as you listen to recordings of this famous work. Approach each practice session with a sound goal already in mind.

➤ Determining the tempo for each section is a primary challenge. Use a metronome to set the tempo for each section. The opening introductory *Andante, alla breve,* shares a similar pulse to the following *Adagio* if one feels the half-note pulse (*Andante*) equal to the quarter-note pulse (*Adagio*).

➤ Count very carefully in mm. 16-19. Play these measures with the metronome and make sure all notes and rests are accounted for.

➤ Student performances of this piece often slow at m. 70. Special practice of the *Alberti* figure may be necessary. What role does the rotating hand play in achieving speed and control over a fast *Alberti* pattern? Avoid (at all cost) excessive activity of the LH fingers.

➤ Use the damper pedal judiciously. Damper pedal is encouraged in the opening *andante* and in chorale-like passages (e. g., m. 21). The pedal should never obscure stepwise melodic passages (e. g., m. 12), two-note sixteenth note phrases (e. g., m. 23), and the clarity of passagework (e. g., m. 34).

➤ Develop a dynamic plan for each phrase. Where are the climax points? When do tension-filled harmonies resolve? What should the balance be?

➤ Mozart's fortepiano had less dynamic range than the modern piano. Be careful not to overplay the *forte* sections, especially the LH octaves in mm. 20-22 and 35-37.

➤ The LH fingerings of mm. 26-27 and mm. 41-43 deserve special practice.

➤ The *Presto* "cadenzas" sound best when all notes are not played with equal speed. Begin the passage at a slightly slower speed, then let the run gain momentum before slowing down at the end.

Wolfgang Amadeus Mozart
Sonata in C Major, K 330 (300h)
(Second Movement) (R32)

Background Information

Mozart's piano sonatas are more predictable in form than those of Haydn and Beethoven. They all have three movements, and (with one exception) the first movement is in sonata form. The slow second movements are in a contrasting key. The lively third movements are in either rondo or sonata form. Mozart's themes are often likened to characters in operas because they have strong personality and provide dramatic contrast.

Exploring the Score

➤ The remarkable aspect of this slow movement is the contrast of mood and color between the F major and the F minor sections. As you listen to the *Celebration Series*® recording of this movement, be receptive to these colorful contrasts.

➤ Mozart achieves an organic unity of all themes in this highly contrasting piece. Find the common element that links all of the themes. [begins with a three-eighth-note upbeat]

➤ Chart the overall form of the movement.

A (F major)	Theme 1	mm. 1-8 (I–V)
	Theme 2	mm. 9-20
		(modulates back to I)
B (F minor)	Theme 3	mm. 21-28 (i–III)
	Theme 4	mm. 29-36 (III–i)
	Closing	mm. 37-40 (i)
A (F major)	Theme 1	mm. 41-48 (I–V)
	Theme 2	mm. 49-60
		(modulates back to I)
	Closing	mm. 61-64 (I)

➤ What is the origin of the closing material (mm. 37-40 and m. 61-64)? [Theme III in F minor]

➤ This movement is meticulously notated by Mozart, with detailed attention to articulations and frequent changes of dynamics. Draw the student's attention to these notational features. The expressive "sigh" of the two-note slur is of special importance in this movement.

Practice Suggestions

➤ Achieving an accurate reading of notes and rhythms is quite straightforward. Of greater challenge is the control of the sound, and the expressive realization of the many score markings. This requires very active eyes and ears.
  - Practice phrase by phrase.
  - Determine the dynamic focus of each phrase. In the beginning, exaggerate the shaping of the phrases and the contrast between your hands.
  - Lift at the end of each articulation and phrase slur.
  - Use touches of pedal to add warmth to the sound and to connect chords. Avoid obscuring the melodic line.

Franz Joseph Haydn
Sonata in E Minor, Hob. XVI:34 (R35, R40, R43)
Background Information

It is difficult to describe a typical Haydn sonata because of the variety in form, style, and number of movements. Haydn's compositions are often humorous. He surprises the listener with a sudden interruption of a theme, an abrupt change of key, an unexpected rest, or a startling new texture or register. Haydn's melodies are usually short and motivic, rather than lyrical and flowing, and this sonata is no exception. The outer movements of Haydn's sonatas have themes with clear motives that are later developed. Looking for the composer's treatment of motives can be an enlightening process for both teacher and student.

Learning an entire sonata is a demanding project for teacher and student. The teacher will want to consider the most appropriate order for learning the movements. Within a movement, reverse practice is a helpful tool to ensure that the final sections are secure.

First Movement: Presto (R35)
Exploring the Score

Label the form in the score:

Exposition	mm. 1-45
Theme 1	mm. 1-13
bridge	mm. 14-29
Theme 2	mm. 30-41 [G major, the relative major of E minor]
closing	mm. 42-45
Development	mm. 46-78 [E major, the parallel major of E minor]
Recapitulation	mm. 79-127
Theme 1 and bridge	mm. 79-94
Theme 2	mm. 95-108
closing	mm. 109-123
coda	mm. 124-127

➤ Haydn starts the piece with a dialogue between the hands and continues this "conversation" until the entrance of the first theme.
  - Note the constancy of the LH.
  - Note the subtle differences in the RH groups of three eighths.
  - Many RH groups are related by a motive of three descending steps:

➤ Note the use of "three steps down" hidden in the sixteenths notes of mm. 19-26. The second theme also contains a similar motive. Can you find the use of three steps in the closing theme?
➤ The appearance of many accidentals in the development section alerts the performer to modulation and harmonic color. Look for the main tonal centers in the development.
  - m. 46 E major
  - m. 51 C major
  - m. 71 B minor
  - m. 78 B major

Practice Suggestions

➤ The greatest technical challenge of this piece is mastery of the various sixteenth-note figures. They can be practiced first, because they will determine the tempo of the piece and the success of the performance.
  - The easiest sixteenth-note patterns are those that have a consistent direction, e.g., mm. 14-18.
  - The most difficult are those that change direction (zigzag). Hand rotation is recommended for such figures, and practicing in crisp dotted rhythms is always helpful.
➤ In the second theme, the RH is responsible for two voices.
  - In mm. 30-31, observe the descending groupings of three notes. Play the top voice *legato.*
  - Isolate mm. 32-34, 38-39, and their counterparts in the recapitulation for special practice. First, play the soprano line with the RH and the alto line with the LH to provide the sound model. Then play the RH as written, carefully observing the notated lengths of notes.
➤ In the development section, Haydn writes few dynamic indications. Develop a dynamic plan for this section. Where will you reduce the level to effectively contrast with the *forte* areas?

Second Movement: Adagio (R40)

Exploring the Score

➤ In this movement, Haydn writes an elegant improvisation over traditional harmonies. Your student will gain understanding of this construction by playing the LH while you play the RH, or by playing the LH along with the *Celebration Series®* recording.

➤ This movement is "harmonically driven." Determine the lengths of phrases and find the peak of harmonic tension in each phrase. Circle the I 6/4 chords (mm. 7, 16, etc.), which constitute the focus of almost every phrase.

➤ Which keys are established in mm. 20, 23, and 31?

➤ If the movement is in G major, explain the harmonies of the final five measures. [They establish B major as the V of E minor; this movement proceeds directly into the final E minor movement—*attacca subito*.]

➤ If the student is insecure with the rhythmic subdivisions, tap and count *1&2&3&* while listening to a recording or while you play selected measures.

Practice Suggestions

➤ Your practice of this movement can have three areas of focus:
  1. harmonic structure
  2. phrase length and focus
  3. rhythmic accuracy

➤ Simple LH harmonies provide the background support for the ornate RH. These harmonies dictate the focus of each phrase. With pencil in hand, practice the harmonies and write in your analysis. When the harmonies resolve (e.g., m. 4, m. 8), the phrase ends. Make a special mark in the score to indicate the focus of each phrase.

➤ The wide variety of rhythmic subdivisions may pose a challenge initially. Devise ways to experience the RH rhythms. Know the location of each eighth pulse.

➤ The florid RH must have dynamic nuance and contour. Remember, however, that the RH is always inspired by the LH harmonies, and the tension and relaxation of the harmonies are the best clue to the shaping of the RH.

➤ Give the extended thirty-second-note passages an improvisatory quality.

Third Movement: Vivace molto (R43)

Exploring the Score

➤ What is the form of this movement?

A	mm. 1-18	E minor
B	mm. 19-40	E major
A1	mm. 41-76	E minor
B1	mm. 77-100	E major
A2	mm. 101-136	E minor

Haydn frequently creates a formal synthesis by combining elements of two forms. This movement has the formal characteristics of a rondo, but lacks the C section found in most Classical rondos. There are also traits of variation form in the piece, with a theme in minor and a theme in major.

➤ As you explore further:
  – Which sections are in binary form?
  – Which sections are in rounded binary?

➤ One of the unifying factors in this piece is the way the phrases begin: with an eighth-note upbeat.
  – Can you find any phrases that do not begin with an upbeat?
  – Can you find any phrases that do not begin with a detached (*staccato*) upbeat?

➤ Name the first eight pitches of the A section theme. Now do the same for the B section. Compare the rhythm of these themes. Notice the unity of Haydn's writing.

➤ In the A theme, the short slur is a clue to Haydn's humor. The first tone of a short slur is played loudest. Observing that rule in mm. 2-3 will shift the emphasis from downbeat to off-beat:

Practice Suggestions

➤ Haydn's good-natured humor is conveyed through the articulation. Practice the sound you find desirable on each two-note slur. Whether the slur begins on a beat or off the beat, the first note is always (decidedly) louder.

➤ You may need special practice on the *Alberti* bass figures, as they must be played very fast. Practicing with exaggerated dotted figures helps stimulate the necessary hand rotation.

➤ Phrases make excellent practice units. Be consistent with fingering. Write any changes of fingering (different from the score) in your music. Add ornaments after the notes and rhythm are secure.

➤ How will the opening term *innocentemente* affect your interpretation? [It primarily impacts the dynamics but not the tempo.]

Ludwig van Beethoven
Sonata in G Major, op. 79 (First Movement) (R47)
Background Information

Beethoven originally suggested to his publisher that his Sonata, op. 79, be titled Sonatine or *Sonatine Facile* because of its shorter length and modest technical requirements. The piece was composed in 1809, when Beethoven was also writing the *Piano Concerto No. 5, op. 73* ("Emperor") and the *Sonata in E flat, op. 81a* ("Les adieux").

Exploring the Score

The clue to the interpretation of this piece is Beethoven's marking *Presto alla tedesca, (Fast, like a German Dance).* This is a country dance, and downbeats receive special emphasis.

➤ Notice that Beethoven's artistry creates rhythmic variety even within the predictable $\frac{3}{4}$ of the beginning:
  - Mm. 1, 7, and 11 have three strong beats which lead to the following measure.
  - Mm. 3 and 5 have weak downbeats, as if the bar line had little meaning. There is no change of harmony and the rhythm flows in continuous eighths.
  - Mm. 2, 6, 8, 9, and 10 have strong downbeats, creating the effect of one large beat in the measure.

➤ What happens to the strong sense of $\frac{3}{4}$ during the bridge section, mm. 12-23? The groups of four eighth notes do not conform to the $\frac{3}{4}$ meter, and the dance is momentarily suspended in a flight of light *(leggiermente)* harmonic improvisation.

➤ Measures 24-46 can be labeled the second theme, but Beethoven surprises us once again: instead of the expected lyrical theme in D major, he writes a swirl of scales supported by harmonies that circle around A or A7. When is the key of D major actually established? [not until the cadence in mm. 45-46.]

➤ How does Beethoven indicate the shaping of the second theme? Which phrases are four-measure units? Which are two-measure units?

➤ More surprises await as we enter the development. One expects the development to begin in D major (established in m. 46), but the second ending leads to E major. Follow the stepwise motion that makes this tonal shift possible.

➤ Beethoven's development sections normally feature extensive thematic development. What is unusual in this development? [the extended repetition of a single motive] Can you find the source of the repeated falling 3rds? [mm. 48-51] What folk element might they represent? [cuckoo calls!]

➤ What harmonies do you find in mm. 59-66? [I and V in E] Notice the clever way Beethoven prepares for C major in m. 66.

➤ Analyze the harmonies found in similar passages of the development.

➤ In mm. 119-122, the harmony clearly prepares for the return of the first theme (m. 123). This important moment is intensified by the LH, which momentarily veers off into duple meter.

➤ The Coda summarizes the movement in a remarkable way. The grace notes of mm. 184 and 188 reinforce the good-humored fun of the piece. The "confusing" four-eighth-note figure of the Bridge is found in mm. 191-198. In the last eight measures, the country dance ends and everyone returns home—the music fades and disappears.

Practice Suggestions

➤ As you practice, keep in mind that this is a country dance *(alla tedesca),* filled with good humor and a strong sense of beat.

➤ A wide variety of touches is necessary for the performance of this piece. Make a list of the contrasting sounds and touches, and practice each passage with a focus on the proper sound.
  - Where do you play very lightly and almost detached?
  - Where are eighth notes played *legato* and require dynamic shaping?
  - How many different articulations do you find for quarter notes?

➤ The extended harmonic passages of the Development (e.g., mm. 59-66) require careful thought. The contrast of pedaled phrases and those unmarked by Beethoven is obvious. On the measures that have no pedal, the performer can pedal beat one into beat two to lengthen the bass tone as the LH crosses. Notice that these are four-measure phrases, with a harmonic change on the last measure of each phrase.

➤ Look for 3 + 4 + 1 rhythmic groupings in the development (e.g., mm. 59-66). These measures may feel a little awkward at first.

Ludwig van Beethoven
Rondo in C Major, op. 51, no. 1 (R52)
Background Information

Beethoven composed three rondos in the late 1790s, around the same time his three *Piano Sonatas, op. 2* were being published. The two rondos comprising op. 51 were published together, but the third, the well-known *Rondo a capriccio, op. 129* ("Rage Over the Lost Penny") has a higher opus number because it was not published until 1828.

The *Rondo in C Major, op. 51* is rooted in the Classical style and features melodies, textures, and formal elements that were common for the time. Even though it is a relatively early work, one finds features that would become part of Beethoven's later compositional style, such as the lengthy coda and the tertian harmonic relationships.

Exploring the Score

This rondo is an extended composition with elaborate transitions, a lengthy coda, and a surprising "false" return of the main theme in A flat major. Label the form in your score. The chart below reveals the variety of keys and the amount of time devoted to transition sections.

A	mm. 1-17	C major
transition	mm. 17-24	
B	mm. 24-34	G major (dominant)
transition	mm. 35-43	
A1	mm. 44-51	C major
C	mm. 52-72	C minor (parallel minor)
transition	mm. 72-75	
"False" A	mm. 76-78	A flat major
transition	mm. 84-91	
A2	mm. 92-104	C major
coda	mm. 105-135	C major

➤ Locate the A, B, and C themes and discuss the way Beethoven creates variety.

➤ The piece starts simply. The A theme is "innocent," and the accompaniment adds to that impression of simplicity. Discuss ways in which Beethoven contrasts this innocent first impression with the elaborate figures and dramatic thematic statements in other sections.

➤ Examine the transition material. Are these measures based on material from one of the themes, or are they new figures?

➤ Note that Beethoven favors the keys on the flat side of the circle of 5ths from C. There is a theme statement in A flat and the *coda* goes to D flat. How might he justify those two keys? [A flat has a common tone with C Major; D flat is the Neapolitan of C major]

➤ The harmonic climax of the entire piece occurs on the downbeat of m. 116. Name the chord. [C 6/4] How do the previous measures build to this intense moment? [RH ascends chromatically to G; LH circles the G]

➤ With the metronome ticking, have the student experience the various subdivisions of the beat. You will find that the beat is divided into 2nds, 3rds, 4ths, 5ths (m. 75) and 6ths. Establish security with all of these subdivisions, and with moving freely between them before home practice begins.

➤ Have you ever used the highest note on your piano in a piece you studied? Find appearances of the highest pitch on *Beethoven's* piano (F). Where does he use this pitch for its delicate quality? Where is it used for dramatic effect?

Practice Suggestions

This *Rondo* has many technical demands. A partial list would include:
- balance of melody and accompaniment
- alternating hands textures
- extended sixteenth passages
- arpeggiated chords between the hands
- chromatic runs
- brilliant *sf*, *f*, and *ff* writing

➤ This piece is rhythmically challenging. Be sure you can subdivide the beat accurately into Beethoven's groups of 4ths, 5ths, and 6ths before you start practicing.

➤ Review chromatic scale fingerings before practicing the C section (see mm. 88-91) and the coda (see mm. 127-128).

➤ Focus on the RH articulation. In the opening A section alone, there are *staccato* notes, slurred *staccato* notes, two-note slurs, two-note slurs with turns, and long groups. Learn the correct articulation and phrasing as you read the piece.

➤ Listen at all times for appropriate balance between your hands. Where do the hands play equal roles? Where does the texture feature melody vs accompaniment?

➤ The damper pedal is used in this piece. However, the A theme needs an innocent, delicate sound. Adjust your pedal accordingly. Avoid blurring stepwise motion.

LIST C – ROMANTIC
Suggested Order of Difficulty

Page	Composer	Title
R67	Felix Mendelssohn	*Lost Happiness, op. 38, no. 2*
R74	Frédéric Chopin	*Mazurka, op. posth. 67, no. 4*
R78	Edvard Grieg	*Notturno, op. 54, no. 4*
R76	Johannes Brahms	*Intermezzo, op. 76, no. 7*
R60	Robert Schumann	*Herberge / The Wayside Inn, op. 82, no. 6*
R70	Frédéric Chopin	*Waltz, op. posth. 70, no. 2*
R63	Franz Schubert	*Impromptu, op. 142, no. 2*
R82	Pyotr Il'yich Tchaikovsky	*June (Barcarole), op. 37a, no. 6*

The late 18th and early 19th centuries bore witness to the beginnings of Romanticism, a movement that swept through all the arts and lasted for more than a century. Romantic music is characterized by extreme individualism and great intensity of feeling. The pieces in List C represent some of the most important Romantic composers and offer a wide variety of styles and textures for exploration and study.

Although Romantic composers wrote sonatas and variations, their interest in creating a concise, intense statement caused them to favor the *character piece,* a relatively short composition most frequently in a simple ternary form (ABA). Expression, mood, and color are at the heart of these short pieces. The extended harmonic palette of Romantic music exploits chromaticism, altered chords, and dissonance, and makes use of more-remote keys. (Notice the variety of flat keys used in List C.) In addition, composers marked their scores precisely, indicating subtle variations of tone quality and dynamic range. Contrasts and extremes of dynamics add to the intense expressivity of this music. Pedaling was an important aspect in the development of 19th-century pianism. Its subtle and varied use helped blend harmonies and enhance tone quality.

The chromaticism, thicker textures, and colorful pedaling that characterize Romantic keyboard music were possible, in part, because of 19th-century developments in piano construction. Greater string tension gave the piano a more brilliant sound. The range of the keyboard was also extended.

A sensitive balance of sound between melody and accompaniment is especially important in Romantic character pieces. If the student can shape and project a beautiful, expressive melodic line, the result will be most rewarding.

Robert Schumann
Herberge / The Wayside Inn, op. 82, no. 6 (R60)
Background Information

Schumann was a prolific composer of short character pieces, which he most frequently grouped in programmatic sets. *Waldszenen, op. 82* ("Forest Scenes") is one such series, composed in 1848–1849. *Herberge* is the sixth piece in this nine-piece set.

Nature was a favorite theme of nineteenth-century writers, painters, and composers. *Waldszenen* is a title typical of nineteenth-century thought; the forest held great fascination for Romantic artists. In this set, Schumann's pieces often focus on scenes of solitude, devoid of human presence and activity (*Entering the Forest, Solitary Flowers, Farewell to the Forest*). *Herberge,* however, depicts hunters meeting at a wayside inn—the most human interaction of all the pieces in the set. Interestingly, compared with the other pieces, it also features the largest number of contrasting moods. Is Schumann making a subtle comment about human nature?

Exploring the Score

Herberge evokes feelings of warm friendship and conviviality. The opening theme welcomes us, and the rising dotted figures are like shouts of joy (or toasts with mugs held high!). There are contrasting moments of sensitive reflection (mm. 19-24). The scene ends with a subdued farewell.

➤ Schumann's themes in this piece focus on descending motion:

- ➤ Do you find other examples of descending melodies?
- ➤ If the descending melodies serve to unify the piece, what features provide contrast? [variety of figures, dynamics, and rhythms]
- ➤ The form of the piece is determined by the repetitions of melodic ideas. Compare m. 1 with m. 25 and m. 19 with m. 48.
- ➤ Discuss ways in which Schumann builds tension in the piece, and ways in which he creates a contrasting, relaxed mood.

Practice Suggestions

The challenge of this piece lies in its quick changes of mood, which are created through articulations, rhythms, and dynamics. Almost every measure requires a different touch from the one that precedes it.

- ➤ Schumann's score features detailed phrasings and articulations. Practice slowly and carefully until his markings are fully realized.
- ➤ When playing the dotted-quarter-sixteenth figures, (e.g., mm. 3, 41, 42) group the sixteenth note and the notes or chords that follow it into a single arm gesture. Avoid two separate forearm motions.
- ➤ Special practice can be devoted to the melody of m. 19. Each tone is notated to be slightly detached. Individual pedals on each beat will help unify the phrase.
- ➤ Pedal to achieve *legato* connection where desired. Use the LH as a pedaling guide. Make note of harmonic changes, rests, and *staccato* markings.
- ➤ Have you found a translation for *etwas zurückhaltend,* m. 24? [*rallentando* or "somewhat holding back"]

Franz Schubert
Impromptu, **op. 142, no. 2** (R63)
Background Information

In his short lifetime, Schubert wrote nine symphonies, numerous chamber and choral works, over 600 songs, and more than twenty piano sonatas. His eight *Impromptus*—four each in op. 90 and op. 142—count among his numerous character pieces for piano. Although all eight *Impromptus* were composed in a burst of creative energy during the fall of 1827, only the first two of op. 90 were published in his lifetime; the others did not appear until 1857. *(Impromptu in E flat Major, op. 90, no. 2 is in Piano Repertoire 10.)*

Exploring the Score

Mark the (ABA) form in your score:

A section	mm. 1-46
A theme	mm. 1-16
B theme	mm. 17-30
A theme	mm. 31-46
B section (Trio)	mm. 47-98
C theme	mm. 47-58
C1 theme	mm. 59-78
C theme	mm. 79-90
Bridge	mm. 91-98
A section	mm. 99-148
A theme	mm. 99-114
B theme	mm. 115-128
A theme	mm. 129-148

Schubert often used the *Trio* designation for the middle section of a larger ternary form. Within this *Trio* is a miniature ternary form with a minor section (mm. 59-76) situated between two major sections.

- ➤ Even though the entire *Impromptu* is in $\frac{3}{4}$, notice how Schubert's themes often emphasize beat two. How is the second beat reinforced in the B section?
- ➤ Observe the way Schubert creates textural variety. Notice the change of register in mm. 9-16. On Schubert's piano, and playing at a *pp* level, this statement of the theme would have had an extremely delicate effect.
- ➤ Explore Schubert's use of chromatic harmony:
  - In mm. 13-15, find the inner chromatic motion leading up to the cadence. [E flat – E natural – F.] Now compare mm. 13-15 with mm. 35-38. [bass line descends from G flat to E flat] Once again chromaticism is used to great effect.
  - Schubert uses chromaticism on his way from the subdominant (D flat) in m. 24 to the dominant (E flat) in m. 30. In mm. 25-27, find the alto line: G flat – G – A flat. In mm. 27-29, find the similar line D flat – D – E flat. Notice how smoothly these half steps bring us back from the remote G flat minor chord in m. 25.
  - Schubert masterfully changes moods as he moves from major to minor. Compare the mood at the beginning of the *Trio* (m. 47) and the restatement of that same material in minor (m. 59).
  - There is a surprising venture into a sharp key at mm. 67-76. To understand the way Schubert arrives at A major in m. 69, think of m. 66 as being written in C sharp minor. The progression then becomes iii-vi-V-I.
  - The return to D flat major shows Schubert's use of chromatic modulation. Block the chords of mm. 76 and 77 and notice the half-step movement. Where else in the piece are these two chords used? [mm. 23-25, but using enharmonic spelling of F sharp minor]

Practice Suggestions

Projection of the melody is essential for a successful performance of this piece:

A section:

➤ Practice the outer voices of the texture (soprano with bass). This polarity is the most important element to hear as you perform the piece.

➤ The opening hymn-like texture requires that the top tones of chords be projected. Slurred melodic notes (e.g., mm. 3, 11) should be played *legato* even if the alto voices must detach.

➤ The fingering you choose for the chords will affect your accuracy. Experiment with the fingering to determine which fingers play the inner notes most accurately and comfortably. Notate your findings in the score.

Trio section:

➤ Blocking the RH in the *Trio* section will help you learn notes, position shifts, and fingerings.

➤ The RH accented tones are almost always played with the fifth finger. Move the wrist and arm in the direction of the line to support the tonal projection.

➤ Schubert's notation of the LH makes it possible to play the *Trio* without pedal. If you choose to use the pedal, be sensitive to each change of harmony.

➤ Notice the consistent LH accents on beat two.

Felix Mendelssohn
Lost Happiness, op. 38, no. 2 (R67)

Background Information

During the 19th century, the piano became an immensely popular instrument. Middle-class families could afford to purchase a piano and pay for lessons. The piano became not only a symbol of culture and good breeding, but also the focus of home entertainment. Families gathered in the evening around the piano, and when guests came to the home, music was the entertainment. The piano was used as a solo instrument, in chamber music, and for the accompaniment of singing.

Lost Happiness is from Mendelssohn's *Songs without Words.* These short pieces were an instant success throughout Europe, not only for their musical value but also because they were accessible to the vast public of amateur pianists. Each piece is based on a single technical figure and mood, and the main melody is always clear. The forty-eight *Songs without Words* were written between 1829 and 1845 and published in sets of six, each set with a single opus number. Mendelssohn gave titles to only five of the pieces (three *Venetian Boat Songs, Duet,* and *Folk*

Song). Additional titles were supplied by editors and friends. For other selections from Mendelssohn's *Songs without Words,* see *Piano Repertoire 7* and *Piano Studies/Etudes 9.*

Exploring the Score

Mendelssohn's songs can be organized into four types: solo song (single melody with accompaniment), accompanied duet, choral song (chorale-like texture), and instrumental. Which type is *Lost Happiness?* [solo song]

➤ Have the student play the melody and bass line, and discuss why a friend might ascribe the title *Lost Happiness* to the piece. [Consider key and melodic shape.]

➤ Slurs in the score show articulation groups, but not the phrase structure. To discover the true phrase lengths, play the melody and sing along. Where do you want to take a breath?

➤ Do you hear one long eight-measure phrase in mm. 1-8? Beginning in m. 9, what phrase organization does Mendelssohn use? [2 + 2 + 4]

➤ Notice that slurs in the bass (e. g., m. 8) give special importance to the line.

➤ Look for accidentals to discover places where Mendelssohn leaves the home key of C minor.

Practice Suggestions

The main issue in this piece is melodic shaping and balance among three separate parts (melody, harmonic accompaniment, and bass).

➤ As a preliminary exercise, play the melodic line in unison, hands together. Concentrate on dynamic shape and inflection of the line.

➤ Play the RH melody and LH bass line (omit the inner voice).

➤ Divide the melody and the inner accompaniment between the hands (LH plays inner repeated-note accompaniment). Project the melody over the accompaniment.

➤ Play the complete texture as written, with pedal, listening carefully for the desired balance.

Frédéric Chopin
Waltz, op. posth. 70, no. 2 (R70)

Background Information

The waltz evolved from the 18th-century *Ländler.* By the 19th century, it had become Europe's most popular dance. Chopin's seventeen waltzes were written as solo piano compositions, not as dance accompaniments. Chopin's waltzes have clearly defined sections with contrasting moods. This particular *Valse* was composed in 1841.

Exploring the Score

➤ In contrast to many Chopin waltzes, this piece has only two themes. Locate the two themes and their repetitions.

➤ Chopin's music is often "tonally ambiguous." In what key does he begin this waltz? [F minor]. In what key does it end? [A flat major]. What other keys are emphasized? [E flat major, C minor.]

➤ Chopin uses chromaticism to switch seamlessly from one key to another. After the much-anticipated E flat cadence in m. 20, why does the sudden shift back to F minor sound so smooth? [half-step progression E flat – E – F links the three chords] Does this type of shift occur elsewhere? [mm. 72-73]

➤ The phrases of this waltz frequently focus on *appoggiaturas.* Look through the score to find examples of these elegant melodic dissonances. Do the ornaments emphasize non-chord tones?

➤ Notice how the opening melody descends directly to a dissonant downbeat. Composers use downbeat *appoggiaturas* for their expressive quality. Trace Chopin's use of downbeat dissonance in this piece.

➤ Play the bass line, mm. 1-20, in four-measure units. Are any phrases alike?

➤ In the lesson, discuss the pedaling. Listen to the *Celebration Series®* recording or other professional recordings to hear different approaches to the pedaling.

Practice Suggestions

➤ Your performance of this piece will be enhanced when you differentiate melody, bass line, and inner harmonies. To achieve this:
 – Practice the melody with the bass line.
 – Practice the LH part divided between the hands. Play the bass line more prominently than the accompanying chords.
 – Play the entire texture, and listen for three simultaneously different dynamic levels.

➤ Where are the goals of the RH melodic phrases? Do you find any phrase focus that is not on a downbeat?

➤ Where are the largest RH leaps? Give rhythmic space to those moments.

➤ Decide on a fingering for the LH chords. Where possible, avoid using finger 5 on the chords. Reserve that finger for the downbeat bass tones.

➤ The double 3rds in the B section (e.g., m. 47) will be easier if played with a slight arm impulse.

➤ Find measures in which there is more than one harmony. For instance, the harmonic rhythm of m. 18 and the zigzag RH indicate intensification. If you play slightly slower, the harmonic and melodic changes will be clearer.

➤ Practice the LH alone with damper pedal. The dance lilt is achieved when the texture is not over-pedaled.

Question: Will you play the multiple grace notes on the beat or before the beat? [on the beat]

Frédéric Chopin
Mazurka, op. posth. 67, no. 4 (R74)
Background Information

The mazurka has its roots in the Polish folk music tradition. It was a "turning dance" for couples, and existed in three forms: the slow and serious *kujawiak,* the moderate *mazur,* and the faster *oberek.* A mazurka is always in triple meter, with characteristic rhythmic stresses on either the second or third beat. Chopin's mazurkas span his entire career (he wrote more than fifty) and contain some of his most ingenious writing. His unique melodic and harmonic ideas brought the mazurka to a new artistic level. This particular piece was composed in 1846, shortly before Chopin left France to tour and reside in England.

Exploring the Score

As with most dances that originate in folk traditions, the mazurka has special rhythmic nuances that are difficult to notate in the score. A performance tradition was handed down aurally.

➤ While you listen to a professional recording, observe the rhythmic nuances. To develop a sense of this style, conduct while listening to several different mazurkas.

➤ Examine the rhythmic construction of the various themes. Notice the frequent pairing of measures in which one measure emphasizes the downbeat, and the following measure avoids that emphasis. Could one consider the "real" meter of this piece as $\frac{6}{4}$?

➤ Notice the melodic contour of mm. 1-16. Downward motion is so often associated with a sad mood.

➤ In the next section, mm. 17-32, the phrases form two huge arches. Notice Chopin's dynamic indications. Listen to a recording to observe how the performer shapes the phrases.

➤ How does the mood change with the shift to the major tonality in m. 33? Does the performer speed the tempo slightly at this point to emphasize the brightness of the major?

➤ Over half of Chopin's mazurkas are composed in a ternary form. The remainder have rondo or binary structures. What is the form of this mazurka? [ternary] Assign letters to the major sections.

➤ Compare mm. 1-8 with 9-16. How does Chopin create variety in the melody and accompaniment?

Practice Suggestions

➤ The successful interpretation of this piece relies on its rhythmic nuance. Where will the downbeat be stretched for special emphasis? How much time will you take between phrases? What rhythmic nuance do you use to project the dance element? Listening to recordings of several mazurkas will be of special assistance as you make these decisions.

➤ Practice the LH alone. If a chord is too wide to play all tones simultaneously, try redistributing the notes between the hands (e.g., m. 4).

➤ Chopin's mazurkas express a wide range of emotions. What descriptive words fit this piece? Is there more than one mood portrayed? Here are some suggestions to get you started: *intimate, wistful, tender, proud, melancholy, longing.*

Johannes Brahms
Intermezzo, op. 76, no. 7 (R76)
Background Information

Brahms was the last of the great German conservative Romanticists. He tended to favor the Classical-era forms and disliked the extreme chromaticism used by his contemporaries, most notably Wagner and Liszt. The *Acht Klavierstücke, op. 76,* composed in 1878, represents a significant evolution in his piano writing, as Brahms limits himself to shorter character pieces, most in ternary form, with the titles *Capriccio, Rhapsody,* and especially *Intermezzo.* The op. 76 is a set of eight compositions with alternating titles of *Capriccio* and *Intermezzo* (four of each). *Intermezzo, op. 76, no. 7* is the shortest piece in the set.

Exploring the Score

➤ The solemn A section of this ternary form is very short (eight measures) compared with the extended middle section. Compare the two sections. How are they different?
➤ A unifying factor throughout the piece is the half-measure upbeat to each phrase. Explore the themes of both sections and note the consistency of this upbeat figure.
➤ The dotted rhythm of m. 1 is also an element of unity. Although the notation is different in the B section, the same dotted feel prevails throughout.
➤ The notes A and E serve as the framework for the construction of melody and bass line:

➤ Find the extension of that idea in mm. 4-8:

➤ The opening RH theme descends, suggesting resignation, pain, or loss. Find examples of descending melodic motion in the middle section.
➤ What effect is created by the "misalignment" and elongation of RH chords in mm. 5-6? [increased harmonic tension, and an extended phrase]
➤ The motive connecting the first two phrases is made of half-step intervals. How does Brahms further use the D sharp–E half step? [upbeat motive of the B theme]
➤ Explore the bass line for its use of chromaticism (mm. 11-16; mm. 17-18). Measures 17-18 feature chromatic lines in both the bass and the alto. Can you identify the chords in these measures?
➤ Note the exchange of melody and bass between mm. 17-18 and 19-20.

Extra Credit Assignment: The opening of this *Intermezzo* is remarkably similar to the opening of Chopin's *Nocturne in F Minor, op. 55, no. 1.* Compare these two compositions. Do you find additional similarities?

Practice Suggestions

➤ Student performances frequently overlook the phrase focus on the downbeat. Notice the time signature (cut time, or *alla breve*). As you begin your exploration of this piece, conduct and count two half notes per measure. Feel the pull of the downbeats. Are some stronger than others? This will be important as you determine the goal of each phrase.
➤ Compare the first two short phrases. The octaves create a somber quality. The chords of mm. 2-3 bring warmth to the theme. As you practice these measures, create contrast in your sound.
➤ What effect does Brahms create in mm. 8-16 with the tied eighths at the beginning of each phrase? [They provide rhythmic anticipation, and they create a feeling of anguish.]
➤ Block the diminished seventh chords and their resolutions in mm. 17-20. Note the direction of the half-step motion, which changes in m. 19.
➤ Damper pedal changes must preserve the clarity of harmonic changes and avoid the blurring of half steps. Listen carefully as you practice with the pedal.

Edvard Grieg
Notturno, op. 54, no. 4 (R78)

Background Information

Grieg's ten sets of *Lyric Pieces* represent a significant contribution to the genre of the character piece. These sixty-six compositions reveal the composer's interest in the folk music and traditions of his native Norway. Many of the pieces are inspired by the natural landscape and activities of daily life. Grieg studied composition in Germany, and his early works reflect the influence of Schumann.

Grieg's *Notturno* is one of his most beloved *Lyric Pieces*. While nocturnes are most frequently associated with Chopin, John Field is generally credited with the development of the nocturne style. There are two other nocturnes in the *Celebration Series®*, one by Field *(Piano Repertoire 8)* and one by Chopin *(Piano Repertoire 10)*. Five other *Lyric Pieces* have been included in earlier albums *(Piano Repertoire 5, 6, 7, 8,* and *Piano Studies/Etudes 8)*.

Exploring the Score

➤ It is best to begin the study of this piece by hearing a polished performance by the teacher or a recording artist. Listen to the way Grieg creates the mood of evening, and to the various events that transpire.

➤ What references to nature do you hear? [m. 2, falling 4th may refer to a bird call; mm. 15-19 are reminiscent of the warbling of a bird; mm. 21-32 create the effect of the rustling wind, etc.]

➤ The A section features a triplet accompaniment against a duple melody. Devise ways for your student to practice the control of two-against-three.

➤ The opening bass line features a chromatic descent from tonic to dominant. Notice how this chromatic descent is mirrored in the ascending RH melody of mm. 5-12.

➤ Chromaticism plays an important role in the harmonies of the piece. Examine the chords created in mm. 5-8. Follow the chromatic bass in mm. 21-27 and analyze the harmonies.

➤ In mm. 9, 11, and 13, Grieg writes a D7 chord. Which of those chords finally resolves to the expected G?

➤ Notice the dynamic plan of mm. 21-32. How does Grieg enhance the climax in m. 29? [reduces the dynamic level in m. 25]

Practice Suggestions

In a final performance, the two-against-three rhythms should sound smoothly flowing. Use the *Celebration Series®* recording as a sound model. These practice steps will assist in developing fluency with the two-against-three rhythm. Using m. 5 as an example:

- Tap and count *without* the LH ties. Count *1 2& 3, 1 2& 3, 1 2& 3.*
- Tap and count *with* the LH ties.
- Play the measure in those same two ways.
- Tap and count the rhythm in mm. 51-54. Do not rush the duple eighths when they are unaccompanied by triplets.

➤ Avoid giving rhythmic emphasis to the chords in the two-against-three sections. They should provide harmonic color only. Listen for the long RH and bass lines in these passages and push through each phrase to its goal.

➤ Mm. 15-20 are a marvel of tone painting. The RH articulations on the duple sixteenths (mm. 15, 18) are crucial, as is the *diminuendo* on the trill.

➤ Avoid reaching with the fingers on the ascending LH broken chords in mm. 21-29. Keep the hand and forearm aligned behind the fifth finger to start, then adjust laterally for the remaining notes.

➤ Did you notice Grieg's directives for use of the "soft pedal" and its release?

Your practice checklist for this piece is:
- projecting the melody in the A section
- clarity of pedaling in the opening chromatic bass line
- correct articulations (e.g., RH two-note phrases, mm. 15, 18; *staccatos,* mm. 27-28)
- accurate rhythm (all triple and duple rhythms)
- attention to dynamic changes

Pyotr Il'yich Tchaikovsky
June (Barcarole), op. 37a, no. 6 (R82)

Background Information

In 1875, Tchaikovsky began working on a set of pieces that was to be gradually released in a monthly periodical beginning in 1876. Each piece represented one month of the year, and the complete suite was called *Les saisons* ("The Seasons"). It became one of Tchaikovsky's best-known piano works. Most of the descriptive titles reflect the time of year. For example, *January* is "At the Fireside," *May* is "Clear Nights," and *November* is "Sleighbells."

A *barcarole* is usually in $\frac{6}{8}$ meter and imitates the movement of a Venetian gondola. You may want to compare this *barcarole* with compositions of the same title by composers Duke *(Piano Repertoire 4)* and Heller *(Piano Studies/Etudes 6)*.

Exploring the Score

➤ Notice the unorthodox meter Tchaikovsky chooses for this barcarole. [common time!]

➤ Play the LH and feel the rocking from beat one to three. Notice how the two-note slurs contribute to the rocking effect.

- How does Tchaikovsky shape the opening phrases in the A section? [intense rising of the RH melody in mm. 3-4, followed by the release of energy through descending phrases in mm. 4-6]
- Which beat is the focus of the RH phrases? [beat one]
- Look for changes of key signature to help you mark the sections on the score. What is the form of the piece? [ABA1] Make note of the differences between the two A sections.
- How is the B section different? Do the double 3rds connote a "duet"? Does the *l'istesso tempo* of m. 40 suggest a dance?

Practice Suggestions

There are several passages where hands separate practice might be helpful:

A sections:
- In the RH, mm. 7-11, play the top tones as *legato* as possible. You may need to adjust the fingering so that octave stretches are played 1–5.
- How will your RH scale in m. 13 sound different from m. 3? (Notice the tenuto marks.)
- In mm. 84-85 and 88-89, play only the RH thumb and name the scale. [G harmonic minor]
- Block each chord (pairs of eighths). Mentally prepare for the black keys in each chord before you play.

B section:
- For the octave stretches in mm. 36-39, check fingerings. One cannot connect top tones, but note the possibility of *legato* inner tones. Practice in short phrase groups. It may be helpful to say the inner-finger numbers aloud.
- Mm. 50-51 feature inversions of the same diminished seventh chord. Memorize this passage as quickly as possible:
  1. Acquaint yourself with the outline of the series of chords by playing open octaves. Which black keys are used? [B flat and C sharp]
  2. Note the relationship between the hands (the LH thumb is always one note "behind" the RH)
  3. Practice the complete chords by alternating octaves with inner tones (octave-middles-octave-middles, etc.).

As you practice the entire piece, consider the following:
- Use the damper pedal to help connect LH shifts.
- Articulate two-note slurs, lifting on the second tone. The longer the note value, the more gentle the lift.
- Listen for imitation between the hands, especially in the A sections.
- Does your practice reflect the dynamics written by the composer?

LIST D – LATE ROMANTIC AND CONTEMPORARY
Suggested Order of Difficulty

Page	Composer	Title
R102	Dmitri Kabalevsky	*Variations in D Major, op. 40, no. 1*
R124	Clermont Pépin	*The Nose*
R114	Alexina Louie	*Distant Memories*
R87	Joaquín Turina	*Sacro-Monte, op. 55, no. 5*
R109	Ewart Bartley	*Dance No. 1*
R100	Octavio Pinto	*Salta, Salta*
R118	Rodion Konstantovich Shchedrin	*Humoreske*
R90	Claude Debussy	*La fille aux cheveux de lin*
R92	Gabriel Grovlez	*La sarabande*
R122	Harold Arlen, arr. Shearing	*Over the Rainbow*
R95	Jean Sibelius	*Romance, op. 24, no. 9*

Music of the 20th century includes a rich variety of disparate trends, movements, and styles, all of which have provided us with wonderful music. Finding common denominators is difficult.

Several pieces in List D employ aesthetic models from previous centuries: Sibelius' *Romance* and Schchedrin's *Humoreske* are reminiscent of the 19th century. Both Kabalevsky's *Variations in D Major* and Grovlez's *La sarabande* draw upon frequently used 18th-century forms. The voicings in Shearing's arrangement of *Over the Rainbow* are rooted in 20th-century jazz, and Pinto's *Salta, Salta* is reminiscent of a scene from childhood. As in all music, characterization and expression are foremost considerations. The crucial question for student teacher discussion is "What is the composer expressing?"

The discussions that follow are arranged in the order in which the pieces appear in *Piano Repertoire 9*.

Joaquín Turina
Sacro-Monte, op. 55, no. 5 (R87)
Background Information

Joaquin Turina (1882–1949) was one of Spain's leading composers in the 20th century. After studying in France under Moszkowsky and d'Indy, he returned to Spain, where he achieved fame as a leading music educator and teacher of composition. His piano music is attractive in the way it incorporates the flavor of Spanish instruments and rhythms.

Sacro-Monte is the final piece in Turina's *Cinco danzas gitanas* (Five Gypsy Dances). The title refers to the famous caves at the Sacro-Monte near Granada. The emphasis in the piece is overwhelmingly rhythmic, and the colorful writing evokes images of strumming flamenco guitars and clattering castanets.

Exploring the Score

➤ Three chords introduce the arrival of the dancers, who quietly begin to clap their hands and stomp their feet. These chords establish a basic harmonic pattern: B flat moving to A. Find the colorful dissonance in mm. 2-4 where Turina writes B flat against A. Is this a recurring sound throughout the piece? [yes]

➤ How many measures of the piece are devoted to the figuration of mm. 2-6? When the dancing intensifies at the *Più vivo* in m. 36, this rhythmic figure changes. Tap the variations of the figure in this section.

➤ What might the louder sixteenth-note phrases of mm. 7-8 represent? [unison guitars] And the eighth-note answers? [castanets]

➤ A technical challenge in this piece is the quick change of registers. Discuss practice procedures for the shifts in mm. 12-13, 17-18, 23-24, and mm. 45-46.

➤ Turina's notation is very detailed and specific. Scan the score for dynamic changes, accents, and *staccato* markings. Circle any indications that might be overlooked.

➤ Why do you think Turina notated the chords in mm. 23-24 as dotted eighths? [to specify a longer sound and sharp release]

➤ How will you articulate notes without slurs or *staccato* markings?

➤ Will you use pedal in this piece? If so, where?

Practice Suggestions

➤ Tap the rhythm of m. 3 (lightly). Observe the natural way in which your RH lifts on the second sixteenth. Incorporate this motion into your playing of this figure.

➤ Tap the rhythm of mm. 36 and 40. You will play these two measures with a distinctly different technique. Measure 36 is played with a lifting wrist; m. 40 is played with hand rotation. Practice the outside notes of the RH, m. 40, before adding the chord tones.

➤ Devote special practice to the shifts in mm. 12-13. Move from one position to the next as quickly as possible, covering the notes of the new position *without playing*: Play – shift – cover. Practice the shift in this way until you can move with lightning speed and cover the new sound accurately.

➤ Dynamics and accents play a crucial role in the effect of this piece. Observe every indication. Do not overplay the passages marked *p* and *pp*.

➤ Hold notes without *staccato* markings for their full value, but release sharply.

Claude Debussy
La fille aux cheveux de lin (R90)
Background Information

Debussy's twenty-four *Préludes* (published in two books, 1910 and 1913) present a variety of musical scenes. Though his preludes are loosely modeled after earlier groups of preludes, Debussy did not follow a key scheme like those found in the preludes of Bach or Chopin. A distinguishing feature in Debussy's preludes is that he placed the title of each at the *end* of the composition, signifying the importance of the music rather than the picture implied by the title. *La fille aux cheveux de lin* (The girl with the flaxen hair) is one of the best-known of Debussy's preludes. The title comes from a poem by the French Romantic poet Leconte de Lisle, in which a young Scottish girl sings a simple, heartfelt song under the light of the summer sun.

Exploring the Score

Students playing a Debussy piece for the first time should familiarize themselves with the variety of French-language tempo and descriptive markings. In this prelude, the student needs to understand these terms:

> *très calme et doucement expressif* – very calm and sweetly expressive
> *cédez* – slowly (ritardando)
> *au Mouvt.* – a tempo
> *très peu* – very little
> *un peu animé* – somewhat animated
> *sans lourdeur* – without heaviness
> *très doux* – very sweet
> *mumuré et en retenant peu a peu* – murmuring, holding back little by little

➤ The form of the piece is not readily seen. However, notice that the marking *au Mouvt.* signals the beginning of new sections.

➤ How does Debussy vary the treatment of the opening theme? [mm. 8, 29]

➤ Discover the variation of the main theme in m. 24. [Melodic intervals are present in a different rhythm.]

- ➤ Compare the opening theme (mm. 1-4) with mm. 28-32. How does the LH accompaniment and marking *(très doux)* change the musical effect of the passage?
- ➤ Compare mm. 3-4 and 10-11. Notice that the top voice is exactly the same.
- ➤ Reading the score with meticulous attention to Debussy's notation is of utmost importance. The exact length of ties and longer tones must be counted accurately from the first day of practice. Examine potentially troublesome rhythms with the student.
- ➤ This piece is pedaled ... carefully! A special challenge to pedal–hand coordination is presented by widespread or rolled chords. Explore these specific situations with the student:
  - In m. 6, roll the chord on the beat (not before). This creates a smooth connection from beat two to beat three.
  - In m. 13, the low G flat is held over from the previous measure. To accomplish this, change the pedal on the last eighth note of m.12 while holding the high and low G flats with the fingers.
  - In m. 16, change the pedal and play the LH grace note before the downbeat. The downbeat chords strike together, and the low bass C flat sounds through the measure. A similar plan can be followed for m. 31. Play the bass fifth with a pedal change slightly before the beat.
  - In mm. 32 and 36, roll the LH chord on the beat.

Practice Suggestions

- ➤ Fingering will play an important role in making *legato* connections.
- ➤ Circle finger substitutions in the score (e.g., m. 10, RH second beat). Practice substitutions carefully to sustain rhythmic values.
- ➤ Spot practice mm. 14, 33, and 34. Play *without* damper pedal to check for finger *legato*.
- ➤ Use the metronome to check for rhythmic accuracy. Be attentive to ties and longer values.
- ➤ After learning notes and establishing rhythmic accuracy, make dynamics a high priority in your practice. Debussy marks his score with great care.
- ➤ Debussy does not write pedaling *per se,* but the length of his written bass notes must be respected. Usually, these bass notes will last their full value only through use of the pedal.
- ➤ Plan the voicing of chords. Which chords carry the melody and require projection of the top tone? Which chords emphasize color and sonority and have equal emphasis on all tones?

Gabriel Grovlez
La sarabande (R92)
Background Information

Grovlez was a prominent French conductor and composer. He conducted the Paris Opéra from 1914 to 1934 and later served on the faculty of the Paris Conservatoire. Grovlez's compositional style was influenced by Gabriel Fauré.

The English translation of the poem on which this piece is based reads:

> *The Sarabande*
>
> *Those who will come here to dance*
> *Will no longer need to have light legs:*
> *It is your turn, marquis and shepherdesses,*
> *In ornaments of the past.*
>
> *The bows under the fingers of the musicians*
> *Loiter enough for the sarabande*
> *And the delicate shoes move without hurry*
> *On the rhythm of this ancient air.*
>
> *A last note dies in the violins*
> *Like a most tender confession;*
> *The fringed dresses on the high heels*
> *Whirl without waiting any longer.*
>
> *And in pairs of tired couples*
> *With little steps, the whole band*
> *Of dancers of the sarabande*
> *Go away.*

Exploring the Score

- ➤ Your student may have experienced a sarabande in earlier levels of the *Celebration Series®* (Zipoli's *Sarabande* in Level 6 and Gallant's *Sarabande* in Level 7). What typical sarabande characteristics can you find in Grovlez's 20th-century sarabande?
  - Is this piece slow and dignified? [yes]
  - Is triple meter used? [yes]
  - How does Grovlez emphasize the second beat? [second beat ornaments, e.g., m. 3, and longer note values in mm. 13-15]
  - Is this piece in binary form? [no]
- ➤ As you peruse the score, you see great contrasts. Compare, for example, mm. 1, 8, 13, and 26. Are these contrasts inspired by the poem?
- ➤ Discuss the elements in this piece that evoke the feeling of a dance.
- ➤ The rhythmic subdivisions of this piece may be as challenging as anything your student has studied. Make sure the student can reproduce the rhythms accurately before beginning work on the notes.
- ➤ "Shadow-playing" on a flat surface and counting subdivisions is a helpful way to experience the rhythm. Ultimately, the student must play the piece feeling the large quarter-note pulses.

Practice Suggestions

➤ One of the challenges of this sarabande is the rhythm complexity:
  - Locate the great variety of RH rhythmic subdivisions.
  - Tap or conduct steady eighths in the LH and reproduce those various subdivisions in the RH or with your voice.
  - Repeat the same exercise, substituting quarter pulses in the LH.
  - "Shadow-play" each measure on a flat surface, counting the "ands," until you have the rhythm learned.
➤ As you start to read the notes:
  - select a small practice unit (one measure will do)
  - tap the rhythm first if necessary
  - review the fingerings
  - count aloud as you play
  - repeat each unit three times

Jean Sibelius
Romance, op. 24, no. 9 (R95)
Background Information

Jean Sibelius (1865–1957) is Finland's most famous composer. Although he wrote a number of piano pieces for students, his primary contribution to music literature was his orchestral writing. Sibelius wrote seven symphonies and numerous tone poems inspired by the folk legends of Finland. The melody from his tone poem *Finlandia* is beloved throughout the world.

Exploring the Score

➤ An effective introduction to this expressive, dramatic piece can begin by hearing the music. Let the lyrical melody, lush texture, and grand climax stimulate the desire to practice.
➤ Tone poems like Sibelius' *Finlandia* are known as "program music" because they depict specific events or moods. What images are conjured by this *Romance*? Encourage the student to develop a program for the piece.
➤ There are two melodic ideas:
  - "x" (mm. 3-4): a written out turn followed by a descending 5th
  - "y" (mm. 10-11): rise and fall of six notes

Search the piece for appearances of "x" and "y."
➤ At the peak of the cadenza (m. 56), a restatement of the A section is initiated. Follow the dynamic plan of this restatement of A.
➤ Sibelius is a master of construction. Foreshadowing of the eventual outburst already begins in m. 19. Follow the course of action from m. 19 through m. 53. How many times does Sibelius reduce the dynamic level in order to achieve a more effective climax?

➤ The entire piece is pedaled. To achieve a peaceful mood in the beginning and maintain delicacy, the pedal can change on each beat. When the LH enters with the "x" melody, the pedal will change on each note.
➤ Note reading and fingering are especially challenging in mm. 26-28. Mark all A naturals in the score, and assist the student to find the best *legato* fingerings.
➤ In mm. 46 and 48, inversions of the same chord occur. Name the chord.
➤ M. 55 is ample justification for all of the scale assignments you have ever made!

Practice Suggestions

➤ Start your study of this piece with the D flat scale as found in m. 55. You may wish to devise your own scale routines to achieve secure parallel and contrary motion playing.
➤ Play mm. 3-10, changing the pedal on every melodic tone. Then practice the same melody as it appears in mm. 56-63. Notice how the pedal is now held to maintain the low D flat.
➤ Fingering and note accuracy are the challenges in mm. 26-28. Practice the intervals in isolated pairs (&2; &3; &1, etc.). What chord is always on the beat? [B flat minor]
➤ Devote special practice to the RH fingerings of mm. 33-35.
➤ When learning mm. 45 and 47, play and name the chords on the main beats (G7, B flat7, A flat7). Then practice the chords as written, but in pairs as described above for mm. 26-28.
➤ Compare the LH of m. 51 with the notes on the main beats in m. 49.
➤ Why will the RH of mm. 51-52 be easy to memorize? [all black keys]
➤ Start the descending tones of mm. 53 deliberately. Notice the *dim. poco* in that measure and the *crescendo* of m. 54. Play the downbeat of m. 55 very loudly, and start the scale ascent quietly.
➤ At the return of the main melody in m. 56, the pedal allows you to avoid unnecessary tension and play the chords detached. Keep the forearms and elbows loose and use arm weight for a full, rich tone.

Octavio Pinto
Salta, Salta (Hobby-horse) (R100)
Background Information

Pinto, originally trained as an architect, was a well-known Brazilian composer who studied with Isidor Philipp and married the prominent pianist, Guiomar Novaes. *Hobby-horse* is the last of five pieces published in the set *Scenas Infantis* in 1932. Take this opportunity to introduce your student to other pieces from this set. (The first piece, *Roda-roda,* is in *Piano Repertoire 8.*) Pinto was not the first composer to create a musical setting of a child's hobby-horse. One only has to look at the *Kinderszenen (Scenes of Childhood), op. 15* of Robert Schumann to find an interesting "Hobby-horse" from the 19th century.

Exploring the Score

Pinto provides the performer with the poem on which the piece is based, and very specific interpretive directions.

➤ Explore all of the markings by the composer that assist the interpretation. Did you include the change of tempo markings?
➤ Notice the *Prancing* indication in m. 16. Apply that marking to the opening theme in m. 1.
➤ Circle all indications of tempo change.
➤ Notice how the composer uses *fermata* and pause (comma) symbols to achieve a slowing of pace or break in the sound (mm. 9, 13, 15, 23).

Practice Suggestions

➤ Notice the similarity between the RH mm. 1-3 and mm. 4-6. The first set is broken and the second is blocked. Practice the broken intervals for the quickest grace note.
➤ For ease in playing mm. 8-9, and 23, use the arm and wrist. One gesture ("lift-ing") plays two six-teenths. This same technique is used in mm. 24-31.
➤ Experiment with the fingering in m. 15. Play each interval with the same two fingers. Try 2-5 in both hands.

Dmitri Kabalevsky
Variations in D Major, op. 40, no. 1 (R102)
Background Information

Kabalevsky's compositions are among the most important 20th-century works for piano students. These works are remarkable in the complete training they give students in technique, style, and form. Kabalevsky wrote ten sets of variations for students. *Variations in A Minor, op. 40, no. 2* is in *Piano Repertoire 10.*

Exploring the Score

➤ Kabalevsky often chose folk tunes as themes for his variations. This theme is quite unique in its simplicity: a descending scale!
➤ Variations stimulate special musical sleuthing. Can the student find evidence of a scale in each variation? **Hint:** Some of the scales may be fragmented; Some may ascend; and be sure to check the LH.
➤ The theme is eight measures long. Do you find

variations lasting more than eight measures? Can you determine how Kabalevsky extends those variations?
➤ Many of the variations are in two four-measure phrases. Look for changes in that phrasing plan.
➤ How many of the variations are not in D major?
➤ What is the purpose of the introduction? [establishes the V of D; creates anticipation]

Practice Suggestions

➤ This piece requires your very best *staccato* touch. Look through the piece and notice the frequent use of *staccato.* The sound of the piece contrasts a very sharp *staccato* against your best *legato.*
➤ Practice the piece "backwards." Start with the coda (m. 172) and practice the last eight measures of the piece (mm. 180–end). Then practice from mm. 172-180. Divide Variation XII into four-measure units and practice them backwards. Continue learning the piece in this fashion or select other challenging variations and divide them into appropriate practice units.

Ewart Bartley
Dance No. 1 (R109)
Exploring the Score

➤ Listen to the *Celebration Series®* recording. Did you hear what you expected, or were you surprised? [tempo? dynamic? variety of sounds?]
➤ If the opening of the piece were played at half tempo, it would remind us of certain pieces from Bartók's *For Children.* Bartley's choice of tempo changes that impression immediately.
➤ It will be helpful to students if they feel the *Alla breve* from the beginning. Even when counting slowly, say *1 & 2 &* instead of *1 2 3 4.*
➤ This piece has an unusual variety of sections. Mark the main sections to find repeating material:

A	mm. 1-12
A1	mm. 13-20
B	mm. 21-28
C	mm. 29-48
D	mm. 49-72
E	mm. 73-92
A	mm. 93-104
B	mm. 105-114
D	mm. 115-138
Coda	mm. 139-149

➤ How does the E section sound similar to the C section? [both hands rhythmically augment thematic material from C]
➤ Do you find other links between sections?
➤ Review with your student how the *sostenuto* pedal is used in mm. 57-60 and 123-126.

Practice Suggestions

Attention to phrasing and articulations will be crucial to a successful performance. To realize the sound intended by the composer, practice under tempo and in short phrase groups.

➤ Consciously relax the hand before playing each three-note slur.

➤ Notice that the repeated-note patterns in mm. 23-24, 27-28, etc. use alternating hands (stems down = LH; stems up = RH).

➤ Practice the quick position shifts in mm. 31-32, 35-36, 65-66, and 31-136 by blocking half-measures.

➤ The LH of mm. 53-54 will be easier to play if you group the quarter notes in pairs and use a down–up motion as if they were marked with two-note slurs.

➤ To avoid an awkward LH leap in mm. 56-57, you may wish to let the RH play the blocked intervals in m. 56. Substituting the thumb on the E will allow you to hold it while playing the intervals above.

Alexina Louie
Distant Memories (R114)
Background Information

Canadian composer Alexina Louie has developed a uniquely personal, expressive style rooted in a blend of east and west. Her music emphasizes craft and imagination stemming from a wide variety of influences: her Chinese heritage; theoretical, historical, and performance studies; and an ongoing investigation and introspection concerning the arts and musical composition. Leading orchestras, including San Francisco, Toronto, and St. Louis, have performed Louie's orchestral works.

Distant Memories is the third of four pieces comprising *Music for Piano,* a work commissioned by The Alliance for Canadian New Music Projects. As requested by The Alliance, the pieces make use of contemporary notation.

Exploring the Score

Combining the freely improvised with the strictly controlled is a pairing of long tradition. The earliest preludes and fugues were such a combination. Many fantasies and toccatas also show this type of contrast in their different sections. In this piece, *senza misura* sections are contrasted with the quiet, metered parts.

➤ Although there is considerable freedom in the way the opening section is to be played, much about this music is controlled and indicated by the composer. Make a list of the elements that are dictated by the composer, then list the elements that are determined by the performer.

➤ If this is the student's first experience with graphic notation, explore the symbols in the *senza misura*

section. Discuss the different note beams and the desired effect of each. What is the meaning of 0", 10", 18", and 30"? [approximate duration of each line in seconds].

➤ In such "freely atonal" music, certain notes will stand out if they are repeated. Which tones does Louie wish to stress in the opening section? [E and C sharp]

➤ How many sections do you find in the middle, measured portion of the piece?
  – mm. 2-9 – changing meters; LH pedal point
  – mm. 10-17 – black keys; LH pedal point
  – mm. 18-23 – RH steady quarters; LH pedal point
  – mm. 28-35 – repetition of mm. 2-9

Practice Suggestions

➤ To gain control over the notes in the *senza misura* section, practice the groups of changing pitches slowly and clearly. When the runs feel secure, add the dynamic plan indicated by the composer. Then add the feeling of *accelerando.*

➤ Think of the longer flourishes as written-out *glissandos* for tiny wind chimes made of metal or glass.

➤ Select your best fingering for the repeated tones. Then practice the *diminuendo,* and finally add the *accelerando.*

➤ The metered portion of the piece has few dynamic indications, and they are subtle. The quiet mood and the constant LH pedal point create a hypnotic spell.

Rodion Konstantinovich Shchedrin
Humoreske (R118)
Background Information

Shchedrin is one of the premier Russian composers of his generation. Since the breakup of the Soviet Union, his music is becoming better known outside Russia, though within Russia he is considered one of the most successful composers of his time. Shchedrin's output includes symphonies, ballet scores (including commissions for the Bolshoi Theater), piano concerti, and film scores. Shchedrin's respect within Russia is evidenced by the fact that he succeeded Dmitri Shostakovich as President of the Russian Composers' Union.

Exploring the Score

➤ A humoresque is a humorous or fanciful composition that sometimes incorporates extreme opposites. Begin your exploration of this piece by listening to the *Celebration Series®* recording. Does it live up to its title?

➤ The tempo marking, *Tempo moderato assai con buffo e elegante,* says much about the humorous character. As you explore this tightly crafted composition, what elements create contrast? In your discussion, consider register, dynamics, and articulations. How do these contrasts contribute to the comic *(buffo)* atmosphere?

➤ Mark the different sections in the score:

Introduction mm. 1-4

A	mm. 5-12
B	mm. 13-20
A	mm. 21-29
C	mm. 30-36
A	mm. 37-44
B	mm. 45-52
A	mm. 53-60
Coda	mm. 61-66

➤ What is this form? [rondo]
➤ Explore the A sections. Does Shchedrin vary the material? For example, compare the RH in mm. 5, 21, 37, and 53. Which measure is slightly different? [m. 5] Notice that the LH changes in m. 37. What other changes can you find among the A sections?
➤ Are the B sections the same? [yes]

Practice Suggestions

This piece is a sound exploration into the realm of dark humor. This is great Hallowe'en music!

➤ The key signature, leger lines, and numerous accidentals make this piece difficult to read. As you practice the RH, check *very carefully* for notes and accidentals that may be misread.
➤ Practice the RH of mm. 5-11 alone until you are completely confident with the notes, shifts and articulations. Then add the LH.
➤ Isolate the RH from m. 13 to the downbeat of m. 15. This passage recurs in mm. 45-47. Find the relationship between the leaping sixteenth notes by lowering the top note two octaves. The interval is a 3rd! Memorize these RH skips. Practice them without looking at the score. Then combine with the LH.
➤ Block the RH two-note phrase groups in mm. 17-18.
➤ The LH uses an *ostinato*-like figure much of the time. When that *ostinato* is combined with a bass melody (mm. 37-40), the LH suddenly becomes complicated. Practice the LH in those measures first. Use touches of damper pedal to help with the connection.

Harold Arlen, arr. George Shearing
Over the Rainbow (R122)
Background Information

Harold Arlen was a well-known American composer and arranger of popular music. His most widely recognized contribution was the 1939 film score for *The Wizard of Oz,* which included the famous song, *Over the Rainbow.* This transcription for piano solo is by American jazz pianist George Shearing, whose writing is best known for its rich extended harmonies and thick chords in parallel motion.

Exploring the Score

➤ Although the texture is thick, Shearing places the melody at the top of chords. As the student listens to the *Celebration Series®* recording, mark the measures that are "filler" between melodic phrases. The student may enjoy playing the melody along with the recording.
➤ You may wish to teach the student the lyrics of the song.
➤ Notice the repetition of melodic and harmonic material in mm. 9-16.
➤ Where does the opening melody recur? [m. 25] How does Shearing vary the texture? [RH an octave higher, use of grace notes, and different LH accompaniment]
➤ The sonorous jazz harmonies are most appealing. To the extent possible, identify chord letter names and the harmonic extensions that add "color" to the harmony. For example, the last chord of the piece is an E flat major chord with an added 9th (F) and 6th (C).
➤ Some students will have difficulty with the large LH stretches of mm. 2 and 10. It is possible to redistribute the inner eighth notes to accommodate smaller hands.

Practice Suggestions

➤ Reading the thick texture accurately will be your biggest hurdle. When learning notes, check all accidentals and key signature notes carefully, practicing in repeated short units.
➤ To gain technical security with chord textures, play the outer notes of any chord followed by the inside tones ("outside-inside" practice).

➤ The most difficult moment is the LH of m. 26.
  - Play the outsides of the chords without the grace notes.
  - Add the inner tones of the chords.

- Practice the grace note going to the top note of the chord (thumb). Say the names of those pitches as you play.
- Play the LH as written, slowly and accurately.

➤ Bring out inner chromatic lines. For example, isolate the LH in m. 28. The interest lies in the inner half-step movement.

➤ Use damper pedal for *legato* connection.

➤ The final performance goal is a smoothly flowing sound and a beautifully voiced melody.

Clermont Pépin
Le nez / The Nose (R124)
Background Information

Pépin has had a distinguished career as a leading Canadian composer, teacher, and administrator. Pépin's composition *Le nez* was inspired by a short story by Russian author Nicolas Gogol: A man wakes up one morning and discovers to his great dismay that his nose has disappeared during his sleep. On his way to look for it he meets his nose, on a bridge. The nose is dressed as a General, strolling along and dancing. Returning home to sleep, the man discovers upon awakening that his nose is back in its original place. He concludes that the entire episode was a silly nightmare. The music depicts the nose as it joyfully goes around town dressed as a General.

Exploring the Score

➤ As an introduction to the sound, listen to the *Celebration Series*® recording of *Le nez* with score in

hand. What elements of the music depict the story? Consider:
- How is the music dance-like? [RH dotted rhythms and skipping texture, natural rise and fall of the RH tune]
- Since the man's nose is dressed as a General, which section of the piece sounds like a military march? [B section, mm. 11-38]
- Where is there a trumpet fanfare? [m. 11]
- Which hand provides the military march rhythm in the B section? [LH]

➤ The LH clearly indicates the change of sections. Note the use of different LH *ostinato* patterns, indicating walking, marching, etc.

➤ What intervals contribute to the slightly dissonant sound? [half-steps and tritones]

➤ In the B section, find and compare passages that are similar. How do they differ?

Practice Suggestions

The fast tempo and frequent shifts of position in the A section are a challenge. To facilitate the quick shifts in mm. 3-9, block the two-note slurs in the RH while playing the LH. Then play as written.

➤ You will learn the piece thoroughly if you practice in short units and gradually increase the tempo. Determine your practice unit (no more than four measures). Aim for three *perfect* repetitions of each unit. When all parts are secure, combine them until the entire piece is learned.

➤ Follow the LH fingerings in mm. 29-30 (also mm. 33-34) to obtain the desired *legato*.

PIANO STUDIES/ETUDES 9
Suggested Order of Difficulty

Page	Composer	Title
Less Difficult		
S18	Hermann Berens	Study no. 8: *Study in F Major, op. 61, no. 10*
S8	Hermann Berens	Study no. 3: *Study in F Major, op. 61, no. 8*
S20	Niels Gade	Study no. 9: *Scherzo, op. 19, no. 2*
S30	Moritz Moszkowski	Study no. 13: *Study in E flat Major, op. 91, no. 17*
More Difficult		
S12	Stephen Heller	Study no. 5: *Study in G Major, op. 47, no. 24*
S14	Felix Mendelssohn	Study no. 6: *Song without Words, op. 102, no. 3*
S6	Hermann Berens	Study no. 2: *Study in A Minor, op. 61, no. 13*
S24	Jean-Baptiste Duvernoy	Study no. 11: *Study in C Major, op. 120, no. 10*
Most Difficult		
S10	Carl Czerny	Study no. 4: *Study in C Major, op. 533, no. 1*
S22	Béla Bartók	Study no. 10: *Bagatelle, op. 6, no. 2*
S4	Johann Baptist Cramer	Study no. 1: *Study in E Minor, op. 39, no. 2*
S16	Moritz Moszkowski	Study no. 7: *Study in E flat Major, op. 91, no. 6*
S26	George Frideric Handel	Study no. 12: *Suite No. 8 in F Minor, HWV 433 (Allemande)*

CHART OF TECHNICAL FIGURES – continued

This chart lists the studies with their main technical focus. A study may be listed in more than one category.

Category	Composer	Study no.
Accompanying figures	Hermann Berens	2
	Hermann Berens	8
	Niels Gade	9
	Jean-Baptiste Duvernoy	11
	Stephen Heller	5
Alternating hands	Béla Bartók	10
	Stephen Heller	5
	George Frideric Handel	12
Arpeggiated figures	Johann Baptist Cramer	1
	Hermann Berens	3
	Niels Gade	9
Broken chords	Johann Baptist Cramer	1
	Hermann Berens	3
	Moritz Moszkowski	7
	Niels Gade	9
	Moritz Moszkowski	13
Extensions and contractions of the hand	Johann Baptist Cramer	1
Irregular change of direction	Hermann Berens	2
	Béla Bartók	10
	Moritz Moszkowski	13
Melody presented in extended positions	Hermann Berens	3
	Hermann Berens	8
	Stephen Heller	5
	Moritz Moszkowski	13
Octaves	Carl Czerny	4
	Moritz Moszkowski	13
Quickly shifting chords	Felix Mendelssohn	6
	Béla Bartók	10
Repeated technical gesture	Hermann Berens	3
	Carl Czerny	4
	Felix Mendelssohn	6
	Béla Bartók	10
Rhythmic complexity	Béla Bartók	10
Rotational figures	Niels Gade	9
	George Frideric Handel	12
Scale figures	Johann Baptist Cramer	1
	Hermann Berens	2
	Moritz Moszkowski	7
	Niels Gade	9
	Jean-Baptiste Duvernoy	11
Two voices in one hand	Hermann Berens	3
	Hermann Berens	8
	Stephen Heller	5
	Moritz Moszkowski	13
	George Frideric Handel	12

Students require a variety of technical challenges to achieve technical growth. Fast passagework alone does not develop control of voicing; finger activity does not develop hand and arm movement; and foot–hand coordination varies with the tempo of the music.

Piano Studies/Etudes 9 provides a wide variety of technical challenges. Although included in a collection of studies, these pieces deserve the same musical investigation and refined interpretation as the selections in *Piano Repertoire 9*. Listening to the *Celebration Series®* recording of these studies/etudes reinforces this perspective.

The following discussions focus on the technical aspect of each study/etude.

Johann Baptist Cramer
Study in E Minor, op. 39, no. 2 (S4)
Background Information
German-born pianist and pedagogue Johann Baptist Cramer was one of the most eminent pianists of his time. For a brief time (1783–1784), he studied with Clementi. During his career, he met many famous composers, including Beethoven. His lasting contribution to the field of piano teaching was his method, *Grosse Praktische Pianoforte Schule,* published in five parts. The last part, *Studio per il pianoforte,* was a set of eighty-four technical studies published in 1804 and 1810.

Exploring the Score
➤ Find the three different figures that comprise the piece:
  "x" – broken octave chords plus a mordent (mm. 1-12)
  "y" – three ascending steps (mm. 9-12)
  "y1"– three ascending notes in wider intervals (mm. 14-23)
  "z" – scale figures (mm. 24-26)

Create exercises to prepare for these technical ideas. Play the exercises in various keys.

Practice Suggestions
➤ The opening gesture will be most successful if the thumb "joins" the hand immediately after it has played. [By the time finger 5 plays, the hand should be in a five-finger position, not outstretched.]
➤ Move the arm and hand in the direction of the line. Rocking the hand will aid in playing 5-4-5 clearly and easily.
➤ "Crush" the grace note with the beat note in one motion.
➤ In mm. 20-23, practice the basic figure in three ascending notes, not in their beamed groups.
➤ Preliminary practice of scales in thirds will facilitate the playing of mm. 25-26.
➤ Alternate *legato* practice with *staccato*.

Hermann Berens
Study in A Minor, op. 61, no. 13 (S6)
Background Information
Hermann Berens was a German pianist and teacher who studied with Czerny. His piano studies, *Neueste Schule der Geläufigkeitwere,* were modeled after Czerny's technical writing. Later in his life, Berens emigrated to Sweden, where he was appointed teacher of composition at the Stockholm Conservatory in 1861.

Practice Suggestions
This is a study in endurance and technical security with rapid passagework. Analyze the direction of the sixteenth note lines. Find:
  – Sixteenth groups that flow in the same direction.
  – Groups that frequently reverse direction or have an irregular change of direction. [mm. 3-4]
  – Repeated fingering patterns.
  – Arpeggiated figures.

➤ In sixteenth-note passagework the grouping of notes does not always coincide with the beaming. For example, in mm. 3-4 and similar passages, the sixteenth-note figures are best practiced in four-note impulses of "2-3-4-1."
➤ If a particular measure or passage is troublesome, try saying the fingering aloud while practicing slowly.
➤ Often with such an active RH, one overlooks the LH. Projecting the LH (especially the bass line) will add a feeling of security to the RH.
➤ Do not forget the metronome. It is a helpful friend when increasing the tempo gradually.

Hermann Berens
Study in F Major, op. 61, no. 8 (S8)
Practice Suggestions
This study has four different figures within a three-voice texture:
  – LH broken chord sixteenth figures
  – RH single note melody
  – RH two-voice texture
  – LH scale-like passages

- ➤ Which figures will profit most from hands separate practice?
- ➤ Berens marks this study *con pedale*. The damper pedal must be used discreetly to avoid blurring the LH scale passages.
- ➤ How should RH two-note slurs (drop-lift motion) be coordinated with the foot and pedal? [Mm. 25-27 will be pedaled the same as in the beginning. The two-note slur effect is mainly a dynamic principle.]

Carl Czerny
Study in C Major, op. 533, no. 1 (S10)
Background Information

Czerny was of Czech heritage but lived in Vienna his entire adult life. He studied with Beethoven for three years. Beethoven entrusted the musical instruction of his favorite nephew, Karl, to Czerny, as well as the premier performance of his *Fifth Piano Concerto,* (The "Emperor"). Czerny became a famous pianist and pedagogue. His students included Liszt, Thalberg, and Kullak.

Czerny is best known for his myriad technical studies (note the opus number of this study.). His 861 opus numbers include not only exercises, but piano arrangements of symphonies and fantasies on well-known opera themes. His études are still of value for today's piano students because they drill the technical figures required for command of 18th- and 19th-century piano repertoire.

Practice Suggestions

This study is all about playing octaves, octaves, and more octaves!
- ➤ Try these preparatory drills:

1) Play octave scales, playing each note three times with a lifting gesture of the wrist.

2) Play octave scales in three-note groups with the same lifting of the wrist.

3) Repeat these drills using groups of six notes. Notice Czerny's dynamics and the *leggieramente* marking. The *forte* level occurs only midway through the piece.

- ➤ Keep the wrist relaxed to avoid tension. Avoid playing successive downward motions.
- ➤ To develop endurance, practice the forte passages quietly with a light touch. Develop a natural "bounce" in the staccato motion.

- ➤ Remember that the thumb is the "eye" of the octave. Practice playing only the thumb notes of the octaves, accompanied by the other hand.
- ➤ Notice how Czerny builds in "relief" by changing the octaves from the RH to the LH, beginning in m. 9.

Stephen Heller
Study in G Major, op. 47, no. 24 (S12)
Background Information

Heller was a famous Hungarian composer and pianist who studied briefly with Czerny. He spent much of his life in Paris, where he became a friend of Chopin and Liszt. Some of Heller's contemporaries actually felt his playing was superior to Chopin's. Heller composed hundreds of piano pieces, many for instructional purposes, of which the collection, *Twenty-Five Studies for the Piano, op. 47,* is well known.

Practice Suggestions

Heller's op. 47 is subtitled "For Developing a Sense of Musical Rhythm and Expression." Melodic projection, voicing within a hand, and clear pedaling are the primary elements in this study. Slow practice will help develop control of the voicing in the RH.

Practice phrase by phrase:

- ➤ Play only the RH melody. Observe the dynamics and contour of each phrase.
- ➤ Combine the RH melody with the sixteenth-note accompaniment. Pause on each melodic tone. Let the accompanying sixteenth notes push weight and tone into the melody notes (the eighth notes).
- ➤ Play the LH of each phrase. Often, the LH phrasing and articulation differ from the RH.
- ➤ Play the RH melody and the LH together (just one phrase at a time). Do you hear the dynamic contour of the phrase? Does the LH have independence from the RH?

Felix Mendelssohn
Song without Words, op. 102, no. 3 (S14)
Practice Suggestions

➤ It is important to find a single wrist gesture to support each group of three eighth notes. Practice the following preparatory exercises, hands separately and hands together.

➤ While playing a triplet pattern, move the wrist up and down without lifting the fingertips from the keys:

➤ Practice a drop-lift motion using the following patterns:

➤ The first note of the two-note slurs, beginning in mm. 9-10, should be slightly louder. To make this easier, lift the wrist on the second note, played with a light *staccato* touch.

➤ In the LH eighth-note pairs (mm. 9-22), play the second chord lighter and quieter than the first chord.

➤ Compare the LH fingering of mm. 54-57 with the RH of mm. 1-2.

Moritz Moszkowski
Study in E flat Major, op. 91, no. 6 (S16)
Background Information

Moritz Moszkowski was a well-known German pianist and teacher of Polish descent. Two of his students, Josef Hofmann and Wanda Landowska, achieved international fame.

Practice Suggestions

Playing scales in intervals of a 10th, a 6th, or a 3rd between the hands is an important technique to master. This study includes scales in 3rds (mm. 1-2 and 9-10) … but that's the easy part!

The unpredictable changes of direction present a greater challenge. When hands move in parallel motion (e.g., in mm. 5-6), the problem can be solved with comfortable fingerings. When parallel and contrary

motion are combined (e.g., in mm. 3-4), the difficulties increase.

➤ Look for groups of notes in parallel motion. Stop on the last note of a group, and prepare your hand for the next group:

➤ Another effective practice technique is to pause briefly on the beat note of each group of three eighths.

➤ For the figures that seem most complex (e.g., m. 7, mm. 18-19), practice hands separately to secure the fingering and clarify the direction of the patterns. Begin hands together practice slowly and deliberately, exaggerating the dynamic levels.

Hermann Berens
Study in D Minor, op. 61, no. 10 (S18)
Exploring the Score

Berens' *Cantabile* marking provides the primary clue for the study of this piece. The sound goal of the piece can be realized when the student plays the soprano melody (without the sixteenth-note accompaniment) and the LH. Enjoy Berens' lovely melody and its natural dynamic contour. Each day's practice can start with this reminder of the basic melodic contour of the piece.

– With your student, examine Berens' phrase lengths:
– Notice that mm. 1-8 are two four-measure phrases.
– What is the phrase organization for mm. 9-16? [2 + 2 + 1 + 1 + 2]
– What is the phrase organization for mm. 17 to the end?
– Compare mm. 1-4 with mm. 17-20. How does the composer vary the LH and inner-voice accompaniments?

Practice Suggestions

This is a study in voicing two lines within one hand. Practice different combinations of the RH melody, RH inner sixteenth note accompaniment, and LH bass line:
– RH divided, playing sixteenth notes in LH and melody notes in RH
– LH with RH melodic tones
– LH with RH sixteenth notes

Develop balance in this type of RH figure by exaggerating the *forte* on each melodic tone while thinking the sixteenths as ***p*** or ***pp***:

- Pause on each melodic tone (played loudly), relax the hand, then play the next three 16ths *pianissimo*. Exaggerate the melodic tone over the inner accompaniment.
- Continue by pausing and playing the next melodic tone *forte*. This practice approach will ensure that you have time to relax the hand to control the quiet accompaniment.
- Use the damper pedal carefully to connect melodic quarter notes (pedal each beat). When possible use "finger *legato*" to connect the top tones.
- Notice how Berens uses *cresc.* and *dim.* marks to highlight peaks of phrases.

Niels Gade
Scherzo, op. 19, no. 2 (S20)
Background Information

Gade was a composer of Danish descent who greatly admired the music of Mendelssohn and Schumann. Gade worked directly with Mendelssohn, serving as the Assistant Conductor of the Gewandhaus orchestra and teaching at the Leipzig Conservatory. Following Mendelssohn's death in 1847, Gade was appointed Kapellmeister of the Conservatory. Shortly thereafter, he returned to his native Copenhagen, where he spent the remainder of his career.

Practice Suggestions

Scherzo has five different technical figures. Isolate each figure for concentrated practice:
- three-note figure (m. 1)
- RH ascending scale and descending arpeggio (mm. 5-6)
- LH broken pattern (mm. 10-13)
- RH turn figure (mm. 14-15)
- RH broken-chord and scale pattern (mm. 27-28)

The LH figure in mm. 10-13 forms a cross rhythm against the RH. Practice the LH separately to establish the proper rolling motion. When the LH is secure, add the RH.

Béla Bartók
Bagatelle, op. 6, no. 2 (S22)
Background Information

Bartók was one of the most famous and distinguished 20th-century composers. He wrote a great deal of piano music for both developing and advanced pianists. Many of his compositions are based on folk tunes from his native Hungary as well as Rumania and Slovakia. Bartók left Europe because of World War II to live in the United States. Two of his most famous piano collections were written for the instruction of young pianists: *For Children* (four volumes) and *Mikrokosmos* (six volumes).

The term *bagatelle* dates from the time of Couperin and is a French term meaning "trifle" or a short piece. The *Celebration Series®* includes bagatelles composed by Beethoven (Levels 6 and 7) and Ann Southam (Level 10). Bartók's Op. 6 (1908) contains fourteen bagatelles, many only one page long.

Exploring the Score

As a sound model, listen to the *Celebration Series®* recording of this piece. Listen for the interpretation of the sharp articulations and dynamic marks. Do you hear changes of mood? Is the effect truly *giocoso* (joyous or humorous)?

Practice Suggestions

Coordination of the independent figures is the main challenge in this piece.
- Practice mm. 3-6, 15-16, and 23-25 on the closed keyboard cover. Use precise fingering and simulate interval relationships and the locations of black and white keys.
- At the keyboard, first practice hands separately, emphasizing the tones that last full value.
- As you practice hands together slowly, exaggerate the difference between legato and staccato touches.

Jean-Baptiste Duvernoy
Study in C Major, op. 120, no. 10 (S24)
Practice Suggestions

The focus of this study is clear passagework in each hand as well as endurance. To learn the various technical figures and to increase endurance, follow these steps:
- Make sure your fingering is secure. Write in additional fingerings if needed.
- Stop on the first sixteenth note of each beat. Slightly raise the finger that starts the next group of sixteenth notes. Then play to the next beat.
- Continue this practice method in groups of eight sixteenth notes.
- Continue in groups of twelve sixteenth notes, stopping on the downbeat of the next measure.
- Practice the sixteenths in dotted rhythms.
- Select larger practice units and rehearse at a minimum of four different metronome speeds, gradually reaching the desired tempo.

George Frideric Handel
Suite No. 8 in F Minor, HWV 433 (Allemande and Gigue) (S26)

Allemande
Exploring the Score
A list of characteristics of a baroque Allemande might include:
- $\frac{4}{4}$ meter
- short upbeat
- imitative, contrapuntal texture
- binary form, each section repeated

Find those stylistic characteristics in Handel's *Allemande.*

There are many articulation possibilities for this piece.
- Upbeats should be detached.
- LH wider intervals are detached.
- Mm. 3, 5-8 can have a slight break between beats.
- In the figure in mm. 7-8, 23-24, detach the step motion between beats (notice the 1-1 fingering on beats three to four).

➤ In m. 14, all beats should sound alike, whether played by one hand or two.
➤ Notice the alto entrance of the subject in m. 17.

Practice Suggestions
This Allemande requires disciplined finger work, and a nearly detached, "fingery" sound.

➤ As a preliminary exercise, practice the sixteenths *staccato.* Listen carefully for the clarity of your sound.
➤ How will you practice the more complex texture at each cadence?
- Practice hands separately at first
- When the RH is responsible for two voices, be attentive to the rhythmic value of notes.

Gigue
Background Information
Although the student has studied other Baroque dances, this is the first appearance of a gigue in the *Celebration Series®.* The gigue was the final core dance of the Baroque keyboard suite: allenmande, courante, sarabande, gigue. Optional dances such as the minuet, gavotte, and bourrée were inserted between the sarabande and gigue. The gigue is lively and vigorous and is associated with triplet figures and compound meters of $\frac{6}{8}$ and $\frac{9}{8}$.

Exploring the Score
➤ Three figures dominant this gigue:
- angular eighth notes (e.g., m. 1)
- four sixteenth notes leading to a beat note (e.g., m. 6)
- repeated bass tone supporting rising stepwise motion (e.g., mm. 10-11)

As you peruse the score, look for the multiple appearances of each of these musical ideas.

➤ When you circle the following harmonies, you have a harmonic "road map" of this piece:

m. 1	F minor
m. 13	A flat major
m. 24	C major
m. 30	B flat minor
m. 47	E minor

➤ Realizing that a harpsichord cannot provide a dynamic accent, discuss the ways in which articulation can help identify the downbeat in measures of eighth notes, e.g., mm. 1-4.

Practice Suggestions
➤ You have one primary decision to make: how to articulate eighth notes. Your decision will help the listener hear the downbeats clearly.
➤ You have one technical issue to solve: how to finger the sixteenth notes. Follow the fingerings in the score consistently.
➤ When learning fingerings of detached figures, it is helpful to practice *legato* at first.

Moritz Moszkowski
Study in E flat Major, op. 91, no. 17 (S30)
Exploring the Score
This study is highly unified. The sixteenth motion in the LH is constant, and the RH presents the melody.

➤ Examine the ways Moszkowski creates variety in this study:
- The LH frequently has a bass line that is marked by the composer to be emphasized.
- The RH melody has a variety of phrase lengths.
- In m. 25, the RH melody is played in octaves.

➤ Does the ending chordal section present new material? [no; it is a harmonization of the opening RH melody]

Practice Suggestions
➤ The LH extensions in the opening four measures present a special challenge. Rotate the hand and arm in the direction of the line, letting the fingers move with the arm as the notes are released. Use arm movement to avoid unnecessary stretching of the fingers.
➤ Practice the LH "melody" in mm. 5-11. Stop on each melodic tone. Hold that tone as you quietly play the sixteenths that lead to the next bass tone. What arm gesture facilitates this passage?
➤ Isolate the RH melody and LH quarter-note countermelody (omit sixteenths) for hands together practice.

➤ Use the damper pedal to help connect the RH octave melody beginning in m. 24. Give priority to the *legato* sound of the top voice (4-5 finger combinations or finger substitution help achieve a *legato* sound).

➤ Should the top notes of the chorale (beginning m. 43) be projected? [yes; this is a harmonized version of the opening melody]

The performance goal of this study is to maintain a smoothly flowing, expressive melody, pedaled to enhance the *legato* and blend the harmonic colors. How will the term *armonioso* in m. 41 affect your sound goals? Listen to the *Celebration Series*® recording to study nuances of phrasing and *rubato*.

Level 9 CONCLUSION

The greatest gift we give to our students is a life-long enjoyment of playing the piano. In its own way, Level 9 has been that gift. Through Level 9, your student has traversed the musical centuries hand in hand with Bach, Scarlatti, Mozart, Haydn, Beethoven, Chopin, Mendelssohn, Grieg, and modern-day Russian, European, and North American composers. Your student has experienced the fascination and thrill of making music.

Our piano lessons provide an opportunity—for both teacher and student—to explore beyond the printed note, to think more deeply about the music, to gain new insights, and to come closer to each composer's thoughts and musical intentions. Level 9 is also, in many ways, a gift to the teacher. Through investigation and involvement with this literature, we grow musically with our students. As our resources and knowledge base increase, so do the musical riches that we can share with our students.

Level 10

The Publications

Level 10 of the *Celebration Series®* includes the following publications:

Piano Repertoire 10
Piano Studies/Etudes 10
Recording of Repertoire and *Studies/Etudes 10*

The Repertoire

Piano Repertoire 10 is divided into five lists.

➤ List A includes a selection of pieces composed during the Baroque period (*ca* 1600 to *ca* 1750).
➤ List B pieces are from the Classical period (*ca* 1750 to *ca* 1820).
➤ List C includes a selection of pieces composed during the Romantic era (*ca* 1820 to *ca* 1910).
➤ List D pieces were composed during the late 19th century and the 20th century.
➤ List E explores more recent 20th-century repertoire.

Musical Development

Piano Repertoire 10 and *Piano Studies/Etudes 10* contain the most difficult material in the *Celebration Series®*. The teacher can appreciate the years of investment necessary to bring the student to this advanced level. The student's experience, progressing from level to level, is similar to climbing. The higher the climb, the more expansive the musical view. With this final step of the ascent, the musical horizon stretches even wider. The music in *Piano Repertoire* 10 and *Piano Studies/Etudes 10* includes pieces by the greatest composers of piano literature.

Organization of Level 10

As in Level 9, the discussion of repertoire and studies is not divided into Study Modules, but rather follows the list order of *Piano Repertoire 10* (A, B, C, D, and E). At the end of this chapter, you will find a discussion of each piece in the *Piano Studies/Etudes 10*.

For each list, there is a suggested order of study based on difficulty, a brief discussion of the general style characteristics, and a detailed consideration of each piece under the following headings:

- *Background Information:* stylistic or biographical information
- *Exploring the Score:* suggested material for student–teacher discussions
- *Practice Suggestions:* addressed to the student to assist in the beginning weeks of practice

Teachers can determine the order of repertoire assigned, based on the individual student's needs and program of study. Teachers are encouraged to formulate units of study, integrating pieces of contrasting style periods from the *Piano Repertoire* album and the *Piano Studies/Etudes* album.

The *Celebration Series®* does not include a student workbook for Level 10. It is our hope that the following discussions will facilitate your teaching of this repertoire, provide material for fruitful discussions between you and your students, and increase their musical enjoyment and technical facility.

The Studies/Etudes

The studies are discussed separately at the end of this section. The pieces in the *Piano Studies/Etudes* album are similar in purpose to the Chopin *Études*. Although each piece has a specific technical focus, these studies have noteworthy musical value and can be considered as repertoire. To assist your choice of appropriate works, we have suggested a difficulty-based order of study and a chart showing the types of technical figures encountered in these studies.

The Recordings

The *Celebration Series®* recording of all pieces in this level is a valuable teaching resource. This professional recording provides a musical sound model, a pedagogical element that words cannot communicate. Listening to the recording with the student can stimulate discussion on topics such as articulation, balance and dynamics, expressive timing *(rubato)* and nuances, and pedaling. Listening to recordings should be a regular part of the student's assignment.

The following chart lists the repertoire and studies of Level 10 according to the order presented in *Piano Repertoire 10* and *Piano Studies/Etudes 10*. Page numbers for works in the *Piano Repertoire 10* and *Piano Studies/Etudes 10* are found in the first column.

Piano Repertoire 10

Page	Composer	Title

List A – Contrapuntal works by J.S. Bach

R4	Johann Sebastian Bach	*Prelude and Fugue in D Major, BWV 850*
R8	Johann Sebastian Bach	*French Suite No. 5, BWV 816, Allemande and Gigue*
R13	Johann Sebastian Bach	*Capriccio sopra la lontananza del fratello dilettissimo / Capriccio on the absence of a most beloved brother, BWV 992, Mvts. Four, Five, Six*

List B – Classical Sonatas

R19	Ludwig van Beethoven	*Sonata in E Major, op. 14, no. 1*
R32	Franz Joseph Haydn	*Sonata in B Minor, Hob. XVI:32*
R43	Wolfgang Amadeus Mozart	*Sonata in E flat Major, K 282 (189g)*

List C – Romantic Repertoire

R51	Frédéric Chopin	*Waltz in E Minor, op. posth.*
R55	Frédéric Chopin	*Nocturne in F sharp Major, op. 15, no. 2*
R59	Johannes Brahms	*Ballade in D Minor, op. 10, no. 1*
R63	Franz Schubert	*Impromptu in E flat Major, op. 90, no. 2*
R72	Robert Schumann	*Intermezzo, op. 26, no. 4*

List D – Neo-classic, Neo-romantic and Impressionistic Repertoire

R76	Sergei Rachmaninoff	*Mélodie / Melody, op. 3, no. 3*
R80	Cyril Scott	*Lotus Land, op. 47, no. 1*
R85	Claude Debussy	*Brouillards / Mist*
R91	Françis Poulenc	*Suite française, Mvts. Three, Six, Seven*
R99	Manuel de Falla	*Danse du meunier / The Miller's Dance*
R102	Amy Marcy Cheney Beach	*A Hermit Thrush at Eve, op. 92, no. 1*

List E – Twentieth-century Repertoire

R107	Béla Bartók	*Rondo No. 1, op. 84*
R111	Aaron Copland	*The Cat and the Mouse*
R117	Clermont Pépin	*Trois pièces pour la légende dorée / Three Pieces for the Golden Legend*
R124	Olivier Messiaen	*Plainte calme / Gentle Sorrow*
R126	Dimitri Shostakovich	*Three Fantastic Dances, op. 5*
R132	Alberto Ginastera	*Róndo sobre temas infantiles argentinos / Rondo on Argentine Children's Folk-tunes*
R136	Harry Somers	*Strangeness of Heart*
R139	Samuel Barber	*Pas de deux*
R143	Lee Hoiby	*Prelude, op. 7, no. 1*
R147	Dmitri Kabalevsky	*Variations in A Minor, op. 40, no. 2*
R154	Robert Muczynski	*Six Preludes, op. 6, nos. 1 and 6*
R160	Ann Southam	*Four Bagatelles, nos. 2 and 4*
R164	Christos Tsitsaros	*Snow Games*

Piano Studies/Etudes 10

S4	Carl Czerny	Study no. 1: *Study in A Minor, op. 740, no. 41*
S6	Stephen Heller	Study no. 2: *Prelude in C sharp Minor, op. 81, no. 10*
S8	Ernst Haberbier	Study no. 3: *Serenade, op. 53, no. 5*
S11	Hermann Berens	Study no. 4: *Study in A Minor, op. 61, no. 32*
S14	Moritz Moszkowski	Study no. 5: *Etude in C Major, op. 72, no. 4*
S18	Alexander Scriabin	Study no. 6: *Etude, op. 2, no. 1*
S20	Carl Czerny	Study no. 7: *Study in F Major, op. 299, no. 12*
S22	Anatol Konstantinovich Lyadov	Study no. 8: *A Trifle, op. 2, no. 12*
S24	Carl Albert Loeschhorn	Study no. 9: *Etude in E Minor, op. 67, no. 5*
S26	Sergei Rachmaninoff	Study no. 10: *Étude-tableau, op. 33, no. 8*
S30	Jean-Baptiste Duvernoy	Study no. 11: *Study in C Major, op. 120, no. 13*
S32	Moritz Moszkowski	Study no. 12: *Study in C Major, op. 91, no. 15*
S35	Béla Bartók	Study no. 13: *Bagatelle, op. 6, no. 5*
S38	Christos Tsitsaros	Study no. 14: *Gallop*

LIST A – CONTRAPUNTAL WORKS OF J.S. BACH

Suggested Order of Difficulty (entire works)

Page	Composer	Title
R13	Johann Sebastian Bach	*Capriccio sopra la lontananza del fratello dilettissimo, BWV 992* (*Mvts. Four, Five, Six*)
R4	Johann Sebastian Bach	*Prelude and Fugue in D Major, BWV 850*
R8	Johann Sebastian Bach	*French Suite No. 5, BWV 816 (Allemande and Gigue)*

Suggested Order of Difficulty (individual movements)

Capriccio, Mvt. Four
Capriccio, Mvt. Five
Fugue in D Major
Allemande from French Suite No. 5
Capriccio, Mvt. Six
Prelude in D Major
Gigue from French Suite No. 5

The pieces selected for List A provide a variety of Baroque forms and represent works from different periods of Bach's life. The *Capriccio sopra la lontananza del fratello dilettissimo* (*Capriccio on the Departure of a Beloved Brother*) is one of Bach's few programmatic works, written when he was in his late teens. *The Well-Tempered Clavier, Book I* and the six *French Suites* were written nearly twenty years later.

When studying Bach, the piano student often learns a predominance of strict contrapuntal works: inventions, sinfonias, and fugues. However, the dance suite was the most important Baroque genre for stringed keyboard instruments. One welcomes the variety of style presented by these two dances from the *French Suite in G Major*, as well as the toccata-like *Prelude in D Major* and the early programmatic works.

If possible, arrange for your students to play these works on a harpsichord to experience the unique touch and sound of that instrument. A harpsichordist uses subtle timing and articulation to emphasize meter and beat.

Johann Sebastian Bach
Prelude and Fugue in D Major, BWV 850 (R4)
Background Information

Each volume of *The Well-Tempered Clavier* contains a prelude and fugue in each major and minor key. *The Well-Tempered Clavier* was not written for a specfic instrument; the use of the term *clavier* simply implies keyboard instruments in general.

The pairing of two contrasting movements has a long and rich history. The prelude, keyboard literature's oldest form, has always been free from the obligations of strict voice limitation or set formal plan. Indeed, its origins lie in the act of improvisation, or warm-up ("prelude" = playing beforehand). This improvised expression was a natural partner for a contrasting piece in strictly controlled style, such as a fugue or *ricercare*. The miracle of Bach's forty-eight preludes and fugues lies in their great diversity. Bach composed slow preludes and fast preludes, free preludes and strict preludes, preludes that dance and preludes that sing. The *Prelude in D Major, BWV 850*, is a technical piece much like a toccata movement.

Prelude in D Major, BWV 850
Exploring the Score

A quick perusal of the score reveals that the RH plays thirty-two measures of sixteenth notes. Several questions immediately come to mind:
1. Are there unifying factors in the sixteenth figures?
2. How does Bach achieve contrast within that rhythmic unity?

Looking at m. 1, one sees that each beat contains a stepwise pattern: D–E–F sharp or F sharp–E–D. The note on the beat provides the variety and surprise (low, then high).

➤ Look through other measures of the prelude. Does each beat have a similar three-note step wise pattern? [yes] This consistency helps to unify the piece.

➤ The LH clarifies the harmonic progression. The strongest harmonies occur when the bass moves down a 5th, creating a V–I progression.

➤ Find examples of bass movement down a 5th. You will find the V most frequently on beat three, and the I on beat one, e.g., mm. 5-6.

A major: V   I

➤ Using the accidentals as your guide, search for the movement to other keys, especially IV and V. [Notice the transposition of the opening measures to G major (IV), mm. 20-22.]

➤ Because the bass line moves around so much, the ear is drawn to the contrast when a bass tone repeats for more than a measure. Find examples of repeated bass tones. Be aware of the tension created by the held bass tone mm. 27-34. This is an excellent example of a pedal point.

➤ How does Bach create tension and climax at the end of the prelude after so many measures of RH perpetual motion and unchanging rhythm in the LH?

➤ What is the quality of the rolled chords in mm. 33, 34? [diminished 7th]

➤ Why would Bach prefer two-handed diminished 7ths over a I or V7 harmony at this point? [greater tension]

Practice Suggestions

Clarity and rhythmic precision of the RH sixteenth notes is all-important.

➤ From your first day of practice, determine the fingering of sixteenth notes that works best for your hand. Write chosen fingerings in the score. Consistent use of the same fingering is an important factor in establishing technical security. Fingerings can be reinforced by saying them aloud.

➤ Note the relationship between the last sixteenth note of a beat and the following beat note. This pairing forms the technical contour of the RH.

➤ Maintain a flexible wrist and hand as you follow the contour of the sixteenth-note patterns. Keep the thumb in a relaxed, natural position and avoid extending it unnecessarily.

➤ For ultimate control of the sixteenths, use these practice techniques:
  - dotted rhythms
  - short group practice
  - *staccato*
  - each note repeated

Fugue in D Major, BWV 850
Background Information

There is controversy over the rhythmic interpretation of this fugue. Is the dotted note to be performed in the style of the French Overture (the double-dotting or "over-dotting" effect used in slow, majestic movements)? The term French Overture and the practice of double dotting originated in orchestral works of the French Baroque. The notation of a double dot was unknown in Bach's day, but the rhythmic practice was traditional for this majestic style. Because of a lack of notational precision, Bach was forced to align the thirty-seconds and sixteenths in the manner shown in the score. To gain perspective, listen to a variety of recordings in addition to the *Celebration Series*® recording of this fugue. What is each performer's decision about the rhythm? Does each rendition create the atmosphere of festive ceremony?

Exploring the Score

Fuga a 4 (the title of this fugue as printed in the score) indicates that this fugue has four voices: soprano, alto, tenor, and bass. Bracket the entrance of each subject and label it as S, A, T, or B.

In much of this four-voiced fugue, the RH plays the soprano and alto, and the LH plays the tenor and bass. Notice the consistent stemming of those voices: soprano = up-stems, alto = down-stems, tenor = up-stems, bass = down-stems. This information will facilitate your reading of individual voices.

The musical materials of this fugue are severely limited and consist solely of the subject "head" and "tail," and even sixteenth notes (mm. 9, 10, etc.).

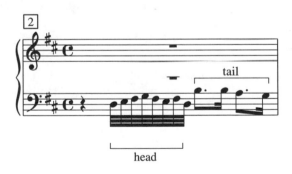

Find the source of the even sixteenths hidden in the "head."

becomes

➤ To find the main cadence points, look for V-I motion in the bass. Mark the cadences on the score and label the keys.

[m. 6 – A major
m. 9 – B minor
m. 17 – E minor
m. 21 and 23 – D major]

➤ Listen to several recordings for ideas on articulation as well as additional ornamentation at cadence points. Is everything played *legato?*

➤ The majestic quality of the final chords may be enhanced by light touches of pedal.

Practice Suggestions

➤ Plan how you will shape and articulate the subject. Here is one suggestion: the last four tones of the "head" (zigzag pairs) provide a special intensity to the figure. Play the "head" with a slight crescendo into the following beat.

➤ Working in sections defined by the cadences, use a layered approach as you practice:
1. Carefully work out the fingerings and notate your decisions on the score.
2. Practice each voice separately, *using the fingering you will use when playing the complete texture.*
3. In short practice units, create combinations of voices, e.g., S and A, S and T, S and B.
4. Add voices until you have the entire texture.

➤ Considering the contrapuntal nature of a fugue, the exposed chordal texture found in mm. 9-10, 17-19, 21 is quite unusual. These chords are to be divided between the hands. Playing the final chord of a measure with one hand can help solve a technical difficulty. For example, the final chord of m. 10 can be played by the RH, which gives the LH time to move to the bass G at the beginning of m. 11.

➤ Rhythmic precision in mm. 25-26 is of the greatest importance. Broaden the tempo to emphasize the majestic ending.

Johann Sebastian Bach
French Suite No. 5, BWV 816 (Allemande and Gigue) (R8)

Background Information

Collections of instrumental dances date back to the Renaissance period. The dances were often paired, a slower dance followed by a faster one, each with its contrasting meter and characteristic rhythms. By the time of Bach, the dance suite had been formalized in north Germany to include four standard dances: allemande, courante, sarabande, and gigue. Newer, popular dances were inserted between the sarabande

and gigue as optional dances. The most frequently used optional dances in the Bach suites are the gavotte, minuet, and bourrée.

The core dances were no longer in vogue in the ballroom, but had an honored position in musical tradition. Furthermore, their origins lent an international flavor to the suite: *Allemande* is French for "German," therefore indicating a German dance; *Courante/Corrente* had both French and Italian forms; *Sarabande* originated in Spain; *Gigue/Giga* had French and Italian forms.

The dance suite was unified by two factors: (1) each dance was in the same key, and (2) the dances were cast in binary form. Otherwise, the dance suite was a study in contrast, as the dances had different meters, tempi, and rhythmic formulas.

Bach's contributions to the keyboard dance suite literature are found in groups of six:

six French Suites
six English Suites
six Partitas

Your student may wish to research the topic of Bach suites further, making a comparison of the suites. How are the *French Suites* different from the *English Suites* and *Partitas?*

Allemande

Although the *French Suites* were not published during Bach's lifetime, several copies exist in manuscript. Bach wrote a finished manuscript from which his students made copies. These sources reveal discrepancies regarding the ornaments, perhaps depending on the capability of the student. In some standard editions of this *Allemande,* there are no trills in mm. 2, 3, 6, and 7, and the ornaments in mm. 1, 4, 5, and 13 are trills without prefix.

Exploring the Score

➤ As you explore this *Allemande,* check for the following characteristics:
– Binary form?
– Modulation to V at the double bar?
– Strict-voiced (as a fugue) or free-voiced (with chords and changing texture)?
– Phrases beginning with an upbeat motive or phrases beginning on downbeats?
– How many different ornaments? How are the signs realized?
– Melody shared by the LH or carried by the top voice?

There are many approaches to the articulation of this movement. A comparison of several recordings will illustrate a variety of choices. Dances must have a strong rhythmic sense, and articulations can enhance the location of main beats. General guidelines to articulation include:

1) Stepwise motion will be played *legato,* and wider intervals will be played detached.

2) The degree of detachment depends on the prevailing mood of the piece and the particular beat. For emphasis, downbeats will be less detached than successive beats in the measure.

3) Detach before a syncopation.

4) Detach at the ends of short phrases, especially when the phrase ends with a long tone.

5) Change of melodic direction may suggest articulated groupings.

Practice Suggestions

Establishing fingerings and articulation from the first week of practice is the greatest time-saver in learning this dance. The primary texture of the piece is three-voiced. Practice each voice separately to train the ear and to facilitate decisions about the articulation.

Gigue

Background Information

Gigues are fast, energetic dances, usually in compound duple or triple time. The triplet motion conjures images of excited whirling. In his suites, Bach includes examples of the Italian Giga and well as this French Gigue. (For examples of the Italian *Giga,* see the *Partita in B flat,* or the *French Suites in C Minor* and *B Minor*).

Exploring the Score

➤ If students have not played a Bach Gigue (French version), a startling revelation awaits them as they compare the opening phrase of each half. [The second half begins with an inversion of the opening theme. Both are unaccompanied.] Does Bach maintain this inverted version throughout the second half of the piece?

➤ Have the student make a further comparison between the first and second half. Are there passages in the first half that are not repeated in the second half? Is there new material presented in the second half?

➤ The organization and repetition of melodic and rhythmic patterns affect how many beats are felt in each measure. Do you see two large beats per measure instead of four in this example?

Do you find measures with four-beat groupings? Could there be a measure with only one large beat?

Practice Suggestions

The drive and energy of this dance preclude a *legato* touch, yet the speed of the movement makes a true *staccato* nearly impossible. The fingers must play cleanly and precisely, using a touch that is sometimes called *non-legato.* Special vitality results when the sixteenth-note upbeat is separated from its downbeat. Two such groups can be found in nearly all measures:

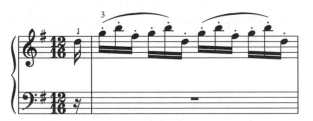

➤ Planning an efficient fingering is important from the beginning.

➤ Before combining the entire texture, practice voices separately in short sections.

Johann Sebastian Bach
Capriccio sopra la lontananza del fratello dilettissimo, BWV 992 (Mvts. Four, Five, Six) (R13)

Background Information

This is one of Bach's earliest surviving keyboard compositions. Note the stylistic differences between this piece and the previous two Bach works, written approximately twenty years later. Each movement has a title describing an event or emotion accompanying the departure of Bach's older brother for Sweden where he was to take up his passion as oboist in the National Guard of the Swedish King Charles XII. As his return to Saxony was unlikely, his departure caused much grief.

This early *Capriccio on the Departure of the Beloved Brother* exists on the periphery of Bach's oeuvre. While program music (music with a story line) was not uncommon—Bach's predecessor in Leipzig, Johann Kuhnau, wrote a set of highly descriptive *Biblical Sonatas*—Bach's fame as a keyboard composer rests on his more abstract compositions like the preludes and fugues and dance suites.

Mvt. Four: Allhier kommen die Freunde
Exploring the Score

The full title of movement four is translated in the text. Notice the predominance of descending pitches, musical depictions of the sadness of a farewell. It is difficult to determine the key of this movement, as the key signature and the final cadence do not correspond. Name as many of the chords as you can, and enjoy the wandering sense of tonal center. (Could it be that the confusion of key is a musical depiction of conflicting emotions felt by the friends at this farewell?)

Practice Suggestions

Blocked chords were arpeggiated by Baroque performers and sound more dramatic when rolled from bottom to top.

➢ Which chords will you arpeggiate in mm. 1-3? Listen to a recording for further ideas. Rolling only the half-note chords may give a desired emphasis to the downbeats.
➢ The descending eighth notes (sadness) will be most effective when played *legato*.

Mvt. Five: Aria di Postiglione
Exploring the Score

The fifth and sixth movements are based on the postilion, the horn call that announces the arrival and departure of the coach. In Bach's time, the octave

intervals of this *Aria* would have been readily associated with the postilion.

Practice Suggestions

➢ Play the sixteenth-note figures slightly detached (*non-legato*), with precise finger activity.
➢ Eighth notes leading to quarter notes (see LH, m. 1) can be detached.
➢ The ornament in m. 1 gives emphasis to the dotted-eighth–sixteenth figure. Find that same rhythm in mm. 4, 6 (LH), and 11. Add an ornament to those dotted eighths if you wish.

Mvt. Six: Fuga all' imitatione di Posta
Exploring the Score

➢ Throughout the fugue you will find descending octaves depicting the postilion horn call. Notice the intensity created by their appearance in mm. 42-46.
➢ Bracket the entrances of the fugue subject (five measures; sometimes four measures). Long fugue subjects are typical of Bach's early compositions. Later fugue subjects tend to be more concise. (Compare the length of the D major fugue subject discussed above.)

Practice Suggestions

➢ Bach fugue subjects can have a variety of legitimate articulations. Experiment with different possibilities. How would this fugue subject sound if played on a bugle? Here is one articulation suggestion:

➢ One assembles a fugue gradually and methodically.
  - Find the fugue subject statements on a given page. Play them with the articulation you have decided upon.
  - Add the other voices, one at a time, to the fugue subject. (You may need to divide your practice units into shorter segments because of the subject length). As you add the voices,

determine the best fingering, write your decisions in the score, and *follow them consistently*.
- Each practice unit should be repeated a minimum of three times.

➤ In a fugue, a reduction of the number of voices signifies less tension. The addition of voices creates thicker texture and greater tension. As you practice, be aware of "thick" *vs* "thin," and plan your dynamics accordingly.

LIST B – CLASSICAL SONATAS
Suggested Order of Difficulty

Page	Composer	Title
R43	Wolfgang Amadeus Mozart	*Sonata in E flat Major, K 282 (189g)*
R32	Franz Joseph Haydn	*Sonata in B Minor, Hob. XIV:32*
R19	Ludwig van Beethoven	*Sonata in E Major, op. 14, no. 1*

Music is analogous to language. It can be discussed in terms of phrases, sentences, punctuation, inflection, accent, and emphasis. Central to the "language" of the Classical style is the principle of contrast. Classical composers used forms with distinct sections—binary form, ternary form, sonata form, rondo. These structures display contrasting themes, keys, textures, and accompaniment patterns. Music in the Classical style has a strong harmonic orientation and a predominantly homophonic texture (melody supported by harmonic accompaniment). Some harmonies have natural tension and receive dynamic stress. Non-chord tones in the melody are a primary means of expression and are often played with extra dynamic or rhythmic stress.

The sonatas of the three great Classical period composers invite comparisons, especially in terms of the way sonata form was approached. The following general observations can act as a point of departure for your student's further examination of the works of Haydn, Mozart, and Beethoven.

➤ Haydn is remarkable for the motivic development of his themes. He often chooses to continue a motive from his first theme and make it the basis of the second or closing theme.
➤ Mozart is known for the lyrical quality of his themes, each with a distinct character.
➤ Beethoven was (for a brief period) Haydn's student, and he carried many of Haydn's ideas to incredible creative lengths. In particular, Beethoven developed the idea of the motive as the core of thematic construction and elaboration. His sonata-form movements are lengthier than those of either Haydn or Mozart, with longer themes and extensive *codas*.

Ludwig van Beethoven
Sonata in E Major, op. 14, no. 1 (R19)
(Movements One, Two Three)
Background Information:

In 1802, Beethoven referred to this sonata in a letter to his publisher, indicating that he had transformed it into a string quartet. The string quartet version of the sonata is in F major and represents some of Beethoven's earliest quartet writing. (Some scholars have even speculated that the quartet was the original medium the composer had in mind.) Acquainting oneself with the sound and style of Classical string quartets would be excellent preparation for the study of this sonata.

First Movement: Allegro
Exploring the Score

➤ Beethoven's compositions were often based on a rhythmic motive or specific interval. (Consider the opening of his *Symphony No. 5*.) When he opens a movement with a prominent interval, one can expect that interval to be featured frequently. Explore uses of a rising 4th (or its inversion, a falling 5th). There are many to be found, both in the LH and the RH. Check these measures:

mm. 4, 5, 22-23, 39, 46, 50, 65-66, 74-75.

➤ Beethoven frequently writes several themes within the first and second theme areas of a sonata movement. The second theme area starts with the upbeat to m. 23. Notice the appearances of new thematic material in mm. 39 and 46.

➤ The *sfz* marking is frequently used by Beethoven for dramatic effect. Often this dynamic accent occurs on a beat other than the downbeat. Make a survey of Beethoven's use of the *sfz* marking in this movement, and the beat on which he places the accent.

➤ The Development section is severely limited to one thematic idea. Its purpose is "modulation" through several keys from the E major of m. 61 to the E major of m. 91. Label the primary harmonies and important cadence points in the Development.

Practice Suggestions

➤ In the opening theme the accompanying chords provide a breathless excitement. Agitation is created when each group of three chords is played with a slight *diminuendo*.

➤ The broken third pattern in mm. 5-6 is challenging. Explore different fingerings to find what works best for your hands.

➤ Practice with rotation.

➤ Practice with "scratching" fingers, close to the key surface.

➤ Beethoven carefully writes the voice leading in mm. 8-12. Practice slowly until all note values are realized accurately.

➤ The octave phrases in the Development section are to sound *legato*. Emphasize the lateral movement of your arm and connect where possible. Subtle touches of pedal will help create the illusion of *legato* as will a well-executed dynamic plan for each phrase.

➤ Keep the texture and balance of a string quartet in mind as you practice.

Second Movement: Allegretto

Background Information

Beethoven indicates neither "minuet" nor "scherzo" for this movement, yet it bears the traditional $\frac{3}{4}$ meter and is a clear reference to those dance movements. His choice of contrasting keys for second movements stood in bold contrast to that of Haydn and Mozart, and was of great influence on the Romantic Era composers of the early 19th century.

Exploring the Score

➤ Discuss Beethoven's choice of key for this movement. [parallel minor]

➤ The principal motive of this movement is the half-step "mordent" figure in the rhythm:

♩. ♪♪

This motive appears at the beginning of each eight-measure phrase, stimulating the forward motion.

➤ Bracket the eight-measure phrases.

➤ Identify the "periodic phrases" (short-short-long), e.g., mm. 17-24. What is their total length?

➤ Find any phrases that do not conform to an eight-measure plan.

➤ A traditional minuet is cast in binary or rounded binary form. This first section (mm. 1-62) has no double bars. What is its form?
[a = mm. 1-16; b = mm. 17-32; a1 = mm. 33-40; a extension coda a2 = mm. 41-62]

➤ Much of the melodic writing of this first section features unison playing between the hands. How will that affect your balance of the sound? Compare the *Celebration Series®* recording of this movement with other professional recordings to determine if the performers play the hands with equal emphasis.

➤ The B section, or *Trio (Maggiore),* "should be" in E major, to contrast the E minor opening section. Beethoven's choice of C major is surprising, yet logical: notice the common tone linking mm. 62 and 63.

➤ Find other ways in which the A section (mm. 1-62) contrasts with the *Maggiore.* [The short groupings of the A section create a dance feeling. The phrases of the B section are long and flowing.] (Note that on the repeat of the *Allegretto,* this section is not played.)

➤ A dance movement in $\frac{3}{4}$ would naturally emphasize the downbeat. A characteristic of Beethoven's rhythm is his interest in off-beat accents. Are the off-beat accents in this movement marked with Beethoven's characteristic *sfz*?

➤ The Coda rounds out the movement by restating the theme of the *Maggiore.* The movement must end, however, in E. How does Beethoven avoid ending the movement in C major? [The A minor chord of m. 110 becomes the iv in E minor.]

Practice Suggestions

➤ Beethoven marks the articulation and dynamics of this movement in great detail. Follow the indications carefully, but avoid overplaying the *sf* markings, which might cause unnecessary thickness. (In the quartet version, a *crescendo* in m. 2 leads to *sfp* in m. 3.)

➤ Notice the slurred groupings Beethoven indicates within the first eight-measure phrase: 1 m. + 1 m. + 2 mm. + 1 m. + 1 m. + 2 mm. Slight breaks at the ends of slurred groups help clarify that construction. (In the quartet version, the opening motive is marked *staccato*.)

➤ The placement of the *sf* in mm. 18 and 20 defines the two-measure units. The absence of *sf* in m. 22 helps create a four-measure phrase.

➤ The melodic line in mm. 5-8, 13-16, and 37-40 needs your best *legato* fingering. Bring out the soprano line.

➤ Hold the LH ties in mm. 51-56 for their full value.

Third Movement: Rondo
Exploring the Score

➢ Analysis of the first movement revealed frequent use of the interval of a 4th. The opening motive of this movement is a rising 4th, outlining the exact notes that started the entire sonata. Can you find other appearances of a rising 4th or falling 5th? [mm. 5-6]

➢ The sections of this movement are found easily:

A = mm. 1-21
B = mm. 21-30
A1 = mm. 30-46
C = mm. 47-83
A2 = mm. 83-98
B1 = mm. 98 = 108
A3 (coda) = mm. 108-131

Note the unequal proportions, especially the longer C section. A rondo with an extended middle section can be labeled *sonata rondo*.

➢ Label the key for each of the sections listed above.
➢ Why does Beethoven move to E minor in m. 38?

Practice Suggestions

➢ To learn the opening LH chord shapes and fingerings, you may find it helpful to block the triads. Then practice the descending beat notes with the *appropriate fingering*.
➢ Isolate the sixteenth-note scales. Practice until the LH scales match the sound of the RH scales.
➢ In the C section (m. 47), Beethoven writes *staccatos* on some of the top tones. Treat those *staccatos* as accents. They are the "melody."
➢ Try this plan for practicing the coda, mm. 108-116.
  - Practice the octaves mm. 112-116 without *staccatos* for even rhythm.
  - Practice the same with sharp RH *staccatos*.
  - Mm. 108-111, play only the LH bass notes with the RH octaves. Listen for an even eighth note rhythm as you play.
  - Mm. 108-111, play blocked triads in the LH and the RH octaves. Maintain the even eighth-note rhythm.
  - Mm. 108-111, play as written, listening primarily for the eighth-note rhythm created between the bass and soprano. Minimize the rhythmic confusion that can result from paying too close attention to the two-against-three pattern. Keep the upper two notes of each triad quiet and precise.

Franz Joseph Haydn
Sonata in B Minor, Hob. XIV: 32 (R32)
(Movements One, Two Three)
Background Information

Haydn wrote approximately sixty-two piano sonatas that span his entire compositional life. His early sonatas were titled "Divertimenti" and "Partitas," and were collections of contrasting movements in the same key. Nearly half of his sonatas were written for harpsichord. When Haydn wrote dynamic markings and accents in the score, his preference for the fortepiano is clearly indicated.

The 18th century was a time of great change in terms of musical forms, types, and styles. Because the "textbook" definitions of sonata form had not yet been written, Haydn's innovative ideas are always of interest. His experiments with multi-movement forms make him an important figure in the development of the Classical sonata structure. The performer is advised to analyze each movement carefully.

First Movement
Exploring the Score

We readily associate humor and surprise with Haydn's keyboard sonatas, but this work allows us to explore the darker side of Haydn's expression. The stark outline of the opening theme (mm. 1-2) may be fate knocking at the door of our lives. We answer (mm. 3-8) with intense pleading.

➢ Label the main formal sections:

Exposition	1st theme group	mm 1-12
	2nd theme group	mm. 13-28
Development	mm. 29-47	
Recapitulation	mm. 48-70	

➢ Find the two main key areas of the exposition and compare the lengths of the thematic groups.
➢ What adjectives could be used to describe the mood of the theme starting in m.13? dramatic? desperate? playful?
➢ Compare exposition and development materials. Does Haydn draw primarily from the first or second theme group in the development?
➢ Find Haydn's dynamic markings. (There are none!) Listen to the *Celebration Series*® recording of this sonata and discuss the choices of dynamics made by the performer. Dynamic planning can be the springboard for a student–teacher discussion of mood, key, and instruments of the Classical period and their expressive range.
➢ As the student scans the score for Haydn's articulation marks, discuss the importance of a careful observation of the slurs.

It is assumed that Haydn expects the performer to continue the two-note groupings of m. 13 in mm. 14-21, bringing out the top tone.

➤ Note the articulation slurs in m. 25. How will they be applied in mm. 26 and 27?
➤ Examine mm. 39-47. They show the same articulation in three different ways:
    mm. 39-40 – the slurs show a slight break of sound before main RH beats
    mm. 41-42 – the *staccatos* show that same lift before the beat note
    mm. 42-47 – the lack of articulation implies that the performer continues the same articulated beat groupings experienced in m. 41.

Practice Suggestions

➤ Dynamics and articulation are the keys to a successful interpretation of this movement. Invest each phrase with details of contrasting touch and tone. It is better to over-dramatize this movement than to play without conviction.
➤ Before practice begins, listen to a recording of this movement, giving special attention to dynamics. Mark in the score where the performer creates dynamic contrast.
➤ As you practice, "edit" your score with your ideas for dynamics. Your score might look something like this:

➤ Detachment of tones in the Classical period is an issue that requires refined musicianship. The wedges are Haydn's *staccato* signs in this movement. They do not imply accent, as is clearly shown by the wedges in mm. 5 and 6. Some detached notes are "sticky," such as the upbeats into m. 3. They sound as if you were trying to play the repeated tones *legato*. The answering repeated accompanying tones in the LH are played with a similar "sticky" touch.
➤ The slurs in m. 13 show (a) that the top descending tones are to be the main melody and (b) that there is slight detachment between each of those top tones.

Second Movement: Menuet
Exploring the Score

For the middle movement of a three-movement sonata, a contrast of key is expected.
➤ Discuss what Haydn's choices for the key of this movement might have been. Speculate why this choice of B major was best. (Consider the contrasting key of the B section as you discuss key choice.)
➤ Compare the wide intervals of the main motive throughout the A section. Find the widest interval. [m. 17] What impact will these varied intervals have on the timing of the second beats?
➤ Haydn is highly creative with varied phrase lengths. This movement starts with two-measure phrases. Discover the extensions of those phrases (mm. 5-10; mm. 13-16; mm. 17-22).
➤ It is normal for two-measure phrases to focus on the downbeat of the second measure. Does Haydn follow this plan? [yes] Are other beats stressed in a phrase? [the surprising high pitch of second beats]
➤ The contrasting *Trio* section changes to B minor. Once again we are confronted with the dark, tragic colors of the first movement. Compare the first part of this *Trio* section to the sixteenth-note figuration of the first movement, mm. 55-56.

> Notice the relationship between a sixteenth figure in the *Trio* section and a theme yet to come in the Third Movement:

(from *Menuet and Trio*)

(from *Finale*)

Practice Suggestions

> A primary consideration for the interpretation of this movement is the contrast between the *Minuet* and the *Trio*. Practice for a light-hearted, good-natured sound in the *Minuet*. Bring definition to the varied lengths of phrases, and contrast *legato* lines with the shorter motives.

> The *Trio* is dark and moody. Let tension mount through the repeated sixteenth figure in mm. 31-33.

> The upbeat figures into mm. 1, 3, etc. are played as four equal sixteenth notes.

> Trills start on the upper auxiliary note.

> Compare the varied rising intervals of mm. 1, 3, 5, 11, 13, and 17. The wider the interval, the more expressive importance it deserves. Give the widest interval (m. 17) special significance. Do not rush into the second beat.

Third Movement: Finale
Background Information

This movement invites comparison to the Mozart *Sonata in A Minor, K 310*, written at the time of his mother's death when Mozart was far from home. Mozart's first movement is filled with a desperate frustration and anger. His opening repeated LH chords are similar to Haydn's repeated notes in this movement.

Exploring the Score

The frantic quality of this movement is projected when the performer emphasizes the smallest phrase units: a dart here, a dash there ... and sudden outbursts of octaves.

> Look through the score for clues to the form:
>   - changes of figures [m. 39!]
>   - repeat signs [m. 70, m. 193]
>   - an exact return of the opening [m. 125]

Label the form and its sections. [sonata-allegro form with exposition, development, and recapitulation]
> Discuss Haydn's choices of articulation. The majority of notes in this *Presto* movement are to be played detached. The slurred notes define the beat. Many of the two-note slurs are across a bar line and create rhythmic tension (LH mm. 2-4, RH mm. 24, 25).

Practice Suggestions

> The character of this piece is created through an accurate reading of each slur and each *staccato*.

> Notice, for instance, that downbeats starting with a slur are preceded by a written *staccato* or detached tone. Notes that are not slurred were referred to as "ordinary touch" and were played detached, e.g., the intervals of mm. 32-36.

> In the Classical period, short slurred groups started with a slightly accented tone.

> The sixteenth notes require facile fingers and utmost clarity. Organize the sixteenths by shapes and figures for practice purposes:
>   - turn figures
>   - scales
>   - broken chords
>   - short trills

Find all appearances of the same figure, and practice each in several different ways (*staccato*, dotted rhythms, each note repeated, etc.). Observe your hand and fingers carefully to determine the movement that creates greatest speed and clarity.

Wolfgang Amadeus Mozart
Sonata in E flat Major, K 282 (189g) (R43)
Background Information

This sonata is unique among the Mozart sonatas in two ways: it is the only sonata that begins with a slow movement, and the middle movement is cast as a pair of minuets. The minuet movement of a sonata is traditionally in the tonic key, but because the minuets function as the contrasting middle movement, Mozart chooses the contrasting key of B flat major.

The three movements are marked *Adagio, [Moderato], Allegro*. Coupled with these changing tempi are highly contrasting moods: seriously expressive, elegant dancing, vigorous and enthusiastic.

Primarily because of its slow first movement, this sonata is regarded as one of Mozart's less technically demanding sonatas. The musical challenges, however, are always evident. Subtle tone control is required throughout.

First Movement: Adagio
Exploring the Score
Your student is thoroughly familiar with sonata form and has experienced variations within that basic framework.
➢ When analyzing a sonata-allegro movement, it is helpful to locate the following:
  - the second theme, naming its key [m. 9, B flat]
  - the second theme in the recapitulation, naming its key [m. 27, E flat]
  - the first theme as it reappears in the recapitulation

And here is where we see the genius of Mozart at work, manipulating the material to create balance and interest. There is no clear restatement of the m. 1 theme.

➢ Discuss the ways in which the concepts of development and recapitulation are synthesized in mm. 16-21.
➢ Mozart marks the score the great care. Note the many changes of dynamics and the precise detail of articulations. Articulation and dynamics are the clues to this movement's intense expressivity.
➢ This movement shows examples of Mozart's "finger pedal." The broken chords with slurs (e.g., m. 4) are an indication by Mozart to "collect" the notes during the beat.
➢ Compare the rhythms of mm. 1 and 16.

Practice Suggestions
➢ In order to gain the maximum expression from the details of Mozart's articulation and dynamic markings, practice without pedal. Cultivate a professional level of beautiful finger *legato*.
➢ Listen carefully to a recording of this movement for the contrasts between *forte* and *piano*. If possible, find a recording of the work performed on a fortepiano and note the dynamic variety on that instrument. To achieve an approximation of Mozart's dynamic intentions, reduce the degree of dynamic contrast on your piano.

Second Movement: Menuetto I and II
Background Information
Paired dances are often found in Baroque dance suites. This tradition was carried into the Classical period in the form of Minuet-Trio-Minuet. Here,

Mozart chooses to label the middle section as *Minuetto II*. As the score indicates, a repetition of *Minuetto I* follows the playing of *Minuetto II*.

Exploring the Score
➢ Analyze the form and keys of the two minuets. As mentioned above, in Classical sonata structure, a minuet is usually in the tonic key. Why does Mozart choose B flat for the key of this section of the piece? [contrast for middle movement]
➢ Throughout this *Handbook,* mention has been made of "short-short-long" phrase construction, sometimes known as a "periodic phrase." Find several of the many examples of this construction to be found in these minuets.
➢ Although some dances do have a characteristic upbeat, minuets most often begin on the downbeat. Note Mozart's unusual use of upbeat in these phrases.

Practice Suggestions
➢ These two dances are notated with an unusual amount of detail which heightens the dance character. A great many notes are marked with a slur or *staccato*. Those not marked are played with "ordinary touch" (slight detachment). Practice with special attention to articulation.
➢ Dynamic contrast plays an important role. The frequent dynamic changes in *Minuet II* are remarkable. When practicing these contrasts, consider the more limited dynamic range of the fortepiano.
➢ You may wish to devote special practice to the rhythm of *Minuet II* mm. 5-8 for accurate subdivisions of the beat.
➢ Pedaling for *legato* connection is not necessary in these minuets. Where might you use pedal to enhance the texture of the sound? [perhaps individual pedals on the chords of *Minuet I,* mm. 13-14]

Third Movement: Allegro
The performance goal for this movement is great energy and enthusiasm. This is high-spirited Mozart. Sixteenth-note figures sparkle, LH *Alberti* bass patterns are played lightly, *staccato* notes are bright and sharp, and the dynamic contrasts are filled with great humor.

Exploring the Score
➢ The double bar at mm. 39-40 is a clue to the form. The material at m. 62 is the "give-away." This movement is in sonata-allegro form. Find the second theme in both the exposition and recapitulation. [mm. 16 and 77] Are the keys

"correct," i.e., is the second theme of the exposition in the dominant key?

➤ Compare mm. 30-33 with mm. 91-94. Why does Mozart change the figure in the recapitulation? [There were not enough notes on his piano to write a transposition of mm. 32-33.]

Practice Suggestions

➤ As the only fast movement of the sonata, the emphasis here is on high spirit and the greatest clarity of sixteenth notes. You will find that RH sixteenths played on the tips of fingers produce this sound most efficiently. Release the fingers very quickly for a sparkling touch.

➤ The LH *Alberti* bass pattern is a challenge for many performers. Speed and lightness are achieved when the fingers are played close to the key, the hand and forearm are relaxed, and the *Alberti* figure is played with a slight hand rotation. The hand rotation can be practiced first by playing only the wide interval (fingers 5-1) in sixteenth notes. Rotation is most easily achieved when the wrist is above the key surface and when the hand and arm are in alignment. When the 5-1 rotation is comfortable, add the middle tone.

➤ Upbeat eighth notes are played with the sharpest *staccato*. Match the RH upbeat *staccato* with its answer in the LH.

LIST C – ROMANTIC REPERTOIRE
Suggested Order of Difficulty

Page	Composer	Title
R59	Johannes Brahms	*Ballade in D Minor, op. 10, no. 1*
R51	Frédéric Chopin	*Waltz in E Minor, op. posth.*
R55	Frédéric Chopin	*Nocturne in F sharp Major, op. 15, no. 2*
R63	Franz Schubert	*Impromptu in E flat Major, op. 90, no. 2*
R72	Robert Schumann	*Intermezzo, op. 26, no. 4*

The 19th century is sometimes referred to as the century of the piano. During those years, the instrument evolved from the early fortepiano to the modern piano we know today. For the first time in music history, traveling piano virtuosos attracted huge crowds at their concerts and became wealthy from their performances and publications. More piano music was written during this century than ever before. The parlors of most middle-class families were arranged around their prized possession—the piano.

Although most of the prominent 19th-century composers who wrote for the piano composed sonatas and variations, the majority of their compositions were shorter pieces with titles such as *Intermezzo, Ballade,* or *Impromptu*. These short compositions, usually in ternary form, are known as character pieces because they focus primarily on a strong expression of character and mood. In an effort to create a larger work, Robert Schumann composed cycles of character pieces. *Scenes from Childhood (Kinderszenen), op. 15,* is one of Schumann's best-known character cycles.

The extended harmonic palette of this music exploits chromaticism, altered chords, dissonance, and modulations to remote keys. In addition, composers marked their scores precisely, indicating subtle variations in tone quality and dynamic range. The use of contrasting tone quality and extremes of dynamics adds to the expressiveness of this music. Tone quality is enhanced with the subtle and varied use of pedaling, which was an important part of the development of pianism in the 19th century.

Frédéric Chopin
Waltz in E Minor, op. post. (R51)
Background Information

Throughout 19th-century Europe, the waltz was the most popular dance. Many composers were commissioned to write waltzes as dance music for special celebrations. Chopin's seventeen waltzes, however, are concert pieces, not accompaniments for dancing. They are sectional and often change keys to lend variety to the pervading $\frac{3}{4}$ meter. This piece was written in 1830, prior to Chopin's move to Paris.

Exploring the Score

➤ Mark the sections in the score. Notice that the introduction is balanced at the end with a coda.

➤ What name would you give to this form? [rondo]

➤ Label the keys of each section. The C section (mm. 57-96) is cast as a rounded binary form. What key changes do you find in that section? [E major – G sharp minor – E major]

➤ Chopin's bass lines often give the impression that he first composed the bass and then added the

RH. Analyze (and memorize) the bass lines in these sections:

    mm. 9-15
    mm. 25-32
    mm. 109-123

➤ Of special interest are the chromatic bass lines. Can you analyze the resulting harmonies?

➤ Chopin's waltzes reveal skillfully-achieved variety within the $\frac{3}{4}$ meter. One finds groupings of two measures into a unit of $\frac{6}{4}$. Often the phrases flow in a convincing four-measure unit, each measure feeling as if it were one beat in a larger (macrorhythmic) four-beat phrase. As you study this piece, be aware of Chopin's changing rhythmic units.

➤ Is there a section in the piece where the melody shifts to the LH?

Practice Suggestions

➤ The waltz accompaniment provides much of the elegance in this piece. LH practice is essential to achieve control over its component parts. The bass line is the most important factor, but notice the two-note slurs on beats two and three. They must also have the appropriate dynamic nuance.

➤ In your first days of practice, determine phrase length and focus. Make the shaping and dynamics of each RH phrase your highest practice priority.

➤ Notice the pedal markings in the score. Listen to the pedaling of professional pianists as they play Chopin waltzes. Dance lilt is achieved when the measures are not connected by pedal. Exceptions are extended harmonies, such as the introduction, mm. 1-8. No pedal is shown on the first two measures because of the low bass register. When the LH plays rolled chords, each measure receives generous pedal. You can experiment with the pedal held for the final three measures of the introduction.

Frédéric Chopin
Nocturne in F sharp Major, op. 15, no. 2 (R55)
Background Information

Chopin's nocturnes are some of the most introspective and subjective of all his works. As was true of the *Waltz in E Minor* discussed above, this piece was written prior to the composer's arrival in Paris. From the Irish composer, John Field, Chopin borrowed the title, character, and certain formal characteristics for his nocturnes. Usually following an A-B-A plan, Chopin's nocturnes feature a middle section in a contrasting tempo and mood. The lyrical melodic lines are vocally inspired, and exhibit many

characteristics of the *bel canto* style: long-breathed phrases, subtle *rubato* over a steady accompaniment, *fioriture* (small-note cadenzas), grace notes, and coloratura runs.

Exploring the Score

➤ It is always helpful to hear a composition prior to studying. Follow the score as you listen to a recording of this remarkable piece. Notice dynamic range, pedaling, tempo fluctuations, and tone.

➤ A quick perusal of the score reveals its ABA form and the detailed notation of rhythmic subdivisions and filigree passage work.

➤ A close look shows the care with which Chopin brought subtle variation to the piece.
- Compare the repetitions of the melody of mm. 1-2 (mm. 3-4, 9-10, 11-12, 49-50, 51-52). Are any of those repetitions exactly alike? Did you notice the differences in dynamic shadings?
- Compare the wide leaps of mm. 6, 14, and 54.
- Compare the rhythm of mm. 25 and 33.

➤ Mm. 7-8 are filled with details of careful voicing and performance.
- Notice the three-voice structure of the LH. Notes must be held their full length to realize the voice delineation of the LH.
- The RH notation of the rolled chords is a specific indication from Chopin to start these rolled chords on the beat. Strictly speaking, there are two moments at which the downbeat of m. 9 occurs in the RH. Both the bottom B and the top A sharp represent the downbeat, yet they are not played at the same time! This is also true for the previous upbeat.

➤ Mm.17-24 serve as a bridge between the A and B sections. Notice the bass line of this section. Our ears tell us that m. 24 should be followed by a D sharp harmony, yet the B section begins with a C sharp 7, the V7 of the home key. Chopin links the two harmonies through their common tone, E sharp.

➤ Find the highest pitch of the piece. The ending is an exquisite experience of sound floating from a high pitch downward to a resting point.

➤ Discuss the rhythmic organization of the B section, comparing mm. 25 and 33. Why would Chopin change the RH rhythm in m. 33? [intensification of the mounting drama]

Practice Suggestions

➤ A meticulous reading of the score is imperative to realize the subtlety and beauty of this piece. Devote special attention to Chopin's dynamic markings and the length of notes. Look up any unfamiliar terms in a music dictionary and mark the translations on your score.

➤ The filigree passages, mm. 11 and 51, can be practiced separately. Memorize the passage and the fingerings. As you listen to recordings, you will hear that performers do not play all notes at exactly the same speed. In passages like this, the beginning and ending notes will generally be slightly slower than those in the middle of the passage. At first, you may find it helpful to divide the RH into groups of notes that line up with the LH. For example, the filigree in m. 11 can be organized into groups of six, eight, nine, then six notes. (Do not accent any RH notes!)

➤ To learn the RH notes in the *Doppio movimento* section more quickly, play the octaves and smaller intervals blocked (alternate: octave, middles, octave, middles).

➤ The stretched hand position in the *Doppio movimento* section can easily lead to fatigue. Keep a relaxed hand and forearm throughout. Avoid articulating the low part of the figure with the fingers.

➤ Play the top notes of the *Doppio movimento* as *legato* as possible. Listen for the long, undulating phrases. The *sotto voce* marking is your clue to create a totally different tone color.

➤ In m. 56, the trill from below will start *on* the beat (play the RH F double sharp and LH B sharp together.)

Johannes Brahms
Ballade in D Minor, op. 10, no. 1 (R59)
Background Information

This early piece is unique among Brahms' instrumental works because it follows a "program." Brahms was well acquainted with the collection of folk poetry *Stimmen der Völker* (Voices of the People) translated into German by Herder. The "Edward" Ballade tells the grim story of a mother who discovers that her son has killed his father. The opening lines of the Scottish ballad *Why dois your brand sae drap wi bluid, Edward, Edward?* (Why does your sword so drip with blood?) are reflected in Brahms' opening melody, almost as if we were hearing the text set to music. (Brahms later set the poem as a duet for alto and tenor.) The entire piece is dark and grim.

Exploring the Score

➤ The A section features two contrasting melodies, as if one were hearing the dialogue between mother and son. Brahms heightens that contrast through the *poco più mosso*. What is similar about those two themes? [rhythm]

➤ The rhythmic motive ♩ ♩ ♫♩ is a unifying feature common to all of the themes in this piece. Look for this motive in each section.

➤ In the A section, the *poco più mosso* theme is stated twice. Compare those statements. What is the origin of the melody in mm. 22-23? [the bass line of mm. 9-10] If the bass becomes the melody, the melody becomes the _____. [tenor] Brahms reverses the parts.

➤ Similarly, what is the origin of the B section melody, m. 27?

➤ The B section reaches a point of ultimate intensity. Discuss the means by which Brahms achieves this effect.

➤ Notice the sudden change of key in mm. 41-42. The B flat harmony is used to restate one of the phrases from the A section. Find those parallel phrases.

➤ Compare mm. 9-12 and mm. 49-52.

➤ The return of the A section, mm. 60-71, restates the melody associated with the mother's question *Why does your sword so drip with blood, Edward, Edward?* There is, however, no answer. You finish the story.

Practice Suggestions

➤ Balance of sound and voicing are challenges to the performer of this piece.
  - Notice that the opening theme is presented in *three*-octave unison.
  - The LH of the *poco più mosso* theme is of equal importance to the soprano lines.
  - The melody of the B section is in the bass and requires special projection.

➤ In mm. 60-64, the LH long values are to be held with the hand, since there is little pedal possible in this section. Brahms breaks up the left-hand triplet rhythm, and the effect is chilling—the LH *staccato* notes seem to represent the drops of blood.

➤ Throughout much of the piece, Brahms writes subdivisions of two against three (see m. 27). You can count that rhythm:

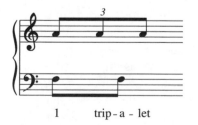

Franz Schubert
Impromptu in E flat Major, op. 90, no. 2 (R62)
Background Information

Schubert's eight *Impromptus* count among the early character pieces, a genre of piano composition that became extremely popular in the 19th century. An earlier collection of impromptus was written by the Czech composer Vor˘ís˘ek and published in Vienna. Schubert knew these pieces, and used the same title for his eight varied works, which were published as opp. 90 and 142.

Viennese society during Schubert's time was completely absorbed with dance music. Schubert was often commissioned to write dances for social events; as a result, we have over 400 dances from his pen. Many of Schubert's compositions use $\frac{3}{4}$ meter and, regardless of their title, a dance lurks in the shadows of that music.

Exploring the Score

➤ As discussed earlier concerning the Chopin waltz, composers writing in $\frac{3}{4}$ often find ways to combine measures into larger metric units or to bring emphasis to beats other than the downbeat. As you look through the score, notice that the RH emphasizes the downbeats with great subtlety, leaving the primary metric definition to the LH. Also, notice the LH's consistent emphasis on the second beat. This is especially prominent in the B section.

➤ Discuss the lack of rhythmic variety in the A section. If the rhythm is unyielding in its consistency, how does Schubert create variety in this section? [the RH figure includes scale passages, chromatic figures, occasional wide intervals, and broken chords; change of tonal center, mm. 25-51]

➤ Notice that Schubert frequently writes a wide interval for the RH at the beginning of measures. What purpose is served? [the interval helps define a changing harmony]

➤ Name the key of the B section, m. 83. [B minor] How did Schubert reach that tonal center, so remote from E flat major? **Hint:** Analyze the final twelve measures of the A section. Note the important role of the tone G flat/F sharp, and remember the concept of common-tone modulation.

➤ The B section is remote from the A section, emotionally as well as tonally. It is rough and vigorous and may reflect Schubert's acquaintance with gypsy music. Beat two is highlighted with accented chords. The sforzando markings (*ffz*) highlight the harmonic clashes in bold relief.

➤ The coda returns to the key of the B section. Analyze the way Schubert moves from B minor to E flat, and note the key of the final measures. [E flat minor, in keeping with the mood of the B section]

Practice Suggestions

There is much repetition in this impromptu. Once a passage is learned, it will be used again.

Fingering of the various figures is a primary focus in the early days of practice.

➤ Isolate the different figures of he A section (scales, chromatic movement, broken-chord section) for fingering practice.

➤ This impromptu can be played convincingly at a variety of tempi. The decisive factor is the clarity of each note. Do not allow speed to detract from precise, clear playing.

➤ Schubert's notation of the LH takes into consideration which notes can be held (without pedal) and which must be released. He writes as if the piece is to be played without pedal. If you decide to use the pedal for color, it must be applied subtly.

➤ Endurance can be an issue in this lengthy piece. As you practice, foster a relaxed hand and wrist. Keep fingers close to the key surface. (Overextending causes tension and fatigue.) When practicing the B section, start each measure with a relaxed hand.

Robert Schumann
Intermezzo, op. 26, no. 4 (R72)
Background Information

This movement is the fourth in a larger work, *Faschingschwank aus Wien (Viennese Carnaval Prank).* The entire work bore an earlier title, *Grande sonate romantique,* which indicates the scope of the individual movements. *Intermezzo* is one of the shorter movements, forming a bridge into the *Finale.*

Exploring the Score

Romantic piano composers were fond of creating a texture that sounded as if the pianist had three hands. *Intermezzo* is an example of this texture. Schumann deftly enables the pianist to create this sound, in part because the sixteenth-note triplets receive assistance from the LH.

➤ Have the student sight-read the piece, playing only the bass line and the melody. The purpose of this activity is to:
  – become acquainted with the key and harmonic progressions
  – hear the phrase groupings (mark them)
  – discover the form [rondo: A (mm. 1-8); B (mm. 9-15); A1 (mm. 16-23); B1 (mm. 24-30); A2 (mm. 31-38; Coda (mm. 38-end)]

➤ Compare the melody of the A sections with the B sections. Which section has the higher pitches and seems more intense? [B]

➤ Discuss the purpose of Schumann's dynamic and articulation marks in the melody. Schumann leaves few questions concerning phrase emphasis and nuance.

➤ Here's an analysis challenge: The key is E flat minor. Find the dominant 7ths in that key (B flat 7). [m. 29, but does not resolve to E flat; m. 34; m. 41] Schumann is a master craftsman, controlling harmonies to serve his expressive intentions. His avoidance of the resolution of the dominant 7th harmony is remarkable.

➤ What purpose is served when a composer avoids the resolution of the dominant 7th? [It creates a sense of urgency, a need to resolve.]

Practice Suggestions

➤ Practice the LH bass line with the RH melody. Observe Schumann's dynamic and articulation markings in the RH.

➤ Add to that bass-melody texture the triplets, played as blocked chords. You can practice with an "event" on each eighth note:

➤ After practicing in this blocked manner for short units, play slowly as written. You may add the pedal from the beginning.

LIST D – NEO-CLASSIC, NEO-ROMANTIC AND IMPRESSIONISTIC REPERTOIRE
Suggested Order of Difficulty

Page	Composer	Title
R91	Françis Poulenc	*Suite française (Mvts. Three, Six, Seven)*
R99	Manuel de Falla	*Danse du meunier/The Miller's Dance*
R80	Cyril Scott	*Lotus Land, op. 47, no.1*
R76	Sergei Rachmaninoff	*Mélodie/Melody, op. 3, no. 3*
R85	Claude Debussy	*Brouillards/Mist*
R102	Amy Marcy Cheney Beach	*A Hermit Thrush at Eve, op. 92, no. 1*

Late 19th-century composers found ways to alter the traditional harmonies of the Classical and early Romantic periods.

➤ They added chromatic notes to help disguise the shift from one harmony to another.

➤ They related harmonies through common tones or through chromatic relationships rather than the traditional I – IV – V7 – I progressions.

➤ Impressionist composers employed scale systems other than major and minor by altering pitches or by equalizing the relationship between the notes in the scale, e.g., a whole-tone scale. The lack of a clear tonic in whole-tone compositions gives the music a weightless, floating quality.

Sergei Rachmaninoff
Mélodie/Melody, op. 3, no. 3 (R76)

Exploring the Score

Rachmaninoff's melodies have thrilled listeners around the world. His music is known for its rich texture and lush harmonies. *Mélodie, op. 3, no. 3* is from a set of five pieces written when the composer was nineteen. Rachmaninoff dedicated the pieces to Anton Arensky, one of his professors at the Moscow Conservatory. The enormously popular *Prelude in C sharp Minor* also comes from the same set.

➤ Locate the different melodies in the piece, and determine the phrase length of each melody.
  m. 2 – eight-measure phrases
  m. 18 – four-measure phrases
  m. 26 – two-measure phrases
  m. 32 – two-measure phrases
  m. 42 – return of beginning melody

➤ Analyze the range of each melody. Is the melody created from scale motion or wide intervals?

➤ Can you name a key for each phrase? Notice how the melodies are entirely diatonic, outlining scales or scale fragments.

- ➤ Chromaticism plays an important role in much of Rachmaninoff's music. Considering all the diatonic melodies, where is the chromaticism in this piece? [the accompaniment]
  - – Starting in m. 18, one sees obvious chromaticism in the RH. (Which voice is creating the chromaticism?)
  - – Find foreshadowing of chromaticism on the first page of music.
  - – Analyze the LH figure starting in m. 26. Where do you find diatonic movement, and where is the chromaticism?

- ➤ The climax of most pieces is to be found near the end. Draw a graph of the dynamics and find Rachmaninoff's unusual dynamic plan.
- ➤ Projecting the long, flowing melodic lines in Romantic music poses a special challenge for the performer. One must think, hear, and "sing" the lines to project them. Creating the illusion of a continuous line while holding a long tone demands a touch of "piano magic." As you listen to recordings of this and other expressive pieces by Rachmaninoff, determine how the performer creates the illusion of a long line. What role does the accompaniment play?

Practice Suggestions

- ➤ Reading this piece is challenging because of the combination of accidentals and key signature. Rachmaninoff writes in complex keys, easily slipping from sharp keys into flat keys. Write in or circle the accidentals that will help you read the piece most accurately.
- ➤ As the main melodies enter (mm. 1, 9, 17), Rachmaninoff indicates a significant dynamic differentiation between the melody and the accompaniment. This contrast is an important clue to your effective practice.
- ➤ In mm. 18-25, circle chords that represent a change of position. Devise a way to learn these measures quickly: position – chromatic top – new position – chromatic top – etc.
- ➤ Pedal changes are dictated by two considerations: melody and harmony. If the melody is in the bass (as in the opening), there will be frequent pedal changes to avoid blur. In other places, the texture and harmony are dictated by the bass note. Rachmaninoff frequently shows the importance of long bass tones (see mm. 14-26). The pedal must hold these bass notes to their notated length.
- ➤ Rachmaninoff uses *tenutos* frequently, providing hints about melodic and rhythmic intensity. Notes marked *tenuto* should not be rushed; hold them for their full value or even a shade longer.

Cyril Scott
Lotus Land, op. 47, no. 1 (R80)
Background Information

Scott received his musical training in Germany as well as in his native England. His compositions cover a broad spectrum of musical genres, including operas, symphonies, concerti, and solo piano works. The composer's ability to evoke exotic images in his pieces earned him a reputation as "the English Debussy."

The basic requirements for playing *Lotus Land* are a LH span of a 10th, fluent octaves, facile five-finger patterns, and flexibility of rhythm. It would be helpful for the student to review the story of Odysseus and the Lotus Eaters.

Exploring the Score

- ➤ Scott creates the effect of exotic allure, a hypnotic seduction into a world previously unexplored. The quarter-note rhythm, be it waving palm trees or the lapping of water on the sandy shores, is enticing. The opening harmony is unstable and "exotic." Few pieces have an E flat minor seventh chord as their tonic!
- ➤ Where does Scott move the bass from the constant E flat (D sharp) of the opening? Note the new texture in the RH at that point.
- ➤ How many white keys are played on p. 80? [none]

Practice Suggestions

- ➤ Scott has written the piece very cleverly, combining both predictable beat (LH) and the feeling of improvised flexibility. With the exception of the cadenza (p. 80), strive to play the LH with a strict, predictable beat. If you realize the RH notation accurately (dynamics, slurs, etc.), that hand will sound free.
- ➤ Check the meaning of *languido.*
- ➤ Observe *tenutos* and accents carefully, paying special attention to inner lines played by the LH thumb.

Claude Debussy
Brouillards / Mist (R85)
Background Information

Debussy's twenty-four *Préludes* (published in two books, 1910 and 1913) present a variety of musical scenes.

Brouillards is from the second book of *Préludes.* In this book, Debussy frequently employs three staves in his notation, showing more clearly the streams of sound that are woven into the texture. (For more detailed information on the Debussy *Préludes,* please refer to the discussion of *La fille aux cheveux de lin* in Level 9.)

"Brouillards" means "mists" or "fogs." Our experience of fog is often confusing and even frightening, for the familiar eludes us and our perceptions are uncertain.

The familiar sounds of tonic and dominant are not present in this harmonically elusive work, with the overlapping of bitonal harmonies obscuring familiar tonal landmarks.

Exploring the Score

➤ Look through the score and discuss the constant use of opposing tonalities.
➤ Mark the sections in the score:
   A – mm. 1-9: opposing white key triads and black key broken chords
   B – mm. 10-17: "bell" tones imposed over the A figure
   C – mm. 18-24: wide-spread octave theme
   A1 – mm. 24-28
   D – mm. 29-37: LH triads act as pedal point to black key arpeggiated figure
   C1 – mm. 38-42
   A2 – mm. 43-52

➤ As one might expect in this harmonically ambiguous piece, no resolution is found at the end. Note the final sound of the piece.
➤ The student may need some assistance with the French terms (the opening directives are translated at the bottom of p. 83):
   - *cédez* – slowing
   - *un peu en dehors* – slightly emphasized
   - *un peu marqué* – slightly accented
   - *en retenant et en s'effaçant* – holding back and fading away
   - *presque plus rien* – almost nothing more

Practice Suggestions

➤ Debussy marks his scores with meticulous care. Dynamics, touch, and tone are notated. The goal of practice is to realize the score with artistic sensitivity.
➤ Most of Debussy's piano scores have no pedal indications. This piece has two. However, every sound of the piece is pedaled, even when they are notated to be played detached (LH chords of mm. 1-3). Practice the sound of those LH chords, playing them detached but connected with the pedal. (Change the pedal with each chord.) Here we see an example of Debussy's great sensitivity to color and touch.
➤ In spite of the fact that the piece explores the moods and vague images of fog, each figure must be played cleanly. Interpreting the idea of fog is no invitation to imprecise finger work.
➤ As Debussy instructs at the beginning, listen for slightly different levels of sound, playing the LH *staccato* chords with more emphasis than the RH arpeggiated figures. In m. 10, you must control three levels of sound: bolder long tones are now projected above and below the previous texture.

➤ You have developed several practice techniques for arpeggiated passages. Mm. 29-30 and 32-37 require two practice approaches:
   - In mm. 29 and 30, discover the logical groupings within each hand. In the RH, stop on the thumb to discover the beginning of each group. In the LH, stop on finger 4. When first practicing hands together, block the patterns.
   - In mm. 32 to 37, only the RH plays arpeggios. Practice RH thumb to thumb. A slight lifting of the wrist facilitates the changing directions.

➤ What LH finger will play the top note of each 32nd note flourish in mm. 29-30?

Françis Poulenc
Suite française (Mvts. Three, Six, Seven) (R91)
Background Information

Originally written in 1935 and scored for brass, woodwinds, and harpsichord, the *Suite française* was later transcribed for piano solo, and was a favorite work in Poulenc's own piano recitals. The dances were originally written or transcribed by the French 16th-century composer Claude Gervais. Poulenc added his "modern" harmonies.

Third Movement: Petite marche militaire
Exploring the Score

➤ What is the key of this piece? Poulenc does not make the answer an easy one. If one were to label the key of the melody, F major would be the ready answer. The frequent insertion of E flats in the harmonics gives the piece the sound of F Dorian. The last two measures are a tongue-in-cheek surprise—the cadence is in G!
➤ How long are the phrases on the first page? [six measures]
➤ Survey the phrases of the B section, which starts in m. 36. Compare the phrases in mm. 43-50 with mm. 51-58.
➤ As mentioned above, Poulenc's first transcription of these dances was scored for woodwinds and brass. From the dynamics and rhythmic figures, one can imagine which phrases were scored for the winds, and which were for the brass. Write in your thoughts on the "orchestration" of the piece.

Practice Suggestions

➤ Not all notes are *staccato*. In mm. 1-12, the LH eighth notes match the RH *staccato,* but the quarters are full value.
➤ Poulenc indicates a projected top melody in the B section starting in m. 36.
➤ The most difficult passage begins in m. 51. Provide

yourself a model of the RH balance by playing the two voices divided between the hands. When you play as written, maintain a flexible wrist and forearm and think in two-note slurs for technical ease. A touch of pedal on each beat will help create a *legato* sound in the melody.

Sixth Movement: Sicilienne

Exploring the Score

➢ If your student is playing a *sicilienne* for the first time, assign research on the origin of the dance and its characteristic meter and tempo.

➢ Survey the dynamic markings and performance directions. With the exception of one phrase, they indicate that this piece is played quietly, delicately, and *mélancolique*.

➢ Somewhat unusual for Poulenc is the literal repeat of mm. 1-12. Find that repetition. Notice how each line in this section has its own theme.

➢ Emphasis is given to the middle and bass register in this section. How might this be "orchestrated" for woodwinds and brass?

➢ Mm. 17-20 feature an ornament reminiscent of French Baroque harpsichord writing. Play the small notes before the beat.

➢ Notice how the downbeats in mm. 1-4 descend by step [C-B-A-G]. Find the descending motion in the coda, mm. 33-37.

Practice Suggestions

➢ A practice goal is to create appropriate contrast between this piece and its companions. Observe dynamic markings carefully.

➢ Maintain a gently undulating feel throughout the piece, and find a dynamic goal for each phrase. Be sure to taper off at the ends of the slurs.

➢ Part of the delicate and *très doucement* (very sweetly) effect of the piece is created by the pedal. Each quarter and eighth note in the LH is pedaled, even when pitches and harmonies are repeated. With the exception of the *forte* in mm. 13-16, *très doucement* should sound as if little or no pedal is used.

Seventh Movement: Carillon

Exploring the Score

➢ Has the student heard a carillon? If the student is unfamiliar with this instrument, assign some research reading. How does the carillon produce its sound? How is it played?

➢ The rondeau was a preferred form in French Baroque music. A refrain (mm. 1-10) was alternated with contrasting sections. A typical form would be ABACA. Poulenc states five different ideas in this piece, three of which are repeated. Chart out the form of this piece, marking the sections in the score.

A – mm. 1-10
B – mm. 11-22
A – mm. 23-32
C – mm. 33-48 (compare RH of m. 33 with LH of mm. 11)
A – mm. 49-57
extension – mm. 58-65
A – mm. 66-75
D – mm. 76-91
A – mm. 92- 101
B1 – mm. 102-113
extension – mm. 114-125
A – mm. 126-end

Of special interest is the unvaried restatement of the A theme.

➢ Name the chord(s) that end the phrases. Is the piece in C or in G?

➢ The different "themes" in this piece are not boldly contrasting. What elements do they share, thereby giving the piece a unified sound?

Practice Suggestions

➢ A primary clue to your practice and interpretation is the *alla breve* indication and the marking *Très animé—très gai*. The phrases flow to their final chord in one breath.

➢ Poulenc's accents represent the striking of the bells. Bring out those top tones. Work out pedaling that will enrich the sonority without unnecessary blurring.

➢ From the structure of some chords, we assume that Poulenc had a large hand. In mm. 58-61, he indicates that the middle tones are to be held into the second beat. For those with a smaller reach, an alternate fingering is to play the two bottom tones with the thumb.

➢ In m. 138, Poulenc writes *sec, laisser vibrer*. The sharp (*sec*) staccato is caught in the pedal, and the sound continues to vibrate.

Manuel de Falla
Danse du meunier/The Miller's Dance (R99)
Background Information

Although his works for piano are few, Falla numbers among the most important Spanish composers of the 20th century. After receiving his training in Spain, he moved to Paris, where he became friends with Debussy, Ravel, and Dukas. Falla spent the final years of his life in Argentina, where he died in 1946. *Danse du meunier* is an arrangement of a flamenco dance from *El sombrero de tres picos (The Three-Cornered Hat)*, a ballet commissioned by Diaghilev for which Pablo Picasso designed the sets.

Exploring the Score

➢ There is little question regarding the provenance of this music—the rhythmic figures and chord structures are graphic imitations of intense flamenco guitar strumming.

➤ Explore the score for melodic figures. There are few, as the main emphasis of this piece is rhythmic.

➤ The dynamics provide much of the flavor. Look through the score for dynamic contrasts. Circle the frequent use of a sudden *pp*.

➤ Notice the wide span of some chords. The piece requires a minimum stretch of a 9th.

➤ If a synthesizer or digital keyboard is available, play the "guitar" figures with the instrument set to an acoustic guitar sound. The clarity and bite necessary for these passages will be obvious.

Practice Suggestions

➤ A successful performance of this piece relies on accurate beat subdivisions. The sixteenths must be distinctly different from the triplets and eighths. From the first day of practice, emphasize the steady beat and its accurate divisions.

➤ Hand rotation will facilitate the broken chords. Practice the top and bottom tones of the broken figures to feel the rotation. (In the RH, they are often octaves.)

➤ The measures that imitate the guitar strumming are marked carefully with accents, yet they are not all alike. Follow the score carefully.

➤ Note the stress on the LH weak beats, mm. 10-15. Which beats are stressed in the RH in those same measures?

➤ Listen to the *Celebration Series*® recording for the interpretation of the final page *accelerando*.

Amy Marcy Cheney Beach
A Hermit Thrush at Eve, op. 92, no. 1 (R102)
Background Information

The list of Amy Beach's compositions is long and comprehensive. She was America's first prominent woman composer. As a child she exhibited prodigious talent in piano and composition. Her *Gaelic Symphony* was the first symphonic work by a woman to be performed by the Boston Symphony. As is illustrated in *A Hermit Thrush at Eve,* her piano works bear the marks of late Romanticism.

Exploring the Score

➤ As has been suggested with previous compositions, it is helpful to start by listening to the *Celebration Series*® recording. From listening, one gains an impression of mood, tone color, voicing, and the sound of the bird calls.

➤ Beach repeats several musical motives in this evocative piece, and the overall form can be determined by the order in which they appear. It is helpful to give the various motives a descriptive character

Slow rising scale (the thrush soars): Although this motive first appears in mm. 2-4, it usually precedes the song of the thrush. Mark these scales in the score.

Triplet figuration (murmuring introduction): This filigree sets the atmosphere, preparing the listener for the themes that follow. Similar triplet figures are used in combination with the "evening theme" later on.

Three descending steps (evening theme): First appears in mm. 10-13. There are three subsequent appearances, two of which are in the tenor. Mark them in the score.

Rapid broken chords (hermit thrush song): Readily recognized by the groups of small notes.

➤ The score appears complicated and dense. But ... what is the loudest dynamic level and how much of the piece is played at that level? Beach uses numerous descriptive words to help communicate the desired sound: *murmurando, dolce cantabile e legato, dolcissimo espressivo, sempre cantabile.* Conclusion: The piece exudes the quietude of a summer evening. We listen ... and wait ... for the song of the hermit thrush.

Practice Suggestions

➤ This is a complex piece in a complicated key. Immerse yourself in E flat minor by playing scales, chords, arpeggios, and cadences in that key.

➤ The outline above shows several distinct recurring motives. You could approach the piece by practicing all appearances of a given theme. A suggested starting place is the "evening theme" of three descending steps:

mm. 10-13: – memorize the theme
  – practice hands separately
  – tap the two-against-three if needed
  – play slowly, hands together

Follow similar steps for other "evening theme" statements: mm. 14-17, 34-37, 38-41. As you learn these measures, you will quickly see the parallels between mm. 10-13 and mm. 34-37. Similarly, you see the parallels between mm. 14-17 and mm. 38-41.

➤ Next, practice the ascending scales (the "thrush soars" theme). These are found preceding the thrush calls: mm. 18-22, mm. 43-47. The piece also begins and ends with these scales.

➤ The "hermit thrush song" is played quietly and delicately, but distinctly. Barely brush the top of the keys with your finger strokes.

LIST E – TWENTIETH-CENTURY REPERTOIRE
Suggested Order of Difficulty

Page	Composer	Title
R147	Dmitri Kabalevsky	*Variations in A Minor, op. 40, no. 2*
R132	Alberto Ginastera	*Rondó sobre temas infantiles argentinos/Rondo on Argentine Children's Folk-tunes*
R164	Christos Tsitsaros	*Snow Games*
R136	Harry Somers	*Strangeness of Heart*
R154	Robert Muczynski	*Six Preludes, op. 6, Nos. 1 and 6*
R160	Ann Southam	*Four Bagatelles, Nos. 2 and 4*
R139	Samuel Barber	*Pas de deux*
R117	Clermont Pépin	*Trois pièces pour la légende dorée (First Mvt.: I. Prélude; Second Mvt.: Interlude; Third Mvt.: Toccate)*
R143	Lee Hoiby	*Prelude, op. 7, no. 1*
R107	Béla Bartók	*Rondo No. 1, op. 84*
R111	Aaron Copland	*The Cat and the Mouse*
R124	Olivier Messiaen	*Plainte calme/Gentle Sorrow*
R126	Dmitri Shostakovich	*Three Fantastic Dances, op. 5*

As noted in the Introduction to List D, Impressionist composers employed scale systems other than major and minor, destabilizing traditional harmonic relationships through the use of modes and the whole-tone scale. Many 20th-century composers continued the trend away from traditional harmony by avoiding familiar chordal functions. The historic "breakdown of tonality" reached its conclusion with the introduction of the twelve-tone system, in which each chromatic step has equal importance. Throughout the 20th century, rhythm also became increasingly complex, featuring shifting meters and irregular rhythmic patterns.

In reaction to these trends, some composers, such as Igor Stravinsky and Paul Hindemith, wrote in a neo-Classic style, using their personal harmonic vocabularies while borrowing from established Classical forms. Some composers integrated jazz and ragtime elements into their compositions. Composers such as John Cage, Henry Cowell and George Crumb extended the color of the instrument by playing directly on the strings with the hand or fingernail, placing nuts and bolts inside the piano, or using the human voice to resonate overtones from the piano.

The pieces in List E represent many of these trends and embrace a wide variety of national backgrounds. The combination of Lists D and E includes compositions from nearly every decade of the 20th century. Some of the pieces are firmly grounded in the traditional tonal system, while others defy a relationship to perceived tonality. In all cases, however, the music is motivated by the same elements we find in the music of Mozart and Chopin: sound flows forward to a point of tension; unity and contrast are the polarities around which all works are conceived; and each piece exploits a unique sonority from the instrument. When the student bears these basic principles in mind, the study of these 20th-century works becomes an extension of the style periods previously studied.

Béla Bartók
Rondo No. 1, op. 84 (R107)
Background Information

In his lifetime, Bartók was the world's leading authority on the folk music of his native Hungary and surrounding central European countries. The three rondos of this set are based on Slovak folk tunes. Bartók's music integrates the sound of folk tunes to such a degree that it is difficult to distinguish the quotation of a folk tune from his own writing. Of special interest in Bartók's music are the colorful accompaniments he creates. These accompaniments augment the mood of the tune and intensify the rhythm of the dance.

Exploring the Score

➤ The rondo form is easily recognizable through the changes of key and tempo. Do you find the reappearances of the A theme? [m. 95, m. 152]

➤ Label the ABACA form in the score, and identify the prevailing keys.

➤ Each theme is stated several times within its section. Discuss Bartók's varied accompaniments. Are the accompaniments of any statements of the theme exactly alike?

➤ Optional *ossia* phrases in a score are usually easier versions of the material. In this case, Bartók writes a more difficult option for the *ossia* phrases.

Practice Suggestions

➤ Passages that present coordination challenges (e.g., mm. 30-34) can be solved most quickly by tapping the rhythm on a flat surface before attempting to play on the keyboard.

➤ Observe Bartók's phrasing carefully. Note places where the hands do not end their phrases simultaneously (e.g., mm. 5-8).

➤ In the C section, mm. 103-110, notice the high and low C's that accompany the stepwise melodies. Project these notes with a rich, bell-like sound. (You may wish to add pedal to these measures.) Practice for the same tone quality (*staccato* quality and dynamic level) for both the bass and treble Cs.

➤ In m. 139 of the C section, the stepwise melody appears as the *bottom* tone of the RH chords.

Aaron Copland
The Cat and the Mouse (R111)
Background Information

The Cat and the Mouse was Copland's first published piece, written in Paris while he was a student of the famous French pedagogue Nadia Boulanger. In style and harmonic structure, it is far removed from his mature works.

This "Scherzo humoristique" is highly programmatic. Developing a story line for each figure and section is an important aspect of the study of *The Cat and the Mouse*.

Exploring the Score

➤ Listen to the *Celebration Series®* recording of this piece and discuss the events which Copland portrays. Urge the student to be specific.

➤ As would be true of a toccata with similar alternating hand figures, it is important that the rhythm be strictly controlled.

➤ In m. 72, the editor suggests the use of the *sostenuto* pedal. (This may be a unique event in the entire *Celebration Series®.*) This middle pedal is depressed while holding the tone that is to be sustained. While holding the *sostenuto* pedal (in this case, from mm. 72-80), the damper pedal can be used to clarify changing harmonies.

➤ Have the student experiment with the *sostenuto* pedal. For instance, play a low C and capture it with the *sostenuto* pedal. While the C continues to sound, play I, IV, V harmonies above it, changing the damper pedal to clarify each chord.

Practice Suggestions

➤ To learn the piece efficiently, isolate all sixteenth-note figures that feature alternating hands (mm. 5, 21, 51, 55, 68). Name the harmonies as you block these

passages until the shifts are comfortable. Practice at graduated tempi with accents on the beats.

➤ The success of the dramatic effects rests on the ability to play convincing dynamics. Strive for dynamic control in mm. 9-12, 20, 34-37, 59, and 65.

Clermont Pépin
Trois pièces pour la légende dorée (First Mvt.: Prélude; Second Mvt.: Interlude; Third Mvt.: Toccate) (R117)
Background Information

Pépin has had a distinguished career as a leading Canadian composer, teacher, and administrator. His development as a composer has led him to highly controlled serial compositions. "To me serial music is not at all intellectual. The more I go into it, the more I find that it opens an entire new world of emotional expression."

La légende dorée (The Golden Legend) was a 13th-century literary work consisting of 177 chapters describing the miracles and martyrdom of the Saints and Apostles as well as heroic deeds of legendary characters. A special Canadian Broadcasting Corporation program on Good Friday of 1956 featured several of the legends, with music provided by Clermont Pépin. *Trois pièces* are three of the pieces written for that program. Although they are not written in serial technique, they avoid tonal references through constant use of 7ths and chromaticism. To establish an aural image for this piece, have the student listen to the *Celebration Series®* recording with the score in hand.

First Movement: Prélude
Exploring the Score

➤ Pépin successfully balances unifying and contrasting elements in this prelude. Find elements that unify the piece. [constant triplet motion; motive of four repeated beat notes in mm. 2, 6, 11, 14, 23, 27, 31, 34, 42, (45); return to opening idea in m. 45; opening LH intervals found mm. 31-37]

➤ What provides contrast? [duple subdivision in the section at m. 23; triplets shift from LH to RH; dynamic contrasts]

➤ Having found the elements of unity and contrast, you now can outline the form. Mark it in the score:
Theme: mm. 1-10
Variation 1: mm. 11-22
Variation 2: mm. 23-30 (with repeat)
Variation 3: mm. 31-40
Variation 4: mm. 41-end

➤ Discuss Pépin's use of dissonance. Prevailing sounds are 7ths and chromaticism. Look through the score to find examples. Notice in m. 3 the "chromatic 7ths": RH B–A sharp, LH A–G sharp.

➤ Variation 2 (m. 23) avoids chromaticism. What are the preferred intervals in the LH in this variation?

Practice Suggestions

➤ Practice first the passages that require attention to fingering. What finger(s) feel best on the F's in m. 4? Practice RH mm. 9, 16, 21-22, 37-38. Practice LH mm. 11, 14-16, 19-22.

➤ Pépin marks the score with a variety of touches. What different touch will you employ on RH phrases without slurs (e.g., mm. 9, 35) and those marked with slurs (e.g., m. 37)? [Pépin gives the clue in m. 35 with his marking *détaché*. Because of his frequent use of *staccato,* one assumes that *détaché* is a touch existing between *staccato* and *legato*.]

Second Movement: Interlude
Exploring the Score

➤ Similar to the *Prélude,* Pépin employs a constant rhythm throughout this movement.

➤ This piece contains considerable melodic repetition, but there are subtle differences that can be brought to life in a performance.

– Lines 1, 2, 4, and 6 are very similar. Notice, however, the rhythmic differences in the second measure of each slur.

– In what ways do lines 3 and 5 provide contrast? [LH accompaniment, dynamics, rhythm, pitch level.]

➤ What role does the interval of a 7th play in this piece?

Practice Suggestions

➤ If you plan to memorize, it is advisable to focus on the subtle changes of rhythm in the A theme (lines 1, 2, 4, 6). Compare each group of two measures. Do you find any pairs of measures that are exactly alike? [only mm. 1-2 and 21-22]

➤ To help with the differentiation of the rhythmic patterns, use these labels:

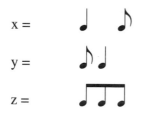

When practicing, call out the pattern ("x," "y," or "z") as you play each half measure.

Third Movement: Toccate
Exploring the Score

➤ In the previous two movements, Pépin used a consistent perpetual-motion rhythm. Harmonically, both movements focused on 7ths and chromaticism. Are those elements evident in *Toccate*?

➤ The opening idea consists of a repeating motive of three eighth notes played by the RH, against

quarter-note octaves in the LH. Because the RH rests in mm. 3 and 5, the alignment between the hands shifts every two measures. First, the LH starts with the bottom note of the RH motive. In m. 3, it starts with the middle note, and in m. 5, the top note. Have the student experience this shifting relationship by playing on the keyboard cover. A wide rotation of the RH is helpful to differentiate the top, middle, and bottom tones to be played.

➤ Find other examples of a three-eighth-note motive in the RH played against quarters in the LH. [mm. 16-19, 45-51]

➤ What musical elements generate excitement in this toccata?

Practice Suggestions

➤ You will learn the piece well if you practice short units slowly with a firm, *legato* sound.

➤ Practice the piece in units from the end, moving forward. For example:

Unit 1: mm. 45-end
Unit 2: mm. 41-44
Unit 3: mm. 36-40
Unit 4: mm. 33-35

Each unit should be played a minimum of three times. When several units are well in hand, combine them.

➤ Compare the sound of mm. 28 and 30. Play clearly defined two-note units in the RH.

➤ Listen to the *Celebration Series®* recording for ideas about pedaling and articulation. What degree of *legato* or *staccato* is used on passages where there are no slurs?

Olivier Messiaen
Plainte calme / Gentle Sorrow (R124)
Background Information

Best known for his organ compositions, Messiaen was one of the premier French composers of the 20th century. His monumental cycle for piano, *Vingt regards sur l'enfant Jésus* (1944) reflects the strong influence of Catholic mysticism on his writing as well as his lifelong experimentation with rhythm, harmony, and notation. *Huit préludes pour piano* (1929), which includes *Plainte calme,* represents Messiaen's early style. They foreshadow, however, the complex chordal texture and unusual rhythmic relationships that became hallmarks of his later style.

Exploring the Score

Nearly half of the piece is a repetition of previously stated material.

➤ Find repetitions of the material stated in mm. 1-6. [see mm. 9-14, 25-30]

- ➤ Find the repetition of mm. 15-19.
- ➤ In m. 15, notice the LH imitation of the RH figure.
- ➤ Compare m. 15 with m. 16. The chords of mm. 15-16 are constructed from 4hs.
- ➤ Label the form of the piece:
    - A – mm. 1-14
    - B – mm. 15-24
    - A – mm. 25-32
- ➤ The harmonies of the piece appear complex, but there are familiar chord structures. It is the functioning of the chords that is unique. The A flat 7 chord, for example, is repeated frequently and assumes the "rest" function usually fulfilled by the tonic harmony. Find the A flat 7 on the downbeats of mm. 1, 2, 4 and as part of m. 5. Label them in the score. Note the final chord. [A flat 7]
- ➤ The chord of secondary importance is the D7. Notice the way the D7 "partners" the A flat 7 in the final line. Find the D7 in mm. 6 and 13.
- ➤ Melodically, notice the frequent use of an "upward sigh" at the ends of phrases. This is an interesting variation on the descending figure that typically communicates sorrow or anguish.

Practice Suggestions
- ➤ Messiaen's music is complicated to read because of the many accidentals. Read slowly and carefully, writing in any accidentals you might overlook.
- ➤ Label and practice the A flat 7 and D7 chords. These serve as harmonic landmarks.
- ➤ Practice the chords of mm. 17-18 hands separately. Can you label them?
- ➤ Practice the chords of mm. 19 and 24 in pairs of eighth notes.
- ➤ As you put the piece together, phrase by phrase, be especially alert as you read stepwise motion. Are the steps half steps, whole steps, or augmented 2nds?
- ➤ It may be helpful to count eighth notes at first; they are the rhythmic "common denominator" in this piece.
- ➤ Despite the complex harmonic language, this piece requires the same subtle phrase shaping and attention to dynamics as any lyrical piece by Mozart, Chopin, or Debussy.

Dmitri Shostakovich
Three Fantastic Dances, op. 5 (R132)
Background Information
Russian composer and pianist Dimitri Shostakovich is one of the most distinctive voices in 20th-century music. A prolific composer, he is considered one of the 20th-century's greatest symphonists. For piano, he wrote a set of twenty-four preludes and a set of twenty-four preludes and fugues. *Three Fantastic Dances* is an early work, written when the composer was just sixteen. These three charming dances continue the 19th-century genre of the character piece.

First Movement
Exploring the Score
- ➤ If one were to look only at the bass notes, the piece might be mistaken for a Classical period work. The bass line is firmly grounded in C major, with moves to F (IV) and G (V). It is the harmonies and figures above these bass notes that lend a "fantastic" nature to the piece.
- ➤ As you look at the score and listen to the recording, list the dance elements.
- ➤ In addition to the harmonies, what else is "fantastic" about the sound of the piece?
- ➤ True or false?—The B section (beginning in m. 9) features converging chromaticism.

Practice Suggestions
- ➤ Accurate rhythm is a challenge for some students who learn this dance. Be precise with the rhythmic details in mm. 3, 10, 14, and 31.
- ➤ The B section is filled with dynamic nuance and surprise. Follow Shostakovich's markings.

Second Movement
Exploring the Score
- ➤ Shostakovich writes a waltz in G major. The chromatic motion of the LH harmonies disguises G major, lending a "fantastic" element:

The penultimate chord is the expected V7 (D7) in G, found on the downbeat of m. 7. The real surprise is the harmonization of the G chord in m. 8. [augmented harmony]

- ➤ At first look, the B section (m. 17) seems to lose interest in chromatic movement. However, each "answer" phrase is highly chromatic. Note the dynamic that is associated with these chromatic phrases.
- ➤ List the ways in which the B section is contrasting. [melody, texture, keyboard range, rhythm]
- ➤ With pencil in hand, listen to the *Celebration Series*® recording and notate the pedaling you hear. Are the dotted half notes in the bass held with the LH or by the pedal?
- ➤ Mm. 17-20 and 25-28 have contrasting articulations. How does the performer create that contrast?
- ➤ As in most waltzes, the downbeat is all-important. How do the different figures of the piece emphasize the downbeat?

Practice Suggestions

➤ Because of the extended hand position and octave writing, the whimsical one- and two-measure RH slurs can be challenging. Use the arm to move smoothly in the direction of the musical gesture. Avoid finger reaching, and listen for the uninterrupted flow of each short idea. The *legato* effect you achieve will be illusory.

➤ The return of the A section at m. 41 includes thicker textures in the same quiet dynamic. Use the same techniques to achieve a *legato* effect.

➤ Practice mm. 37-40 without the downbeats to understand the chromatic and oblique motion, listening for the usual shaping of a two-note slur. When you add the downbeats, secure the leaps by making them silently; practice from beat three to beat one using a "throwing" gesture to create exclamatory downbeats.

➤ Never forget the underlying motion of an elegant waltz as you work to master the challenging textures of this piece.

Third Movement

Exploring the Score

➤ This piece smiles! It is energetic, high spirited, and full of fun. One could picture a group dancing a polka.

➤ This dance is full of the harmonic surprises that characterize Shostakovitch's musical style. Read slowly through each hand's part, making note of traditional chord structures and shapes.

➤ Using subtle melodic relationships, Shostakovitch cleverly connects chords that seem unrelated in terms of traditional harmonic progressions. For example, in the RH of mm. 1-4, look for the descending line: A flat–G–F–E flat–D–C–B (**Hint:** play the thumb notes!) Find similar relationships throughout this piece.

➤ Perhaps the most difficult passage of all three dances is the chromatic sixteenth-note movement of mm. 13-20. Discuss practice approaches for these measures before home practice begins.

Practice Suggestions

➤ Let your first week of practice address the double notes of mm. 13-20. Releasing the thumb will reduce tension and promote a relaxed hand position. On the downbeat of mm. 14 and 16, lift the thumb during the tie.

➤ To practice the RH of mm. 17-20, keep the wrist and thumb loose and play the eighth notes as if they were *staccato* sixteenths. Release the notes by tipping the hand away from the thumb. You can capture this feeling by playing a zigzag rocking gesture outlining the bottom note of each blocked chord and the single sixteenth that follows:

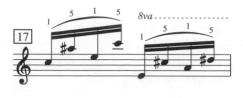

➤ Here is another fingering suggestion for the RH sixteenth notes in m. 17: 4-3-4-5-4-3-4-3

➤ The pedal can be used to bring color and contrast to this piece. The *quasi campanelli* (like bells) requires pedal to create that image in m. 21. Experiment with the pedal held for two measures. Are there places where you will not use the pedal? Where are the most extended pedals?

Alberto Ginastera
Rondó sobre temas infantiles argentinos/Rondo on Argentine Children's Folk-tunes (R132)
Background Information

Ginastera was the most prominent Argentinean composer of the 20th century. His works evoke the flavor of Argentinean life, with its dances, scenes of the vast hinterland *(pampas),* and the songs of the cowboys *(gauchos).* His early compositions, of which this rondo is an example (1947), are nationalistic in nature and have wide general appeal through their melodies, rhythms, and creative sonorities.

Exploring the Score

➤ The term rondo implies that the first theme will be restated. Search for reappearances of the opening theme, mm. 5-12. (Keep in mind that several factors can "disguise" a return statement: tempo, texture, key.) [mm. 67, 108, 116]

➤ Find other children's folk-tunes in the piece.

➤ Between statements of folk tunes, Ginastera writes interludes, providing the music with connective tissue. Find those interludes and discuss their importance in the piece. Will they be played as prominently as the folk tunes?

➤ Make a "flow chart" of the sections and keys. Are there common-tone links between keys?

Practice Suggestions

➤ Acquaint yourself with the different themes. Play them, hands separately if necessary, and listen to a recording so you can hear them at performance tempo.

➤ There are several passages which deserve immediate practice:
  – Mm. 56-65. The extended scale is easy when you realize that both hands play identical finger groupings (groups of four, groups of three). Block the patterns first.

- Mm. 67-74 and mm. 116-131. These chords are played staccato, with a "knocking" motion of the hand. Resist the temptation to play successive down motions of the arm. Several chords may be included in a single arm gesture.
- Mm. 74-88. Of first importance is the RH fingering. Next, block the LH harmonies. Then practice hands together slowly.

Harry Somers
Strangeness of Heart (R136)
Background Information

Harry Somers was one of Canada's most famous composers. Recognized internationally, his music has been performed in the USA, Central and South America, Europe, and the USSR. Somers' list of compositions is extensive, ranging from film and television scores to opera and symphonies. A gifted pianist, Somers initially intended to pursue both performance and composition as a career. *Strangeness of Heart* was written in 1942, when Somers was studying composition with noted Canadian teacher and composer, John Weinzweig.

Exploring the Score

➤ It would be helpful to listen to a recording of *Strangeness of Heart* prior to discussion and practice. The student may wish to play the bass line (double-stemmed quarter notes) quietly as you listen.
➤ A hypnotic lull settles over the LH. The rhythm and figure undulate predictably for lengthy periods. Have the student play a few LH measures to experience the rocking effect.
➤ A characteristic of Somer's writing is the prominent use of a falling 2nd in his melodies. Look through the score for these "sighs." You will also be able to find descending intervals in the bass line.
➤ Somers uses dynamics to great dramatic effect. Find the loudest moment in the piece.
➤ Is there a tonal center to this piece? Can you name the key? Somers rejects traditional chord relationships. He is able to create resting places (cadences), but avoids any sense of traditional tonality. Notice the final chord: a D7 that remains hovering in midair.

Practice Suggestions

➤ Somers favors 7th and 9th chords in his compositions. As you learn the notes, identify these harmonies, and listen to their individual sonorities. Watch for changing accidentals and key signatures.
➤ Practice the LH separately until you are confident with the chords and lilting rhythm.
➤ Invest your most sensitive musicianship into the shape of the RH lines. There is great longing and pleading in this piece.

Samuel Barber
Pas de deux (R139)
Background Information

Samuel Barber was one of America's leading composers, perhaps best known for the extremely popular *Adagio for Strings*. Barber's prestigious commissions include *Anthony and Cleopatra*, written for the opening of the Metropolitan Opera House in New York City's Lincoln Center, and the *Piano Concerto*, which was premiered at the opening of Philharmonic Hall in New York. Barber's *Piano Sonata, op. 26*, is the most famous contemporary sonata written by an American composer.

Barber's works are known for their lyricism and lush colors. His style of writing is referred to as neo-Romantic. *Pas de deux* is from the ballet suite *Souvenirs*. It exists in arrangements for piano solo and piano duet.

Exploring the Score

➤ In ballet music, one expects to find a rigorously steady beat. The dance gestures flow from beat to predictable beat.
➤ A *pas de deux*, as the name implies, is danced by two people. Choreography frequently calls for one of the dancers to appear on stage alone, later to be joined by the supportive partner. Find the moment in the score where the RH becomes responsible for two interweaving lines.
➤ The texture and dynamics from mm. 41-50 show dramatic tension. Make a chart of the dynamic plan of the piece. Notice the overall arch form that starts quietly, rises to points of tension, and returns to quiet.

Practice Suggestions

➤ Barber's elegantly flowing lines are masterfully crafted. Your goal is to create the most beautiful *legato* sound possible. Experiment with an extended flatter finger, and slightly roll the hand from finger to finger, transferring the weight.
➤ Shaping two melodic lines in one hand is challenging—one voice frequently tapers off while the other grows. Divide the two RH voices between the hands to model the sound, listening carefully for a quiet beginning and end to each slur. Try to achieve the same interplay when playing with one hand.
➤ In mm. 29-30, you may wish to let the LH take the first two eighth notes of the middle voice.
➤ As you approach the dynamic peak of the piece (mm. 46-50), do not over play. Barber's directive sostenuto allows you to take additional time on the full-handed chords, preventing a harsh accented tone.

Lee Hoiby
Prelude, op. 7, no. 1 (R143)
Background Information

Lee Hoiby received his undergraduate music degree in his native Wisconsin. He studied composition with Gian Carlo Menotti at the Curtis Institute. Hoiby has written extensively in many areas: opera, ballet, theatre, choral, songs, and chamber music. An accomplished pianist, he has also made significant contributions to the piano repertoire, including two piano concertos and numerous solo pieces. Hoiby is the recipient of numerous awards and grants. His music has been described by critics as "conservatively neo-Romantic."

Exploring the Score

➤ Hoiby's use of three staves facilitates the reading of the score. As mentioned earlier with regard to some 19th-century compositions and the *Debussy Preludes, Book II,* this is a "three-handed" texture. The RH plays the top staff and the LH the bottom staff. The middle staff is shared between the hands.

➤ For most of the piece, the main melody is notated on the middle staff. Those notes are divided between the hands. Notice that the small notes in the middle staff are melodic tones that are played as part of the RH figuration.

➤ What gives the prelude its contemporary sound? Where do you find simple major and minor triads? Look for the figures and chords that are built of stacked 4ths and 5ths.

Practice Suggestions

➤ It is important to become thoroughly acquainted with the melodic lines in this piece. Focus on the middle staff first, playing as notated (small notes will be played by the RH). Notice how the melody sometimes moves to the lower staff for ease of reading.

➤ Next, isolate the melodic lines that come out of the RH figuration in the top staff (double-stemmed notes).

➤ Finally, play all the melodic lines together. One voice often answers or imitates the other.

➤ Technically, the RH is the obvious "star of the show." Much of the RH deserves special practice:
  – mm. 5-7, 15-18, 27 for arpeggio crossings
  – mm. 7-13, 23-24 for double-stemmed held tones

➤ Practice the two lower staves together, focusing on the LH shifts and the division of hands required by the middle staff.

➤ When you are in control of each hand, slowly practice short sections of one or two measures, playing all three staves. Keep listening for the melody tones.

➤ Hoiby indicates *legato con ped.* How do you determine the pedaling? [The low bass tones are the "pedal markings."] When playing at performance tempo, you may wish to "flutter" the pedal occasionally for clarity in the middle and upper parts (the bass notes should still ring because of their low register.)

Dmitri Kabalevsky
Variations in A Minor, op. 40, no. 2 (R147)
Background Information

Kabalevsky's contribution to the piano student's repertoire is unsurpassed. He was devoted to the field of music education, and through his compositions, the student experiences the gamut of technical figures and musical forms. Kabalevsky wrote nine sets of variations on folk-tunes, and two sets on themes of his own creation.

Exploring the Score

➤ Kabalevsky creates a theme filled with possibilities for variation.

"x" = rising octave, descending a 4th by steps

"y" = rising 4th in stepwise motion

"z" = descending scale. In mm. 10-14 find these pitches.

➤ Kabalevsky uses these motives in each of the variations, sometimes more obviously than others. Find the different ways in which Kabalevsky varies the motives. Consider LH participation in your analysis.

Practice Suggestions

➤ As you begin your practice, read the score with meticulous care. Kabalevsky marks his scores very carefully. Each phrase mark, slur, *staccato,* and dynamic level will help you create a convincing performance.

➤ From the first day your goal should be a slow but finished performance of each practice section.

Robert Muczynski
Six Preludes, op. 6 (Nos.1 and 6) (R154)
Background Information
Chicago-born and -educated, Robert Muczynski has contributed significantly to the field of contemporary piano literature. He has written three advanced sonatas as well as many intermediate-level teaching pieces. Rhythm and sonority are hallmarks of his style.

Prelude No. 1
Exploring the Score
➤ This tightly crafted piece is unified by a rhythmic motive. Find the frequent appearance of:

➤ Contemporary composers frequently employ quartal harmonies (chords made of 4ths.) See mm. 5-8 for examples of both tertian and quartal harmonies.
➤ Note the wide keyboard range used in *Prelude No. 1*. What are the highest and lowest tones?

Practice Suggestions
➤ Muczynski marks every tone with a *staccato,* accent, or slur. Articulation is extremely important and every tone is played with a bright, intense sound. The staccatos are to be played very short, and the sixteenths with crystalline clarity. In your slow practice, focus on the distinct quality of each sound.
➤ You have already become acquainted with finger substitutions in other pieces. Note the substitutions in the LH, mm. 11 and 15. *Hand* substitution may be a new experience: in m. 31, the LH octave B becomes a RH octave B.
➤ Keep the wrist, hand, and thumb very loose while sustaining the long notes in mm. 11-13, 15-18. Play the *staccato* notes by gently rotating the whole hand; avoid lifting individual fingers.

Prelude No. 6
Exploring the Score
➤ As you listen to the *Celebration Series*® recording, have the student describe the mood. What effect is created with the *forte, staccato* bass sounds, frequent accents and fast tempo?
➤ This piece creates the impression of darkness, with the RH scored in the bass clef for much of the piece. Notice the extreme keyboard range outlined by the very last sound.
➤ The rhythm is predictable and stable, and the beat is always obvious. Find the frequent accents on beat two, and the few uses of syncopation.
➤ This piece focuses on the tone B flat.
  – On the first page, have your student quickly find all B flats.

  – Analyze the RH pattern of mm. 7-9. Find the black key minor 3rds on B flat and E flat. Note the white key half-step relationship surrounding those minor 3rds.
  – In the lesson, memorize the RH of mm. 7-9.
  – Block the black key minor 3rds in mm. 16-17.
  – Discuss the pattern and memorize it in the lesson.
  – Explore the remainder of this prelude (RH) for more black key 3rds.

➤ Find B flat major 3rds in the LH. What effect is produced by the LH continuing to play major 3rds? [tension and dissonance are created with the cross relation of the LH D natural against the RH D flat]

Practice Suggestions
➤ Muczynski writes the LH octaves of mm. 36-46 with three different accent patterns:
  – accent on downbeat (m. 36)
  – accent on downbeat and *sf* accent on beat 2 (m. 38)
  – no accents (m. 40)
➤ Practice each of these accent patterns. How will you achieve the desired results? (Lift the hand before playing an accent. Play unaccented octaves close to the key.)
➤ Memorize the octaves in mm. 42-45, hands separately.
➤ Practice the final two measures for the extensive RH shifts. Keep the hand close to the key surface.

Ann Southam
Four Bagatelles (Nos. 2 and 4) (R160)
Background Information
Canadian composer Ann Southam is known for her electronic works as well as compositions for piano and chamber ensembles. Her music has been described as "lyrically atonal," and *Bagatelle No. 2* is a representative example. Southam was a founding member and first president of the Association of Canadian Women Composers.

Bagatelle No. 2
Exploring the Score
➤ Listening to the *Celebration Series*® recording would be a helpful beginning to the study of this short piece.
➤ An analysis can start with m. 12.
  – The prevailing motive of this piece is the accompaniment figure found in the RH of m. 12. Two black keys move outward to form a 4th.
  – Find that motive, divided between the hands, in mm. 13-16.
  – Return to the beginning of the piece and find appearances of the motive in mm. 1-4.

➤ Half steps and outlined 4ths are prominent in this piece. Search for them:
  – in the opening melody
  – in the repeating accompaniment pattern, m. 1 inner voices, m. 12, RH
  – in the middle section (mm. 5-11)

➤ An inverted 4th becomes a 5th. Notice the LH chords made of 5ths in mm. 5-7.

Practice Suggestions

➤ As you heard on the recording, the melody is the most prominent feature in *Bagatelle No. 2*. Much of your practice will be focused on balance, projecting the melody.

➤ Rhythmically, you play subdivisions of the beat in eighth notes, triplets, sixteenths, two-against-three (m. 7), and three-against-four (m. 10). In all cases of beat subdivisions, the primary issue is to maintain your feeling of the pulse. Devise practice methods to learn the rhythms of mm. 7-11:
  – Can you accurately move from duples to triplets to sixteenths, keeping a steady beat?
    (Use the metronome to reinforce the pulse while you practice switching rhythms.)
  – Tap and count only the duple eighths and sixteenths.
  – Tap and count only the triplets and sixteenths.
  – When playing two-against-three and three-against-four, strive to hear the hands independently of another.

➤ The pedal is necessary to enhance the sonority and color of the piece. However, the harmonies are not to be blurred. In general, the pedal will change frequently, often on individual eighths. Practice without pedal for the discipline of *legato* playing.

Bagatelle No. 4
Exploring the Score

➤ If half steps and 4ths were the primary intervals of *Bagatelle No. 2,* those same intervals appear in bolder relief in *Bagatelle No. 4*. If you were to circle all half steps and 4ths (and their inversions, 5ths), would there be any tones not circled?

➤ The piece has constant sixteenth-note motion, yet rhythm becomes the special challenge. Notice the asymmetrical beamed groupings in the $\frac{5}{8}$ measures:

  – Tap and count each sixteenth note in the beamed groupings: *123 12 123 12*
  – Find other examples of this asymmetrical rhythm.

➤ The mixing of three sixteenths and two sixteenths occurs in m. 16 with the RH playing groups of three sixteenths against LH eighths. In m. 17, the sixteenths change from groups of three to groups of two. What RH groupings do you feel in m. 25?

➤ The eighth note serves as the main pulse in the other meters ($\frac{6}{8}$, $\frac{3}{8}$, $\frac{9}{8}$, etc.). Those measures can be counted *1&2&3&*.

➤ Work with the various rhythms in the lesson and make a decision on the approach to counting before home practice begins.

Practice Suggestions

➤ Divide the piece into short practice units. Write in the fingerings that give you the greatest speed and control. Make special note of the composer's dynamic plan.

➤ Practice the $\frac{6}{8}$ and $\frac{3}{8}$ measures. Count aloud as you play.

➤ Practice the $\frac{5}{8}$ measures counting the sixteenths: *"123 12 123 12."*

➤ Practice mm. 16 and 25, feeling the RH groups of three sixteenths.

➤ As you increase the tempo, feel the music in wave-like gestures. Follow the dynamics carefully and keep the fingers close to the keys.

➤ Practice the performance tempo by playing an entire measure or half-measure in one "impulse." (Hear the sound in your mind before playing.) Gradually build longer sections by connecting one impulse to the next.

Christos Tsitsaros
Snow Games (R164)
Background Information

Tsitsaros teaches at the University of Illinois, where he received his Doctor of Musical Arts degree in Piano Performance with a Minor in Piano Pedagogy. While studying at the École Normale de Musique in Paris, he was awarded the prestigious Diplome Supérieur d'Execution. "I write in an extemporaneous, eclectic idiom which is infiltrated by folk and jazz influences," writes the composer. Tsitsaros's shorter pieces are characterized by vibrant rhythm, distinct melodic patterns, and contrapuntal lines.

Exploring the Score

This piece incorporates a considerable variety of rhythms, harmonies, and textures.

➤ Circle the changes of meter. Make special note of the meter signatures at the beginning of the piece.

➤ Compare these contrasting harmonies:
  m. 1 (bitonal)
  m. 25 (minor chord with added 6th)
  m. 37 (minor and diminished harmonies in
    unison)
  m. 59 (chromatic 4ths)

➤ Discuss your ideas on the consistently thin texture of the piece. Does the title give you a clue?

➤ Although the tones in the first section are played together, there is a rhythmic "confusion" between the $\frac{2}{4}$ and $\frac{6}{8}$, evoking a picture of swirling snow. Groups of six sixteenth notes can be divided as 3 + 3 (triplet subdivisions in $\frac{2}{4}$) or 2 + 2 + 2 (normal subdivision in $\frac{6}{8}$). Tsitsaros creates a RH figure that is clearly in $\frac{6}{8}$.

At some points, he allows the RH to engage in hemiola:

Hemiola occurs in the LH in mm. 21-24:

A further complication of the rhythm occurs when the RH figuration contains four-note scale fragments:

➤ Formally, the piece is divided into two sections. Mark the beginning of the B section. [m. 25]
➤ List ways in which the A and B sections are contrasting. (Check the dynamics!)
➤ Look for unifying motives in the B section. For example, in mm. 25-27, Tsitsaros writes broken chords and four-note descending patterns. Can those figures be found throughout the section? Are there other unifying devices you can identify?

Practice Suggestions

➤ If you begin practicing the A section hands together, the RH will easily fall under the influence of the LH $\frac{2}{4}$. To establish the independence of the RH $\frac{6}{8}$ rhythm, practice it separately counting *1 2 3 4 5 6*.
➤ The shape of the RH figure is the primary consideration. When the composer writes the RH in groups of four sixteenths (m. 9), let that become the accent pattern.
➤ Before playing hands together, play the RH (in $\frac{6}{8}$!) and tap the LH.
➤ The B section of the piece falls nicely in the hands and presents no rhythmic or technical difficulty. Practice the B section in short groups, observing the dynamics.

PIANO STUDIES/ETUDES 10
Suggested Order of Difficulty

Page	Composer	Title
S6	Stephen Heller	Study no. 2: *Prelude in C sharp Minor, op. 81, no. 10*
S20	Carl Czerny	Study no. 7: *Study in F Major, op. 299, no. 12*
S30	Jean-Baptiste Duvernoy	Study no. 11: *Study in C Major, op. 120, no. 13*
S18	Alexander Scriabin	Study no. 6: *Etude, op. 2, no. 1*
S38	Christos Tsitsaros	Study no. 14: *Gallop*
S8	Ernst Haberbier	Study no. 3: *Serenade, op. 53, no. 5*
S22	Anatol Konstantinovich Lyadov	Study no. 8: *A Trifle, op. 2, no. 12*
S24	Carl Albert Loeschhorn	Study no. 9: *Etude in E Minor, op. 67, no. 5*
S11	Hermann Berens	Study no. 4: *Study in A Minor, op. 61, no. 32*
S32	Moritz Moszkowski	Study no. 12: *Study in C Major, op. 91, no. 15*
S4	Carl Czerny	Study no. 1: *Study in A Minor, op. 740, no. 41*
S26	Sergei Rachmaninoff	Study no. 10: *Étude-tableau, op. 33, no. 8*
S14	Moritz Moszkowski	Study no. 5: *Etude in C Major, op. 72, no. 4*
S35	Béla Bartók	Study no. 13: *Bagatelle, op. 6, no. 15*

CHART OF TECHNICAL FIGURES

This chart lists the studies with their main technical focus. A study may be listed in more than one category.

Category	Composer	Study No.
Accompanying figures	Ernst Haberbier	3
	Sergei Rachmaninoff	10
Alternating hands	Anatol Konstantinovich Lyadov	8
	Christos Tsitsaros	14
Arpeggiated figures	Carl Czerny	1
	Carl Czerny	7
Broken chords	Carl Czerny	1
	Stephen Heller	2
	Carl Czerny	7
	Sergei Rachmaninoff	10
	Moritz Moszkowski	12
	Christos Tsitsaros	14
Extensions, contractions of the hand	Carl Czerny	1
	Moritz Moszkowski	5
Irregular change of direction	Hermann Berens	4
	Moritz Moszkowski	12
Melody presented in extended positions	Sergei Rachmaninoff	10
	Alexander Scriabin	6
Octaves	Moritz Moszkowski	5
Quickly shifting chords	Anatol Konstantinovich Lyadov	8
	Carl Albert Loeschhorn	9
	Béla Bartók	13
Repeated technical gesture	Moritz Moszkowski	5
	Béla Bartók	13
Rhythmic complexity	Christos Tsitsaros	14
Rotational figures	Hermann Berens	4
	Jean-Baptiste Duvernoy	1
Scale figures	Stephen Heller	2
	Sergei Rachmaninoff	10
Three-note mordent figure	Carl Albert Loeschhorn	9

Celebration Series® Handbook for Teachers

The following discussions focus on the technical aspect of each study/etude.

Carl Czerny
Study in A Minor, op. 740, no. 41 (S4)
Background Information

Czerny was Beethoven's favorite student, and they enjoyed a long-term friendship. Beethoven entrusted the instruction of his nephew to Czerny, as well as the premier performance of his *Emperor Concerto.* Czerny wrote an amazing number of technical studies. (Note this opus number!) His studies are important because they drill the technical figures required for command of the Classical and early Romantic piano repertoire. His metronome markings require ultimate speed. (This study is marked by Czerny to be played ♩ = 100.)

Practice Suggestions

➤ This is a study for LH expansion/contraction and quick changes of direction. Prior to each octave stretch, Czerny writes a mordent figure. Isolate this five-note pattern, practicing with *fermatas* on either side of the low note. Do not stretch and prepare the octave. Keep the hand together and practice the quickest possible extension to the octave.

➤ The zigzag motion of mm. 21, 23, 25 can be practiced in dotted rhythms (short-long, short-long). If the hand is relaxed and the wrist is slightly above the key level, a natural rotation will result.

➤ Create your own E major and A minor arpeggio exercises in preparation for this study.

Stephen Heller
Prelude in C sharp Minor, op. 81, no. 10 (S6)
Practice Suggestions

➤ There are three primary technical figures in this study:
    1) four-note scale fragments (e.g., mm. 1, 21)
    2) full scales (e.g., mm. 31-32)
    3) broken chords (e.g., mm. 7, 41)

➤ The figures listed above occur in reverse order of difficulty. You may wish to start with the most difficult (broken chords). Find measures of broken chords and create your own practice steps for that figure. Group the broken chords into patterns of four ascending tones (as opposed to their beamed grouping). Allow the thumb to leave its tone and follow the fingers as you move to higher pitches.

➤ Next, find the scale passages for special practice. Check the fingering.

➤ Your last practice category is the four-note scale fragments. They appear in both hands.

Ernst Haberbier
Serenade, op. 53, no. 5 (S8)

Changing fingers is the usual procedure when playing repeated tones. It is obvious, however, that Haberbier intends for the repeated tones at the bottom and top of the LH figure to be played by the same fingers. This complicates the tonal control of the accompaniment.

Practice Suggestions

➤ Find the larger gesture encompassing an entire LH measure. Try the following:
    With your LH fingers resting on a flat surface, rotate the wrist in an oval shape. One complete rotation is an "out–around." The wrist drops as you move from finger 1 to finger 5 ("out"). The wrist lifts as you move from finger 5 to 1 ("around").

➤ As you play the LH notes at the beginning of the piece, let the wrist complete one "out-around" gesture per measure. The wrist is constantly, freely moving. The tones at the top of the figure coincide with the wrist starting to drop. The tones at the bottom of the figure coincide with the wrist starting to lift.

➤ Follow the LH fingering carefully. If none is written, or if you wish to substitute your own fingering, write the chosen fingering in the score.

Hermann Berens
Study in A Minor, op. 61, no. 32 (S11)

The primary figure of this study features "interrupted stepwise motion." For contrast, Berens also writes diatonic and chromatic scales.

Practice Suggestions

➤ A helpful practice approach to the main figure involves preparation for playing fingers 2–1. In this study, finger 2 represents a change of direction. When you first start practicing, pause before you play each finger 2. Lift that finger with a slight tilt of the hand and play to the note that next precedes finger 2. The hand helps you play the figure.

➤ There are several fingerings possible for chromatic scales.

Decide which fingering gives you greatest clarity and speed, and write your fingering in the score, mm. 38-44.

Moritz Moszkowski
Etude in C Major, op. 72, no. 4 (S14)
Practice Suggestions

The repeated intervals and chords in this study require a highly developed technique. The octaves of mm. 25-28 pose their own challenge in playing double notes.

➤ Throughout your practice, keep a loose hand and wrist. Practice quietly with a light touch.

➤ Do not add the loud dynamic levels in mm. 25-43 until you can play these passages lightly and easily.

➤ To avoid tension, keep the hand in straight alignment with the forearm. (Tension results when the hand is turned at an angle.) Also, for endurance and ease, practice a slight drop-lift of the LH wrist on each beat. A single wrist gesture with tiny "afterbounces" can provide momentum for up to four sixteenths.

➤ Create special practice techniques. For example, in mm. 1-2:
1) Play the LH top notes separately.
2) Play the pairs of sixteenths quickly, with a rest after each pair.
3) Practice groups of four sixteenth notes with a rest after each group.
4) Play the moving top LH notes louder than the repeated lower LH notes.

➤ Special octave practice for mm. 25-28:
  – m. 25: form short practice groups of black keys which end on a white key. Lift the wrist slightly as you approach the white key.
  – m. 26: practice in groups of four sixteenths
  – m. 27: practice in groups of four descending pitches
  – m. 28: practice in pairs of ascending pitches

➤ The RH also has its challenges in this piece. Moszkowski writes the chords so that the top tones can be played *legato*. Practice playing *only* the top RH tones *legato;* the other chord tones can be lightly detached.

➤ The score is marked *con pedale.* Experiment with different levels of pedaling each eight-note pulse to achieve a pleasing blend without sacrificing clarity. Where are there passages in which pedal *cannot* be used?

Alexander Scriabin
Etude, op. 2, no. 1 (S18)
The *Three Pieces, op. 2* date from Scriabin's student years at the Moscow Conservatory. His early works reveal the strong influence of Chopin.

Exploring the Score

➤ There are two themes in this short study. Both are highly lyrical and are carried by the top voice.
  – List the similarities found in mm. 1-2 (A theme) and mm. 17-18 (B theme). [two-measure phrases in which the melody of the first measure is primarily eighth notes and the downbeat of the second measure is a dotted rhythm]
  – Find the restatement of the A theme. [m. 26]
  – The B theme is marked by a change of key signature. Mark the theme (m. 17) and find its restatement (m. 34).

➤ The student can play the melody and mark the phrases in the score. Do you find the phrase plan of 2mm. + 2mm. + 4mm. in both the A and B themes?

Practice Suggestions

➤ As a product of the late Romantic period, Scriabin places greatest emphasis on melody. The "etude" aspect of this piece involves projection of the melody above the thick texture. That projection is your primary practice goal.

➤ This study is supremely *legato.* The sound never stops. Melodic phrases come to an end, but the accompaniment continues the flow. *Legato* connections between melodic tones are extremely important. Work on RH fingerings that will enable you to play as many connected tones as possible.

➤ Pedaling of the LH rolled chords may be a challenge. Of primary importance is the capturing of the low bass tones in the pedal. One solution is to play these bass tones *with* the RH (not before).

Carl Czerny
Study in F Major, op. 299, no. 12 (S20)
Czerny's *School of Velocity, op. 299* is one of the most famous technical exercise books. Each study focuses on a single technical figure, exploring its various manifestations. This piece is a study in arpeggio and broken-chord playing.

Exploring the Score

➤ Is this piece entirely in unison? [yes, except for the blocked chords]
➤ Do the hands stretch wider than an octave? [yes, beginning in m. 13]

Practice Suggestions

➤ Because of the unison construction, the piece is easy to read. As you approach the piece, your initial focus will be on fingering. Circle any fingerings in the score that you might overlook.
➤ As the spans become wider in m. 13, let the hand carry the fingers to the notes. Reaching and stretching with the fingers create unnecessary tension in the hand. Czerny marks *staccatos* with his accents in mm. 13-16, giving permission to disconnect some tones.

Anatol Konstantinovich Lyadov
A Trifle, op. 2, no. 12 (S22)
Practice Suggestions

➤ This piece is to be played *prestissimo,* and should sound playfully "tossed off" in performance. (Notice the dynamic level: the piece never becomes dramatic.)
➤ The clue to success is quick and easy playing across the bar line. To accomplish this, try the following:
  - practice in segments of three-eighth notes, starting with the last eighth of each measure.
  - play the RH consecutive eighths with one arm gesture: "throw-lift." One gesture = two chords. (Half the work; double the speed!)

Carl Albert Loeschhorn
Etude in E Minor, op. 67, no. 5 (S24)
Practice Suggestions

➤ This study is based on a three-note mordent figure, utilizing the two possible directions. The piece is light, fanciful, and fast. Although there is a *forte* in mm. 29 and 57, the overall effect should be one of extreme lightness and delicacy.
➤ Practice the sixteenth-note figures as they appear in both hands. Experiment with the fingerings. Consider using, for example, 243 for the RH m. 1; and 321 for the LH in m. 5. In m. 23, you may wish to use the traditional mordent fingering of 231. The goal of the fingering is to produce clear, fast, consistent sounds.
➤ Play the repeated eighth notes (e.g., LH m. 1, RH m. 3-4) with one arm gesture: "throw-lift." Use that same gesture for RH chords (e.g., mm. 5-8), "throwing" on the eighth note and "lifting" on the quarter note. One gesture = two chords.

Sergei Rachmaninoff
Étude-tableau, op. 33, no. 8 (S26)

Much of the appeal of Rachmaninoff's music lies in its sumptuous texture and luscious harmony. The melodies spin long lines, and are often accompanied by countermelodies that intensify the texture and expression. Rachmaninoff's superb skill as a pianist is evident in his works, all of which pose considerable challenge to the performer.

Exploring the Score

Although we are aware of an echoing countermelody, close inspection reveals that this is a monothematic work. Furthermore, this melody adamantly clings to the same pitches throughout:

➤ Look through the score to find all appearances of the melody and its faster-moving "echo." Can you see a pattern to the use of A flat *vs* A natural? [A natural is used mainly in the echo.]
➤ The "cadenza" is easily identified. Speculate on its role in the piece.
➤ The constant reiteration of the same pitches forces Rachmaninoff to stay close to the home tonality (G minor). The cadenza comes to a climax with a great harmonic surprise at m. 30. Name this chord. Follow the progression from the "surprise chord" to the I6/4 – V7 in m. 35.
➤ One senses the return of the A section in m. 36, and there is, indeed, a literal repeat. But which measures are repeated? [compare m. 36ff with m. 10ff]

Practice Suggestions

➤ Tonal variety and projection are the primary challenge in this piece. Great performers of late-Romantic works create an entire orchestral palette of sound on the piano. Each day, focus your attention on the various colors and tone qualities you produce:
  - Accompaniments are extremely hushed and gentle.
  - The primary melody rings with a lovely, projected sound.
  - The "echo" motive fades like a sigh.

Jean-Baptiste Duvernoy
Study in C Major, op. 120, no. 13 (S30)
Practice Suggestions

Just what you've been waiting for—an entire study devoted to rotation! When you master this study, many passages in the standard literature will suddenly be easier to play.

➤ Taking Duvernoy's staccato notes as your clue, practice in a sharp dotted rhythm as if the staccato notes were grace notes. The release of those bottom fingers is created by the hand rotation.

➤ When an entire piece is unrelentingly fast with no pause for relaxation, endurance becomes a challenge to the performer. Suggestions for building endurance include the following:
  – In the beginning, practice lightly with focus on ease and relaxation.
  – Practice one-measure units with a *diminuendo* and slight *rit.* This creates the feeling of "impulse-relax." Programming moments of relaxation into your practice will facilitate endurance during a performance.
  – Plan a slight break before each new figure, e.g., mm. 5, 7, 9, 13, etc.

Moritz Moszkowski
Study in C Major, op. 91, no. 15 (S32)
Exploring the Score

This study is primarily for the LH. Discuss the different figures you find and the specific challenge for the hand.

Practice Suggestions

A major difficulty of this piece lies in the fact that the figures change frequently.
➤ Your study of this piece is best served if you isolate each figure and devise several ways to practice that figure. For example, in mm. 1-4, isolate the turn-arounds:

1) practice with high, lifted fingers
2) practice *staccato*
3) practice with fingers close to the keys and a slight hand rotation
4) experiment with alternate fingerings
5) practice in larger units, stopping on finger 1

➤ Devise several ways to practice the rotations in mm. 6, 8, 9.
➤ Does that rotation practice have impact on the way you will play mm. 17-20?
➤ In m. 33, include stopping on finger 1 as part of your RH practice.

Béla Bartók
Bagatelle, op. 6, no. 5 (S35)

Bartók's interest in folk music is legendary. The melody of *Bagatelle No. 5* is from a Slavic folk song: *Before our door, the abandoned young lad, beautiful as a painting, plants a white rose.*

Practice Suggestions

➤ Acquaint yourself with the folk tune (LH, mm. 5-18). As you play, make note of Bartók's articulations (on every note!). The quarter notes are played long, but still detached.
➤ The chords in the piece require endurance and accuracy. A preparatory practice could be done on a flat surface. With the fingers of both hands in a loose five-finger position, play continuous "throbs" of four eighth notes as in m. 1, with a slight emphasis on the downbeat. Let the wrist reflect a slight "throw [the hand] and lift-ing; throw and lift-ing," relaxing the hand as you lift.
➤ The most difficult measures of this *Bagatelle* are those in which the chords change, e.g., mm. 21-24, 79-84.
  – Practice only the outlines of the chords (fingers 1-5).
  – Play again, adding the second finger (fingers 1-2-5).
  – Write in your fingering for the RH next-to-top tone. You must decide if that finger is 3 or 4.
  – Practice full chords in pairs, played very quickly from one chord to the next.
➤ As you work for accuracy of the chords, avoid reverting to four downward gestures per measure. One gesture per measure is your goal.

Christos Tsitsaros
Gallop (S38)
Exploring the Score

➤ Much of this piece features an independence of hands in direction, rhythm, and texture. Find the measures where the hands play in unison.
➤ Engage the student in tapping exercises:
  1) Mm. 1-4: LH taps constant sixteenths; student says the RH rhythm in groups of three, saying only the notes printed: *1 2 3 - 2 - 1 - 3 1 - 3 1 2 3 1* etc.
     Then add the RH tapping the rhythm.

2) Mm. 9-12: for your counting, use only *1-2* or *1-2-3* and count the sixteenth groups. (The 5/16 would be 1 2 1 2 3 .)

3) Mm. 22-25: tap and count using numbers (for eighths) and "&" for off-beats.

➤ Examine the opening figure in the LH. How many beats is the figure? The LH will be easier to play if you feel it in two pulses per measure.

Level 10 CONCLUSION

Students who reach and complete Level 10 demonstrate an unusual dedication and accomplishment. They will have accumulated not only a rich background of music literature, but also an understanding of the harmonic and formal structures of music, and information about composers and the history of musical styles. This musical experience becomes an integral part of the student's life. As far as the *Celebration Series®* is concerned, the goal has been achieved. The summit has been reached, and the view is glorious. You, the teacher, know that Level 10 is similar to a graduation ceremony. Finishing Level 10 is commencement into a lifetime of making music at the piano.

Returning to the analogy of the climb, the student's ascent has been made easier through the expert assistance of a guide—you, the teacher. You have nurtured your student at every step, planning the smoothest path for the journey, avoiding potential pitfalls, and offering constant encouragement. Your gift to the student has been your affirmation and guidance. Because of your effort, the student will cherish classical music for a lifetime. What a gift you have given!

Appendix 1: Composer Catalogue Numbers

"Opus" (Op.) is a term used with a number to designate the position of a given work in the chronological sequence of works by the composer. However, these numbers are often an unreliable guide, and may have been assigned by a publisher rather than the composer. Sometimes a single work will have conflicting opus numbers. Certain genres, such as operas and other vocal works, were not always assigned opus numbers.

For these reasons, individual works by a number of composers are identified by numbers assigned in scholarly thematic catalogues. The catalogues referred to in the *Celebration Series®, The Piano Odyssey®* are listed below. (Some catalogue numbers include the prefix "Anh." (for example, BWV Anh. 121). "Anh." is an abbreviation for *Anhang*, a German word meaning appendix or supplement.)

Works by Carl Philipp Emanuel Bach are often identified by "Wq" and/or "H" (Helm) numbers (for example, *Morceaux divers pour clavecin, Wq 117/39, H 98*). Alfred Wotquenne (1867-1939) was a Belgian music bibliographer and author of *Thematisches Verzeichnis der Werke von Carl Philipp Emanuel Bach* (Leipzig, 1905, revised 1964). Eugene Helm is an American musicologist and author of *A New Thematic Catalogue of the Works of C.P.E. Bach* (New Haven: Yale University Press, 1989).

Works by Johann Sebastian Bach are identified by "BWV" numbers (for example, *Allemande in G Minor, BWV 836*). BWV is the abbreviation for *Bach Werke Verzeichnis*, the short title of the *Thematisch-Systematisches Verzeichnis der musikalischen Werke von Johann Sebastian Bach* (Leipzig, 1950), a monumental thematic catalogue of Bach's complete works compiled by the German music librarian Wolfgang Schmieder.

Works published during Ludwig van Beethoven's lifetime were given opus numbers. In the thematic catalogue of Beethoven's works, *Das Werk Beethovens* (Munich and Duisburg, 1955, completed by H. Halm), compiled by German musicologist Georg Ludwig Kinsky (1882-1951), works which were published posthumously were designated "WoO". WoO is an abbreviation for *Werk ohne Opuszahl* (work without opus number).

Works by George Frideric Handel are identified by "HWV" numbers (for example, *Gavotte in G Major, HWV 491*). HWV is an abbreviation for *Handel Werke Verzeichnis*. The full title for this thematic catalogue, compiled by Margaret and Walter Eisen, is *Händel-Handbuch, gleichzeitig Suppl. zu Hallische Händel-Ausgabe* (Kassel: Bärenreiter, 1978-1986).

Works by Franz Joseph Haydn are identified by Hoboken numbers (for example, *Sonata in D Major, Hob. XVI:37*). Anthony van Hoboken was a Dutch

musicologist. His thematic catalogue, *Joseph Haydn: Thematisch-bibliographisches Werkverzeichnis* (Mainz: B. Schott, 1957-1971) divides Haydn's works into a number of categories. The piano sonatas are in category XVI.

Works by Wolfgang Amadeus Mozart are identified by "KV" numbers (for example, *Sonata in C Major, KV 545*). KV stands for *Köchel Verzeichnis*. Ludwig Ritter von Köchel (1800-1877) was an Austrian professor of botany who devoted his retirement years to collecting all the known works by Mozart. He created a chronological catalogue in which these works are listed and numbered.

Works by Domenico Scarlatti are usually identified by two numbers, one beginning with "L" and one beginning with "K." The L numbers are from *Opere complete per clavicembalo* (Milan: Ricordi, 1906-1908), compiled by Alessandro Longo. K stands for Ralph Kirkpatrick, an American harpsichordist and scholar who provided a revised and more exact chronology and a new numbering system for the sonatas in his book *Domenico Scarlatti* (Princeton: Princeton University Press, 1953, rev. 1968).

Works by Franz Schubert are identified by "Deutsch" numbers (for example, *Waltz in A Flat, Op. 9, No. 12, D. 365*). These numbers were assigned by Otto Erich Deutsch (1883-1967) in his thematic catalogue of Schubert's works, *Thematisches Verzeichnis seiner Werke in chronologischer Folge* (*Neue Schubert Ausgabe* Serie VIII, Bd. 4, Kassel, 1978).

Works by Georg Philipp Telemann are identified by "TWV" numbers (for example, *Fantasia in D Minor, TWV 33:2*). TWV is an abbreviation for *Telemann Werkverzeichnis*. This thematic catalogue – *Thematischer-Systematisches Verzeichnis seiner Werke: Telemann Werkverzeichnis* (Kassel: Bärenreiter, 1984) – was compiled by Martin Runke.

Composer Index

André, Johann Anton
Sonatina in A Minor: 3rd mvt. [3R/20, 3SW/34], 81

Anonymous
Bourrée in D Minor [2R/4, 2SW/4], 56
Minuet in D Minor BWV Anh. 132 (attr. J.S. Bach) [4R/4, 4SW/4], 97–98

Archer, Violet
Jig [5R/38, 5SW/65], 117

Arlen, Harold
Over the Rainbow (arr. George Shearing) [9R/122], 235–36

Aubry, Leon
Woodland Scene [1S/16], 35–3

Babell, William
Rigadoon in A Minor [4R/5, 4SW/7], 91

Bach, Carl Philipp Emanuel
La Caroline, Wq 117/39, H 98 [5R/12, 5SW/24], 116–17
March in D Major, BWV Anh. 122 [4R/9, 4SW/18], 101
Sonata in C Minor, Wq 48/4, H 27: 3rd mvt. [9R/25], 217

Bach, Johann Christoph Friedrich
Allegro in C Major [5S/4], 117

Bach, Johann Sebastian
Allemande in G Minor, BWV 836 [5R/5, 5SW/8], 122–23
Capriccio sopra la lontananza del fratello dilettissimo, BWV 992: mvts 4, 5, and 6 [10R/13], 250–51
French Suite No. 5 in G Major, BWV 816: Allemande and Gigue [10R/8], 248–49
French Suite No. 5 in G Major, BWV 816: Gavotte [7R/12, 7SW/19], 168
Invention No. 1 in C Major, BWV 772 [7R/4, 7SW/4], 171–72
Invention No. 6 in E Major, BWV 777 [8R/11, 8SW/14], 193
Little Prelude in C Major, BWV 939 [5R/4, 5SW/4], 111–12
Little Prelude in D Major, BWV 936 [8R/6 , 8SW/7], 205
Little Prelude in D Minor, BWV 926 [6R/4, 6SW/4], 147
Little Prelude in E Minor, BWV 938 [8R/4, 8SW/4], 197
Little Prelude in F Major, BWV 927 [7S/17], 162
Minuet III in G Major [1R/6, 1SW/8], 34
Prelude and Fugue in C Minor, BWV 847 [9R/17], 214–15
Prelude and Fugue in D Major, BWV 850 [10R/4], 246–48
Prelude in C Minor, BWV 999 [6S/4], 150
Sinfonia No. 6 in E Major, BWV 792 [9R/4], 212
Sinfonia No. 11 in G Minor, BWV 797 [9R/6], 212–13

Bach, Johann Sebastian (attr.)
Minuet in D Minor, BWV Anh. 132 [4R/4, 4SW/4], 97–98
Musette in D Major, BWV Anh. 126 [3R/9, 3SW/14], 77–78
Polonaise in G Minor, BWV Anh. 119 [3R/10, 3SW/17], 69–70

Balázs, Árpad
Game [4S/7], 89
A Sort of Rondo [7S/18], 174

Barber, Samuel
Pas de deux [10R/125], 271

Bartley, Ewart
Dance No. 1 [9R/104], 233–34

Bartók, Béla
Bagatelle, op. 6, no. 2 [9S/22], 241
Bagatelle, op. 6, no. 5 [10S/35], 280
Children at Play [2R/16, 2SW/34], 54
Children's Game [4R/28, 4SW/56], 89
Evening at the Village [8R/58, 8SW/71], 188
Jest [5R/30, 5SW/49], 112–13
Little Dance in Canon Form [2R/36, 2SW/68], 45
Minuet [3S/7], 76
Pentatonic Tune [7R/44, 7SW/69], 161
Play [3R/29, 3SW/54], 65
Rondo, op. 84, no. 1, 267–68
Syncopated Dance [4S/19], 93

Beach, Amy Marcy Cheney
A Hermit Thrush at Eve, op. 92, no. 1 [10R/150], 265

Beethoven, Ludwig van
Bagatelle in A Minor, op. 119, no. 9 [6R/27, 6SW/40], 133
Bagatelle in G Minor, op. 119, no. 1 [7R/18, 7SW/30], 172
Für Elise, WoO 59 [7R/25, 7SW/39], 179–80
Rondo in C Major, op. 51, no. 1 [9R/52], 222
Sonata in E Major, op. 14, no. 1 [10R/19], 251–53
Sonata in G Major, op. 49, no. 2 [8R/28, 8SW/32], 197–98, 201
Sonata in G Major, op. 79: 1st mvt. [9R/47], 221

Beethoven, Ludwig van (attr.)
Sonatina in F Major [5R/20, 5SW/34], 119–20, 123
Sonatina in G Major [3R/18, 3SW/29], 74–75, 78

Bender, Joanne
Inuit Lullaby [2R/27, 2SW/54], 44–45

Benedict, Robert C.
Shallows [4R/34, 4SW/65], 92–93

Benjamin, Arthur L.
Romance-Impromptu [7R/38, 7SW/57], 160–61

Berens, (Johann) Hermann
Study in A Minor, op. 61, no. 13 [9S/6], 238
Study in A Minor, op. 61, no. 32 [10S/11], 277–78
Study in F Major, op. 61, no. 8 [9S/8], 238–39
Study in F Major, op. 61, no. 10 [9S/18], 240–41

Berkovich, Isak
Mazurka [2R/17, 2SW/37], 54
Study in C Major [1S/8], 42–43

Berlin, Boris
The Haunted Castle [3R/30, 3SW/57], 72
March of the Goblins [2R/20, 2SW/41], 41
Monkeys in the Tree [4R/30, 4SW/59], 92

Bernstein, Leonard
For Susanna Kyle [6R/44, 6SW/72], 141

Bernstein, Seymour
The Elegant Toreador [3R/34, 3SW/66], 76

Bertini, Henri
Etude in C Minor, op. 29, no. 7 [7S/14], 170
Etude in E Minor, op. 29, no. 16 [7S/4], 166
Study in E Minor, op. 29, no. 14 [6S/14], 155
Study in G Major, op. 166, no. 6 [2S/5], 55

Blok, Vladimir
The Bear in the Forest, op.11, no. 6 [1R/30, 1SW/56], 16–17
Happy Times [1R/24, 1SW/44], 29
Two Ants [3S/11], 79

Bolck, Oskar
Sonatina in G Major, op. 59, no. 2: 3rd mvt. [7R/20, 7SW/33], 164

Bonis, Mel.
The Sewing Machine [1R/16, 1SW/29], 27

Brahms, Johannes
Ballade in D Minor, op. 10, no. 1 [10R/59], 259
Intermezzo in A Minor, op. 76, no. 7 [9R/76], 227
Waltz in G sharp Minor, op. 39, no. 3 [7R/42, 7SW/62], 161

Burgmüller, Johann Friedrich
Arabesque, op. 100, no. 2 [3S/5], 72–73
The Gypsies, op. 109, no. 4 [8S/16], 204
The Hunt, op. 100, no. 9 [5S/10], 124
Morning Bell, op. 109, no. 9 [8S/14], 195
Progress, op. 100, no. 6 [4S/13], 102–3
Sweet Sorrow, op. 100, no. 16 [5S/9], 117–18
The Wagtail, op. 100, no. 11 [4S/10], 96

Chatman, Stephen
Beaver Boogie [1R/22, 1SW/40], 35
Game of Hypnosis [4R/38, 4SW/74], 96
Ginger Snaps [7R/46, 7SW/73], 165–66
Kitten [7S/12], 177–78

Chopin, Frédéric
Mazurka in A Minor, op. 67 posth., no. 4 [9R/74], 226
Nocturne in F sharp Major, op. 15, no. 2 [10R/55], 258–59
Prelude in B Minor, op. 28, no. 6 [8R/41, 8SW/42], 187
Prelude in E Minor, op. 28, no. 4 [7R/31, 7SW/46], 164–65
Waltz, op. posth. 70, no. 2 [9R/70], 225–26
Waltz in E Minor, op. posth., B 56 [10R/51], 257–58

Christopher, Renée
The Snake [1R/40, 1SW/77], 35

Cimarosa, Domenico
Sonata in B flat Major [8R/20, 8SW/25], 190

Clarke, Jeremiah
Minuet in D Major, T 460 [1R/4, 1SW/4], 16

Clementi, Muzio
Sonatina in C Major, op. 36, no. 1 [3R/12, 3SW/23], 64, 67–68, 71
Sonatina in C Major, op. 36, no. 3: 1st mvt. [7R/22, 7SW/36], 175–76
Sonatina in F Major, op. 36, no. 4 [6R/18, 6SW/31], 139–40, 143–44
Sonatina in G Major, op. 36, no. 2: 2nd and 3rd mvts [4R/10, 4SW/22], 88, 91–92
Sonatina in G Major, op. 36, no. 5: 1st mvt. [8R/24, 8SW/29], 187
Sonatina in G Major, op. 36, no. 5: 3rd mvt. [5R/16, 5SW/31], 126

Copland, Aaron
The Cat and the Mouse [10R/101], 267

Coulthard, Jean
Star Gazing [5R/32, 5SW/52], 124

Couperin, François
Allemande in D Minor [7R/10, 7SW/15], 178–79

Cramer, Johann Baptist
Study in E Minor, op. 39, no. 2 [9S/4], 238

Crawley, Clifford
You're Joking! [4S/12], 106

Creston, Paul
Pastoral Dance, op. 24, no. 4 [6R/36, 6SW/60], 148–49

Crosby, Anne
Robots [1R/27, 1SW/49], 24–25

Czerny, Carl
Study in A Minor, op. 740, no. 41 [10S/4], 277
Study in B flat Major, op. 599, no. 83 [4S/6], 102
Study in C Major, op. 261, no. 3 [2S/7], 45
Study in C Major, op. 533, no. 1 [9S/10], 239
Study in C Major, op. 777, no. 3 [1S/5], 25–26
Study in D Minor, op. 261, no. 53 [3S/9], 73
Study in F Major, op. 299, no. 12 [10S/20], 278–79
Study in G Major, op. 599, no. 45 [4S/4], 96

Daquin, Louis-Claude
Le coucou (Rondeau) [9R/22], 215–16

Debussy, Claude
Brouillards [10R/83], 262–63
La fille aux cheveux de lin [9R/90], 230–31
Page d'album [8R/68, 8SW/86], 203

Diabelli, Anton
Sonatina in F Major, op. 168, no. 1: 1st mvt. [4R/16,
4SW/31], 95
Sonatina in F Major, op. 168, no. 1: 3rd mvt. [6R/28,
6SW/43], 152

Dolin, Samuel
Little Toccata [8S/24], 200

Duke, David
Barcarole [4R/35, 4SW/68], 98–99
March (Lydian Mode) [1R/23, 1SW/42], 17
She's Like the Swallow (arr.) [1R/34, 1SW/64], 32

Dussek, Jan Ladislav
Sonatina in G Minor, op. 20, no. 1: 1st mvt. [6R/16,
6SW/27], 136

Duvernoy, Jean-Baptiste
Study in C Major, op. 120, no. 10 [9S/24], 241
Study in C Major, op. 120, no. 13 [10S/30], 279–80
Study in C Major, op. 176, no. 24 [4S/14], 100

Eben, Petr
Bird on the Windowsill [3R/33, 3SW/63], 75

Elliott, Carleton
Canon [2R/39, 2SW/72], 52

Eurina, Ludmilla
Blues [5S/8], 128

Falla, Manuel de
Danse du menuier [10R/107], 264–65

Fiala, George
Postlude (à la Shostakovich), op. 7, no. 6 [5R/36,
5SW/58], 128

Field, John
Nocturne in B flat Major, H 37 [8R/51, 8SW/61], 202

Filtz, Bohdana
An Ancient Tale [6R/40, 6SW/66], 149

Finch, Douglas
Cancan [6R/48, 6SW/84], 150

Finney, Ross Lee
Playing Ball [6S/20], 146

Fiocco, Joseph-Hector
Suite in G Major, op. 1, no. 1: 2nd mvt. [7R/14,
7SW/23], 175

Fitch, Gem
Chinese Kites [3S/13], 79–80

Frid, Grigori
The Jolly Fiddler [1R/32, 1SW/60], 22

Fuchs, Robert
A Little Song, op. 47, no. 4 [6S/22], 137–38
Timid Little Heart, op. 47, no. 5 [3R/28, 3SW/52],
64–65

Gade, Niels
Scherzo, op. 19, no. 2 [9S/20], 241

Gallant, Pierre
Dorian Invention [1R/38, 1SW/72], 17
Jazz Invention No. 1 [2R/39, 2SW/73], 55
Jazz Invention No. 2 [2R/40, 2SW/75], 42
Sarabande [6R/45, 6SW/75], 141
Sur le pont d'Avignon (arr.) [1R/38, 1SW/74], 19–20
This Old Man (arr.) [1R/29, 1SW/54], 29–30

Garścia, Janina
The Clock [2R/32, 2SW/62], 41–42

Garztecka, Irena
A Ball [1R/35, 1SW/66], 30

Gedike, Alexander
Fugato, op. 36, no. 40 [2R/37, 2SW/70], 48
A Happy Tale, op. 36, no. 31 [1R/33, 1SW/62], 32
Military Trumpets, op. 36, no. 53 [2R/15, 2SW/31], 51
A Sad Song, op. 36, no. 39 [1R/18, 1SW/31], 34
Sonatina in C Major, op. 36, no. 20 [3R/22, 3SW/37], 72
Study in C Major, op. 32, no. 16 [5S/17], 114
Study in E Minor, op. 32, no. 12 [3S/15], 83
Study in G Major [2S/4], 52
Study in G Major, op. 36, no. 26 [4S/5], 106

George, Jon
Dialogue (Canon) [1R/37, 1SW/70], 22–23

Ginastera, Alberto
Rondó sobre temas infantile argentinos, op. 19
[10R/118], 270–71

Goud, Stella
Moon through the Window [2S/14], 58–59
Spider on the Ceiling [8S/18], 207

Graupner, Christoph
Bourrée in D Minor [1R/5, 1SW/6], 18–19
Intrada in C Major [5R/8, 5SW/15], 115–16

Grechaninov, Alexandr T.
After the Ball, op. 98, no. 13 [3R/26, 3SW/46], 75
Fairy Tale, op. 98, no. 1 [1R/15, 1SW/26], 32
Horse and Rider, op. 98, no. 5 [3R/24, 3SW/43], 78

Grieg, Edvard
Arietta, op. 12, no. 1 [6R/32, 6SW/52], 140
Elfin Dance, op. 12, no. 4 [7R/36, 7SW/54], 169
Little Bird, op. 43, no. 4 [8S/4], 191
Notturno, op. 54, no. 4 [9R/78], 228
Puck, op. 71, no. 3 [8R/42, 8SW/45], 201–2
Waltz, op. 12, no. 2 [5R/28, 5SW/47], 123–24

Grovlez, Gabriel
La sarabande [9R/92], 231

Gurlitt, Cornelius
  Canon [2R/40, 2SW/77], 42
  The Hunt, op. 117, no. 15 [1R/14, 1SW/24], 19
  Morning Greeting, op. 117, no. 6 [1S/6], 23
  Sonatina in G Major, op. 188, no. 3: 1st mvt. [4R/20, 4SW/39], 104
  Study in E Minor, op. 132, no. 1 [6S/10], 145
  Study in G Major, op. 132, no. 7 [7S/15], 166–67
  Undaunted, op. 197, no. 7 [3S/12], 66

Haberbier, Ernst
  Serenade, op. 53, no. 5 [10S/8], 277

Handel, George Frideric
  Allemande and Gigue (from Suite in F Minor, HWV 433) [9S/26], 242
  Allemande in A Minor, HWV 478 [6R/6, 6SW/7], 139
  Bourrée in G Major (from Sonata in G Major, op. 1, no. 5, HWV 363b) [4R/6, 4SW/10], 94–95
  Capriccio, HWV 483 [8S/6], 203–4
  Entrée in G Minor, HWV 453 [6S/8], 142
  Gavotte in G Major, HWV 491 [3R/11, 3SW/20], 74
  Impertinence, HWV 494 [2R/6, 2SW/9], 50
  Suite No. 8 in G Major, HWV 441: 4th mvt. [7R/8, 7SW/12], 163–64

Hansen, Joan
  Irish Jig [2S/10], 49

Haslinger, Tobias
  Sonatina in C Major: 1st mvt. [4R/18, 4SW/36], 98

Hässler, Johann Wilhelm
  Minuet in C Major, op. 38, no. 4 [1R/9, 1SW/12], 24

Haufrecht, Herbert
  Tick-Tock Toccata [5R/34, 5SW/55], 127

Haydn, Franz Joseph
  Divertimento in G Major, Hob. XVI:8: 1st mvt. [5R/14, 5SW/27], 112
  Divertimento in G Major, Hob. XVI:G1: 1st mvt. [6R/13, 6SW/23], 148
  German Dance in G Major, Hob. IX:22, no. 3 [1R/11, 1SW/17], 21
  Quadrille [2R/8, 2SW/15], 53–54
  Sonata in C Major, Hob. XVI:1: 2nd mvt. [7R/16, 7SW/26], 160
  Sonata in F Major, Hob. XVI:9: 3rd mvt. [4R/15, 4SW/28], 101
  Sonata in B Minor, Hob. XVI:32 [10R/32], 253–55
  Sonata in E Minor, Hob. XVI:34 [9R/35], 219–20
  Sonata in G Major, Hob. XVI:27: 3rd mvt. [8R/16, 8SW/21], 193

Heller, Stephen
  Abenddämmerung, op. 138, no. 3 [6S/18], 137
  The Avalanche, op. 45, no. 2 [4S/8], 99–100
  Barcarole, op. 138, no. 5 [6S/11], 154
  Etude in D Minor, op. 45, no. 15 [8S/26], 195–96
  Etude in E Major, op. 47, no. 16 [8S/20], 189
  Etude in G Major, op. 47, no. 24 [9S/12], 239

Fluttering Leaves, op. 46, no. 11 [6S/15], 145–46
Grief, op. 47, no. 15 [7S/8], 162
Prelude in C sharp Minor, op. 81, no. 10 [10S/6], 277
Study in D Major, op. 125, no. 12 [5S/16], 121

Henderson, Ruth Watson
  Lullaby in Black and White [3R/36, 3SW/70], 78–79
  Toccatina [6S/12], 142

Hoiby, Lee
  Prelude, op. 7, no. 1 [10R/129], 272

Jaque, Rhené
  Lutin [7R/54, 7SW/82], 181

Kabalevsky, Dmitri
  Clowns, op. 39, no. 20 [3R/27, 3SW/49], 82
  Dance, op. 27, no. 27 [7S/22], 182
  Etude, op. 27, no. 3 [7S/24], 167
  Etude, op. 27, no. 24 [8S/30], 191–92
  A Little Song, op. 27, no. 2 [2R/21, 2SW/43], 47
  A Porcupine Dance, op. 89, no. 8 [1S/4], 20
  Prelude, op. 39, no. 19 [5S/5], 113–14
  Rondo-Toccata, op. 60, no. 4 [7R/50, 7SW/79], 173
  Toccatina, op. 27, no. 12 [6S/6], 134
  Variations in A Minor, op. 40, no. 2 [10R/159], 272
  Variations in D Major, op. 40, no. 1 [9R/105], 233
  Warrior's Dance, op. 27, no. 19 [6R/34, 6SW/58], 153

Kadosa, Pál
  Allegro, op. 23/f, no. 5 [2S/28], 207–8
  Study in A Minor [2S/6], 48–49
  Vivo [5S/18], 121

Kalinnikov, Vasili Sergeievich
  Chanson triste [8R/54, 8SW/65], 198

Karganov, Génari
  Game of Patience, op. 25, no. 2 [6S/24], 138

Karp, David
  Sailing Along [4S/16], 90

Khachaturian, Aram
  An Evening Tale [2R/18, 2SW/39], 57
  Skipping Rope [2S/12], 55

Kossenko, Viktor
  Melody, op. 15, no. 11 [7R/40, 7SW/59], 176

Krausas, Veronika
  The Alligator [1R/28, 1SW/52], 34–35
  Kangaroos [2S/9], 58

Krebs, Johann Ludwig
  Bourrée in A Minor [6R/10, 6SW/17], 135–36

Krieger, Johann
  Minuet in A Minor (from Partita No. 6 in B flat Major) [1R/13, 1SW/22], 26–27

Kuhlau, Friedrich
  Sonata in A Major, op. 59, no. 1: 1st mvt. [8R/36, 8SW/38], 206
  Sonatina in C Major, op. 55, no. 3: 1st mvt. [7R/28, 7SW/43], 168–69

Kuzmenko, Larysa
Mysterious Summer's Night [8R/69, 8SW/89], 198
Romance [5R/40, 5SW/68], 113

Last, Joan
Sailing by Moonlight [2R/22, 2SW/46], 51–52

Lea, William
Snoopy [3R/32, 3SW/61], 68–69

Lebeda, Miroslav
Miniature [6R/47, 6SW/81], 136

Lefeld, Jerzy
Little Mouse [1S/15], 30

Lemoine, Antoine Henry
Study in A flat Major, op. 37, no. 44 [5S/6], 121

Liszt, Franz
Consolation No. 1 [8R/50, 8SW/59], 194

Loeschhorn, Carl Albert
Etude in E Minor, op. 67, no. 5 [10S/24], 279
Song of the Waterfall [8S/22], 189
Study in D Minor, op. 65, no. 40 [5S/14], 125

Louie, Alexina
Distant Memories [9R/100], 234
O Moon [8R/60, 8SW/75], 206–7
Shooting Stars [7R/48, 7SW/76], 169

Lyadov, Anatol Konstaninovich
A Trifle, op. 2, no. 12 [10S/22], 279

Maikapar, Samuil
Staccato Prelude, op. 31, no. 6 [5S/20], 118
Toccatina, op. 8, no. 1 [7S/6], 177
The Young Shepherd's Song, op. 28, no. 3 [3S/8], 82

Markow, Andrew
Teapot Invention [1R/39, 1SW/76], 25

McKinnon, Gordon A.
The Argument [2R/38, 2SW/71], 58
Swirling Leaves [1R/36, 1SW/68], 27–28

Melartin, Erkki
Sonatina [4R/22, 4SW/43], 105

Mendelssohn, Felix
Andante sostenuto, op. 72, no. 2 [8R/46, 8SW/51], 206
Lost Happiness, op. 38, no. 2 [9R/67], 225
Romance in G Major [4R/25, 4SW/48], 95
Song without Words, op. 102, no. 3 [9S/14], 240
Venetian Boat Song, op. 30, no. 6 [7R/32, 7SW/48],
180–81

Messiaen, Olivier
Plainte calme [10R/110], 268–69

Moszkowski, Moritz
Etude in C Major, op. 72, no. 4 [10S/14], 278
Study in C Major, op. 91, no. 15 [10S/32], 280
Study in E flat Major, op. 91, no. 6 [9S/16], 240
Study in E flat Major, op. 91, no. 17 [9S/30], 242–43

Mozart, Wolfgang Amadeus
Fantasie in D Minor, K 397/385g [9R/28], 217–18
Minuet in F Major, K 2 [1R/12, 1SW/20], 31
Minuetto I in C Major [2R/12, 2SW/23], 41
Sonata in C Major, K 330 (K 300 h): 2nd mvt.
[9R/32], 218–19
Sonata in E flat Major, K 282 (189g) [10R/43], 255–57

Muczynski, Robert
Six Preludes, op. 6: no. 1 and no. 6 [10R/140], 273

Nakada, Yoshinao
The Song of Twilight [3R/31, 3SW/59], 68

Neefe, Christian Gottlob
Allegretto in C Major [2R/10, 2SW/17], 47

Niamath, Linda
Butterflies [2S/11], 49
Hallowe'en Night [1R/19, 1SW/34], 24
Kites [1S/12], 25
Penguins [2R/28, 2SW/56], 57–58
Robins [1S/4], 28

Norton, Christopher
Blues No. 1 [4S/20], 93
Chant [2R/29, 2SW/58], 45
Coconut Rag [3R/40, 3SW/76], 69
Dreaming [5R/37, 5SW/62], 120–21
Duet for One [1R/26, 1SW/46], 19
Inter-City Stomp [1S/6], 65–66
Play It Again [4R/40, 4SW/76], 105–6
Tram Stop [2S/16], 52

Oesten, Theodor
Hunting Horns [1S/8], 20

Owens, Terry Winter
Prelude for Aries [1S/13], 30

Papp, Lajos
Martellato and Forte-Piano [1S/7], 17

Paterson, Lorna
Rush Hour [3S/16], 69–70
Scherzo [4S/18], 103

Peerson, Charles
The Mouse in the Coal Bin [2R/24, 2SW/49], 44

Pépin, Clermont
Berceuse [7R/43, 7SW/65], 176–77
Le nez [9R/124], 236
Trois pièces pour la légende dorée [10R/133], 267–68

Pescetti, Giovanni Battista
Sonata in C Minor: 3rd mvt. [8R/14, 8SW/18], 186–87

Peterson, Oscar
The Gentle Waltz [8R/70, 8SW/92], 199

Petzold, Christian
Minuet in G Major, BWV Anh. 114 [3R/4, 3SW/4],
63–64
Minuet in G Minor, BWV Anh. 115 [3R/6, 3SW/7], 67

Piazzolla, Astor
Milonga del ángel [8R/62, 8SW/78], 188

Pinto, Octavio
Roda-roda! [8R/56, 8SW/68], 191
Salta, Salta [9R/116], 232–33

Poole, Clifford
Spooks [1R/20, 1SW/37], 22

Poot, Marcel
Across the Channel [4R/32, 4SW/62], 105

Poulenc, François
Suite française: mvts. 3, 6 and 7 [10R/93], 263–64

Previn, André
Roundup [6R/46, 6SW/78], 153–54

Purcell, Henry
Hornpipe in B flat Major, Z T683 [3R/8, 3SW/11], 81

Rachmaninoff, Sergei
Étude-tableau, op. 33, no. 8 [10S/26], 279
Mélodie, op. 3, no. 3 [10R/74], 261–62

Rameau, Jean-Philippe
Deux rigaudons (from Suite No. 1) [5R/6, 5SW/12], 126
Minuet en rondeau [2R/5, 2SW/6], 40–41

Raphling, Sam
Bike Ride [3S/4], 65

Rebikov, Vladimir Ivanovich
The Bear [1S/10], 32–33
In the Forest, op. 51, no. 4 [5S/21], 114
Miniature Waltz, op. 10, no. 10 [6R/33, 6SW/55], 133
Waltz [7R/34, 7SW/51], 172–73

Reubart, Dale
March of the Buffoons [6R/42, 6SW/69], 149–50

Scarlatti, Domenico
Aria in D Minor, L 423, K 32 [4R/8, 4SW/15], 104
Minuet in C Major (from Sonata in C Major, L 217, K 73) [2R/7, 2SW/12], 43–44
Sonata in A Major, L 31, K 83: 2nd mvt. [6R/12, 6SW/20], 151–52
Sonata in C Major, L 104, K 159 [9R/8], 213
Sonata in D Major, L 463, K 430 [9R/14], 214
Sonata in D Minor, L 413, K 9 [9R/11], 214

Schmitt, Jacob
Study in G Major, op. 3, no. 3 [7S/16], 173

Schubert, Franz
Écossaise, D 299, no. 8 [2R/13, 2SW/26], 54
Impromptu in A flat Major, op. posth. 142, no. 2 [9R/63], 224–25
Impromptu in E flat Major, op. 90, no. 2 [10R/62], 260
Sentimental Waltz, op. 50, no. 13 [6R/30, 6SW/45], 152–53

Schumann, Robert
Fantastic Dance, op. 124, no. 5 [7S/20], 181–82
Herberge, op. 82 no. 6 [9R/60], 223–24
An Important Event, op. 15, no. 6 [8R/45, 8SW/48], 190–91
Intermezzo, op. 26, no. 4 [10R/70], 260–61
A Little Romance, op. 68, no. 19 [5R/25, 5SW/41], 127
Melody, op. 68, no. 1 [2R/14, 2SW/29], 51
Waltz in A Minor, op. 124, no. 4 [6R/31, 6SW/49], 144–45
The Wild Horseman, op. 68, no. 8 [4R/26, 4SW/51], 102

Scott, Cyril
Lotus Land, op. 47, no. 1 [10R/78], 262

Scriabin, Alexander
Etude, op. 2, no. 1 [10S/18], 278

Shchedrin, Rodion Konstantinovich
Humoreske [9R/123], 234–35

Sheftel, Paul
Ins and Outs [1S/14], 23

Shostakovich, Dmitri
Dance [6S/16], 134
Three Fantastic Dances [10R/112], 269–70

Sibelius, Jean
Romance, op. 24, no. 9 [9R/95], 232

Smetana, Bedrich
Song, op. 2, no. 2 [8R/48, 8SW/55], 202

Snowdon, Judith
Adults [4S/11], 96–97

Somers, Harry
Strangeness of Heart [10R/122], 271

Southam, Ann
Four Bagatelles: no. 2 and no. 4 [10R/146], 273–74

Starer, Robert
Bright Orange [6R/38, 6SW/63], 133–34
Crimson [8R/66, 8SW/83], 194–95
Pink [8R/65, 8SW/81], 194

Stölzel, Gottfried Heinrich
Minuet in G Minor [6R/8, 6SW/10], 132

Szelényi, István
Changing Bars [4R/36, 4SW/71], 99
Faraway Regions [2R/26, 2SW/52], 57

Takács, Jenö
In a Great Hurry, op. 95, no. 3 [7S/10], 170
The Little Fly [5S/12], 124–25
Toccatina, op. 95, no. 1 [8S/8], 199

Tan, Chee-Hwa
The Land of Nod [2R/30, 2SW/60], 47
The Wind [2S/13], 46

Tansman, Alexandre
  Both Ways [1S/9], 28
  The Doll [3S/14], 76–77
  Melody [4R/27, 4SW/54], 88–89
  Skating [4S/15], 106–7

Tarenghi, Mario
  Dance of the Marionettes [8S/11], 207

Tchaikovsky, Pyotr Il'yich
  June (Barcarole), op. 37a, no. 6 [9R/82], 228–29
  Mazurka, op. 39, no. 11 [5R/26, 5SW/44], 120
  Morning Prayer, op. 39, no. 1 [3R/23, 3SW/40], 81–82

Telemann, Georg Philipp
  Fantasia in C Minor, TWV 33:35: 2nd section [5R/10, 5SW/18], 119
  Fantasia in D Minor, TWV 33:2 [8R/8, 8SW/10], 190
  Fantasia in E Minor, TWV 33:21: 3rd section [4R/7, 4SW/13], 87–88
  Solo in F Major, TWV 32:4: Bourrée [7R/6, 7SW/8], 159–60

Telfer, Nancy
  Crocodile Teeth [2R/33, 2SW/64], 48
  Monté sur un éléphant (arr.) [1R/31, 1SW/58], 27
  A Sioux Lullaby (arr.) [2R/34, 2SW/66], 42
  The Sleeping Dragon [3R/38, 3SW/73], 72

Tsitsaros, Christos
  Gallop [10S/38], 280–81
  Snow Games [10R/155], 274–75

Turina, Joaquín
  Sacro-Monte, op. 55, no. 5 [9R/87], 230

Türk, Daniel Gottlob
  Arioso in F Major [1R/10, 1SW/14], 29
  Contentment [2R/11, 2SW/20], 44
  Having Fun [3S/10], 79
  The Hunting Horns and the Echo [1R/8, 1SW/10], 16

Weber, Carl Maria von
  Waltz in G Major, op. 4, no. 2, J 16 [4R/24, 4SW/46], 102

Zipoli, Domenico
  Sarabanda in G Minor (from Suite in G Minor) [6R/9, 6SW/13], 143
  Verso in E Minor [5R/11, 5SW/21], 116

Subject Index

Alberti bass, 136, 190, 218, 220, 258

allemandes, 126, 139; by J.S. Bach, 122–23, 248–49; by Couperin, 178–79; by Handel, 139, 242

animals in music: alligators, 34–35; bears, 16–17, 32–33; beavers, 35; birds, 28, 52, 75, 96, 191, 265; cats, 177–78, 268; crocodiles, 48; dragons, 72; elephants, 27; horses, 78, 102, 232–33; insects, 49, 79, 124–25, 207; kangaroos, 58; mice, 44, 267; monkeys, 92; penguins, 57–58; porcupines, 20; snakes, 35

arias, *ariosos, ariettas:* by Grieg, 140; by Scarlatti, 104; by Türk, 29

articulation: in Baroque music, 132, 139; breath mark, 30; double notes, 127; for independent voices, 215; *portato,* 113, 121; slurred notes, 114, 123, 136, 148, 164, 213; *staccato,* 20, 52, 166; *staccato* wedges, 148, 254

bagatelles, 133; by Bartók, 240, 280; by Beethoven, 133, 172; by Lyadov, 279; by Southam, 273–74

barcarolles: by Duke, 98; by Heller, 154; by Mendelssohn, 180–81; by Tchaikovsky, 228–29

Baroque music, 211; articulation principles, 132, 139; binary form dances, 21, 74, 94, 122, 139, 159, 168; *continuo,* 205; contrasting textures, 104, 116; dance suite movements, 248, 263; detatched notes, 95, 98, 116, 160, 164; keyboard style, 179; key signatures, 179; musical tension, 150; ornaments, 56, 67, 147; phrases and phrase structure, 95, 97; syncopation, 95, 116, 160; terraced dynamics, 151; trio sonata texture, 205; unequal rhythm for eighth notes, 41, 247

binary form, 18, 160; in Baroque dances, 21, 74, 94, 122, 139, 159, 168; rounded, 23, 26, 87, 101, 115, 135, 193

bitonality, 96, 114, 154

black keys, music using only, 49, 80, 124

blues. *See* jazz

bourrées: anonymous, 56; by Graupner, 18; by Handel, 94–95; by Krebs, 135; by Telemann, 159–60

cadences: deceptive, 165, 187; imperfect vs. perfect, 143–44; ornaments at, 116, 171; rhythmic and harmonic activity preceding, 63

cadenzas, 147, 218, 279

cancan, 150

canons, 19, 32, 42, 45, 52

cembalo, 217

chorale texture, 73, 81–82

chords. *See* harmony and chords

chromatic scales, 155

circle of 5ths, 135, 187

Classical period: dynamic levels, 148, 216; elements of style, 251; principle of contrast, 112, 216

drones, 77, 99

dynamic levels: contrast between hands, 117; in early Classical music, 148, 216; with five-finger pattern, 35–36; on fortepiano, 47; with long notes, 203; on repeated notes, 57; terraced, 151

Eastern European folk music, 99, 121, 188, 266 *écossaises,* 54

Empfindsamer Stil, 116

fanfares, 51

fantasias, fantasies, 87; by Mozart, 217–18; by Telemann, 87–88, 119, 190

fioriture, 258

five finger warm up, 48–49

fortepiano, 47, 216, 218

French musical terms (Debussy), 230, 264

fugues: fugatos, 48; by J.S. Bach, 214, 215, 246–48, 250

gavottes: by G.F. Handel, 74; by J.S. Bach, 168

German dances: by Beethoven, 221; by Haydn, 21

gigues, jigs: by J.S. Bach, 248–49; by Handel, 241; by J. Hansen, 49; by V. Archer, 117

glissando, 58–59

Gypsy music, 204, 230

harmonic rhythm, 87

harmony and chords: analysis of, 166; apreggiated chords, 133, 189; augmented 6ths, 145; bitonal, 96; chromaticism, 82, 199, 201, 223, 224, 257, 262; harmonic extensions, 141, 199; in jazz, 120, 141, 199, 235; Picardy 3rd, 91; quartal, 207; rolled chords, 250; tetrachords, 106

harpsichord, 116, 151, 216, 217, 246

hemiola, 138, 141, 275

hornpipe, 81

humor, musical, 68, 89, 106, 144, 149, 201–2, 234–35, 241

instruments imitated on the piano, 163; bagpipe, 77, 99, 117; bells, 121, 169, 195, 264; guitar, 104, 151, 230, 265; horn, 16, 20, 250; trumpet, 51; violin, 22, 117

inventions: by Finney, 147; by Gallant, 17, 42, 55; by J.S. Bach, 171, 193, 212–13; by Markow, 25

jazz: blue notes, 42; blues scale, 55, 69, 106; blues style, 93, 105–6, 128; boogie bass, 35; characteristic harmonies, 120, 141, 199, 235; characteristic rhythms, 45, 65–66, 69, 134, 199; walking bass, 128

jota, 213

Ländler, 225

lullabies *(berceuse)*: by Bender, 44–45; by Bernstein, 141; by Henderson, 78–79; by Pépin, 176–77; by Tan, 47; by Telfer, 42

marches: by C.P.E. Bach, 101; by Berlin, 41; by Duke, 17; by Poot, 105; by Poulenc, 263–64; by Reubart, 149

mazurkas: by Berkovich, 54; by Chopin, 226–27; by Grechaninov, 75; by Tchaikovksy, 120

mechanical sounds in music: city rush hour, 69; clocks, 41–42, 127; marionettes, 207; perpetual motion, 134, 200; sewing machines, 26; trams, 52

minuet(s): and trio, 254–55, 256; characteristics of, 34; six-beat dance sequence, 16, 40, 63, 97; to dance, 16; by or attr. J.S. Bach, 34, 97–98; by Bartók, 76; by Beethoven, 201; by Clarke, 16; by Hässler, 24; by Haydn, 254–55; by Krieger, 26–27; by Mozart, 31, 41, 257–58; by Petzold, 63–64, 67; by Rameau, 40–41; by D. Scarlatti, 43–44; by Stölzel, 132

modes: Dorian, 45, 89, 117; Lydian, 17, 148–49

musette, 77–78

night music: moon and moonlight, 51, 58–59, 206–7; nocturnes, 202–3, 228, 258; stars, 124, 169–70; summer night, 198; twilight, 68, 137, 265

octaves, drills for, 239

organ, 116, 151

ornaments: *appoggiatura,* 31, 41, 95, 104, 193, 226; Baroque, 56, 67, 147; at cadences, 116, 171; functions of, 175; mordents, 111, 112, 279; use to create musical tension, 56, 111

ossia, 266

ostinato, 17, 19, 27, 33, 35, 41, 58, 114

overtones, 17

passepied, 197

pastorals, 148

pedaling, 223; direct, 123; finger, 256; flutter, 272; pedal-hand coordination, 231; *sostenuto,* 268; syncopated, 82; *tre corde,* 170; *una corda,* 141, 170

pedal points, 140, 147, 150, 162

pentatonic scales, 80, 154, 161

phrases and phrase structure: balanced pairs, 16, 21, 40, 54, 71, 120; in Baroque music, 95, 97; breath test, 27; endings, 66; focus of, 30, 54, 91, 188; length of, 76; "out of four, go for three," 26, 105; *rubato* at ending, 194; short-short-long, 24, 32, 41, 47, 52, 75, 97, 193

poetry, music based on, 47, 230, 231, 259

polonaise, 70–71

preludes, 147; by J.S. Bach, 111–12, 147, 150, 162, 197, 205, 214–15, 246–47; by Chopin, 164–65, 187; by Heller, 277; by Hoiby, 272; by Kabalevsky, 113–14; by Maikapar, 118; by Messiaen, 268–69; by Muczynski, 273; by Owens, 30; by Pépin, 267–68

quadrille, 53–54

quartal harmony, 207

rhythm: analysis of, 93; assymetrical beamed groupings, 274; bending in blues style, 42, 93, 105–6; changing meters, 121; downbeat, 31, 153; irregular meters: 5/4, 198; 5/8, 48; 7/8, 194–95; learning through movement, 70, 173; rocking motion, 51, 78–79, 98, 176, 228–29; scat syllables, 69, 105–6; *senza misura,* 206, 234; "short notes go to long," 50, 67, 123, 166; syncopation, 69, 95, 101, 116, 160, 175, 199; triplet patterns, 187, 240; two vs. three, 162, 175, 176–77, 197, 259, 274; unequal eighth notes (Baroque), 41, 247; words or rhymes for, 51, 67, 73, 105, 126, 166

rigadoon, *rigaudon,* 126; by Babell, 91; by Rameau, 126

romances: by Beethoven, 78; by Benjamin, 160–61; by Kuzmenko, 113; by Mendelssohn, 95; by Schumann, 127; by Sibelius, 232

Romanticism: character pieces, 201, 223, 257; importance of piano, 225, 257; programmatic music, 124; use of common tones, 145

rondeau, 264; by Daquin, 215–16; by Rameau, 40–41

rondos and rondo form: by André, 81; by Balázs, 174; by Bartók, 266–67; by Beethoven, 123, 179–80, 201, 222, 253; by Chopin, 257; by Clementi, 126, 144; by Diabelli, 152; by Ginastera, 271–72; by Haydn, 220; by Kabalevsky, 173

rubato, 113, 167, 194, 258

sarabandes: by Filtz, 149; by Gallant, 141; by Grovlez, 231–32; by Zipoli, 143

scale passages: analysis of, 167; to practice, 64; studies for, 102–3, 117, 173

scherzos: by Gade, 241; by Haydn, 101; by L. Patterson, 103

sequences, 27, 95, 101

sicilliene, 265

skeleton, musical, 30

sonata form, 98, 119–20, 136, 139–40, 148, 164, 168, 175–76, 187, 197, 206, 219

sonata rondo form, 253

sonatas, 252; by C.P.E. Bach, 217; by Beethoven, 197–98, 201, 221, 251–53; by Cimarosa, 190; by Haydn, 101, 112, 148, 160, 193, 219–20, 251, 253–55; by Kuhlau, 206; by Mozart, 218–19, 251; by D. Scarlatti, 213–14

sonatinas: three-movement structure, 81, 144; by André, 81; attr. Beethoven, 74–75, 77–78, 119–20, 123; by Bolck, 164; by Clementi, 64, 67–68, 71, 88, 91–92, 126, 139–40, 143–44, 175–76, 187; by Dussek, 136; by Gedike, 72; by Gurlitt, 104; by Haslinger, 98; by Kuhlau, 168–69; by Melartin, 105

Spanish and Latin music, 104, 151, 188, 213, 230, 232–33, 264–65, 270–71

techniques for: contrary motion with mirror fingering, 20; hand substitution, 273; repeated notes, 57; rotation, 106–7, 279–80; shifting positions, 58, 92, 118; sixteenth-note passages, 73, 107, 177, 215, 238; three-handed (three-stave) texture, 260, 262, 272; *tremolo,* 170; unison, playing in, 127; warm-up drill, 192; zigzag figures, 64, 79, 204

ternary form, 88, 102, 201, 223, 224

toccatas, toccatinas, 200; by Dolin, 200; by Henderson, 142–43; by Kabalevsky, 134; by Maikapar, 177; by Pépin, 268; by Takács, 173, 199

20th-century composition techniques, 229, 266; absence of key and time signatures, 114; aleatory (chance) music, 96; contemporary notation, 234; contemporary piano techniques, 266; different RH and LH key signatures, 199; twelve-tone music, 124, 266

variations, 112, 153, 220; by Bartók, 188; by Haydn, 193; by Kabalevsky, 233, 272

waltzes: bass and accompaniment, 26, 45, 57, 102, 123, 133, 258; jazz rhythm for, 199; by Brahms, 161; by Chopin, 225–26, 257–58; by Czerny, 25–26; by Debussy, 203; by Grieg, 123–24; by Peterson, 199; by Rebikov, 133, 172–73; by Schubert, 152–53; by Schumann, 144–45; by Shostakovich, 269–70; by Weber, 102

whole tone clusters, 25, 57

whole tone scales, 33, 57, 90, 169, 261